Creating

DISCARD

for

Authors

and

Inquirers

Kathy G. Short
UNIVERSITY OF ARIZONA

Jerome C. Harste
INDIANA UNIVERSITY

with
Carolyn Burke
INDIANA UNIVERSITY

&

*contributing
teacher
researchers*

GLORIA KAUFFMAN
Maldonado Elementary School, Tucson, Arizona

KATHRYN MITCHELL PIERCE
Glenridge Elementary School, Clayton, Missouri

TIM O'KEEFE
Lonnie B. Nelson Elementary School, Columbia, South Carolina

KATHY EGAWA
Echo Lake Elementary School, Seattle, Washington

Creating Classrooms

for

Authors

and

Inquirers

HEINEMANN

Portsmouth, NH

Heinemann
A division of Reed Elsevier Inc.
361 Hanover Street
Portsmouth, NH 03801-3912
Offices and agents throughout the world

Every effort has been made to contact the copyright holders for permission to reprint borrowed material where necessary. We regret any oversights that may have occurred and would be happy to rectify them in future printings of this work.

The authors and publisher wish to thank the students and teachers who granted permission to reprint borrowed material in this book.

Library of Congress Cataloging-in-Publication Data
Short, Kathy Gnagey.
    Creating classrooms for authors and inquirers / Kathy G. Short,
Jerome C. Harste, with Carolyn Burke ; and contributing teacher
researchers, Gloria Kauffman . . . [et al.] — 2nd ed.
        p.   cm.
    Rev. ed. of: Creating classrooms for authors / Jerome C. Harste,
Kathy G. Short, with Carolyn Burke. c1988.
    Includes bibliographical references and index.
    ISBN 0-435-08850-5 (alk. paper)
    1. English language—Composition and exercises—Study and
teaching.   2. Language arts.   I. Harste, Jerome C. (Jerome Charles)
II. Burke, Carolyn L.   III. Harste, Jerome C. (Jerome Charles).
Creating classrooms for authors.   IV. Title.
LB1576.S38   1995
372.6—dc20   95-18854
                                                       CIP

Editor: Leigh Peake
Production: Melissa L. Inglis
Cover design: Jenny Jensen Greenleaf
Interior design: Joni Doherty Design Studio

Printed in the United States of America on acid-free paper
99 98 97   RRD   2 3 4 5 6 7 8 9

Contents

Planning New Inquiries Through Reflection and Reflexivity

Taking Thoughtful New Action Through Invitation and Reposition

Conclusion

Preface

This book presents a curricular framework for teachers based on what we know about learning. Teachers who are familiar with the first edition of *Creating Classrooms for Authors* will immediately note that the title is different. *Creating Classrooms for Authors and Inquirers* is meant to signal what is new. The essence of the first volume is still intact, but what has been added is how we have taken our work in reading and writing and philosophically reconceptualized it as inquiry.

When we wrote *Creating Classrooms for Authors* we assumed readers would come to our text having first read *Language Stories and Literacy Lessons* (Harste, Woodward, & Burke, 1984). With time, this assumption no longer holds so we have included in this book some of the basic principles of language and learning from which we operate. We have also included more curricular engagements in Section Two because of requests from teachers who read and used the first edition of this book.

Hindsight is wonderful. In the first edition of *Creating Classrooms for Authors* we shared how we went about creating classrooms for authors based on our work with classroom teachers. What we didn't tell were the problems we faced or points at which we had reservations. The result was that teachers looked at us as experts. In this book we are more modest. Not only have we organized the book in terms of how we developed—by working on the writing curriculum first, the reading curriculum second, and then rethinking curriculum as inquiry—but we have shared our lingering concerns and questions in addition to our successes. Rather than posing as experts we have attempted to position ourselves as inquirers.

The two sections of this book are organized around key processes of inquiry and their realization within the authoring cycle as a curricular framework. Chapter 1, "Visions of Literacy," overviews the entire book as well as establishes a theoretical frame for what follows. Chapters 2–4 focus on the authoring cycle and the ways in which we and other teacher researchers have used the cycle as a curricular framework in our classrooms. In Chapter 2, we explore how to begin an authoring cycle in writing; in Chapter 3, we examine how to extend this framework to reading; and in Chapter 4 we share our recent efforts to use the cycle to rethink the whole curriculum as inquiry. Chapter 5 focuses on critical and practical issues related to maintaining a community of inquirers and raises our lingering questions about inquiry. Throughout this book, we invite readers to become teacher researchers and further explore curriculum as inquiry with us.

In between each of the chapters in Section One are articles by teachers. Each of the teachers we invited to write in this volume use the authoring cycle as a conceptual framework for thinking about curriculum. Tim O'Keefe (Columbia, SC) is clearly one of the best observers of children we know. Not surprisingly, we asked him to contribute an article on kidwatching. Kathryn Mitchell Pierce (St. Louis, MO) recently moved from the university to an elementary classroom. We asked her to share her trials, tribulations, and successes in getting the authoring cycle started in reading and writing. Gloria Kauffman (Tucson, AZ) is simply one of our heros. She not only has worked with us over many years, but she also continues to push us to grow and learn. In her article she focuses on the first three days of school and how she begins to create a sense of community in the urban classroom in which she teaches. Kathy Egawa (Seattle, WA) is a teacher researcher interested as much in her own development as she is in the development of the children whom she teaches and the colleagues with whom she works. In her article she shares how she and a group of teachers formed a study group to reform parent-school relationships and report cards.

In each chapter of this book we elaborate specific curricular engagements which we and other teachers have used within the authoring cycle framework. Curricular engagements that are capitalized in Section One are discussed in much greater detail in Section Two. Readers should also note that Section Two contains extensive book lists as well as other resources that they will find helpful.

Readers who would like to see what classrooms for authors and inquirers look like will find the videotape series *Visions of Literacy* helpful (Harste & Jurewicz, 1991–1994, Heinemann). Included in this series are videotapes entitled "Literature Circles," "Literature Guilds,"

"Education as Inquiry," "Multicultural Education," "Children at Risk," "Early Childhood Education," "Teachers as Learners," "Whole Language and the Library Media Specialist," and "Multiple Ways of Knowing."

The ideas and experiences in this volume are the result of a group of people who have worked, thought together, and built from the work of others over time. Ludwik Fleck ([1935]1979) calls such a like-minded group a "thought collective." Thought collectives hold some values in common, but this does not mean that everyone thinks exactly alike. That's why we must assume responsibility for this book and the curriculum it presents, though within it you will meet and see reflected the theory and practice of many others. Throughout the chapters, we continuously reference the many teachers without whom this book would not have been possible. Readers should note that our work with several of these teachers has spanned more than ten years and so examples from their classrooms come from different teaching contexts and grade levels.

To highlight as well as to acknowledge Carolyn Burke's conceptual input we elected to list her as a contributing author for the volume. In addition, you will note that Kathy Short is the first author of this volume and Jerome Harste is second author. Since we have shared equally in the development of both books, this arrangement seemed fair and timely. When we refer to ourselves in this volume we use our first names, Kathy and Jerry.

In closing we wish to acknowledge all of the teachers who have shared their language stories and literacy lessons with us and who have allowed us to become part of their lives and work. We are especially grateful to the children who have shared their work with us and who have in turn allowed us to share it with you.

The Authoring Cycle: Let's Think Curriculum

Chapter One

Visions of Literacy

Introduction

As part of a course exploring reading/writing connections, Jerry asked teachers to examine their existing curriculum, find some component where they could add writing, and then observe what happened. Teachers used their observations of these writing engagements and their impact on the curriculum and children's learning to reflect on and develop their own personal theories of reading and writing.

Anne Williams, one of the teachers in the course, decided to add a science journal to an activity she was planning to do with plants. Every year, just prior to Mother's Day, Anne collected milk cartons from the cafeteria, bought some seeds and a bag of soil from the local nursery, and had the children plant and grow flowers as part of her science program. When this activity was timed just right, the flowers made a nice Mother's Day gift just as the science unit was ending.

This year, instead of business as usual, she decided to add a science journal and invite children to record their observations of their plants. Micah's first entry read: "I planted my plant. I put soil in there. Three seeds in it. I watered it." To complete his page he added a picture.

Micah's second entry reflected his impatience with this project: "I watered my plant. I don't see a thing, but I hope I will soon." By Day three, May 3, Micah was getting a little disgruntled with the whole project: "I watered my plant again. A lot of them were growing but not mine." He again added a picture, although this time the character in the picture was noticeably less happy.

The fact that his plants were not growing as rapidly as others so disheartened him that he did not make another entry until May 8, but at this point he almost waxes poetic: "I had one plant growing, but today I saw two more! I wonder how they grow so fast! But now there is three at last!" His illustration is next to ecstatic with stars, hearts, and streamers surrounding the plant. In his illustration he has even included a smiling face and the word *good*, leaving little doubt as to his frame of mind.

On May 9 he reported, "One of my plants is really big, one is really little, one is just right. I wonder what it's going to look like every night." May 11 was the last day of the project and Micah wrote, "My plant is beautiful. This will be my last day to water it and it is doing well."

At this point Anne had children share their journals and suggested they take both their journal and their plant home to give to their mothers on Mother's Day. In the back cover of his journal, Micah wrote his mother a note. He obviously had second thoughts, however. In the front cover he wrote his mom a letter (see Figure 1.1).

Anne—influenced by Micah's reservations—used this experience to think about her teaching and her beliefs about learning. When she shared this story with other teachers in the course, they thought the activity was fine, but that Anne should not have tried to establish the context of what was to happen with the plants. Micah knew more than she did on this count. Had the disposition of the plant been left open, Micah could have taken his plant home and enjoyed it himself rather than being trapped into giving it as a Mother's Day gift. From a reading and writing standpoint, there is lots of evidence that writing made Micah reflective, so much so that when asked to give the plant as a Mother's Day gift he illuminates a weakness in Anne's current curriculum. But that is okay. Teaching is never about "getting it right." It's about inquiry: using children as our curricular informants to continue to grow and learn as professionals.

This experience expanded Anne's visions of literacy. She's now convinced writing supports more careful observations of the world as well as reflective thinking. She thinks about her curriculum differently. Not only is she making connections between reading, writing, and the content areas, but she is interested in how her curriculum interfaces with what is going on in her children's homes. How we envision literacy makes a big difference.

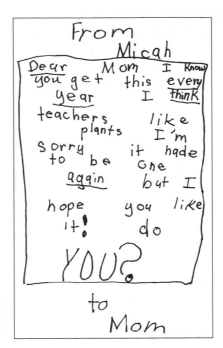

We invite you to envision and re-envision literacy, schooling, and curriculum as we share our experiences with children and with teachers in classrooms over time. Not everything is settled. While we know a great deal about the role that language plays in learning, we still have much to learn. Taking what we know and using it to form curriculum is also work in progress. We provide no surefire answers, only invitations to join us as inquirers in this exciting work.

This chapter is the story of how our notions of literacy, schooling, and curriculum have developed over time. We begin with some language stories and literacy lessons. These stories—from our own, as well as others' work—helped us to come to an understanding of language and language learning. What we learned evolved into a set of guiding principles which we upheld as we worked with teachers in exploring classrooms that supported natural language learning.

The second major section in this chapter relates to teaching and tells the story of how we used "authoring" as a curricular frame to rethink, first, the writing curriculum, second, the reading curriculum, and last, sign systems and other content areas. The final section of this chapter shares our latest thoughts. As a result of our work with teachers in reading and writing, we have come to see the authoring cycle as a framework for rethinking schools and schooling. This section introduces curriculum as inquiry and identifies what we see as seven key

Chapter One
Visions of Literacy

underlying processes in inquiry. Throughout this chapter we will share with you our thinking as well as our lingering questions and concerns.

Language Stories and Literacy Lessons

In 1967 Kenneth Goodman did a very simple thing which revolutionized the teaching of reading. Instead of building a model of the reading process based upon adult logic, he handed readers a book, asked them to read and then tape recorded their readings. Based on his observations and analysis of their reading, he devised a psycholinguistic model of the reading process (Goodman, 1967).

Kenneth Goodman defined a miscue as the difference between an expected and an observed response during reading. Figure 1.2 shows a miscue. In this case the reader, John, has read a section of the story as: "Jim opened the attic door. There were amazing, magnifying, magazines and boxes of clothes. . ."

The little *c* in the circle means that the reader corrected the miscue. What is significant about this miscue is that given the letters in magazine—M, A, G, A, Z, I, N, E—the reader came up with two words, within the period of about two seconds—amazing and magnifying—with many of the same letters. This feat, repeated again and again as people read, gives us pause. The mind is truly a marvelous thing. Although we have difficulty explaining the rapidity of the miscues, we do know that letter-sound or graphophonemic information was involved in the production of the miscue.

Notice also that the reader adds *-ing* to the ending of each miscue. The helping verb *were* sets up the expectation that an *-ing* word will follow. Here's proof that the reader is using syntax, the structure of language, to make predictions while reading. Proficient readers unconsciously ask themselves, "Does what I read sound like language to

me?" If it doesn't, they self-correct based on their intuitive sense of the grammatical rules which govern word order and the flow of language.

Another thing to notice is that the reader corrects his miscue. Obviously *were magnifying and* doesn't make sense. The reader goes back, resamples from the text and aligns what is being said with what is on the page. Proficient readers also continually ask themselves, "Does what I read make sense to me?" In this case, the linguistic system that triggered the rereading is called semantics or meaning.

All three systems of language—graphophonemics, syntax, and semantics—work together when we read. This is why we give children in the classrooms in which we work whole books and stories to read rather than lists of words. When word lists are used, readers cannot rely on their knowledge of syntax and semantics to predict or to self-correct. They are forced to depend upon the graphophonemic system alone to get the information that they need. This causes a lack of additional cues to support the reader and makes reading in school a harder task than it is in the real world.

Understanding Process Approaches to Reading

The discovery that the subsystems of language work together in reading led to the creation of what has been called a whole language view of reading. Figure 1.3 illustrates what a whole language model of reading looks like.

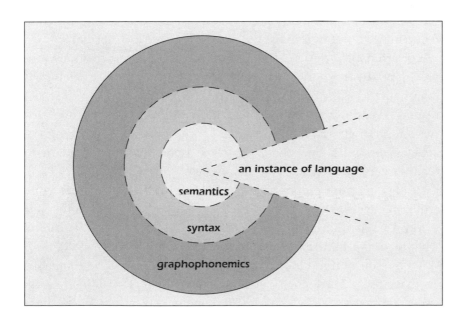

FIGURE 1.3
Whole Language Model of Reading (Harste & Burke, 1977)

Chapter One
Visions of Literacy

Notice that semantics or meaning is the core of reading. The flow and structure of language, or syntax, surrounds and maintains this core. On the outside is letter-sound relationships. These outer systems—what earlier models of reading called phonics and grammar—need to be transparent. If reading is to be successful, readers need to be able to see through these systems while maintaining their focus on meaning. When these outer systems become opaque the reading process breaks down. When the wedge in the model is labeled reading, it is meant to suggest that any instance of reading for authentic purposes involves all three systems. When the wedge in the model is labeled instruction, it suggests that whole language—language having all three systems intact—should always be used in teaching. The secret is in choosing whole, meaningful chunks of language and introducing strategies which proficient readers use to overcome problems when children experience difficulty. A fourth system of language, pragmatics, deals with the rules of language that operate in a setting and is the basis for why children learn language by using language for real reasons.

For now it is important to note that this model of reading differs from Phonics and Skills Models of the reading process (Harste & Burke, 1977). A Phonics Model of Reading assumes that reading is accessed by decoding letter-sound relationships. A Skills Model of Reading presents proficient reading as the sum total of a variety of subskills, each of which needs to be studied independently and mastered in a progressive fashion. In this approach meaning is viewed as being important, but it is not the central focus of instruction.

Unfortunately, these older models of reading instruction are still prevalent. Instructional materials derived from these models still dominate too many reading programs. The graded stories in the basal readers do contain selections from children's literature, but these stories are often altered or are selected for the purpose of teaching vocabulary or skills. Such programs focus upon teaching children to read—a very different purpose than why we normally pick up a book to read. Literature proponents argue that children's literature gives children new viewpoints by which to see and to appreciate their world. Using children's literature to teach reading, they say, distorts what reading real literature is all about (Peterson & Eeds, 1990).

As a result of Ken Goodman's work we now understand that readers make use of three cueing systems as they read. The difference between proficient readers and less proficient readers lies in the flexibility displayed in the use of the three systems. Less proficient readers use all three systems upon occasion but tend to overuse one system at the expense of others.

Whole language is not a specific approach to teaching reading as much as it is a philosophical understanding that language cannot be simplified for purposes of instruction. In this view grammar and phonics should not be taught in isolation but rather within the context of language. When instruction focuses on meaning, all the systems of language—semantics, syntax, and graphophonemics—are then available for both attention and use.

In 1989, Jerry reviewed the instructional research on reading for purposes of proposing new policy guidelines for the teaching of reading (Harste, 1989). This review revealed that children do learn what teachers teach. If children are taught to sound out words, they then perceive reading as a sounding-out process. If flash cards and word identification are stressed, children perceive reading as word calling. If inferencing is stressed, children learn to inference. The strategies of instruction become the strategies of use. This pattern, seen over and over again, forces us to conclude that teachers' beliefs about reading impact the teaching of reading as well as what students learn.

Understanding Language Use and Learning

In 1975, Michael Halliday did for language what Ken Goodman had done for reading. Using his son, Nigel, as a case study, Halliday documented that oral language was learned functionally through use (Halliday, 1975). This research demonstrated that language is first and foremost social. By using language in authentic and functional settings Nigel "learned language" (that is, he learned to use language in order to accomplish those things he wanted done), "learned about language" (that is, he learned how to talk about language as an object in its own right), and "learned through language" (that is, he increased his knowledge of the world and how it worked). Instructionally, Halliday's findings were revolutionary as they suggested that children learn language best when everyone is paying attention to something else. Parents don't have the teaching of language as their goal. Their goal is to teach living. In the process, language is learned naturally (Edelsky, 1992).

Curricularly, these ideas are significant. They are why our curriculum focuses on meaning. Instead of using basals and other materials designed to teach children how to read, we use stories and tradebooks that hold their interest and capture their attention. Instead of using grammar exercises, we write letters to pen pals and community leaders about topics of personal importance.

Halliday offers other important lessons as well. One of his most powerful ideas is the notion of "text in context." Text in context is the concept that language users produce texts that reflect the context in which they find themselves. RAILWAY STRIKE AVERTED is a piece of text that signs its context—a newspaper. ON YOUR MARKS, GET SET, GO is a piece of text that signs its context—a race. We know what is happening (Halliday called this the Field), we know that it is oral language (the Mode), and we know or can infer the relationship of the parties involved, who is saying what to whom (the Tenor). Every text signs its context. Change one element and you have a new text! Curricularly, the message to teachers is "create the context and the rest will follow." Instructionally, the implication is that if you want a child to sound like a lawyer, have her associate with lawyers. If you want her to sound like a teacher, have her associate with teachers. If you want her to become an inquirer, create an inquiry curriculum.

In one school in which we worked the teachers planned a focus on poetry. Following Halliday's lead they decided if children were to be poets that they needed to be immersed in poetry. As a result, they read poetry to them on a daily basis, and poets were brought into the classroom. The context was contagious. Children as young as kindergarten age perceived themselves as poets. One of our favorite pieces is a narrative poem by Katie.

Our invitation and Katie's response offer another literacy lesson. As educators we can set the process in motion, but we cannot predetermine the outcome. Katie is literate, but in some ways she takes her literacy too far, using it to defy the very system that supported her in her growth. Most teachers, for instance, might hesitate to put Katie's poem up at an open house, not because it isn't literate, but because it goes beyond and challenges the status quo. Failing to understand education as a process—that one puts into motion rather than as a specific end point—is exactly what is wrong with the use of behavioral objectives, national standards, and other efforts that try to straight-jacket education.

Language has both a maintenance and a generative function. Listen to young children as they talk. They are always using language in new ways. Upon arriving home from school, first-grader Alison,

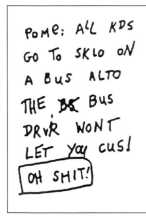

Poem; Katie, Age 6

Jerry's daughter, announced, "Megan is not my friend anymore. I fell down. She was being so 'unconcentrative,' she didn't even notice!"

Convention—"correct" speech, "correct" spelling and "correct" grammar—is the counter force. The generative nature of language is a force which no one ever seems able to stop. Despite the efforts of lexicographers and other guardians of proper usage, language is dynamic and forever changing. Think of the way that change has enriched our vocabularies. Old words are used in new ways ("bad," "cool"), and each generation leaves its own mark through a set of words that mean like never before!

Understanding Written Language Use & Learning

Building off of Ken Goodman's and Michael Halliday's work, from 1978 to 1984, Jerry, Carolyn Burke, Virginia Woodward, and a host of other colleagues engaged in a series of studies that looked at what young children know about reading and writing prior to going to school (Harste, Burke, & Woodward, 1981, 1983a, 1983b; Harste, Woodward, & Burke, 1984). One of the most impressive and easily interpreted sets of data that Jerry and Bob Carey gathered came from four-year old children with different cultural backgrounds (Harste & Carey, 1979). Each child was given a blank sheet of paper and asked to write a story. Afterward they were asked to read what they had written.

Dawn, a four-year old from the United States, wrote in unconventional script using a series of wavy lines. Each line is written left-to-right. Dawn created a page of such lines starting at the top of her page and finishing at the bottom. When she completed her writing she read her piece to us. "My name is Dawn. I go to University School. My brother Tommy goes to Children's Corner, but he is going to go to University School too," making sure that her finger was on the bottom right-hand mark as she finished reading her text. In contrast to Najeeba and Ofer's scribbles, Dawn's writing looks decidedly English.

Najeeba, who is from Saudi Arabia, said as she completed her piece, "Here, but you can't read it . . . I wrote it in Arabic and in Arabic we use a lot more dots than you do in English." Ofer is an Israeli child whose writing looks decidedly Hebrew, though his grandmother affirms that, "It looks like Hebrew, but it's not. He wrote it backwards."

What these samples of children's writing demonstrate is that long before receiving formal instruction the young child is actively making

Uninterrupted Writing;
Dawn (United States), Age 4
(Harste & Carey, 1979)

Uninterrupted Writing;
Nejeeba (Saudi Arabia), Age 4
(Harste & Carey, 1979)

Uniterrupted Writing;
Ofer (Israel), Age 4
(Harste & Carey, 1979)

Chapter One
Visions of Literacy

sense of the world, including the world of print. Each of these children understands that language is functional and that its purpose is to convey a message. How these children organized their message reflected the print they saw in their environments.

At the time of this discovery, most kindergarten programs were organized around letter A day, letter B day, and so on. The assumption seemed to be that children learned oral language naturally, but written language needed to be taught. Our data suggested a different reality, one that built off the written language information that children already possessed.

Frank Smith (1981) coined the term "demonstration" to explain a fundamental social process in language learning: "The first essential constituent of learning is the opportunity to see what can be done and how. Such opportunities may be termed demonstrations . . . The world continually provides demonstrations, through people and through their products, by acts and artifacts" (p. 101). Deborah Rowe (1986) elaborates on this notion:

> When participants at the literacy centers authored their own texts, talked about their work, or left physical traces of these activities in the form of books, pictures, or songs, they provided demonstrations for their audience. These demonstrations added to the meanings which may potentially be constructed and to the learning which may potentially take place. Observing and talking with other authors has a powerful impact on learning precisely because the audience has the opportunity to see demonstrations of content information and process information linked in uses which are meaningful to both audience and author. That is, in literacy events they are constructing together, the audience has the opportunity to see demonstrations of what authors might say/write/draw/play/etc. coupled with demonstrations of how it might be said/written/drawn/played/etc. as well as demonstrations of why or to what ends these engagements serve. (p. 102)

Many educators equate demonstrations with modeling, but these concepts are not identical. Modeling assumes that children simply imitate, in an unthinking fashion, what has been shown to them. Teachers who hold this view assume that all they have to do is show children how to do something and learning takes place. Demonstration assumes that mentally active learners consciously pick and choose what it is that they will attend to out of what is shown to them. We may demonstrate how something is to be done to children, but they will attend to only those demonstrations that make sense to them given their current inquiry questions and what it is that they already know. Kathy's distinction between these two terms emphasizes that how educators talk about learning makes a difference: "Demonstration shows what might be done. Modeling shows what must be done."

Within any literacy event, then, multiple demonstrations are available. This book, for example, not only demonstrates the content we think teachers need to know about language, but it also demonstrates how we think about teachers and children. Further, it stands as a testimonial to how it is we think about curriculum and the kinds of decisions that govern our thinking. In it are demonstrations of our humor or at least what it is that we perceive to be funny, informative, and striking instances of language learning. There are, in short, multiple demonstrations available. Engaging in any literacy event—reading this book, listening to a public lecture, or having a discussion with colleagues—provides multiple opportunities to learn. Not every language learner will learn the same thing, however. Which demonstrations we attend to is a function of how the environment is structured as well as what we are ready to learn.

If you understand the notion of demonstrations, then you will understand why reading a book for a second time is not a waste of time (Pappas & Brown, 1988). You learn new things during the second reading by attending to demonstrations that you may not have noticed the first time. That is why *how* you teach is just as important as *what* you teach (Barnes, 1975). As is evident from the multicultural examples of Dawn, Najeeba, and Ofer, each has attended to different demonstrations depending on the written language in their culture. Interestingly, all have learned that written language is intentional and is designed to mean. None treat it as if it were meaningless or decorative like the print that they have probably seen on materials such as wallpaper.

Understanding Literacy

At six years of age, Alison had a telephone conversation with her friend Jennifer (Harste, Woodward, & Burke, 1984). They decided to get together after church on Sunday and play ballerina. Alison would get her leotard, slippers, and hair ribbons from her dresser, and

Jennifer would bring her leotard, slippers, and hair ribbons with her in a bag from church. When Alison got off the phone, she went to her room and recorded her conversation. She used art, math, and language to do so.

Alison forced us to rethink literacy. She showed us that literacy is much broader than language. If we define literacy as the processes by which we, as humans, mediate the world for the purpose of learning, then this language story demonstrates that Alison is clearly engaged in the stuff of "real" literacy. To mediate the world is to create sign systems—mathematics, art, music, dance, language—that stand between the world as it is and the world as we perceive it. These sign systems act as lenses that permit us to better understand ourselves and our world.

Four-year old Michelle was asked to write her name and anything else that she could write (Harste, Woodward, & Burke, 1984). She wrote three sets of letters in three rows. When we asked her to read what she had written she pointed to the first set of letters and said, "This says Michelle; [moving to the second set of letters] Jay, that's my daddy's name; [moving to the third set] and Nancy, that's my mother's name." Michelle paused at this point, thought a moment, then snatched up the pen and drew a circle around the names. Putting down the pen she announced, "And together they say Morrison"—her family name.

We like these language stories because they not only demonstrate key processes in literacy, but they also teach us that no one becomes literate without personal involvement in literacy. Both Alison and Michelle are engaged in a sophisticated study of language. Alison's fi-

**Uninterrupted Writing;
Michelle, Age 4 (Harste,
Woodward, & Burke, 1984)**

*Section One
The Authoring Cycle:
Let's Talk Curriculum*

nal product is an elegant summarization of a complex literacy event. Michelle is reflecting on what she knows about language. She knows what she wants to say, but she doesn't quite have all of the conventions that she needs to say it. Grouping names and linking them by circling those that belong together as a set is an option that we could have invented to signal family names. How to retain the individuality of persons, yet write about one's family, is no easy feat, even for us. Importantly, both Alison and Michelle teach us that reflexivity is not something in which only older, wiser, more mature language learners engage. It is not a "higher level thinking skill," but rather part and parcel of the learning process for each of us.

Experiences such as these teach us to trust children and the learning process. These lessons are important ones for teachers to have firsthand. We can't help but think that most of what is wrong with instruction in schools is a failure to trust learners and the learning process. Failing to trust learners and the learning process results in the wrong kind of structures—structures that restrict, not support learners. When children are not permitted to consult with peers or to choose what aspects of content to engage in, they can't "wiggle" the structure so as to have it make personal sense to them (Erickson, 1985).

Understanding Teaching as Supporting Literacy Learning

It is important to note that both Michelle and Alison address literacy on their own terms, around topics of personal interest to them. If they are to grow as literate persons we must learn to "lead from behind" (Wells, 1986) using "the child as our curricular informant" (Harste, Woodward, & Burke, 1984). Marie Clay (1985) has called this "working in the known." Regardless of the term, language instruction cannot be prepackaged if it is to connect with children's personal agendas.

Children can learn new things only by building from where they are. This means that we must accept the language that children bring with them to school as well as the experiences they have had. When teachers say, "The children I work with don't have experience," what in actual fact they are saying is that they don't value the experiences that these children bring to school (Harste, 1989b).

In one sense you don't need to teach anyone to be literate. We, along with other researchers (Goodman, Altwerger, & Marek, 1989), found that children as young as three can read STOP on the stop sign and McDONALD'S when they see the golden arches. If this is all that they can read, we start there. To create additional materials to read, we can, like first-grade teacher Vera Milz (1980), invite children to bring in labels of the things that they can read at home. By adding a predictable patterned text ("I can read Stop," "I can read McDonald's," "I can read Crest," and so on) we have created a text that builds from but extends what the child already knows.

Together these language stories and literacy lessons confirm one fundamental truth. The first task of a teacher is to become what Yetta Goodman (1978) calls "a kidwatcher." There are several ways to become a kidwatcher, but our advice is not to delay. Hand a child a book to read and a blank sheet of paper on which to write. The secret to teaching is in asking yourself "What's there?" and using what you find to support the child in the inquiry project in which he or she is currently engaged.

Kidwatching is an alternative to testing. A score on a standardized reading test tells you very little. There is no way to know what instruction to provide if a child receives a 67 on a reading test. However, point out a particular miscue and we'll be happy to talk about the possible instructional decisions which can be made. To demonstrate this point, let's revisit John's miscue in Figure 1.2 ("Jim opened the attic door. There were amazing, magnifying, magazines and boxes of clothes"). To begin with, let's ask ourselves, "What's there?," "What do we know about this child as a language user and learner?"

We know we are dealing with a good reader. John uses graphophonemic information, but he does not rely solely on one strategy. When all else fails he goes back to resample the text. He also operates very differently from someone who calls out words or "barks at print" in the name of reading (Sherman, 1979). His reading has a flow; that's why he anticipates and adds -ing to amazing and magnifying. He understands that what he knows about oral language is a valuable resource for him in dealing with written language. (In this regard, show us a word-by-word reader with no flow to his reading, and we will show you a reader who is in trouble and who likely will not get out of trouble until this important connection is made between how oral and written language work!) More importantly, we know that John has his priorities in order. He sees reading as a meaning-making process, and he monitors what he says in terms of whether it makes sense. The miscue assures us that here is a powerful reader with self-correcting strategies that will keep him growing long after the reading of this selection. Provide us with a sample of twenty-five miscues from John, and we will be even more sure of what we know based upon the patterns that we see (Goodman & Burke, 1972; Goodman, Burke, & Sherman, 1980; Goodman, Watson, & Burke, 1987).

Over the years we have continued to visit and revisit the samples of children's work that we have collected. There always seem to be more demonstrations to uncover. When we first analyzed Alison's sample it forced us to come to grips with the fact that all literacy events are multimodal, involving the orchestration of a wide variety of sign systems. Only later did we come to see it as an extension of Halliday's notion that to be successful in today's world a literate person has to create a multimodal text that is appropriate to the present context. And while this realization is clearly the case with Alison and her ballerina text, it is also true of the book that you are reading replete with its pictures, diagrams, and children's samples. Flexibility in using sign systems to create a successful text for a specific context defines as well as expands our notions of literacy.

Understanding Written Language Learning as Authoring

In our studies of young children's reading and writing, we often asked our informants to write a story. When five-year old Beth was given a pen and a piece of paper she produced the product seen in Figure 1.5.

On first glance Beth's product looks like a scribble. However, partly because of the technology of video recording, we arrived at a different conclusion; namely, that Beth is—in every sense of the word—an author.

By examining Beth's story as it looked at different points in the writing process, it is easier to see how we came to this conclusion. Beth began her story by drawing a picture of a sun and a house (Figure 1.6, Point A). Then she proceeded to write her name, first near the top of the page and then near the center as she announced, "I can write my name another way."

Near the bottom of the page she wrote *David Dansberger* and told us that it was her brother's name (Figure 1.6, Point B). Shown in Figure 1.6, Point C is Beth's attempt to write her other brother's name, *Jeff*. Saying "That doesn't look right!" she tried to erase the *J* with her finger. Farther down the page she drew a picture of David and announced, "This is David." Next she began to draw a picture of Jeff, but remembered that she hadn't finished his name earlier. With an exclamation of "Oops!" she decided not to finish his picture either.

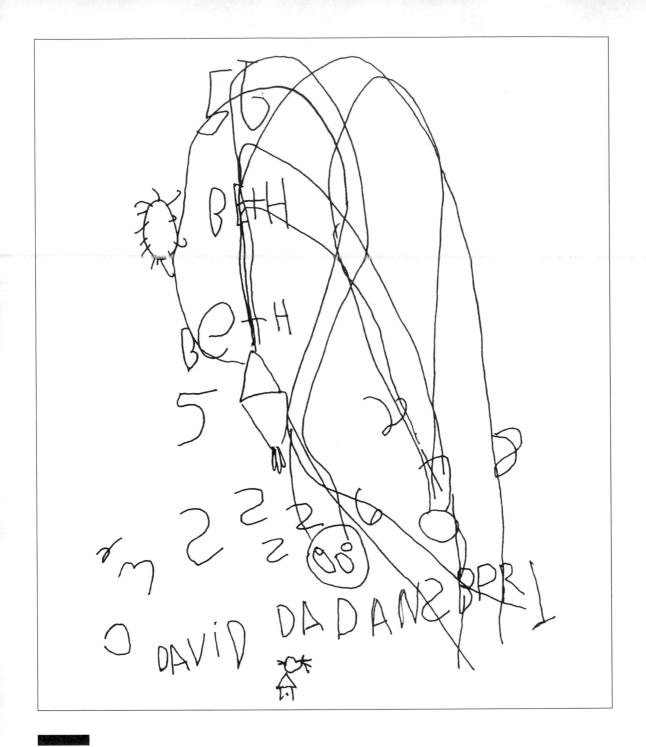

FIGURE 1.5
Story Writing; Beth, Age 5
(Harste, Woodward, & Burke,
1984)

FIGURE 1.6
Story Writing; Beth, Age 5
(Harste, Woodward, & Burke,
1984)

Her next effort was an attempt to write her age, 5, near the abandoned J at the top of the page, but once again she was dissatisfied with the product. Immediately she produced the 5 located near the middle of the page.

After a pause, Beth began saying and writing her numbers backward: "Eight, seven, six, five" (Figure 1.6, Point D). Once again she was displeased with her 5 and said "Five, five, five, five" as she made a series of forms in an attempt to produce one that she could accept. Finally she shrugged her shoulders and continued by saying and writing, "Four, three, two, one, zero, blast off!" At this point Beth drew the rocket seen in the center of the page complete with plumes of smoke and accompanied by sound effects, "Varoom! Varoom! Varoom! Varoom!"

Upon request, Beth read her story: "Well, this is a story about what me and my brothers do at home, play rockets and things like that."

The processes Beth used in writing her story share much in common with those of older authors whose finished texts appear more conventional. She is not merely transcribing pictures and words in her head onto paper. Like adult authors (e.g., Eisner, 1982; Graves, 1983), what she has written influences what she *will* write. Her decision to abandon writing Jeff's name has the effect of eliminating his picture as well!

We are fortunate that Beth gives us so many clues to her meaning-making processes. Her spontaneous verbalizations serve both a social and a personal function. At times she directs her comments to the adult researcher to clarify and extend her work, as in her comment, "I can write my name another way." This serves to share her newest discovery about language with us (i.e., *Beth* and *BEth* both spell "Beth"), and to clarify her intentions and action. Language also serves to fill in details that are not signed in the text, such as the fact that *David Dansberger* is her brother. At other times, her comments seem to accompany the realization that her product is not meeting her intentions and needs to be revised.

Though many researchers (e.g., Piaget, 1976; Vygotsky, 1962; Hakes, 1980) have suggested that five-year-olds have limited knowledge of language as an object, or what linguists call "metalinguistic awareness," Beth seems to us to demonstrate many of the same kinds of awareness of both language features and processes that are observed in adult writers. All of us have muttered to ourselves, "That doesn't look right," as we have attempted a difficult spelling or tried to address a complex concept. And whether or not our "Oops!" has been expressed aloud, we have also experienced the necessity of deleting an idea because it did not fit in the current text.

Beth uses other strategies that demonstrate her engagement in authoring. First, she shows that she understands and uses "keep-going" strategies. By this we mean that she keeps foremost in her mind the task of getting the meaning down and refuses to get hopelessly sidetracked in details. While dissatisfaction with her 5 leads her momentarily to test several ways of creating a more pleasing symbol, after a few tries she returns to the main task of writing her story. She marks this decision with a shrug that seems to mean, "I'll have to return to that later." Her decision reminds us of strategies that we also use to keep going.

Beth uses and orchestrates several sign systems while producing her text. She creates a unified meaning using written language, oral language, art, and math. Her first act is to use art to produce the setting for her story—home. She then deftly identifies herself using written language and the mathematical symbol 5. Using both writing and drawing she adds a second character, her brother. Finally Beth completes her story by combining mathematical symbols to stand for the countdown and by using a swirl of energetic drawing to represent the rocket's blast-off.

What may not be particularly noticeable is that her story—though scripted unconventionally from an adult perspective—was created using components of a well-formed story. She begins by drawing a setting (Figure 1.6, Point A), then introduces characters—herself and her brothers (Figure 1.6, Points B & C)—and ends with an event sequence (Figure 1.6, Point D). From hearing stories read to her, she has internalized the structure of a story, what linguists call "story grammar" (Stein & Glenn, 1978).

There is an ever bigger lesson to be learned here. Because Beth's writing sample looks like a scribble, it is easy for adults to describe her efforts using pejorative labels. As teachers of young children we need to learn to look beyond the surface of the text to the deep meaning if we are to take children and their early involvement in literacy as seriously as is merited.

DeShonna is an inner city six-year old with whom we met over a three-day period. On Day One we asked DeShonna to write her name and anything else that she wished to write, on Day Two we asked her to write a story, and on Day Three we invited her to write a response

Uninterrupted Writing;
DeShonna, Age 6 (Harste,
Woodward, & Burke, 1984)

The is DeShonna shonna nanana
DESHONNA is jirg roid

Story Writing; DeShonna, Age
6 (Harste, Woodward, & Burke,
1984)

to a letter that she had received from Linda Crafton, who at that time was a research assistant and who wasn't there for Day Three.

On Day One, DeShonna created an uninterrupted piece of drawing. If we ask ourselves, "What's there?," "What do we know about DeShonna, given this single piece of writing?" some important discoveries take place. We know, for example, that DeShonna can write her name using upper- and lower-case letters. We also know that she feels comfortable enough to move this task to a place where it makes sense to her. Instead of writing, she draws. After drawing a picture of herself, she adds a Christmas tree and a pumpkin, two objects that are related through a holiday theme. Given DeShonna's self-portrait and her comfort in negotiating our writing request to one of drawing, we suspect that she is a happy and well adjusted child. The details in her drawings and the precision of her name alert us to the fact that this is probably not a representative sample of what she is capable of doing in writing. With our familiarity of children at this age, we suspect DeShonna knows more about writing than this sample suggests. Instructionally, as an extension of this activity, it would be interesting to encourage DeShonna to write something about what the pictures she has drawn mean to her.

When DeShonna was asked to write a story on Day Two, she wrote, "This is DeShonna-shonna-nanana. DeShonna is jumping rope."

So, what's there?

First we notice her name. Now instead of perfect upper- and lower-case mixed caps, DeShonna seems to have randomly mixed capitals and lower case letters. Some might interpret this as a sign that she has regressed. We, however, would say "Not so." The difference between her first writing sample and this one is complexity. In the second sample, DeShonna needs to concentrate on her message in order to create a story. Her mind is apparently ahead of her hand, so to speak, and it is this mind-hand gap that causes us, like DeShonna, to write *their* instead of *there* and to make a host of other such errors when we clearly know better. You will notice that DeShonna also has some sight word knowledge. She knows how to write *this*, and *is* in standard conventional form. Given the way she has written *jumping* and *rope* we suspect DeShonna is using initial, and maybe also final consonant sounds, as her dominant writing strategy. What goes in between these sounds defies DeShonna at the moment, though her tendency is to placehold these sounds with the vowel letter *i* and some other letter. You may also notice the curly lines on top and over the first line of print. As DeShonna created this sample she dramatized jumping rope with her pen, the result of which is this curly line. Read her text again. Notice that it almost has a jump rope rhythm to it.

On Day Three DeShonna wrote a letter to Linda who couldn't be there. We initially read DeShonna the letter that Linda had written to her and then invited her to write back. Her response reads, "DeShonna. Love Linda. I like to do the things for you." DeShonna began by writing her name on the top of the page. She then wrote her text and finally squeezed in the closing, "Love Linda," on the top line beside her name.

This sample, too, is interesting. DeShonna has learned her school lessons well. Give her a sheet of paper and regardless of the task, her first response is to write her name in the upper left-hand corner! This single finding should alert teachers as to why they need to think carefully about the routines and rules they establish in their classrooms. At age six, DeShonna knows how schools work.

What seems obvious is that DeShonna knows less about letter writing than she does about other genres of writing. We suspected, though we don't know for sure, that this may have been the first letter she had ever received. Under such circumstances it is interesting to note that she attended to the salutation and decided to include one in her letter to Linda. Her decision was to copy Linda's closing for her own letter. Since she had already written DeShonna, "Love DeShonna" may have seemed odd to write. In attempting to understand children, we have found it always best to assume sense. Although this may lead to error, it gives the child the benefit of doubt.

In addition to *this* and *is*, this sample shows that DeShonna knows several other words by sight: *I*, *like*, *to*, *do*, *the*, *for*, *you*, and *love*. Her spelling of *things* is almost conventional. Not only does she get the initial consonant sound but also the middle sounds in the word. What defies her is the ending.

Although spelling things the way they sound has been called "phonetic" or "invented spelling" by several researchers (Gentry, 1987; Zutell, 1978), we prefer the term "functional spelling." Sight enters into spelling very early. All of DeShonna's words contain English letters. Where did these come from if not from her experience as a reader?

To keep the writing process flowing, writers use a wide range of functional spelling strategies (see Bean & Bouffler, 1987). In this instance, there is evidence that DeShonna is spelling things by sight as

DeShoNNA LoVe LioPS
I LiKe To Do The Thin
for You

Letter Writing; DeShonna, Age 6 (Harste, Woodward, & Burke, 1984)

Note; Robin, Age 6 (Harste, Woodward, & Burke, 1984)

TRANSLATION
Patty
in the
morning
come
in my
room

THE WRLDSGRNTS
MY doG   DOG
TEENA
AND MY FENDS
doG RooBe   by
ACr VArY NIS   Robin
doGS OAN.DAY
A LTL GRIL
FAL IN THE
WOTR ROOBY AND
TEENA SAVTARE
THE END

Story; Robin, Age 6 (Harste, Woodward, & Burke, 1984)

TRANSLATION
The World's Greatest Dog
My dog
Tina
and my friends
dog Ruby
are very nice
dogs. One day
a little girl
fell in the
water. Ruby and
Tina saved her.
The end.

Section One

The Authoring Cycle:

Let's Talk Curriculum

well as by sound. Lots of English spellings are not phonetic. To say that DeShonna is "spelling the way words sound" is to show a lack of respect for the complexity of the processes in which she is engaged. Carolyn Burke says that anyone can talk about a process simply but to do so does not change the underlying complexity of the real process.

"Phonetic spelling" and "invented spelling" have been used in such a way that it gives people the impression that these are something little kids do that they will outgrow. While this is true to some degree, the processes underlying "invented spelling" and "phonetic spelling" are more general. We all invent spelling every day and every time we write. To focus on spelling and correctness would be to lose sight of what it is we want to say. Once we get the ideas down, it is easy to go back and clean up our text.

Functional spelling is the holistic alternative to the direct instruction of phonics (Mills, O'Keefe, & Stephens, 1992). By inviting children to write—"Do the very best you can"—children are actively engaged in using their current graphophonemic information. Rather than being the passive recipients of rules, children have to remain active, intuiting rules of how our language works, as they write messages of personal importance to themselves.

In contrast to her letter, DeShonna's story may now look better to you than it did when you first encountered it. Interestingly, she seems to have an intuitive feel for story. Notice that her story begins with a setting ("This is DeShonna") and contains an initiating event ("DeShonna is jumping rope"). One can't help but wonder, if she had more time and encouragement, she might have been able to develop this text into one that contained all of the elements of a well-formed story. If we were DeShonna's teachers, we would encourage DeShonna, over the course of the next day or two, to finish her story and to illustrate it. Such a curricular invitation would provide us with more information about DeShonna as a written language user, as well as support her personal growth and development in literacy.

By six years of age, children's stories sound like stories, look like stories, and function like stories. Similarly their letters sound like letters, look like letters, and function like letters. Notes often not only sound like notes, look like notes, function like notes, but also need to be written on note paper. ("Patty, In the morning come in my room. Robin"). This is why we recommend a writing center in classrooms with lots of different kinds of pencils and papers so that children can select the instruments they need for the task at hand.

Clearly, the practice of using what a comedian called "Grade Z paper"—"that's the stuff you find in schools with the blue lines on the lower half and the dotted line in the middle" so that children know the height to make their letters—is questionable. This paper doesn't exist in the outside world. It signifies school and its format says to children that the first order of business in writing is to get your letters right, which is the absolute opposite message from the one we should be sending.

Children like DeShonna and Beth have forced us to reconsider many of the things we do in schools. From watching these young language users it is apparent that there is never a pure act of reading or writing. Writing always involves some amount of reading during production, and reading always involves speaking and listening to either real or imagined audiences. Beth and DeShonna demonstrate to us that alternate sign systems such as language, art, mathematics, movement, and music are commonly combined to create meaning. Children, naturally, see the potential usefulness of combining these various sign systems. For us, as adults, this recognition comes harder, probably because we were taught to see each system as a separate "subject" in school.

To sum up, we have seen that both Beth and DeShonna create meanings as they write. Both use the literacy tasks at hand to test their current language hypotheses. Both see language as social and use this knowledge to help them define the task. Both seem aware of language as an object and as a convention. This awareness allows Beth and DeShonna to self-correct and to redirect energy. Both orchestrate art, oral language, written language, and other sign systems to produce statements that cohere or form a text. Beth and DeShonna have taken ownership of the literacy process. They are authors.

Understanding language and the role language plays in learning is fundamental to good teaching. These language stories are just a beginning. As professionals we are committed to children and to the continued study of how children learn. Each response a child makes is fodder for thought and potential for growth. As is evident by the ways in which we interpret and reinterpret these samples, we too continue to grow and learn.

Young children started us on our journey of language learning and curriculum development. Using what children taught us, our next step was to work with interested teachers in exploring and creating

Letter; Robin, Age 6 (Harste, Woodward, & Burke, 1984)

TRANSLATION
Dear Dad
I love you. Is the cat okay? The puppies already have their eyes open. Tina had 7 puppies. Grandma's puppies are 1 month old. Willy said Hi. My mom painted my room. We got an apple tree. Oops, it's a pear tree. Marcie said Hi. I went to see Gulliver and The Great Muppet Caper. Love Robin.

supportive classroom environments for language learning. Our only concern was that we not violate what we had learned about language and learning.

The Authoring Cycle as a Curricular Framework

An understanding of curriculum is at the heart of what we do as educators. For us, curriculum involves putting our beliefs about learning, language, and social relationships into action (Short & Burke, 1991). Our understandings about curriculum allow us to connect theory and practice and make day-to-day decisions with our students in order to create powerful learning environments.

When we first began teaching, curriculum meant the content and skills prescribed by textbooks, teachers' guides, and school curriculum guides. Curriculum was a program which was mandated by "experts" outside the classroom and imposed by teachers onto students. When we found ourselves frustrated with the current curriculum, we went to conferences and read professionally to try and find another program. It never occurred to us that as teachers we could create curriculum with our students.

Curriculum as Acting On Our Own Beliefs

Through our experiences, we now realize that the first step in creating curriculum is reflective consideration and reconsideration of what we currently believe so that we can consciously act on those beliefs in consistent and generative ways. As long as curriculum consists of acting out someone else's beliefs and practices, neither we nor our students have the understandings to keep the curriculum alive and growing. We are dependent on someone else to create the ideas and programs which we then impose on our context. When we act on our own beliefs, we can make decisions by reflecting with our students about what we know and what is happening in the classroom. The knowledge of outside experts becomes part of what we reflectively consider in forming our beliefs and planning curriculum with our students, not what we automatically implement in our classrooms.

Carolyn Burke believes that the function of curriculum is to give perspective. For curriculum to work, teachers have to have an understanding of the strategies and processes of successful learners and of the specific children in that classroom. Curricular experiences become invitations for children to engage in, see demonstrated, and come to value the social and mental strategies of successful learners. If a particular curricular engagement does not support a child's learning, a new invitation needs to be offered. This process is called curriculum development. It's why children, not activities and tests, must be the teacher's curricular informant. It's why curriculum is negotiated and why curriculum must be in the hands of teachers and children.

It's also why it is not good enough if the teacher is the only person in the classroom who understands how an activity relates to proficiency or success as a learner. Children need to have a curricular perspective, too. They need to understand the relationship between what they are doing in the classroom and becoming a strategic user of literacy for various purposes. In short, curriculum needs to be made visible to both teachers and students in classrooms.

Curriculum is thus not a set of unchanging mandates that are imposed onto classrooms, but our best predictions about how people learn, what people should be learning, and the contexts that support that learning (Short & Burke, 1991). It is an organizational device that we use as teachers to think about our classrooms. When we take time to write down our current curriculum on paper, we are better able to reflect and adjust curriculum as we are involved in classroom life and envision new curricular possibilities. A curriculum operates in the present by interpreting the past and predicting the future.

Creating a Curricular Framework to Link Theory and Practice

While our beliefs and theories provide the underlying assumptions of the curriculum, we still have to put those beliefs into action in the classroom. We need some kind of curricular framework that will support us in making decisions about the specific learning engagements that comprise our day-to-day living in that classroom.

When we started teaching, that framework was a linear sequence of skills from the teachers' manuals that needed to be taught in a particular order. As we came to understand more about learning and literacy, however, our beliefs changed and we moved away from these programs. We began to really observe and talk with our students in order to figure out the kinds of experiences to pursue in the classroom.

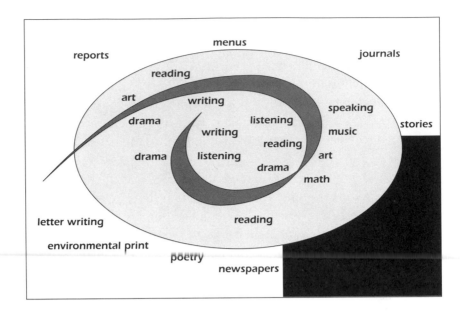

While we found these new ways of thinking about classrooms and learning exciting, we were also frustrated. We had spent long hours thinking and rethinking our beliefs about learning and teaching and had developed a strong, although constantly growing, theory base. We had also gathered together a range of activities, such as shared reading, writing workshop, journals, theme units, and literature circles, that were theoretically consistent with our beliefs. The frustration came because there was no framework to connect the theory and the practice. We did not want to go back to a program with a linear framework and step-by-step procedures. By default, the curriculum became a grab bag of activities from which we pulled randomly every day without a framework to tie those activities together over time or to support negotiation with our students. Developing curriculum became an endless cycle of coming up with new theme units, new projects, new reading and writing activities and new "experts" who could provide us with yet more activities. We needed a curricular framework that would support us in thinking, planning, and evaluating curriculum *with* our students instead of *for* our students, not a program where an "expert" had already made these decisions for us and our students.

Toward Theoretical Practice and Practical Theory

Given the shoulders on which we intellectually stood as well as our studies of young children, we began our work with teachers by assuming that authoring was a form of learning. The diagram in Figure 1.7

depicts the natural language learning we observed in our studies of what young children know about reading and writing prior to coming to school (Harste, Woodward, & Burke, 1984). Learners bring a stock of life experiences to the cycle that are the basis for engaging in personally meaningful communicative events. The oval that surrounds the cycle represents the situational context in which all instances of authoring are embedded, and the activities listed outside the oval represent the multitude of culture-specific contexts in which literacy events can be enacted.

The path of the cycle crisscrosses between the alternate sign systems of language, art, music, mathematics, and movement. This is a recognition that both authoring and learning are multimodal processes and that authors shift stances from reader to writer to artist to speaker and so on. As authors move between and among sign systems they are able to expand the range of meanings they can express.

Eisner (1982) has cogently reminded us that not "everything can be said through anything" (p. 49). Sign systems have varying potentials to express particular ideas. If we encourage only those forms of literacy that highlight language, many types of meanings will necessarily be neglected because they simply cannot be said in language. Attempts to express messages in alternate media also encourage authors to generate new meanings and to expand existing ones because learners are required to take a new psychological stance toward their knowledge. They are encouraged to reflect on their concepts in the process of inventing forms to express them. A final aspect of the cycle depicted in this diagram is the regenerative nature of authoring. Neither authoring nor learning is seen as having an end point. When meanings are expressed or created, they metaphorically become fuel for the next cycle. On the basis of our current understandings, we approach tomorrow's literacy events.

Figure 1.8 represents Carolyn Burke's first attempt at depicting the authoring cycle as a curricular frame. In this instance the focus is on writing and publishing. This framework was developed and refined through use with students and has benefited immeasurably from our collaborative relationships with several excellent teachers who have implemented and revised this model to fit their classroom needs (Harste, Short, w/ Burke, 1988). We want to stress at the outset that, like learning, curriculum is context-specific; it must be modified to address the needs of teachers and students in particular situations (Mills & Clyde, 1990).

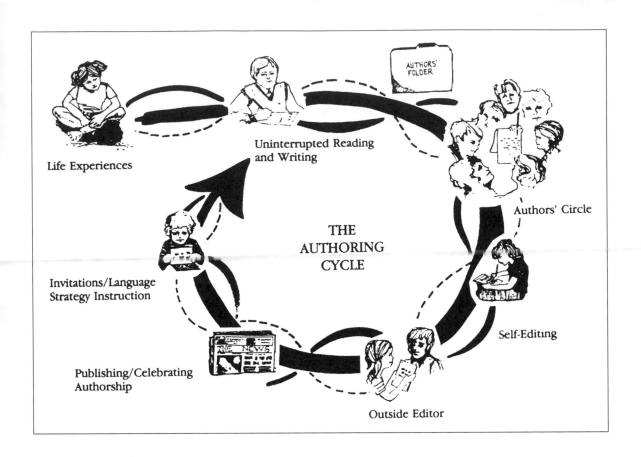

Life Experiences

Uninterrupted Reading and Writing

AUTHORS' FOLDER

Authors' Circle

THE AUTHORING CYCLE

Self-Editing

Invitations/Language Strategy Instruction

Publishing/Celebrating Authorship

Outside Editor

FIGURE 1.8
The Authoring Cycle:
Publishing (Harste & Short
with Burke, 1988)

The cycle begins by immersing students in writing for many different purposes. Children write letters to pen pals, notes for the classroom Message Board, reflections in Personal Journals, responses to their reading in literature logs, and observational notes in a science log. They write entries and drafts as they interview another student for a class newsletter, tell a story about an experience they had when they were little, or research and write about a topic of interest to them. They use writing to inquire about their world as they work through personal issues and reach out to explore new ideas and questions. Many of these uninterrupted experiences with writing do not continue through the cycle; they are published as soon as the note is passed on to a friend or the writer rereads a journal entry. Other pieces of writing, however, are ones that students want to continue working on and develop as drafts to possibly share with other readers; these are placed in their Authors Folder. When students have drafts that they want to think about with other authors, they gather in small groups we call Authors Circles. Each author, including the teacher, reads his or her piece aloud and engages in a dialogue with other authors about its content. Meaning is the focus of the Authors Circle. Concerns about conventional form (spelling, punctuation, and so on) are left for later editing.

After receiving responses from peers, authors usually engage in revision and self-editing. They may respond directly to their listeners' comments, but because they maintain ownership of their piece, they need not follow their suggestions. After revision and self-editing, they make decisions about whether to publish their piece and how to publish it. They may choose to publish it informally through sharing their draft with others. If they want to publish it formally through a book or newspaper article, the piece goes into the editors' box to be read by students and teachers acting as outside editors. The job of the outside editors is patterned after the responsibilities of editors at publishing companies. They serve primarily as a final check to see that the piece makes sense and is in conventional form. Authors always have the final authority to make (or refuse to make) changes that affect the sense of their pieces. After typing, the piece is put into a formal form, often either as a book bound with sturdy covers or as a newspaper that is copied and distributed in the classroom and school.

The cycle continues as authors reflect on their writing processes and strategies in order to plan new inquiries. They set goals for themselves as learners which in turn can lead to teachers offering strategy lessons that focus on a particular aspect of written language or the writing process. The cycle begins again as students explore new invitations and continue to take action through writing—sometimes for themselves, and sometimes for publication. The cycle is not only continuous, but it is recursive with authors constantly moving back and forth within the cycle.

As we use language, art, or drama to communicate ideas, the process of working with the words, paints, or gestures allows us to construct and generate meanings for ourselves as well as for others. Literacy is a process of outgrowing our current selves to solve our communicative problems. Reading and writing are transactions whereby language users begin with concepts and beliefs, but in the process free themselves from what they presently think, feel, and perceive.

In the writing process, authors often produce multiple, mental drafts even before they begin the document that is usually considered the first rough draft. Some researchers (e.g., Donaldson, 1978) believe that forms of language which produce lasting traces are especially important in the learning process because they allow us to work analytically on our present understandings. For example, as readers of our own writing or the writing of others we can check the logic, fine-tune the message, or even overcode the message with yet another layer of meaning. When we write, the text is never wholly conceived beforehand (Murray, 1984). The authoring process allows us not only to clarify and add details but also to produce an interim text that serves as the basis for forming new ideas and discovering new connections between existing ideas. In a real sense, through reading and writing we often outgrow both the author and ourselves—gaining new understandings in the process. The generative aspect of writing is what we call learning. That's why it is so important.

A Guided Tour Through the Authoring Cycle with Corey

Gloria Kauffman began using the authoring cycle to organize writing experiences for her first-grade students. In her classroom, children were involved in many different kinds of reading and writing experiences, including Personal Journals, Pen Pal Letters, the Message Board, note taking, Shared Reading, class read-aloud sessions, Literature Circles, written stories and reports, and the publication of class books, newspapers, and individual books. Although much of the children's writing was informal and so never went through a revision process, children selected some of their writing to go through the authoring cycle and be published in some way.

To illustrate how the authoring cycle was developed in Gloria's classroom, we will follow one piece of writing through the entire cycle. Corey, the author, was repeating first grade and so began the year with little confidence in his ability as a learner and as a language user. As the year progressed, Corey's confidence in his own learning increased, and other children came to admire his work and to borrow ideas from him for their own writing and illustrating.

One day in February, after finishing a story, Corey could not think of any ideas for a new piece. He looked at books in the classroom and talked with others, but still he could not find an idea he liked. Finally he sat down with Gloria and together they generated a list of topics and experiences about which he might be able to write.

During the next month, Corey wrote stories based on several of these ideas, as well as on other topics. When, in the middle of March, he again needed a new story idea, he consulted his list of topics in his Authors Folder and decided to write about the time he had "smashed my toe on the door." Corey quickly produced a short story about his smashed toe (see Figure 1.9, above).

Corey took the piece to Gloria, who was informally conferencing with children as they wrote. She read his story and commented that she hadn't known that he had once stubbed his toe and that she would find the story more interesting if he told more about what had happened. As Corey returned to his desk, Gloria began talking with another child. He reread his story for a few minutes, then got some paper and began writing.

Corey continued writing on the piece the next day. He excitedly read his story to several children and to Gloria and then put it in

Chapter One
Visions of Literacy

I Smashed my toe in the door
One day I came in from
reeses. then the door smashed
my toenell. I had to go
to the nises offes.

I thet I just spraned my
toe untell I looked at
it? it was bleeting and
it had little bits of
toenell peeses in my sok.
Wen I saw it I tried
not to cry "but" I cudet
help it. filly Chuck and
I went down to the nrsis
offes. they called my mom.
My mom came and sied,
what did you do to your
self? and I dident say
inny thang. and then I
had to go home. I had
to have it banchej up for
munth.

the revision box. An Authors Circle for writers to discuss their pieces with each other would meet as soon as three or four pieces of writing were in the box.

The next day four pieces were in the box, so Gloria met with Corey and the other writers. When it was Corey's turn to share, he read his story aloud to the group. As he read, he realized he wanted to say "Then they called my mom" instead of "They called my mom," so he quickly added the word *then* and continued reading.

After Corey had finished, Jessica commented that she liked the way he described the pieces of toenail stuck in his sock. Sherri added that she liked the way he said that he tried not to cry but couldn't help it.

After the children had commented on what they had heard in his story, they began asking questions about parts that were unclear. "How did it happen that the door hit your toe?" asked Erin. "Well, I was opening the outside door to come in from recess. It started shutting. I was trying to be sneaky and go in the other door when the teacher couldn't see me, and it shut on my toe," Corey explained to the group. Sherri suggested that he might want to add how he had gotten home with his mom. Gloria pointed out that the first page didn't make sense to her because he had written about going to the nurse's office and then described the door shutting on his toe.

Corey reread his story and realized that he no longer needed the sentence that had been the first ending of his story and so crossed it out. He talked about the revisions he planned to make after the Authors Circle and decided he would add the part about how the accident happened, but not how he had gotten home.

After he left the Authors Circle, Corey read through his piece again and added a section about sneaking in the door. He then put the story in the editors box, but just before it was time to go home he reclaimed his story to write another section describing what had happened when his mom took him home. He decided he wanted more response to his story because he had made so many changes, so he put his piece back in the revision box.

The next day, Corey again met in an Authors Circle. As he read his story aloud to the group, he realized that he had written "she could carry my" when he meant "she could carry me," and that he wanted his story to end with "I haven't broke my toenail," not "I have broke my toenail." After he made these changes, the other authors in the group commented on what they had heard as they listened to his

FIGURE 1.11
Third Draft of Smashed Toe Story; Corey, Age 7 (Gloria Kauffman's classroom)

I Smashed my the in the door
One day I came in from
reeses. then the door smashED
my toenell. ~~I had to go~~
~~to the nrsis offes~~
I was going to sneek
in the other door wen
it hit my toenell.

I thot I just spraned my
toe antell I looked at
it? it was bleeting and
it had little bits of
toenell peeses in my sok.
Wen I saw it I fned
not to cry "but" I cudet
help it filly Chuck and
I went down to the nrsi's
offes. ~~they~~ then → they called my mom
My mom came and sied,
what did you do to your
self? and I dident say
inny thang " and then I
had to go home* (I had
to have it bandij up for two
munths.)

FIGURE 1.12

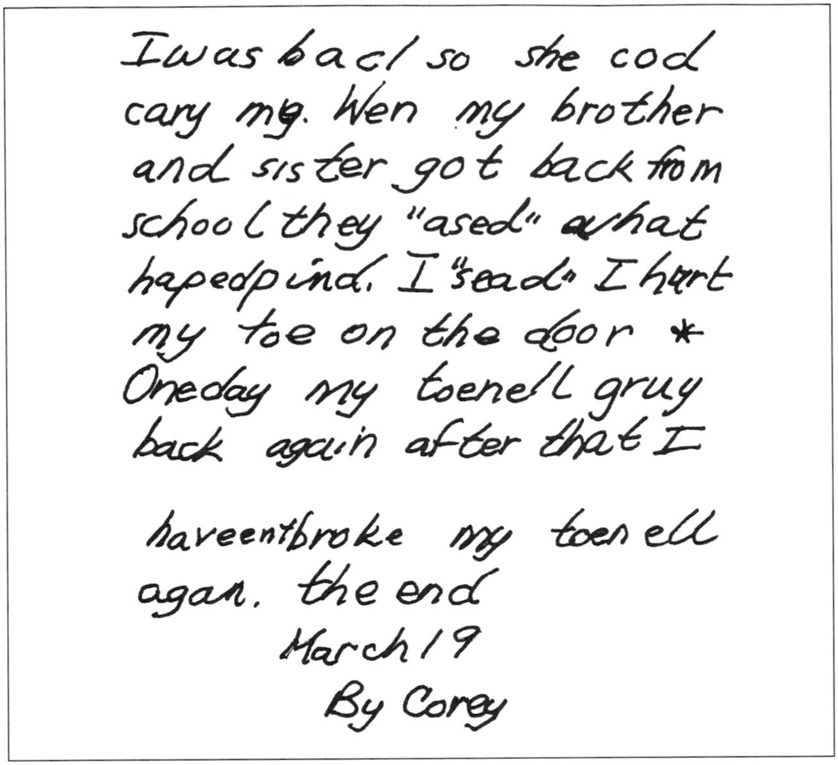

> I was bacl so she cod cary my. Wen my brother and sister got back from school they "ased" qhat hapedpind. I "sead" I hart my toe on the door * Oneday my toenell gruy back again after that I
>
> haveentbroke my toenell agan. the end
> March 19
> By Corey

story, and then Sheila asked him why he had written this story. "I wanted to remember it all the time," he responded. Amy said that she was confused by the part about "two months." "It should be at a different place in the story," she commented. Gloria pointed out that this was where he had ended the story before, and suggested that he might either cross it out or move it if he didn't think it made sense. Corey decided to move this sentence to a position just before the section describing his toenail growing back. He also decided that he did not want to make any other changes in his story. Because of the other authors' enthusiastic responses to his story, he decided he wanted to publish it as a book and so he placed it in the editors box.

The story was edited for meaning and conventions such as spelling and punctuation by an outside editor. Each week, three children from the classroom served as outside editors for any pieces submitted that week for publication. After editing, the story was then typed by a parent volunteer and returned to Corey. He cut his story apart according to what he wanted on each page and glued the parts into a book. The next step was for Corey to work on his illustrations. Illustrating his published books was an important part of the cycle for Corey, and he

Chapter One
Visions of Literacy

I smashed my toe in the door

One day I came in from recess. Then the door smashed my toenail. I was going to sneak in the other door when it hit my toenail. I thought I just sprained my toenail until I looked at it.

It was bleeding and it had little bits of toenail pieces in my sock. When I saw it, I tried not to cry but I couldn't help it.

Finally Chuck and I went down to the nurse's office. Then they called my mom. My mom came and said, "What did you do to yourself?" I didn't say anything.

And then I had to go home. I was 6 or 7 so she could carry me. When my brother and sister got back from school they asked, "What happened?" I said, "I hurt my toe on the door."

I had to have it bandaged up for two months. One day, my toenail grew back again. After that I haven't broke my toenail again.

By Corey

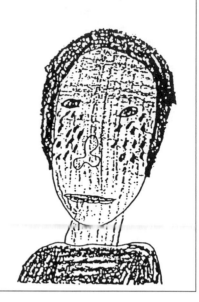

■■■■■■

FIGURE 1.13
Final Draft of Smashed Toe Story; Corey, Age 7 (Gloria Kauffman's classroom)

often spent a great deal of time creating pictures that extended his story. His illustrations were usually brightly colored and filled the entire page. Other children in the room admired his illustrating style and emulated it in their own books. For this book, Corey tried a new art medium, using colored pencils rather than crayons.

After Corey had illustrated his story, he read his finished book to the entire group during the class read-aloud time. They responded by telling him their favorite parts and asking questions about how he had written it and what he liked about it. This was a time of celebration as Corey proudly presented his book to the class. After this, the book went into the classroom library for the rest of the school year, and children often read it during their shared reading time.

Following the publication of his book, Gloria talked with Corey about the processes he had used to extend his story and make it more interesting for others to read. This discussion of these strategies constituted a strategy lesson which was intended to help Corey reflect on the processes he had used in authoring the "smashed toenail" book so that he would become aware of writing strategies he could use in later experiences. Gloria chose to focus on his strategies for extending and developing his story because she felt they constituted his current interest and inquiry question. However, she could have also explored the function of quotation marks or question marks with him, as there

Section One
The Authoring Cycle:
Let's Talk Curriculum

was evidence that he was trying to sort out how these things worked in writing.

As this example illustrates, the authoring cycle provided a framework which the children in Gloria's classroom used to guide their activities as they authored their own books. It allowed them to connect their life experiences with their school experiences and in the process have their voices heard. During many periods of uninterrupted writing and reading, they wrote for both private and public purposes and chose some of their public documents to be rethought and revised in order to be published for others to read. As they shared their stories with others through informal interactions and Authors Circles, the children shifted from taking the perspective of an author to taking the perspective of reader and critic. These shifts occurred as they read their pieces aloud and listened to the comments other authors made about their stories. As children became aware of their audience, they were able to see their writing in a different light.

The presence of an outside editor at the end of the cycle helped children put aside concerns about convention until later in the cycle and to focus, instead, on meaning. Because conventions exist to support readers, not writers, it was important that the editors were outside readers. Authors already know what their pieces say and so issues of spelling, punctuation, grammar, and capitalization do not interfere with their understanding of the story. Readers, however, need these conventions to construct meaning for the story.

The celebration of authorship created a purpose for publication. Children saw others reading the books they had written, and their work took on new importance. The opportunity to reflect on their learning processes during and after writing helped them to gain greater control and understanding of these processes so they could continue to grow and to push themselves as authors.

Using the Authoring Cycle as a General Framework for Curriculum

Originally the authoring cycle served only as a framework for the writing curriculum in our classrooms. As we experimented in our own college classrooms as well as talked and worked with other teachers and colleagues, however, we came to see the authoring cycle as a metaphor for learning and as a general framework for curriculum. Initially we began by using the authoring cycle as a framework for rethinking specific curriculum areas such as reading.

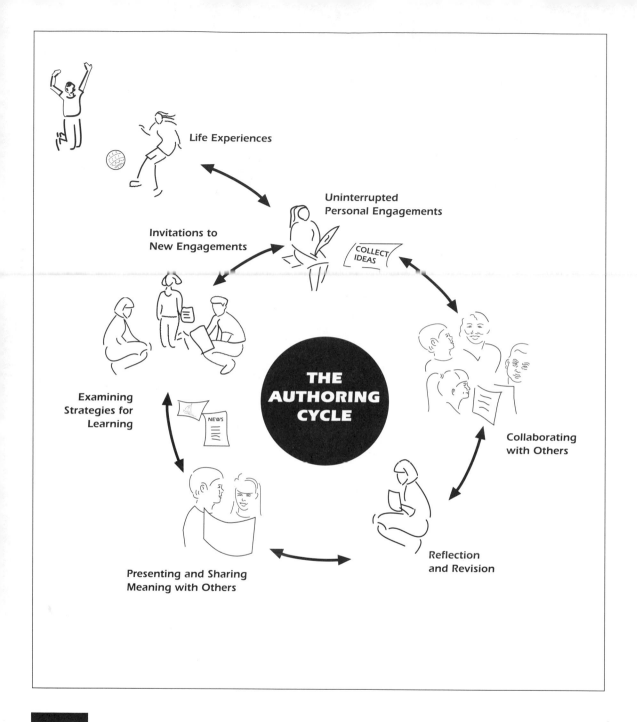

Life Experiences

Uninterrupted
Personal Engagements

Invitations to
New Engagements

COLLECT
IDEAS

THE
AUTHORING
CYCLE

Examining
Strategies for
Learning

NEWS

Collaborating
with Others

Presenting and Sharing
Meaning with Others

Reflection
and Revision

FIGURE 1.14
The Authoring Cycle as a
General Curricular Frame
(Harste & Short with Burke,
1988)

Reading as an Authoring Process

Conceptually during this period a great deal of work was being done in the area of reading comprehension (Harste, 1989a). In lieu of reading models that viewed good readers as those who read a text and regurgitate everything back verbatim, reading comprehension was now seen as an interaction between a text and a reader. Reading was no longer viewed as the transfer of the text into the reader's head, but as a process where readers actively interact with a text using their background experiences to comprehend that text.

Cognitive psychologists attempting to get computers to read found that in order to answer even the simplest of questions they had to preprogram the computer with up to 5,000 pieces of information (Spiro, Bruce, & Brewer, 1980). The knowledge and experience the reader brought to the text strongly affected what the reader got out of the text (Anderson & Pearson, 1984). Other researchers studied texts in terms of basic meaning units, called propositions. They watched readers to determine which bits of information were discarded and which were retained (Kintsch, 1977). Verbalizations during reading allowed still other researchers to study the kinds of inferences that readers made during reading. These research studies provided powerful explanations of how readers cognitively process texts.

When researchers went into the real world of classrooms, however, they found that teachers taught quite differently from how the same information was structured in the textbooks children read (Tierney, LaZansky, & Schallert, 1981). In order to be successful in such a setting, readers had to comprehend the text and adjust their comprehension according to what the teacher wanted. Pragmatics—the rules of language use in particular settings—became a popular area of research, showing that different classrooms had different rules and, depending on the rules, quite different messages were being taught about reading (Edelsky & Smith, 1984).

The work of Louise Rosenblatt (1978) and Ken Goodman (1984) pushed educators to consider reading as a transaction between a text and a reader in which the result is a new text. Interactional theorists recognized that readers have a role in comprehension but still assumed that there were particular meanings in the text to be comprehended by readers. Transactional theorists argued that readers construct their own understandings and interpretations as they engage in "lived through experiences" with text. While a text has particular potential meanings, each reader constructs his or her own under-standings. Readers construct their own understandings in light of their experiences and rethink their experiences in light of the text so that they bring meaning to and take meaning from a text. Both the reader and the text are thus changed in the transaction. Reading, like writing, is therefore a form of authoring.

We realized that if reading is an authoring process, then the authoring cycle would also serve as a curricular frame for supporting readers in classrooms. We encouraged children to connect to their own life experiences and interests by giving them choices in what they read and in how they responded. We immersed children in reading a wide range of books and other reading materials for many different purposes. We brought many different kinds of reading engagements into the classroom including wide uninterrupted reading (SSR), Readers Theater, Shared Reading, and read-aloud. The classroom library became the focal point of the classroom, and students were given time each day to self-select books to read during wide reading. They didn't have to write a book report about these books. They just read books of their choice alone or with a partner. With younger children, we read predictable books, often in the form of "big books," and then encouraged children to use the author's structure as a way to compose their own texts. With all children, we read aloud many pieces of literature which pushed their understandings and connected to their inquiries. Through these many extensive reading engagements, they gained fluency and flexibility as readers and built a repertoire of reading strategies and experiences.

Students no longer read to practice reading or to learn reading skills so that someday they could read for their own purposes. They used reading to pursue their personal questions and interests, to explore class themes and topics, and to think about language. Through conversations and dialogue with others, they gained new perspectives on their reading that pushed them as inquirers. One way in which we encouraged their inquiry was through Literature Circles, where small groups of children gathered together to talk about their understandings and personal and literary connections to what they had read.

In Corey's first grade classroom, these Literature Circles played an important role in encouraging children to view reading as a critical thinking process of constructing meaning. They not only gained proficiency as readers through Shared Reading and wide reading, but also learned to think deeply about what they read. The texts they discussed in Literature Circles were often picture books that were read aloud to them.

Kathy and Gloria Kauffman also experimented with showing films of children's books like *Rosie's Walk* (Hutchins, 1968) and then inviting children to select their favorite film for a literature discussion. Once they selected the film group they wanted to join, children were asked to write thoughts or sketch images that crossed their minds as they watched the film and later looked at the book. They then came together in a Literature Circle to share what was on their minds. One of our favorite classroom videotapes is a group of first graders huddled around *Rosie's Walk* trying to figure out if Rosie knew that the fox was trailing her around the barnyard. The discussion was heated.

> "She looks like she knows—the expression on her face," says Erin. "I thought she would run," Amy says excitedly. Sherri argues, "If she knew the fox was following her, then she wouldn't have looked back so he wouldn't know that she knew." Sheila asks, "Couldn't she hear all that stuff coming down behind her like the flour, the splash, and the wheelbarrow?" "Maybe she's deaf," comment both Amy and Michael. "She might have had an earache," explains Jessica. "I had one once and I couldn't hear," contributes Billie Jo. "She doesn't look like she has any ears," says Sheila. Kathy asks if any of them know if hens have ears and Michael, a farm child, explains, "They have ears behind their heads. You can't see them in the pictures" (Short, 1986, p. 311–312).

Many children were initially reluctant to talk about what was really on their minds in these discussions because their previous school experiences led them to believe that teachers want right answers, not the child's thinking about the meaning of a story. Over time, however, these Literature Circles have become a place for students to think deeply and critically with other readers as they engage in collaborative inquiry about their transactions with books.

One of the surprising things that Kathy and Gloria found from their work with Literature Circles was that often children who could not handle the text prior to the experience of viewing the film, having the book read to them, and discussing it intensely, could read the book by the time the experience had ended. Meaning rather than phonics was their access point to reading.

In first grade, these Literature Circles usually lasted two to three days while circles with older children can last several weeks. Through these discussions, students revise their understandings by gaining new perspectives and attending to differences in how others think about the world and that particular piece of literature. As their circles come to an end, they share insights they have gained through their discussion of that book by putting together a presentation, often in a sign system other than language. Depending on the story, children create drama, write a piece of music, paint a mural, or develop a Readers Theater. These creations are shared and celebrated with other members of the class. The children use these experiences to reflect on themselves as readers and to plan goals for where they want to go next. These goals become the basis of strategy lessons on specific aspects of the reading process or authoring cycle and lead to new invitations as readers move into new experiences and actions.

We frequently begin our college methods classes by having students experience this same authoring cycle in reading. Jerry has often used adult short stories that are far from easy to understand on a first reading. *Granta,* a quarterly literary magazine which prides itself on publishing new authors and can be found in good bookstores everywhere, is an excellent source. Students are asked to read the selected story, write about their understandings, and then represent their meaning in art, music, sculpture, movement, or some sign system other than language. The next period they share in groups of five or six using Save the Last Word for the Artist. After each sharing, students are asked to jot down the insights they gained and to indicate if these were new insights or confirmations of insights they already had. Most times, ideas take on more saliency and significance after discussion. Once everyone has shared, students are asked to look over their initial understandings, the notes they made after each student shared their interpretation, and write about how the meaning of the story has changed for them. After doing this with three or four stories, students are asked to create an Insights into Reading paper discussing how these experiences have changed their conception of reading and what they see as the implications of these experiences for the teaching of reading in their future classrooms. If you have never participated in an experience like this, we suggest you try it. We have found no engagement that more quickly alters adult views of the reading process.

Adult Sketch to Stretch after reading *Grandad's Gifts* (Jennings, 1992); (Indiana University, Purdue University, Indianapolis [IUPUI] Summer Workshop on Multiple Literacies, Indianapolis, IN, Summer, 1994)

Section One
The Authoring Cycle:
Let's Talk Curriculum

Sign Systems and Interdisciplinary Studies as Authoring Processes

The authoring cycle can also serve as a curricular framework for other sign system processes. In Ray Levi's second-grade classroom, children authored texts in music and art as well as in language (Levi, 1991). Using the authoring cycle as a curricular frame, Ray reconceptualized his art and music program. Building from the notion of Written Conversations in which children take turns "talking on paper" (Clyde, 1986), Ray provided pairs of musical instruments in the Music Center and invited children to have a musical conversation with each other by playing the two instruments. Ray also provided paper and pencils and suggested that some children might wish to try their hand at recording their creations. Many children took up this invitation, sharing and discussing their musical creations at Authors Circle time later in the week. Ray, an elementary teacher trained in music education, introduced the vocabulary of music as well as musical notations as the need arose. Visitors to his classroom were often amazed to find that children who had requested an Authors Circle were as likely to bring a piece of art or a musical composition to the circle as they were a piece of writing. After discussion, children would return to their projects, often to revise them following the suggestions they had received. We were impressed with the fluidity with which children were able to talk about both art and music.

Song; Darcy, Age 7
(compliments of Mary Hill)

In South Carolina, Tim O'Keefe, Heidi Mills, and David Whitin began using the authoring cycle as a framework for thinking about mathematics. Building off the life experiences of children in Tim's classroom (losing teeth; the number of walkers as opposed to the number of bus riders) children were invited to think like mathematicians, deciding for themselves how to collect data as well as how to organize and display these data. Envisioning mathematics as a set of concepts which allow us to think about our world quite differently, children were invited (often through the reading of a key piece of children's literature) to explore and share their world in new ways (Whitin & Wilde, 1993; Whitin, Mills, & O'Keefe, 1990).

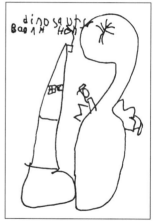

Comparison of a dinosaur to a house; Jerry, Age 7
(Tim O'Keefe's classroom)

In addition to using the authoring cycle to construct meaning in a variety of sign systems, several classroom teachers have been using the authoring cycle as a way to conceptualize interdisciplinary units of study. In Tom Wendt's fifth-grade classroom in Arlington Heights, Ohio, children did a unit on canals which grew out of their interests

Chapter One
Visions of Literacy

in local canals and Ohio history (Harste & Jurewicz, 1991–94). Tom began by collecting as many tradebooks as he could, such as books on the construction of canals, stories about people who came to Ohio as a function of the canals, and Civil War tales that include the use of canals. He introduced the unit through an engagement called Pass. Each child was given a book and allowed just thirty seconds to look through it before it was passed on to the next child. After playing several rounds of this, children were invited to find a book they would like to read that had passed through their hands. If two children selected the same book, they became partners. Tom said he used this engagement because often the large stacks of books he brought into the classroom went unexplored. By opening the cover and scanning the table of contents, children got a sense of the resources available in the room. Following reading, children identified topics they wished to explore. Tom webbed these on the blackboard, forming and reforming the web to create groups of children who might collaborate together on their projects. In doing their research children were encouraged to interview community members, build models, and visit museums in addition to reading about their topic.

As part of the unit Tom read aloud *Zoar Blue* (1978) authored by Janet Hickman, a local Ohio author, about the Civil War and the people who were brought to Ohio because of the canals. Later in the study, Tom invited the author to the classroom. She not only read favorite sections of her book but became a resource for groups of students who were engaged in research on different dimension of canals. Several field trips to the sites of old canals were taken as a class. As a culminating activity, children were invited to share their insights using whatever sign systems they wished. One group built a model of a canal lock, another created their own story, while a third group made up a trivial pursuit game on canals which stumped many a parent and other visitors. Final projects were shared during Authors Circle, revised, and displayed publicly at an open house to which parents came and rotated from group to group hearing what their child and others had learned.

These experiences with authoring through writing, reading, art, mathematics, and other content areas allowed us to see the authoring cycle as a general framework for curriculum and to expand our definition of authoring. We observed that, regardless of the knowledge system or sign system involved, children had:

1. constructed meaning from their experiences;
2. engaged in many uninterrupted attempts to construct meaning;
3. informally explored and negotiated some of their constructions with others;
4. revised and reflected on their constructions;
5. shared and presented their authoring to others in a public form;
6. examined through reflection the processes they used to construct meaning; and
7. moved ahead to accept new invitations to form still other texts.

Both children and teachers came to see these activities as a learning cycle, not just a writing cycle.

One of the advantages of the authoring cycle as a curricular frame is that it gets played out differently in different settings (Mills & Clyde, 1990). Despite this strength what bothered us, as we applied the authoring cycle to ever new curricular areas, was that the basic structure of schooling was not being changed. The traditional school subject areas—mathematics, reading, science, social studies—reigned supreme. Seeing authoring as inquiry provided us with a frame for re-thinking schooling and curriculum more generally. The section that follows shows how our current work in schools builds from the authoring cycle as well as establishes an evaluative framework for curriculum development more generally.

Curriculum as Collaborative Inquiry

There are several ways to think about curriculum. In the past curriculum was seen as a course to be run. Some state departments see curriculum as a listing of the skills that should be taught. A lot of commercial publishers present curriculum as if it were nothing but a set of cute activities, as if the key to good teaching was to make sure everyone was having a good time. Where these activities take teachers and children, other than keeping everyone busy, is questionable.

Curriculum is too important to be destroyed through misuse. By way of contrast, we see curriculum as a metaphor for the lives we want to live and the people we want to become. That is why we start this book with a chapter on visions of literacy. How we envision children, how we define literacy, how we see education, makes a difference. In a way curriculum is our invitation to imagine a different future as well as create classrooms where children create a new reality—a reality that we think will make a significant difference.

In this regard, there are three aspects of the authoring cycle that bear particular notice. First, the cycle calls attention to the underlying processes of inquiry. If the cycle is our framework for thinking about education, then curriculum should focus on and support the underlying processes of inquiry. Activities that are planned should do more than keep children busy. They need to go somewhere. While they might highlight a particular process (help children build from the known, find their own inquiry question, gain a new perspective, and so forth), they need to fit a larger purpose.

Second, the cycle's focus is on learning or inquiry. This is the larger purpose. Education, first and foremost, is about learning. It is about outgrowing ourselves through inquiry.

Inquiry, given the authoring cycle as a curricular frame, is not a technique but the very focus of the curriculum. Inquiry is not a skill children should learn, but a framework for viewing education. In the past we taught problem solving as part of a unit in mathematics and inquiry as part of a unit in science or history and then we were done. In contrast, the authoring cycle as a curricular frame puts inquiry at the center of what education is all about.

Third, the authoring cycle is a model for professional education too. Teaching is a matter of inquiry. Children need to be our curricular informants and collaborators, but there is no getting teaching right. As professionals we too are always learning and growing. That is why the authoring cycle keeps changing. As we engage in teacher research we learn more and we grow.

Many teachers feel that what happens at universities is irrelevant to their lives in classrooms. All that theory has nothing to do with teaching. But this is a misperception. The whole of education is of one cloth. Theory and practice go hand in hand. What teachers do in classrooms makes a difference in the theories being developed. By the same token, how academics think about education makes a practical difference in classrooms. When experimental research was king, classrooms focused on the teaching of isolated skills, controlled vocabulary, and correct answers. As researchers observed young children learning in natural language settings, the value of creating these contexts in classrooms also became apparent and many educators began to explore more holistic and collaborative learning environments.

Recently, there has been a new shift. Instead of seeing research as objective and language as value free, researchers are now realizing how subjective the whole process is. Research doesn't stand in some exalted position. Good research has to unpack issues as well as interrogate the values inherent in the project itself. The only thing research can do is help a learner or a community of learners interrogate their values. It can't say what is truth and what is not. But, this is good enough. Despite the fact that researchers can't make some claims they used to make, the more limited things research can do makes it valuable in its own right.

What makes this latter shift so significant is that inquiry is changing its stance in education. It has gone from being a skill to being a philosophical position on what both teachers and children do in the name of learning. This shift parallels the changes we have made in the authoring cycle over time too, and it's also why the authoring cycle gets at what is basic about school reform as we move to the twenty-first century.

Currently there is a lot of talk about school restructuring. Unfortunately, much of this talk deals with surface changes to the nature of classrooms. Instead of one grade level, schools are moving to multiage classrooms. Instead of moving children to a new teacher each year, schools are experimenting with multiyear classrooms. While reforms of this sort are long overdue, they do not in themselves constitute real change in education. If interaction patterns in classrooms don't change, then nothing is really different. One can have multiage and multiyear classrooms and still have dreadful instruction. To change education requires a shift in the nature of teacher-student, student-student, student-content area interaction.

That's why the authoring cycle as a curricular frame is so important. It gets at basic change. Its intent is to transform the interaction patterns in classrooms—how teachers talk to children, how children talk to each other, how teachers and children position themselves relative to sign systems and knowledge systems. In the past these were subjects teachers and children studied but did not make their own.

As we looked at our use of the authoring cycle over time, we realized that regardless of the various permutations we had created of the authoring cycle for different curricular areas, the focus of the cycle

FIGURE 1.15
Curriculum as Inquiry (Short, 1993)

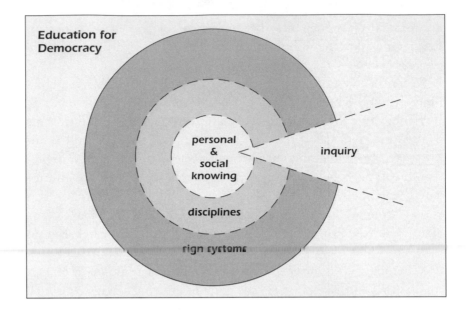

was always on inquiry. Given these connections we proposed *collaborative inquiry* as the focus of our new curriculum, arguing at a practical level that the only thing we can guarantee for children is that they are going to face problems of great magnitude which they are going to have to solve collaboratively.

Figure 1.15 shows how we are now envisioning curriculum given this recent change in thinking (Short, 1993). From studies of language learning we know that no one can become literate without personal involvement in literacy. Curriculum begins in voice. Learners not only have the right but also the responsibility to name and theorize their world. There is no place for learning to begin other than by making connections between the known and unknown. Personal and social knowing is the heart of the curriculum.

Subject areas have a stranglehold on curriculum right now. Even "the integrated curriculum" begins from the assumption that the subject areas are rightfully the center of curriculum, and the only real problem is that we need to integrate them more. Instead of emphasizing the facts and skills of subject areas, we focus on knowledge systems as perspectives which inquirers might take in exploring a topic of interest to them. In some ways knowledge systems are like syntax in language. Just as syntax is an explanation of how language is structured, so knowledge systems represent various perspectives or ways of structuring knowledge about the world. Each knowledge system has its own focusing question. Historians are interested in how the past might inform the present and future. Ecologists are interested in how what we do affects the balance of nature. By rotating our questions through the knowledge systems we gain new insights. In our curricular model, knowledge systems become research perspectives used by inquirers rather than dead bodies of knowledge that must be mastered.

Language, art, music, drama, mathematics, and movement are sign systems. They represent ways humans have learned to mediate the world in an attempt to make and share meaning. The wedge in Figure 1.15 represents inquiry. It cuts across all of the other systems, thereby suggesting that an alternative way to organize curriculum is around inquiry questions of personal and social interest. Knowledge systems and sign systems become tools that inquirers flexibly use in collaboration with others to explore, share, and make meaning. From our perspective the smallest unit of curriculum is a focused inquiry.

It is important to understand that what meanings get made, shared, and explored is determined in part by the context of situation in which education is embedded. Education in our society means education for a democracy. If some sign systems and ways-of-knowing are valued over others or if some forms of inquiry are privileged over others the whole model is changed. In this way both multiple ways-of-knowing and inquiry become tied to issues of access, equity, and justice.

Curriculum as inquiry is not something that happens from one o'-clock to three o'clock in the afternoon in school. It is not a clever device for integrating the curriculum through themes. Nor is it a skill we can teach by doing a unit on the experimental method in science.

Curriculum as inquiry is a philosophy, a way to view education holistically. Inquiry is education; education is inquiry. Teaching reading as inquiry is quite different from teaching reading as comprehension. All of a sudden we are more interested in the tension different interpretations offer than we are in arriving at consensus as to what the story means. Writing as inquiry is different from teaching writing as a skill that is to be mastered. Inquiry is more than problem solving. Problem solving suggests a right answer; inquiry suggests alternate answers as we unpack the complexity of issues. Problems are not something to be avoided, but opportunities to inquire. The very act of teaching itself becomes a process of inquiry. Teachers and students are all inquirers.

If the authoring cycle is to serve as a powerful framework for curriculum, it must be anchored in the underlying processes of inquiry.

Chapter One
Visions of Literacy

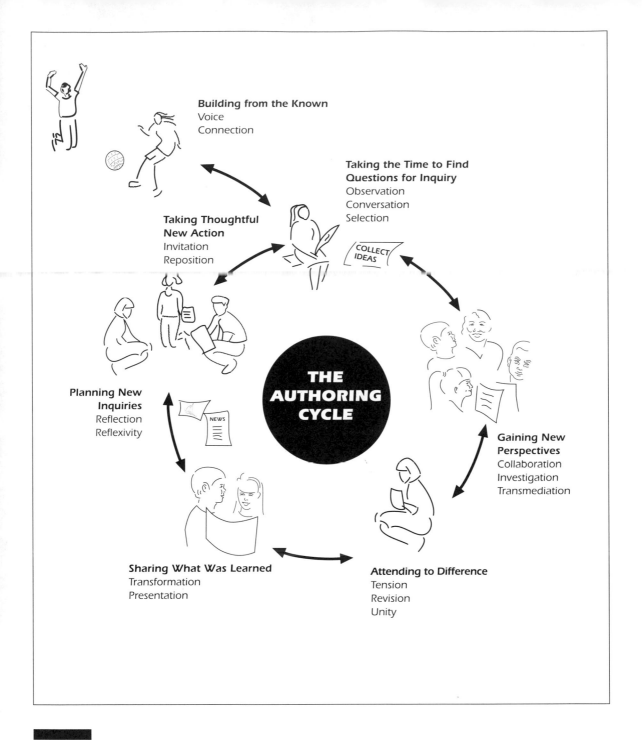

FIGURE 1.16
Underlying Processes of Inquiry
in the Authoring Cycle

Figure 1.16 highlights the seven key processes that we believe underlie all learning. These processes evolved from our teaching and research on language learning and represent characteristics of language and language users. They are the conditions for natural language use and learning that we believe must become part of classroom settings. We assume these same conditions are essential to the use and learning of other sign systems although we are still engaged in researching these systems.

Instead of a single literacy we need to think in terms of multiple literacies, where various ways of knowing and being are encouraged and enhanced. By defining literacy as the use of language, art, music, movement, and other sign systems to explore and expand our world, each of these underlying processes is enhanced as a potential of schooling to serve a democratic multicultural society. What rules operate pragmatically in our society—whether art, music, mathematics, movement, and so forth, are seen as legitimate ways of knowing—determine the kind of democracy we have as these decisions affect who participates and whose voice gets heard.

The following section overviews our most recent thinking about inquiry and briefly introduces each of the seven key processes. We will return to these processes as we discuss the authoring cycle in Chapters 2, 3, and 4 and examine them in depth in Chapter 5. You may not understand them completely at this point. The rest of the book is organized to extend and explore these processes in greater depth both theoretically and practically. Because an inquiry curriculum is set up to support these processes, an understanding of these processes is essential to curriculum development.

Building from the Known: Voice/Connection

All children come to school with experiences and language. Although some educators may not personally like the particular experiences and/or language children bring with them to school, it is this base from which children grow. Seeing the world from the back of a pick-up truck may very well be a more vital experience than seeing it from the back seat of a Volvo. Regardless, it is a different experience, and it is these differences that set up conversation as well as reflection. Children need to be assured that what is on their mind is legitimate. Voice means that curricular invitations need to be open-ended and provide choice.

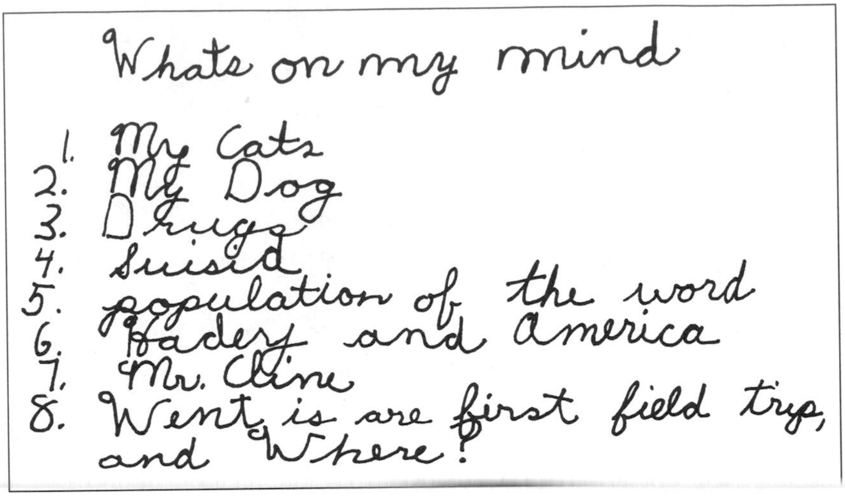

FIGURE 1.17
List of Possible Inquiry
Questions (Rise Paynter's
classroom)

Whate on my mind

1. My Cats
2. My Dog
3. Drugs
4. Suisid
5. population of the word
6. fader and America
7. Mr. Cline
8. Went is are first field trip,
   and Where?

Children also come to school with strengths in various areas. Some may be good in art, others in language, still others in music. Although what children know in one area can be used to support growth and development in other areas, a good curriculum expands the communication potential of each learner. Language, art, music, mathematics, and movement are all ways of knowing. We do a disservice to children and to ourselves if schools limit our ways of knowing by valuing one form of knowing over others.

Students need to feel free to recontextualize what it is they think teachers want in terms of their own experience and in terms of what makes sense to them. The goal of school is not so much to get children to outgrow their commonsense ways-of-knowing as it is to legitimize and make real connections with these literacies. Throughout life these experiences are our anchor and touchstone. When life gets difficult, the connections most of us seek are to our homes and the forms of making sense we learned there. The agenda ahead for educators is to learn to successfully negotiate family and school literacy rather than to assume that the function of schooling is to estrange one from one's roots.

Taking the Time to Find Questions for Inquiry: Observation/Conversation/Selection

Inquiry does not occur on demand or when learners are forced to pursue someone else's topic or question. They need time to find the questions that really matter in their lives. To do so requires time to immerse themselves in observing the world and in conversations with

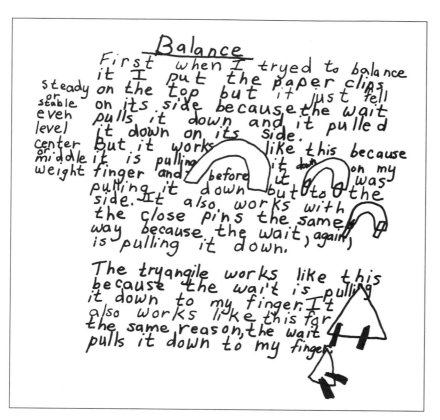

FIGURE 1.18
Journal; Melissa, Age 8 (Gloria
Kauffman's classroom)

other learners so they can find those questions that are significant to them. They need to time to read, write, observe, talk, listen, paint, sing, and dance as they explore their worlds.

To be declared a writer one not only has to know how to write but has to have something to say. Writing really begins in observation. Noticing things that others haven't and then writing about them is what sets one in position to be recognized as a writer. Writing as inquiry begins by inviting learners to observe the world in new ways.

Observation is the key to all learning. All new learning, all advances in the knowledge systems, begins by someone noticing something new through observation. What makes this even more remarkable is that we only have five senses; we only have five ways of gathering new observational data. The implications of this insight is what is behind Elliot Eisner's observation that to become educated is to educate the senses (1982).

The creation and use of sign systems, of course, supports the educative process. Language did not develop because there was one language user, but two, and they wished to communicate. Some would go so far as to argue that it is language that makes us human. We agree, if language is taken to mean the language of art, of music, and more. These languages or sign systems are what connects us to others. They are ways that we have found to mediate and make sense of the world. Susan Langer (1980) says they represent humankind's finest accomplishments. Often we do not even know what we believe until we have heard what others believe.

Conversation is key. Knowledge, formerly considered static, is now seen as socially constructed. Conversation is informal, free-flowing. Through conversation we make connections with what we already know as well as identify new possibilities for exploration. Learning begins on our own terms, with the connections that we personally make to the life experience we have had. Learners need to be given time to find and select their own inquiry questions. Curriculum invitations which allow children to construct, ask questions, converse, and find ways to express what they already know support the inquiry process. Conversation allows us to wander and wonder, to find our way, to observe, to identify a personal thought collective. Through conversation we can try different stances on for size and in the process select an inquiry question that is of personal interest to us. This selection process should not be rushed as it represents commitment to a intellectual position without which we cannot grow.

Gaining New Perspectives:
Collaboration/Investigation/Transmediation

Learners gain new perspectives on their experiences by taking the risk to state what they believe. This process makes thinking public so others can help by providing critical challenges through dialogue. Unlike conversation, dialogue is intense and purposeful. Participants

FIGURE 1.19
Learning Log; Miranda, Age 9
(Gloria Kauffman's classroom)

Section One
The Authoring Cycle:
Let's Talk Curriculum

When I came in I didnt know many kids and I was shy but when we did a interview I felt better. I've changed as a writer beacause I can share ideas with everone in the room. Beacause I accept everyone in my class it is easier to understand and accept people in the world for their differences join in for the purpose of understanding, critiquing, exploring, and constructiog meaning. Ideas, not people, are at risk. Others are used to gain new perpectives and to help one outgrow one's very self.

Another way to gain perspective is by taking what we know in language and recasting it into another sign system, a process called transmediation. How different does the Vietnam War look through music rather than through language? What new perspectives on Vietnam do we gain as a function of looking at it in this new way? The feelings and messages we get about war from listening to songs about the Vietnam War are usually very different than the images we get from reading about that war in a book. More often than not, transmediation allows us to get in touch with the qualitative dimensions of a topic.

Rotating a topic under investigation through various knowledge systems is a third way to gain new perspectives. Each knowledge system has its own focusing question as well as its own tools and way of thinking about a topic. What do historians have to say about this subject? How does how they go about their research affect what they have to say? What do psychologists have to say? What is the ecological impact of doing things this way? Researchers know that seeing the topic of their investigation with as many eyes as possible from as many perspectives as possible expands their outlook as well as increases the odds that they will both see something new and have something new to say.

Attending to Difference: Tension/Revision/Unity

The mind has been envisioned by Gregory Bateson as a pattern finder and a pattern maker (1979). From this perspective comprehension and learning are explained as processes involving the finding of patterns that connect. When what we observe matches what we know, comprehension occurs. When what we see doesn't match with what we know, tension results. To find a new unity we have to revise our existing theory of how the world works.

A theory of difference is a theory of learning. Difference, not consensus, propels the learning process. The mind gravitates to the new and the different. That is why you often remember the asides rather than the main points in a lecture. Differences cause tension and put an edge on learning. Differences force us to revise what we thought we knew and to seek a new unity through the use of logic. Learners have nothing to learn by concentrating on what they already know. Attending to difference as well as focusing on the new, the anomaly, the surprise is more efficient. When the surprise makes sense, learning has occurred.

Story ("The tooth fairy took my tooth. No dime."); Justin, Age 7 (compliments of Joby Copenhaver)

Chapter One
Visions of Literacy

If you understand the role that tension plays in learning, then you can begin to understand what is wrong with standardized testing, behavioral objectives, national standards, and other educational movements that see like-mindedness and conformity as the goals of education. Democratic societies are enhanced through diversity. Strong democratic communities work best when differences are acknowledged and members of the community see diversity as a potential rather than a problem.

Sharing What Was Learned: Transformation/Presentation

Although one is rarely done revising a piece of writing, rethinking a piece of literature, or completely researching a topic of personal interest, there comes a moment when it is time to share what was learned. Presenting is never just a matter of pulling together what was learned. Different audiences call for different presentations. How you talk with colleagues about education as inquiry is very different from how you talk about education as inquiry with a friend who is not in the field of education. What we know has to be transformed. In one case we may use an overhead, in another we need a concrete example or a nice folksy metaphor. In one case we may do a lot of talking—language is used to carry the major message; in another case a picture or a quick sketch will do.

Presentation is never a form of regurgitation. From the storehouse of what is known, learners pull and transform information for purposes of creating just the right multimodal text for a specific context. This is why the process of presentation can be very generative. How does the old adage go? You never really know something until you try to teach it. What you thought you understood often needs further clarification when presented to others. While learning always involves finding patterns that connect, new insights often signal needed new conversations to be started. Because presenting involves connecting what we know to particular issues at hand, it calls for new thinking. Transformation and presentation provide learners the opportunity to clarify for themselves and others the contributions their work has made to the functioning of the various thought collectives of which they are a part.

Planning New Inquiries: Reflection/Reflexivity

Learners take time to reflect—to think about what they have learned for purposes of planning new inquiries. Careful reflection begins by reconstructing the process of inquiry for purposes of bringing what

Begging

They beg to you for a penny.

One little penny. What is so wrong with that.

The government and presadent were here to make high dessissions and help.

So who are they helping throwing people on the streets.

They can't afford taxes.

Give them a penny to survive the streets.

Dominois

Dominois hit one by one Til they all have fallen down.
One by one they dissapear Like people when they die They hit each other to make them fall
It's just like people They push and push until everyone is down including themselves.
They do not care because the job is done.
Theres nothing left to do.

Poems; Tara, age 11 (Gloria Kauffman's classroom)

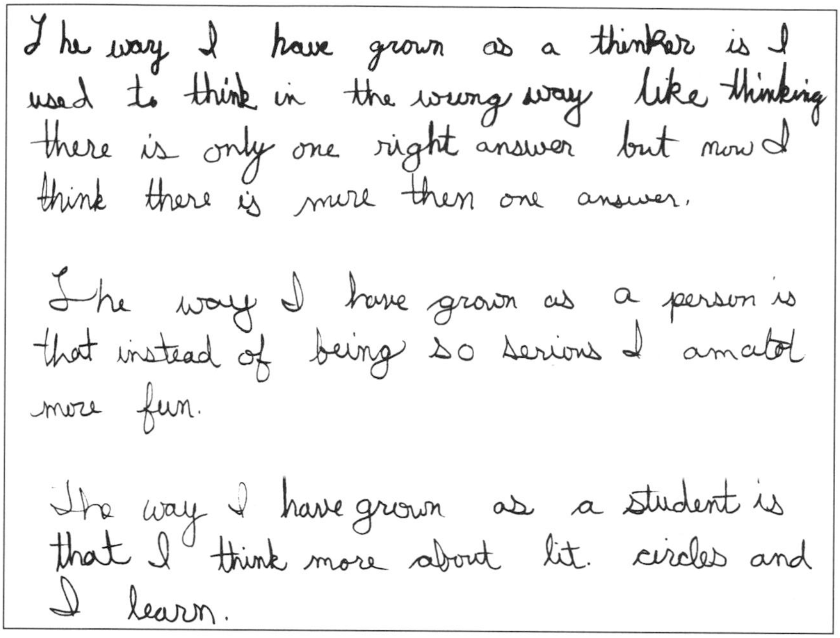

> The way I have grown as a thinker is I used to think in the wrong way like thinking there is only one right answer but now I think there is more then one answer.
>
> The way I have grown as a person is that instead of being so serious I am alot more fun.
>
> The way I have grown as a student is that I think more about lit. circles and I learn.

FIGURE 1.20
Reflection; Lynn, Age 9
(Gloria Kauffman's classroom)

worked and what didn't work in clearer focus. By retracing the mental trip that was taken as well as by assessing each component of the process, learners become consciously aware of what worked, thus increasing the likelihood that what was learned about both the content and process of inquiry will be of use in the future.

Because the only thing that inquiry can do is help a learner or a community of learners interrogate their values, reflexivity means that learners are forced to reexamine, if not interrogate, the very constructs they are using to make sense of the world. As inquirers and authors of this book, for example, we need to ask ourselves why is it that we see meaning and inquiry as the core of language and learning. By prioritizing these constructs, what other ideas can't surface? Who benefits and who gains if education is conceived as inquiry? What new voices get heard? What new conversations get started? What conversations and voices get stopped? Can we morally and ethically live with these outcomes? Assuming we can withstand this sort of interrogation, what new inquiries should we be pursuing?

Taking Thoughtful New Action: Invitation/Reposition

As a result of inquiry, learners literally reposition themselves both mentally and physically in the world for purposes of taking thoughtful new action. What we have learned has to cause us to interact differently in the world. From a social perspective we have to position ourselves

Chapter One
Visions of Literacy

Letter; Marianne, Age 6
(Vasques, 1994)

TRANSLATION:
Dear John Watson
Next year I
Don't want to
go in a portable
because when it [is]
hot it [is] very hot
and when it [is] cold it [is]
very cold so I don't
want to
Marianne

differently. Our identity as well as the identity of others has been affected. We simply are not the same people. The ground has shifted in terms of how we stand in relationship to friends and knowledge systems. Business cannot go on as usual. If, in the final analysis, interactional patterns do not change, nothing very much has happened.

Now is also the time to take thoughtful new action in the world. Now is a time to consider what new invitations you want to offer others as well as explore for yourself. Here is the opportunity to invite yourself and others to live a different curriculum—to live the life you really want to live and to become the people you really want to be.

Conclusion

We have a new vision of literacy, schooling, and curriculum. When we envision curriculum as inquiry, we see a community of learners in the process of collaboratively constructing knowledge as they continually seek understandings of personal and social significance from new perspectives—new sign system perspectives, new knowledge system perspectives, new social perspectives—for purposes of creating a more just, a more equitable, a more thoughtful world. Our vision for literacy does not discriminate against severely labeled children, minority groups, or children born to parents who happen to reside in the inner city. From what we can tell, there is only one learning process and it is the same for rich kids and poor kids, African Americans and Hispanic Americans, gifted and talented as well as for children labeled learning disabled.

We are not alone in these beliefs. The experts, teachers, classrooms, and programs featured in this volume and the videotape series *Visions of Literacy* (Harste & Jurewicz, 1991–94) demonstrate what curriculum as inquiry looks like with various populations (at-risk learners, teacher-researchers) as well as in various subject areas (reading, social studies), and settings (multicultural education, early childhood education, the library).

We wanted to begin this volume by overviewing our current thinking about curriculum. By turning Figure 1.16 into a series of questions, we have created a basis by which we currently critique our work in classrooms as well as make curricular plans for the future.

Voice/Connection: Does the engagement build from the known so that all voices get heard?

Observation/Conversation/Selection: Have learners been provided the time to find their own inquiry questions?

Collaboration/Investigation/Transmediation: What new perspectives will be gained and what new conversations will be started?

Tension/Revision/Unity: How are tensions being used to put an edge on everyone's learning?

Transformation/Presentation: Have opportunities for sharing what is learned been put into place?

Reflection/Reflexivity: Are learners being supported in planning new inquiries?

Invitation/Reposition: Have structures for continuing new conversations been planned so that thoughtful new action can be taken?

These questions represent conditions for learning given our current theories. You may find, as we and other teacher researchers have found, that these questions help you and the learners in your classroom devise as well as select new strategy lessons and curricular engagements for your classroom. Together they constitute a set of beliefs about how best to restructure schools to support literacy learning in democratic classrooms. Theory is a self-correcting device. Not only does it provide guidance, but it forces us to grow when, using children as our curricular informants, we encounter data that do not correspond with what we currently know.

Good learners assume that one tenet in their theory is wrong. The big problem is that they don't know which tenet it is! Over the years our model of curriculum has grown and expanded though some ideas have remained intact. We wanted to begin by sharing our latest thinking. In the sections that follow we trace our journey as well as explain in some detail what we see as the key elements of each of the curricula we created. This book was not written to convince you that our model of curriculum is right; rather, our purpose is to start some much needed new conversations in education. We acknowledge one fundamental truth: What educators believe makes a big curricular difference for themselves and for the children they teach.

■ Tim O'Keefe has been a teacher for sixteen years and has taught all grades from Head Start through sixth grade in self-contained and alternative settings. He is the co-author of two books, **Living and Learning Mathematics: Stories and Strategies Supporting Mathematical Literacy** (Heinemann, 1990) and **Looking Closely: Examining the Role of Phonics in One Whole Language Classroom** (NCTE, 1992) and has published numerous articles and chapters on education and young children. He lives in South Carolina with his wife and co-researcher, Heidi Mills, and his two young children, Devin and Colin.

Teachers as Kidwatchers

TIM O'KEEFE

It was getting close to Halloween and our second grade class was finally feeling like a community. It had taken a while but, just like every year, by mid October enough of a routine was established that the children were becoming independent and working well together. At this time of the year when everything seemed to be running so smoothly, a new student appeared at the door.

He came at the beginning of writer's workshop, and so I had some time to get to know him. He said as little as possible, answering my questions with single words. He totally avoided eye contact with me. When he wrote his name on a folder, it was clear that he didn't know how to spell his first name.

I immediately jumped to conclusions about him. I began thinking selfishly that our class was becoming crowded after all and that he would require a lot of my already thinned out attention. I had him pegged as a problem from our first conversation.

After I explained our workshop routine and showed him around the room, he seated himself at his desk and quietly wrote in his new notebook. He worked deliberately and rarely looked up from his writing. After about half an hour he walked up to me, notebook in hand.

When he softly read his Halloween poem, he showed me what a fool I was to judge him. I realized later that he didn't know how to spell his name because he had always gone by a nickname and he was, in a sense, experimenting with a new name in his new school. His unconventional writing was used to create a beautifully descriptive poem with clear images that demonstrated a wonderful understanding of language. When he read it to the class just over an hour after he arrived I was deeply moved. Moved not only from the sheer beauty of his poem but also because he unwittingly put me in my place. How could I call myself a whole language teacher and fall into the trap of making judgments about someone based on his use of conventions?

The lessons I learned from that little boy will always stay with me. He showed me the disproportionate amount of importance I place on correctness. He showed me what a mistake it is to use conventions to make assumptions. He showed me the importance of risk taking (he was, after all, sharing a new piece of writing with a strange group of people less than ninety minutes after arriving at his new school). He reminded me that our best teachers in the business of education are our students. And he reminded me to practice what I preach.

While this story is somewhat embarrassing to share, I think it captures the essence of kidwatching for it is through kidwatching that we can more effectively and honestly evaluate and plan for our students and, perhaps, become better people ourselves.

What is Kidwatching?

Educators have been watching students as long as classrooms have been in existence. As classroom teachers, we cannot live and learn with students without observing important events that affect how we look at our students. But merely watching students does not significantly alter classroom practice. Yetta Goodman (1978) defined kidwatching and how it can be used effectively to monitor and report student progress and development. "The best alternatives to testing come from direct and, in most cases, informal observation of the child in various situations by the classroom teacher. Since the process itself is somewhat informal, perhaps the term 'kidwatching' is preferable to the more formal 'observation'. Either way the process is the same" (p. 43).

Put simply, kidwatching is learning to see what's there and using that information to create a better classroom (Burke, 1991). Watching children carefully to inform the curriculum is a part of many teachers' classroom routine. Like an authoring cycle curriculum, kidwatching is necessarily put into effect differently from classroom to classroom. It may also look different within the same classroom from year to year. It is a continuous, systematic look at the process of how students learn. It is taking what we know about students and turning that knowledge into effective instructional invitations. It is reporting to students and parents about authentic learning. It is valuing the contributions each child makes within the learning community that is our classroom. It is helping children to realize who is an expert at what and who they can turn to when they need assistance. It is giving voice to students who might otherwise be silent. It is getting to know each child in as many different contexts as possible—to know each child as a person unique in all the world. It is the fuel for our desire to know more about the learning process as well as the continuous refinement of our craft as teachers. Kidwatching is not something apart from the curriculum but rather it is what holds it together and pushes it forward into new and often unexplored territory.

The only way to write this chapter is to divide my stories into categories for explaining the role of kidwatching in my classroom. This is a paradox that cannot be escaped. While describing the connecting thread throughout the curriculum I must write about *events* which may seem disjointed when viewed this way. With this in mind the following stories and anecdotes come from my most recent teaching experience, a second-grade self-contained classroom.

Conditions for Kidwatching

The power of kidwatching lies in the fact that each year—indeed every day—is remarkably different from any other. Obviously, in order to be an effective kidwatcher there must be something worthwhile to observe. Part of the teacher's job then becomes making sure that exciting things can and do happen in the classroom by creating a rich, stimulating environment in which students can truly inquire. Along with an environment which sparks curiosity the classroom must also be a forum from which the young learners can make their discoveries and hypotheses known to their peers. The classroom should be a truly public place where the students and teacher wonder aloud, eliciting feedback from the rest of the group.

To have an effective classroom where kidwatching can occur, there must be authentic conversation within an atmosphere of trust. Students must trust that the teacher and their peers will value their contributions, find their questions interesting and worthwhile and provide them with genuine, thoughtful feedback. The teacher must trust that children are self-motivated and are the best judges of what they need to work on. The teacher must also trust that the students' interests are valuable enough to actively pursue and that the students are capable teachers themselves. Indeed, if one truly believes in the inquiry process, then there is no learning in a social situation without also teaching (Watson, Burke, & Harste, 1990).

The Course of Inquiry

I cannot remember being a teacher without also being a kidwatcher. I have always taken meticulous notes about student work as well as in-process observations. The very act of recording insights makes me a more observant teacher. It wasn't until I became involved in a four-year research project with Heidi Mills and David Whitin from the University of South Carolina that I carried kidwatching into the big picture of curriculum development (Whitin, Mills, & O'Keefe, 1990).

While the second graders in our class all had their own inquiry projects independent of school, I found that, by being mindful of their interests and "hot topics," kidwatching can serve as the connecting element across the year leading us from inquiry to inquiry. In retrospect, the direction of our course of study this year seems like a series of careful maneuvers. In actual fact it was simply following a logical track from one topic to the next based on what the class found fascinating.

I often begin teaching in the fall with a unit on animals. This year was no different in that respect. I have many materials and books on animals, and know a lot about their classification, characteristics, and habitats. We have several class pets and the children are always excited about animals and have much to share from their own experiences.

During our study of gorillas we discovered some interesting books on Koko the gorilla (Patterson, 1987) in our school library. Koko is unique in that she continues to "speak" to humans through sign language. At that point I brought in some articles I had collected complete with photos of Koko and her trainer. One student discovered what we thought was an address for Koko and Dr. Patterson in the back of one of the books. During our next workshop everyone wrote letters with artwork.

The children became fascinated with sign language and the manual alphabet. Because of their obvious interest and because becoming familiar with another language could serve to strengthen their own, I extended their inquiry. I brought in a large manual alphabet chart to display in the room and one child, Sara, found a small copy in a children's magazine to duplicate for everyone. Soon we were inundated with books on sign language and the chalkboard ledge was filled to capacity. Students challenged each other by signing and spelling out words and sentences when they wanted to converse quietly. The entire class learned many signs and almost everyone learned the finger alphabet. Because of their interest, children brought in many additional materials for us to explore.

Corey Leigh brought in an easy-to-read biography of Helen Keller and suggested that I read it to the class since Helen Keller had to learn sign language to communicate. I read it gladly, marvelling at the connections being made by the students. After returning from the media center, several students noticed that there were other biographies of Helen Keller written for "big kids." I checked out two of these and proceeded to read them as our next read-aloud books.

Sara brought in *The Miracle Worker*, an academy award-winning movie that her parents had recorded from TV. In this age of high tech and action movie heros I would never have imagined that seven and eight year olds would have enjoyed a thirty-year-old, black-and-white film clearly made for an adult audience. They were riveted. Some of the fast-paced dialogue and unfamiliar vocabulary went by without complete understanding. This only made them hungry for more details. "Stop the video and let's talk!" became a frequent refrain as we watched the film over the course of three days. Many students started taking notes in their learning logs; they recorded ideas and questions they wanted to bring up during the the breaks.

Not only did we learn all about Helen Keller and her amazing accomplishments but we also learned about biography as a literary form. It was after all of this that I suggested writing biographies. It seemed like the perfect instructional invitation given the course of events of the year so far in school. Together we wrote a biography of Helen Keller as a class. For the next couple of weeks, afternoons were devoted to trips to the media center, reading and writing, Authors Circles, revisions, more reading and writing, drawing, discussion, debate, and more reading and writing. The biography projects culminated with presentations to the class and to many parents who came to school to watch their children present their work. After the children published their reports three of their peers and I filled out an

Biography Report Evaluation Form

Presenter's Name Matthew

Evaluator's Name Mishcie

This biography is about Martin Huther King

EFFORT ___+___   LENGTH ___+___   CREATIVITY ___✓___

INTEREST ___✓+✓___   ACCURACY ___+✓___   NEATNESS ___+___

VOICE ___✓+___   AUDIO VISUALS ___+___

Comments: I think he did goo on his report. I like his pechr. I I wndr wiy he waniu to do martin luthr King

Biography Report Evaluation Form

Presenter's Name Matthew T.

Evaluator's Name Mr.D.

This biography is about Martin Luther King (Junir)

EFFORT ___+___   LENGTH ___+___   CREATIVITY ___+✓___

INTEREST ___+___   ACCURACY ___+___   NEATNESS +

VOICE ___+___   AUDIO VISUALS ___+___

Comments: I could tell that you practiced. You must have read a lot! I knew a lot about Mr. King but now I even know more. You had a lot of important facts in your report. You really know about Dr. King! I'm proud of you.

evaluation form designed by the students. The children also filled out forms for themselves (see Figure TA1.1). The evaluation procedure and the form were collaboratively designed by the class and myself.

The course of our inquiry was clearly influenced, if not determined by, the interests of the students. That is not to say that I didn't make any curricular decisions. There could have been other directions taken based on what surfaced as interesting to the class. The biography was ultimately my request, but we all felt part of the progression of our inquiry. We progressed from a general study on animal classification, habitats, and characteristics to a more specific study of gorillas and on to an in-depth study of one particular gorilla (Koko). This led to an extensive study of sign language (which lasted the entire year), to learning about Helen Keller, and then to the study of biography as a literary form and the completion of individual biography reports. Our course of study was largely determined by the books, pictures, articles, and tapes the children brought in, the experiences and questions the children shared and what seemed logical to examine next. Each of our units were unique because the participants personalized them with their input. While my classes in the future may study gorillas, there is no way that I can simply look back at my lesson plans and bring out my "gorilla unit." The unit belongs to the children who helped to create it at that time and place.

For me to plan each unit of study or inquiry project before the year even begins seems ludicrous now that I realize the importance of student input. What a teacher *doesn't do* in his or her classroom may be just as important as what the teacher *does do*. Sometimes it is essential for us not to interfere with the natural curiosity and excitement within a group by imposing our agendas. Often the students' agenda is not only more important but also provides much more potential for authentic inquiry. This act of paying attention to the students' agenda is kidwatching. Kidwatching is the difference between planning *with* children and planning *for* them.

Kidwatching Through Journals, Notebooks, and Logs

There are many opportunities for kidwatching in my classroom including carefully examining the journals, notebooks, and logs that students keep as part of our ongoing inquiry. At the beginning of this school year, Mary was thinking like a scientist. Sitting near the window in the science area she recorded her thoughts in the science journal. She shared her entry during the morning meeting the next day.

Mary's Science Journal Entry

MARY	I do not know where you got that greenish, brownish bug from Mr. O'Keefe. Where did you get it? And I just saw a big hornet and now I see a little bug crawling on the window. Now I know what you mean when you say "When you think like a scientist everything is science."
O'KEEFE	Tell us more about what you were thinking, Mary.
MARY	I mean like I saw a big hornet and I say to myself "how do hornets fly? How do hornets sting? What other stuff do they do?"
O'KEEFE	Do you think that thinking like a scientist means asking lots of questions?
MARY	Yeah!
COREY LEIGH	Scientists observe things like she was doing.
MCKENZIE	How do scientists do things like figure out how wasps can do things like fly?
O'KEEFE	Good question.
MARY	I think they find interesting things to study, and they just look at it with a microscope and stuff.

Teacher Article One
Teachers as
Kidwatchers

O'KEEFE	So Mary thinks that scientists sometimes examine animals' bodies to find out how they do what they do.
MARY	And they see how they do all their stuff without trying to hurt them.
O'KEEFE	I notice that other children have been wondering in the science journal as well. Corey wondered the other day what bees use to make honey. Amy wondered how frogs swim. Cortney wondered why birds sing, and Matthew wondered why Bingo (our class pet, an African water frog) jumps up and down in his water.

I was greatly impressed that Mary and her classmates shared their musings by publishing in the science journal. For years I have been aware of the value of public journals for discussion, recording the ideas of the class concerning certain topics and mapping our progress as we think through questions and record observations. By encouraging these young scientists to record and share their questions and observations, the forum is set for a public exchange of ideas in which the children and myself become collaborators in the learning process. Everyone may add something that they know or may have observed for the benefit of the entire group and our collective understanding.

As a kidwatching teacher part of my responsibility is being sure that students have avenues to make their questions and discoveries known. Simply observing the wonderful, informative entries students make in the science journal does not make me a kidwatcher. My role in the process is to participate (I add journal entries almost every day) and to formalize the process by setting aside time each day at our class meetings for the children to wonder together about our world. In this way I become more familiar with the scientist within each child. By listening to and recording their responses to each other's entries, I can better prepare invitations. For example, if many children wonder about animal behavior, then the literature I share, the experiences I prepare, and the field studies I plan may help children follow through with these questions.

Creating classrooms where children's voices are valued is my quest as a teacher. By watching, listening, recording, encouraging, and extending the sharing of public journals—like the science journal—I become more aware of who the students are and how they think. Through this process all of the students become teachers. Concerns, queries, and experiences of individuals become the property and responsibility of the group.

Section One
The Authoring Cycle:
Let's Talk Curriculum

Kidwatching and the Reading Process

There are several ways in which I observe and record information regarding the learning process and development of students. Providing opportunities for students to write and publish journals is important. I also tape-record many large group conversations, individual reading samples, story discussions, Authors Circles, and celebrations of authorship. I have come to realize that the more I make my kidwatching explicit, the more the children realize how carefully I am thinking about what and how they are learning. I am convinced that they become more reflective and take more conscious control of their own learning. We become coresearchers: the children and I research *together* instead of my doing research on them. The very act of taking notes about what they are saying and recording tapes of our conversations highlights how important their thinking is to me.

Our tiny tape recorder is used to capture different kinds of events. When I replay a particularly effective Authors Circle for the class to hear, for example, the importance of effective questioning, positive and sincere response, and thoughtful listening all become apparent to the group. We can stop the tape and discuss certain aspects of the Authors Circle that really went well and why. During future Authors Circles the class becomes more mindful of their purpose.

In discussing literature I often take the time to record students' reactions. Holding the small tape recorder up to the students encourages them to be polite and to take turns, but more importantly it seems that the children are simply more thoughtful about *what* they share—often adding to or disagreeing with previous statements. At times, listening to the tapes during my drive home in the afternoon, I discover connections and insights missed during the original discussion. I also get a better sense of their understanding and analysis of literature. Listening to myself on the tapes also helps me to become a better questioner and clarifies for me what my role is in discussions. Occasionally, I find that I do too much of the talking.

A strategy I use to help me to know students better as readers is to periodically tape reading samples while recording anecdotal notes about their strategies. Yetta Goodman (1978) suggests that "tapes can be kept of a child's oral reading and retelling of a story or article at different times during the year. Together, the child and the teacher (and parents if possible) can examine the development that has taken place during the year and select areas that need more work" (p. 45). When the children have read for a few minutes or there is a natural break in the story, I rewind the tape, let the students listen, and then record comments they make concerning their own reading (Goodman, 1992). Their reactions range from a few words, "I think I'm pretty good," to great long explanations and revelations about the reading process. Below is a transcript from one such reading interview. Hart chose to read one of his favorite books, *The Wizard of Oz* by L. Frank Baum.

O'KEEFE   Now that you've listened to yourself what do you notice about yourself as a reader?

HART   I notice that my voice isn't too good. It doesn't sound like the Wizard should sound or like Dorothy would say it.

O'KEEFE   What about when you're reading by yourself or just reading inside your head?

HART   When I'm reading inside my head, I can just go SO fast.

O'KEEFE   I noticed how fast you are. Is the way you say the words inside your head just the way you want them to be?

HART   Sure!

O'KEEFE   How do you account for that? The fact that when you're reading out loud it doesn't sound the way you want it to.

HART   My voice isn't perfect as Cowardly Lion and Dorothy and the Tin Woodsman and Scarecrow. It might be good for one of them, but it's probably not good for all of them.

O'KEEFE   Is there anything else that you notice?

HART   I notice that I can read very, very, very fast in my head and I can't read very fast out loud.

O'KEEFE   Well, Hart. One way I can tell about how you're doing is to listen to you and to talk about what you're reading with you. I know that you are a fast reader and that you aren't looking at only a letter or even one word at a time. It seems like you look at whole groups of words. That's one thing that good readers do. You don't seem to need to sound out words much anymore.

HART   There are some words that are hard for me though. Like there was this dinosaur word that my sister and my mom didn't even know.

O'KEEFE   Believe me, every reader comes to unfamiliar words. What do you do, Hart, when you come to a word that you don't know?

HART   I kind of just skip it and keep reading on.

O'KEEFE   Do you understand what those words mean even if you can't say them out loud?

HART   Yeah.

This kind of kidwatching is a wonderful, evaluative tool. By discussing the reading process with individuals, I get a much clearer understanding of the cue systems they rely on and the strategies they use when they encounter unfamiliar words. The audio tapes along with the reading notes I take while "coaching" (see below) assist me in selecting materials to use for reading with individuals and help in designing strategy lessons. If, for example, I notice some children substituting words that are graphically similar but semantically distant from the text, I can prepare lessons to aid in focusing on meaning such as cloze or synonym substitute.

In addition to discussing and taping reading samples, I have developed a system of taking notes that helps me keep track of reading development and students' use of strategies. Included in my notes are: The student's name, the date of the sample, the text (most often self-selected), a subjective comment on the difficulty of the material for that individual, and any miscues that I notice. After each miscue I write down whether it was self-corrected and if the miscue seemed to change the meaning of the text. I also keep track of any spontaneous comments made during the reading sample and anything else that lends insight into the students' reading process such as, "points with right index finger," or, "pauses, looks at pictures for support," or, "stuck on 'impatient' and looks up for help." My recording strategies grew out of what I learned about the Reading Miscue Inventory from my undergraduate reading methods courses (Goodman & Burke, 1972).

I attempt to record at least one fairly lengthy reading sample from each student every month. From that data I can give individual feedback on reading during my response. My students and I call this time coaching. By knowing the predominant reading strategies my students use, the type of literature they enjoy reading, the difficulty of the material they select, and so forth, my responses to them as readers can be individualized. My coaching may range from agreeing that the student should select material that is interesting but a little more challenging, to asking the student to be aware of the meaning of the story so that it all makes sense, to helping the students to be more consistent in their use of letter sounds as well as word order to make meaning out of text. The information from my coaching notes informs me about my students and also serves as a rich source of information for reporting to parents.

Kidwatching During Writing Workshop

At the end of every workshop time we celebrate authorship. Those who have finished pieces of writing read their material to the class. The young authors read their pieces to their peers with greater ease as the year progresses. The listeners are more eager to hear their friends publish as they become familiar with characters being developed throughout the year and the writing styles of their peers. By using a microphone when the students publish, everyone, no matter how quiet their voices are, can be clearly heard. In my notes I keep an up-to-date class chart of all the titles, dates, and types of texts published (poem, story, song). My clipboard also contains many pages of anecdotal notes about how the children read, summaries of each piece, and a few sentences verbatim from each text which demonstrates the kind of language used.

> Jim W. 5/24 The Jungle In Mon-X—Two animals battle to see who is the real king of the jungle. Nicely read. Lots of intonation. . . ."I'm telling my king on you," said the lion. "I am too," said the gorilla. The last battle about to happen but the gorilla sets a mine. The lion's mane is burned off. At last the lion retreats. Spies, wizards, armies of animals. . . ."They were longing for another adventure!" Very much like an Oz story. One of the longest and best developed of his stories.

I often include comments about the length of the piece and characteristics of the book that make it unique in form (a dedication, an about the author section, a text divided into short stories or chapters, etc.) and any intertextual tics. My notes are a specific, long-term record of each child's writing accomplishments and development. I often refer to these when conferencing with children and parents and when each child presents finished books to the class and asks for comments and questions.

The ritual of getting my thoughts down on my clipboard helps me to internalize characteristics of the students as writers. Even if I never referred back to my notes for progress reports or conferences, by listening and watching carefully enough to write I come to know the students better. My notes make me aware of their strengths, favorite genres, elements of style, fluency, and their use of grammar. I use these insights to formulate plans for writing strategy lessons.

Kidwatching as an Invitation to Parent/School Partnerships

Unfortunately, I am saddled with an old-fashioned report card with discrete subject areas and A-F grades with a 1–3 effort scale. Part of my job is to keep parents informed of current trends in education and my own philosophy of education. While I must use the traditional re-port card in reporting student progress, I continually encourage parents to come and discuss how their children are doing, to review writing samples over time and to listen to reading samples and examine my record-keeping notes. In this way parents may become better kid-watchers themselves and, at the very least, they will come to better understand my methods and philosophy.

When I came to this school three years ago, I found that the teachers were using an interim report (the progress report between report cards) that was similar to the report card only with percentages instead of letter grades. I opted to write a letter instead and much of the information I write about comes from the kidwatching I do in the classroom. In writing letters to parents I use the notes, writing samples, and other information I collect to describe learning strengths in detail. In this way, my progress-reporting, supported by extensive kidwatching, is much more than letter grades or number scores for subject areas which largely show what children do not know and cannot do well. It becomes a way of rejoicing about the accomplishments of individuals.

Interim Report for Ashley K. 2/23

I enjoy having Ashley in our class this year. She is sensitive and caring and takes school very seriously. Ashley has become a much more confident reader. I can see this in the kinds of books she likes to read on her own. Sometimes, she picks books that seem too difficult for her, but I am proud that she is challenging herself. The types of "mistakes" or miscues that she makes when reading aloud show me that she is really paying attention to what she reads because they often don't change the meaning (light for lamp post and Harry for Harold). Please spend time reading to her and listening to her read at home. I can never overstate the importance of getting children to read for pleasure. I would like to see Ashley be a little more logical in her spelling. In other words, her writing would be much easier to read if she would try to pay attention to the sounds of the letters in the words she writes. The content of her writing is meaningful and very creative. I can really see this in the letters she writes to her university pen pal. . . . Thanks for all of the time you give to the school by coming in for Workshop. This makes the time so much more productive.

I think you have achieved your goal of instilling the love to read-with Ashley. She picks up books and things with words on them all over the house and reads or tries to read them. She talks about the stories she's reading and wants to read parts to me. She reads till she gets sleepy some nights. I love to read, too and its nice to have someone to read to, to read with and to read to me. Thanks! Jan

Kidwatching and Teacher Reflection

I have no formula for my teaching journal. I write, as regularly as I can, about the important events and stories that could possibly affect my teaching. In my journal this year I wrote about lessons I learned from students, funny stories, invitations that went particularly well (and lessons learned), invitations that went poorly (and lessons learned), important questions, important student reactions to literature, notes about the public journals, rough drafts of stories I wanted to publish during workshop, notes on class experiments, ideas for publishing, important events that could shape future curriculum, notes on classroom routines and rituals, and parent involvement.

This notebook is only for me. Its purpose, like that of kidwatching, is to make me a more watchful teacher and allow me to know my students better. I keep a notebook each year with varying degrees of success. I usually begin the year with entries on many consecutive days and end the year with only occasional entries. Making the time for writing becomes more difficult as responsibilities accumulate during the year, but I find that by writing and reflecting, my decisions as a teacher become more thoughtful and it saves me time and energy in planning.

By December our class had become interested in creating visual models to explain fairly abstract ideas. I read aloud the book *The*

Wednesday Surprise by Eve Bunting (1989), hoping that our discussion on models might become focused on reading. The following is an excerpt from my teacher's journal on December 4:

> I read *The Wednesday Surprise*. Got interesting comments throughout. Jim insisted that this book was a mystery. "Not all mysteries are scary, you know!" he said. Great discussion about the reading process and how we learned to read. I need to go back and listen to that tape again. One thing that stands out in my mind is that no one mentioned school as being important in learning to read until I mentioned it about ten minutes into the discussion. Until this most kids talked about being taught by friends, parents, grandparents, and older siblings. As soon as I pointed out that school had not been mentioned, almost everyone began talking about the effect school had on them. Now I think I shouldn't have said anything. After the discussion I asked the children to write down something about learning to read. Among my questions were: How did you learn to read? What is reading? How would you teach someone to read? Some kids were stumped and opted to read quietly. Others fairly flew. I think I would have gotten closer to their real models if I hadn't mentioned school. A lot of phonics and little-word-to-big-word stuff. Overall impression of their products: 1) The power of DEMONSTRATION (MT) I would read the book and then let the other person read it. 2) Similar to 1) . . . MENTORS and APPRENTICESHIPS (MW) My mom made me read to her every day and every night. 3) The SKILLS mentioned are almost always connected to school. Some were conflicting within individual pieces. (JW) I learned how to read BY reading . . . If I had to teach someone I would tell them what the letter sounds made.—I LOVE his ending . . ."Reading is everything. If you know how to read then you know how to live." This would be a great class motto. . . .

Writing about the day's events always makes me more reflective about my teaching. It forces me to pay attention to what I do with a little more clarity and definition. It also makes me more mindful of the insights of the students. Creating at least ten minutes each day for reflection is a luxury that I try to afford myself. This kind of analysis may be the most important personalized staff development I have ever undertaken.

A Letter from Phil

At the beginning of March a terrible thing happened to one student. He was badly bitten by his family's German Shepherd. At first we thought Phillip might be out of school for a long time; for a while he had to be tutored as a homebound student. Phillip managed to come back to school in about two weeks, but while he was gone, he wrote to his classmates and responded to all of the cards, letters, and pictures he received from us, telling us about the very unsettling event.

Phil's letter to the class (see Figure TA1.3) revealed a great deal about his feelings and about his ability as a writer to convey his thoughts and ideas in a clear and concise way. This letter, read aloud and posted on the bulletin board, let everyone know about Phillip's physical progress and how he was feeling about his pet. We *all* came to know Phillip better, as a writer and as a friend.

In Lucy Calkins' *Living Between the Lines* (1991) she remembers a conversation in which the author Avi said, "If you can convince your children that you love them, then there's nothing that you can't teach them" (p. 11). Ultimately, in classrooms where teachers are kidwatchers they get to know their children well personally, as well as professionally. Beyond notes and tapes and portfolios, beyond rubrics and report cards, kidwatching teachers come to know and care deeply about their students.

When teachers are kidwatchers then everything becomes information upon which to build an understanding of children. Kidwatching is not a method or a way of teaching. It is not a set of materials or activities. It is not a computer program. It is not a bag of tricks or a destination. It is a way of thinking about children from a learner's perspective. It transforms teaching into an interactive process in which the teacher is a student as well as a mentor. Good teaching to me is the art of weaving my agenda—what I want the class to have achieved by the end of the year—with the continuously emerging agenda of the children. Kidwatching is the means to this end.

Dear Class

How are yall dowing? I am doiwing better. I want you to know about Beethovan my dog He was sick with a brain tumor. His brain was bleeding and he lost control and he didn't know who I was. Beethovan lovs me and is in heaven now. I still love him. I want to say thank you for all your letters and presets. I am gong to the docter today and my mom hopes he well let me come to school on Monday. I look realey good today. On Thirsday I was felling bad.

I hope I have not mist much of class. Mrs. Miller has been coming to my houes. She is cool. My mom will give y'all a pesd party win I come back to school.

your Frend Phillip L.

S-UAM

S-CUK

S-TUHA

S-KUPJUWI

S-NALASA

S-WEG

Gakimdag Masad

JANU

5 6 7

12 13 14

19 20 21

26 27 28 29

Sunday
Monday
Tuesday
Wednesday
Thursday
Friday
Satur

The Authoring Cycle as a Curricular Framework for Writing

Introduction

The authoring cycle is our attempt to make curriculum visible to both teachers and students. It connects theory and practice, supports planning, and predicts teaching by providing a framework to guide instructional decision-making. It helps us anticipate where we want to be and what we want to know. It provides us with a structure, not a sequence, for our work together in classrooms. It doesn't tell us how to spend our time, but creates a structure that suggests ways to use that time. The authoring cycle is a curricular framework that keeps all of us, teachers and students, moving ahead as lifelong learners because it supports and reflects our own learning processes.

The authoring cycle as a curricular frame (see Figure 2.1) builds from the theoretical insights we discussed in Chapter 1 but moves one step further to a curriculum. Using the major components of this cycle as a frame, what follows is a detailed description of how we first began using the authoring cycle to organize the writing and language arts curriculum in school settings. The components of this cycle are not a set of skills or procedures to be taught in sequential order, but a broad framework that supports learning and teaching. The

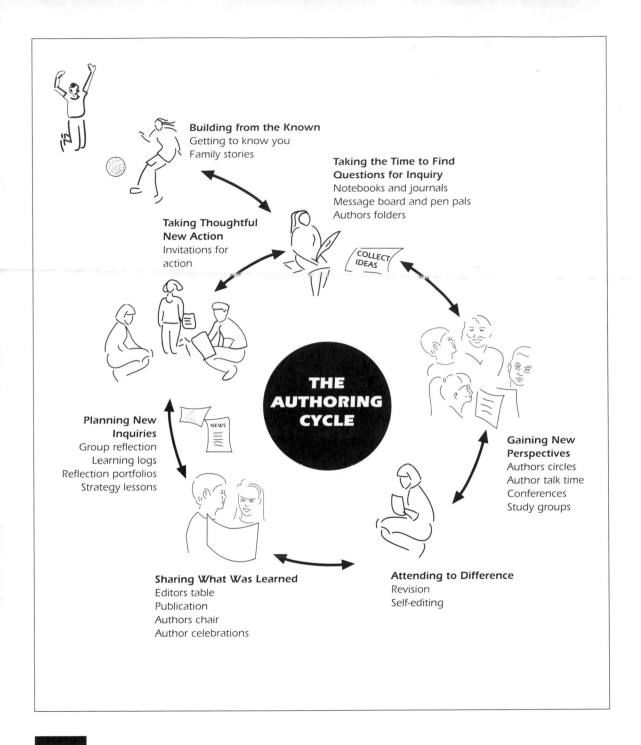

Building from the Known
Getting to know you
Family stories

**Taking the Time to Find
Questions for Inquiry**
Notebooks and journals
Message board and pen pals
Authors folders

**Taking Thoughtful
New Action**
Invitations for
action

COLLECT
IDEAS

**THE
AUTHORING
CYCLE**

**Planning New
Inquiries**
Group reflection
Learning logs
Reflection portfolios
Strategy lessons

NEWS

**Gaining New
Perspectives**
Authors circles
Author talk time
Conferences
Study groups

Sharing What Was Learned
Editors table
Publication
Authors chair
Author celebrations

Attending to Difference
Revision
Self-editing

FIGURE 2.1
The Authoring Cycle as a
Curricular Frame for Writing

components of the cycle are recursive as authors move back and forth and across the cycle to meet their purposes and needs.

Some educators talk about teaching without ever mentioning the word learning, while others talk about learning without talking about teaching. Both of these perspectives are incomplete. Teaching and learning are a relationship—one cannot be discussed without the other. Curriculum is a reflexive look at the relationship between teaching and learning. Although we have a responsibility to plan activities to foster the kinds of learning we see as central to literacy, we have no right to do so without regard for children. What children know—their life experiences—becomes *the* touchstone upon which curriculum is negotiated. By keeping our focus on life experiences, our curriculum is made vital and ever alive.

When teachers build curriculum upon experience, their classrooms all look different. No formula or magical set of activities guarantees an authoring curriculum. In fact, to the extent that teachers purchase and use published materials without regard for the specific children they teach, the whole process movement in education is in jeopardy. The curricular engagements we suggest in this book are open and allow teachers and children to take ownership of the literacy process.

Building From the Known: Connecting to Life Experiences

Children must begin any learning experience with what they currently know, perceive, and feel. Curriculum has no other place to begin than with children's current concepts and language. In starting the authoring cycle it is important, therefore, to select open activities that permit all students, from the least to the most proficient to connect; they should be able to begin and achieve, given their current levels of understanding and proficiency. The question that we need to ask as educators is not whether children are ready for school, but whether schools are ready for children. Have we created schools and classrooms that will connect with the experiences and voices of our students?

Getting to Know You
One way we start the cycle is by announcing that the class will be publishing a class magazine or newspaper and that the first articles will be

written interviews of everyone in the room. These interviews, we explain, are articles written to introduce someone to others who haven't had the pleasure of meeting that person. At the beginning of the year, these articles are a way for everyone in the classroom to get to know one another. The class magazine can also be distributed to parents and placed into the Visitors Corner. The final product includes each child's article introducing someone in the class and a drawing or a photograph of that person taken at school or brought from home.

An engagement called Getting to Know You supports the children's development of their interviews. In this engagement, the class examines published interviews and children jot down questions that they wish to ask the person they have elected to interview. We used to ask children to interview someone they didn't know, but discovered that better articles often resulted when friendship pairs were permitted to interview each other. Therefore, we now let children choose who they want to interview. Children are encouraged to take notes during their interviews and to use the notes in writing their rough drafts.

Once the activity has been introduced in this fashion, students pair up, conduct interviews, and begin drafting their articles. As teachers, we are also part of this process and pair up with a student or another adult in the room. By the end of the first day, some children will have finished their rough drafts while others may still be interviewing each other or writing their drafts. At sharing time, which we call Author Talk Time, it is important to assure students that it does not matter where they are in the process. Children can be invited to talk about their first drafts with the class or a small group whether they have finished them or not. Students who have finished their rough drafts place them in their Authors Folders and, on the second day, either select their own topic to write about or choose another writing invitation.

As children finish, they meet in groups of three to four for an Authors Circle where they read their article out loud to the group, ask whether or not their interview makes sense to others who do not know that child, and take notes of suggestions. Following the Authors Circle, each child makes any needed revisions and meets with another child for peer editing. The draft then goes to the teacher or another adult for typing. We realize that, at this point, children will make few, if any, revisions or editing suggestions, but we want them to get an overall sense of the authoring cycle.

Meet Denise

The person I interviewed is a girl. I really like her. She eats pizza and she is beautiful. I asked her name, and she said, "Denise." I asked her if she was married or would like to be. She said "No," I asked, "Are you active?" She said, "No." I asked, "Who is in your family?" She said, "My mom, dad, bro-ther and me." I asked her to tell me all about her pets. She has one dog, a cat and a turtle. I asked her how playful she was. She said, "Really well." I asked her how loving she was. She said, "Really well." She has not published books.

By Gabe

Getting to Know You published interview; Gabe, Age 8 (Gloria Kauffman's classroom)

Section One
The Authoring Cycle:
Let's Talk Curriculum

Using Getting to Know You with Young Children

A variation of Getting to Know You for young children was developed by Kathy and Gloria Kauffman. First-grade children were introduced to the engagement on the second day of school as a way to create a newspaper about themselves to send to a class who were going to be their pen pals. After a discussion of questions to ask in an interview, each person, including the teachers, chose a partner and went off to conduct the interviews. The children were asked to take notes during the interviews that they could then use to dictate their interview to Gloria or Kathy. When several children said, "But I can't spell," Gloria answered that they were the only ones who would read their notes and they could use words, letters, or pictures—whatever would help them remember what had been said in the interview.

When children began dictating their articles, Kathy and Gloria were excited by how well they were able to use their notes to retrieve the information shared with them. Children had freely moved across sign systems using various combinations of written language and pictures in their notes.

Once an interview was dictated by a child, it was read back to the author and several other children sitting nearby to see if they thought it made sense to other readers. Following these informal Authors Circles, the interviews were typed and published in a newspaper that was distributed to the children and their pen pals. Using the interviews to

Chapter Two
The Authoring Cycle
as a Curricular
Framework for Writing

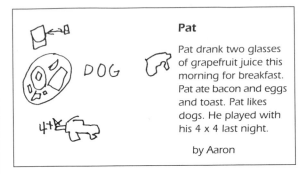

Pat

Pat drank two glasses of grapefruit juice this morning for breakfast. Pat ate bacon and eggs and toast. Pat likes dogs. He played with his 4 x 4 last night.

by Aaron

Miss Kauffman

Marvin: What is your name?
M.K.: Miss Kauffman
Marvin: How old are you?
M.K.: 30
Marvin: What color eyes?
M.K.: Green
Marvin: How many children do you have?
M.K.: Zero
Marvin: What do you do?
M.K.: Teach first grade

by Marvin

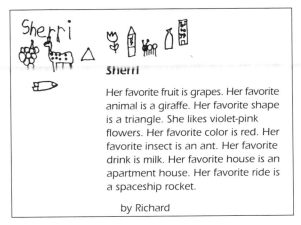

Sherri

Her favorite fruit is grapes. Her favorite animal is a giraffe. Her favorite shape is a triangle. She likes violet-pink flowers. Her favorite color is red. Her favorite insect is an ant. Her favorite drink is milk. Her favorite house is an apartment house. Her favorite ride is a spaceship rocket.

by Richard

FIGURE 2.3
First-grade Interview Notes and Articles; Marvin, Aaron, and Richard, Age 6 (Gloria Kauffman's classroom)

produce a newspaper for their pen pals gave this activity a purpose that went beyond the immediate classroom. The children got to know each other better, and they introduced themselves to their new pen pals. This engagement could be used anytime a classroom begins exchanging letters with a new group of pen pals.

Family Stories

Later on in the year, when Getting to Know You may no longer be appropriate because the children already know each other well, an engagement that can be used to introduce the authoring cycle is Family Stories. We developed this engagement as a way for children to explore the stories that their families tell over and over again about important events in their lives. After reading and orally discussing *Aunt Flossie's Hats* (Howard, 1991), we point out that these "remember when" stories are often shared at family gatherings and reunions. We ask children to interview their parents or other family members to begin gathering their own oral family stories.

When Kathy and Gloria Kauffman introduced this engagement to first graders, children brought in their notes from these interviews on scraps of paper and spent several weeks sharing their stories orally with the group. Many children forgot to interview family members for the first several days, but the oral sharing encouraged everyone to get involved. Each day, several children had new stories to tell, and their stories always reminded others of stories they had to tell. A "broken arm" story generated all kinds of "broken bone" stories.

The children were then asked to make a list of their stories and to decide which ones they wanted to write. We talked about which of their stories were private and not meant to be shared with others and which ones they wanted to publish for others to read. The number of stories children wrote also varied by how interested they were in family stories. Some were ready to go on to other topics and so wrote only one story from what they had collected, while others wrote many more. Once they had written their family stories, they took them to Authors Circle and published individual collections. Each child then chose one favorite family story to include in a newspaper of family stories that was published to share with parents.

If we were using this engagement to begin the authoring cycle midyear, we would have children first write their favorite family story and publish these in a newspaper so they could quickly experience an entire cycle. Their list of family stories would go into their Authors Folders so they could decide whether to continue writing family stories to create individual books or go on to other writing invitations. The engagement can be introduced to older children as an invitation to collect historical family stories by providing multiple copies of *Sarah, Plain and Tall* (Maclachlan, 1985). Students can read the book with a partner using Say Something, where students read aloud a chunk of text and then stop and "say something" to each other.

Jean Schroeder introduced family stories to her multi-age primary class by having students construct personal time lines of their own lives. They collaborated with their parents to record significant events in their lives and then used this research to construct individual time lines. On these time lines, they indicated important events that had occurred for each year of their lives. Later, they worked with their families to construct family time lines that ranged from six years

My Sister Lisa

My sister Lisa always sucked her thumb when she was little. One time when she was fishing, she put the worms on the hook. Afterwards, in the car, she was sucking her thumb without washing her hands. My dad turned around and said, "Oh, Lisa. That's awful!" Then Lisa said, "Try it, you'll like it."

Remember When Story; Karen, Age 8 (Jean Schroeder's classroom)

FIGURE 2.4
Family Story; Rocky, Age 5
(Julie Larird's classroom)

Mt. Lemmon

We drove to Mt. Lemmon, when we got there we made a snowman. They let us go through up to the snow. When my hands were freezing, my dad let me warm my hands on his stomach. We were in the clouds. We brung home snow, and took it out of the truck. When we took it out, my brother threw snow at me. We had fun. My Dad took us to get hot chocolate.
Our snow melted.

The End.

to several hundred years. The process of researching and creating these time lines resulted in many students becoming interested in and collecting their family stories, both "remember when" stories and historical stories.

Another type of family story can be introduced by reading and discussing *The Relatives Came* (Rylant, 1986). We then initiate a discussion of stories about particular family experiences that reflect that family's culture: who they are, what they value, and how they live. Students are invited to write stories about what it is like to grow up in their family and what experiences define who they are as a family. In order to write these stories, students spend time observing and taking notes about their family life as well as reflecting on past experiences that might capture what life is like in their family and community. We read other pieces of literature and share our own family stories about events such as a family camping trip that capture our sense of family culture and identity.

Both Getting to Know You and Family Stories invite children to make immediate connections with their past experiences and their lives outside of school as they explore authoring through writing. They are also important in creating a sense of community, a valuing of the differences that exist among students that strengthen that community by providing resources that all can use. Because these writing activities build so directly on their past experiences and lead quickly to a publication, children come to understand the cycle as a curricular frame for authoring in the classroom. They need an overall sense of writing for many purposes, creating rough drafts, sharing with others, revising, editing, and publishing to support them as they take future writing through the cycle. Students understand the value of this process only after they have experienced it.

About My Grandpa

When my grandpa was a small boy, he crawled in the thrashing machine to see how it looked inside while the men were fixing it in front. My grandpa could not get out by himself anymore.

The men said it was all right to go ahead and thrash. Straw was coming down on his head. His dad was coming around the back and saw his hand hanging out. He reached in and pulled him out and explained what could have happened.

My grandpa always wondered how a thrashing machine looked on the inside. But he found out. But he never crawled in unless he was asked to! He was glad his dad pulled him out.

Historical Family Story; Lorene,
Age 9 (Gloria Kauffman's
classroom)

Section One
The Authoring Cycle:
Let's Talk Curriculum

Taking Time to Find Questions for Inquiry: Uninterrupted Writing and Reading

Once Getting to Know You or Family Stories have been introduced, children need uninterrupted time to conduct their interviews and to begin drafting their articles. Having a long block of time each day for uninterrupted reading and writing is the key to a successful reading and writing program (Graves, 1983). Because children can learn a process only through engagement in that process, they must be given invitations to read and write each day. Without invitations and time, there will be limited engagement and conversation. Without engagement and conversation, children cannot make connections. Without making connections, children cannot grow as reflective learners.

Invitations and choice are important in learning. A true invitation, however, is more than just a choice between two activities proposed by the teacher. An invitation means that the children have the right to turn down an option and to justify how their own idea is an equally valid experience. Choice is the propeller that gets the whole process started. It is in making the decision to read this book rather than that book, or to write this story rather than that story, that ownership of the process occurs. To make any decision, the learner needs to weigh and think about a variety of issues. This thinking about available options is crucial; it allows one to focus on a topic and, because alternatives have been weighed and rejected, to know what can be done with a topic before really beginning.

When topics and books are assigned rather than chosen, no such personal weighing has taken place. The orientation of the language user is other-directed (what does the teacher want?). By providing real choices, students have to decide and then begin composing. In so doing, they take ownership of the literacy process and can engage in observations of their world and conversations with others in order to select their own topics and inquiries for exploration through writing. These writing engagements are authentic because they have meaning and purpose in students' lives instead of being imposed as assigned topics to be completed for the teacher.

Writing as a Tool for Thinking and for Publication

Children need to be informed that although they will be reading and writing each day, only a small portion of what they read or write will be presented to others. The language arts curriculum in the classroom is far more than publishing. The primary message we want to send to children is that writing is a powerful tool for observing and exploring their world, and it is a way for them to begin conversations with themselves and others. While selecting some pieces for formal publication is an integral part of the cycle, the vast majority of what children write will remain private or be shared informally with others.

Uninterrupted time for reading and writing allows readers and writers the opportunity to test, confirm, and revise their latest inquiry questions and hypotheses about language and the world. Through time for uninterrupted reading and writing, language users try various strategies and come to see written language as a tool for inquiry. In a curriculum organized around an authoring cycle, first drafts are valued as much as final drafts. Students need time to observe the world and explore meaning before they are expected to present meaning. Without a first draft there can be no second draft or formal published draft. Without risk there is no growth. Carolyn Burke says it this way, "Within every professional there once was an amateur." We also recognize that even when a piece of writing is published, it is not a final draft. The author has gone public and put together a formal draft to be shared with others. Authors continue revising their ideas even if those revisions occur only in their heads and not on paper.

Lucy Calkins (1991) points out that the purpose of many classroom writing programs is to send pieces through an assembly line of producing a rough draft, fixing it up, and publishing it, rather than using writing as a tool for thinking. In reality, professional authors spend the majority of their time observing life, gathering ideas, and thinking through writing short entries before they begin a rough draft, and many of those drafts are never published. According to Donald Murray (1989), authors spend seventy-five percent of their time in rehearsal, getting ready to write a draft. They search for topics, conduct research, read favorite authors, take walks, write observations and memories, and talk to friends and informants. Students in schools have been misled to believe that the majority of their time should be spent writing a draft for publication.

When we first began working with writing, we overemphasized the role of publication and presented an assembly line picture of the authoring cycle in practice. Our recent experiences in classrooms have made us realize that we needed to place a much greater emphasis on uninterrupted reading and writing within the cycle. The cycle depends on children having time to observe the world and explore reading and writing for a wide range of purposes, both personal and social. Through these explorations, they have time for conversations with themselves through writing and with other learners through oral and written language. These conversations allow them to make connections to what they already know and to identify new possibilities and ideas.

Ralph Peterson (1992) defines conversation as an "unrehearsed intellectual adventure" that involves the lively participation and enjoyment of learners. There is no particular purpose or task to be accomplished. It is a time to engage, play, and think. Just as in any conversation, writing must include time for play and the choice of what to "talk" about. In most classrooms, students engage in discussions where the topic and responses are determined by the teacher and they fill in the oral blanks. Writing should be a conversation, not a discussion.

Brainstorming Topic Lists

We have used several curricular engagements to support students in choosing and writing on their own topics during uninterrupted writing. One is to have students create a list of possible writing ideas. We use the technique suggested by Donald Graves (1983) and Nancie Atwell (1987) of demonstrating how we make our own list of experiences and topics we are interested in from our lives. We talk about playing with the cat, taking a walk in the early morning, memories of our first day of school, wondering why coyotes howl at night, and spending time with friends. We highlight the everyday, rather than the "big" events that children often think should be the focus of writing. We brainstorm with students about possible topics and experiences from their lives and ask them to make their own lists. After giving children time to write, we ask them to share their lists with a small group or partner. This sharing often gives them additional ideas to add to their individual lists.

Students can then use these lists to choose a topic for their first piece. One way to support them in making this choice is to have students describe each of their ideas to a partner. After they have shared all of their ideas, they choose the one they want to begin with and talk about why. The conversations and the process of describing each of their ideas often enables them to make a decision about where they

Topic Idea List; Mardell, Age 9 (Gloria Kauffman's classroom)

Chapter Two
The Authoring Cycle
as a Curricular
Framework for Writing

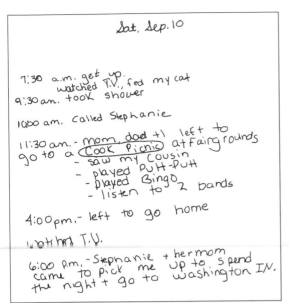

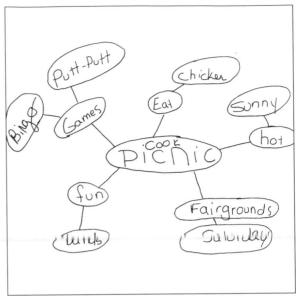

FIGURE 2.5
Life Story Time Line including time line of day, selection of topic, expansion of topic through webbing; Natalie, Age 11 (compliments of Carol Hardin)

want to begin. These lists of possible writing topics are then kept in the student's Authors Folder for later reference and to add new ideas.

At the Whole Language Umbrella Conference in San Diego, Donald Graves (1994) shared a strategy which we call Life Story Time Lines. What he did was walk us through his day, recalling what he did from the time he awoke to the time he went to bed. On an overhead he noted the time and wrote phrases which reminded him of these events. At 6:00 he awoke and started his morning routines, some of which are rituals, others of which were unique to this particular morning. At 7:00 he sat down to work and began his usual practice of devoting a portion of each day to writing. He shared his latest topic with us and some of the strategies he uses to keep himself writing. At 8:00 he left for the airport. On his overhead he noted the time and wrote key phrases to remind himself of the events on the plan—who he sat by, the conversations he had, and the significance he made of these events.

Once he finished talking his way through his day, he went back and used another color of pen to highlight all of the things he might write about—a humorous piece on getting up in the morning, an essay on strategies he employs to keep himself going during writing, a reflective piece on the importance of education based on a conversation he had with the person who sat next to him on the airplane, and so on.

Section One
The Authoring Cycle:
Let's Talk Curriculum

Since the conference we have used this strategy with several groups of students. To introduce the strategy, we talk students through our day, noting times and writing phrases that signal key events as well as related contexts and stories. We then look over our lists and highlight different essays and stories we might write about from this list. Once we have provided this demonstration, we invite students to pair up and do the same. Students use their Life Story Time Lines to identify potential writing topics from their personal lives.

This engagement can also be used to introduce students to reflection. Once students have produced their own Life Story Time Lines, identified potential writing topics, and actually taken several of these to draft form, they can use this experience to understand and keep a reflective journal. In keeping a reflective journal we recommend they use the Life Story Time Line strategy. After class each day, they take out their journal and walk through all of the events that happened, taking note of key ideas they associate with these events. Once they have created this list, they go back and highlight several powerful ideas. They then take what they see as the key ideas and write a reflection about how these ideas affect their lives and what it is they believe. We suggest that they leave the page facing their reflective writing blank so that as they read through their reflective journals they can note implications and identify other topics that need exploration and expansion through writing.

Writer's Notebooks

Instead of creating a brainstormed list of topics for drafts, educators at the Teachers College Writing Project (Calkins, 1991) developed Writer's Notebooks as a place where children use writing to observe their world. These notebooks contain entries, notes, lists, drafts, observations, ramblings, and quotes. They are similar to the journals, diaries, bureau drawers, and files from which the published work of professional authors eventually emerges. These authors spend much of their time collecting "bits of life"—observations, memories, ideas, favorite quotes, and clippings of articles from newspapers and magazines. While the notebooks may take the form of a looseleaf notebook, composition book, bound book, or spiral notebook, they are always a place for authors to rehearse. Lucy Calkins believes that these notebooks are a more natural place for children to grow and uncover topics that they want to develop into drafts than creating topic lists.

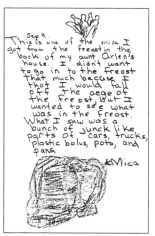

Writer's Notebook Entry;
Michelle, Age 10 (Gloria Kauffman's classroom)

Chapter Two
The Authoring Cycle
as a Curricular
Framework for Writing

Instead of students feeling that they need to work on a draft of a complete piece, they can write short entries each day which might involve a memory, a family story, an unforgettable scene or image, or favorite quotes from books they have read. They can also clip excerpts and illustrations from magazines and newspapers or note observations of people or objects around them. While the notebooks are highlighted during uninterrupted writing, students keep these notebooks with them throughout the day at school and at home so they can capture ideas and images as they occur. About once a month, students read and reflect on their entries to find something they want to pursue further. They read through their entries looking for themes, connections, interests, or a particular image that they want to use as a topic for writing a draft. They usually do not take a particular entry and revise it, but use the entries as a place to discover a topic or idea for a draft. These entries give students many opportunities to use writing as a tool for thinking and to develop fluency as writers without the pressure of immediately producing a complete story or draft. They also provide students with a reflective way of uncovering topics they want to pursue in their writing.

Sketch Journals

Sketch Journals play a similar function to Writer's Notebooks in that they are also a collection of bits and pieces of daily life and are carried by students as they move through their day at school and at home. Sketch Journals differ from Writer's Notebooks in that students use art to express their thoughts, ideas, and experiences and add occasional written comments in the margins. Students gather a variety of pens, colored pencils, and other art materials that they can use to record and reflect on their experiences. In these journals, students sketch out the images, feelings, and meanings that are significant in their daily lives. The focus is not on finished drawings to be shared with others, but on recording something new students have observed in the world that day.

Because art as a way to observe life is not usually part of children's experiences in schools, they need support in maintaining these journals. This support includes encouraging them to share their entries with each other, providing strategy lessons such as how to draw figures, and offering invitations such as sketching anger or joy (without human figures) and creating a Song Map (a visual map of the underlying patterns or deep structures of a musical selection). An art studio

Sketch Journal: Sketches of emotions; Michelle, Age 9 (Gloria Kauffman's classroom)

Section One
The Authoring Cycle:
Let's Talk Curriculum

with many different kinds of art materials and invitations and illustrator studies are important supports. Children's books such as
A Crack in the Wall (Haggerty, 1993) where characters use sketch
journals will also support students as they explore the potentials of
viewing the world through visual images. Just as with the Writer's
Notebook, Sketch Journals and Illustrator Studies become places to
collect short entries over time from which ideas for drafts of either
artistic or written pieces may later emerge.

Sketch Journal: Portrait of a
class member using Picasso's
style; Lynise, Age 8 (Gloria
Kauffman's classroom)

Invitations for Writing

Some students find it difficult to initially create their own list of ideas
and need the support of writing invitations. We offer invitations that
allow students to build from their own life experiences but give them
some support in generating story and language structures. As soon as
some students finish the rough drafts of their interviews, we have
them make topic lists so they can begin other pieces while they are
waiting to meet in an Authors Circle on their interviews. We also offer writing invitations so students can decide either to write on their
own topics or to accept one of the invitations. These invitations can
become short entries in a Writer's Notebook or Sketch Journal or a
rough draft in their Authors Folder.

One such invitation, Picture Setting, is introduced by suggesting
that students having difficulty thinking of something to write can
look through magazines at home to find a picture of a setting (devoid
of people or animals) that reminds them of an experience in their
lives. They will add their own characters to the setting. To make sure
they understand, we share picture settings we have selected from
magazines and tell children what we are reminded of by these settings. It is important to assure children that they are free to write
about anything they wish, and that they need not accept this invitation if they already have another idea.

On the next day we begin "work time"—our official name for uninterrupted reading and writing—by finding out how many children
are still drafting their written interviews. We then ask how many accepted our invitation to find a background picture setting to create a
new story; these children are invited to bring their pictures and assemble at a table in the back to cut out characters for their story. We
also find out how many others have their own ideas and are ready to
begin drafting new selections. Students who have not taken our invitation, who have finished the rough draft of their interview, and who

Chapter Two
The Authoring Cycle
as a Curricular
Framework for Writing

do not feel they have a story just waiting to be written, are reminded of other writing opportunities available in the room—such as Pen Pals, Message Board, and Journals—or are invited to look through the books in the classroom library to find something to read. During uninterrupted time for reading and writing, everyone is expected to be engaged, although the particular reading and writing engagement is a matter of choice.

There is nothing magical about Picture Setting as a first invitation. Instead, many teachers offer an invitation to write a text for a wordless book or to write a Group Composed Book based on a predictable patterned language book. The key is to offer students specific invitations to get them started while providing them the option of turning down the invitation and going with their own ideas.

Having a variety of writing and drawing utensils, papers, and blank books in the writing-reading center allows children to choose the ones that meet their needs and purposes; they signal different invitations for writing. Wordprocessing capabilities should also be available. Technology has opened up new possibilities for children who find the actual physical formation of letters difficult. For these children, the computer can be a liberating experience because they can focus on what they want to say instead of working so hard at letter formation. For all children, the computer makes the revision and editing process less cumbersome and opens up the potential for multimedia texts with audio, video, and wordprocessing.

One type of strategy for rough drafts that should be available to students are Storyboards. Peter Catalanotto, an illustrator of picture books, points out that the traditional format of a written draft on a piece of paper does not allow him to see the flow of the story and the interweaving of text and picture. Instead he makes a Storyboard which shows all the pages of a book, greatly reduced, on a large sheet of paper. The Storyboard allows the maker of a picture book to create a plan for the book just as an architect draws a plan for a house before building it (Shulevitz, 1985). Catalanotto uses white squares of paper (or large Post-it notes) for each page of the story and tapes them on a large sheet of paper so he can move them around as needed. As he works, the pictures often come before the words and the storyboard format allows him to quickly sketch pictures in rough draft form. It is ironic that most classrooms encourage children to write rough drafts of their text but pictures are added only in the final draft. Storyboards support children in exploring both picture and text through rough drafts.

Gloria Kauffman found that young children worked better with a Storyboard that consisted of a long strip of paper because they were confused by the directionality of the usual storyboard format. The Storyboard was a powerful tool for these children in allowing them to move back and forth between picture and text and to change the organization of the story as needed. Information on how author-illustrators use Storyboards can be found in Uri Shulevitz's book *Writing with Pictures* (1985).

Supporting Student Choice During Work Time

During work time, students are seldom involved in the same engagement. Instead they are immersed in various kinds of reading and writing experiences as well as in Authors Circle and Editors Table. Teachers who have conducted only whole-group instruction may feel uncomfortable starting with so many options. They may want to begin by offering students two or three options, while remaining open to children who have their own ideas and can go ahead on their own. Students bring a history of literacy instruction with them and may need time to get used to taking an increasing amount of responsibility for their use of time. More options can be added to work time as both teacher and students are comfortable with making a wider range of choices.

Chapter Two
The Authoring Cycle
as a Curricular
Framework for Writing

Teachers have supported students in making these choices through pocket charts listing the different options available in the room. Students place their name cards in the option they are choosing. Other teachers list all of the available engagements on the board as a ready reference for children as they plan their morning. Kaylene Yoder has her sixth grade students use this list to plan their own schedule for the morning in individual schedule books. During author talk time at the end of the morning, achievements and intentions are compared and discussed.

Many teachers find it helpful to begin work time with a group meeting which often involves reading aloud a picture book or excerpt from a longer book or having a class discussion about some aspect of reading and writing. The meeting typically ends with some kind of check-in about what students are currently working on during their work time. Sometimes the check-in is simply a short general discussion about what is happening during work time. Other times, teachers do a "status check" (Atwell, 1987) where each student reports quickly on what he or she is currently doing in writing, and the teacher records these comments on a form. The group meeting creates a sense of focus and purpose as students move into work time. Some teachers have found that this sense of focus is enhanced if work time begins with ten to twenty minutes of quiet writing. Authors Circles, collaborative writing, peer conferencing, and other group activities do not begin until quiet writing ends. Work time ends with author talk time where authors come together in small groups or as a whole class to share ideas and strategies that have developed during their work time.

Another advantage of beginning with a group meeting is that it is also a time when teachers and students can offer particular writing invitations to encourage students to try a greater variety of genres and topics in their writing or to explore a wider range of writing strategies. Uninterrupted reading and writing invitations can include Pen Pals, Personal Journals, Message Board, Shared Reading, Readers Theatre, Getting to Know You, Family Stories, Picture Setting, Written Conversation, Learning Logs, Literature Logs, and Group Composed Books. In many classrooms, it may be more meaningful for children to begin exploring writing through informal communication with others or through personal writing that reflects the ways they have observed language being used outside of school.

Using Journals to Explore Purposes for Writing

Writing plays many different functions in our lives, and writing in schools should reflect that range. Journals fulfill an informal, personal function that is often not met in schools. Although we used to think we knew how journals should be used in a classroom, that confidence has been shattered through experience. Our notion was that the teacher made journals available and invited children to use them as a personal diary, with the sole stipulation that entries be made daily; sharing entries was left to student discretion. We saw journals as a contrast to other writing done in the classroom; their function was to create a very low-risk, informal means for children to explore, among other things, the recording function of language. They served as a personal record that could be consulted as needed to refresh children's memories when reviewing the week or year, or attempting something in writing (such as responding to a pen pal). Because the content was open, each child decided what function and purpose the journal would serve.

Few teachers we know use journals in exactly this way. Mary Lynn Woods explored a communicative function by creating Dialogue Journals where each evening students wrote about topics that interested them and then exchanged journals with another student or with the teacher the following morning. Not only did these journals encourage children to engage in personal written conversations with each other, but they also provided demonstrations in the home setting.

Gloria Kauffman has focused on the more personal function of journals in the different classrooms she has taught. In first grade, Personal Journals were introduced as diaries in which the children could write about events and feelings related to school or home. A diary written by a grandparent was shared with them, as were several books, such as *Dear Mr. Henshaw* (Cleary, 1983), that used diary entries. Initially children had a difficult time understanding this personal function. We realized that writing for yourself to explore feelings and to record experiences is a function that is not used to its potential in our society and is not visible because of its private function. Many children have not observed adults using these journals. Children were more familiar with writing to communicate to someone else. Many of the children's early journal entries consisted of drawings with a few words—"I love" messages, and an occasional

10/4

Yesterday I went to Kings Island I went with lots of girl scouts. We all went by bus. It was fun I rode on almost everything. From the Beastie To the Backward Racer

I like Kings Island Too Its the only one with really good rides. I think its even better than Walt Disney World.
Mrs. Wood

Dialogue Journal; Alison, Age 10 (Myriam Revel-Wood's classroom)

Chapter Two
The Authoring Cycle
as a Curricular
Framework for Writing

sentence about something that had happened. Many of the children did not enjoy journal writing and did not use it to explore personal meaning. Gloria persisted, however, in having a journal time and accepting whatever children chose to write. She did not respond to their journals but did read through them about once a week to see what children were doing. Near the end of November, Personal Journals finally clicked, and children whose entries had remained brief and unfocused suddenly began writing and sketching long entries about their lives. Children no longer complained about journal writing, unless, for some reason, there was no time to write in them.

In January, Gloria introduced the option of Dialogue Journals. She did this because a number of children had indicated a need for more attention and interaction with her. She felt comfortable introducing this option in January because the children understood and valued the personal function of journaling and so could really make a choice. Each day when children wrote, they either left the journals open for her response or put them away. The majority of children chose to continue keeping their entries personal, with an occasional request for a dialogue. On Mondays, more children wanted Gloria to read and respond to their descriptions of their weekends. A few children switched to using their journals almost entirely as Dialogue Journals and having Gloria respond each day.

Later, when Gloria taught third grade, she again introduced journals as a diary in which children could write about experiences and feelings. She also immediately introduced the option of leaving the journals open for her response. She found that nearly everyone wanted a response and used journals as a way to send her messages and to complain about other children rather than to explore the personal function of writing. Gloria felt that this occurred because the option of Dialogue Journals was introduced before the children had a chance to explore the personal function of journaling. Because the children's past experiences in other classrooms had been limited to Dialogue Journals, journals signaled a way to send messages. Since Message Board and other engagements where students used writing to communicate were already available, she wanted journals to highlight personal writing.

This experience led her to return to Personal Journals. Children write their journal entries each morning as they arrive and then put their journals away. Once in a while Gloria reads through their journals, except for the pages the children have indicated that she is not

Journal Entry; Corey, Age 7 (Gloria Kauffman's classroom)

Dialogue Journal Entry between a student and his teacher; Ben, Age 10 (Myriam Revel-Wood's classroom)

Section One
The Authoring Cycle:
Let's Talk Curriculum

to read, but she does not respond. Initially children find her lack of response difficult, but Gloria knows from her previous experiences that she needs to give them enough time to explore the personal function. She does not provide specific topics or a certain amount to write, but she does have a short sharing time as students complete their journals. Anyone who chooses can read an entry to the class. This sharing meets the needs of children for whom journals are a way to share with others rather than for private thinking. It also provides demonstrations to children who are having difficulty. Gloria found that spiral notebooks, rather than paper stapled between covers, make these journals seem more "real" to children.

Exploring Different Kinds of Learning Logs

Some classrooms use other forms of journals, particularly various kinds of Learning Logs. When Kittye Copeland taught in a multi-age (K–6) classroom in Columbia, Missouri, she had children keep a Learning Log where they recorded what they had learned each day. This log encourages children to be reflective and to bring to conscious awareness their school experiences. Both Myriam Revel-Wood and Tim O'Keefe use science logs where children record observations about self-selected topics within science units they are studying. Other teachers use math logs where students can write their thinking about the meaning and strategies they are using in math explorations, or teachers place community or class logs next to an area where students can observe a plant or animal. In one first-grade classroom, community logs were permanently placed outside the terrarium and gerbil cage. Children were invited to record, date, and sign their names to entries indicating what they observed as they spent time in these centers. These logs were later used as the basis of a class discussion.

Another type of log that is frequently used is a Literature Log. In some classrooms, students use Literature Logs to write about their reactions to books they are reading for Literature Circles or in response to the class read-aloud book. Other teachers use logs developed by Nancie Atwell (1984) where students write letters to the teacher or another child about books they are reading independently. This log is similar to a Dialogue Journal and has a real purpose because the books are ones they are reading on their own and do not have an opportunity to discuss with others.

I leaned there are diffrent ways in math to do things. I like the game we plaged. I learned there are games you can make and it can have math in them. I am begening to like math. I think we are learning som thing. I want to learn how to carry and when you don't need to carry. I want to Learn how to divid and mltoply.

Math Log; Sherri, Age 9
(Gloria Kauffman's classroom)

These various forms of journals and logs can provide students with more functional views of writing and reading processes. Many teachers have introduced several different kinds into the classroom. Sometimes they are in separate notebooks and, other times, one notebook is used for all of these functions. In deciding how many and which kinds to try, the needs of the students and the classroom learning environment must be considered.

Journals may be the most misused curricular engagement in many classrooms today. Some schools mandate their use, and others use them because they are *the* thing to do, not because they meet the needs of the children and the curriculum. Many students view journals as a school task to be completed that has no purpose in their lives as learners or writers. In some classrooms, assigned topics are written on the board and entries are graded and corrected. The basal companies that produce literature anthologies have put together booklets of comprehension worksheets and labeled them "Journals" or "Literature Logs." In still other classrooms, journals have reached the overkill stage, and each student has a stack of different notebooks to use throughout the day. Just saying the word "journal" can bring groans of dismay.

Journals are *not* an automatic part of an authoring classroom. They are included only when they play a function within the curriculum and in the writing processes and needs of students. If other curricular engagements, such as Writer's Notebooks, are in place and meet the same needs, then journals are not needed. The questions that teachers can ask as they make decisions are, "What functions might journals play in the curriculum that currently are not being met through other engagements?" and "What needs do my students have that particular forms of journals might meet?" It also helps to know what students have already experienced in other classrooms. There are no right or wrong answers whether or not to use journals. Teachers and students need to make these decisions together based on their specific learning context.

Writing to Communicate with Pen Pals

Although journals focus on using writing as a personal learning tool, Pen Pals are a form of informal writing to communicate with others. Before you say, "I tried that once, and it didn't work; kids lost interest," let us discuss why this might have happened and why Pen Pals is worth a second try. First, if the class pen pals are in Australia or some other exotic spot, no matter how rapidly teachers set up a pen pal exchange in September, it is often mid-November before the class actually gets responses. Under these conditions only the most tenacious students maintain interest. What one ends up with is a hit-or-miss pen pal program. Some children have a great experience; most do not. Under these conditions it's hard to think of the pen pal program as a serious and integral part of a language arts curriculum.

But this need not be the scenario. There are alternatives. Keep the infrequent long-distance pen pals, but also have pen pals who live nearby. We have found, for example, that having pen pals in the same town solves the problem of turnaround time without seriously detracting from the function of Pen Pals. We identify a willing teacher—in the same city but in a different school who lives nearby—and set up a weekly exchange schedule. When letters arrive, students are given several days to put their response in the mail bag. Students who don't get their letters in miss out and have lots to write in their next letter. Getting the pen pals together in Meet Your Pen Pal parties adds to the success of the program. Sometimes these pen pal meetings are author teas where both pen pals bring pieces to share, or the two pen pals have a writing session to co-author a story.

In one fourth-grade classroom, three sets of pen pals were going concurrently. One set was with children in a fourth-grade class in a neighboring school, another set was with a first-grade class in the school, and a third set was with college students in a language arts methods class at the university. Copies were made of the letters before they were sent and students kept both their own letters and the letters from their pen pals in a pocket folder. Later in the year they were invited to contrast the letters written to the fourth graders with those to the first graders, and both of these with the letters to the college students. This led to a discussion about similarities and differences between the various sets of letters in terms of length, topics discussed, language used, handwriting changes, and such features as the use of art. This discussion led to insights into how successful language users vary language by the circumstances of use, a discussion on language variation within the community, a dialect dictionary project, and a general sensitivity and understanding of culture and language diversity. The university students, by the way, used the pen pal letters they had written and received to conduct their own child-as-informant language studies. Everyone benefitted intellectually.

In another classroom a pen pal program was set up with residents in a nursing home that happened to be located between the teacher's

First and Ninth Pen Pal Letter;
Jenny, Age 8 (Vargas, 1982)

home and school. One day, Maura, a fourth grader in Myriam Revel-Wood's classroom, excitedly commented, as she finished reading her pen pal's letter, "I can hardly wait to tell her." Having overheard her enthusiasm, Jerry [Harste] was surprised when seconds later she put the letter away and began working on something else. Never willing to leave well enough alone, he asked, "Well, if you're so excited, why aren't you writing her back immediately?" To this, Maura said, "I don't want to right now. I don't have any stationery. I'll get some at home and write her tomorrow." We had never thought about the fact that the children, like the adults with whom they were corresponding, would like special stationery, and we immediately decided to remedy the situation. Students were soon taking turns designing stationery for the class.

Message Board is another curricular engagement that uses writing to communicate and legalizes notepassing between friends in school. The Message Board is often a bulletin board in a central location in the classroom where children and teachers send messages through written notes and sketches to each other. Personal messages are folded and addressed with the recipient's name; class announcements are posted for all to see. Another version of Message Board is a school-wide postal system where mail is collected and delivered by children who serve as mail clerks to each classroom. Within the classroom, another child is in charge of delivering the mail to individual boxes.

Written Conversation also highlights writing as communication and involves two children having a conversation through writing using one piece of paper and one pencil. As students engage in a wide range of writing experiences, they become flexible and proficient writers who use writing for a variety of functions in their lives. Writing becomes both a way of thinking and discovering new ideas as well as a way of conversing with others.

Authors Folders

As children write on a daily basis, they need ways to keep track of writing they want to think more about. Some of their writing, such as letters, messages, and lists, is immediately "published" when they pass it on to someone else or use it for their own purposes. Other writing, such as Learning Logs, take place in a specific notebook and play a particular function within the curriculum. Children need other places where they can collect ideas, notes, drafts, and exploratory

I am goen to Be with Monica for farMars Market. We are goen to sell oredaMents and hair Boes.

Message Board, Note to Teacher (Kittye Copeland's classroom)

who do you like?
No one
who do you like?
some body at my church
what is her name?
Soffea
you don't have to yell!

Written Conversation; Paul and Miguel, Age 10 (Sandy Kaser's classroom) writing that they can revisit in order to select drafts to consider for publication. The most common way we have seen children keep track of their writing drafts is in Authors Folders (Graves, 1983). The purpose of these folders is to allow children to collect and organize their writing and to revisit and reflect on that writing over and over again. Authors Folders send the message that first drafts are valued and that children can follow leads and explore possibilities. They allow children to select and separate out the writing that has potential and to accept the tentativeness of the writing process. Children are able to gain a greater depth in their writing and thinking and to search for connections and insights that run across their work.

An Authors Folder usually holds their brainstormed lists of writing topics and various in-process rough drafts, but can also contain memories, observations, and quotes on bits and pieces of paper. Often children return to their folders while in the midst of a new piece to revisit an idea or check how they did something that is now giving them problems. Sometimes, in this process, they identify a piece that they had forgotten and decide to carry it forward to publication. Sometimes they laugh at things they used to do when they "were littler." Authors Folders thus provide the organizational support that authors need for writing over time.

Some teachers have two sets of folders for each child. One set contains writing entries and rough drafts that the child is using or working on at that time. These pocket folders are stored in a cardboard box that is always available for children on a counter or table in the classroom. The second set are expandable hanging folders that hold drafts that are completed and have been published, drafts that the student has decided not to publish, and previous writing entries that the child is currently not using. They may also contain notes or lists that the child wants to keep. These hanging folders are kept in a cardboard box or a file cabinet that children have access to at all times, so they can freely move entries and drafts from one folder to the other. Young children find that boxes with lids, such as file folder boxes, often work better for storing the different sizes and shapes of papers they like to use.

Authors Folders support the role of the author as a decision maker in selecting what to write, how to write, and how long to write. The folders provide a cumulative record of an author's writing entries and pieces—formal and informal, published and unpublished—throughout the year. Both students and teachers can use these folders as a way to monitor growth over time in writing processes and conventions. As students look back through their writing, they are able to see how much they've grown as writers. Students look through their folders or notebooks on a regular basis to reflect on themselves as writers and to write self-evaluations of their writing growth.

Both student self-evaluations and teacher evaluations will be more insightful and complete if a system is developed for recording observations about the student's processes and understandings as a writer. This system should include ways to collect observations during writing, conferencing, and editing as well as on the actual pieces of writing. Routines need to be established so that evaluation becomes part of the curriculum, not something extra tacked on at the end of the term. At parent conferences these folders are a useful document for explaining the curriculum and for helping parents understand how they might support their child's growth in reading and writing. Teachers need to remember, however, that Authors Folders must serve a function for children and not simply become a way for teachers to evaluate children and justify the writing program.

The drafts and ideas in their folders are a source of possible publications. About once a month authors are asked to look through their current folder or Writer's Notebook to find entries or pieces they want to write as a complete draft to take to an Authors Circle for response and then possibly move the draft to a publishable form.

Gaining New Perspectives: Authors Circles

As students move the drafts of their interviews through the authoring cycle, we introduce them to its various components. The next part of the cycle, Authors Circle, is introduced as soon as three or four students have a rough draft that they want to think about with other writers. The drafts that students bring to an Authors Circle are either an in-process draft where the author needs response to solve a problem or figure out where to go next or a rough draft that an author has completed and wants an audience perspective. In Authors Circle, authors read their pieces to the group for their response and suggestions. The focus is always on responding to the meaning of the piece, not to the spelling, punctuation, or neatness.

While authors continually engage in conversations about their writing with others during work time, Authors Circles are a context for more in-depth inquiry and critique of their writing. Authors who come to these circles have a sense of purpose and focus that allows the talk in these small groups to move from conversation to dialogue. They think together to support each other, and so they are encouraged to take different perspectives on their own work as well as the work of others. The major focus in a dialogue is understanding and constructing meaning with each person putting forth the best they have to offer and listening thoughtfully and carefully to bring out the best in others (Peterson, 1992). These circles are *not* cooperative learning groups where different members are assigned particular tasks, but they are collaborative groups where authors inquire together.

Authors Circles facilitate growth by capitalizing on the social nature of learning and authoring. Just the presence of listeners encourages the author to take a different perspective on the piece of writing. Authors shift to a reader's perspective as they read their pieces aloud to the group and receive comments about their pieces from other authors. As detailed in Chapter 1, Corey spontaneously edited his story about his smashed toe as he read it aloud to the rest of the group; then he later made revisions in response to the group's comments.

Through dialogue with others in the group, authors begin to develop the sense of audience that is so essential to becoming a writer who can successfully communicate with others. They gain a sense of what their story is like from that audience's point of view. Because one intent of writing is to communicate a message to others, every author needs to develop a reader's perspective and the awareness of what the audience does and does not know. Authors Circles give children access to readers they know and trust as they continue thinking and working through how they can communicate their meaning through writing.

Authors Circles also capitalize on the social nature of learning because authors see a wide range of writing strategies demonstrated. As they share their drafts, ask questions, and respond in an Authors Circle, they see how other authors handle suggestions, solve problems, revise their pieces, and have an opportunity explicitly to discuss writing strategies. Authors gradually begin to use these strategies in their own writing and to ask themselves the questions they predict other authors will ask in Authors Circle as they work through their early drafts.

Participating in an Authors Circle

The first criterion for coming to Authors Circle is that everyone who comes should have a draft of writing. When we first started these circles, we saw them as a place where authors brought completed drafts rather than partial in-process pieces. We found, however, that when children brought completed drafts, they often saw them as finished and were not open to the comments of other authors. Authors Circle became part of a procedure children went through to get their writing published rather than a vital part of their process of thinking and writing. We wanted Authors Circles to be places where children thought collaboratively and found that if children brought partial drafts at points where *they* felt the need for response, Authors Circles became more productive.

The second criterion is that the author likes the piece but wants to think more about it with others. Authors Circle is different than authors chair. At Authors Circle, authors come to receive help from other authors on what is and is not working in their piece and what, if anything, they might consider doing next. Participants come to Authors Circle for the expressed purpose of supporting their own and each other's authorship. If a child has a piece that he or she likes as is, we recommend that the child take it to authors chair, a special chair designated for various kinds of sharing and read-aloud experiences.

To facilitate these intents, Authors Circle is under the direction of whichever author is presenting a piece. The presenting author indicates what kind of response he or she needs, reads aloud the piece of writing, and asks for response from other authors. The other authors listen carefully, receive the piece by telling what they heard, and then offer supportive criticism. Although authors generally find it difficult to hear criticism of their work, they nonetheless find such criticism helpful. The strategy, from the presenting author's perspective, is to not get defensive, but rather to take notes and later decide what to do with the information gathered. Because the author is the owner of the piece, the final decision about what changes will or will not be made rests with the author. The strategy, from the collaborator's perspective, is to be helpful, take cues from the author, and never challenge the author's ownership of the piece.

Introducing Authors Circle

Authors Circles begin as soon as three or four authors have pieces they want to think about with other authors. Some teachers have a sign-up sheet where students place their names when they are ready for Authors Circle. Others have a basket where students put their drafts to signal that they want to meet. During the class meeting before work time, the basket or sign-up sheet is checked to see who will be meeting that day.

One way that we introduce Authors Circle is by sharing a piece we have been writing, such as a professional article or a children's story. We discuss how we went about getting other authors to read and react to it and indicate the kinds of criticisms we found helpful, the kinds of questions we were asked, and the specific kinds of help we requested. We talk about what we did with this information (tried to be accepting and took notes) and show how the new version does or does not incorporate the suggestions. If teachers do not have a revised piece of their own writing, they can share a rough draft and a revised piece written by a previous student. Another option is for teachers to share their own rough draft, have students ask questions, and then write and share a revised draft with students, telling them what was helpful and talking through revision decisions.

Throughout our introduction we stress ownership and the kinds of comments we find supportive and not so supportive. We also point out that too much good advice can overwhelm the author, making the task of revision appear unmanageable. The criterion for a successful Authors Circle is that the authors leave feeling they had a chance to think collaboratively about their writing and gained some ideas about what to do next.

After setting a frame, we begin our first Authors Circle by asking the first author to tell why he or she brought the piece to the circle before reading it aloud to the group. For example, the author might say, "I don't really like my introduction. It's too boring. I want to make it more exciting so people will want to read my story." By having the author identify the area of difficulty, the author's agenda is given top priority. Our assumption is that the author's interest will largely determine what he or she learns from and uses in the revision process.

Don't be concerned if initially many authors have difficulty identifying where they want response. They may need to begin by reading their pieces aloud to the group and listening to their responses and comments. As they gain experience in thinking and talking about their writing through author talk time and Authors Circle, they will be more specific in identifying specific parts of the piece needing group response and suggestions.

Reading their pieces aloud to the group allows authors to retain physical control of the draft, thereby maintaining ownership of the rough draft both in the circle and later as they decide whether to accept suggestions for changes. As listeners, the other authors are forced to focus on the meaning of the piece rather than on conventions such as spelling or punctuation.

After listening to the piece, the other authors are asked to receive the piece by saying what they heard. We assume the author already likes the piece because the author selected it to bring to the circle, and so we inform children that telling an author merely that they like a piece is not particularly helpful. Having the children first state what they heard in the piece lets the author know what is working and creates an atmosphere of collaboration. If the children move immediately to asking questions, the author often feels more defensive about the piece. The author, first and foremost, needs to feel that the other participants have really listened to *what* he or she had to say before they discuss *how* it was said. Authors need to know that their thoughts matter.

The questions and comments about unclear areas, however, are what really push the author to reconsider a piece in a new way. As Amy, a third-grade writer, told us, "When they tell me what they like, that doesn't really help me, but when they ask me questions, that really makes me think." During this part of the circle, children first make suggestions on the parts where the author asked for response and then ask questions about things they didn't understand or want to know more about, offering other suggestions on how the author could improve the piece. It takes a while for children to understand how to receive and give constructive criticism. Initially many students will respond with "I like it," "It was fine," or "Make it longer." They are inexperienced in receiving and reacting to another author's writing, and so it takes time for them to learn how to respond in a specific and constructive manner.

If the listeners criticize the author's sentence structure or grammar, we simply remind them that before authors can edit (i.e., worry about grammar, spelling, and so on), they have to be sure they have included everything they want to say. We further remind them that often authors themselves realize they could have said something in a better way and that typically some of these changes will occur as they revise for meaning. At this point in the authoring cycle, authors are

Irene

1. I need to write 2 stories one about Jamies party and one when Monique and Cecelia sleped over.

2. I could write my stories in to letters.

3 I could write my stories as journals.

4 I can read books with letters and journals

5. I will read I hate Ronald Roberts.

6 My choice is I want to make my 2 stories into letters.

7. I need to know who I am going to write to.

Notes from Authors Circle; Irene, Age 11 (Gloria Kauffman's classroom)

Section One
The Authoring Cycle:
Let's Talk Curriculum

interested in working on a particular problem area in their draft or in whether they have included everything needed to communicate their story to others. The focus of Authors Circle is on thinking about meaning. Editing for conventions is the function of Editors Table.

When the other authors ask questions or identify unclear areas, the author takes notes on the rough draft or a small piece of paper to refer to later. We tell students that taking notes does not mean the changes will be made, only that they will have the information to consider later. The other authors in turn read their pieces, and the listeners tell them what they heard in the pieces, ask questions, and make suggestions. Because reading and discussing writing takes time, Authors Circles should be kept small and discussion and turn taking should be kept moving. Remind students who received help that it is their responsibility to give help when others want it. Even if they like the ending of someone's story but the author does not, they are obligated to offer other ways the author might explore ending the piece. Although it does not hurt for them to say they like the ending the way it is, they should respond to the author's request.

If authors come to an Authors Circle to share rather than to gain new perspectives on their piece, we remind them that they can share in author talk time or authors chair; Authors Circle is for seeking advice and thinking with others. Authors are responsible for deciding what to work on to improve their writing each time they come to a circle. Authors are never "done"; they just finally quit. The real issue is not perfection but, rather, "Of all the things in need of improvement, what will I work on this time?" The teacher and other authors need to remember that the author makes these decisions, rather than others imposing their beliefs about what they think is good writing. Some writers choose to make few revisions in a current piece but use the comments from Authors Circle in their next piece of writing.

Students often need a great deal of support in their first Authors Circles so that every author walks away feeling the circle has helped them as authors. Teachers will find that less and less discussion of how to conduct the circle has to take place over time. During the first circles, teachers provide important demonstrations of the kinds of comments and questions that authors can use to support each other. Misconceptions can cause problems that undermine the very function that Authors Circle is designed to serve. As students gain experience, teachers find that they need not—and, in fact, should not—be present at every circle and only join one or two circles that they feel could particularly benefit from their presence.

Whenever possible, teachers should participate in Authors Circles as an author with a piece of writing. This allows teachers to participate with other authors, both receiving and giving suggestions, without imposing their judgments on students' work. Because the teacher is a participant, students feel freer to collaborate with the teacher and to reject suggestions that the teacher makes for revision instead of feeling that "I have to change it because the teacher said so." When teachers participate as authors, they can demonstrate the strategies that a more experienced writer uses. Students come to see that all writers, including adults, produce drafts that need revision—a revelation to students who think that adults produce perfect drafts the first time through. They realize that revision is a natural part of authoring for everyone and so begin to value the process of conferring with others.

Many teachers use the whole group meetings before work time as a place to provide further demonstrations of how to respond in an Authors Circle. Instead of trying to be present in every circle, teachers can use the group meeting to read aloud from children's literature and encourage group response, to read their own work for response, and to have a particular author share an in-process piece for whole class response. By carefully observing the needs of authors and the ways in which the Authors Circles are and are not functioning, teachers can determine the particular aspects needing discussion. A student can be asked to share a particular piece of writing so that a real context is established for discussing the aspects of the writing process or the Authors Circles that need to be addressed.

The first circles may seem unproductive, but, given the chance, children will gradually discover the power of consulting with their fellow authors. We have found that many children need to participate in the entire authoring cycle before they understand the purpose of Authors Circle. Once their pieces are edited by an outside editor and then published and shared with the class, they realize how helpful it is to receive input from other authors. This is why we begin with an engagement such as Getting to Know You that will quickly lead to a publication.

Changing the Format of Authors Circle

The procedures for how to conduct an Authors Circle should be adapted to fit the needs of the group and so change over time. By understanding at a general level how Authors Circle supports authors, teachers can use this understanding in making adjustments so that these circles are productive for particular authors. Because there is no one way to conduct an Authors Circle, teachers should constantly evaluate these circles with their students so that they stay effective.

We have found, for example, that sometimes authors have to read their pieces aloud twice when circles first begin because students have not yet learned how to listen and respond to another person's writing. Students need the first reading to get a frame for the story and the second reading to identify areas that are unclear. Young children particularly seem to have difficulty listening and responding to others' stories. Gloria Kauffman found that sharing drafts on Storyboards significantly increased the amount of interaction because young children can visually and aurally follow the story and reference the Storyboard in their discussions.

Jerry found that having students read aloud their piece often seemed to shut down discussion when they first brought it to Authors Circle. He introduced a variation where an author talked about the piece and the strategies he or she had tried during writing. The listeners then challenged the author to think about other strategies that might be used. The author left the circle, without ever reading the piece to the group, and returned to writing. Only at the second Authors Circle on a piece did authors read their pieces aloud to the group. This variation encourages authors to play with language in new ways.

When authors begin writing lengthy pieces, teachers may need to provide copies of their drafts for the receiving authors to look at because they cannot keep the entire story in their heads. This should be considered only after a tone has been set that focuses on content, not convention. We have also found that when pieces get longer, it is important to limit circles to three authors, or they get too long and students lose interest.

As students understand and value the role that other authors play in the revision process, they will take charge of these circles themselves. Before long students who have pieces they want to revise will wait until one of their favorite authors also has something ready, so they can be in the same group. These author friendship groups should be encouraged. All authors have fellow authors to whom they prefer to read their rough draft efforts, in part because they have proven trustworthy and in part because they intuitively seem to know each other and what is the most helpful thing to say at a certain point. In some cases, the other students do not bring a draft, but simply gather to support the author and then disband as a group.

Bringing drama into Authors Circles can provide new perspectives through transmediation across sign systems. Authors can choose other students to act out particular roles, briefly explain the plot, and then begin reading the story aloud while the students act out their parts. Following this drama, the students meet to discuss the author's observations and the actors talk about what they would have liked to do that wasn't in the story. The author can also give a description of the story, then stand back and watch the others create dialogue and act out their interpretation of the story. Another variation is to assign narrator and character parts and have the story read aloud as a Readers Theatre.

Author Talk Time

While teachers generally think of Authors Circles as formal groups of authors who meet during work time, the most significant talk about writing may occur during author talk time at the end of work time. During author talk time, authors gather—in small groups, with a partner, or as a whole class—to talk about what they consider significant or problematic from their work that day as readers and writers. As they talk, they often gain new perspectives on in-process pieces of writing that result in much more significant rethinking and re-visioning than when they take a completed draft to an Authors Circle. In this context, they are not reading their drafts to each other but are talking about their writing with other authors. The comfort and demonstrations they receive through this talk are critical to the success of Authors Circles and their thinking as writers.

Kathleen Crawford organizes her fourth grade students into writing groups of four students who stay together over a period of time. Twice a week, these groups gather during author talk time to share and respond to each other's writing. Because the same children stay in the same groups, they become comfortable and familiar with each other's writing. These groups have been an effective introduction to Authors Circles.

Preserving the Function of Authors Circle Through Authors Chair

Authors chair is where the reader sits to share either a child-authored text or a professionally authored text (Graves & Hansen, 1983).

Children and teachers come to authors chair to share texts with a group by reading that text aloud to a group. Children are invited to use authors chair throughout work time or whenever they have something to share and can find an audience to listen. Unlike author talk time, at authors chair children can read their whole text.

Authors chair differs from Authors Circle in that children come to authors chair to share their writing through reading the text rather than conferring to see what is and is not working in the piece. The talk at authors chair is similar to the talk about a read-aloud book; children might respond to the author by talking briefly about their connections and understandings of the piece. They do not suggest revisions or critique it. Their presence is all that is really required from the author's perspective. The presence of authors chair helps preserve the function of Authors Circle. If children are coming to Authors Circles wanting to share rather than to think about or revise their pieces, this may be occurring because no time is available for children to share a piece with others.

Authors chair encourages children to reread what they have written. Even though the focus is on sharing and not on rethinking their text, the change in perspective from writer to reader may highlight things in need of revision. It is not uncommon to see children stop while reading, change a spelling, add a word, or even shrug their shoulders when it appears that their thoughts have been too far ahead of their writing. Like all writers, children like to share their first draft efforts with others. We often read what we have written to a family member or a graduate student. Sometimes we are not as interested in response from our listeners as we are in finding out how it "sounds" and "reads." Children have these same needs. Authors chair meets those needs so that children will go to Authors Circle for different purposes.

Children can indicate they want to share simply by walking over to authors chair during work time. Anyone who wants to can go and join the author for sharing. Some teachers use a sign-up sheet where each morning children who want to share sign their name and what they want to share. Other children in the classroom can then decide whether they want to join a group during that morning. For some authors, authors chair serves as a form of informal publication, and they put the piece away after sharing. Other times, they continue working on that piece and taking it through the authoring cycle.

Other Forms of Collaborating with Authors

While Authors Circle is the major form of dialogue with other authors, collaboration can occur in other classroom settings. These include student-to-student conferences that are more intimate and spontaneous due to the influence of Authors Circles. Students may also quickly gather an informal group of authors to respond to something they have written rather than waiting for a formal Authors Circle. When authors take their pieces to an Authors Circle as they write, they often do not return to a formal Authors Circle once the piece is finished; instead they share the piece informally in student-to-student conferences.

Sometimes students form a study group to research the particular genre or content they are writing about in their own work. If a group of authors is writing mysteries, members spend some of their writing time reading and discussing mysteries. Or, if a group of authors is writing about pollution, members may form a study group to research the topic.

Another setting is a student-teacher conference where students have the opportunity to interact individually with the teacher as an author with more writing experience. This type of conference also gives the teacher a chance to do a strategy lesson based on an immediate and felt need of the student. Lucy Calkins (1994) describes these conferences in great depth and reminds teachers that their first role is to listen and ask questions so they understand the writer and the writer's process. The teacher focuses on the writer, not the specific piece of writing, and so suggests strategies that students can add to their repertoire, instead of specific solutions for that piece.

Another variation is an activity called Writing in the Round. When authors suspect that they have a "hot piece" that they want to publish, a blank sheet of paper can be attached to the end of the draft and the draft left at the writing-reading center. Those who read the piece (classmates, teachers, parents, visitors) are asked to write their comments and recommendations for revision on the attached sheet, dating and signing their comments. Authors are encouraged to make the first entry on the blank sheet telling their readers what they particularly like about the piece and the areas they see as problematic (e.g., "I don't like my ending but I can't think of anything else").

These variations do not replace Authors Circles but augment them. Any engagement used in this part of the authoring cycle involves authors in dialogue about their writing and gives them response from their readership for the purpose of reconsidering their writing from new perspectives. Nancie Atwell (1987) points out the goal of conferences is not to get students to revise but to help them grow to independence as writers. She reminds us that we are teaching the writer, not the piece of writing.

Through collaboration with others, authors learn how to explore meaning with an audience and how to think critically about their writing. They become part of a thought collective in their classroom that expands their world as they hear others' ideas and express their own. Authors Circles grow out of a real need for authors to communicate with others, to understand readers' perspectives, and to expand and clarify the ideas they want to express through writing. Through this dialogue, learners gain new perspectives and outgrow their current selves. Even though they may not revise a particular piece, authors are learning a way of thinking and are gaining flexibility and awareness of their writing process. While some authors find revising their current piece an overwhelming or threatening task, they do not necessarily ignore others' comments. They simply use these comments in their next piece of writing.

These same needs are present when students author meaning in other sign systems, such as art, drama, movement, mathematics, and music. Authors Circle supports authors of all kinds of meaning to think about and explore their ideas with others. Decisions about how to respond to the suggestions and comments of others, however, are made in private by the author.

Attending to Difference: Semantic Revision and Self-Editing

When authors leave an Authors Circle, they often feel a tension between their vision of their writing and the responses of other authors. They must make decisions about how they will respond to these tensions through revision in order to create a piece of writing that has unity for themselves as well as for other readers. Authors may occasionally decide that they no longer want to revise and publish a piece and return it to their Author Folders. Most authors, however, make semantic revisions of their writing based on the suggestions from Authors Circle and then edit for conventions such as spelling that they have noticed as they read their piece to themselves and others.

An Author's Right to Control Revision

Authors wait to revise their pieces until they leave the Authors Circle so they can consider in private the comments and suggestions that were made and not feel forced to make changes. They need not follow the advice of other authors, but instead they can make revisions based on their vision of what the piece should say and on the issues they feel ready to deal with in their writing. Although excellent suggestions may have been given in Authors Circle, the author may not yet know how to deal with these issues or may have another agenda that is more important for that particular piece. Authors may also decide to act on suggestions in their next piece of writing instead of revising the current piece. The right to make decisions about semantic revision is imperative for authors to retain their vision for a particular piece of writing and to allow them to create their own unified meaning for that piece.

We have observed classrooms where students turn out wonderful writing, but that writing is the teacher's rather than the students'. The teacher wants students' writing to be the best possible and so pushes students to make many revisions instead of allowing them to focus on the revisions they are most interested in and feel capable of handling. Teachers need to be sensitive to what the author is interested in exploring because those are the areas in which growth and learning are most likely. If the author's inquiry question is how to better end the story, this will be a productive area to explore even though the teacher can identify other parts of the story that could also be improved. Although the teacher or other students may mention some of these other areas in the Authors Circle, authors will find comments on the area they want to improve most helpful and will probably use only those suggestions during semantic revision. No author can work on improving all aspects of writing at one time. When teachers try to get authors to make many different kinds of revisions, they end up taking over the writing of the piece.

That authors must have ownership of their pieces and make decisions on revisions does not mean that teachers no longer have a role in students' growth as authors. Teachers influence the growth of the authors in their classrooms just by establishing the authoring cycle structure. Teachers also influence authors by the invitations and suggestions they offer in informal conferences, Authors Circles, and class meetings. The teacher uses what the author is exploring to make suggestions and invitations, connecting with that author instead of taking control of the piece. Because the teacher is offering suggestions and invitations, the author retains the right to make final decisions about semantic revision.

Teachers should demonstrate to students how to write a revised section on a new sheet of paper and to insert it into the text by cutting and pasting or by drawing arrows to another part of the paper where the insert is written. We also suggest that rough drafts be written on only one side of the paper and that students skip every other line on the paper when writing to make revision easier. Students are often reluctant to consider revisions because they believe that they will need to recopy their entire piece, and so these techniques for quick revisions affect their willingness to rethink and revise their writing.

The kinds of revisions which authors explore change over time as they gain more experience with writing. Initially, revision for young children simply means adding missing information or changing the order within a piece. Their focus is on learning to write fluently and independently rather than to write well and so revision does not play a key role for them. Some authors do not revise a piece, but take the suggestions and write a completely new version. Only as authors gain experience and maturity are they able to move from revision as correcting and "fixing up" a piece of writing to using revision as a process of discovery. Lucy Calkins (1994) points out that revision may even make the writing worse, but that what is important is not the specific revisions themselves but the habits of mind that authors learn.

Revision and Self-Editing Process with Young Children

Some educators believe that young children do not understand revising for meaning and so Authors Circles are not essential in their classrooms. An experience in Gloria Kauffman's first-grade classroom demonstrated to us that young children can and do think in these ways. During the second week of school, Gloria read aloud *Ten Little Bears* (Ruwe, 1971) and the children brainstormed ideas about other activities the bears might do. They were then handed a piece of paper on which Gloria had written the repeating part of the sentence with a space for them to write what their bear would do. Once the

children had completed their pages, they were stapled together to make a Group Composed Book called *Eighteen Little Bears*.

The class wrote several Group Composed Books based on patterns from predictable books during the first two weeks of school. With Parents' Night coming up at the school, we suggested that they publish one of their books for their parents to take home. The children selected *Eighteen Little Bears* as their favorite, and we made photocopies of their original pages to take to Authors Circle. The children met in Authors Circles and then revised their pages. These were typed, illustrated by each child, and reduced on a copy machine to produce a book that each family took home on Parents' Night.

As we read through the children's revisions of their pages, we were excited to see that all of the children revised for meaning rather than for conventions. These first-grade children understood the need to focus on meaning before having to attend to conventions and were able to use their classmates' comments to make these revisions.

Attending to Conventions Through Self-Editing

As authors read and reread their pieces to themselves and others, they also begin to self-edit their writing. Self-editing involves attend-

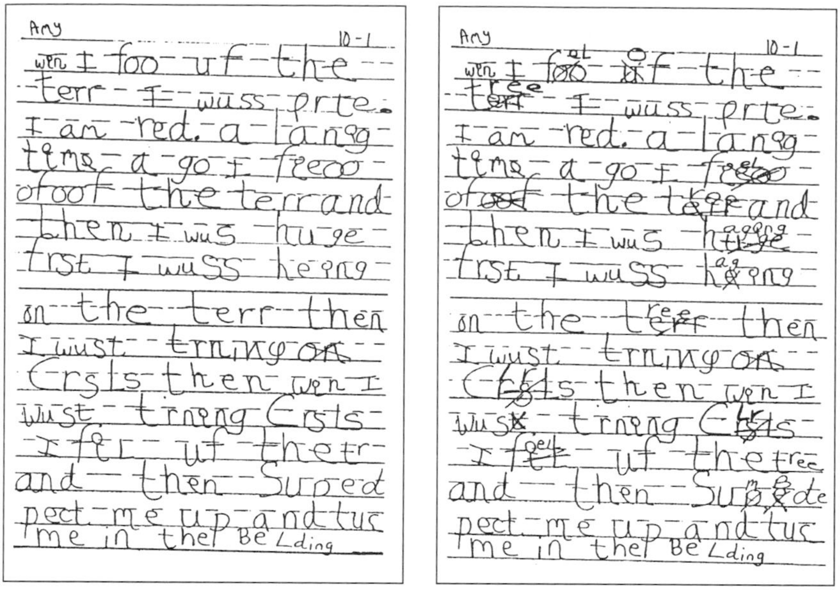

FIGURE 2.8
Original and Revised Leaf Story; Amy, Age 6 (Gloria Kauffman's classroom)

TRANSLATION
When I fell off the tree I was pretty. I am red. A long time ago I fell off the tree and then I was hanging. First I was hanging on the tree then I was turning colors. Then when I was turning colors I fell off the tree. And then somebody picked me up and took me in the building.

ing to conventional aspects such as spelling, grammar, punctuation, and capitalization. Once authors serve as outside editors for other authors, they often begin to do more self-editing of their own work. Although the major responsibility for editing occurs at Editors Table, authors are encouraged to clean up any conventions they notice before submitting their writing to be edited by outside readers.

When authors revisit their writing, they are able to take a different perspective and use their understandings about story and language. The areas of the cycle labeled self-editing and Editors Table represent points that highlight editing for purposes of moving a draft document to formal publication. The issue thus is not one of convention or meaning but rather a shift in focus. Authors use conventions all the time, but their focus is not always on those conventions. During the writing of the rough draft, when authors are focusing on constructing meaning, they intuitively use conventions and operate with their best current control of conventions. If they are required to focus on conventions during these early stages, the communicative and discovery aspects of writing suffer.

An example of this shift in focus from meaning to convention occurred when Amy, a first grader, finished writing a story about leaves and was waiting for an Authors Circle to meet. As she waited, she read back through her story and made corrections in spelling. The self-editing Amy did five minutes after she finished writing her story

Chapter Two
The Authoring Cycle
as a Curricular
Framework for Writing

shows that she had more knowledge about spelling than she was able to use when she was focusing on meaning. Once she got that meaning down, however, she shifted her focus and used her knowledge of conventions.

The shift in focus allows authors to not only use their knowledge about conventions such as spelling but also their understandings about story structures and genre. One day during the class meeting, Caroline Mattson invited the children in her kindergarten classroom to write their own stories for wordless picture books. She had made photocopies of the pages of several wordless books so that children had room to write their text on the pages themselves. The books were stapled and available as multiple sets in the writing reading center. Kammi chose to write a story about a group of children finding and burying a dead bird. Thus drafted, Kammi's story was added to the classroom library as a form of informal publication.

About a week after Kammi had contributed her book to the library, one of Kammi's classmates, Stephanie, read her book. When she got done she commented, "Oh, Kammi, I like your book." "Oh," reflected Kammi, "I don't think I much care for it anymore." Overhearing the conversation, Caroline Mattson remarked, "And why is that?" "Oh, I made a mistake. I shouldn't have just described the pictures. I should have written about what they [the characters in the pictures] were thinking." "Well, there are more copies of the book at the writing-reading center. You might like to redo your story now that you've got a better idea. Most writers have to rewrite things several times to get them the way they want."

Kammi accepted the invitation and created a new story. What is impressive about Kammi's revision is that she speculates on what the characters were thinking about, explicates several key causal relationships, semantically elaborates all the elements of her story structure, reduces semantic redundancy by combining several sentences, cleans up many of her misspellings, and develops a clear voice in her writing. Even before the revision, Kammi's involvement in the authoring cycle permitted her to test her growing understanding of stories, of how one separates ideas in writing, of how the sounds of language are mapped onto written letters, of how one uses writing to mean, and more. She was able to orchestrate what she already knew by taking the stance of a reader as well as a writer.

Authors should not be asked to copy over their work before submitting it for editing. Only on the rare occasion when it is impossible

1. WANS APNATIM ~~ThAiD~~ ThAIR WAS A DED BRD.

2. ThAT BRDA ~~si~~ is DED, SED TOMMY.

3. OH WAT A POR BIRD.

4. The giry is ~~SAD~~ CRING

5. ThAiR WOKING TO THE FORIZT.

6. ThAIR BAiRiNG THE BiRD.

7. THEY R BRiNGiNG flowRS.

8. THEY R SAD.

HERE LIES A BIRD THAT IS DEAD

9. TOMMY LOOKt UP AT THE SCi.

10. THEYR PLAIN BLL.

FIGURE 2.9
Original Story; Kammi, Age 6
(Caroline Mattson's classroom)

WANS A 1PON1ATIME thaair woAS A DEAD BriD.

Tommy sied Look AT tht 1 Por BriD.

I WUN DER How THEat BirD Got KilD.

Lests BARE THe BiRD, SAiD TORY.

So Tory KAMMi Tommy AND Dirk To BARE All SET owt out To BARE THE BIRD.

So Tommy PUFt THE BiRD oN THE MAPLE LEFE So THAT THAY DiNt HAf to KARRY HIM.

KaaMMi's 1BriGN Bringing I Lots of flowrs.

THEY JCRATZEt A SINE no A ROOK.

HERE LIES A BIRD THAT IS DEAD

Theey all Lookt up At The SkY To see How The BiRD Got KilD.

THEY WERE GLAD THAT THEY BAI3RED the BiRD.

FIGURE 2.10
Revision of Original Story;
Kammi, Age 6 (Caroline
Mattson's classroom)

to follow a revised copy is an author ever asked to recopy anything. If the revised draft is difficult to read, we usually have authors read their piece to the editor or typist rather than recopy it. Making authors recopy their writing can quickly kill their interest in revisions. Young children who use few conventions generally read their pieces to the typist.

Sometimes, after extensive revision, authors will want to take their piece through Authors Circle a second time, as Corey decided to do with his "smashed toe" story. This is encouraged and is evidence that Authors Circle is becoming a natural part of the authoring process. Once authors are satisfied with their revised drafts, these drafts are submitted to Editors Table if the author is creating a formal publication or go directly to publication if the author is publishing it informally.

Sharing What Was Learned: Editors Table, Publication, and Celebration

When authors decide to share what they have learned with others through writing, they need to examine readers' needs and the ways they might present their work to others. Through this process they are able to determine what they currently know and celebrate their accomplishments as authors. Pulling together a piece of writing for presentation to others transforms their understandings as authors and clarifies what they do and do not know. Curricular engagements which support students in sharing what they have learned include Editors Table, a publication program, and ways to celebrate authorship in the classroom.

Shifting in Perspective from Author to Reader to Editor

Because the purpose of written language is to communicate a message, authors focus on getting their meaning down during the early parts of the authoring cycle. When authors decide to take their pieces to formal publication, they edit them for convention to show their regard for readers. It needs to be stressed, however, that editing does not begin at those points labeled self-editing and Editors Table on the authoring cycle. As students reread their in-process rough drafts, or read their pieces at Authors Circle, they commonly correct many surface features of their texts.

Editors Table is usually the first point at which someone other than the author reads the piece and so the focus shifts to conventions. Conventions exist to support outside readers as they construct meaning through reading. The author already knows what the piece says, and so misspelled words or other conventional miscues do not interfere with the author's reading of the piece. Adults as well as children find it more difficult to proofread their own work than to proofread the work of someone else. Although both revision and self-editing help authors develop the perspective of a reader, Editors Table involves an outside reader who edits for meaning and conventions. This type of editing is needed only when something is going to be formally published for an audience. Informal writing often has no reason to be edited.

When authors serve as editors of others' writing or have editors talk to them about their own work, they begin to understand the importance of conventions for reading. This shift in perspective from author to reader to editor produces a learning situation in which authors discover new conventions. Marvin, a first grader, was writing a story about leaves when Kathy stopped by his desk for an informal conference. She noticed that he was exploring the concept of where to put spaces in his writing and so commented to him, "You know, it would really help me as a reader if you put your spaces between the words." Marvin looked at her and said, "Oh, okay," and went back to his writing. Marvin immediately began leaving spaces between his words. Although this was not a formal editing conference, this experience demonstrates that a shift in perspective from author to reader allows an author to discover new conventions.

Marvin's ability to immediately use spaces between words occurred because he was already exploring spacing. An author begins using conventions when they do not take the author's attention away from creating meaning. This was obviously true for Marvin as he continued his story. The convention of putting spaces between words did not cost him a great deal of mental energy. He realized that it would support the reading of his story by other people, and so this convention entered naturally into his writing.

Marvin's exploration of spacing demonstrates that authors need the chance to explore alternatives to conventions and to use their best current knowledge. This exploration of alternatives makes authors more receptive to learning the convention. Giving authors the chance to explore alternatives is not putting off learning conventions

Story Writing; Marvin, Age 6
(Gloria Kauffman's classroom)

TRANSLATION:
I am a leaf. A long time ago
I was on a tree. I
don't have food.
I am red. I fell
off the tree. The
sun was shining
on me.

but rather is a necessary part of this learning. Although authors use their best current knowledge of conventions as they write, through editing they are able to go beyond their current understandings.

Editing is a social event and a natural part of authoring. All authors need outside editors—no writer singlehandedly controls the authoring process. This is one misconception that past approaches to reading and writing have perpetuated. The result is guilt, when the simple fact is that almost every piece ever published has had the benefit of outside editing by others.

The Role of Editing in the Authoring Cycle

We have found that many teachers hesitate to start Editors Table in their classrooms. They feel that editing is beyond the capabilities of their students, that the focus on editing will inhibit students as they write, or that they do not have time to spend with both Authors Circles and Editors Table. They believe that they need to edit with the child, a position that may reflect their unwillingness to completely let go of a skills model. Editing is their chance to teach directly the skills they believe all children need, and they do not want to turn over this function to children.

The physical presence of the Editors Table is a signal to students just beginning to draft a piece that they can take risks, that their concerns for spelling and grammar are important, that this classroom is a safe environment that supports authors, and that when and if they decide to "go public," their concerns about conventions will be handled. Understanding the function and place of editing in the authoring cycle is important. The very presence of an Editors Table allows real authoring to start.

Even if students use many functional spellings, editing is beneficial for both more and less proficient writers in helping them take a reader's perspective and in gaining control over conventions. Rather than reserving the process of editing for themselves, teachers simply make adjustments in the amount and type of conventions students are expected to look for as they edit. Teachers should not expect or wait until students can do the same quality of editing that the teacher is able to do. Students should begin editing right away at whatever level they can handle. Just as we do not expect young children immediately to produce adult language as they learn to talk, we should not expect students immediately to meet adult standards for conventions in written language. They need time to explore and discover these conventions gradually.

Teachers do not need to be present at both Authors Circles and Editors Table. Once these groups are functioning, teachers should only occasionally join the groups. If the teacher is always present at each group, this is an indication that the teacher is controlling too much of the process and making students depend on teacher input rather than allowing students to take over the process themselves. Students who need more support can initially edit with a partner rather than with the teacher. Editors Table recognizes that students learn best through actually using skills for purposes that make sense to them. Editing the work of other authors has a real function in the classroom. Sitting beside the teacher while he or she corrects your work does not. Little is learned by the author, other than a feeling of defeat.

Gloria Kauffman discovered the important function that editing plays when she postponed beginning Editors Table with her first-grade students, feeling they were not ready to handle it. She noted late in the year that few were using punctuation in their writing and realized that the children did not understand the importance of conventions such as punctuation because she or another adult always served as the editor. She did not need to ask the authors about invented spellings or punctuation because she already knew what the piece said. If students had served as outside editors, they would have been faced with reading someone else's piece or with an editor coming to talk to them about parts that were difficult to read. As argued earlier, conventions are important to *readers* who need them to construct meaning. When Editors Table is omitted from the authoring cycle, authors do not fully realize the function of conventions.

In studying the process of editing during Mary Lynn Woods's summer program, we found that editors during the first week were aware of approximately sixty-five percent of conventional changes, a statistic that would please any English teacher. By the end of the third week, editors were aware of eighty-nine percent of the conventional changes needed in a given text. This observation was interesting enough. The real finding, however, was that over time the function of the editor changed. As the authors gained experience, knowledge, and confidence, they began to assume more responsibility for self-editing, both for content and convention. Thus, outside editors needed to make fewer conventional changes, and, in turn, found the quality of the changes to be increasingly complex, calling for a finer understanding of English syntax.

Setting up Editors Table

In the classrooms in which we have worked, once a student has revised and self-edited a piece to submit for publication, it is put into the editors box to be taken to Editors Table. In most classrooms, the editors work with the handwritten, revised, rough draft. In some classrooms, students type the text on the computer, look over the typed copy for one final proofing, and place it in the editors box.

Editors Table is a physically identifiable area in the classroom. It often includes a typewriter or computer, a set of basic reference books (thesaurus, spelling dictionary, regular dictionary, English stylebook, and so on), visor hats or buttons for the editors to wear, a "ready for typing" box, an in-box, a managing editor box, pens, pencils, colored markers, a sign reading "Quiet! Editors at Work," a poster of various editing marks, a chart showing what this week's editors have decided specifically to look for when editing, and so on.

Usually students volunteer to serve as outside editors for one week, although the length of time can vary with the type and frequency of publication. Some teachers have three to five students serve as editors for a week. Everyone, from the best and most proficient writer to the least proficient writer, gets a turn. Sometimes teachers think that only the better writers will be able to handle the demands of editing. We have found, however, that although the less proficient writers make fewer editorial changes, they tend to learn more from the experience. The less proficient writers use conventions the least and so benefit from focusing on conventions in someone else's work.

During the week that students serve as editors, they have limited opportunities to work on their writing. Keeping authors away from their writing may conceptually bother a conscientious teacher. However, this change in perspective—from writer to editor, from user to critic—often is quite beneficial as well as motivating. After a week's hiatus students are anxious to get on with their writing. They have new ideas as well as new perspectives on the writing process and understandings about conventions.

Introducing Editors Table

In introducing Editors Table, we walk the first group through the process. We begin by sharing documents similar to what the class is

Editing Marks

☰	capitalize
⊙	make a period
∧	add something
⋏	add a comma
⌄	add quotation marks
↶	take something away
◯	spell correctly
¶	indent the paragraph
/	make a lower case letter
∿ tr	transpose

Editing Guidelines

going to publish (e.g., books or newspapers) and talking about what an editor of this publication does. After listing the responsibilities of an editor, the group examines copies of a rough draft piece of writing. They discuss to whom this draft belongs to stress the author's ownership. The group uses this draft to decide on the editorial markings that they will use for editing. These rules are written on a blackboard or chart, and the editors then begin their first round of editing. At the end of this first round, the editors suggest changes in their rules. The second group of editors the following week proceeds from the list generated by the first group and makes any changes they consider important. For the most part, little consultation with the first group is needed, because by the time the first set of editors complete their week, authors have been consulted so often that everyone knows what one does at Editors Table.

The amount and kind of editing varies according to the current level of control students have over conventions. With young children, an editor usually needs to have the author read the story; the author and editor together circle several words they think might be misspelled and want the typist to check. With all ages of children, it helps to have students work as partners in editing a particular piece when they first begin. The editing chart on which the group indicates what they will look for during editing can begin with only one or two conventions and other conventions can be added as students are able to deal with them.

Editing for Semantics and Conventions

Editing generally involves both semantic editing and editing for convention. The first task of the outside editor is semantic editing—reading the piece to make sure it makes sense. Editors do *not* have the right to make meaning changes in the texts they read because editors do not own text; authors do. If something does not make sense, the editor finds the author, explains the problem, and lets the author decide whether to change the text. Minor changes in text that do not change the intended meaning of the piece can be made by the editor. We usually suggest that editors not bring more than three questions regarding meaning to the author so that the author does not feel overwhelmed.

Once editors have read the piece for sense and consulted with the author, the piece is ready to edit for conventions. Editing for conventions includes editing for grammar and spelling. During this editing, editors reread each piece several times, paying particular attention to conventions they as a group have decided to worry about, such as run-on sentences, capitals and periods, quotation marks, commas, and paragraphing. They also check for spelling. We suggest that the editor read through the piece and highlight any word that looks questionable; then editors work together, consult each other on spellings, and use resource materials if they are unsure. One strategy that we have suggested to editors is that they write the word several times, trying out different spellings, and then choose the one they think looks correct.

After a document goes through semantic editing and editing for conventions, it is ready to be sent to the managing editor. This is typically the classroom teacher or the person doing the final draft typing. If the rough draft was earlier typed into the computer, the corrections can be made on the computer. If errors in convention remain, the managing editor makes those changes, just as any typist in an office would. The managing editor does not have the prerogative to make changes that affect the meaning of the piece.

Depending on the type of publication, editors may have other responsibilities beyond editing texts. If the publication is a newspaper, editors can be involved in deciding on layout, organization, assembly, and distribution of the publication. Readers can be invited to write letters to the editors giving their suggestions on how to improve a publication. When we were involved in producing a newspaper in a summer reading program in Indianapolis, readers wrote letters suggesting the addition of cartoons, jokes, page numbers, and different kinds of articles. They also wrote letters complaining about typing mistakes that had changed their articles. The editors printed these letters with their answers in future publications and made changes in the newspaper. Everyone became more interested and involved in the newspaper because of these letters to the editors.

We want to stress that every piece of writing does not need to be edited. Students should be involved in many informal writing experiences (journals, pen pal letters, stories, and so on) that never go to publication. Only pieces that have been selected for formal publication go through editing. Editing may not be necessary for all pieces in a publication, such as letters to the editors or personal ads. It may also not be needed for more informal publications. Some children choose

Letter to the Editors and Editors' Reply; Mai Xia, Age 12 (Indianapolis summer program)

Letter to the Editors; Keith, Age 7 (Indianapolis summer program)

to share their pieces as a rough draft at authors chair, by posting them on a classroom bulletin board, or by making their own informal books; these pieces go through minimal or no outside editing.

Publication and Celebration of Authorship

Although there are many forms of celebrating authorship, publication is clearly one of the most important. In fact, we would go so far as to say that to establish an authoring cycle in the classroom, the first thing that is needed is a publishing program. Publishing creates a purpose and audience for authors to move documents through the entire authoring cycle.

Several criteria define a published document. First, there must be a real audience for the document and a recognized need for publication. Second, there should be a continuing use of that publication to keep it alive and functional in the classroom. If a document is read only once and then disappears, why publish it? We have found that when published books become part of the class library, they are read over and over; students then see a purpose for publication.

Publication can be both informal and formal and can include group and individual books, newspapers, class magazines, displays in classrooms and hallways, posters, games, invitations, and announcements. The kind of publication, informal or formal, that occurs in a classroom is determined by the projected audience. In addition to classroom publications, students can submit their work to the school paper, the local newspaper, trade magazines that publish student writing, or writing contests.

Informal Publication for an Immediate Audience

Displays of student work on bulletin boards in the classroom and hallway are a form of informal publication. By having students create posters or large murals on which their writing and art has been cut into interesting shapes, these displays can be visually attractive. Students can share their drafts informally with peers at authors chair as a form of publication. They can also write a page based on a patterned language book for a Group Composed Book to put in the class library. Many of these publications use students' first draft efforts.

These informal publications work well in the secure environment of the classroom. Depending on the school, displaying such student work in the hallway may or may not be wise. This decision rests with the teacher, but the guideline to follow is that the teacher is there to support the students' use and exploration of writing, not to embarrass them when they engage in such exploration. If either the teacher or the students will be judged negatively by the work displayed in the hall, or if parents and administrators do not understand the program, then we recommend that teachers not display first drafts outside the low-risk environment of the classroom.

We use the same rule in deciding whether first draft work will go home. We generally do not send rough drafts home until we have had a chance to talk with parents. At Parents' Day we explain the writing cycle and recommend that the home environment be a low-risk environment so that children can feel free to share first drafts. If, later on, parents come in wondering when their child is going to attend to spelling and grammar, we remind them that they are reacting to first drafts and show them some of the child's writing that has been published.

Formal Publication for an Outside Audience

As student work moves further and further from the supportive environment of the classroom, a more formal publishing program is needed. To create such a need we recommend that teachers set up a class magazine or newspaper and a book-publishing program in addition to any more formal student publications that exist at the school or district level.

In setting up a bookmaking program, we work with parent volunteers to develop a stockpile of book covers and blank pages through either a Parents' Work Night or sending materials home for parents to make covers and pages for the classroom. We particularly like hardcover books because they signal "you are an author" to students. Bookmaking in Section II has diagrams and detailed information on how to make these books from typing paper, cereal boxes, and contact paper.

Usually formal copies of books and articles in the Classroom Newspapers and Magazines are typed. Books are recopied only when they are informally published by the child for a small audience or when the design of the book is enhanced by handwritten print. One strategy that has worked well for us is to have a parent come into the classroom to type materials for publication. This strategy is especially helpful when typing the drafts of young children because the parent can ask the child to come to the computer and read the draft aloud. Typically, formal copy of stories that are to go in books are typed

Cover, Classroom Newspaper
(compliments of
Dennis Windrim)

Chapter Two
The Authoring Cycle
as a Curricular
Framework for Writing

double-spaced with triple-spacing between paragraphs. When the formal copy comes back, the author has to decide how to break the story to lay it out in the book. Once this decision is made, the text can be cut apart and glued into the book at the locations selected. Illustrations can also be done on another sheet of paper and then put into the book.

For authors who are producing a picture book, the process of illustrating their book is a significant part of the publication process as they construct meaning through art. In many classrooms, children rush through the illustrations and treat the pictures as decorations, not an essential part of the meaning of a book. As children illustrate their books, they should be invited to engage in Literature Circles on illustrators, spend time consulting with published books, and conference with favorite illustrators from the room. They also can take their rough draft illustrations to Authors Circle for response.

Cheri Anderson worked with other teachers in her school to set up an illustrators' studio. The school already had a publishing center with blank books, covers, computers, typewriters, and a binding machine. They added an illustrators' studio with paints, pastels, and art materials as well as art prints and examples of books illustrated with different media.

The design of a picture book is also a key decision point. One disadvantage of the hardcover books we use is that they result in books which look quite similar. Children can become quite creative in designing books with different shapes, sizes and types of paper, flaps, and foldout sections. Paul Johnson has written two excellent books, *A Book of One's Own* (1992) and *Literacy Through the Book Arts* (1993), that teachers and students can use in exploring alternative book designs.

In addition to publishing books, some type of regular Classroom Newspaper or Magazine gives children many more opportunities to publish their work formally for others. In some classrooms, teachers publish a range of student work in each issue and, in other classrooms, the articles are all related to a particular class inquiry focus. Computer software programs, like The Writing Center (1994), greatly facilitate layout and publication of a class newspaper. Classroom Newspapers and Magazines in Section II gives specific information on ways to establish this type of publishing program in the classroom.

There is no specific guideline for all classrooms on how frequently children should publish. The major issue is that authors need to present their writing through informal and formal publication on a *regular* basis. It's important to take the needs of students into account in deciding how often to encourage students to move their writing into formal publication. However, we think it is important to keep some kind of publishing process going and to talk with students about how often and where they publish their work. When children move to publication, they look through their Authors Folders to identify rough draft efforts that they want to publish or read through their Writer's Notebook or Sketch Journal for topics to pursue in a draft. Given the number of invitations to write, the problem usually isn't having something to publish, but deciding which pieces are worth the extra investment of time and energy to take them to publication.

If students wish to publish more they may do so, but on their own time and with their own materials. We take this firm stand because we do not want publishing to be the entire language arts program. Although it is crucial that students have an outlet for their work and a ready audience, not everything written merits publication. We want children to have time to write daily, to explore using writing as a vehicle for learning, to experience the generative nature of the writing process, to learn how to support themselves and others in the process, to read like writers, and to use reading and writing as vehicles for exploring and expanding their world. Publishing is a central feature of the authoring process, but it is only one feature. It cannot and should not overshadow everything else.

Celebrating Authorship

Once a newspaper or book is formally published, we take time to celebrate the authorship of that document. The publication of a newspaper is greeted with fanfare and everything stops while students take their newspapers and scatter around the room to read and enjoy them with one another. These newspapers are then taken home and shared with parents and other family members.

When a child publishes a book, the entire class comes together in celebration to listen to the author read the book aloud at authors chair. Once the author has read, the listeners receive the book by telling what they heard, talking about what they liked about the book, and asking the author questions about the writing and publishing.

The questions and comments of the listeners differ from those in Authors Circle in that the purpose is not to help authors think about or revise their stories but to celebrate authorship. The listeners respond as they would to published literature or to a visit by a children's author to the classroom. The book is in formal form and the author wants to celebrate the book and what they have learned about life and writing, not receive suggestions for revision.

Authors are in their glory as they proudly share their publications with their friends. These books are taken home to share with family members and then brought back to school and placed in the classroom library until the end of the year. We have found that these books are often the most frequently read materials in the classroom.

Other Types of Author Celebrations

Other ways that teachers have involved authors in celebrating their authorship include having authors go to other classrooms to share a published book and having author teas. In one school a third-grade and a sixth-grade classroom paired up, and students from these grades took their published books to the other classroom to read. Author teas can involve inviting other students, the principal, or parents to celebrate authorship. It is better if these occur several times during the year, rather than at the end of the year, because they motivate students to want to continue to write and publish. Usually the tea begins with authors briefly describing the authoring cycle and then meeting in small groups to share their entire book with guests. The guests also have time to walk around and look at the various publications and to enjoy refreshments.

Young Authors Conferences provide a formal way for students, parents, and teachers to celebrate authorship. These conferences are usually organized by a county reading association or school district, and they occur on a Saturday morning. Children register for the conference and bring a book they wrote. The conference usually consists of listening to a professional children's author in a large group session and meeting in small groups with other children. Parent sessions are held to give parents ideas on how they can encourage their children in reading and writing.

If the authoring cycle has been operating, students should have many books from which to choose. In school systems where students write one book a year to take to Young Authors Conference, this conference is often a negative experience. Another problem arises when only several authors from a school are selected to attend. This reinforces the notion that writing is a special gift for only a few select people. When organized to include all authors and to give them a chance to celebrate their own authorship as well as listen to others, Young Authors Conferences can play a vital role in communicating the importance of authorship to students, parents, and the community.

Publication and celebration of authorship give students the chance to present their documents to other class members and to feel the satisfaction of successfully communicating with an audience. The thrill that authors experience as they present their work to others encourages them to continue writing and moving through the authoring cycle. Celebrating authorship is also essential in providing demonstrations to other authors of new ideas and strategies that they might use in their own writing. This, in turn, encourages other authors to move through the authoring cycle. We have found that as soon as a few authors get their work published and celebrated, there is a sudden surge of rough drafts being written and taken to Authors Circle by authors who had been relatively unproductive. The entire cycle finally fits together for them. Some students need to go through the whole cycle several times before they become fully engaged in it. The celebration of authorship brings both an end and a new beginning to the cycle as it offers invitations to engage in the cycle anew.

Planning New Inquiries: Strategy Lessons and Self-Evaluation

Throughout the authoring cycle, students continuously move between action and reflection. They actively engage in reading and writing for real purposes and reflectively consider their language processes and the meanings they are constructing. Particularly as they engage in conversations and dialogue with others, they become more reflective about themselves as meaning-makers. While reflection is a continuous aspect of the authoring cycle, it plays a different function at this point in the cycle. The reflection that occurs as students move through the cycle is usually tied closely to the specific context and piece of writing. Because the process of publication requires authors to pull together what they know, they are able to reflect on their learning from a more distant perspective. They need to be encouraged to reflexively take a much larger step back and examine what they learned, how they learned, and their goals for learning before moving on to other pieces of writing.

Through reflexivity, authors examine the strategies and understandings they have gained from working with specific pieces of writing and take these to a broader level to become part of the knowledge base they use to make decisions as a writer. They ask themselves "What have I learned from this piece of writing and this experience that I want to remember and use another day?" "How does the strategy I used (e.g. putting in dialogue) affect my writing? What is gained? What is lost?"

This part of the cycle encourages students to relive the mental trip they took as authors moving through the cycle so they can identify their needs and inquiry questions as writers. A wide range of engagements can support students in taking a more reflexive stance on their learning. Sharing their work at authors chair is an opportunity not only to celebrate the current work but also to talk about what they have learned and where they want to go next. Some teachers have students write self-evaluations about their learning, either as part of a Learning Log or on a separate sheet of paper that goes into their Authors Folder. Occasionally group meetings are focused more broadly on discussing what children are learning through authoring.

Using Portfolios as a Tool for Self-Reflection

One curricular engagement that can encourage a reflexive stance on learning is portfolios. Gloria Kauffman has used Reflection Portfolios to have students reflexively consider who they are as writers (Short & Kauffman, 1992). She encourages students to constantly reflect on their learning on a daily basis through short oral reflections (five to ten minutes) that occur frequently throughout the day and a written reflection journal which children use each morning to reflect on the previous day. These daily reflections support students in using the portfolio to reflexively look at their work as writers over time. Typically students put together a portfolio three times a year by going through their collections of writing—logs, notebooks, journals, notes, messages, rough drafts, publications—and gathering all of their writing into a large pile. They spend time reviewing their piles asking themselves the question, "Who am I as a writer?" The class then meets together to brainstorm what students have discovered about themselves as writers.

FIGURE 2.11
Tag on Rough Draft for
Reflection Portfolio;
Mardell, Age 9 (Gloria
Kauffman's classroom)

I chose this story because I did a lot of reivison on it and now I feel proud of it. I put a lot of work into it and I expected it to be good.

Mardell

One thing I learned is while I read my story I can edit. At the end of a sentence your voise goes down. You can tell that's where you put a perieod
Some things I have started doing in revision are story's are getting focuseds Better meanings,that I can stay on track with the main idea. I have started getting ideas from my journal and I have the ideas wrote down incase of writers block. I have also been doing some cutting up. It helps get my story to make sence.
Almost all my ideas come from frinds or my own experence.

A) Make my story's very intresting so people get exsighted.
B) I would like to emprove in paragraph

After the class discussion, students go back to their piles and select the pieces they feel reflect who they are as writers. It is important that students be selective so they really have to make decisions and think through what is most important to them. The criteria for these choices are determined by the child, not the teacher. *These portfolios*

Chapter Two
The Authoring Cycle
as a Curricular
Framework for Writing

are a chance for children to think about what they value, not to evaluate themselves according to teacher or school values. To make sure that students do not confuse the portfolios with grades, the portfolios are scheduled so they do not occur at the end of a grading period or quarter.

Once they have made their selections, they share these with a partner, explaining how these choices reflect who they are as writers. They then go back and make their final decisions about the pieces and write a reflection for each item on a half sheet of paper. In this reflection, they explain why they selected a particular piece and what it shows. When all of the pieces are tagged, children share them with a partner and talk more broadly about who they are as writers (see Figures 2.11 and 2.12). The class then comes back together to share their descriptions of themselves and to brainstorm possible goals for where they might go next. After this class discussion, students write a one-page reflection describing themselves as writers and establishing their goals. These one-page reflections are shared with parents and put into the child's cumulative file. The portfolio itself remains in the child's control, and the child makes decisions about whether to share it with others.

While there are many other types of portfolios, this one highlights student voices and encourages students to examine themselves as writers and learners. They evaluate the content and process of their writing from a more distant reflexive stance by looking at their work over time. Because of this stance, they are able to evaluate their purposes for learning and to establish goals for where they want to go next. Through this process, teachers also gain valuable insights into children's inquiries.

The value of reflexivity in learning signals a different relationship between teaching, learning, and evaluation. Traditionally, teachers teach, students engage (and supposedly learn), and then teachers test students to see if they have learned what was taught. This teach, engage, and test sequence highlights the teacher's agenda and excludes student voices. The authoring cycle changes this relationship and highlights, first and foremost, student engagement in learning through uninterrupted writing experiences. As students engage in these experiences, both teachers and students reflect and evaluate what students are learning. We highlighted evaluation as part of Authors Folders because we believe in examining these processes in action. Out of these experiences and evaluation come opportunities for teaching—for offering particular engagements and strategy lessons that will support learners in their continued inquiries. The teach, engage, and test sequence becomes an interdependent cycle of engaging, evaluating, and teaching.

Exploring Language Through Strategy Lessons

A missing component in many reading and writing process classrooms is the strategy lesson. Strategy lessons are instructional engagements designed to highlight some aspect of literacy that the student or teacher sees as important in relation to students' current use of writing for inquiry. They are generated by students as well as by the teacher. These lessons include both the psychological and sociological strategies employed by learners during authoring and help students become aware of how to support their own learning as well as the learning of other students. Learners are invited to distance themselves from the immediate experience for purposes of offering new invitations for their own and others' inquiry.

While curricular engagements involve settings that call for students to use a variety of language strategies, strategy lessons have a more limited focus. They typically highlight one particular cognitive or social strategy that a successful language user might employ. Dorothy Watson (1982) defines a strategy lesson as an instructional episode or event in which all appropriate cueing systems of language and life are used to strengthen the language user's ability to process language.

We believe that strategy lessons make conscious the processes and strategies of "good" writers. They allow students to learn from their engagements with writing. Unlike minilessons, they are not an excuse to teach skills teachers think children need but represent that point in curriculum where both students and teachers are given the opportunity to be reflective. If the student used dialogue for the first time to engage readers, he or she might ask, "Wow! This really worked. Why?" Strategy lessons are a time to explore options; to make unconscious strategies conscious for purposes of control and empowerment. They serve as self-correcting invitations to inquiry and curricular planning.

Our intent here is to make children strategic rather than rote learners. With conscious awareness comes choice, and with choice comes empowerment. Unlike direct instruction, insights and discussion evolve from language in use, rather than from a predetermined skill sequence. Strategies are not formulas or rules to be applied, but options that can be used to construct meaning so that students develop a repertoire of strategies. For a strategy to be useful, students must understand how the strategy relates to what proficient readers and writers do, as well as the conditions under which its use is appropriate. The lessons should relate to what successful learners do as they engage in reading and writing processes and include psychological strategies (e.g., self-correction, monitoring for meaning during reading), and sociological strategies (e.g., talking with a neighbor during writing, reading drafts aloud to someone else, getting someone to brainstorm initial thinking).

Strategy lessons are chosen because they meet the current needs and inquiries of specific learners in the classroom. The safest place to start strategy lessons is not with the needs that teachers identify, but with the inquiry questions that children ask as they reflect on their writing and learning. When Jason says he wants to figure out how to "stop killing characters" in his stories, we need to listen and offer a strategy lesson so he can explore this question.

The strategy lessons teachers develop—based on the student needs they identify through careful observation and kidwatching—should be offered as invitations to students. These teacher-identified lessons may not be as successful as when students identify their own needs because they don't match children's inquiries. We need to remember that it is human nature that we attend to our own questions and ignore what others think we need.

Strategy lessons have three parts (Goodman, Burke, & Sherman, 1980; Goodman, Smith, Meredith, & Goodman, 1987). They begin with an actual engagement in reading and writing in a setting where the strategy of interest is highlighted. Students are then asked to talk about their thinking and strategies during this engagement—they make their strategies conscious. In the final part of the lesson, teachers and students talk about the strategies they are using and suggest ways these strategies can be used in their work. If students want to add details to their stories, we might read aloud excerpts from a book that has many details in its storyline. After discussing the book, we invite students to try writing their next piece with more detail or to go to their Authors Folder and find a selection they believe would be improved by adding more details. At author talk time, we ask students to reflect on how adding more detail helped or failed to help make their writing better. We also ask students to share the strategies they used for deciding what kind of details to add as well as where to add those details. Finally, we tie together what they have shared and suggest other possible strategies.

Students also generate their own strategy lessons. This often occurs through sharing. "Did you notice what Miguel did when he got stuck and couldn't figure out where to go next with his story? The next time you have a writer's block, you might want to try his strategy." Amy, a first grader, wrote a story involving a new adventure with Peter Rabbit. During sharing she commented, "What I learned was that you can take an idea from another author and change it to write your own story." The class discussed her strategy of borrowing in creative ways from other authors and literature; during the next several months students used Amy's strategy for beginning their own stories. When Jason, a third grader, shared his published book with the class, students talked about how much suspense he had in his story. Jason decided to offer a small group strategy lesson for anyone who wanted to learn about creating suspense (Kauffman & Short, 1990).

In listening to students' questions, we also need to ask ourselves about the beliefs behind those questions and whether we need to first challenge those beliefs. One device that we have found helpful in providing insights into students' beliefs is the Burke Writing Interview (Burke, 1980). When Maria, a third grader, wrote that her goal was to "learn how to spell," we did not automatically teach strategy lessons on spelling. We first needed to know whether Maria's inquiry came from an overconcern with spelling and misunderstandings of its role in the authoring cycle. Our observations indicated that she and others in the class understood the role of spelling and so we did offer lessons on strategies such as checking in reference books, searching for root words, sounding out words, trying different spellings to see how they look, discussing possible spellings with peers, and learning and applying a few basic spelling rules and generalizations (Gentry, 1987; Wilde, 1991).

In another case, we taught a strategy lesson on functional spelling to first graders who kept asking about spelling. This lesson simply reinforced their already dysfunctional beliefs about spelling correctly. We should have first addressed those beliefs. When we realized that these students saw writing only as handwriting and spelling, we introduced Written Conversation to challenge those beliefs and help them see writing as communication. Tim O'Keefe challenged his students' beliefs about spelling by focusing on when spelling matters.

He showed them several kid spellings and an adult spelling of *snow*. He asked them to write down how they each spell *snow*, and these spellings were added to the list. Students then discussed when particular spellings were appropriate such as *sno* in the word *sno-cone*. Diane Stephens took the examples of young children's functional spelling that we shared in Chapter 1 and showed these to children as a demonstration of strategies they could use in their writing.

Other strategy lessons might include Schema Stories for students who are exploring story structures or Generating Written Discourse to figure out how to create a unified meaning for a text, particularly when writing informational reports. Many times, however, we have found that rather than planning a specific strategy lesson, teachers use their observations of students to offer particular engagements. They may choose specific books to read aloud during the group meeting or encourage children to take on a particular role. Corey indicated in his "smashed toe" story that he was asking questions about punctuation. Taking on the role of editor allowed him to explore punctuation through others' writing and was probably more effective than offering a specific strategy lesson on this topic.

Students must first have experiences using language before they can consciously reflect on that use. They must be writers before they can be taught about writing. Strategy lessons help students become consciously aware of their strategies; this awareness makes choice possible and allows learners to be strategic. Strategic behavior involves some element of conscious awareness so that learners can think about their options when they run into trouble. Just experiencing strategies may not be enough as learners often fail to use that strategy in new situations. They need to be encouraged to reflect on their language strategies. Carolyn Burke reminds us, however, that "a little awareness goes a long way." We see these strategy lessons as brief focused engagements that can occur with the whole class during group meetings and author talk time or with individuals and small groups during work time.

Taking Thoughtful New Action: Invitations for Authoring

The reflection and celebration that are part of publication, strategy lessons, and portfolios naturally lead to new invitations for writing and inquiry. As students celebrate each other's writing, they receive many demonstrations about new genres, topics, and writing strategies that they can use in their own writing. Through strategy lessons and portfolios, they become more reflective about their own decisions and processes as authors and reposition themselves as writers by establishing goals for where they want to go next. In classrooms where sharing, celebrating, and reflecting are daily occurrences, students invite other authors to take new actions and choose to accept others' invitations for their own actions. In Chris Collier's classroom, Eugene wrote a Family Story that took on a ghost story quality. Tommy saw the potential and made an invitation, "Let's all write ghost stories," which caught on quickly.

We rarely hear "I don't know what to write" once the authoring cycle is in place in classrooms where conversation and dialogue are present. Students who do make this comment usually need some time off to read and reflect before moving to another piece of writing.

Invitations for action can also be offered by the teacher, but it must be remembered that students always have the option of turning down an invitation. The teacher's invitations can provide a starting point for students at the beginning of the year, especially in giving them a sense of the kinds of writing they can pursue. Teachers can also use invitations to challenge students to take a risk and try new genres, topics, and strategies. These invitations need to be based in careful observation of students and allow them to connect to, yet go beyond, their current selves. Many teachers believe that the move to process writing means that they can no longer suggest possibilities for writing. They silence their own voices, believing that students need complete control over their choice of topics. They move from assigning writing to providing no support. Part of the teacher's role is to create both a supportive and a challenging learning environment.

When Leslie Kahn, a sixth grade teacher, grew frustrated with her students' reliance on "gang" stories and "mall" stories, she offered invitations to encourage students to explore new genres. To introduce the genre of information books, for example, she brought in a range of information books and shared how these authors wrote about topics they knew about from their own life experiences or through research (Graves, 1989). She asked students to brainstorm topics they knew a lot about because of their experiences, share these with their small groups, and then put the lists in their Authors Folders. She also put together sets of information books by particular authors and encouraged students to explore and discuss these sets. In addition, she read aloud information books during group meetings. To introduce the genre of poetry, she immersed her students in poetry through read aloud, choral reading, and invitations to write particular types of poetry (Graves, 1992). In the past, Leslie might have assigned students to write information books or poetry. Now, she puts forth a range of invitations that provide students with the demonstrations they need to challenge them to take thoughtful action as writers.

Authors Meeting Authors is an ongoing invitation that introduces professional authors to children so they realize that the books they read are written by real people who work hard at their authoring, rather than by a machine that impersonally prints books. As students research the lives and writing of favorite authors, they become more aware of their own authoring processes and of options they may not have considered before. These insights are even more dramatic when professional authors are brought to the classroom. Some classrooms also choose an "author of the week," displaying and reading the writing of a classroom author and interviewing the child on his or her writing process. The author's books are used in one of the Literature Circles and the author is invited at some point to join the group to answer their questions.

Another invitation that can encourage writers to reposition themselves as authors is to explore authoring across other sign systems. Randy Beard, a singer and guitarist in a local band, visited School 39 in Indianapolis to share his authoring through music. He first sang a song he had written and shared how it had evolved and the revisions he had made to get the song to its current form. Students were then invited to work in groups to write a song which he would put to music. Even though the children had been writing all year, it was quickly obvious that they were having great difficulties. Randy pulled everyone back together and had them talk about what they were thinking. As they threw out ideas such as "sick of school," he wrote them down on the board. After working in this fashion, he asked if they wanted to move the lines around. Once students had the lines in an order that made sense to them, he asked what kind of music they had in mind and tried out several versions, including country and blues, and the children chose the one they felt fit the meaning of their song. Over the next several days, many children began writing their own songs, and by the end of the year they had produced two songbooks that included musical notation (thanks to the help of the school music teacher). This invitation allowed children to explore new mean-

Original Song; Amy, Age 6 (Gloria Kauffman's classroom)

ing potentials through language and music and to connect authoring across both sign systems.

Children's illustrator Molly Bang introduced us to another engagement which we use to offer invitations for authors to take new actions through art. We first share a few basic concepts about using shape, color, and size to communicate visual messages using Molly's book *Picture This: Perception and Composition* (1991). Students are then given black, white, red, and purple paper and asked to make a scary picture. We talk a bit about things that are scary to them, such as birds and sharks, and then students are given five to ten minutes to use the four colors and their scissors (no glue) to cut out shapes and create a scary picture. At the end of ten minutes, amidst many groans of "I'm not finished," everyone brings their picture and places it on the floor. We gather in a circle around the pictures and ask viewers to choose pictures they think are scary. We talk about what makes them scary. We also talk about pictures we think could be made even scarier and, because the shapes are not glued down, we can move them around to see how different arrangements give different perspectives.

Scary Story; Sam, Age 7
(Jean Schroeder's classroom)

Students then take their pictures and revise them to make them scarier. Again we return to the center of the room to talk about the ways in which their pictures visually communicate "scariness." This invitation provides authors with more complex understandings about revision as a process that cuts across sign systems, and with new understandings about how "pictures come to mean" that they can use in their own illustrations.

Each engagement in the cycle ought to expand participants' understandings about authoring, renewing their faith in the learning process and in themselves as learners. One day Ben exclaimed, "I just love my poem. Who would have thought I had it in me." Such comments are living proof the cycle is working.

Conclusion

How we teach writing affects what students come to believe about the writing process as well as the strategies that they use. David Wray and Jane Medwell, teacher researchers from England, interviewed students as to what they knew about writing. Nine-year old Kelly's responses are typical of what researchers found in England as well as in the United States and elsewhere (see Figure 2.11).

FIGURE 2.13
What I Know about Writing;
Kelly, Age 9 (Wray & Medwell,
1991)

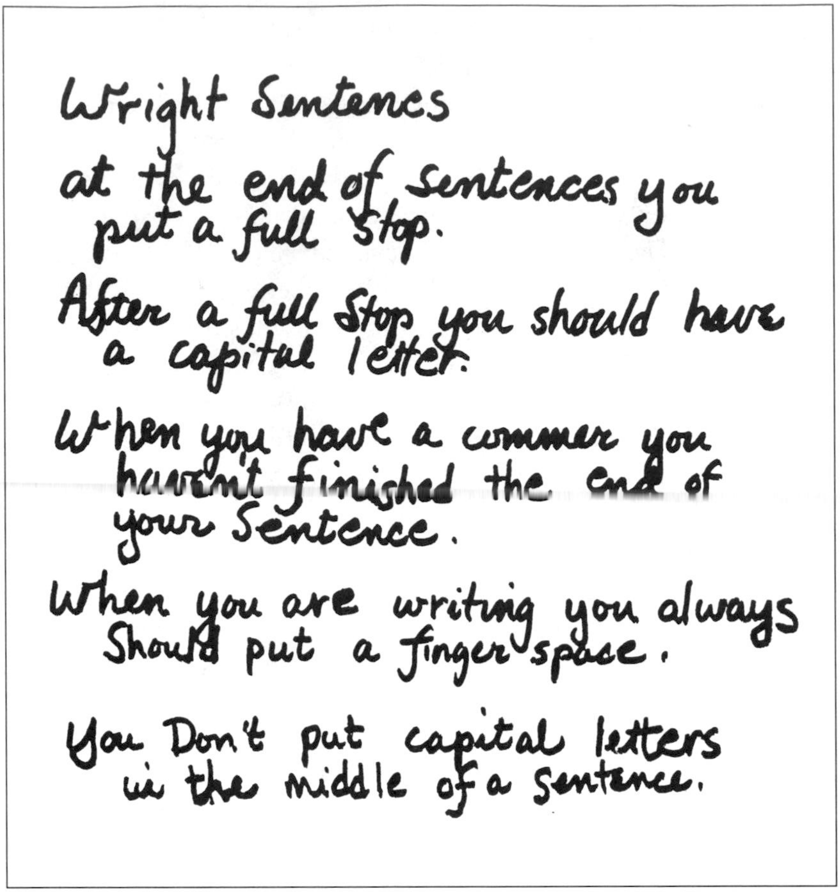

Wright Sentencs

at the end of sentences you put a full stop.

After a full stop you should have a capital letter.

When you have a commer you haven't finished the end of your Sentence.

When you are writing you always Should put a finger space.

You Don't put capital letters in the middle of a sentence.

Fortunately, this scenario is changing. In more and more classrooms children are invited to write in a classroom environment designed around what we know about real authors and how they work. This is the value of the authoring cycle as a curricular frame. Instead of isolated activities, teachers and students using the authoring cycle come to see writing as a holistic process which results in reflection, growth, and learning. In the past the writing programs in schools created secretaries—people who could spell and punctuate—but writing itself was seen as a gift, something some people had but others didn't.

Today we understand the travesty of instructional programs which do not support each and every child in experiencing for themselves the power of writing as a tool for learning. Spelling and punctuation are important, but they are not prerequisites for engaging in the writing process. While they have a place in the authoring cycle—at that point when we wish to make our ideas public—too much attention too soon puts children off. They edit their ideas before they ever permit themselves to have any. Teachers can do the same thing. Given the world in which we teach, we can edit our dreams for how to create a supportive environment for writing in our classrooms before we ever try to create the supportive environment we know children need. There are always tests and tradition to intimidate us.

This chapter is the story of teacher researchers on the move. Consider it your invitation to create, dream, and write a new future for writing and education too. Powerful writers have always taken our breath away. Six-year-old Victoria said it best, "What do you mean, you don't like stories where animals talk. You can make them talk, Alicia. Use your imagination. That's why you need to write."

■ Kathryn Mitchell Pierce teaches in Clayton, Missouri in a multi-age, multiyear primary classroom for children ages six through eight. She recently returned to full-time elementary teaching after working in teacher education programs for twelve years. Her previous publications reflect her work with teachers exploring talking and learning in small groups, particularly literature discussion groups. She is co-editor of **Talking about Books: Creating Literate Communities** (Heinemann, 1990) and **Cycles of Meaning: Exploring the Potentials of Talk in Learning Communities** (Heinemann, 1993). In addition, she and Kathy Short served as co-editors of the Children's Book Department in **The Reading Teacher**, published by the International Reading Association. She lives with her husband, Don, and their two young daughters, Jennifer and Courtney, in Belleville, Illinois.

Getting Started
Establishing a Reading/Writing Classroom

KATHRYN MITCHELL PIERCE

A visitor walks in and looks around our multi-age classroom of six to eight year olds. At first glance, the teacher isn't visible and the children appear to be "all over the place." A slow scan of the room, however, reveals that the children are actively engaged in a variety of literacy experiences. In the reading area, two girls have made a tower of the floor pillows. They are comfortably perched on top of their tower, reading side-by-side from two copies of the same book. The class guinea pig is not-so-comfortably perched between them.

Maurice is reading out loud to Jered at the base of the tower from *Goodnight Moon* (Brown, 1947). Jered is playing with small objects on the nearby shelves, but he turns periodically to look at the illustrations, to ask a question, and to let Maurice know when he has read something incorrectly. A.T. and Martin, both new to our country and our classroom, are writing pen pal letters on the computers. A.T. is writing his letter in German, Martin in Spanish.

Emily, Natalia, Tracie, and Sara are kneeling around a low table working with a pile of books from a plastic basket. They are using a comparison grid that Emily and Tracie invented during their work

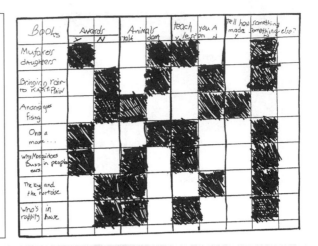

Afrcain folK tales 5-19

Most of them dident tell how somthing made somthing else We wrote about 8 books. We learned that most afreain folk tales are about animals that talk.

with an earlier Text Set. The grid lists the book titles down the side and various characteristics across the top. They are using a complicated code for filling in information on their grid to show the comparisons they are exploring.

Seth, Evan, Ted, and Chris are working at a hexagonal table with spiral notebooks used for writing and an impressive collection of colored markers. Several X-Men comic books and transition chapter books along with action figures are spread out on the table. The boys are writing and illustrating their own X-Men adventures, but discussing them in the group as they go. At times, one or another lifts several of the plastic figures into action with the help of a partner to show how the battle proceeded before writing about it in his spiral. Animated discussion continues throughout the writing, punctuated with "yeah," "cool," and "no, wait, wait," as they explore alternatives and offer suggestions to one another. These stories are often enacted on the playground and at home. For this group, packing a writing spiral notebook for an overnight visit with a classmate is as important as bringing a soccer ball.

Catie is working alone at a table "doing portfolios." Her mother is coming in next week for a regular conference, and Catie is getting her materials in order. She'll take her portfolio home in the next day or two to share with her mother prior to our three-way conference. Catie has her working file of important papers spread out on one side and her three-ring binder opened out on the other side. As she sorts papers into different piles, she calls over to another child, Natalia, to ask her opinion. Natalia moves back and forth between Catie's portfolio work and her own group's work at the nearby short table. Even-

Ted has 6 hermet crabs. And Ted had a turtle and 20 fish. Ted got his hermet crabs at the shore. That is where his gramma lives. They like to drink. Ted has a travel cage and a home cage. The bighest is the fastest. Ted has goten pincht 1s. Ted had one that pinchats alought. Ted has 2 hermet crabs that dont pinch. And Ted makes homes for the hermet crabs. Ted's hermet crabs are very acuteve. Evry year he gets a new cage for them. The hermet crabs die evry year. And he gets 3 at the most. The hermet crabs food is made of corn mix. Every hermet crab come with a food boul. and a spunge.

All about Rusty

Rusty is our new pet guinea pig. Rusty came to us from our friend, Mrs. Gwyn. We get to keep him for a year. He is a brown rusty color. He is a very cute guinea pig. We think he is going to be a good class pet. Rusty eats carrots and lettuce. He is a great guinea pig.

We have 22 cubes. She hide 11 and I new that because I had 11 in my piel and so I just conted on from 11 to 22

He hide 12 and I new that becase befor he did 11 and 11+11=22 and so I new when he gave me ten all I had to do is plus 1.

Shoping for our hamster

Seth, Sara, Emily, Ted, Natalia, Dr. perce, My Mom, and me are going to get our class hamster. I don't now the name of the petstore and don't now if the petstore has the hamster's. I think the petstore only has dwarf hamsters, but I am not sure, I hope they do have hamsters. We are going to have to wait to see the hamster's color to name it.
The End.

Wednesday, 24th, we are going to Forest Park to plant things. That is our Service Project. It's like helping people.
By Jiayi

Today we went to the light and shadow station. We studied on light and shadow and we looked at books. Sara and Shatara made a little maze with mirrors. It looked neat when you put a light in it. It was fun because we could play with the flashlight.

Kana did a rabbit. It was very hard to cut. Tired, my fingers! Thinking to cut a grass or rabbit or flowers. Make teeny tiny piece of paper for sun's rays. We put it on the wall. Back there, on the tape—on yellow paper, the yellow big paper. Don't step on it. Very tired, what you make or thinking
Dictated by Kana

FIGURE TA2.2
Excerpts from Classroom Newsletter

tually, Natalia pulls up a chair beside Catie to work with her on the portfolio, serving as a sounding board, critic, and supportive friend.

Two girls are putting the finishing touches on a display about trees. They've attached excerpts from their research to large sheets of construction paper and added leaves, twigs, and seeds from their partner inquiry. Also included are illustrations depicting the growth cycle of trees and the parts of a tree. They have studied trees several times throughout the year, each time from a new perspective and with greater depth.

The visitor is invited to walk down the hall into the Learning Resource Center where four children are working on the class newsletter. It's Thursday, so they are revising and editing one another's work on the bank of computers available in the LRC. The group is working without adult assistance, although the librarian is nearby with a group of kindergartners.

Farther down the hall, Lauren is sharing her read-around book with the school nurse. She has already read it with three other people

Teacher Article Two

Getting Started

and can almost read it on her own. When she feels comfortable reading the book on her own, Lauren will write a letter to her kindergarten teacher and ask for a time to read her book to a small group of children.

For the moment, I'm standing near the entrance to our room trying to see the room through the eyes of our visitor. I'm amazed that several students aren't standing in front of me waiting for direction, or throwing Unifix cubes over the low shelf at the "enemy" at the next table, or a million other things they have done at different times. As our visitor comments on how independent and focused the children seem to be, I celebrate for a moment how far we have come this year. I think back to the first few weeks of school and wonder how we got to this point.

Beginning the School Year

My thinking and planning before beginning the school year were guided by what I knew was possible or desirable based on my twelve years of working in teacher education and in other teachers' classrooms. I felt comfortable establishing the "what" for the classroom, but more unsure than I wanted to admit about the "how." Even though I had worked intensely in and read about many outstanding classrooms, these experiences had all reflected what classrooms look like once they are up and running. Most teachers invited me into their classrooms only after the first six weeks of school when the getting started process was over. I hadn't gotten an elementary classroom started up from day one for twelve years! I also felt under a certain amount of scrutiny as a new teacher to the district and the teacher in a pilot program to explore multi-age classrooms. I wanted to be sure that I took on only what I could manage fairly well.

Our first few weeks of school were devoted to establishing the routines and procedures that I hoped would enable the children to work independently. By that I don't mean I wanted them to work by themselves as individuals, but that I wanted them to be able to make decisions about what they would do, where to store and locate materials, how to spend their time, and where to get help. Our first schedule included four major work times of approximately forty-five to sixty minutes each: Reading Work Time, Writing Work Time, Math Work Time and Inquiry Lab. I felt the need to have recognizable blocks of time as a way to shape our day. During these times we focused on reading, writing, math, and content area inquiries respectively. By the sixth week of school, the first two blocks were combined into a longer Reading/Writing Work Time. Class meetings, read-aloud time, recess, lunch, special subjects and school-wide quiet reading filled in around our work times.

Math Work Time was organized as a math workshop during which students engaged in mathematical problem-solving, worked with the district curriculum materials, created math games, and participated in focus lessons on mathematical concepts. Inquiry Lab was the time we worked on content area inquiries primarily focused on science, health, and social studies. During this block of time students worked with mobile labs filled with resource books and materials related to core topics, engaged in independent projects where students became experts on topics of their own choice, and participated in focus lessons on strategies and procedures related to the core topics.

Essential to my survival were the teachers in my new school and the network of support teachers I had established prior to beginning this adventure. The network of teachers with whom I had previously worked and studied helped me focus on my theoretical beliefs and my long-term goals for the classroom. The experienced teachers around me offered invaluable assistance in getting to know the district, the community, and the culture of the school itself. I needed both groups. In time, the lines between the two groups have blurred as my teaching colleagues and I have created and merged our questions into a shared focus on curricular issues.

Reading Work Time

At the beginning of the school year our class moved from morning meeting directly into Reading Work Time. I used the meeting to establish the list of invitations, introduce a new invitation, share a new book or set of books, and help the students think through what they wanted and needed to spend their time doing. During or before the meeting, I would list various invitations and work time choices on our chart paper.

About six weeks into the school year, after our routines were in place, I called on several students and asked what they had decided to work on. Sara, Catie, and Natalia said they needed to edit their articles for the upcoming newsletter. After recording their names next to *newsletter*, I encouraged them to go to the library to begin working.

Next I called on Chris because I knew he would either choose partner reading or writing spirals and that two or three other children would follow his lead. After calling on several students in this way, generally those who seemed self-directed or who had their hands up indicating that they had a choice in mind, only a few students were left sitting in our meeting area. These students had heard others make their decisions and had had additional time to think through their own options. This extra time helped Kana make up her mind: she wanted to practice on her cursive writing. Martin, Emily, and Tracie were still left. Since the other students were already busy with their own work, having trickled away from the meeting area a few at a time, I could spend some additional time talking with these three students about their options and helping them establish goals for their work.

Partner Reading Engagements

To get the routines in place, we started Reading Work Time with partner reading for the first few weeks of school, varying the directions as students seemed ready to consider alternatives. Sometimes I would say, "Tracie, pick a partner and then you two select a book and a place to work." This procedure for establishing partners helped ensure that the same children were not the last to be picked. Other times, I introduced a crate of thematically related books or new books and asked students to select a book from the crate before choosing a partner.

I chose partner reading as our dominant, getting-started reading engagement for several reasons. This was an engagement with which I was very comfortable and in which I had great confidence. I *knew* this would be successful with all of the children. Eventually, I wanted to have students engaged in literature discussion groups, and I saw partner reading as a way to work up to this. For these younger children, the ability to work in a group and to collaborate with others was something we would develop throughout the school year. Working in twos was a manageable starting place. Talking about books with another person is also a common reading experience for all readers in and out of school. I assumed most of the children in the classroom had had similar experiences at home, in preschool, or in earlier school years. Partner reading also played a significant role in the "getting to know you" process essential to building a learning community.

Partner reading time lasted anywhere from ten to forty-five minutes, depending on how long the students seemed actively engaged in the reading and talking. At the end of partner reading in late September, we gathered back in our meeting area to talk about their responses to the books and to the experience. This time, however, I also asked them to reflect on and discuss their strategies for selecting and sharing the reading of the books. Evan explained that sometimes he chose books he had read before because he already knew he liked them. Shatara chose books about pets because she was an expert on pets while Catie chose books being read by friends in neighboring classrooms. Often, these discussions about books and strategies gave me ideas about books to offer in the future or variations on partner reading that we might try. Based on Catie's comments, for example, Sandy Miller—the teacher who shared an adjoining room with us—and I introduced several shared reading experiences that were available to students in both of our classrooms so these students could work together.

During partner reading and the follow-up discussion, I studied the children carefully. I looked for insights into their reading strategies and preferences, their ways of interacting with others and of getting started with their work. I looked for those children who seemed to need additional support in working cooperatively with others, getting settled into their work, or making transitions. At times I joined partners for a few minutes, participating with them in the reading and discussion and highlighting for them the successful strategies they were using as they read and talked about their books. When Evan and Lauren were discussing the illustrations in an informational book, I shared with them how I often use the pictures to help me know what a book is about. I tried to help them see "reading the pictures" as a valuable reading strategy used by both beginning and proficient readers. Other times I chose a partner, usually someone I wanted to get to know better or to observe more closely. When I worked with Maurice, we read aloud together from the same text. I adjusted the speed and volume of my own voice to support Maurice's reading. When he was reading confidently, I read more softly. When he began to struggle, I let my voice come in stronger to help maintain the rhythm of the reading. During these opportunities to observe a reader closely, I made mental notes of their reading strategies and topics of interest. My kidwatching was best during this time of the day because I could concentrate so closely on the children. Their reading and work habits were more visible because they were working—and talking—in pairs.

Partner reading moved from our ritual opening reading experience to an ongoing invitation during Reading Work Time. Later, when we joined other classes for reading experiences, partner reading was an easy way to mix two groups of children and get them involved right away in reading and talking about books.

Literature Discussion Groups

From partner reading we moved very slowly into small group discussions of literature books and Text Sets of five to ten conceptually related books. I tried after our sixth week of school to get students involved in Literature Circles. Initially, I asked partners to join partners in creating groups of four. Each group of four worked at a table or on the floor with a basket of books—either shared titles or Text Sets. Groups were asked to browse and skim the books, read some of the books any way they wished, and then talk about them. During our first round of book baskets I was disappointed that three out of five groups seemed to have nothing to talk about. The group looking at sports-related texts flipped through the pages of their books quickly and then announced that they were finished. On subsequent days this group spent more time talking about after-school social plans than they did about the books. This was in stark contrast to the ways these boys pored over similar books during partner reading.

The "pets" group, on the other hand, began talking about their own pets and making connections both to the books and to the stories shared by members of the group. They quickly accepted my invitation to write their own pet stories and generally seemed to stay busy with their books throughout the time. I tried to highlight the successful aspects of this group's work during the reflective discussions of the whole class, but the next day I couldn't really tell that much had changed. I found myself wanting to assign response forms, to dictate the focus of their discussions, to force them to defend their use of time. I never felt the need for these mandates during partner reading.

After several failed attempts to get these group experiences working, we returned to partner reading. Our class had not established a strong sense of community and the small group experiences were driven by social agendas rather than reading or inquiry agendas. I spent far more time helping students resolve significant social problems than observing their reading and discussions. While one or two groups could work without major disruptions, I still felt the agenda was imposed on them, that it wasn't a natural outgrowth of their interest in reading and sharing books.

This caused particular tension for me. I had devoted almost ten years to the study of literature discussion groups and had worked with a number of outstanding teachers in learning about the potential for such groups. Yet, in my own classroom these Literature Circles weren't working. Worse, I felt I was pushing something because I valued it, not because it extended what I saw the children doing. Partner reading could, at this point in the school year, operate without me. That signaled to me that the children understood and valued the engagement as relevant for their purposes. Literature Circles, however, were a constant struggle even into November. By this I don't mean to imply that I was only willing to do what came easily in the classroom. Rather, I felt that I was using the engagement because I knew it was good for kids, not because it was right for *these* kids at *this* time.

As I retreated, licking my professional wounds, to reflect on this problem, I realized that text set discussions were taking place with amazing ease during Inquiry Lab. As children explored their interests during our exploration of the solar system, they created their own small groups, Text Sets, and agendas for discussion. During our study of the systems of the human body, Anton, Martin, and Emily formed their own focus group and spent weeks exploring the various systems of the body and their interdependence. As we explored various physical science concepts (light and shadows, magnets) Ted, Jiayi, Chris, and Andreas combined books and apparatus from our science tubs into multimedia text sets. I would not have recognized these as Text Sets had I not been familiar with Debbie Rowe's work creating Book and Toy Sets. Because I knew what she had seen in her research, I began to see the potential in what I observed the children doing in our room.

I resolved the issue, for this year, by focusing attention on shared discussions of Text Sets during our Inquiry Lab, by continuing to expand the potential of partner reading during the mornings, and by offering literature discussion groups as an open invitation during our Reading/Writing Work Time. This meant that only one or two groups of children were involved in an extended Literature Circle at a given time in the classroom. At times, but not until later in the year, Literature Circles formed between students in my classroom and in Sandy Miller's second-grade classroom with whom we shared an open wall.

In the spring, after careful study of the ways Text Sets had functioned in our Inquiry Lab, I returned to Text Sets during Reading/Writing Work Time. This time, they worked much more smoothly. I attribute the difference in success to four factors. First, the children knew one another much better and could negotiate shared agendas in larger groups. Second, most of the children were comfortable reading independently but also valued working with others. Third, I was a more astute observer and could pull together sets of books with strong appeal to larger numbers of children. Fourth, we preceded this experience with a discussion of the ways we had used Text Sets in our content area inquiries and the reasons why they had been important to us.

Other Engagements with Literature

In addition to partner reading, I pulled small groups together for guided or shared reading experiences and conferenced with individuals about their independent reading. Maurice and I read short stories from *In a Dark, Dark Room* (Schwartz, 1984), a short chapter book. Within two days our partner reading experience had grown into a small group of six children and myself reading and talking about scary stories. Once they seemed hooked into the book and their discussions, I was able to move in and out of the group without concern that the group's momentum would dwindle. The group stayed together for six or seven days, rereading stories from the book, discussing scary stories and scary personal experiences, retelling ghost stories learned through scouting and camping experiences, and writing their own scary stories. Next they discovered the R.L. Stine Goosebumps series and started a classroom passion for these books, expanding their numbers until almost half the class was involved with the books in some way. Almost overnight, children who had been content with transition books were working with partners and small groups to make their way through these more challenging scary stories.

Children also created literature extension projects as an outgrowth of their reading experiences. Shatara and Natalia invited three other girls to help them stage a simple play based on a book they had read. This experience grew into a series of informal skits and plays, puppet experiences, and new invitations for our Wednesday morning choice times. Other times, art seemed to be the dominant form for extension. For several weeks bookmaking became a passion as children from our classroom and Sandy Miller's room made their own books modeled after commercially published books they had read. Once the first group shared their books with the class, others were eager to learn how and to participate in making their own books with spy windows, moving parts, special flaps, fold-outs, and other paper engineering feats.

Pierce—Read Around

Date

My Name

Title

Author

I will have the following people read my book with me or to me so that I can learn to read the book by myself.

1.

2.

3.

4.

5.

6.

7.

8.

9.

10.

When I finish this Read Around, I will read my book to Dr Pierce and then I would like to read it to:

While all students seemed to enjoy partner reading experiences, read-arounds were perhaps the most popular choice for a small group of younger students during the first quarter of the school year. Carol Gilles first shared the strategy with me, though I'm sure that we have modified it from her description. Early in the year, Evan and Seth often worked together on read-arounds using simple predictable texts. After completing the top portion of the read-around form, they took their book and form all around our classroom and the building asking others to help them practice the book. When they could each read it independently, they signed up to share the book with me and then with their former kindergarten teacher or a few of her students. The end of each read-around experience was marked by placing the completed read-around form in their working portfolio file. Later, during conferences, these forms helped to provide a record of the books students had read and the amount of support necessary to be able to read a book aloud to others.

In a multi-age classroom, reading abilities and interests vary widely. With the particular range of ages represented in our classroom, those who could read longer chapter books had achieved special status in the classroom. When Andreas started reading chapter books, his friends and younger children who admired him began to carry around their own chapter books, moving their bookmarks from page to page like Andreas did as he read his books during independent reading times. The chapter book discussion club that Sandy Miller and I had started provided opportunities for small group discussions among those students who were independently reading various chapter books. On Wednesday mornings, eight to ten students from our classrooms signed up to meet together for about thirty to forty-five minutes. During the club meetings, students talked about the different books they were reading independently and any reading strategies they were aware of using or needing as they worked through their different books. Some of Andreas's followers occasionally signed up for Chapter Book Club discussions with him. Students also read quietly for a portion of the time devoted to club meetings. Sometimes they talked about their books in order to interest others in reading the same book. Other times they read aloud portions of their books to celebrate outstanding examples of the writers' craft. Sandy facilitated these discussions, but also participated by discussing children's books she was reading.

Interest in the Chapter Book Club dwindled as children became more intensely involved in literature discussion groups, expert projects and class inquiries. For next year, I'd like to continue exploring various formats for the Chapter Book Club in an effort to sustain it throughout the year. I felt it filled an important need for students to talk informally, but regularly, about the books they were reading independently.

Writing Work Time

For the first few weeks of school, our Writing Work Time began like Reading Work Time with a brief discussion of the available choices listed on the chart paper easel near our group meeting area. We had lots to write about from the very first day of school when Lauren initiated a class inquiry by asking if we were going to have a class pet.

Written Conversations, pen pal letters, and writing notebooks or "writing spirals" were introduced during the first week of school and were added to our list of choices. A typical list might also include writing on computers, working on the class newsletter, corresponding with persons special to our class, making baby books and cards for new siblings, and completing library research relating to an ongoing inquiry.

On any given day, four to six children could work on the computers in or near our classroom suite. We corresponded with pen pals in Tucson, Arizona, and during the two to three days after our letters arrived, students worked alone or in pairs writing responses to their pen pals. Writing spirals were used as a place to write daily entries, stories, or personal narratives. In addition students recorded research notes, Written Conversations, and other kinds of writing in their spirals. Illustrations, charts, and figures were always welcome. During the afternoons, we focused on content area inquiries that often filtered into our work the next morning as students chose to use their Writing Work Time to continue some aspect of their work: notes, reports, news articles, letters requesting information, interviews of resource persons.

Our class published a newsletter about once a week, although we generally missed one week each month. On Mondays, three to five students volunteered for the newspaper committee. They spent their writing time that entire week writing, revising, editing, and publishing the newsletter that went home on Fridays. The articles included information about classroom inquiries and ongoing projects, upcoming events of interest to families, personal interest stories about students and their pets, and interviews of students and adults (college practicum students) new to our classroom. At times, I added curriculum notes of my own and professional journal articles of interest to families. A special computer camera was used to add photographs of students, classroom pets, and visitors.

Our class sharing times at the start of each day often revealed important family stories—Jiayi's new baby brother, Emily's former nanny's baby, Ted's hermit crab adventures, Catie's new hamster. Sometimes, these important stories would lend themselves to invitations for our Writing Work Time. We created baby cards for Jiayi's new brother, get well cards for Mrs. Ruth—our community volunteer—thank you letters to parents for sharing information about a Jewish holiday, notes to the school nurse about school health rules

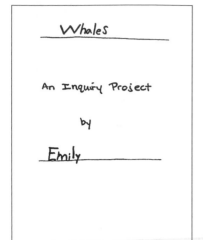

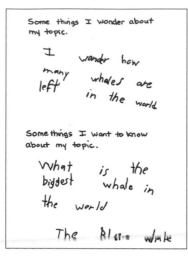

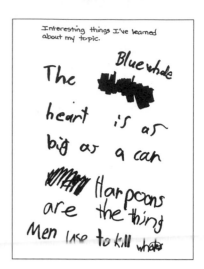

Letter to Get Information for Inquiry

affecting pets in the building, and so on. Writing notes and letters was an important part of our writing experiences, providing an authentic reason for writing as well as a realistic setting for learning how to convey important messages across time and space.

Most of the writing in our classroom was either student-choice writing during Writing Work Time, or inquiry-related writing. While we published many newsletters and inquiry reports, sent letters, created displays including writing as well as art, and performed plays written by students, we published very few books. Over several years' time, my emphasis on classroom writing had shifted from writing for publication to an overemphasis on writing as a tool for inquiry and nonbook celebrations of writing. One of my goals is to use what we have learned about writing as inquiry to inform our personal writing, encouraging more publication of students' personal writing.

Outgrowing Our Schedule

The schedule remained basically the same throughout the year, but children quickly blurred the distinctions between the various work times, particularly the Reading and Writing Work Times. During a class meeting, we talked about combining these into one larger block so students could focus on reading and writing as it suited their needs and purposes. For the remainder of the year, students made decisions about the work they wanted to engage in and how best to use this first work time of the day. We still started each morning with a list of invitations, usually taken from our planning discussions the previous afternoon. At times, I limited the options for students who seemed to need help making good use of their time or managing long-term projects. For example, the day we were scheduled to mail our pen pal letters back, I listed *pen pals* on the easel. Students who hadn't completed their letters by this last day would do so before moving on to other choices.

Another change in schedule occurred in late October, growing out of our success with the Chapter Book Club. On Wednesday mornings, four teachers, three specialists, and our teaching intern along with any practicum students offered Wednesday Morning Choices. Initially, this choice time was designed to give all of us an opportunity to work with a multi-age group and to provide specific literacy and math experiences to meet the needs of individuals. At times, we felt the younger members in the group, usually the less proficient readers, were missing out on literacy experiences they might have had in a regular first-grade classroom. For example, I didn't spend as much time exploring big books and predictable books as patterns for reading and writing as I might have done in a conventional first-grade classroom. On the other hand, these youngsters were involved in sophisticated research using more complex research tools and procedures than I would have considered in a regular first-grade classroom. Wednesday Morning Choices permitted us to reduce the number of children working with each adult, to increase the number of invitations we could extend to all children, and to create groups of children from across four classrooms that might have similar needs and interests.

While we planned invitations with specific children in mind and geared toward different levels of experience and proficiency in reading, writing, or math, children made their own choices. As a result, some Chapter Book Readers signed up for big book experiences and some of our "just emerging readers" signed up for Chapter Book Club. Similarly, children who were still learning one-to-one correspondence in math signed up for the logic games planned to challenge some of the older students in our groups. Each time a student broke out of our "ability" expectations, we were forced to rethink the nature of the invitation and the ways we were continuing to think about children in terms of ability. We made a commitment to adjust the invitations so that they were accessible for all students. In doing so, we identified many of our previously unexamined assumptions about working with multi-age groups and thinking about ability groups.

A typical invitation list for Wednesday Morning Choices included seven to nine of the following options:

- Chapter Book Club
- Big book experience
- Skits and improvisation
- Unstructured computer time
- Computer games
- Various math centers
- Strategy lessons
- CD-ROM and laser disk
- Cursive writing clinic
- Literature extension
- Readers theater
- Puppets
- Book making
- Logic games
- Newspaper activities
- Story starters
- Author study
- Poetry reading

Children were also free to reject all of the invitations for a given Wednesday in which case they remained in their own classrooms and worked on a reading/writing/math choice of their own. Students constantly had input into the list of invitations as it was being developed. I hope next year that we'll get better at letting them create more of the invitations themselves based on their own inquiries, interests, and special hobbies.

At different times of the year, particularly when our content area inquiries were at their most intense, Reading/Writing Work Time looked more like Inquiry Lab. As we neared our culmination of work on mechanical systems, students seemed to spend as much time working with their mechanical projects as they did reading, writing, and talking about their inquiries. The children were successfully pushing the boundaries as needed to carry out their work. These divisions of time, however, signaled to students that I valued spending time engaged in reading and writing, mathematical thinking, and content area studies. I continue to search for new labels for our chunks of time that better describe how we are using that time. Right now I'm considering the implications of labels such as (quiet) independent work time, (noisy) project work time, small group discussion/planning time, and whole class meetings.

Looking Back to Look Ahead

My attention returns to the present as the visitor in our classroom asks, "How did you get them to do this?" Such questions are important because they invite teachers to reflect on their teaching decisions and the beliefs which guide those decisions. In answering our visitor, I discover new insights into our journey. I recognize that I am not the one who got us to this point: we arrived here together. Right now in spring, this is a comfortable place and as summer looms near, I wish for a longer school year so we can enjoy this place we have created for ourselves. But because there is a next year, which brings opportunities for revisions and refinements, we look ahead.

I'm comforted to know that most of these children will be returning to our room again next year. Now that we've reached this temporary but comfortable plateau, we can begin to consider the questions we couldn't seem to ask earlier. We can talk from experience about creating a learning community and use our insights to rebuild this sense of belonging and caring more quickly, more efficiently next year. We can reflect on our experiences with partner reading and literature discussion groups so that we can work more collaboratively in our reading next year. We can celebrate the ways writing supported our content area inquiries in order to expand the ways we use writing to support our personal growth. We can search out ways of structuring our day to meet our needs rather than letting the structure of the day dictate the ways we will pursue our agendas. And we will probably find ways to make better use of our visitors because we have come to value the questions they ask and the reflections they invite. Because we have lived and reflected on this year, next year holds new potential for us.

Chapter Three

The Authoring Cycle as a Curricular Framework for Reading

Introduction

Kathy remembers sitting with a reading group listening to her students read the basal story, and finding herself falling asleep. At that point, she knew she had problems because she was probably the most active thinker at the table. The need for change also came from listening to her first-grade students dictate what they considered significant about that day's experiences at the end of each afternoon. Day after day, students talked about the afternoon theme units and the reading they were doing as part of those units. The morning, which was when Kathy taught reading using the basal reader, was never mentioned. According to the school district, the basal reader program was where the "real" learning went on, and yet that time period was insignificant in children's minds as purposeful learning. Reading for these children was a time of the day, a set of skills, and a basal reader, not a way of making meaning about their lives and worlds.

Along with many other educators, our first attempts at changing how we approached reading was to immerse children in many experiences with literature. We flooded the room with books through read-aloud experiences, big books, listening centers, author studies, and time for independent reading of self-selected books. Our goal was that children would learn to love books and to see reading as a process of enjoyment and learning. This "book flood" approach worked—children read constantly—but we knew something was still not right. It was when we returned to the authoring cycle as a framework for curriculum that we realized what was missing. We were providing students with many engagements where they could read broadly and extensively, but we were not providing engagements where they could explore some of what they read more intensively (Peterson & Eeds, 1990). We had stopped the authoring cycle at uninterrupted reading, and so we were not seeing students engaged in critical, in-depth thinking about their reading.

Students were becoming proficient readers without also becoming literate readers who thought critically and reflectively. We wanted to deepen their understandings about literature. Our experiences with Authors Circles made us see that when learners talk together for a purpose, they begin to examine and reflect on their authoring. About this time we met Karen Smith, who was teaching sixth grade in Arizona, and her descriptions of the literature groups she used in her classroom gave us some ideas about how we could begin to work at authoring circles in reading. Our experiences with publication also made us realize that readers needed opportunities to pull together their thinking and present their understandings to others. In this chapter, we will examine the components of the authoring cycle as they operate within a curricular framework for reading.

Building from the Known: Children's Choices as Readers

We found that the best way to begin the authoring cycle in reading is to fill a room with books, read aloud to children, give them uninterrupted time to read, watch to see which books they select, and listen to their responses. Using our knowledge of the community and the children, we provide books and reading materials that connect closely to *their* life experiences, not ours or the school's.

Just as writing engagements must be open-ended and encourage children's voices through choice, so must reading engagements connect to, and build from, children's life experiences inside and outside of school. To connect with the experiences that are significant to them, children need to have choices in what they read for wide

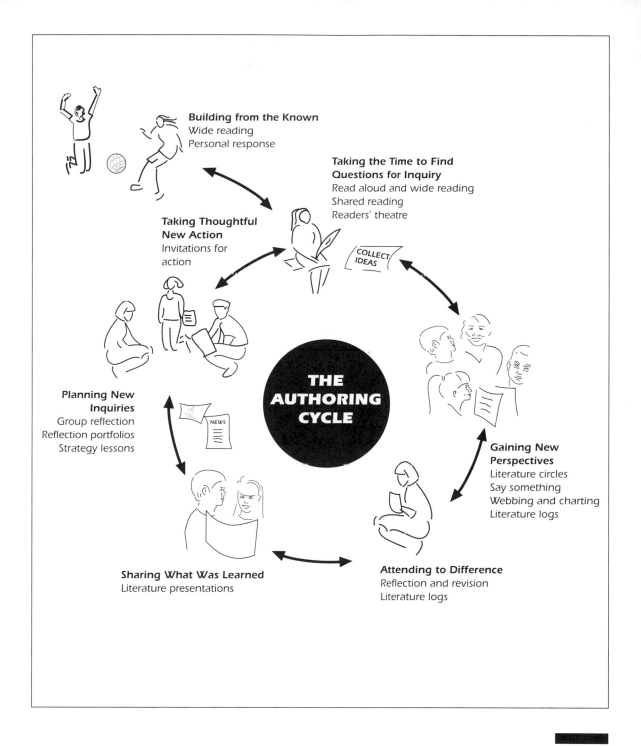

Building from the Known
Wide reading
Personal response

Taking the Time to Find Questions for Inquiry
Read aloud and wide reading
Shared reading
Readers' theatre

Taking Thoughtful New Action
Invitations for action

COLLECT IDEAS

THE AUTHORING CYCLE

Planning New Inquiries
Group reflection
Reflection portfolios
Strategy lessons

NEWS

Gaining New Perspectives
Literature circles
Say something
Webbing and charting
Literature logs

Sharing What Was Learned
Literature presentations

Attending to Difference
Reflection and revision
Literature logs

FIGURE 3.1
Authoring Cycle as a Curricular
Framework for Reading
(Short & Harste, 1995)

171

reading and Literature Circles. Choice assumes that there are a wide variety of books and other reading materials available for children. While sometimes the choices are more limited, such as when children are choosing from a set of books for Literature Circles, at other times they are able to choose from a tremendous range.

Connecting to life experiences also means that children have choices in how they respond to their reading. When children find it difficult to answer teacher questions about a story, teachers often assume that the student is not comprehending. Teachers need to consider that they may be asking the wrong questions for *students'* understandings and connections. This point was evident in the responses of first graders in Kathleen Crawford's classroom when Kathy read aloud *The Wednesday Surprise* (Bunting, 1989) early in the year. As the children discussed their favorite parts, they talked warmly about their many experiences with grandparents. No one mentioned the young girl teaching her grandmother to read. Instead of asking questions to see if they understood that part of the book, Kathy simply shared that her favorite part was the grandmother learning to read and the difference that was going to make in her life. The children nodded—and then went back to discussing their connections to grandparents. When Kathy and Kathleen discussed this later, they realized that these children did not yet see themselves as readers and did not come from homes where books were important literacy events. For them, the literacy connections were not yet important, while grandparents were.

The work of Denny Taylor (1983, 1988) with families in suburbs and inner cities reminds us that all families use reading and writing, but for many different purposes. All children come to school with literacy experiences. While some children may not have children's books in their homes, we should not assume that they are deprived and lack experience. In fact, Taylor's research shows that these children often have had many rich experiences with literacy, but they have had different experiences than schools normally expect. Our role as teachers is to understand and build from those life experiences. When we say that children are not literate, it is often because we are starting with topics that are not part of their lives. The problem is our understanding, not theirs.

Young children come to school able to read fast food signs, toothpaste cartons, road signs, and cereal boxes (Harste, Woodward, & Burke, 1984). Their literacy experiences in schools need to build from their knowledge of environmental print. Books such as *Signs*

(Goor, 1983), *I Read Signs* (Hoban, 1983), and *I Walk and Read* (Hoban, 1984) serve as demonstrations to children of their abilities to read environmental print. We have taken young children on environmental print walks around the school or local neighborhood to find something they can read. After the walk, children draw pictures of what they can read to create a Group Composed Book. Children then bring labels from home which they glue in individual blank books, write captions, and then read the book to others in the classroom. We also have set up a classroom grocery store and invited children to create their grocery lists using the logos from environmental print.

Other experiences have included gathering commercial and environmental print jingles in a Group Composed Book and creating individual recipes for the cooking center that use logos and drawings to indicate the ingredients and procedures. These environmental print materials involve students in reading the print that constantly surrounds them as they go about their daily lives. These experiences with environmental print can be extended into other areas of children's literacy. We have invited children to collect jump rope rhymes and favorite songs and dictate these to the teacher to put onto charts and in books for children to read. Language experience charts were created from shared experiences in school and became another source of reading materials with which children feel successful because the charts reflect their language and experiences.

Another important point of connection is understanding children's beliefs about reading. The Burke Reading Interview (Goodman, Watson, & Burke, 1987) has been a powerful tool in giving us insights into what children believe about themselves as readers and the reading process. While it takes time to interview students individually, we find that the understandings we gain are worth the time investment. When children have such dysfunctional views of the reading process as a process of sounding out and reading every word accurately, we need to be aware of these beliefs in order to involve children in experiences that will challenge them.

Taking the Time to Find Questions for Inquiry: Uninterrupted Engagements with Reading

If children learn about writing through engaging in writing whether or not they are spelling conventionally, it makes sense that children learn to read by engaging in reading. It is more important that they immerse themselves in reading experiences where they come to see themselves as readers than that they read the exact words on the page. Just as with the writing process, the conventions develop over time. Children often tell their own stories to go with the pictures in a book and gradually come to read the print itself (Holdaway, 1979). What is significant is that they have many engagements reading a wide range of reading materials for many different purposes. As adults, we do not read to practice reading; we read for purposes important in our lives such as following directions, enjoying a good story, or occupying our attention while waiting. We go to the bookstore to buy the latest self-help book hoping that we might get our lives in order or to find the book version of a great movie we just saw with a group of friends.

When we look at our lives as adults, we also realize that we read a variety of materials on a daily basis—newspapers, magazines, pamphlets, maps, menus, food labels, and signs. Schools have limited reading to literature and, although these books are essential to our lives as readers, the reading materials in school need to be greatly expanded to reflect children's lives outside of school. Everyday reading materials should play a much greater role in schools than they have in the past. We have not only tended to limit reading materials in school to books, but also have focused on fiction to the exclusion of other genres, particularly information books. Consequently, we have failed to connect to many children as readers.

Through extensive reading experiences, children are able to develop flexibility and fluency as readers and to integrate their reading strategies. As they read for many different purposes, they become proficient readers who are able to use reading efficiently and effectively in their daily lives. Engagements such as authors chair, wide reading, Readers Theatre, and Shared Reading support children in developing this proficiency.

Reading Aloud at Authors Chair

In addition to serving as a place for students to celebrate their writing, authors chair is also where teachers read aloud to the entire class. Although authors chair may occur at different times throughout the day, the rule to follow is simple: read aloud every day. Reading aloud is not a reward—something you do if the kids are good—but an ongoing part of each classroom day. Teachers often begin the morning by

"I put myself in the character's place to feel what they feel. I want to understand. What happens in this book makes me understand how to deal with my family."

Amber, Age 11 (Gloria Kauffman's classroom)

reading a picture book aloud and then read from a chapter book right after lunch. They also have another time of day, often in the group meeting before work time, where they read aloud books by particular authors or illustrators whom the class is studying. Although the teacher most often reads aloud at authors chair, children also share a favorite book that they have practiced so that it is effectively presented to the group.

Reading aloud is just as essential for older children as it is for young children. Through read-aloud times at authors chair, children experience book language, the patterns of stories, and different types of literature. They develop an interest in books and are introduced to quality literature that might be beyond their current reading proficiency but not their comprehension. Reading aloud encourages children to grow as readers and broadens the types of literature they choose to read.

When reading aloud to children, it is especially important that teachers savor the words, using their voice to orally interpret the story. Children should not have to tolerate listening to a story that is poorly read. We believe in this so strongly that we have recently begun working with theater educators who are teaching us to use our voices more effectively. This oral interpretation extends to storytelling as a way to share oral literature and make connections to the rich oral traditions of many children. By telling their own family stories and orally interpreting folklore from a range of cultures, teachers invite children to use storytelling as a form of oral authorship.

A variety of written and oral literature should be shared during read-aloud, including literature written by authors from the classroom as well as by professional authors. When teachers choose to read children's work to the class, they show that they value children's authorship. In choosing the work of professional authors, teachers should read picture books, poetry, chapter books, short stories, and information books to all age levels. Many fine picture books, for example, are appropriate for older children and can provide them with a wider variety of reading experiences (Benedict & Carlisle, 1992).

We suggest reading a book that is slightly beyond where most of the class is reading independently or that is a different type of book from what the majority of the class is reading. In first grade, for example, we introduce short chapter books that first graders can understand and enjoy. If children are not reading historical fiction, we choose historical fiction to read to the group. Reading new materials aloud helps children form a mental expectation for how such materials are organized and prepares them for reading such books on their own. If teachers need specific recommendations for read aloud titles, we recommend they consult Jim Trelease's *The New Read-Aloud Handbook* (1989), *The New York Times Parents' Guide to the Best Books for Children* (Lipson, 1991), or *Books Kids Will Sit Still For: The Complete Read-Aloud Guide* (Freeman, 1992).

One benefit of literacy is information. To understand this benefit, children must experience it. Information books and fiction based on true events are rarely used as read-alouds even though these materials form the bulk of what students will be expected to read in high school and in daily life. Because students have not experienced informational books, they have difficulty understanding these materials when they are asked to read them on their own. Not only should teachers read information books during authors chair, but they should also monitor the news to find items of interest to the children. Various newspapers from the local area can be perused so that the sharing of news items related to children's inquiries becomes a normal part of authors chair.

After the teacher brings in several newspaper clippings on classroom topics, children can be invited to bring clippings to share. In one fourth-grade class, this invitation led to a daily newscast. Three students each morning signed up to share items they found relevant to the topic. As children presented their newscast (the class decided on a five-minute maximum program length) a videotape was cut that, after a replaying in the class, was available to other classes in the school throughout the day. Written versions of these newscasts led to a publication entitled "The Week in Review," which was distributed throughout the school. Many children in this class began reading the newspaper daily. All had a pretty good idea of the types of information in area newspapers as well as an understanding of what newspaper reporters could do that television newscasters could not.

Although parents occasionally may read a newspaper item or a story with their children, poetry is almost never read in homes. It is crucial that teachers share favorite poems with children on a regular basis. Many adults do not enjoy poetry or value it as an important literary form. In pursuing this issue with parents, we find that many parents (and teachers) do not know how to read poetry. Rather than following the interpretations suggested by the rhythm and words of the poem, they read poetry as they would read an encyclopedia: namely, in terms of the facts the poem teaches. To ensure that children do not develop these faulty notions, teachers might ask students to close their eyes and concentrate on the images and feelings that the poem creates. They can then sketch the meanings of the poetry using Sketch to Stretch.

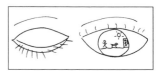

Children need to understand that reading strategies vary by context of situation and that they have a responsibility when reading poetry to discover the allusions, to use their past experiences as a working metaphor in comprehension, and to enjoy the lived-through experience. In other types of reading, the contract is different, but to enjoy poetry one cannot be textbound. Sharing poetry can lead to invitations for children to find poetry to share as well as writing their own poetry. Teachers may want to pair their favorite read-aloud books with poems, actually gluing a poem in the back of the book so that they remember to share the poem whenever they read the book aloud to a group.

When children find a book exciting, teachers should consider reading other books by the same author, thereby setting up an environment where children begin to recognize an author's work by his or her style (see Authors Meeting Authors). Any teacher worried about creativity just needs to bring in a Chris Van Allsburg Text Set and then watch children take off. Teachers can also bring in other books that are the same genre or have similar themes. They can either read them aloud or give a short introduction to the books and then put them into the classroom library corner. In many classrooms, teachers and students keep lists of their read-aloud books on large charts according to authors and themes so they can return to these books in discussions during later read-alouds.

The books that teachers read aloud are usually placed in the classroom library because they are in high demand for students to read on their own. When reading a longer chapter book, some teachers make a number of copies available because of student interest. Debbie Manning purchases multiple copies of a short chapter book which she reads aloud to her first graders while they follow along, sitting in pairs. If they lose their place, they simply turn the page when she does. This experience helps them develop listening strategies and understandings about the structure of chapter books.

Because read-aloud books are such significant experiences in children's lives, they provide a natural point of connection for further explorations through talk, drama, and writing. Many teachers use dis-

Chapter Three
The Authoring Cycle
as a Curricular
Framework for Reading

cussions of the class read-aloud to demonstrate to children the kinds of talk that occur in Literature Circles. Although fewer children can participate in whole group discussions, these discussions offer multiple demonstrations about talk. Karen Smith (1990) invites her students to gather in a circle to talk about the class read-aloud while she sits outside the circle taking field notes of their discussion. She then joins the group and talks with them about their discussion, using examples from her field notes to help them become aware of the kinds of connections they are making and the behaviors that are supporting their discussion.

Read-alouds are also an opportunity for teachers to offer children invitations to extend their experiences as writers. Children can be invited to write the same type of story, such as a memoir or a "Choose Your Own Adventure." Many children enjoy taking a language pattern that an author has used and writing their own story (e.g., "Brown bear, Brown bear, What do you see?" [Martin, 1970]). If the book is rich in descriptive language or dialogue, children are invited to try this in their own pieces. Many children put dedications and "curtains" (endpapers) in their books or use certain styles of illustration after noticing these in books shared at authors chair. Invitations to extend the story through drama are another possibility as children work through their understandings by taking on the roles of particular characters and creating actions and dialogue that reflect their interpretations of that story. Since these are invitations, an author can decide whether to accept, ignore, or put on hold any invitation that is offered. No matter how an author responds, however, read-alouds continually put new invitations and demonstrations on the floor so that students continue to grow and to be challenged as authors.

Authors chair gives both teachers and students the chance to take the role of an author sharing a text with other authors. Although there are different reasons authors read aloud from their own or other's texts, authors chair gives all authors the chance to share whole texts with others and to offer new demonstrations and insights to other authors through this sharing. The use of authors chair by teachers to read aloud a variety of literature to the class is one engagement that no class should ever be without because of the tremendous impact these experiences have on children as writers and readers.

Classroom Libraries and Wide Reading

An essential ingredient in a classroom where children are active readers and writers is a classroom library. When children have easy access to a variety of books, they more frequently read and refer to those books. We believe strongly in the principle of accessibility—the more accessible something is, the more likely it is to be used. If we want to highlight the importance of literature in our classrooms, then classroom libraries must be a prominent and permanent feature. In focusing on the importance of having a library in the classroom, we are not deemphasizing the significance of the school library. We have found that having an active classroom library increases children's use of the school library because they become more interested in books and more aware of the kinds of books that are available and so go in search of them in the school library.

Children need to be assured access by putting books easily within their reach, creating attractive displays of books related to a certain theme or author, providing time for children to browse and read, and encouraging them to share what they are reading with each other. Simply putting books in the classroom does not create a library. Teachers can further increase the chances children will read the books available in the classroom by reading aloud to the class and giving short introductions or book talks about the books on display. Try a little experiment sometime and introduce some of the books on display and not others and see which books the children interact with the most.

The easy access to books that a classroom library provides is important not only in encouraging children to read more widely but also in facilitating their responses to literature. Janet Hickman (1981) found that the direct accessibility of a book was of primary importance to children's willingness to express any response to that book. They needed to be able to return to the remembered books as they wrote, created artwork, or discussed literature with others. Some children were not willing even to talk about a book unless they were able to touch the book as they talked. The books that generated the most responses were the books the teacher had introduced or read to the class and the books organized around a theme or in some way related to one another. These related books got children involved in making comparisons among books and helped them see similarities and connections.

Fill the classroom library with all kinds of books, focusing on both the quality of the literature and on variety in genres, topics, themes, authors, and illustrators. Classroom libraries should not consist of out-of-date castoffs. With the tremendous amount of books available today for children, it is possible for children to read only substandard books and never read a significant piece of literature. Quality literature provides children with "lived-through experiences" and supports rereading and reflection. Teachers can also collect Text Sets, sets of books that are conceptually related, so that children begin to build connections between literature. In addition, one section of the library should display children's own published books.

Many teachers create rotating author and illustrator displays in their classroom (see Authors Meeting Authors). As children come to know authors and illustrators, the library seems less overwhelming as they search for books by "old friends." First graders created an "I recommend" file for their classroom library. Alphabetized by author, the file consisted of cards on which children recommended a particular author's books. We have found that if we tell parents whom we are focusing on, they may help their child find that author's books at the public library.

The books in a classroom library at all grades should range from picture books to chapter books and from highly predictable books that provide easy reading experiences to more difficult and challenging books. Teachers need to look closely at their students and provide the kinds of books they need to support their current levels of reading proficiency. We found out the importance of supportive reading materials several years ago in Gloria Kauffman's first-grade classroom. Early in the year, many easy-to-read predictable books had been brought into the classroom and the children were soon active readers who constantly had books in their hands. In January, Kathy returned most of the predictable book sets to the library from which we had borrowed them. The children were left with the existing classroom library, which contained few predictable books. To our amazement, the same group of children who had been reading anything in sight almost stopped reading. Kathy quickly started bringing back ten to twenty predictable books a week from the library and started checking out more books from the school library for the room. The children soon returned to being avid readers.

We learned several lessons from this experience. One is that if children are not choosing to read, it may be that the available reading materials are not supportive for them. For young children, this means having many familiar predictable books for fluent reading experiences as well as more challenging materials. For older children, this means having picture books and short stories available, as well as series books and difficult chapter books. Older children often

"I Recommend" card;
Lanny, Age 6 (Kathy Smith's classroom)

respond better to "soft" materials such as paperbacks, magazines, comics, and newspapers because these books look so different from the hardback textbooks they associate with boring reading.

Teachers sometimes feel that letting children read a book below their reading "level" is cheating. What we found is that children use these books to "take a break" after they finish a particularly difficult book and to build fluency in their reading. As adults, we do not read only books at a particular level of difficulty. We develop strategies for reading materials that range from easy to difficult and children need this same range in their reading. In fact, we believe that children should be encouraged to read "hard" books because they are pushed to develop new reading strategies and to engage in conversations with others to make sense of their reading.

Building a good classroom library does not happen overnight. We have used a variety of sources including paperback book clubs such as Scholastic and Trumpet Club and grants from parent-teacher organizations. Many teachers have their own personal collections that they share with children, and they also borrow extensively from libraries. We have been known to wheel a cartload of books from the school library to take to the classroom for several weeks and then later to exchange those books for another load.

While children will interact with the books in the classroom library throughout the day for different purposes, they need one time of the day when they can engage in uninterrupted reading for their own purposes. Wide reading goes by many names such as SSR (Sustained Silent Reading) and DEAR (Drop Everything and Read), but what is important is that children are free to choose from books and other reading materials—such as newspapers and magazines—and that they read for their own purposes with a primary focus on enjoyment. They do not have to write responses or discuss the books; they simply read. They are encouraged to share informally in author talk time and many teachers have students keep records of book titles, but beyond those requests, children read for themselves.

Although research on almost everything else is inconclusive, the amount of uninterrupted reading in which children engage is consistently related to their growth as readers (Morrow, 1991). Despite this finding, children spend most of their "reading" time filling out worksheets and workbooks, which have *no* correlation to reading growth. One study showed that fifth graders read an average of zero to four minutes a day outside of school and seven minutes a day in school

(Anderson, Wilson, & Fielding, 1988). Students who are labeled "poor" readers by schools have even less time for reading because they receive more skill sheets. Some of the most important teaching that teachers can do is to provide time in the daily schedule for wide reading.

It often works well to schedule wide reading at transition points in the day because it provides a time of quiet reflection and gradual coming together. Many teachers schedule it right after recess or lunch so that as students come into the classroom, they grab their books and quietly begin reading. Other teachers start the day with journals and, as students finish writing, they move into wide reading and then to a group meeting. Whenever it is held, it is rarely a time of silence. Some children will want to partner read with another child and others will quietly share a comment or favorite page. It's a natural response to turn and share with a friend when something touches us with humor or deep connection.

Janet Hickman (1981) notes that the "impulse to share" is one of the most frequent responses that children make to literature. This impulse to share should be scheduled into wide reading. Susan Hepler (1982) spent a year examining responses to literature in a fifth- and sixth-grade classroom and found that, for a majority of readers, the single most influential factor in children's selection of books was the recommendation of another person. These recommendations primarily occurred during the group sharing time we call author talk time at the end of the morning work time. Students meet with a partner, in small groups, or as a whole class to share the books they are reading and writing. Since everyone is reading different books, this sharing takes the form of a conversation between readers rather than the dialogue that occurs in Literature Circles.

Authors Meeting Authors

Another curricular engagement that supports students as they engage in wide reading is introducing them to professionally published authors including writers, poets, and illustrators of children's books. Through author studies, children develop a warm, personal feeling for particular authors and search for their work in the library. When they realize that books are written by people just like them, they begin to more critically respond to books as one person's story rather than "THE truth." They also come to recognize the style of particular authors which facilitates their understandings of new books by those authors.

We usually devote one of our daily class read-aloud times, often the one occurring at the beginning of work time, to a writer, illustrator, or poet. On the first day of a particular focus, we talk about the author, relate any interesting stories we found in our research, and then briefly introduce the books in the display. On the following days, we read aloud from that author's books. If the author writes chapter books, we choose one to read to the class and briefly introduce the others or read excerpts. As we read, we tell any additional stories we know about the author or quote what the author has said about the particular book or about his or her work. Sometimes the class also becomes involved in drama, art, and writing projects related to that author's books.

The author study can be a natural outgrowth of ongoing theme and inquiry studies. Sandy Kaser's fifth graders became interested in Jane Yolen because of their study of birds of prey. They came across a number of her books during this study, and their interest in her work led them to search for other books and to a class focus on Yolen. They went to several libraries and gathered every book they could find to create a display of her books. Students browsed through these books and then divided them into different categories according to genre and topic. These Text Sets were used for wide reading and Literature Circles. As they read these books and listened to Sandy read aloud from other books, they created a chart with categories of the characteristics of Yolen's books, such as her writing style, the topics of her books, and kinds of characters. They also read from Yolen's short stories and used engagements such as Say Something and Save the Last Word for Me as a way to become more comfortable with talking about literature.

Because Yolen writes on so many different topics in books that range from picture books to complex novels, Sandy's students were able to find books that connected to their interests and reading proficiencies. They created posters to "sell" their favorite books and placed these around the school as well as prepared presentations on their connections to a particular book. These presentations were displayed in the school library. In addition, Sandy shared excerpts from articles that Yolen had written for adults about her work, and students read from an autobiographical article. Yolen's comments about

> "In the beginning of the book, the author's note says that this book is based on things that really happened. I think that's interesting the way he puts it in there. He puts a lot of his personal feelings and personal life in his stories."

Discussion of **Baseball Saved Us** (Mochizuki, 1993); Renee, Age 11 (Gloria Kauffman's classroom)

Chapter Three
The Authoring Cycle
as a Curricular
Framework for Reading

her writing techniques led them to new realizations of what it means to write from experience in their own writing.

We also invite children to research their favorite authors, illustrators, and poets. We realize that the research process in which we engage when preparing an author's study for the classroom is where the most exciting learning takes place. Children do not gain as much from our sharing as they do if they are engaged in researching and exploring authors themselves. We encourage children to do this research by bringing many author reference sources into the classroom and by familiarizing children with what is in the school library. Sometimes the class becomes involved in a more formal study of particular authors through Literature Circles where each circle reads and discusses a particular person's work, explores resources about their life and work, and presents what they have learned to the class. The best source of information about children's authors is a large set of encyclopedias called *Something About the Author* (Commire, 1971–present) which adds new volumes each year. Many additional sources are available and some of these are listed in Section II. Books such as *How Writers Write* (Lloyd, 1987) and *Talking about Artists* (Cummings, 1992) include comments by the authors on their writing and illustrating processes.

A common activity is to have children write to favorite authors and illustrators. Beverly Cleary, in her children's book *Dear Mr. Henshaw* (1983), points out that having children write simply for the sake of writing, as an imposed assignment, is not beneficial to either the child or the author. Letters to authors should grow out of a child's desire to communicate with that person rather than to complete an assignment. As children ask questions about a particular person or talk about how much they like that author's work, we encourage them to write to that author. Once several children receive responses, other children become interested in writing to an author they particularly like. Vera Milz concludes an author study by having one or two children who particularly connected to that author volunteer to create a card and write a message; then the other children sign their names. Her children also send cards to their favorite authors on the authors' birthdays or on holidays. It is best to send correspondence to authors in care of whichever publisher is currently publishing their hardcover books.

It is particularly exciting if an author can actually visit a classroom or school. The author can be a community person publishing

roses are red,
violets are blue,
your the best auther
I ever now

from
Erin
+ Amy

Letter to Children's Book Author; Erin and Amy, Age 7 (Lynn Manning's classroom)

Section One
The Authoring Cycle:
Let's Talk Curriculum

through a local press or a more well-known author. A retired teacher who self-published a book of poetry at a small press visited Gloria Kauffman's first-grade classroom. The children prepared for her visit by reading and discussing her poetry in Literature Circles. They brainstormed questions they wanted to ask her, and each child wrote down several questions they wanted to remember to ask. When the author visited the classroom, she brought in her rough drafts and talked about her writing and illustrating, showed the different stages in the publication process, and answered the children's questions. The children then moved into work time. They each put their own favorite published work out on their desks. As they worked, the author walked around, and each child author briefly shared a piece of his or her own work with the visiting author. Several children listed this experience as the highlight of the year for them. It validated for them that they were involved in the same process of authoring as adult authors.

The elementary schools around Columbus, Ohio, benefit from the many authors who visit The Ohio State University. They arrange for those authors to come a day early and visit their schools, thus keeping the cost of the visit down. Kathy visited Highland Park Elementary School as they prepared for a visit from children's author Eve Merriam. For several weeks before she came, the entire school was involved in units developed around her poetry. Individual classrooms carried out projects related to her work, and copies of her books were available for student purchase. Many classrooms were involved in poetry units in which children read poetry, wrote their own poetry, and responded to her work through murals, dioramas, giant books, and displays. Teachers also worked with students in helping them generate questions they wanted to ask Eve Merriam during her visit.

In addition to the individual classroom projects, there were a number of school-wide projects based on her poetry and books. The front lobby of the school was converted into a museum where displays related to a particular poem were set up; the school faculty put on a play for the children from one of her books; a school poetry-reading assembly was held; and a poem on pizza led to making giant pizzas that were wheeled around the school with each classroom adding something to them.

One morning minicourses on activities related to Eve Merriam's poems were offered by each adult in the school. The children signed up so that one or two children from each class attended a particular workshop. When children returned to their classrooms after the workshops, they shared what they had done, providing new ideas for ways of responding to literature for the other children. The mini-courses included making mobiles, stuffed objects, pocket poems, windchimes, and monster masks as well as examining sea shells, taking field trips to a pizza shop, and working on a drama.

On the day Eve Merriam came to visit, the entire school was filled with murals, posters, dioramas, books, and displays related to her work. Her day at the school began with a tour of each room. Each class had fifteen minutes to share some of their responses to her work and to ask several questions. She then had lunch with a group of children (one child had been chosen from each room) followed by lunch with teachers. After lunch, she met with small groups of children who had been chosen to share special projects with her. A school assembly was then called, where she read from her poetry and talked about her writing. The day ended with an autograph session in the gymnasium. Booths were set up around the perimeter of the gym with activities to do as the children waited in the long autograph line. Each child received a number to reserve their place in line. It was an exciting day for both Eve Merriam and the children.

Although arranging a major author to visit your school is expensive, there are ways to offset the costs. Check with the publisher to see if the author will be near your area for another engagement so that you could share the transportation costs. See if you can split the costs with another group, such as a local college or your area's Young Authors Conference. Publishers are often willing to pay the costs for new authors whom they are trying to promote. Some schools have fundraisers to get the money they need for these visits. Finally, do not forget the authors who may live near your area. In addition, many authors today are willing to do telephone conference calls. These can usually be arranged through the author's publisher.

Authors Meeting Authors provides children with many different demonstrations on authoring as a central process in bringing meaning to their lives. This engagement should not be limited to authoring through writing and illustrating. People who author in other sign systems should be featured in our classrooms for the same reasons authors of children's books need to be featured. A focus on mathematicians, dancers, musicians, artists, and others should be considered an essential part of Authors Meeting Authors.

Section One
The Authoring Cycle:
Let's Talk Curriculum

Readers Theatre

Another important uninterrupted reading engagement is Readers Theatre. To conduct Readers Theatre, we gather multiple copies of picture books and old basal readers or copies of short stories and excerpts from longer books to mark as the script. Once a story is selected, the various reading parts are marked with highlighter pens to indicate those to be read by the narrator(s) and those that are the speaking parts of characters. The performance involves reading the story without props or costumes so that the focus is on oral interpretation. Once students understand how the parts are assigned, they are able to read from stories that have not been highlighted and create their own Readers Theatres.

Stories with dialogue, poetry, and stories to which sound effects can be added work well for Readers Theatre. Sometimes background music can set the stage for reading. We created an audiocassette tape with four-minute segments of ten different styles of music ranging from classical to country. As children read various stories, they use these segments as background music and discuss how the music either contributes or fails to contribute to the meaning of the selection.

Theoretically, Readers Theatre allows stories to come to life. Many written texts need to be read orally to be appreciated. The sound of the language adds a new dimension of meaning. Further, interpretation is highlighted in Readers Theatre through the voice and facial expressions. Inevitably, discussions ensue as to how a group might have read something differently. The group takes a look at other ways to divide the story into speaking parts and to use their voices in interpreting the story. These discussions lead to new readings and to reflecting on how the various readings create different meanings. One student, who had difficulty deciding when to read and when to be quiet asked, "How did everyone know when to stop reading?" This led to a discussion of quotation marks and the response, "Oh, that's what those things do, huh?" We never try to second-guess problems. Sometimes such emergent problems set up the best learning situations. What we found particularly interesting was that after this "aha experience," the questioner's written stories were full of dialogue. His latest language discovery was what he was most interested in exploring As adults, we experience this same phenomenon when we continually insert a newly learned term into almost every conversation.

Readers Theatre helps children confirm the fact that a good text allows multiple interpretations, that language is open, and that interpretation is what distinguishes a good reader from a poor reader. It also helps children realize that reading is an active process of composition, and that although all interpretations are good, some are more powerful than others. Readers Theatre supports all kinds of readers. Individual children are not put on the spot, and less capable readers find support in reading along with the group. Because key characters see their parts ahead of time, they can practice and perform as well as anyone else when it comes time for them to read. Interpretation centers on the expressiveness of the voice.

After the teacher has selected a few stories, it's time to invite someone in the class to choose and prepare the next story for Readers Theatre. The students, rather than the teacher, need to own this activity if it is to be successful. A sign-up sheet in the Readers Theatre area will allow others to volunteer as individuals or in pairs. To get the right to select a story for Readers Theatre, the teacher signs up just like the rest of the class. True engagement and commitment come when children are given choice in deciding what to read as well as what not to read. These decisions must then be honored by teacher and students. We have found that having stories that work as well as stories that don't work only adds to the richness of the Readers Theatre experience. As Readers Theatre becomes a familiar part of classroom life, we see children spontaneously using it during their work time as a way to do Shared Reading. They gather as many people as they need to read the story and have their own Readers Theatre off in a corner. Many times these are not shared with the class, but as a way to enjoy the story together.

Choral Reading engagements are similar to a Readers Theatre but involve the oral interpretation of poetry and nursery rhymes. To introduce students to different kinds of Choral Reading, Leslie Kahn and Kathy invited sixth graders to take a familiar nursery rhyme, "Hickory Dickory Dock," and develop as many different ways to arrange and read the rhyme as possible. They tried reading solo and in groups as well as reading staccato and in the style of rap and opera. These students then created their own choral readings for various poems throughout the rest of the year.

Once children have experienced Readers Theatre, it is time to give invitations for further authorship. The focus on oral interpretation provides a natural invitation for children to become oral storytellers of their own stories or of folklore based in oral traditions. Through Readers Theatre they learn how to use their voices effectively while having the security of a script to read. Oral storytelling brings them even closer to their audience as they use their voices and faces to communicate their interpretation of the story. Another extension is to encourage children to move into other types of drama where they use props and create their own dialogue and actions based on familiar stories or their own ideas. One way to encourage drama is through Acting It Out where a story box is put together that includes a wordless book such as *The Bear and the Fly* (Winter, 1976) and clothing that might be used as costumes for the characters. The box becomes an immediate invitation for children to engage in dramatic interpretation.

Shared Reading

A learning environment needs to be organized to provide maximum support for readers. Shared Reading is a curricular engagement that provides this support by involving language users in sharing with each other in the reading of meaningful, predictable texts. Reading and rereading familiar and predictable stories with others provides successful and enjoyable reading experiences that can then lead to other kinds of responses that cut across sign systems. Less proficient readers especially benefit from this engagement because it supports their initial reading experiences and encourages them to take risks and to make predictions based on meaning and structure.

Shared Reading can involve whole group and small group experiences where the teacher and class read together, either in unison or in choral reading, from books that are highly predictable for that group of children. Shared Reading also refers to several children who decide to read together during wide reading. Although Shared Reading can take place in many different ways, the essential criterion for Shared Reading is that the reading experience is set up so that readers support and share with each other using a predictable text setting.

The books used in Shared Reading provide highly predictable text settings through text organization and connections to reader experiences. Although many teachers tend to think of predictable books only as books for young children, predictability can be a characteristic of books for all age levels. What is predictable varies according to the particular age and experience level of the specific children in a classroom.

Some books are predictable because they reflect life experiences about which readers have a great deal of knowledge. A child who has grown up on a farm will find a story about farms more predictable than a story about the city. Books that have already been read aloud to children at home or at school are predictable, especially if children have heard them over and over, because they already know the plot, language, and characters. Children who have seen television shows and movies based on children's books, especially chapter books such as *Charlotte's Web* (White, 1952), often find the books predictable. If children have had many reading experiences with a certain type of book such as mysteries or folklore, they often find other books of the same type predictable. Books by the same author, in the same genre, or in a particular series often have common structural elements.

Lynn Rhodes (1981) points out that elements such as repetitive patterns or refrains, the match between text and illustration, the rhythm of the language, familiar sequences, rhymes, and cumulative patterns help to make books predictable for young readers. Stories such as *The Very Hungry Caterpillar* (Carle, 1969), *Brown Bear, Brown Bear, What Do You See?* (Martin, 1970), and *It Didn't Frighten Me* (Goss & Harste, 1985) are examples of books that use these organizational devices.

We found that series such as Babysitter Club books or Sweet Valley Twins books provide for easy fluent reading on topics of interest to older children in a format that is predictable and easy to understand. While these books do not support critical, in-depth dialogue, they are high interest books that can be read easily and quickly. These books are especially popular with third and fourth graders as they make the transition to chapter books. After reading several books in a series, the reader can predict the plot of the next book because they follow a similar format. The predictability of series books helps students figure out how to read longer books.

One type of Shared Reading experience occurs when the teacher or another child reads a predictable book to an entire class of young children and invites them to join in the reading. We usually begin this experience by reading the title of the book and having the students predict what the story might be about based on the title and the cover illustration. We then read the story to the children, inviting them to join in on any repeating phrases or parts of the story whenever they feel ready. We often stop at certain points and have the students predict what the next word or phrase will be or what will happen next. Depending on the predictability of the text, most students will be reading the most predictable parts of the text by the end of the book.

If students have responded enthusiastically to the story, we ask if they want to read it again. On the second reading, many more students usually join in on reading the text, and the teacher's voice can be phased out so that the children are actually doing the reading. Multiple rereadings of books help children gain control over the story content, language, and organization. After the first or second reading, students can share their feelings about the story, confirm their predictions, and talk about parts of the story they especially like. The number of times we reread a story depends on whether the students enjoy it and request the book and on how well they are able to join in on reading the story. If students do not enjoy a story or the story is too difficult, we may read it only once or twice and then no longer use it during Shared Reading. The stories that are reread over and over often later become the focus of strategy lessons on the reading process because children have experienced these as a whole text first in a meaningful context.

These whole group Shared Reading experiences often involve the use of big books—books with enlarged print so that all the children can see the print as well as the illustrations. These books can be purchased commercially but can also be made by having the children draw the illustrations and an adult write the text. Songs and poems can be put on large charts so that all the children can see. An alternative is to put the story on overheads. The same procedures can be used in reading predictable books with small groups of children who need extra support as readers. The small group version of Shared Reading is usually called guided reading.

We follow Don Holdaway's (1979) recommendation in making our Shared Reading a time of sharing old favorites as well as a time of introducing new poems, songs, and stories. We begin with some old favorites, taking requests from the students as well as using our own choices, and then move on to a new story, song, or poem. The unison rereading provides support for readers at different levels of proficiency—ranging from children who have no difficulty reading the print to children who are following the group's lead but are unable to read the print on their own. Children are not made to feel embarrassed or inadequate, and everyone joins in as able. As the story is reread, more and more children are able to read it with the rest of the group. During these rereadings, children become familiar with the language and story structure of the book, gain fluency in their oral reading, and begin to notice certain visual features. Each rereading allows children to attend to new demonstrations. The old favorites that are read repeatedly become the stories children draw from in their writing and in other response activities. Following rereading, the book is placed in the classroom library so that students can continue to read it independently. Sometimes the book is placed in a listening center for students who need to continue hearing the story.

Shared Reading is based on the model of lap or bedtime story reading (Doake, 1986; Holdaway, 1979). This model was developed from noting that young children naturally learn to read books when their parents read and reread the same stories to them and that the children then independently explore these same books for long hours during play. In Shared Reading, therefore, we give equal emphasis to the group reading, rereading, and the independent exploration times in helping children gain control of a particular story.

Variations of Shared Reading

Other types of Shared Reading occur during wide reading when children can choose either to read alone or with other children. If they decide to partner read with another child, the two children must then decide how they will share the reading. The most common ways of sharing the reading are to take turns reading pages or parts of the story or to each read a different story to the other person. Sometimes readers decide to read in unison. If one reader is more proficient than the other, the more proficient reader may read the less predictable parts and the less proficient reader the repeating refrains, or the more proficient reader may read the first part of the story and the less proficient reader may read the second part. Either strategy provides support for the less proficient reader because having the proficient reader read first introduces the characters, author's style, and story structure. Classrooms with listening centers of books and taped readings provide another way that children can read along with someone else.

Harmony, a first-grade child who was experiencing difficulty in reading, taught us another strategy. She approached several proficient readers and asked them to read her a book before she attempted to read it herself. Children in Harmony's classroom began approaching each other asking, "Do you want to learn to read my book?" or

"Will you teach me to read your book?" They read both trade books and books they had published.

These variations of Shared Reading build on the social nature of the learning process and allow children to support each other as they gain proficiency in reading. Although Shared Reading tends to be associated with young children, the many variations described support Shared Reading as a curricular engagement that is also useful with older children. Because Shared Reading involves rereading predictable books, these books are a natural choice for a variety of response engagements including drama, art, music, and writing.

Students often choose to use the language or structural patterns of these books in their own writing or to create Group Composed Books. Group Composed Books are usually offered as an invitation for each child to write one page using the patterns and structures of a particular predictable book and then gathering the pages together into one book. Another option, however, is to make the writing of the book truly a group process. Those interested in writing a story gather together, and either the teacher or another child serves as a scribe to write down the story on the blackboard as the group develops it together. Although each child still decides what his or her page will say, that child does so knowing what the other pages will say and with the support of the rest of the group. Once the group has finished the story, each child copies his or her own page from the board and illustrates it for the group book. This activity of shared writing offers an excellent opportunity for children to observe and discuss the composing process as they work together to create a Group Composed Book. Both Group Composed Books and Shared Reading thus provide learning environments that highlight the support that language users can provide for each other in reading and writing with predictable text materials.

All of these experiences—authors chair, wide reading, Readers Theatre, storytelling, read-aloud, and Shared Reading—support readers as they immerse themselves in reading materials and books. Through these extensive experiences, readers gain proficiency and a broad knowledge base that they can draw from in other reading experiences. Responding to these books in a variety of ways is a natural part of this process. Over a period of time, students may be involved in several different ways of responding to the same piece of literature as they talk about the book, write about it in a Literature Log, use the

Whistle Richard
whistle
And you shall have
nieces. I can't
whistle teacher
Because I'm
falling to pieces.

Page from Group Composed Book Based on Whistle, Children, Whistle (Martin, 1982); Richard, Age 7 (Gloria Kauffman's classroom)

Chapter Three
The Authoring Cycle
as a Curricular
Framework for Reading

literature in some way in their own writing, and draw or in some other way represent the book in art. Each response deepens their understanding of that literature. Janet Hickman (1981) observed how children responded to literature in three elementary classrooms and identified the following categories of response:

1. Listening behaviors (body stances, laughter and applause, exclamations, joining in refrains)

2. Contact with books (browsing, showing intense attention, keeping books at hand)

3. Acting on impulse to share (reading together, sharing discoveries)

4. Oral responses (retelling, storytelling, discussion statements, free comments)

5. Actions and drama (echoing the action, demonstrating meaning, dramatic play, child-initiated drama, teacher-initiated drama)

6. Making things (pictures and related artwork, three dimensional art and construction, miscellaneous products such as games, displays, collections, cookery, and so forth)

7. Writing (restating and summarizing, writing about literature, using literary models deliberately, using unrecognized models and sources)

Although these ways of responding are not the only possibilities, they show the range of responses in which children can be involved. The absence of sign systems such as music from this list indicates that these are areas that teachers and students need to explore more fully as possible ways to respond. Through these different ways of responding, readers have the chance to revisit past readings in a new light so that each response is more complex and more reflective and supports readers in gaining new perspectives on the book and their lives.

Gaining New Perspectives Through Literature Circles

Literature Circles provide a curricular structure to support children in exploring their rough draft understandings of literature with other readers (Short & Pierce, 1990; Pierce & Gilles, 1994). While they often exchange a few comments as they partner read or during large group discussions of class read-alouds, these conversations are brief and rarely move to dialogue. Literature Circles involve children in expanding and critiquing their understandings about their reading through dialogue with other readers. These circles support reading as a transaction which Louise Rosenblatt (1978) describes as a process in which readers actively construct understandings by bringing meaning to as well as taking meaning from a text. They are not trying to extract information from a text, figure out the interpretation the teacher wants to hear, or learn about literary elements. They enter the world of literature to learn about life and to make sense of their experiences and feelings.

In Literature Circles, readers must think with each other collaboratively, not simply work with each other cooperatively. Cooperative learning formats where tasks and roles are divided among the members of the group shut down the thinking and talk which is at the heart of dialogue. Learners do not simply contribute their part of the work to the Literature Circle, they listen carefully and think critically and deeply with other group members to create understandings that go beyond those of individual members. The dialogue in these circles leads to new perspectives on literature, their lives, and their reading processes. Learners come to know their own voices as well as those of their classmates. Children's voices are valued for their diversity because new perspectives push the group to deeper understandings and investigations of life. Chris, a third grader, explains the process,

> Everyone has a chance to give their own opinion and even if you don't agree with that person, you keep on talking because you know that you will get more ideas. You aren't trying to figure out one right answer. In reading groups, when someone gave the right answer, we were done talking. In Literature Circles, we keep on going. We try to come up with as many different directions as possible.

From the first day that we used Literature Circles in the classroom, it was evident that these circles gave readers the opportunity they needed to explore half-formed ideas with others and to revise their understandings of a piece of literature through dialogue. The books

> "I think it makes a good discussion when everybody gets to talk and share ideas with each other."
>
> **Travis, Age 11 (Gloria Kauffman's classroom)**

they discussed in Literature Circles became significant parts of their life experiences. They returned to these books in making connections in later reading and writing experiences. The children's thinking about literature became more complex and generative. These discussions helped them revise their understandings about literature, which they shared with other children through some type of presentation. The children also changed in their ability to reflect on their own reading processes, on how they read as well as on what they read.

For us, Literature Circles are usually small groups of four to six students who meet together to think deeply and critically about a shared book set (multiple copies of the same title) or Text Set (different titles of conceptually related books). We recognize that many of the books and reading materials that students read in school are never discussed in this depth. But some of what students read are books that they want to think more about with others because of connections to their own lives or to the curriculum and these become the basis of literature discussion. There is no magical formula for how to organize and conduct a Literature Circle. There are many different options that teachers and students can choose that change the potentials for talk in these groups (Hanssen, 1990; Short & Klassen, 1993). These choices are made according to students' needs and the particular curricular focus.

Establishing a Context to Support Literature Circles

In our work in classrooms, we usually find that because students have not been given an opportunity to think deeply about their reading their first discussions are often not successful. Both teachers and students struggle with how to really talk and think *with* each other about their reading. With older children, the circles are largely silent as they wait for the teacher to ask questions or, if the teacher is absent, they talk about their social lives. Younger children can usually find plenty to talk about, but little of it relates to the book. If the students coming into a classroom have not read widely and have negative attitudes toward books and reading, then they may need many uninterrupted experiences with books before moving into Literature Circles. Karen Smith (1990) found that she needed to spend the first six to nine weeks of school immersing her sixth graders in as many read-aloud and extensive reading experiences as possible. As they developed a knowledge base and enjoyment of literature, she began offer-

> "I've gotten new perspectives talking with others. I get whole new ideas to think about. I've realized what I didn't think about it. I assumed it wasn't important and I've missed whole ideas in books."

Tara, Age 11 (Gloria Kauffman's classroom)

ing invitations to explore literature in more depth in small groups. Kathleen Crawford found that her first graders had few previous experiences with books and so she increased the amount of time for read-alouds, browsing books in the room, and gathering for informal talk and sharing before she moved into Literature Circles.

Gloria Kauffman takes a different approach. She introduces her students to Literature Circles by the third week of school, knowing they will have difficulties with these groups. As they experience problems, she pulls the class together and asks them to talk about what is happening and to think through ways they can make the groups work better. She is willing to put up with some chaos and confusion because she wants to establish an attitude of inquiry for working through problems.

The class read-aloud is often a very important time to introduce new ways of talking and thinking about books. Junardi Armstrong and Kathy found that if they read a related picture book aloud to students and had a short discussion right before moving into circles, children had much more success (Short & Armstrong, 1993). Teachers of young children often call one of their class read-aloud times Literature Circle and the children know that they will take time to really talk about this book. Later in the year, as they move into small group Literature Circles, they know what kind of talk is expected.

Often a chapter book read-aloud provides a powerful shared experience for a classroom. Leslie Kahn (1994) builds on this experience with reflective literature circles. After finishing the reading of a chapter book that her students particularly enjoyed, she asks them to brainstorm a list of issues and connections that came up during their discussions of the read-aloud. She and the students then take this list and group related items together to create categories of issues. Students sign up for a Literature Circle on one of the categories of issues and connections. After Leslie read aloud *Building Blocks* (Voigt, 1984) as part of a class focus on family, the class created categories such as caves, fighting in families, time travel, relationships, pollution, and pain. Students discussed a particular set of issues for several days and then shared their insights with the rest of the class in presentations. Students are supported in their talk in these groups by the shared context of the previous class discussions of the chapter book.

Because of their instructional histories, children often edit what they say about books and only share what they think teachers want to hear. Encouraging them to share their actual connections and

"What I do when I'm in a literature circle is after I read the book, I try to see what our group is like. I give different ideas about what I think about the book. I talk about things I like about the book and things I hate about the book, and the things I would really like to be changed."

David, Age 11 (Gloria Kauffman's classroom)

thoughts can be a major challenge—they are absolutely sure that teachers only want right answers. Jerry and Carol Hill ask children to choose a book from a stack of picture books which have already been read aloud. During the second reading they place an easel next to the authors chair and, as they read aloud, they stop periodically and ask children, "What's on your mind?" Children's comments are quickly jotted down on the chart. At the end of the read-aloud, the children choose several of the comments to discuss in greater depth. This engagement not only communicates the message that books are read more than once but also signals that we value what children are thinking.

Sandy Kaser found that her fifth graders would not talk about books in whole class or small group discussions, not only because of the newness of this talk, but also because they were afraid that their peers would make fun of them. She began reading aloud picture books and short stories to the class and asking children to talk with a partner about the book. To support them in their talk, she introduced a particular engagement such as Say Something, Sketch to Stretch, Save the Last Word for Me, Webbing, and Written Conversation. As they became more comfortable with talking and working in pairs, they moved into small groups.

Sandy's experience reminds us that if children do not trust each other and have a sense of community as a group, Literature Circles will not be successful. You don't tell others what's really on your mind and important in your life if you don't trust them. In many cases where we are struggling with literature discussion, the problem is the lack of trust and community, not just that children don't know how to talk about books. Literature Circles both depend on community and are one of the best ways to develop a sense of community in the classroom.

Engagements where children choose their own partners have worked well for other teachers in creating low-risk environments to encourage talk. Working with a partner almost guarantees that children cannot sit silently as they do in whole group or small group discussion. Say Something has probably been the most effective partner engagement we have used in encouraging children to take an active stance as readers. Two students take turns orally reading chunks of text to each other. Whenever one reader stops, both say something about their connections, questions, predictions, and observations of the story, and then the other person reads. Another partner engagement, Written Conversation, where children write to each other about a book using one piece of paper and one pencil, encourages children to really listen to each other, a frequent problem in discussions.

In some schools, class sets of thirty books have been purchased and everyone in the class reads and discusses the same book together. While this kind of discussion can be effective in introducing students to ways of talking about books or creating a shared context, it takes away student choice and creates a context where only a few get to talk. These class sets should be used only occasionally and, when they are used, students should move between small groups and the whole class in their discussions. For example, students can first meet in small groups and then each group share what they discussed with the class. Purchasing class sets seems like a waste of money to us. For the amount of money needed to buy thirty copies of the same title, multiple copy sets consisting of six copies of five different titles can be purchased and used much more flexibly and frequently in the classroom.

While all of these engagements can provide students with experiences and demonstrations about how to talk about books and work in groups, it's a mistake to delay Literature Circles too long. Even though students may initially struggle, they learn from engaging in the process and come to value the kind of thinking and talk that occurs when they dialogue with others. These circles can help build the sense of community that is so important to a classroom learning environment.

Selecting Literature for Literature Circles

The literature used in Literature Circles should have enough depth to support good discussions. We use picture books, poetry, short stories, and chapter books and cover all different genres from folktales to information books. We have also used films of children's books, especially those produced by Weston Woods. The literature discussed in Literature Circles should be connected to other parts of the curriculum or to children's personal inquiries. It can be related to class inquiries, author or illustrator studies, a particular genre, or children's writing. The depth of discussion in Literature Circles depends on a rich history of stories to which children can make connections. When we first started these circles, we chose what we considered quality pieces of literature. We found that even "good" books do not stand alone. When we started organizing the circles so that they were related to each other, such as each circle reading a shared book set on the theme of survival or Text Sets on different aspects of families, the discussions took on more depth. We could introduce read-alouds, create book displays, and offer experiences throughout the day that supported children's connections in Literature Circles.

The connections across Literature Circles can highlight literature as a way to learn language, a way to learn content, a way to critique the world, or a way of knowing about the world. Students may engage in author studies in order to learn more about language through examining a particular author's style, or the circles may focus on the environment or the Civil War so that students learn more about that content. Sometimes literature supports children in critiquing their world as they explore issues such as racism or homelessness. Literature is also its own way of knowing about the world and may be read to think more deeply about life and literature. While these perspectives are not mutually exclusive, one is usually highlighted during a particular focus. Our concern is that, over time, all of these perspectives are available to meet students' needs in making sense of the world.

One problem is obtaining multiple copies of shared book sets for everyone in the group to read. Our solution varies with the type of literature being used. Because picture books are short, several copies can be shared among the members of the group. Poetry and short stories can also be shared, although we often make extra photocopies of these for children. We also put together Text Sets, small sets of books that are related by theme or topic. For example, six different books on friendship might be placed in a Text Set that will be read and compared at Literature Circles. Only one copy of each book is needed.

Chapter books are a more difficult problem because each student needs a copy to read. We borrow books from the library, from other teachers, and from the children themselves. We hunt in closets and check with resource teachers for sets of books that they might have. We use the bonus points offered when children buy from paperback clubs to purchase sets of books. We talk to the parents' organization about providing money to buy multiple copies of books and to the school about letting us use workbook money to buy books instead.

"What I wish is that parents wouldn't do anything to their children and that they would keep them as their own kids. Some people and their children should spend time together. What's important is your child because they might need more help than you know."

Discussion of The Pinballs (Byars, 1977); Elsa, Age 10 (Kathleen Crawford's classroom)

We have written grants to foundations that support grassroots change in classrooms.

We also look through both old and new basals for good pieces of literature that we might use in these groups, because these are often available in multiple copies. However, we prefer to stay away from the basal in the first circles because of the past history that children bring with them regarding these basal stories. Children bring negative attitudes and expect the discussion to involve a series of closed questions (questions with only one right answer) about the story. This is frustrating when we are trying to encourage children to open up and explore meaning with each other. We find it better to begin with other kinds of literature; once discussions are going well, particular basal stories can then be used occasionally. We have also learned to check these stories to see if language has been changed and simplified in the basal version or if the basal has faithfully rendered the original piece of literature. If we use a basal story, we always bring in the actual piece of literature.

Organizing the Literature Circles

To begin Literature Circles the teacher, in consultation with students, selects quality literature of interest to the students and related to class inquiries. Enough choices are provided so that only four to six children will be in each group. One effective way of identifying books for circles is to think about the books to which students respond thoughtfully in class read-alouds and to observe students during wide reading to see what books seem to have the most significant connections for them. Some teachers begin a particular thematic or topical focus by filling the room with many books, observing students' responses as they browse through these books, and using their responses to choose books for shared book sets or Text Sets. Leslie Kahn put out all of the possible multiple copy sets of novels about the Holocaust from the school and her own collection as part of a broader theme set of Holocaust materials. After several weeks, she asked students to identify the six multiple copy sets that they wanted to use for Literature Circles. Previously she had always chosen the options herself, but this process involved the students in these decisions although they were still limited by what was currently available in the school.

Once the literature has been chosen, it is introduced through book talks to the class, and students individually decide which group they want to join. To help them make their choices, we generally give a short talk on each book or reading selection and then put the items on display for the children to browse for a day or two. Some children read each choice, while others browse through the books. Kathy found out the importance of browsing when she introduced the shared book sets to second graders and had them sign up immediately for the book they wanted to read. Students grabbed their choices and found comfortable places to read. Thirty minutes later, she was surrounded by students who wanted to change groups. She realized that students had signed up for a book they wanted to read, not necessarily a book they wanted to discuss. When students are given time to browse for a day or two, they have time to see all of the books and choose more wisely.

Children can make their choices of literature and group by signing up on a chart under the book title on a first-come, first-served basis. Another option is to write their top two or three choices on a ballot and hand it to the teacher, who then assigns the children to groups, making sure everyone gets one of their choices. Several groups may be formed to discuss a popular book, or the book may be repeated in later weeks. We do not attempt to divide the children according to ability in these groups. Even if we feel a book might be difficult for a particular child, children are allowed to choose. Because the book was their choice and because they wanted to be with a particular group of children, we find that they are generally able to find a way to read the book. If not, they read with a partner or listen to the story on a tape recording. The exact method of forming the literature circles is less important than preserving the crucial element of student choice, for with choice comes student ownership in the process.

When the books being used are longer chapter books, children sign up a full week ahead of their discussions and read the books during their work time in school or as homework. When children come to a Literature Circle, we usually want them to have already read the book all the way through, even though they often reread parts as they discuss the selection. Prior reading facilitates the discussion and avoids problems with children being at different points in the reading.

To support students as they read, we often have mini-circles. The mini-circles meet each day as students discuss what they read the previous day and agree on how much they will read for the next meeting. They usually talk about their favorite parts and clarify confusions. These discussions are brief so that students have enough time to read the book each day. When they finish the book, the group takes several days for longer, more in-depth discussions. These mini-circles are especially important when students first begin reading chapter books or with groups that need more support and encouragement.

Even if students do not meet in mini-circles, it helps if they meet the first day and figure out how many pages they need to read each day in order to be finished in one week. Students who do not reach their goal for the day must take the book home as homework. We have learned to avoid letting the reading of the book drag out over time so that students lose interest and perspective on the story. For those students who finish the book ahead of time, we have other books by the same author or on similar topics available so that when the group does begin meeting that student has more to contribute to the group. If they read unrelated materials, often they find it difficult to return to the book for discussion.

There are times when students meet in their Literature Circles during the reading of the book instead of after finishing the book. Usually these circles occur when students need more support because they are reading a particularly difficult book such as when a group of fifth graders were in a Literature Circle on *Johnny Tremain* (Forbes, 1946). By the end of the first chapter, the boys in this group knew they were in trouble understanding the story, but they wanted to continue with the book. They decided to read for several days and then meet; they continued this pattern until the book was finished. Charlene Klassen found that her fourth-grade students also needed the support of meeting during reading because, for many of them, English was their second, third, or fourth language. They needed to clarify the plot and discuss concepts that were unfamiliar to them by meeting as they read. Even in those cases, we suggest that students meet for several intensive discussions once they have finished the entire book.

Sometimes only half the class meets in various Literature Circles at one time. The rest of the class reads extensively from books of their choice or works on response activities. This way, both extensive and intensive reading continue in the classroom. For example, if the circles last for a week, half the class meets in Literature Circles, and the

> "Like some people may read a book and they think a certain thing about the book and I want to know everybody's thoughts and what's going through their minds after they read this book."

Tara, Age 11 (Gloria Kauffman's classroom)

Chapter Three
The Authoring Cycle
as a Curricular
Framework for Reading

rest read books of their own choice or work on presentations. The next week they switch places. Fridays are often a sharing day, with groups presenting their book to the other children. Other times, the whole class has Literature Circles for several weeks and then takes a week or two off to read extensively.

Participating in Literature Circles

Literature Circles usually begin with conversation as students share their impressions and personal responses to the book. They talk about favorite parts, retell sections, discuss parts they found confusing, make connections to their own lives or to other literature, and engage in social chatter. This time for "mucking around" (Short, 1992) allows them to share, converse, and wander around as they explore a wide range of ideas without focusing on any particular one. Children do not necessarily listen closely to each other because they are eager to share their own connections. This type of talk is often frustrating to teachers who want students to find a focus and talk in depth. In order to find that focus, however, and to create a sense of community as a group, children need time to share and converse. They should not be expected to write summaries, answer comprehension questions, or analyze literary elements. They need time to first share their enjoyment of the book. If teachers attempt to move students to a focus too early in the discussion, they can do so only by imposing their focus on the group. Readers need time to find their own inquiries.

Once readers have had a chance to share their initial responses, questions, and connections, they move to a more specific focus in the discussion. The talk begins to move back and forth between sharing personal stories and engaging in critical dialogue. Dialogue depends on readers being willing to share their thinking, to listen, and give careful consideration to the ideas of others. The actual focus of the dialogue should grow naturally from the group process. When teachers are participants in the group, they have an impact on the focus, but they do not have the right to determine the focus. Sometimes critical issues emerge from the discussion and the group moves easily into dialogue. Other times, however, students need support in moving from "mucking around" to "focusing in." Often the comment by students, "We're done talking about this book" is a signal that they may have shared their initial responses and are not sure how to move into a deeper discussion.

Section One
The Authoring Cycle:
Let's Talk Curriculum

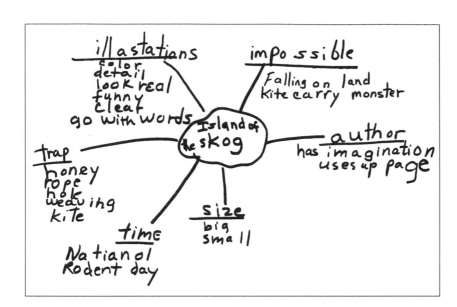

FIGURE 3.2
Webbing What's on Your Mind;
Third-grade Literature Circle
(Gloria Kauffman's classroom)

One strategy that provides a useful structure for moving to an in-depth focus is Webbing What's on Your Mind. Students place a large sheet of paper in the middle of the table and list all the different issues and connections that came up as they shared. They are asked, "What could you talk about with this book? What ideas, connections, and questions do you have related to this book?" We often serve as scribes for the brainstorming early in the year, but students gradually take over the process themselves. As members of the group, we can also add our ideas and questions to the web for consideration. This allows us to push the group to consider issues they might not have developed on their own, but it does not impose those onto the group because they still have the right to decide which of those ideas they will actually discuss. Webbing occurs only after sharing.

Kathy was working with Literature Circles in Kaylene Yoder's sixth-grade classroom when a group of students who had each read a different Betsy Byar novel announced they were done talking after twenty minutes. All they had really done was to describe their books to each other, but they were unsure about how to proceed and so assumed they were done. Kathy brought a large sheet of paper to the group and asked them to talk about the connections they had noticed as they listened to each other's descriptions. As they talked, she wrote their connections on the web and then asked them to choose one of these connections to discuss the next day. After some negotiation, the group decided to talk about the problems of the characters and spent the next day in a vigorous discussion about these problems. They then went on to discuss parents and relationships with peers that become enemies. They made many connections to their own lives and explored these in great depth.

We find that it is important to have each circle decide at the end of one meeting what their focus will be for the next. They are then responsible for thinking about what they want to discuss in relation to their focus, and the next discussion already has a place to start. Donald Murray (1989) notes that writers don't stop writing at the end of a thought but in midstream, so they can start again the next day. This strategy works the same way for the talk in circles.

Students often prepare for their next discussion by rereading sections of the book, writing a log entry, or doing further research and investigation. Children may need a day off to reread or to research before their group is ready to meet again. These re-engagements with a book are important and need to be encouraged. Each day, as they meet for their Literature Circle, they put the web in the middle of their table, so they can refer to it as they make decisions about what to talk about next or add other issues that develop from their discussion. They do not discuss everything on the web, but it gives them a range of possibilities.

Connections to children's own experiences is an integral aspect of productive literature discussions. Children build off of their past experiences, classroom inquiries, movies, books, and each other in exploring their understandings of a story. As part of a broader class focus on rights (Short & Kauffman, 1995), a group of fifth graders discussed the picture book, *Baseball Saved Us* (Mochizuki, 1993), the story of a young Japanese American boy in an internment camp during World War II who deals with prejudice through playing baseball. Ruben related the story to the movie, *Field of Dreams*, while Rudy noted that this book "can go back with our slavery study. They were put into concentration camps just because of their color." Arthur pointed out that "the concentration camps were in *Devil's Arithmetic*, not this book." John commented that, "people didn't like him because of his color, but the teammates just tried to help him." His comment reminded Tino of his experiences with baseball, "like when we play, we try to make our smaller players feel good." The boys went on to talk about the guard in the story which Tino connected to his feelings of "I can't believe I did it" when he hit a home run in front of his dad.

Betsy Byars Text Set
Characters are same age
Characters all have problems
Parents are gone
Kinds of solutions to problems
Enemies that cause problems
Endings - Things are better, not perfect
Are adventures in books
About everyday life today

Brainstormed List of Connections in Betsy Byars Text Set; Sixth-grade Literature Circle (Kaylene Yoder's classroom)

Ruben talked about being new, "I had to prove myself and that's when they started liking me," as he tried to understand how the boy felt when he was taunted at games. John pulled from his experiences as a Tohono O'odham to comment, "It's like a comparison. Like some people don't like black and Mexicans don't like whites sometimes. The white kids in the book, they're saying that they're better than him." "He didn't do nothing at all," Rudy commented, "but they thought that they (Japanese Americans) were gonna do something bad so they might as well put 'em in camps."

In this discussion the children explored a variety of connections and hypotheses about the characters' actions rather than deciding on only one right interpretation. Because Literature Circles involve exploring half-formed ideas, children need time to share their connections and to decide whether to accept, modify, or reject their hypotheses, rather than having the teacher immediately correct any misinterpretations. These circles also support students in their investigations. In this case, the group was involved in an inquiry on rights and the book provided them with an historical perspective.

In Literature Circles, children are encouraged to expand and support their comments and to build off what other children say. Different potential meanings for a story are explored and accepted as long as a reader can support that interpretation. When Pat, a first grader, announced that he thought the witch was really the stepmother in disguise in the folktale of "Hansel and Gretel," the group responded with skepticism and interest. They challenged Pat to explain his thoughts, and he pointed out that the witch and stepmother never overlap in the book. When the witch dies, the children return home to find the stepmother dead also. Pat's interpretation allowed the other children and the teacher to see this familiar folktale from a new perspective and to accept an alternative interpretation of the story.

In addition to Webbing What's On Your Mind, curricular engagements such as Sketch to Stretch, Save the Last Word for Me, Say Something, Cloning an Author, Anomalies, Graffiti Board, and Written Conversation can be used to support students, both in sharing their ideas with others and in moving to dialogue. Sketch to Stretch is particularly effective because students transmediate between language and art, as they create a sketch of the meaning of the book. The role of these engagements changes depending on when they are used within the circle—they can support sharing or dialogue. These options can be introduced during class read-aloud

Sketch to Stretch for Sylvester and the Magic Pebble (Steig, 1969); Whitney, Age 7 (Leland & Harste, 1994)

Chapter Three
The Authoring Cycle
as a Curricular
Framework for Reading

Literature Log Entry; Mark, Age 7 (Margaret Ferguson's classroom)

Crosing The Troll Brige
It made me thingk of when me and my mom went to the Super Market and got komkqots.+ think The book is veary funy. My faveret part is the part whare he yells dont be so load I ¢end my butey rest! It was ditrent becuse in verson 12 and thay eat grass and in 4 thay eat to komkqots. ¢ liked It a Lot.

Sketch to Stretch on **Devil's Arithmetic** (Yolen, 1988) in a Literature Log Entry; Tara, Age 11 (Gloria Kauffman's classroom)

Section One
The Authoring Cycle:
Let's Talk Curriculum

experiences and then students can choose to use them within their groups as needed.

Literature Logs can also be used to facilitate discussion. As children read their books, we ask them to make entries in their logs several times a week. These entries are not summaries of the reading but reflections on what they liked or didn't like, predictions, meanings they thought about, and connections they made to other books or experiences as they read. The logs are helpful in several ways. The process of writing helps students organize their thinking and think more deeply about the literature. In addition, the logs can be used to begin discussions in Literature Circles. At the beginning of the circle, students can share from their logs, and the discussion continues from this sharing. Sometimes it works better to ask students to reread their logs right before the group begins so that their thinking is fresh in their minds, but not to actually read them to the group. Because these logs have a real function within the circles, teachers usually do not respond to them.

While we believe in the supportive nature of these logs, many children have come to view them as a punishment for reading a book. For them, these logs are assignments which they complete for the teacher rather than a way to support their thinking. When teachers assign topics and questions, require children to write every day in a particular format, and grade the logs, children accurately read their purpose as "making sure I read the book." We carefully tie the logs to Literature Circles so students see a purpose for themselves and their group. While we ask children to write twice a week, they can decide when to write based on when they have something to think about. We need to be careful about sending messages we don't intend. Sandy Kaser initially asked her students to write in their logs during the last ten minutes of their literature time. She found that her students saw these logs as a time to report to her rather than a place to think about their books and discussions. She began encouraging them to read their logs before going to their groups so they would realize the connection between the logs and their discussions; this introduced more flexibility in what they wrote in the logs.

We also open up the logs to a wide range of types of response. Children put sketches, webs, charts, time lines, and quotes in their logs as well as write about their connections and thoughts. Gloria Kauffman introduces children to these ways of responding by having the children use their logs to record responses to her first chapter book read-aloud. Several times a week, she introduces a response strategy such as Sketch to Stretch or Save the Last Word for Me and has students try it out in their logs. They come back together as a group to share their responses and then talk about the strategy. These logs then become part of the Literature Circle experiences and the entries from the class read-aloud at the beginning of the logs are reminders of options that students can choose to use as they reflect on their books for literature groups. For some students, having options such as sketches and webs is much more supportive for sharing their thinking than having to write a response.

Some teachers encourage students to use Post-it notes to record short responses for a particular page. This works especially well during the first reading of the story as students prepare to share with others. Jerry has had students make Little Books (see Bookmaking) which they can use as a bookmark and a place to record "what's on their minds" as they read. The function of logs is to support students in reflecting on their reading, and any of these forms are appropriate if they fulfill that function for a particular group of students.

Types of Literature Circles

Many different variations of Literature Circles are possible. We first began circles where the small group read and discussed the same book. In these circles, multiple copies of the same title are needed so that each student has a copy of the book to read. Using these shared book sets, students within a group are able to explore their different interpretations and connections in greater depth because the book creates a shared context. Often these discussions lead children to talk about their differing understandings of the characters, themes, plot, and other literary elements of the book and their response to the author's or illustrator's style.

Another type of circle involves Text Sets—sets of individual books that are related to each other in some way (Short, 1992). These Text Sets can be composed of books or poetry by the same author or illustrator; different versions or variations of the same story, such as Cinderella stories; books on the same theme, such as living at peace with others; books on the same topic, such as survival or friendship; books that are the same story but are illustrated by different people, such as: "I know an Old Lady who Swallowed a Fly" variations; books of the same genre, such as mysteries or folktales; books with similar story structures, such as the same type of cumulative pattern; books with the same characters, such as Ramona; and books from the same culture or country. Sometimes everyone in the group reads the whole set of books, and other times each person reads only one or two books in the set.

Debbie Rowe has created Text Sets with two- and three-year old children which combine books and toys. Instead of keeping the book center separate from the toys, children put books about machines with their bulldozers and dump trucks, and books about zoo animals with their animal collections. Debbie's research (1993) has shown that children continually move back and forth in their play between the books and toys, thus creating an intertextual experience.

Text Sets are carefully chosen and contain anywhere from five to fifteen books or materials. They are not the large theme sets of every book available on a topic which are often put together when beginning a new theme unit. Text Sets are chosen from theme sets and are more focused to support discussion. The major criteria for selection is that the books and materials in the set reflect a variety of perspectives on the topic. We look for materials of different genres and cultures as well as materials that connect in different ways with children's experiences.

Whenever possible, we create sets that include a wide variety of reading materials. Our Text Set on the homeless for example, includes a book of poetry, an information book, several folktales, picture books, chapter books, and autobiographical accounts from children living in shelters as well as magazine and newspaper articles and brochures from local agencies. This range of types of materials and genres helps students explore a topic from many different perspectives and supports their development of more flexible reading strategies. We also include one or two texts from other sign systems—such as an art print or song tape—so that children are encouraged to transmediate as they connect.

Text Set discussions usually begin with students telling each other about the different books they read and then looking for comparisons and contrasts across the books in the set. Students need a period of time to share and read from their set before they are able to move into discussing the connections across their books. Although these discussions rarely go into great depth on any one book such as occurs in circles that discuss a single book, they highlight the process of making connections, both to other books and to children's lives.

We have also found Text Sets helpful with older students who are reluctant to talk. Because students have each read a different but related book everyone has information to share. Kaylene Yoder used Text Sets of common fairy tales such as "The Three Pigs" and "Snow White" with her sixth graders as their initial Literature Circle experience. She asked them to sign up for a story they remembered reading when they were little. Each student read one book in a set and then the group came together for a discussion in which they compared the different versions and created comparison charts. Because each had read a different book, each person talked even if only to share a retelling of the book. The entire process of reading, discussing, and charting took only one week.

Text Sets have also been useful in bilingual classrooms where children are often separated into groups according to language. Caryl Crowell found that by putting together Text Sets that had books in both languages, her second and third graders could join the group that most appealed to them. Interestingly, she also noted that children in these groups read from all of the books in the set, regardless of language. During the discussions, children spoke in both English and Spanish and were able to understand each other because of the shared context.

An easy way to begin Text Sets is to put together Paired Books, two books that are related to each other on some dimension but are oppositional in another. For example, the paired books of *Thy Friend Obadiah* (Turkle, 1969) and *Amigo* (Baylor, 1963) allowed a group of second graders to talk about the similarities in the friendships between humans and animals as well as the differences in the ecosystems of the desert and the sea coast. Two children became partners to read and discuss one of the books in each pair. After several days, the partners became a group of four, sharing and comparing the two books. After discussing the Paired Books, other books can be added to create more complex Text Sets with a wider range of connections.

We also have had circles on a local author whom we then invite to visit the classroom. One of the more exciting variations is to have circles on literature written by authors from the classroom. The group discusses the book and then invites the author to join their group. Sometimes children from different classrooms or grade levels form

> "A good discussion is when people argue; when people have different opinions. Like when one persons say I think this and another says I don't think you're right. Then you get in a big conversation."

Tara, Age 11 (Gloria Kauffman's classroom)

Chapter Three
The Authoring Cycle
as a Curricular
Framework for Reading

groups for several days to discuss literature. These variations keep Literature Circles interesting, fresh, and invite different kinds of insights and discussions.

Literature Circles with Young Children

Many teachers of young children assume that Literature Circles are only for children in the upper elementary. We believe that Literature Circles need to be part of all children's experiences so that they see reading as a critical thinking process of constructing meaning. We do run into some special issues when working with young children that require us to make adjustments, but the central focus on exploring interpretations and engaging in conversation and dialogue is still central.

The first issue is that the majority of first-grade and kindergarten students cannot independently read the books used for Literature Circles. We want books that have enough depth for good discussions. Because most of the predictable books these children are able to read on their own do not have that depth, we choose picture books and read them aloud to students. Each of the choices is read aloud over a several-day period and then children sign up for a literature group. The books are placed in the listening center and also read aloud to the group at their first meeting. If the children have older buddy readers from another classroom, they read the books aloud to the child. The majority of children are able to read these books independently by the end of their Literature Circle. Linda Sheppard (1990) sends the literature book home with her kindergarten students and asks family members to read the book aloud to the child over several days. The child is given a Post-it note to place on a page they want to share and a piece of paper to write or draw their response to the book. The child then brings the book, Post-it note, and response back to school to meet with a Literature Circle.

We have also found that young children have more productive discussions of books they have heard several times. When they have only heard a book once, they often have not put their understandings of the story together in such a way that they can discuss it with others. They tend to focus on isolated aspects of a story or cannot initially put their response into words. We try to create situations where they will have multiple readings of a story before discussing it; we often use old favorites that have been frequently read aloud in the classroom for their first Literature Circles. We also encourage chil-

The goats killd the Troll and got veary fat.

birds eye veiw

Literature Log Entry;
Mark, Age 7 (Margaret
Ferguson's classroom)

dren to respond through art and drama before coming to Literature Circle.

We usually start with many whole class discussions of read-aloud books before moving to Literature Circles. As mentioned earlier, we found that if we call one of those read-aloud times "Literature Circle" and use that as a discussion time, students have a better sense of what to do when we move to small groups. When we do move to small groups, we keep the size of the group to four because children are eager to talk and have great difficulty waiting for others to share. Kathy remembers sitting in a group of seven first-graders that quickly became a group of three and a group of four despite her efforts to keep everyone together.

When young children begin a Literature Circle, they often spend a great deal of time talking about favorite pages and telling stories about related incidents from their lives. Once they have run out of stories, we use webbing and engagements such as Sketch to Stretch to encourage them to focus on one or two issues. These discussions usually last only a couple of days. When Kathy met with a Literature Circle of first graders on *The Three Bears* (Galdone, 1985), the first day's discussion consisted of students eagerly sharing their favorite illustrations from the story and talking about why they liked that part of the

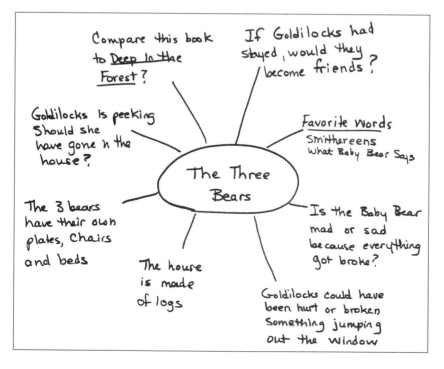

FIGURE 3.3
Webbing What's on Your Mind for "The Three Bears"; First grade Literature Circle (Pamella Sherman's classroom)

*Chapter Three
The Authoring Cycle
as a Curricular
Framework for Reading*

story. After about thirty minutes, the discussion died out and Kathy asked the children to talk about what they thought was interesting and important about this story. She put their ideas on a web and then asked them to choose one of their ideas to discuss the next day (see Figure 3.3). After some negotiation, the group decided to discuss whether the bear was mad or sad. They were concerned about whether Goldilocks should have stayed and become friends with the bear, but they knew that depended on the bear's feelings. The group discussed this issue the following day and then planned a way to share their story with the class. Before inviting students to join these Literature Circles, their teacher, Pamella Sherman, had engaged them in many Shared Reading and drama experiences with different variations of this story. Students then chose their favorite version for a discussion.

We also have found that shared book sets are more successful than Text Sets because of the difficulty of getting the books read. In the shared book sets, young children can focus together on the one book. When we do use Text Sets, we read one book a day from the set to the whole class and then have students discuss the book and how it relates to previous books in either a whole class or small group discussion. We use a chart to list the connections they discover. Another way we've used Text Sets is to begin with shared book sets on an author such as Pat Hutchins or folktale versions such as "Little Red Riding Hood." After students have discussed these in small groups for several days, the groups are reformed so that one child from each group forms a new group that is a Text Set group. Because they have already discussed their books with others, they are better able to share their book with their new group. In addition, Paired Books is often successful in encouraging connections across books without the engagement becoming overwhelming for young children.

The Role of the Teacher in Literature Circles
In the initial Literature Circles, the teacher often plays a more active role in sharing connections and encouraging students to talk about their favorite parts and connections to get a discussion going. This provides children with a demonstration of the kinds of talk and behaviors involved in a Literature Circle. More than with Authors Circles, children bring with them a past history that leads them to believe that there is one right interpretation of a story, and the teacher

FIGURE 3.4
Categories to Analyze Teacher's
Response to Children in
Literature Study; Karen Smith
(1993)

Attending to meaning makers
    Making sense of rudimentary responses
    Dealing with confusions
    Making the story world accessible
    Making learning visible
    Giving students status

Attending to students' interpretations
    Answering students' questions
    Validating students' understandings
    Extending students' understandings

Engaging students in interactions
    Putting students in the lead
    Taking the lead
    Supporting students' lead

has it. They do not know how to talk about a story and to explore meanings with each other, and they don't expect to be given the chance to do so.

In supporting children's talk in these groups, much of the teacher's role occurs outside the group by building a strong sense of community, establishing a rich context for the circles by connecting them to the classroom theme, and providing demonstrations of talk during class read-aloud. By introducing students to supportive structures and ways of responding in these groups such as Webbing, Sketch To Stretch, and Save the Last Word for Me, they are able to use these on their own to sustain their discussions. The structure, for example, of starting by talking about favorite parts and personal connections and then moving to a web of possible issues to discuss, has been one that students of all age levels have used on their own. If Authors Circles are operating in the classroom, these structures help children in their discussions of reading. Gradually students begin opening up and exploring their interpretations with each other.

When teachers are members of the group, it is important they come as readers and participants ready to talk about personal connections, not as leaders and question-askers. When we first started exploring these circles, we saw our role as asking open-ended interpretive questions such as "Did the story end the way you expected it to?" or "What kind of person is the main character?" This type of questioning was a major shift away from the closed-ended questions usually asked in reading groups ("What was the color of the girl's dress?"), but it still kept us effectively in control of what could be discussed. The only difference was that there was more than one answer to our questions. We've learned to move away from these questions, instead making comments as readers. Stating that we thought the story was going to end in a different way opens up the possibility of discussing the ending without students feeling that they must answer our questions, not explore their issues. They can choose to ignore our connections as the first graders did to Kathy in talking about *The Wednesday Surprise* (Bunting, 1989). We do still ask questions, but as readers, because we want to know what others think about a particular issue or because we are genuinely puzzled.

Initially students do expect the teacher to take the role of the "question-asker." When we join in the discussion with comments about what we think rather than only asking questions, this signals to students that we are participants rather than evaluators. We make sure that our comments are very tentative, "This is what I thought. But I'm not sure. What did you think?" We also have to discipline ourselves not to fill every silence but to wait, contributing an occasional comment or question. Students have learned that if they don't talk, teachers will jump in and take over for them. As long as we fill all silences, they can remain passive.

We constantly challenge the children—and they challenge each other and us—to support the statements made in circles. Many "why" questions are raised. These discussions do not involve just accepting whatever a child says. We find instead that it means both accepting and challenging each other. Children have learned from past school experiences to give short responses, and so they make statements such as "I liked it" or "It was a stupid book." It is difficult to have much of a discussion unless we know why the reader felt the book was stupid or what the reader liked about the book. As a participant in the group, we ask the reader these "why" questions so they will expand on their comments. We are often impressed with the thinking behind children's comments that at first seem "off the mark" such as Pat's comment about the witch in "Hansel and Gretel." Other participants in the group soon take over this role because they want to understand.

Teachers should move in and out of Literature Circles. As a member of the group, teachers facilitate the group process and bring experiences that allow them to introduce ideas children may not have considered on their own. When teachers are not present, children learn how to handle these dynamics on their own and are able to focus on issues of "kid culture" (Kaser, 1994) that would not be discussed in the presence of adults. These contexts often result in different kinds of conversations and dialogue which are important to children's thinking. If teachers set up the groups so that their constant presence is not needed, they can join groups they think need their support or are discussing books in which they are personally interested. Some teachers rotate among the groups, joining them for short periods of time to facilitate the brainstorming of the web and to listen to the talk, so they have a sense of what is going on and what they need to do to support the groups in their discussions.

Literature discussion groups are currently receiving a great deal of attention by reading educators who create programs and procedures for "training" children and teachers. They want to do away with the messiness of the process that we have described here, but in doing so they change the very nature of Literature Circles. The potential for dialogue is lost as students and teachers follow a set of procedures to make sure they "do it right." Even when teachers are not present in the groups, student behavior is regulated through charts listing what kinds of literary talk should go on in groups and the kinds of social behaviors that are appropriate. Students are so focused on making sure they discuss character or theme and wait their turn that they have little attention left to focus on meaning.

> "When I work with a group, my discussion goes better. I can build off of others and they build off of me. I am pushed to go further. I create better ideas."
>
> Rudy, Age 11 (Gloria Kauffman's classroom)

Attending to Difference: Reflection and Revision

As students think with each other in Literature Circles, they revise their rough draft understandings about their reading. Literature Circles force them to attend to difference as they listen to other interpretations and connections and put their own understandings into words. Often children feel tension between their own and others' perspectives. They are confronted with different interpretations of a story that cannot be easily brought together to create a unified understanding for that story. As they struggle with these differences in what, at first, may have seemed like a simple story, they try to pull their understandings into a more complex unity for the story. These struggles and tensions change them as readers and thinkers. Karen, grade three, says it this way, "Literature Circles changed me in my eyesight and in my brain too." David, grade three, found that he even thought differently when he was reading a book by himself. "I had

Chapter Three
The Authoring Cycle
as a Curricular
Framework for Reading

a literature circle in my head. One side of my brain said one thing about the story and then the other side said, 'No, wait a minute. What about this?' "

Students need time for quiet reflection so they can make sense for themselves of these different interpretations and perspectives. They need to sort out their own understandings away from the group just as children need to make the final decisions on revisions in their writing away from the Authors Circle. Literature Logs can play a key role in giving them the opportunity for this kind of quiet reflection through sketching and writing. This is one reason why we encourage children to continue making several entries a week in their logs during and after their discussions.

Sharing What Was Learned: Literature Presentations

Literature Circles can last anywhere from two or three days to several weeks depending on the length of the book and the productiveness of the discussion. As the discussion comes to an end, the group needs an opportunity to pull together their thinking about the book and celebrate their authorship. They have worked hard in thinking and talking with each other. So many ideas have been discussed, discarded, and considered that some students are no longer sure what they believe. Taking the time to share informally or to prepare a formal presentation of their thinking and talk during their Literature Circle supports them in clarifying their understandings and gives them an opportunity to celebrate their meaning-making.

Because each small group has read a different book or set of books that are related to ongoing class inquiries, students are eager to hear from each other. Sometimes students share informally with the class during author talk time by telling about their book or Text Set and showing their discussion web. Other circles lead to presentations as a way to celebrate authorship in reading. Students work as a group to create their own original Readers Theatres, paint murals or dioramas, write new endings or versions of the story, put together a comparison chart, set up a learning center with an interactive experience, make a gameboard, or compose a piece of music (Kauffman & Yoder, 1990).

These presentations are not just "cute" activities based on a book. They must in some way reflect what the group talked about or felt they learned as a result of their discussion and should invite other children to explore something the group felt was important. One of the problems we have found with presentations is that students often make quick decisions on the type of presentation according to whatever is the current fad. If skits or bookmarks are "hot," they automatically choose that format for their presentation whether or not it will communicate their meaning. When a group is ready to work on a presentation, we have learned to ask, "What do you want others to understand about your book and discussion? Make a web or list of what you think is most important for others to understand." Through making this list, they pull together their discussions and have a basis for decisions about their presentation. We then ask them to brainstorm a list of ways they could present their understandings to the class. Skits or bookmarks usually go on the list first, and our response is simply to say, "Great. Now what else could you do?" until a whole list of ideas have been brainstormed. The group is then asked to go back and consider their list of what they want others to understand and see which of their ideas for presentations will best communicate those understandings by showing rather than telling.

In Sandy Kaser's classroom, Kathy sat with a group of fifth graders who had just finished their discussions of *Sarah Bishop* (O'Dell, 1980). "We want to do a skit," they immediately announced. "That's one idea," Kathy replied, "but we first need to make a list of what you think other people should understand about your book, and what you talked about." As the group talked, Kathy webbed their comments and then asked how they might communicate these ideas to others. "Skits," of course, was the first word out of their mouths. Kathy wrote it down and asked, "Okay. What else?" The students paused for a minute, thinking they were done, but as Kathy waited, they finally came up with another idea. "Great. What else?" The group continued on in this way with Kathy also adding ideas to the list. When the page was full, she put the web of what they wanted to share next to the list of ideas and asked them to talk about what would be most effective in communicating their ideas. After much discussion, the group decided to put together two survival kits, one with items for surviving in today's world and the other in Sarah's world. They would have the class come up with different problems that children might face and then see if either of the kits would provide a way to survive.

The process of deciding what is most important, coming up with an idea, and making it work often moves the group to more intense dialogue than they engaged in during their actual Literature Circles.

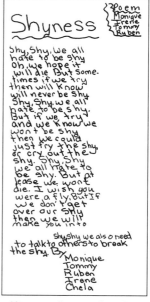

Literature Presentation: Poem about a Text Set on Self-Concept; Monique, Tommy, Ruben, Irene, & Chela, Ages 10 and 11 (Gloria Kauffman's classroom)

Chapter Three
The Authoring Cycle
as a Curricular
Framework for Reading

FIGURE 3.5
Webbing What's on Your Mind;
Fifth-grade Literature Circle
(Sandy Kaser's classroom)

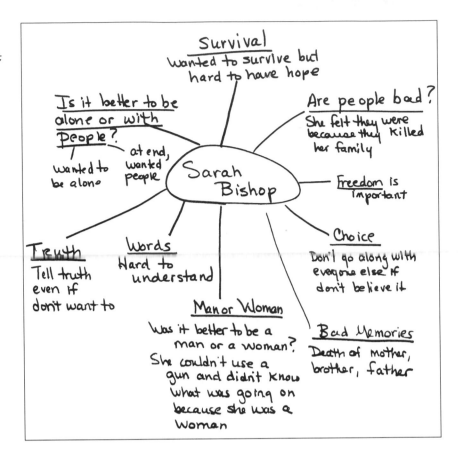

Students do not do all of their thinking about a book and then put on a presentation. The presentation is often what allows them to move to deep and critical thinking. Because many of the presentations involve a transmediation to another sign system, their understandings undergo a transformation, and they make new connections. When a group of third-graders decided to use color and shape to tell the story of how relationships changed in *Sarah, Plain and Tall* (MacLachlan, 1985), they developed new insights into the complexity of these relationships.

Just as in the publication of writing, a presentation encourages readers to make connections and transform what they explored through their reading and discussions. The actual presentation itself celebrates their authorship as readers and pulls the immediate experience to a temporary closure that facilitates reflection on themselves as readers. The sharing and presentations, in turn, serve as invitations for other readers to discover new books they might want to read

---

Presentation Ideas

Record voices and act out parts – use lip sync

Act out parts + have narrator on tape

Dance – No speaking, move to show action
      or use a narrator

Skit of parts of the story

Diorama – boat, snake
           fire + Bible
           Cave with bats

Make a game like Chutes + Ladders

Show ways to survive on a chart
      or in a box

Survival Kit – Now vs Them
      Give class the problem and they
      come up with a way to survive

---

or to see new ways of presenting their ideas to others across a wider variety of sign systems.

Planning New Inquiries: Reflecting on Reading

The balance of action and reflection is essential throughout the authoring cycle. Teachers can encourage students to reflect on their participation in extensive reading engagements and Literature Circles by pulling the class together for short oral reflections. For example, when students first try partner reading, we come together to talk about the ways in which they shared the reading with their partner and their observations of how it affected them as readers. As students meet in Literature Circles, especially at the beginning of the year, we have students come together for ten minutes after their groups have met that day to reflect. Our first question is, "*What* did you discuss in

Chapter Three
The Authoring Cycle
as a Curricular
Framework for Reading

your groups today?" so that the focus is on meaning, not their behaviors. We then ask, "*How* did your groups go today?" and ask students to talk about what is and is not working for them in their groups. If students bring up problems, the class brainstorms ways these might be solved.

As students pull together and share their thinking by going public in literature presentations and author talk time, they are able to step away from their immediate experience and reflectively and reflexively consider their strategies as readers. Fifth graders' discussions and presentations of different biographies of Christopher Columbus led them to an awareness of perspective and how different perspectives bring different "truths." For this class, perspective became an "inner eye" that they used as they read other books and as they interacted with others in the classroom and at home. They realized that there was not just one way to view the world or their lives and that they needed to understand another person's perspective before accepting what others told them or what they read in a book.

As with writing, Reflection Portfolios can be a tool that students can use to examine their reading strategies and establish goals for future inquiries. The portfolio process is similar to the one described for writing in Chapter 2 except that students are focused on asking "Who am I as a reader?" Another difference is that more time is needed to gather a collection of artifacts related to their reading. They gather literature logs, reading lists, projects, webs, charts, and any other evidence of their reading. Because actual artifacts of significant reading experiences do not always exist, they often web favorite Literature Circles, write about powerful books, or illustrate part of a literature presentation. They then repeat the process they used with writing of choosing examples, sharing with others, selecting for their portfolios, writing and sharing reflections, discussing as a class, and writing a one-page reflection with goals (see Figure 3.7).

This process allows them to relive the mental trips they took as readers moving through the cycle so they can identify their needs and inquiry questions. As teachers, we need to support students by setting up contexts that encourage them to take a reflective and reflexive stance on their learning. Only as we understand their inquiries can we offer strategy lessons or invitations for further engagements.

As part of his inquiry on foster families, Derrick was reading materials that often had words he couldn't figure out. He wanted to know what to do about those words. Because we had listened to Derricks's

What Kind Of Reader am I?

If a story is written well I am able to guess and predect what will happen next. I then get excited when I read the authors explanation of what happend. I think about probolems that our world faces and I notice how authors solve the problems in thore storybook worlds. I am a sereaise reader struggling for answers to solve my personel problem, my sister.

Ugly duckling roally had an effect on me. I learned something veary important if you ugly outside and beotyful inside you will probily change and turn beotyful outside and ugly inside My favorite book is The Horse That Came To Breefest I like horses and I think people should respect them more.

What do I need to read to challenge Myself as a reader?

a) Solve the problem before the story does

b) Read some more nonfiction.

c) Read so that I can read a chapter book without picturs and with the words I can make my own pictures

miscues and interviewed him using the Burke Reading Interview, we knew that he understood the reading process as the construction of meaning and used a variety of cue systems while he read. We offered an invitation for a strategy lesson on synonym substitution (Goodman, Burke, & Sherman, 1980) which supported him in developing the strategy of substituting another word that made sense. Many additional examples of this type of reading strategy lesson can be found in *Strategies in Reading: Focus on Comprehension* (Goodman, Burke, & Sherman, 1980).

Schema Stories, a strategy lesson found in Section II, highlights the ways in which various types of print genre are organized. We've used it to help language users understand that they already have information that they can access and use when reading materials in a genre they feel they didn't know anything about. Cloning an Author, also in Section II, introduces a strategy readers can use to create a unified meaning from a text they have just read and are struggling to understand.

Authors Meeting Authors is another source of reading strategy lessons. When children are introduced to a series of books by the same author or illustrator, they begin to recognize an author's work by his or her style. As part of a research study, Jerry identified those strategies used by proficient readers to comprehend texts and found that author recognition played a significant role (Harste, 1986). Once readers had identified the authorship of a selection, comprehension was greatly facilitated. When readers were unable to identify the author, they puzzled and speculated about possible authorship throughout their reading.

Strategy lessons focus on a particular cognitive or social strategy that is used by proficient readers. They provide a context where students can engage in the strategy and then reflect on its use within their own authoring processes as readers. As children gather for oral reflection and sharing at author talk time, they frequently offer strategy lessons for other readers such as when Harmony shared her strategy of having different readers read the same book to her over and over again or when Mardell showed how she used webs and charts in her Literature Log to reflect on her connections.

Strategy lessons are positioned at this point in the cycle because students must be readers before they can be taught about reading. Through these lessons, they become more strategic readers with a conscious awareness of the range of strategies they can use during reading and discussing.

Taking Thoughtful New Action

As students take a reflexive stance on their learning, celebrate their authorship, and attend to invitations from other students and teachers, they are able to take new actions in their lives as readers. They reposition who they are as readers and move forward to take new risks and so push their learning in new directions.

Our experiences with reflective drama are one example of an invitation that allowed readers to reposition themselves in relation to the world of the book. Gloria Kauffman and Kathy took the work of Cicely O'Neill (O'Neill & Lambert, 1982) and adapted it to fit their context. They wanted to invite students to "live within" the stories they were reading and discussing in a more complete and involved way. After reading and discussing *Airmail to the Moon* (Birdseye, 1988) over several days, they invited students to participate in a reflective drama experience. Students were first asked to pair off and one of them became a journalist while the other chose a character from the book and became that person. After several minutes of interviewing, the journalists were asked to think of everything the person had told them. Each journalist arranged the person he or she had interviewed in a pose that summed up the interview. The journalists then walked around and looked at the posed characters, commenting on what message they got from the pose. The children frozen in the pose could not talk, even when they disagreed with what was being said about them. They were unfrozen and the class met to talk about what they had felt while listening to the talk.

The children were then asked to form groups of four and create a still life from the book. They were encouraged to talk first and find some kind of contrast for their still life where characters in the book were feeling or doing opposite things. Once they had created their still life, half of the class walked around and observed and talked about the other's scenes. The final experience involved gathering together for a family meeting on what to do about the character's problem. Following these experiences, the students took out their Literature Logs and wrote and sketched their responses to the experience; then they met in small groups for discussions of the book. They also met as a class to talk about the concept of "living inside a story world" and how drama had affected their ability to become part of the story and yet detached from it. This experience gave them a different understanding of how they could use reading as inquiry in their lives.

In working with reflective drama with other groups, we have found that we need to choose literature that is open and ambiguous so that students can bring a wide range of interpretations to the text. Poetry works particularly well because so much is left unsaid that students can fill in through the drama reflections. If using a narrative picture book or story, it is often best to ask students to situate the various experiences either before the story or after the story rather than staying

within the time of the story. This essential criteria for the different poses and types of reflective drama engagements that are used with any one piece of literature is that each one allow students to take a different perspective on the literature.

The fourth graders in Kathleen Crawford's classroom read and discussed Mildred Taylor's novels about African-American experiences in the South during the Depression. Their discussions led them to many issues about culture, race, and prejudice in their own community. These discussions transformed the ways in which the children in this classroom interacted with each other. Instead of viewing difference as a problem, they came to understand and accept difference as a strength to be valued. They took action within their own context to change their relationships with others. Their interest in culture also led them to new invitations as they searched for other books about cultural diversity. Their definitions of culture began to broaden as they considered other aspects of culture such as family, community, and religion as well as race and ethnicity. They used reading to continue to inquire about their lives and world and the authoring cycle supported their continued search.

Conclusion

If we want our students to be truly literate individuals, we must provide intensive reading experiences through which their understandings about reading are deepened and extended. They also need experiences where they gain fluency and proficiency through reading extensively. As students engage in reading widely and deeply, they are encouraged to be critical thinkers who see reading along with writing as processes of authorship.

Through both extensive and intensive reading experiences, children develop new eyes for viewing and making sense of their world. Yetta Goodman tells the story of her young grandson who loved to smell the flowers in *Pat the Bunny* (Kunhardt, 1940) and asked to have this interactive board book read over and over again. When he took his first steps outside, he saw some flowers and immediately bent over to smell them. He had learned ways of interacting with the world from books.

Sometimes books can cause children to question their world. A sixth-grade girl who came from a traditional farm family with a strict separation of female and male roles was in a Literature Circle on

Sarah, Plain and Tall (MacLachlan, 1985). After several days of discussion, she created a web in her log on which she wrote "men can do some of women's work," "men and women can share work," and "women can do men's work." She was obviously looking at the world from a completely new perspective and considering possibilities she had not known existed. Through their engagements in authoring through reading, readers create the possibility for transforming their lives and taking action in the world. They use reading as inquiry to change the potentials in their own lives and those of others.

■ Gloria Kauffman currently teaches in an intermediate multi-age classroom for children ages nine through eleven at Maldonado Elementary School in Tucson Unified School District, Tucson, Arizona. Previously she moved with her fourth graders to fifth grade which then led her into a primary multi-age classroom at Maldonado. Before moving to Tucson, she taught first grade through third grade in Goshen, Indiana. She has published numerous articles and chapters about her work with the authoring cycle, literature circles, and reflection portfolios.

Creating a Collaborative Environment

GLORIA KAUFFMAN

Creating a learning environment where children think together to create new ideas that go beyond the potentials of any one person is a challenge. In a collaborative community, both teachers and students openly live as learners and make their learning available to others (Short, 1990). I believe a community of learners is formed as learners come to know each other and value what each other has to offer. We commit to sharing responsibility and control, establishing a learning atmosphere that is predictable and yet full of real choices. As we learn through action, reflection, and demonstration, the focus is on being problem posers as well as problem solvers through the process of inquiry.

My beliefs about community are based in my first twelve years of teaching grades one, two, and three in rural northern Indiana. The school served a working-class community where families lived on small farms and worked in local factories. These families included a small population of Amish. When I moved to Tucson, Arizona, I was still working with children from a working-class community, but their families held a different set of beliefs, values, and cultural traditions. I began teaching fourth graders in Tucson and then moved with this class to fifth grade. I moved from there into a primary multi-age

■ I did work out of books. I was hoping for a good education. I could not tell I was not getting what I wanted. I was wild all the time. I was getting in trouble. I was worrying too much about my friends.

Now I like to move around and work with others. I don't like to be alone because I need others to understand me and my ideas. When I work with others, I learn. I need to learn. I need to get along. I share my ideas even if they are not good. I ask questions. The atmosphere in the class has changed my thinking. Others have started to want to learn. I knew if I would try, I would get somewhere.

■ Jennifer, grade 4

(grades one, two, three) position and then continued with my third graders into fourth grade, adding new fifth graders and creating an intermediate fourth and fifth grade multi-age classroom. These experiences at various grade levels in different communities have pushed me to think about how I set up the classroom learning environment and create a sense of community with students.

Each year before school begins, I spend time "planning to plan" (Watson, Burke, & Harste, 1990) and setting up a classroom environment that will facilitate social interaction and dialogue. I organize the physical environment and think about possibilities for the curriculum and classroom daily schedule. The first three days of school are essential in establishing our life together as a community of readers, writers, and inquirers. Then comes the difficult task of maintaining and continuing to develop our community of learners across the school year.

Organizing the Physical Environment

Before the children arrive each school year, I spend considerable time organizing materials and arranging space in the classroom to support curriculum and encourage social interaction. I try to create resource areas in the room so children are able to use the entire room and have supplies readily available during their learning engagements.

I design spaces in the room for whole group, small groups, and individuals to meet for a variety of reasons. We need space for whole class meetings where we can listen to each other without raising our voices. Amy (age six) shared that she was not used to being heard and so talked to everyone using an "outside" voice even if they were sitting right beside her. To create a sense of respect and of being heard, we concentrate on normal voice tones for conversation as we gather together to share our work and thinking.

Ricky (age ten) played with everything he could find—baskets to wear on his head, puppets to entertain the class—so I now plan the group meeting area with the least amount of distractions. We need to be able to sit together to view picture books with enough room left to lie down and relax while listening to read aloud chapter books. This tends to be the largest area in the room and is close to a blackboard for note taking and brainstorming.

With my move to Tucson, I lost the use of the music teacher's choir risers for class meetings. After watching children roll on the rug, swing on chairs, and hide under pillows, I built my own risers from plywood so we have theater seating where everyone can see and sit for longer periods of time. I surround this area with bookshelves and the books forming our classroom library. The risers signal a quieter place to work and many individuals, partners, and small groups use them for private work times. Pillows can be brought into the area for chapter book read-aloud but remain stacked in a corner at other times. I have to remind children that we share the pillows: they do not belong to the biggest or toughest.

Supplies are labeled and stored in a central location so they can be shared by everyone. All kinds of lined and unlined writing paper, drawing paper, scrap paper, and blank books encourage children to become writers and creators of meaning. Markers, crayons, pens, paints, scissors, and glue are available for community use. Wallpaper, colored paper, and art supplies are kept in the cupboards and labeled but can be used whenever needed.

Valuing the diversity of children's ways of knowing is supported through planning an area and times where children have access to many tools and artifacts, just as in an artist's studio. Musical instruments, puppets, dress up clothing, and hats are placed in a corner beside a listening center. In this area are tape recorders, tapes, song books, and books, which invite explorations using multiple sign systems to make and share meaning related to children's questions and explorations.

During free reading and studio time, folders of published Readers Theatres and folktales are made available as well as children's literature with poetry, rhyme and patterns, music and movement, and dialogue between characters—anything which lends itself to singing, chanting, and oral expression. Musical staff paper and drawing paper are accessible to children who want to write their own music.

I take close-up photographs of each child on the first day of school and arrange them on the wall in a graph according to the month of our birthdays. This graph notifies everyone as to who is a member of our class and also serves a clerical role. The pictures signal the order for secretarial duties, which are rotated weekly, and the making of individual birthday books.

Picture books on celebrations, birthdays, and family stories, along with class photo albums (past and present) and address books are on a small shelf to support the need to record our history and stories. Creating a sense of history together makes the group more cohesive. Our

Visitors Corner holds class-published books including a book that introduces each child through Getting to Know You interviews. Visitors, parents, and especially new children entering the room use this book. I started a guest book so children would feel less shy about having others in the room. We brainstorm questions from the class for guests and include a section inviting guests to respond to what they have observed and learned by sharing with us. My older students felt more comfortable knowing they were being accepted by visitors. Amber (age ten) told me that meeting my friends and family was the hardest thing she had done. She was afraid of new people. The guest book feedback helps children to accept others and feel accepted by them.

Communicating with others is not always easy but is a strategy that children need for life. They will not always be able to verbalize what they want to communicate so I encourage children to put their actions into words and pictures. This also helps others appreciate the learning taking place in our classroom. We post our class newsletters, newspapers, and school events on the Message Board. To initiate communicating through written messages, I put a message to each member of the class on the Message Board for the first day of school. This open invitation invites children to write back and forth to me and to each other.

Boxes house reflection journals, literature logs, and math logs. For easier access by me, the children's names are put on the logs in alphabetical order, but I change the color of the notebook every sixth log. I can then take home all the red literature logs on Monday, blue on Tuesday, and so forth to read and review. The color coding also helps children use many strategies to pass out the logs, one being putting all like colors on the same table. Children only have to remember the color of their log.

Three baskets are labeled so that there is one for rough drafts to be revised for meaning, a second for revised pieces to be edited for conventions, and a third for revised/edited pieces for publication. Next to these baskets are picture books and my professional books on illustrating, bookmaking, and making pop-ups to support children as they decide how they want their pieces published. I also include photographs or copies of books published by children from past years.

A letter inviting the children to become part of the class is sent home a couple weeks before school begins. I include a list of supplies

Dear Juliett,
Welcome! I hope you have a good day today. I'm looking forward to working and thinking with you.
I wonder what kind of things you like to do?
Make yourself at home ☺
mox

Welcoming Letter on Class Message Board

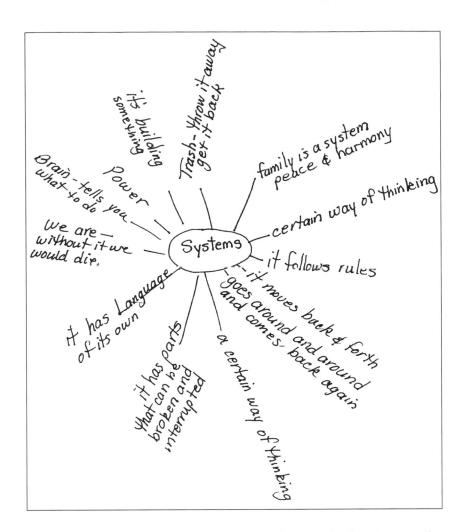

The brainstorming web contains the central concept "Systems" with the following connected ideas:
- it's building something
- Power
- Trash - throw it away get it back
- Brain - tells you what to do
- family is a system peace & harmony
- We are - without it we would die.
- certain way of thinking
- it follows rules
- it has Language of its own
- it moves back & forth goes around and around and comes back again
- it has parts that can be broken and interrupted
- a certain way of thinking

and ask children to bring something to share with the class on the first day to help us all better understand each other as individuals. As I organize the classroom, I think about the curriculum, keeping in mind the authoring cycle as my broad curriculum framework. I also think through a daily schedule and possible initial engagements that will allow children's voices to be heard in negotiating the actual curriculum that is implemented in our classroom. One of the key issues for me is thinking about a broad umbrella concept to give us a starting point for this negotiation.

Thinking about the Curriculum

In my initial planning to plan, I think about a possible umbrella concept such as change, a sense of place, systems, connections, or discovery that will weave in and out of the curriculum allowing us to make connections throughout the entire year. This broad concept helps me focus and plan initial engagements. To introduce such a concept into the curriculum I gather tools and materials, create invitations, and put together sets of literature that give multiple perspectives on that concept so children can begin to establish where their interests and questions might develop. Their interests and wonderings usually lead to a whole class focus within which students pursue small group projects or research on an individual level.

I do not teach the broad concept but, rather, these initial experiences are planned to help children make their own connections to the broad concept. Children now have a context to voice their needs and help plan the curriculum, engage in powerful strategies, and dialogue with peers and teacher to maintain a collaborative environment that supports all learners.

I also think through a daily schedule that is predictable and will support the engagements of children throughout the day. The schedule is based on past years and is adjusted each year according to student needs. I've found that it works well to have students take down chairs and help to set up the room when they arrive at school each morning. Children then move into writing in their reflection journals. This quiet time gets us focused for the day and helps us learn more about each other. We then come together for a class meeting and sharing time; from there we move to various reading, reflecting, and writing engagements in large blocks of work time. Chapter book read aloud is just before lunch to calm us down. I choose a book to read that connects to our morning discussions and Literature Circles. Since the morning hours are spent in conversation and dialogue, I plan the afternoon as a time of many hands-on explorations. We end the day with physical activities outdoors. As the year moves on we modify and arrange the schedule to meet our needs. We are able to change our routines because once the process is understood, then our roles and responsibilities become more fluid.

I also prepare evaluation tools so that I am ready to begin observing as soon as school starts. I use simple checklists created with the names of the whole class down one side and the top boxes left blank. I then decide what to name my checklist and am better able to quickly record my observations. I make many copies of these so I am ready to start kidwatching (Goodman, 1978) the moment the

	Mon.	Tues.	Wed.	Thurs.	Fri.
8:00	Reflections	→			→
8:30	Class meeting				Studio Time
	Reading	Reading	Reading	Reading	·art ·music ·dance ·drama ·reading ·writing ·library ·computer
10:15	Writing — integrate social studies	Writing — integrate social studies	Writing — integrate social studies	Writing — integrate social studies	
11:30	11:30	Chapt. Bk read aloud	11:30	Chapt. Bk read aloud	11:30
12:00	12:00	LUNCH	12:00	LUNCH	12:00
12:40	Math — integrate science P.E.	12:45–1:45 D.A.R.E. / Reflect on day	Math — integrate science P.E.	Math — integrate science & P.E.	12:40 / 1:00–2:00 Computers

2:08 HOME

children walk into the room. I look for children who are shy, self-assertive, helpers, strugglers. I then use these notes to help children be successful by pairing them up with other children, encouraging those who understand to help those who are lost.

I also take field notes about what children are saying and doing throughout the day. These notes help me hear and understand the voices of children. I share these notes with the class to review

Teacher Article Three

Creating a

Collaborative

Environment

discussions and ideas. At the end of each week I remove the checklists from my clipboard and store them in a three-ringed binder. About the second month of school I introduce recording sheets, stapled in manila folders, so children are responsible for recording the books they have read, their free writing pieces, and choices made during studio time. Around the ninth week of school I introduce a process of self-reflection so children create a Reflective Portfolio on themselves as learners (Kauffman & Short, 1993). It is difficult not to use every evaluation tool I read about. I caution myself to choose a few tools to gather the information I need, so that I can make wise choices about my curriculum and inform myself about my learners.

Establishing Our Life Together as a Community

The first three days of school are critical in encouraging children to go beyond cooperation and collaborate together as they are introduced to an overview of the authoring cycle as our curricular framework. I organize my room around engagements that involve children in talking and interacting with each other from the moment they enter the room. I plan engagements that involve learners in thinking and sharing their thinking as individuals, as partners, in small groups, and with the whole class.

As children enter the room the first day of school, I find jobs for them to do. When other children arrive they see that everyone is busy and assume they should get busy also, forgetting the shyness and fear of being in a new class with strangers. I ask several children to take the chairs off the tables and tell others to find a place to sit, anywhere, since there are no assigned seats. I show two more children the cubbies for storing their supplies, and then have those children be in charge of helping everyone in the room find their cubbies. I start another two children passing out reflection journals. A few more will get the date stampers ready, and some will start handing out pencils. I talk to small groups at tables and ask them to begin writing about home, their families, vacations, anything to introduce themselves to the rest of the class.

When everyone has arrived and seems settled, I invite some children to stand and read their entries. I mention the instructions again, and let those who are confused know that the children who are sharing are really explaining what to do. If they are still confused, I suggest they go and ask other people what they are writing about.

I ask a child to turn off the lights, mentioning this will be our signal for announcements, and give directions for everyone to take their journals and meet on the risers. This first morning meeting is to share journals, taking time to listen and ask questions of one another. I always make sure children know that they may choose to keep their journals private. We then discuss the strategies we used to write our entries, talking about our struggles and successes. We start a brainstormed list of strategies for writing in their journals that will continue. If someone doesn't understand what to do, they can refer to this list. As I get out some instruments and games, several children collect the journals and put them away.

Forming a Community of Readers

In our class meeting, we discuss the daily schedule, talk about their questions and concerns, and then engage in some physical activity. The first three days we play name games and sing some songs before moving into reading experiences. Children are not used to sitting for long periods of time, listening, talking and being quiet, and so we move between sitting together and physical activities.

Children find out quickly that literature plays a major role throughout the curriculum all day long. I want to be able to give them an overview of the authoring cycle as a reading cycle so I read a picture book aloud and then invite a discussion of the story. As students discuss, I take field notes, writing down who made what comment. We then talk as a class about the strategies they used for listening, discussing, and talking with each other. I mention, by name, what each child said about the story, pointing out the strategies I observed during the discussion. I explain how these strategies added to the discussion and kept it moving forward by children building off each other's comments, adding details, retelling when we needed clarification, asking questions when we didn't understand, referring back to the text, and so forth. Again I start a brainstormed list of discussion strategies and explain we will refer back to these throughout the day.

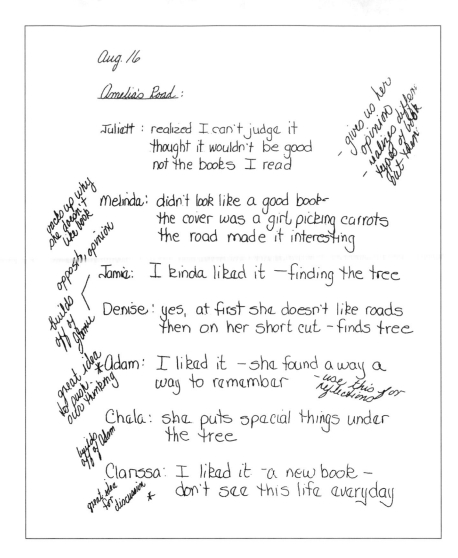

Aug. 16

Amelia's Road:

Juliett : realized I can't judge it
thought it wouldn't be good
not the books I read

— gives us her opinion
— realizes different
types of books
but when

Melinda: didn't look like a good book—
the cover was a girl picking carrots
the road made it interesting

picks up why
she doesn't
like book

opposit, opinion

Jamie: I kinda liked it — finding the tree

Denise: yes, at first she doesn't like roads
then on her short cut — finds tree

builds
off of Jamie

*Adam: I liked it — she found a way a
way to remember

great idea
to push-
onto thinking

use this for
reflections

Chala: she puts special things under
the tree

builds
off of Adam

Clarissa: I liked it — a new book —
don't see this life everyday

great idea
for discussion *

Because we have to learn to work with everyone within the next
few days of school, I plan many different short engagements with
small groups or partners where children read and talk with each
other. For support we always report back to the whole group. These
engagements are crucial to creating community. I first invite them to
find a person they know well and read with that friend. We come together as a whole class and talk about what it was like to read with
someone you know well. When children are feeling comfortable with
each other, we discuss the reading strategies they used, such as when
they came to something they didn't know, again making a list for future reference. I always take field notes during these discussions to

Brainstormed list of strategies as a reader:

J- I like to read books cause when you start them you want to know what happens in the end.
M- I like to read books to learn things.
B- I like to read books I want to read
A- Reading is having words in front of you.
B- having fun with a partner
L- looking at the pictures
C- wondering what will happen next
D- when you are reading, you should have fun
J- should learn to do it alone

C- thinking about my brother when I read
M- what connects to me
J- I read pictures then words
M- I skip words -don't know - read on-then reread
A- if the word is important -I figure it out
M- I know it by other words
C- I break it up into smaller words
J- I sound it out
D- I ask someone
M- I sound it out —skip it —read on —reread
C- I read pictures to figure it out.

- I read a page, my partner reads
- take turns
- helps me to listen

help children remember what was said. I also use my checklists to mark down partners so I am aware of children who are shy or not being included. Some children will never make the move to choose but wait to be chosen (a self-filling hypothesis), believing that no one wants to be their partner.

Each day I offer a new context for reading, followed by reflecting and recording our thoughts. For example on the second day, children are invited to find a partner, someone they do *not* know well. By the third day of school, children are asked to choose a partner of the opposite sex. We repeat the engagements again, reading and coming together as a whole class to reflect on our strategies and add to the brainstormed list.

Teacher Article Three
Creating a
Collaborative
Environment

FIGURE TA3.5
Getting to Know You Newspaper (primary multi-age classroom)

When we have worked through reading in various situations and with almost everyone in the room, we review all of the strategy lists. We discuss our working and thinking strategies, talking extensively about how to make wise choices with partners who will support us as workers and thinkers.

Forming a Community of Writers

Over the first three days we focus our writing on interviewing each other. Using the engagement of Getting to Know You, we interview someone we don't know in the room, work through the authoring cycle as a writer, publish a newspaper by the end of the week, and share it with each other and our families.

First, we read some articles and interviews, discussing how to interview a person. We then brainstorm some initial questions as a group, writing them on the board for reference; we record more questions on our own that we want to ask our partners. We do not choose partners until we have a plan ready—in this case, some questions on paper. Some children move too fast into finding a partner instead of re-membering the need to plan and rehearse before writing.

Still with no partners chosen, we share our questions with some-one we know well, then with the whole class. We discuss the best way to choose a partner—in this case, someone we don't know well—and move into the interviews. When working with intermediate students, I asked that they choose a boy/girl partner. Many times children have in their minds the misconception that boys and girls have certain roles to play in society and that friendships are based on criteria like fashion or being "cool." The message I try to convey is that all of us matter: we have voices and need to be heard. The issue of being equally valued needs immediate attention if the class is to become a community. We need to work on this issue all year long.

We share out loud about every twenty minutes during the inter-viewing and writing so that everyone can remain on task, know what to do, and find support from each other. Students find some-one else to read over their notes and discuss what might be missing from the interviews. As revisions are made, children share with the whole class. We reread and discuss newspaper and magazine articles to see what catches our attention. This helps with finding more questions, adding details, and supporting the writing of our inter-views. I do not expect great pieces of writing this first time around. The focus is to experience an overview of the writing process and authoring cycle.

Forming a Community of Inquirers

Children are naturally curious and delight in manipulating their en-vironment. We all know that children love to ask millions of ques-tions. Using a broad concept such as discovery, change, or cycles helps focus and set a purpose for observing our immediate world. En-gagements are planned to create an environment for inquiry. Strate-gies for inquiry challenge children to search for multiple perspectives, pose their own problems, and develop new questions.

One of my goals is for children to take another look and gain a new perspective on finding out as much as they can about some-thing they think they already know well. One strategy I've used is to have children sit in groups at tables, and take off one shoe to observe all they can about their shoes. This first encounter is filled with squeals, jokes about foot odor, comparing brand names, and looking around to see if everyone has a shoe off. After about ten minutes groups share what they are talking about and discovering. If any group is lost about what to do, they now have some ideas and questions to begin their investigations of their shoes.

The second encounter includes creating a web in small groups. Groups put everything they can think of that relates to their shoes on paper. As they share with the class, I look for questions and ideas that require experimenting to find multiple solutions. For me, problem solving never means coming up with one right answer but refers to exploring many strategies for researching questions and problems. I encourage groups to share the many ways they have recorded information and observations.

In the third encounter with shoes, children choose some questions or wonderings and find ways to pursue them. Children are usually interested in looking at how many different name brands are in the room, comparing the lightest to heaviest shoes, how many shoes have laces or Velcro, or how high a person can jump in their shoes. We continue to explore and share our findings in as many ways as possible, for example, making graphs, writing descriptions, drawing, making comparison charts, measuring, weighing, or sharing orally.

Essential to life as inquirers is constant reflection on what and how we are learning. All year long, we have brief class meetings throughout the day. Sharing, reflecting, and taking action become major strategies to help children come to know each other and know the ways in which we think. We have short sharings and reflections almost every twenty minutes all day long at the beginning of the year. I usually ask different children, throughout the day, to turn out the lights and call the class to the risers for sharing. Sometimes we share briefly without going to the risers. When the lights go out, everyone freezes and listens to the person who wants to share.

Having children turn out the light is a message that the class shares control—that they have a strategy for communicating with others, just like I do. They too have a voice and will have many opportunities to be heard. This takes a long time to establish for some children. There are always a few children that no one wants to listen to. As Chela (age nine) mentioned, "I want to share. It gives others ideas and helps others to remember." But Adam (age nine) added, "No one listens when I share."

Maintaining the Curriculum and Supporting Collaboration in a Community of Learners

Because I currently work with diverse groups of children and large class loads, I have had to take another look at how to support children in a collaborative curriculum and classroom. The first three days of the curriculum are usually successful, but then comes the challenge of maintaining the curriculum. I have had to make adjustments in strategies to help children work toward a new perspective of school and their potentials as learners. I first had to reconsider my perceptions and the standards for behavior I considered acceptable. I set high goals and expect continuous growth in children as learners and individuals. I have come to see discipline as inquiry instead of punishment or adult control over children.

Discipline as inquiry was a difficult concept for many children. The students with whom I work have their own habits and ways of interacting with each other. They feel at times that they have to prove themselves, and that takes precedence over talking things out. Adam (age nine) reflected, "It's better to hit first, than to have others think they can whoop you."

There isn't a quick fix so we have to learn to work through the process and be content with making very slow progress over time. Through talk, mediation, and action planning, children develop new strategies for dealing with each other and handling themselves in more diverse situations. The steps are small, and my focus is to acknowledge those steps by helping children reflect and see the steps and progress they are making. For many months, I invite individuals or small groups of children to have lunch with me so we can talk together and make a plan of action.

During a meeting with Adam, he let me know how difficult it was for him to let things go. He was able to discuss how he admired Chris for having inner strength and walking away from fights. What Adam admired was that others viewed Chris as tough, and Chris never had to prove himself. Adam made much progress in verbalizing his frustrations and setting some goals, but he had less success in his actions.

Teacher Article Three
Creating a
Collaborative
Environment

With time, we very slowly moved towards more positive and socially accepted actions.

I planned an initial experience for the class to get our feelings and frustrations in the open. We spent one week making a list of problem areas that were occurring throughout the day, such as pencil stabbing and name calling. The children then met in groups of four to brainstorm ways they might handle these different problem areas. We shared suggestions from small groups and brainstormed additional ideas for dealing with these situations. We talked about mediation, role playing, self reflection, and creating plans of action. When problems did occur, children worked through their plans—changing them when appropriate. This helped them feel ownership while becoming more self-disciplined.

Following this initial brainstorming, we continued several times a month to list issues that were problems for the class that prevented our working together effectively. Small groups of four each took one of these issues and came up with many ways to take action. The issues and solutions were posted, and the class agreed to try to help each other make changes in behavior and attitudes.

Behaviors change and attitudes improve when children find supportive friends and can play together. In P.E. we play games that highlight everyone feeling successful and participating; even those with asthma try their hardest. Girls are recognized as having physical talents; new strategies develop to help teams get along and work together. Ruben (age ten) decided that weaker players could be put between good players so they could get to home base without striking out. If children do strike out, I have them finish their runs so they know the feeling of making it to home base. I encourage them to keep trying until they are able to hit the ball. Gabe (age eight) decided that shortening the field space helped children make home runs.

We are able to put aside enough of our differences to value each other as collaborators. All year we take the time for talking, planning, and taking action towards being more positive and healthy as individuals and as a community. In time we are able to work together without major confrontations. Taking turns using pillows, joining literature groups without friends, and listening to others we thought we didn't like or respect are issues we deal with on a daily basis.

Maintaining a Community of Readers

We spend a lot of time reading, exploring literature, and making decisions as readers. Daily we demonstrate strategies for each other, such as skipping a word we don't know and reading on; then we discuss how the strategy works for us as readers. The message is that there is always someone in the room who can help when we are confused and don't know what to do. If anyone doesn't understand an engagement, they can go and ask someone who does understand to be their partner. No one is alone. The children learn that we can overcome our fear of failure. The goal is for all of us to value what others have to offer.

Each day a new invitation for readers is introduced during their free reading time. Eventually children will choose and explore potentials in reading plays and Readers Theatre, creating their own dramas, using puppets and costumes, listening to and making music, and browsing or reading from the classroom library. Management, organization, storage, and cleanup need to be part of every option. Over time, the concept of choice, sharing and having a purpose as readers is successful and is maintained through our sharing and reflecting.

Once children have the concept of free reading and making choices, they are independent and can use their time more wisely. This is an ongoing issue because if children are not authentically engaged, trouble brews with hitting, playing around, and disrupting others. As children become more independent in their reading choices they are open to moving into discussing books in small groups.

About the third week of school I start the first Literature Circles. I don't expect these circles to be the best discussions; rather we take the opportunity to learn together and get excited about sharing ideas and opinions by discussing issues found in Text Sets. For example, when our broad concept was Connections, we began with a focus on relationships. I took notes on the students' issues about relationships and used these to develop Text Sets around themes such as anger at family and friends, knowing your culture, fear, and security.

Most Literature Circles continue using the list of strategies for talking about books which the class earlier brainstormed from the class read-aloud experiences. The groups are able to at least share their favorite parts of the book, talk about the illustrations they liked, give a short retelling of the story, tell what they didn't like, and sometimes express what they found confusing about the story. To support these initial discussions, we take the last fifteen minutes of their literature discussion time for groups to share with the whole class what they have been talking about. I put their ideas and strategies for talking about books and working in groups on a list on the board so any group having trouble can refer to the list.

Maintaining a Community of Writers

Looking through our reflection journals from the morning, we begin a brainstormed list of possible ideas and interests that might become possibilities for stories, articles, pictures, cartoons, or poems. Children are also encouraged to bring in artifacts, pictures, collections, or hobbies as further ideas for writing—just like the idea files that authors use. We create lists from these multiple sources that are kept in our Authors Folders so we are able to refer to them anytime we need an idea. During the second week of school, children collect information about their families and homes to be shared orally.

I make up a booklet children can use for a variety of ideas. The accordion-folded paper can be used to draw the houses on their street, a bird's-eye view of their bedroom, a close up of something important like an heirloom, portraits of their family, and so on. These collections are ideas for future writings and are brought back to school daily for sharing oral stories. The more we are able to tell others about ourselves, the more we can accept ourselves and others. This shared oral storytime is important in building community.

We continue all year working together as writers and finding ways to support each other. Writers quickly take off in all directions and find their own reasons for pursuing projects, interests, and making meaning. As children learn to schedule their time more wisely, it is necessary to plan for longer periods of work time. This extended studio time encourages children to work on personal inquiries. Children are invited and encouraged to explore their questions, which sets a purpose for exploring and creating meaning through multiple sign systems.

Maintaining a Community of Inquirers

Through research strategies that support inquiry, children pose ideas and problems that interest them, eventually finding significant questions to pursue as inquirers. Children come to school with many questions; once they are engaged with other learners they have even

Request for Studio Time;
Juliette, age 10

more. I plan engagements that involve observations and encourage a variety of ways for children to record their observations. Over the years, we've observed a wide range of artifacts including gum, ice cubes, sugar cubes, vegetables, plants, and animals. Often the focus of our observations comes from the children.

One year during the first two weeks of school, children would jump up from the risers and race across the room to rescue small frogs jumping out of their cubbies. I was very irritated at these animals being kept in pockets and stored until recess break. Finally I told the children to return them to the outdoors and not bring any more to school. Since Nicole had spent seven years studying frogs, she ignored me and continued bringing in frogs daily, sharing their wonders with me and the class. Even with outdoor temperatures of 101°, it finally occurred to me that we needed to spend some quality observation time with these frogs. Nicole had now brought in ninety frogs for the class to observe. I was being given the message that the children had an engagement that needed to be part of the curriculum.

We began in the afternoons with each child observing a frog. Some groups tried to have their frogs sit on their pencils, fingers, or noses. Melissa was very upset that her frog wouldn't sit still while other children delighted in jumping with their frogs across the carpet. Through all the noise and excitement, we managed to share and found that many questions naturally emerged: How far can frogs jump? Can they do tricks? How long can they sit still?

For the rest of that week's afternoons the class continued observing their frogs, sharing experiments, trying to teach their frogs tricks, and recording information about their frogs through words and pictures. The focus was on being engaged, asking questions, trying out ideas to explore the questions, using primary sources, using measuring tools, recording information, sharing the results with others, and reflecting on their research strategies.

Conclusion

Both the children and I come to school with so many experiences that need to be recognized, connected with, and built from. Our curriculum has to extend those experiences while exploring new engagements. As learners we deepen our understandings when we come together to dialogue, share ideas, and form opinions. Working with each other builds community. Building a community of learners is an

Dear Ms. Kauffmann

Do you like the PHOENIX SUNS? I do. I hope that you have a good summer. I hope that **you injoyde** your frst year at scool and I am srey for ben bda at scool and I hope you like your secit year of scool and I like **you and thac** you for helepen me werk and you are a nice tecer. **Also**, my mom and dad really appreciated the letter that **you sent me.** I told them that I was going to miss you next year.

Your Friend,
Brad

PHOENIX VS CHICAGO
SUNS   BULLS

ongoing process throughout the entire year for all of us. The students and I meet many obstacles, but it is when we work as a team, arriving at consensus, that we find satisfaction and success. Working together, sharing our ideas, and asking questions builds our self-worth, and we become learners for life. In time we find ourselves working at our best and making our classroom an exciting place to learn.

I used to have centers. I didn't have a good attitude. I had to work with the same group. I couldn't get to know others. I didn't have a choice. I was assigned the work and it had to be done a

Michelle

Plan Studio Time

1. Art: because doing stuff on humming birds, doing medas, Draw different humming birds.

2. Writing. writing informashin about hummingbirds.

3. Reading: reading informashin about hummingbirds.

4. Drama: do anther play and wiithe body move ment with Adam, Juliett, and Cekelia.

What I did was art. I drew some pictures of hummingbirds and different medas. Then I did writing informashin about hummingbirds. I read informashin on hummingbirds and we didn't get to do drama because we didn't have enuff time. We couldn't deside what play to do. Next Friday I'm not going to do the play. I used color pencils and crayons for the different medas.

certain way, in a certain order. Now I have freedom to work. I sit and talk and work with others. Everyone is possible to work with. I have freedom and a good attitude. I talk to others in a different way. I encourage them to do work, to try even if they are not right. It only counts that you try. (Amber, age ten)

The Authoring Cycle as Curricular Framework for Inquiry

Introduction

The longer we explored the authoring cycle as a framework for a reading and writing curriculum, the more we became convinced that something wasn't right. Some of our tension came from intermediate grade teachers who saw the power of the authoring cycle in supporting reading and writing processes, but asked the question, "What about content? Doesn't it matter *what* students are reading and writing about?" Our first response was that it did matter, but that the content would emerge from student interests and needs; it should not be dictated by the mandate that all fifth graders study the Civil War. Our response was obviously inadequate, but their questions forced us to bring to consciousness our own uneasiness about theme units. Two parallel curricular structures had emerged in our classroom contexts. The authoring cycle was our framework to think about reading and writing along with other sign system processes. Theme units were the curricular framework for content investigations. While there were connections across these frameworks, we were troubled by the lack of integration and connection, and by our growing feeling that theme units were still tied theoretically to traditional theories about knowledge and teacher role. We were also troubled by the separation between sign system processes and knowledge systems in classroom experiences.

We began to closely examine theme units and to think about whether inquiry might provide a different framework for curriculum. Was it a new framework or another version of a theme unit? Did inquiry make a difference theoretically or practically from what we were already doing? It was Carolyn Burke who suggested that it might be productive to go back to the models of the reading process, the Phonics Model, Skills Model, and Whole Language Model, and see if they would allow us to explore whether these differences actually existed. As we played with these models, we realized that they visually portrayed major theoretical differences between theme units and inquiry and also allowed us to see why sign systems and knowledge systems needed to be integrated in inquiry (Short, 1993). The models helped us put into pictures and words the ideas and tensions we had been feeling but had been articulating poorly. More and more we found ourselves moving from the authoring cycle as process to an inquiry cycle which integrated process and content. The models also reflected major changes in the teaching of content which we saw in our own teaching and in the broader educational field.

Curriculum as Fact

Figure 4.1 represents the curriculum model which we had experienced as students from elementary through the university. Each sub-

FIGURE 4.1
Curriculum as Fact

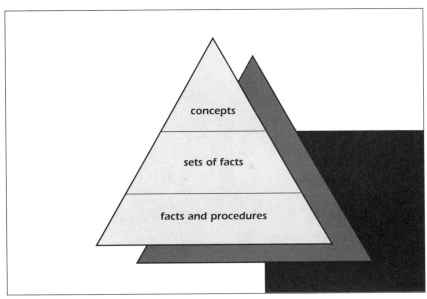

ject area consisted of individual facts and procedures which needed to be drilled and memorized. Once we mastered these pieces of information, we put them together in sets of facts and then combined these sets to form concepts. These isolated facts, sets of facts, and concepts were taught in a predetermined sequence with facts as the basic foundation and building blocks for everything else. We never even got to the point of forming broad generalizations that cut across the different subject areas. We learned each topic and each subject area in isolation. The assumption was that each subject area consisted of a common core of known knowledge which needed to be broken down and taught sequentially to all students. Reading, writing, mathematics, science, and social studies were all labeled as subject areas. In this model, the smallest unit of curriculum was a fact.

Instructionally, this curricular model translated into a textbook-dominated classroom. We read the textbook, filled out worksheets, tried to guess the answer wanted by the teacher in class discussions, and took the test to see if we had mastered the facts. The textbooks which dominated our classrooms were distillations of already known knowledge, written to inform us, but without enough evidence for us to recreate the inquiry process of the author. Often this knowledge was so condensed that we could make few connections between the different facts, and so our only recourse as learners was to memorize. We read about the topics we studied and rarely became involved in the doing of subject areas such as science. We memorized dates, events, formulas, science facts, and procedures. Solving a math problem consisted of memorizing and following an exact set of procedures without variation. Science experiments had one right procedure and answer. Research consisted of copying information from the encyclopedia. We "covered" lots of topics and facts, few in any depth—most were forgotten within forty-eight hours of taking the test. We ended up with superficial knowledge and little desire to keep learning about that topic. "We had covered it; we were done with it" was our perspective.

Curriculum as Activity

As teachers, our frustration with this way of teaching subject areas led us to explore units and thematic approaches. Instead of facts, these approaches were built around activity as the smallest unit of

FIGURE 4.2
Curriculum as Activity

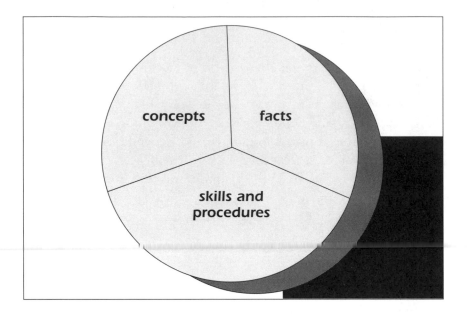

curriculum (Figure 4.2). We no longer believed that particular facts and concepts had to be taught in a particular sequence for each subject area. Each subject area took the form of a pie with different wedges representing the same facts, concepts, skills, and procedures that needed to be taught, but not in a particular sequence. We taught these through activities rather than isolated memorization. Sometimes activities were chosen because of the facts that could be learned from the activity. Other times activities were chosen according to particular skills and procedures that we felt students needed to learn. Still other times, activities were chosen because they allowed students to develop broader concepts related to the topic of study.

To build connections, we connected each pie or subject area around a theme such as bears or the Civil War so that students read about bears, wrote about bears, did science activities on bears, and solved math problems involving bears. In planning, we took a theme, and then listed activities by subject area and the facts, procedures, and concepts that would be learned through that activity (Figure 4.3).

When we grew frustrated with this tight structure of tying activities to specific objectives, we argued that what really mattered was whether children enjoyed the activities, not whether they learned a specific objective. Curriculum became a grab bag of activities. We put units together with a group of fun activities and didn't worry about how they related to any broader whole. "As long as the kids have fun" became our motto.

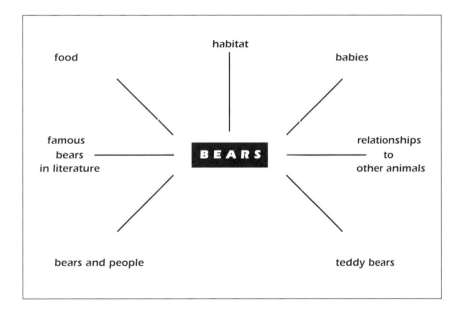

FIGURE 4.3
Webbing a Theme Unit by
Subject Area

FIGURE 4.4
Webbing a Theme Unit by
Issues and Topics

This focus on activity for the sake of activity began to lose its appeal. It was tiring to constantly develop new activities and to have no sense of how things fit together. We moved to brainstorming and webbing out a theme by topics and issues rather than by subject areas. This kind of webbing did not artificially separate activities into subject areas, but grouped together activities across subject areas that were all related to a particular issue or topic (Figure 4.4). The activities had a

Chapter Four
The Authoring Cycle as
Curricular Framework
for Inquiry

connection to each other and to the broader theme which allowed both us and our students to have a greater sense of direction.

Students responded positively to the units and activities. The topics grew out of school curriculum, teacher experiences, and student interests. The textbooks were replaced with literature, both fiction and nonfiction. In contrast to textbooks, the information books were more modest and focused on a particular topic—they didn't cover five centuries in one chapter. They gave a more intimate and personal perspective and were written by authors who wanted to share some of their inquiry with another interested person from the stance of one enthusiast to another. They also usually included enough data so that students could see the author's inquiry process and form their own opinions. The fiction transported students to other countries, cultures, and time periods, allowing them to explore moral and social issues related to technology and science. Literature became the backbone of our curriculum. We gathered books and planned activities based on these books.

Gradually, however, tensions began to arise. We realized we were over-relying on books. Students were still primarily reading *about*, not doing, science and social studies. Our units were more exciting and interesting, but they were still a way to teach predetermined facts. We often did activities at the expense of critical and in-depth knowing. The topics were frequently trite with forced connections. At the end of a two week unit on kites, none of us wanted to hear about kites again. Doing math computations on kite shapes and spelling kite-related words didn't seem especially meaningful. We were still covering topics and supplying information, just in more interesting ways. Children were continuing to focus on facts; now they gathered facts instead of memorizing them.

Our theoretical stance had not made a significant shift from our textbook model of curriculum. We were the ones in charge of the units. We assumed we knew what the students would discover and that they would unearth what others already knew through the unit. Because we developed the units, students were limited by our own knowledge of that topic. The class stayed safely within what we already knew. Our units were still based on a deficit model of learning—a focus on what kids didn't know.

We assumed they would go from more confused to less confused through their involvement in our activities. We still spent hours developing those activities. Because all of the creativity came from us, we ended up exhausted. All we had really accomplished was a move from a curriculum in which the subject areas were completely isolated from each other to a correlated curriculum, not to an integrated curriculum. Knowledge was still compartmentalized.

Curriculum as Inquiry

It was these tensions that led us to think more about curriculum as inquiry. Theoretical concepts about inquiry had intrigued us for some time, but connecting that theory to practice was another issue. We realized that one of the problems with our old models of curriculum as fact and curriculum as activity was that they were both models of how to *teach* content, not of how people actually inquire about something they want to understand. Ken Goodman had been able to move away from phonics and skills models of how to teach reading by looking at how readers actually read and then thinking about instruction. We decided we needed to look at how learners actually go about inquiry in their lives outside of schools.

As we looked at young children, we were impressed with their lives as inquirers. They live in a constant state of curiosity and learning. For them, inquiry comes from exploring and being interested in the world. Through their active explorations of their world, tensions arise and they ask questions about aspects of the world that puzzle them. They then systematically investigate those questions or tensions and create new understandings, new questions, and issues that they want to explore further. As we thought about our own experiences, we realized that we spent at least as much of our time exploring broadly and trying to figure out what our question really was as we did actually researching that question. Sometimes we couldn't figure out our question until we had done the research. For us, a good portion of the inquiry process was being able to put our feelings of tension and questioning into words so that we could focus on that question through further inquiry.

Paulo Freire (1985) argues that inquirers need to be *problem-posers*, not just problem-solvers. We saw that in our classrooms we posed the problems; our students became problem-solvers of our questions. We also realized that problem-solving and research are empty processes when the question is not one that matters in the life of the inquirer. While there are many research strategies that support our lives as inquirers, putting all of our focus on learning those strategies is a waste of time if we don't first put time into finding a significant question. The focus of an inquiry is not always in the form of a specific question, but can be a "wondering" about something we want to

> Why do people think they need everything?
>
> **Inquiry Question;**
> **Karen, Age 8 (Jean Schroeder's**
> **classroom)**

Chapter Four
The Authoring Cycle as
Curricular Framework
for Inquiry

pursue. As we work through inquiry, we do not usually end with one answer or even a set of answers. Our problem-solving does not narrow our perspective but gives us more understandings, questions, and possibilities than when we started!

As we examined our lives as inquirers and those of children and adults around us, we identified three sources of knowledge that inquirers draw from in their search for significant questions and their investigation of those questions. These sources of knowledge include personal and social knowing through our life experiences, knowledge systems as structures of knowledge and alternative perspectives on our world (history, biology, psychology), and sign systems as alternative ways of making and creating meaning about the world (art, music, movement, language, mathematics). Knowledge systems and sign systems are not reduced to subject areas with a focus on mastering specific facts and skills. They are seen as perspectives, ways of thinking, and stances one can take in the world.

At the heart of inquiry is personal and social knowing. Learners bring the knowledge they have gained from their personal experiences of living in the world and being part of specific cultural groups and social contexts. Inquiry can only begin with what learners already know, perceive, and feel.

Knowledge systems refer to the ways in which humans have structured knowledge to make sense of the world, just as grammar emerged as the structural system of language so we can communicate. Knowledge systems developed because a group of scholars shared a set of questions and a domain of intellectual inquiry and, over time, created a body of knowledge, a certain perspective and set of questions about the world, and particular ways of researching and tools for going about that research. Knowledge systems are human inventions that change constantly. The divisions between the systems are arbitrary, for convenience sake, despite the way these divisions have been institutionalized in universities.

There are two major differences between knowledge systems in inquiry and the content areas as traditionally taught in our schools and universities. The first is what is considered significant. The content areas in schools reduce knowledge systems to sets of isolated skills, facts, and concepts. What is significant about knowledge systems is *not* the specific pieces of information, but the alternative perspectives these systems provide about the world. Each knowledge system looks at the world through a different lens and asks a different set of questions. What is also signficant is that these systems provide different ways of investigating and exploring our questions and different kinds of tools to use for researching and sharing what we learn with others. For example, historians look at the world and ask how we can use the past to understand the present and change our future. As part of their inquiries, they use primary sources, interviews, notetaking, time lines, and many other strategies and tools.

The second major difference is that content areas are taught as separate entities. Science has its content and history its content. Inquiry involves the use of multiple knowledge systems at the same time. What we want to do is bring multiple perspectives to a particular topic by asking what questions an historian, biologist, economist, or psychologist would have about this topic and what tools and ways of researching can be used to explore the topic.

Sign systems are alternative ways of creating and sharing meaning with others such as language, mathematics, music, art, and movement. In schools, language has been overemphasized as *the* way of constructing meaning, and the other systems are treated as frills or talents of only a few. All of these sign systems are basic ways of creating and sharing meaning; each allows us to know and communicate different meanings. When we are unable to use a particular system, there are meanings we can never know or communicate to others. Elliot Eisner (1982) argues that every way to communicate and make meaning ignores some aspects of experience and highlights others.

If we think about the ways we construct and communicate meaning outside of school, we realize that we usually use several systems in combination. This book is one example of using both language and visual images to more effectively communicate with others. It is only in school that we insist that students use only one at a time which results in incomplete and inefficient meanings. Inquiry involves having all sign systems available so that students can use the ones that best meet their purposes at any point in time. The significance of sign systems is in the authoring processes that learners can use to make and share different kinds of meanings with others, not the specific set of skills and procedures to be mastered.

Learners will not pursue the questions that really matter in their lives unless they are in an environment where their ideas and lives are valued. Not just any learning environment will support inquiry— only environments that move beyond hierarchy to a democracy where all people are equally valued. Pat Shannon (1993) defines a

> What was the first bug they discovered?
>
> **Inquiry Question;
> Miranda, Age 8 (Jean
> Schroeder's classroom)**

FIGURE 4.5
Curriculum as Inquiry

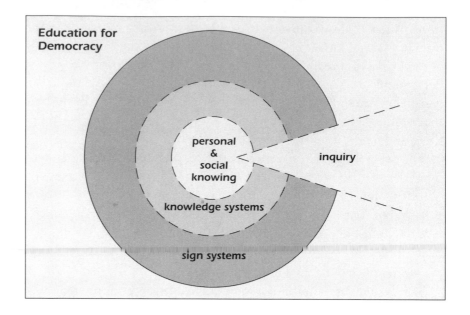

Education for Democracy

personal & social knowing

knowledge systems

sign systems

inquiry

democracy as a system in which people participate meaningfully in the decisions that affect their lives. It involves participation and negotiation among equals—a participation that must be significant. Participants are not just given the choice among options determined by others behind the scenes; they are part of the thinking behind the scenes.

As Figure 4.5 tries to demonstrate, the smallest unit of curriculum is therefore the inquiry itself. Inquiry is a whole process that cuts across and integrates personal and social knowing, knowledge systems, sign systems, and an environment based on education for democracy.

Progress in inquiry is having new understandings and new questions to ask. The term *understandings* highlights the temporal nature of what we learn in contrast to "answers" which signal that what we learn from one experience will never change. Carolyn Burke argues that understandings last only until learners have time to ask new questions or more compelling theories come into existence. The field of education provides ample examples of this type of constant change! We don't inquire to eliminate alternatives but to find more functional understandings—to create diversity, broaden our thinking and ask more complex questions (Short & Burke, 1991). We can end up *more* confused, not less confused, but our confusions reflect new questions that are more complex and based on deeper insights. Teachers can't already know exactly what kids will learn when they begin a focused study in the classroom, because the questions can't be framed ahead by teachers and experts. Children have to be part of creating the questions. John Dewey (1938) states that teachers have a responsibility to establish classroom learning environments and select experiences that have the most *potential* for raising anomalies and questions for a specific group of students. They cannot, however, determine exactly what those anomalies will be for students or else they become the problem-posers.

Instructionally, curriculum as inquiry means that instead of using the theme as an excuse to teach science, social studies, mathematics, reading, and writing, *these knowledge systems and sign systems become tools for exploring, finding, and researching student questions.* Instead of curriculum focusing on activities and books, the focus is on inquiry. Literature comes into this process as it supports inquiry, not as the focal point of all curriculum.

The shift from curriculum as fact to curriculum as activity involved a major change in how the classroom looked. It required many more materials and lots of teacher time in planning activities and gathering materials. Instead of students sitting quietly in desks, they moved around the room engaged in a wide range of pursuits. The shift from curriculum as activity to curriculum as inquiry is a much more subtle shift because the classroom doesn't look different on the surface—the same materials and activities are often there. Many of these materials are now being gathered by the entire classroom community—not just the teacher—and the students are not engaged in as many activities because they are setting up and creating their own sites for exploration. The major difference, however, is in the beliefs underlying those materials and activities, and the functions they serve. That's a much more difficult change for all of us as teachers to make.

As we reflected on these models, we knew that in order to move from our theoretical beliefs and insights about inquiry to curriculum, we needed a curricular framework. Carolyn Burke pushed us to reconsider the authoring cycle as a cycle of inquiry (Figure 4.6) and, with this framework in mind, we began to further explore the potentials of inquiry in our college classrooms and in elementary classrooms with teacher researchers. In the remainder of this chapter, we want to revisit the components of the authoring cycle, but from the perspective of a cycle of inquiry that integrates personal and social knowing, knowledge systems, and sign systems within a social context based in education for democracy.

The inquiry cycle is set in motion as the class moves into a focused study on a particular topic or theme. Just as in theme units, these

> What would it be like if we discovered another planet?
>
> **Inquiry Question; Miranda, Age 8 (Jean Schroeder's classroom)**

*Chapter Four
The Authoring Cycle as
Curricular Framework
for Inquiry*

Building from the Known
Browsing, talking and listening

Taking the Time to Find
Questions for Inquiry
Wandering and wondering
Experience centers
Observing and exploring

Taking Thoughtful
New Action
Invitation for action

COLLECT
IDEAS

THE
AUTHORING
CYCLE

Planning New
Inquiries
Group reflection
Reflection portfolios
Strategy lessons

NEWS

Gaining New
Perspectives
Inquiry groups
Indepth researching
Tools for inquiry
Studio time

Sharing What Was Learned
Inquiry presentations

Attending to Difference
Revision on inquiry
Learning logs

FIGURE 4.6
The Authoring Cycle as a
Curricular Framework for
Inquiry

topics involve a negotiation between the school curriculum, teacher interests and experiences, and student interests and experiences. Sometimes students initiate a focused study, such as when Julie Laird's kindergarten students kept bringing up their issues and connections about families and change over time despite her efforts to move them into a new focus. Sometimes the focused study is initiated by the teacher in response to students' needs such as when Leslie Kahn began a study on the Holocaust because of her concern about the racism in the lives of her sixth-grade students. Even when the focus is mandated by the school, as it was for Kathleen Crawford who had to teach Arizona history in fourth grade, there is still room for negotiation with students. Kathleen's students were interested in culture and so Kathleen began the study of Arizona by bringing in primary sources and literature so they could continue their inquiries through exploring the diverse cultural groups in Arizona.

The most important consideration is that a class focus should not be established without negotiation with students. Within that focus there should be plenty of room for students to find and explore their own inquiries from many different perspectives. The topic may be a class focus, but the problem-posing and inquiry questions are determined by students. The authoring cycle is also set in motion when students engage in individual expert projects that grow out of a personal focus for each student that is not connected to a particular class focus, but it is personally significant to that student's life.

Building from the Known

Because we believe so strongly that we can only learn by connecting to and building from our life experiences, we plan initial experiences that support students in making connections to what they already know. Their first engagements need to be open-ended so they can respond with the connections that are most important to them. We are less concerned with teaching students particular kinds of information than with giving them the time to explore and connect. We choose read-alouds on topics that are close to their own experiences. We set up blocks of time for browsing books, materials, and artifacts. For example, when Junardi Armstrong began a focus on insects with second and third graders, she set up observation areas where students could observe and interact with a wide variety of insects. The only instruction she provided was on how to hold insects without crushing them.

Chapter Four
The Authoring Cycle as
Curricular Framework
for Inquiry

She also put out many books, art prints, posters, insect models, and written materials for student browsing.

Time for students to share their connections and hear each others' voices is absolutely essential in these early engagements. The role of the teacher is to *listen*, not to teach at this point in time, in order to get a sense of children's connections and voices.

Debbie Rowe (1993) found in her research with two- and three-year olds that the typical one to two week preschool unit interferes with children's pursuits and themes. Some children had themes that they pursued for months and so developed sophisticated understandings and questions. Others pursued several themes at one time; still others were samplers who moved from theme to theme. The topics typically covered in preschool units were often unrelated to children's own themes and interrupted their inquiry. Another issue was that the materials and activities in these units were usually put away at the end of the week and so children who had developed an interest in these materials could not continue to engage with them.

The first step taken by the preschool teachers in this classroom was to listen. They took time to find out the children's themes. They scheduled themselves into the book corner during free play where they read aloud and recorded the books that children requested. They also noted the kinds of play in which children were engaging and sent home parent surveys about children's interests. In addition, they recorded children's comments and connections during class meetings.

They began to transform their curriculum by supporting multiple themes. As they became aware of children's themes, they collected books, toys, and other materials related to these themes and put them together in Book and Toy Sets that were located around the room. They continued the class units but always had the Book and Toy Sets available for children. When talking with children, they focused on children's interests instead of pushing their own agenda related to the class unit.

Instead of predetermining the themes for the year, the teachers chose larger themes that encompassed a number of the themes that children were already exploring. The units were scheduled for longer periods of time; materials and books from these units remained in the classroom when the class moved to a different theme. Gradually, the children's themes took over the classroom curriculum as the teachers realized the power of children's interests. For preschoolers, inquiry involved having someone to answer their questions, to provide ma-

> "How do clouds move around?"
>
> **Inquiry Question; Amy, Age 6 (Kathy Smith's classroom)**

Section One
The Authoring Cycle:
Let's Talk Curriculum

terials and books, and to let them play. First and foremost, however, they needed teachers who were willing to let them explore and who listened to their interests and connections.

The talk at the beginning of an inquiry focus takes the form of a conversation, not an intense dialogue. It's a chance to share personal connections after participating in read-alouds, browsing books, listening to music, or observing in a science area. These engagements highlight personal and social knowing as the heart of inquiry. Students' own experiences must be the base from which further exploration of the topic occurs. As they continue their exploration, students are pushed to extend their learning into new areas and gradually develop focused issues and questions to pursue in inquiry.

> "Why does the ocean have waves?"
>
> **Inquiry Question; Richard, Age 7 (Kathy Smith's classroom)**

Taking the Time to Find Questions for Inquiry

Eve Merriam helped us understand why slowing down and taking the time to explore is so important to inquiry. In *The Wise Woman and Her Secret* (1991), a group of villagers travel to an old woman's house to demand that she tell them the secret to her wisdom. When she refuses, they search everywhere but finally give up and return to their village. One little girl, Jenny, lags behind and excitedly explores cobwebs and twigs. She finds a penny that has turned green from years at the bottom of the well and shows it to the old woman, asking her a string of questions. The old woman smiles and tells Jenny that *she* has found the secret to wisdom. Jenny looks at her in amazement and asks what that secret is. The old woman replies that it is taking the time to look, listen, smell, and observe the world around her; to "wander and wonder" about the world.

We have come to see this part of the cycle as highlighting "wandering and wondering" (Short, 1993). It is a time when students have time to wander and explore a topic from as many different perspectives as possible and to wonder about all kinds of ideas as they wander without feeling pressured to immediately develop a question for investigation. We used to begin a focused study by urging students to quickly find a question to research. We had students brainstorm what they knew and what they wanted to know at the beginning of a focused study. Our goal was to get the students into their questions as soon as possible so they could "do research." The problem was that their questions often were the superficial "How many legs does an

Chapter Four
The Authoring Cycle as
Curricular Framework
for Inquiry

insect have?" variety which could be answered quickly. Many times they didn't even ask a question but simply decided to gather information on a topic, such as Jupiter or horses. Their research involved gathering facts on these topics without any real sense of tension and desire to know driving them into inquiry. They were simply covering the topic by putting together interesting, but isolated, facts. Often they didn't even get to develop their own questions, we simply provided the questions for them; they felt the pressure of coming up with answers to please us.

Barry Lopez (1992), a naturalist, argues that to go out into nature and immediately ask questions is disrespectful and inappropriate. Before humans have the right to ask questions, we need to take the time to observe and listen. Through that observation, an interest or feeling of tension begins to grow, we discover what we want to pursue, and that interest gradually forms into a focused question or issue.

While we have spent a great deal of time as educators developing instructional strategies for research, we have not thought much about how to support the search for questions in the first place. As we explore wandering and wondering in classrooms, we have begun to get a sense of the kinds of structures and engagements that give students support in "mucking around" a topic, but we still have a lot to understand. We aren't used to encouraging students to explore without having to focus on a question. We have learned that wandering and wondering must include examining a topic as broadly as possible from many different perspectives and through conversations and observations. These experiences push students to go beyond what they already know and to develop broader understandings from which their own inquiries can then develop.

Creating classroom environments that support observation and wandering and wondering often takes us beyond our classroom doors. Myriam Revel-Wood worked with her students to establish a wildlife area between the different buildings that make up the complex of their elementary school. Over the years, this area has been planted with bushes and shrubs that attract various birds and wild animals. Students continually use this area to make observations. Debbie Manning involves her first graders in a garden and recycling center on the school grounds.

When Junardi Armstrong and Kathy Short explored the Sonoran desert with second graders, the desert was right outside the classroom door. Students took walking trips into the desert outside the

"Why are we still arguing over color?" "Why don't adults want to tell their age?"

Inquiry Question; Grade 5 (Gloria Kauffman's classroom)

school, observed birds at the feeding station on the window, browsed through books, posters, and desert artifacts in observation centers, listened to desert sounds on tapes, viewed art prints, participated in class read-alouds, and shared their observations and wonderings with other students. After one week of this wandering and wondering, they brainstormed individually and as a group on what they knew and felt about the desert and what they wanted to know. These questions became the basis for their inquiries (Short & Armstrong, 1993).

Desert Brainstorming; Thomas, Age 8 (Junardi Armstrong's classroom)

In contrast, Leslie Kahn (1994) and her sixth graders spent five weeks wandering and wondering about the Holocaust before they moved to focused inquiry. The difference in time was because Junardi's second graders knew a great deal about the desert as their own environment, while Leslie's students had never heard of the Holocaust. Leslie filled the room with all of her resources on the Holocaust. She gave students time to listen to read-alouds, watch documentaries, browse through fiction and nonfiction, examine primary documents, talk with Holocaust survivers who came to the classroom, and discuss Holocaust novels in Literature Circles. She read aloud from *Journey of the Sparrows* (Buss, 1991), a contemporary novel about Central American refugees and their life and death struggle when they enter the United States illegally, to remind students that issues of oppression and racism were not limited to one period in time. Students then met in reflective literature circles on issues from this novel. Working with a drama specialist, her students used improvisational drama to take on the roles of victims, aggressors, rescuers, and bystanders. Throughout these engagements, students shared their insights and wonderings.

Many of these engagements are ones that we normally associate with theme units. The difference was that the goal of these engagements was not to cover the Holocaust but to provide students with a rich context and diverse perspectives from which their own inquiries could emerge. *Leslie continually thought about how she could introduce a new perspective on the Holocaust into the context, not how to teach the Holocaust to her students.* Another difference is that Leslie did not gradually bring out these materials and books. She filled the room with everything she could find on the Holocaust and gave students time to find the connections that were important to them. One of the materials she put out were all of the multiple copy sets of novels related to the Holocaust. Students could then choose the ones that

Chapter Four
The Authoring Cycle as
Curricular Framework
for Inquiry

most interested them for a Literature Circle experience instead of Leslie determining the choices.

The initial wonderings of students were about how many people died, how they were killed, and the kinds of weapons used. Gradually, however, questions began to emerge that connected their lives to the Holocaust and racism. The move to focused inquiry was facilitated by the Literature Circles on the Holocaust novels. As students discussed and then presented their novels to the class, their questions moved to a deeper level because they felt the need for more information and understandings. Rosa became interested in whether children in the school were racist in their choice of friends, and she developed a questionnaire that she took to different classrooms. Manuel, for whom gang membership was a positive value, began comparing gangs to the Nazis and questioning gang membership for the first time. Students wanted to know about the art of children, the games they played in the camps, ways of surviving, issues of hunger and starvation, and how Hitler was able to persuade so many people to come to him. The students had moved to inquiries on questions and issues that really mattered in their lives and allowed them to critique their world.

Teachers have found that the engagements they offer as invitations during wandering and wondering are the same kinds of activities they used in the past for theme units. This allows them to build on what they were doing previously and not feel that they are throwing everything away. Just as in Leslie's classroom, the goal of these activities has changed; they serve as a context within which students can find their own inquiries rather than as a way to cover the content. They provide a way to encourage students to explore the topic broadly from many different perspectives and not stay too easily within what they already know. Another difference is that many of these activities become invitations set up in experience centers around the room instead of whole class activities in which everyone must participate. Teachers open up their file drawers and boxes and pull out everything they have on a particular topic so students can find the connections that are significant for them. Much of what they learn as they explore is shared informally through conversation, sketching, and journaling rather than presented formally. A structure that supports continous sharing and conversation is essential to this process of exploration.

Sue Robinson found a way to support students in finding a question during a summer school program where time was short. She began by announcing that each student could select something they wanted to explore and that the topic they selected was important because they would become the resident "expert" and share what they learned in a School Learning Fair. She opened the files of the theme units that she had collected through her years of teaching and used them to a create a multimedia blitz around the room. Multimedia blitz consisted of learning centers with books, filmstrips, pamphlets, posters, buttons, artifacts, and other materials on topics ranging from China to lizards and pollution. Students were encouraged to think about the topics, discuss them with friends, and finally choose one they wanted to pursue. Sue asked them to consider topics not presented in the centers by talking with parents, naturalists, friends, and other adults who might have good ideas. By the end of the first week, students had moved from exploration to inquiry on a focus that interested them.

As students explore, "I wonder" statements and questions constantly emerge. We found that it was important to have some way to record these as they occur. Just as students needed their Authors Folders to keep track of their writing drafts, inquirers need places to store their inquiry questions so they can select the ones they want to pursue. We learned this the hard way after listening to wonderful questions in class discussions for several weeks and then, on the day when everyone seemed ready to move into inquiries, asking students to list their questions, only to be met by puzzled looks. They no longer remembered most of their questions. We began using large wall charts where students' questions and wonderings are recorded as they arise or providing "I Wonder" books for students to record their questions.

Rise Paynter and Joby Copenhaver gave fifth graders Wonderful Questions Journals where they could record their questions on a regular basis (Copenhaver, 1992). On each page, students recorded a question and why it was important to them. These questions were recorded each evening; the next day each student chose one question to read to the group. The students responded using a variation of Save the Last Word for Me. After reading the question, the others in the class speculated on why they thought it a powerful question. The author then had the last word on why he or she found that question

> If I could study anything in the world it would probably be how electric things work. I'd like to discover some new things.
>
> Keegan's dog, because she died and it was sad.

Inquiry Questions (Rise Paynter's fourth/fifth-grade classroom)

Chapter Four
The Authoring Cycle as
Curricular Framework
for Inquiry

personally important. Through this process, students were able to identify the questions they wanted to investigate and to find questions they shared with a partner or small group.

Students may need support in finding a focus for their inquiry as well as demonstrations on the strategies they can use in organizing and moving ahead with their inquiries. In the insect focus with second and third graders, Junardi Armstrong invited students to explore insects and books for several days, record what they were seeing and wondering about in their journals, and share these ideas in class sharing times. After a week, she asked the students to look through their journals and star the three questions they thought were significant. These questions were listed on the board and then the class worked together to group these questions into six related categories. The categories became six inquiry groups, and the students signed up for the group that most interested them.

Before they began their inquiries, however, Junardi was concerned that they have some demonstrations on how to develop their own experiments. She did not want to hand them experiment cards but wanted them to develop experiments for their questions. They began by first looking at experiments they had done as part of earlier class experiences and talked about the materials, procedures, and experiments that helped them explore what they wanted to know.

The class went back to their list of questions and chose one they thought they could answer in class, "How far does a grasshopper hop?" The students brainstormed how they might find this out and the kinds of materials they would need. Junardi brought in the materials and insects and the children broke up into groups to carry out their experiment. After they had shared their results and averaged them together, they critiqued the procedures they had used in the experiment. Reflecting back on this experience, Junardi wishes she had added a step where the class chose another question and formed groups, with each group developing their own experiment for the same question. They could have then shared the different ways they could answer the question and why some had worked better than others.

Another strategy that Junardi used to help the students think about how they could go about answering their questions in their inquiry groups was to brainstorm a list of the ways they learn something they really want to know at home. These strategies were put on a wall chart for student use as they went about their small group inquiries.

These experiences gave students the possible structures and strategies they could use in finding and investigating their own focused questions.

As the students moved into their small groups, they looked at their questions and talked about whether they wanted to make changes or additions. Junardi found that it was important that their questions be related to a broader theme or issue so they did not get so caught up in looking for specific information that they lost sight of bigger issues. She visited each group and asked them to think about what kind of theme or issue tied all of their questions together. The children came up with themes such as the interdependence of insects with other living things. As they went about their inquiry, they had a broad point of reference and did not focus too narrowly only on information.

We have struggled with the role of facts in children's inquiries. Children love to collect information and we now realize that wandering and wondering provides the opportunity they need to immerse themselves in exploring interesting facts, but not as their focus of inquiry. Our initial attempts at inquiry led to student research on topics that essentially involved the collection of pieces of information about animals or space but without any broader framework or purpose. Leslie Kahn's students first explored facts about weapons and death; it was only later that they began to ask the "why" questions that really made a difference in their lives. When students have time to explore and find their focused questions, they move from facts to questions that are significant in their lives.

Gaining New Perspectives: Inquiry Groups

As students move into focused inquiry, they need others to think with in order to explore their issues more deeply and intensely. Because we believe that it is through collaboration that students gain new perspectives and outgrow their current selves, we wanted to encourage students to form groups where they are pushed to consider new ideas and to explain their thinking to others. Many of the group processes and strategies which we discussed under Authors Circles and Literature Circles are needed to support student talk in these groups as well. Say Something, Save the Last Word for Me, Sketch to Stretch, and Written Conversation are not tied to literature but can be used to discuss an observation, a diagram, or an informational text.

We also know that students can gain new perspectives on their inquiries through using different sign systems to explore their questions and investigating across the perspectives of different knowledge systems. The learning environments that would support focused inquiry therefore need to facilitate collaboration and provide many different resources, materials, and tools from a range of sign systems and knowledge systems.

Taking on Knowledge System Perspectives

In the insect groups described above, scientific research strategies and tools were central resources for their inquiry. During their first meetings, Junardi asked them to look at their questions and make a list of what they would need to do to find out what they wanted to know, listing the materials they would need. The children and Junardi worked together in getting these materials. As children worked in their groups, Junardi continued to offer whole group demonstrations. Sometimes she talked about background information on insects that children needed, or she and the class did an experiment together or a class observation of a particular insect, and still other times she showed observational movies or read-aloud literature. In addition, she introduced scientific drawing so they could use this research strategy during their observations. She also encouraged the groups to meet together frequently for sharing so they could hear what other groups were doing and borrow strategies they could use in their own groups.

Literature played a peripheral role in the insect study. It was available as a resource and used for read-alouds, but the inquiry primarily involved the doing of science. When we first began working on inquiry, we realized that we were depending too much on literature instead of thinking through the kinds of strategies and tools that are used by researchers within knowledge systems. Kathy was a member of a group of teacher researchers who were looking at children's understandings of history and time (Crawford, Ferguson, Kauffman, Laird, Schroeder, & Short, 1994). Children in the five classrooms were examining different topics including families, change over time, space, culture, slavery, Arizona history, and events surrounding Christopher Columbus's "discovery" of America. When we shared some of what we were doing with an historian from Canada, Joan Irwin, her comment was that we were relying too much on historical fiction. While she valued these books and encouraged students to read them, she pointed out that sending students to the school library was bypassing the actual doing of history. She argued that historians base their work on primary sources and that we needed to immerse students in doing history, not just reading a fictional account that someone else had constructed from their own historical research. She encouraged us to involve students in community studies so they could take notes and interview informants as well as use primary sources such as newspapers and diaries. Her words made us rethink what we were doing in our classrooms.

Gloria Kauffman's fifth graders were pursuing a focus on slavery which grew from their study of Columbus. They had been reading only historical fiction. Gloria brought in diaries and books which included the oral and written accounts of actual slaves, adding them to text sets as well as reading them aloud. As children explored these primary sources, their questions and concerns changed; they became much more aware of the historical research process. They realized that authors bring a particular perspective to their writing which changes what they choose to write about history. Because of this experience, students asked about the research in other pieces of historical fiction and whether the author was really showing different people's perspectives.

Another way we can encourage children to take on different perspectives is to ask them to find a "fact" that is not true from the perspective of another knowledge system or sign system. We can't stop children from their interest in collecting lots of facts as part of their inquiry, but we can challenge their conception that facts are unchanging. The fifth graders inquiring about Columbus, for example, found that many historical "facts" about the encounter of Columbus with American Indians were misconceptions and myths when examined from American Indian perspectives instead of European perspectives.

Organizing to Support Student Questions

While the inquiry groups are connected by a class focus and students within these groups have related questions, there still needs to be room for students to ask their own questions within these structures. Sandy Kaser (1994) involved her students in a class focus on families and culture. While students were part of a wide range of small groups during this yearlong study, Sandy found through her teacher research that many children had specific cultural connections that they

> At first I wasn't going to believe it when Bill said that Columbus had slaves sent to Spain. I only knew that Columbus discovered America. I wrote a poem about Columbus being a good hero. Then I did my own research. I started to believe. When I found out it was true, I went with it. I was wrong.

Inquiry Group Discussion; Rudy, Age 11 (Gloria Kauffman's classroom)

Chapter Four
The Authoring Cycle as
Curricular Framework
for Inquiry

FIGURE 4.7
Family Story; Kinesha, Age 5
(Julie Laird's classroom)

My Dad

When my Dad and Mom brought me home from the hospital, my Dad would not put me down. My mom said that I was Daddy's little girl. My Dad would get up in the night to see if I was ok. He would also give me my bottle and change my diaper.

When I was older my Dad would help me plant flowers and let me water them. Sometimes I would water Dad too.

I am now 5 years old and my Dad and me still work together in the yard. I know my Dad loves me because he tells me when I'm a good girl and when I'm a bad girl. My dad still checks on me at night to make sure I have my covers on.

I love my Dad.

explored in each inquiry group. Each child had a particular aspect of culture that was most significant to them, and they used the different inquiries across the year to keep exploring those issues. Erwin was concerned about his ethnic heritage, Brian focused on his religious orientation, and Christina on issues of family life. Whether the focused study was on grandparents, cultural groups in Arizona, immigration, or biography, the openness of the group process supported these students in using the focus to explore their own questions.

When students shared their family stories and time lines, Sandy noted that some of their stories involved family members who were associated with various wars. Since fifth grade is traditionally American history (better known as the "year of the wars"), Sandy saw this as an opportunity to connect children's questions and interests to the school curriculum. The class focused on issues of conflict; students broke into various groups to research the different wars of American history.

In many classrooms, students break into inquiry groups within the class focus and so the small group inquiries can be supported through whole class experiences and sharing. Julie Laird found that many of her inquiry experiences with kindergarten children continued at the whole group level. Her students were very interested in how families change over time. Much of their inquiry occurred during class read-aloud discussions of picture books that were Family Stories and through gathering and orally sharing their own Family Stories and personal time lines. Their use of small groups tended to occur for a short period of time. For example, they might work and talk in small groups after a read-aloud and then come back to the whole group to share. She also created center invitations based on their inquiry that children could choose to do with others. Throughout these inquiries,

I want to know about...

1) How did the moon and sun get in the sky?
2) How did the tree grow money on it?
3) When did they start school?
4) What was it like when Columbus was not born yet?
5) What will it be like if we disoverd another planett?
What will it be like in the future?
What was it like when Mrs. S was little?

Miranda

children used historical research processes and tools to explore their questions.

Sometimes inquiry groups form around student questions that are only broadly related to each other. The students in Jean Schroeder's multi-age primary classroom spent the fall semester engaged in inquiries around the broad concept of discovery. They explored space, Columbus, and related Text Sets on topics such as ownership, living in harmony with nature, change over time, and cultural encounters. As they discussed and explored these sets, students kept lists of their questions and then revisited these in January to form inquiry groups. One group decided they wanted to know more about how discoveries

Chapter Four
The Authoring Cycle as
Curricular Framework
for Inquiry

occur in space, another group wanted to know who was the first person to discover bugs, and still another wanted to know what their teacher was like when she was a little girl. Two other groups investigated boatbuilding and the homes of American Indians at the time of Columbus. The final group wanted to know the locations of the seven seas.

These groups had to use many primary resources. For example, the group interested in Jean as a little girl wrote her relatives, interviewed Jean, looked at her scrapbooks and photograph albums, and browsed books she had read as a child. Even though these groups went in quite different directions, they had similar needs in terms of exploring primary sources and needing to know how to write letters and conduct interviews. They were also still connected to the class concept of discovery, and so Jean could provide support that cut across the groups.

For other students, the inquiry groups are based around Literature Circles. When Gloria Kauffman's fifth graders began asking questions about the rights of Blacks, women, children, and animals following their focused study on slavery, she put together shared book sets around the rights the students had identified. Each group read a book such as *Shiloh* (Naylor, 1991), *The Goats* (Cole, 1987), *A Circle Unbroken* (Hotze, 1991), and *One Eyed Cat* (Fox, 1984) and then met together to engage in dialogue about the book and the issue of rights. Their reading and discussion of these books gave them a context for continued inquiry on these issues. They went on to interview people and locate primary sources.

Beth Berghoff and Sue Hamilton used invitations to make resources available to first grade students during their inquiry (Berghoff, 1993). After journal writing and sharing time, students spent the morning in a work block. They met in literature, writing, or inquiry groups; wrote and read independently; and worked at invitations around the room. These invitations provided experiences and demonstrations on how they might further their inquiry. The invitations involved creating meaning in multiple sign systems through open-ended explorations of the class focus. For example, during an inquiry into Colonial America, children were invited to be museum curators, to make quilts and explore patterns, to read poetry and beat drums in rhythm to the poetry, to view portraits of the era and draw portraits of themselves and their friends, to tell math stories with Pilgrim cutouts on the flannel board, and to paint with dyes made from squash and berries. These invitations encouraged children to use a wider range of sign systems in their own inquiry and provided other possible connections and knowledge system perspectives that they could consider. These invitations were also designed to move students beyond traditional stereotypes of American Indians and Pilgrims.

Using Tools from Different Knowledge Systems

As students work on focused inquiries, one of their needs is to have ways of collecting and organizing ideas and data related to their questions and issues. They need places to think and reflect as well as places to preserve and organize ideas. One of the mistakes we have made is to rely too heavily on children writing in journals instead of taking a look at the tools that scientists and historians use in their investigations. Junardi Armstrong and Kathy Short found that students needed to use webs, charts, graphs, and diagrams to gather and share what they were learning about ecosystems. Beth Berghoff and Sue Hamilton found that time lines were an important historical tool in their study of Colonial America. The class constructed a time line for organizing and sharing new information; students also used time lines in their small group and individual inquiries.

We did not fully realize the importance of data collection tools until Kathleen Crawford's first and second graders taught us an important lesson. After several students went to San Diego over spring break, Kathleen's students initiated a classroom focus on the ocean, a fascinating topic for many students who had only experienced the desert. The students spent time browsing books and prints, watching films about ocean life, and looking at ocean specimens. As they observed and talked, they recorded their observations and questions on

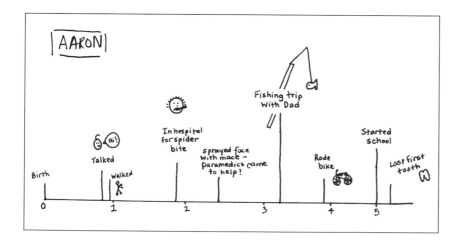

FIGURE 4.9
Personal Time Line; Aaron, Age 5 (Julie Laird's classroom)

Chapter Four
The Authoring Cycle as
Curricular Framework
for Inquiry

a chart. When Kathleen sensed that their questions were becoming more focused, she had them create a web of their most important questions. She and the students looked at the web and grouped questions together to form six groups. The students were excited and eager to begin their inquiries. Kathleen put together Text Sets for each group which included reference materials with many photographs and gave each group a journal where they could record what they were finding.

Within several days, the groups had lost their focus and seemed to be recording isolated information on their topic. Kathy and Kathleen observed each group, trying to see if they could figure out why the process had broken down. Kathy watched one group whose questions had focused on the differences between mollusks and jellyfish. They were writing down facts about these two ocean creatures in their journal, but the facts were completely mixed up because they were written in the order they found them.

As Kathy and Kathleen talked, they realized that the groups needed to develop organizational devices that helped them sort out what they were learning, and the journals were not playing that function. The next day, Kathleen sat down with each group and asked them what they were trying to find out and then helped them develop some type of chart or graph that they could use to record what they were finding. The mollusk and jellyfish group developed a Venn diagram where they could record what was distinctive about each and what was the same. The groups quickly re-immersed themselves successfully into their inquiries. They had literally become lost in a "sea of facts" and couldn't sort out what they were finding.

We have found that once students get to this point in the cycle, they usually take over the process as long as they have had time to find questions that are significant for them. Their questions and need-to-know drives them as learners. They quickly become involved in gathering the resources they need as a group to continue inquiry. These inquiry groups need time to really think through their questions and issues without being pressured to produce a product too quickly. At some point, however, they need to pull their experiences together to share with others.

Attending to Difference

Through their interactions with others in inquiry groups, children are constantly faced with perspectives and ideas that challenge their thinking. They come to understand their own perspectives through having to explain their thinking and to consider new perspectives through listening to the ideas of others in the group. They also encounter other perspectives through reading literature, interviewing informants, and exploring a wide range of primary sources. They feel tension as their understandings and ideas are challenged, and they need quiet reflective time to reconsider what they believe and understand related to their inquiry.

The inquiry groups are often a time of intense dialogue where many ideas and issues are raised. Students need a quiet time away from their group when they can think and consider those ideas. Having quiet time to sketch or write in their inquiry journals becomes an integral part of the inquiry process because it is during these quiet reflections that they are able to make the ideas their own. These reflections also support them in pulling together their ideas into some kind of unity to share with others through presentations.

Sharing What Was Learned: Inquiry Presentations

At some point, children need to go public with what they currently know and understand about their inquiry. While inquiry is a never ending process, students create new understandings through their investigations that satisfy their immediate desire to explore their original question. They are ready to move on to other topics and questions. Through their presentations, they pull their ideas together to present formally to others. These presentations reflect formal, but not final, drafts of their thinking about their inquiries. The process of pulling together their understandings allows them to figure out what they currently know and to move on to new questions and issues. Through presenting, they transform what they and others know.

Sometimes inquiry groups share informally with others, with each group describing their process of inquiry and what they came to understand. Other times, the inquiry groups spend time putting together a presentation for their classmates, parents, or others in the school. These presentations take many forms including Readers Theatres, skits, murals, pieces of writing, displays, songs, webs and charts, and experience centers. A group of sixth-grade boys in Kaylene Yoder's classroom had begun an inquiry on World War II excited about war and killing. As they read through a text set of books including *Rose Blanche* (Innocenti, 1985) and *Hiroshima No Pika*

(Maruki, 1980), their discussions suddenly grew quiet. They began to discuss the pain and suffering of war. Their presentation to the class was a skit about the pain of war and ended with an invitation for the class to talk about their perspectives on war. Students in Gloria's third-grade classroom spent time working in inquiry groups around topics such as soil erosion, plants, rocks, and glaciers as part of a class study and field trip to an environmental center. Their presentations were experience centers with demonstrations, experiments, diagrams, informational reports, and artifacts which required an active response from other class members.

Margaret Ferguson involves her students in a range of presentations to various audiences. Students present informally to their classmates on a continuous basis. About once a quarter, students pull together presentations on their inquiry studies for children in two other grade levels. The students in these classrooms also present to the first graders. Following these presentations, Margaret's students discuss and write evaluations of the presentations which they share with the other classrooms. In return, they also receive response on their own presentations. Twice a year, students put together a much more formal presentation for their families. These presentations occur in the evening and usually involve food provided by the parents that relates to the inquiry study. Students work hard on songs, skits, and other ways of presenting what they have learned in interesting ways. These presentations involve rehearsals and revisions which are not important when the presentations are more informal.

Through sharing and presenting, students are able to celebrate their new understandings. This sharing also provides learners with demonstrations about new topics and questions they might pursue and strategies they can use in their inquiry.

Planning New Inquiries

As students engage in inquiry, they need opportunities to reflect on what they know (content), how they come to know (process), and why they inquire (purpose and goals). The sharing and presentations provide an important context for taking a reflexive stance as inquirers on how they approach learning. They can go beyond the immediate experience to broader meanings for their life. Following the presentations, we have found it helpful to gather together several times as a class to talk about what was learned about the processes and tools of inquiry and which of these might be used in other contexts. We also talk about their new understandings and how those understandings relate to broader sociopolitical issues in their world as well as to their personal lives in their own communities. These reflections are both oral and written; the discussion can move into a Reflection Portfolio of who they are as learners. Portfolios on who they are as learners encourage students to move beyond just gathering written artifacts for their portfolio. They often bring objects from both school and home experiences, creating tags for their self-reflections by using large Post-it notes. Through these reflections, students are able to examine their purposes as inquirers and establish goals for where they want to go next.

Margaret Ferguson's first graders keep an Inquiry Journal during a particular class focus. The journal has a pocket where they can keep maps and other materials that are part of their research. At the end of the class focus, they look through their activities, pictures, webs, questions, and written entries. They then put together a portfolio in which they select the items they consider the most significant from their inquiry and write a reflection about their learning.

In addition to these reflections at a broader level, strategy lessons on research strategies they need as inquirers are also important. Strategy lessons on conducting an interview, taking notes during an observation or interview, reading and understanding informational materials, or using time lines, graphs, and charts to record data are all possibilities, depending on student needs. In two fifth-grade classrooms, students were using many informational books as part of their inquiries about conflict and war. They were having difficulty understanding these materials and so Kathy talked to them about their strategies as readers. She realized that they thought that they could not predict, question, or make personal connections as they did with fiction because informational books are about "real" facts. Over the next few weeks, the teachers taught short lessons on strategies for reading informational materials, including the ways in which these materials are organized.

In another classroom, students needed to know the tools that historians use to record data and so we gathered many informational books written by historians and looked through them to see what kinds of diagrams, charts, or time lines were being used. Whenever a child found a new tool, we made a photocopy of the tool and put it on a chart, listing how and why it was used. This list was extensively used by students as they went about their inquiry.

> "We have independence here. We get to figure out what we know, what we want, too. We are trusted to learn, to talk, and to share. We are expected to ask more questions and to find out more."
>
> **Amber, Age 11 (Gloria Kauffman's classroom)**

Another type of strategy lesson occurred when first graders were researching particular animals as part of an annual field trip to the zoo. They needed ways of organizing the data they were finding through books and their observational notes from the zoo trip. Using a variation of Generating Written Discourse, the class created their own chart where they could record the sources on one side of the chart, their questions and categories on the other side; they then filled in their information in the boxes. When they began to write about their research, the information and ideas they had located were already organized.

Taking Thoughtful New Action

The inquiry cycle is a never ending process. We have found that as one set of inquiries come together through presentations and reflection, a sense of direction on where to go next emerges. Students always end a particular inquiry experience with new questions about the topic they have been pursuing. Sometimes these questions become the basis of the new inquiry focus as a class, but other times the class is ready to move on to a new focus. If individual children want to continue with the old focus, they are encouraged to do so during their personal inquiry time.

Pursuing Individual Inquiries

We believe in having a class focus because of the depth of inquiry that is possible when students think together and teachers create rich supportive contexts for shared inquiry. However, we also know that students have personal agendas and inquiries that they need to pursue. One of the purposes we see for maintaining a work time when students engage in their own choice of reading and writing experiences is that they can use this time to pursue their personal inquiries. We do not take over uninterrupted writing and wide reading with the class focus. Students can choose to bring that focus into their work time, but they do not have to do so. While the Literature Circles usually relate to the class focus, wide reading remains a time when students have a broad choice of reading materials. Occasionally, the writing time involves working on the class focus, but the majority of the time students choose their own topics and uses of writing.

Initially we saw uninterrupted reading and writing as the time of the day when students focus on language itself by engaging in the process and using those engagements to learn about language and how it functions. When we looked closely at what students were reading and writing, however, we realized that they were pursuing their own personal agenda through what they chose to read and write. Some were working through family or peer issues while others were pursuing information on favorite artists or snakes or dinosaurs. By maintaining the open-ended nature of work time, teachers can support children's explorations of "kid topics." While teachers may feel that pursuing these topics is not productive for a whole class focus, children still need the opportunity to pursue personal interests in the classroom. As teachers, we see our role as both supporting and pushing children as learners. The uninterrupted reading and writing time supports children's interests while the class focus challenges them to consider new perspectives and issues.

We have also come to believe, however, that this work time needs to become a studio where students can explore their personal inquiries through a range of sign systems. Art is probably the easiest system to add to a workshop time so that students can use both art and writing to create stories and meaning. Gloria Kauffman and Richard Foster schedule a studio time every Friday morning. During studio, children can use any sign system—art, music, drama, language, and mathematics—to create meaning. The studio runs for the entire morning to give children a large chunk of time. The two teachers open the wall between their rooms and children flow back and forth between the rooms. Studio begins with the two classes gathering for a group meeting where Gloria and Richard ask them what their goals are for the morning and do a quick status check on who is moving to what areas in the classrooms. The check-in is accomplished quickly because children fill out a planning sheet on Thursday so they are ready to use their time well on Friday morning. Areas with tools for the different sign systems have been established. Children often have ongoing projects that they work on every Friday morning. Halfway through the morning, the group meets for sharing; several children or groups share what they are working on and then go back to studio until the end of the morning, when they again gather for sharing. They end the morning by writing about what they accomplished on their planning sheets.

Sometimes the invitations which come out of a particular inquiry lead to the entire class pursuing individual and small group inquiries, rather than a class focus. We used to believe that teachers

"I want to learn more about snakes. How they move, where are their tongues, where do they spit out the poison?"

Inquiry Question; Jason, Age 10 (Joe Turner and Chris Collier's classroom)

Chapter Four
The Authoring Cycle as
Curricular Framework
for Inquiry

Why don't they have
color comics on
weekdays?

The invasion of Haiti; why
did they invade Haiti?

When was the first pizza
made?

Abortion; what do other
people think about it?

**Inquiry Questions (Rise
Paynter's fourth/fifth-grade
classroom)**

should schedule expert projects at least twice a year where students could pursue any topic they chose. The problem we ran into was that these expert projects often seemed more like our old units; students chose a topic, then collected facts and information, without any real sense of broader issues or questions to drive their inquiry. Instead of assuming that these expert projects need to be scheduled, we listen to our students. Sometimes, as they share and present their inquiries, it becomes obvious that their new questions are extremely diverse, and it is important for children to pursue individual questions. At that point, we encourage them to move into small group and individual inquiries, rather than moving into a class focus right away.

Rise Paynter and Joby Copenhaver used a different organizational strategy, Explorers Club, with a class of fifth graders (Copenhaver, 1992). Students in this classroom knew that after each class-focused study, they would be given time to work in Explorers Clubs on their own questions. They collected these questions using their Wonderful Questions Journals. Each time they moved into Explorers Club, they spent time sharing their questions and the reasons they found these questions important using Save the Last Word for Me. Children could choose to work together on similar questions or pursue individual questions. The materials needed for each topic were collected in crates by teachers and students. Each crate contained books, tapes, and computer printouts from the library as well as books, photographs, newspaper clippings, magazine articles, and artifacts from home. Students were supported in their research through strategies they learned in class-focused studies.

As students completed their research, they were encouraged to share their work using bulletin board displays, graphs, photographs, skits, video, and overheads. Each member of the audience responded to these presentations with a form on which they listed three plusses and a wish. The presenters also filled out the same form as a self-evaluation. In addition, students wrote reflections on what surprised them about Explorers Club and what they would do differently the next time. Explorers Club was a structure they could use to find and pursue personally important questions. Because they knew they would have another Explorers Club in four to five weeks, they immediately begin thinking about and searching for personal questions they might want to pursue.

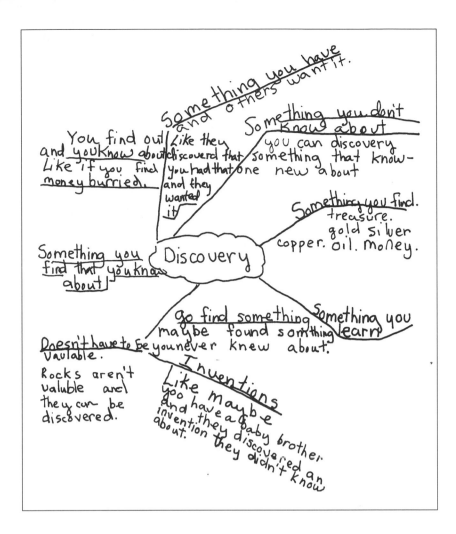

FIGURE 4.10
Discovery Web; Tara, Age 11
(Gloria Kauffman's classroom)

Weaving Inquiries Together Through an Umbrella Concept

The use of broad umbrella concepts that weave across the year is another curricular structure that facilitates the movement from one inquiry to another. Along with other teacher researchers in Tucson, Kathy has found it helpful to use a broad umbrella concept such as change, cycles, systems, and a sense of place as a thread or touchstone that weaves in and out of class and individual inquiries across the year. Their interest in umbrella concepts came from feeling that each focused study was a separate entity and, while the inquiry within a particular focused study was powerful, students did not necessarily make connections across the different focused studies, nor did the studies flow into one another. They wanted to establish an environment

Chapter Four
The Authoring Cycle as
Curricular Framework
for Inquiry

where students expected connection, but without forcing or restricting those connections.

The definition of a good broad umbrella concept is one under which a class can study virtually anything; the topics for focused studies are not restricted and can be negotiated with students. The broad concept gives a sense of continuity, connection, and focus to the different inquiries that are pursued throughout the year. Therefore, the inquiry never ends, but flows from one point to another.

Leslie Kahn used the concept of cycles to connect her students' experiences across the school year. She introduced the concept at the beginning of the year by having her students explore cycles in their everyday lives, looking at various cycles in nature, and focusing on cycles in poetry. Through these initial experiences students developed an understanding of the concept of cycles which they put on a large web on the wall. Throughout the year, as they moved through different focused studies as a class, the concept of cycles was woven through their conversations and experiences. The connections to cycles were not the major focus nor were they taught as a lesson. The connections were simply mentioned and explored at various points throughout the year.

Using broad umbrella concepts supports teachers in planning-to-plan before school begins. It helps teachers brainstorm possible focused studies, engagements, materials, and Text Sets. This thinking allows teachers to be more flexible when actually planning with students and makes teachers aware of possibilities they can suggest to students. While teachers choose the broad concept, each class defines it in a way that makes sense to them. When a group of teachers used the concept of discovery to connect inquiry across the year, each class defined the concept in ways that made sense to them (Crawford, Ferguson, Kauffman, Laird, Schroeder, & Short, 1994). Several classes defined discovery as change over time, another as history and time, and two other classes focused on culture and perspective.

The broad umbrella concept gives a sense of connection across the year and supports movement from one class focus to the next as well as between the class focus and individual inquiries. Students begin to expect connection across the school day and year as well as between home and school. This expectation of connection continually opens up new invitations for inquiry and thoughtful new actions.

The broad focus also provides a way to begin the year and to think together about possible topics of study. Asking students to brainstorm the topics they want to study that year during the first week of school does not provide a context for thoughtful consideration. Students have not had time to explore and really think through the issues and questions that are important to them. Instead, Kathy and other teacher researchers are exploring beginning the year with a concept such as change, by involving students in exploring changes in their home and school contexts during the first several weeks of school. These initial engagements are designed to connect them closely to their past experiences in their families and community, using free writes, sketches, oral sharing, and brainstorming. For example, the class might focus on moving through discussing their own moving experiences as a family or as a student. Personal and family time lines can help them examine changes in their lives. They might talk about issues of moving into a new classroom and working with a new set of classmates and teacher. They also usually meet in some type of Literature Circles with books that explore different aspects of moving. Through these initial engagements, students develop a sense of community in the classroom.

Based on this initial focus, the class creates a concept web which reflects their current understandings about change. To broaden their understandings of change and to begin thinking about possible topics that might be the focus of class inquiries, teachers place experience centers, observation centers, and Text Sets in the classroom to encourage students to explore change as broadly as possible. The ideas for these centers come from teachers thinking about all of the possible topics that might be pursued and from listening to students' interests and issues as they explore change. They are often put together by going through old units and files to pull out activities that reflect these different topics. The goal is to encourage students to think as broadly as possible about topics they could explore. Students have a week to engage in these centers and share their ideas. Through this process, the class adds to their web about the concept of change; they also create webs of possible topics of study and questions that concern students. From these webs of possibilities the first class focus of study is chosen through class negotiation and discussion.

When Gloria Kauffman's multi-age primary students began exploring systems, she first engaged them in a mini-unit on batteries and electrical systems, then encouraged them to think about the concept of systems. The class went on to look at family systems, mechanical systems, body systems, and environmental systems through science centers and text sets. From their explorations and discussions of different kinds of systems, a focus on economic systems and being a consumer emerged as the class focus.

As students share, listen, and reflect, new potentials for taking action are created. One of the mistakes we have made is to assume that children are finished with an inquiry when they give a presentation and that they are ready to go on to another focus and set of questions. Instead we are beginning to encourage students to present and reflect on what they have learned with the expectation that they will take action in their lives and the world based on their new understandings. An inquiry on racism or pollution that ends with presentation and reflection may raise student awareness and acceptance of difference. It won't, however, lead to real change in how students act in the world if we don't challenge students to consider what kinds of action they now want to take based on their inquiries. We must then give them time to take that action. Sometimes action involves rethinking perspectives, but many times that action is an actual project in which students become involved on an individual or class basis. Our current inquiry is on how we can create structures in the classroom that support students in this move to thoughtful action that will go beyond the classroom door.

Exploring the Role of Sign Systems within Inquiry

As we have explored curriculum as inquiry, one of the major questions that has emerged has been the role of sign systems within inquiry. In our early work, we fell into the trap of studying sign systems separately from inquiry in much the same way that schools had previously asked students to read and write without having a purpose that made sense to them. Students use sign systems to create and share meaning about something; that something comes from knowledge systems and from personal and social knowing. The sign systems are not meant to be studied in isolation, but in relation to inquiry topics. We became aware of this misconception as we talked through Jerry's experiences in teaching a course on sign systems.

A Study of Sign Systems

Jean Anne Clyde and Jerry organized a graduate course to explore how teachers might set up environments in their classrooms to support a multiple ways-of-knowing curriculum. They became interested in offering this course after observing that sign systems were being used, but never explored in-depth by children in theme-based inquiry classrooms. From their work with teachers they decided that while the use of sign systems was interesting, few children walked away with a real sense of what it felt like to make meaning about the world from the perspective of an artist, a musician, a mathematician, and so forth. In an effort to explore other alternatives, Jean Anne and Jerry developed this course. They invited teachers who already understood process reading and writing and, rather than just talk about literacy as a multimodal event, explored what such a curriculum might look like in classrooms. Teacher-researcher teams—full time graduate students and classroom teachers—were paired for purposes of data collection and in-depth data analysis. This course was a serious attempt to understand and explore a multiple ways-of-knowing curriculum.

The course met full days for six Saturdays. Because participants came from both Bloomington, Indiana, and Louisville, Kentucky, the course met in Columbus, Indiana—about an hour's drive for all fifty people involved. Educators had to be both dedicated and extremely interested to enroll in this course.

Jean Anne and Jerry had planned each session so that full days were spent exploring a particular sign system. On "music day," for example, each participant was responsible for developing a curricular invitation that would support children in a hands-on understanding of some important dimension of music. The curricular invitations were set up and actually explored by the course participants. Participants didn't just browse the invitations, they had to actually do the invitations during Exploring Time. This was a lived-through curriculum. No observers allowed.

At each session Jean Anne and Jerry planned a whole class activity. Ray Levi from Shaker Heights, Ohio, was both the guest speaker and the experience for music. He led the group through a series of rounds in which everyone moved to feel the rhythm. They then created their own "map" of the song in mathematics by using Cuisenaire Rods to represent the underlying structure in the music. Through these experiences, the group began to sense what it meant to create meaning as a musician. In the afternoon he shared the curriculum he had developed for his classroom using the authoring cycle as a metaphor for conceptualizing music as a composing process. His students created musical pieces, which they took to Authors Circles and later published. He had spent the year in his own first grade class-room exploring what music and art as ways-of-knowing might look like as a curriculum.

The days were packed. The class spent an hour critiquing the curricular invitations that had been brought in. They took another hour in Literature Groups discussing the professional reading. In a third hour they looked at videotapes of children engaged in various curricular activities highlighting the sign system of the day and spent time thinking through possible ways to analyze data of this type.

During one sharing time, Vicki Bumann, an ungraded primary teacher from Louisville, and Darlene Horton, a graduate student from Louisville, told about the data they had collected from an engagement they had incorporated into Vicki's program. They got the idea for this engagement by reading the text for the course, Dan Kirby and Carol Kuykendall's book *Mind Matters* (1991). One of their course assignments was to create a series of at least three curricular engagements that would support children in thinking in some other sign system. They had decided to explore thinking like an inventor. While inventing is not a sign system, they had rationalized after reading Howard Gardner's *Multiple Intelligences* (1993), the other course text, that inventing would support visual and mathematical literacy.

Rather than talk in generalities they shared their curriculum by telling the story of Victor, a second grade Chapter I student. They had introduced their curriculum by inviting a local inventor into the class to share his inventions and talk about what it meant to "think like an inventor." His advice was that they identify recurring problems they were having and check with friends to get other ideas. Then he suggested they assume other people had the same problem, focus on that problem, and brainstorm with others as to how it might be solved.

Vicki and Darlene had prepared Inventor Notebooks for the children in which they could record information they collected and sketch possible inventions. Victor had done everything the inventor suggested. He had first written a list of his problems, he then checked with his teacher and his mother to see what they thought his problems were, and finally decided on a topic.

The problem that Victor chose was personal and very real. He kept losing his pencil; this was driving him and his teachers nuts. Together with the members of his family he had brainstormed ideas for how to solve the problem and came up with the solution of using two pieces of Velcro. One piece he wrapped around the top of his pencil, the other piece he stuck to his desk. At the time of the sharing, Victor had not lost his pencil for over a week.

Vicki and Darlene reported that several other children in the class decided they wanted Victor's invention. Victor's solution was to begin to sell his invention to others for twenty-five cents. Further, because of his success, other children began to see him as a marketing expert and consulted with him as to whether their inventions were worth marketing.

Victor had not been a very popular child in class and was not a proficient user of written language. To some degree he had always been perceived as an outsider. Within one week, given this set of curricular invitations, he had begun to gain a new identity for himself in the class by using visual and mathematical literacy to think about inventions. Vicki, Darlene, and his Chapter I teacher couldn't believe the change they noted in Victor and his attitude toward school.

The last full day of the course was devoted to presentations. It was only then that Jean Anne's and Jerry's enthusiasm began to fade. For the most part, the teacher-reseacher pairs had created a series of activities that were loosely related. Although the activites had been enjoyed by teachers and students, they didn't go anywhere. It was as if the engagements teachers had developed had been dropped into the curriculum from the sky. There was little evidence that music, art, mathematics, or movement had become a way of knowing that significantly affected the life space of the children or the classroom.

This is not to say that the course was not an enjoyable experience. Everyone had fun, the teachers, the children, Jean Anne and Jerry. The problem was this wasn't curriculum. To plan a curriculum focusing directly on the sign systems themselves didn't seem to work. This was play, probably, but no functional context had been set. Students engaged in the planned activities but with no intent. It was as if students were invited to explore sign systems like teachers used to invite children to study English grammar because "it would be good for them."

Jean Anne and Jerry met for several debriefing sessions to retrace the lived-through experience of the class by looking through the artifacts they had collected and the student self-evaluation reports that had been written. They also talked with other colleagues and finally decided they had the right intent, but they had failed to frame the course properly.

Sign Systems within an Inquiry Focus

Jerry had already agreed to repeat the course in Hawaii the following summer because he thought he had a curriculum structure, but now he knew he had to rethink that structure. Learning from his mistakes, Jerry reconceptualized the course in terms of inquiry. He framed the course around the theme of Hawaii knowing that all teachers in Hawaii are required to teach something about Hawaiian culture to their children each year.

The course began by inviting participants, some thirty-eight Hawaiian elementary teachers, to take a moment to write about their relationship to Hawaii—how they got there, what aspects of Hawaii were significant to them. Specifically they were asked to think of a story that would "show, not tell" what Hawaii meant to them at a most heartfelt level.

The teachers wrote for about thirty minutes, then shared what they had written with the class. As they shared Jerry webbed the various relationships represented. Charlotte Yuen shared a story about being a little girl at the bombing of Pearl Harbor. In her story she related how she and her friends loved the war and all of the games they played using discarded gas masks and shell casings. Few class members had ever thought of WWII as having been "fun." Jan Kihl talked about her family's involvement in the fishing industry. Hers was a sad story of tragedy and loss of many near and dear family members. As each participant told their story, the web became more and more complex. The number of aspects of Hawaiian life covered was incredible. It was much different from any state department curriculum guide on the teaching of Hawaii and its culture.

Using Carolyn Burke's model of sign systems, Jerry invited the group to explore first among themselves and then as a whole group what it was they thought Carolyn was trying to say with this model. As a group they decided that the model said two things. One, that each and every sign system contributes something unique to the making and sharing of meaning. Two, that every instance of making and sharing meaning is a multimodal event involving many sign systems in addition to language.

The group talked about sign systems as ways of viewing the world and shared what they thought it would mean to make meaning like a musician, an artist, or a mathematician. That evening Jerry asked each participant to think about their relationship to Hawaii in terms of a sign system of their choosing. "What would your relationship to

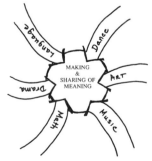

The Role of Sign Systems in the Making and Sharing of Meaning (Burke, 1991)

Section One
The Authoring Cycle:
Let's Talk Curriculum

Hawaii look like if represented in some sign system other than language?" There was only one catch, they had to do more than think about it; they had to bring in an actual artifact. For example, if art was the sign system chosen, their job was to find a picture that reflected or in some way captured some dimension of the relationship to Hawaii they had written about in the opening activity. Then they were to actually bring it to class. Jerry also reminded them that their "Relationship to Hawaii" stories were going to be published and that they would have their first Authors Circle the next day.

The course had been designed as a one-week intensive, meeting from 8 a.m. to 2 p.m. each day. The word *intensive* had not been used casually in the course title and Jerry warned teachers that they should drop any other plans for the week. He suggested that they might just tell any family members whom they were responsible for feeding that this would be a good week to get reacquainted with the fast food world. Jerry knew what he had planned was going to take every minute of their waking day.

The next day Jerry declared the classroom—a library at one of the local elementary schools—to be a museum. He invited teachers to work in small groups to arrange the artifacts they had brought by looking for relationships among them. After the museum had been set up, the class spent an hour or so exploring each area, discussing artifacts, listening to music, contemplating pieces of art, and watching videotapes of dances.

Participants were then asked to sit at the table in the area where their artifact had been placed thus forming groups who had similar interests. To begin to encourage them to collaborate, Jerry announced that their first task was to have an Authors Circle on the drafts of the stories that had been written the day before.

After Authors Circle, the whole class met and Jerry introduced another model which Carolyn Burke had drawn to illustrate the role that knowledge systems play in learning. Participants again first discussed among themselves what they thought the model was trying to say and then pulled back together to share with the whole group.

During this sharing time the class talked about how each knowledge system represented a particular perspective on the world and was governed by a particular focusing question. Ecology's view of the world was people in relationship to nature; geology's view of the world was its mineral composition, and so on. They also talked about tools, and how each knowledge system had developed its own tools to

The Role of Knowledge Systems in Taking Alternate Perspectives on the World

Chapter Four
The Authoring Cycle as
Curricular Framework
for Inquiry

293

enhance the kinds of observations it wished to make. While the tools that each knowledge system use enhance the observations, they also limit, if not predetermine, what becomes known. Different tools provide different data and hence different information. Tools are both an aid and a restriction. The session ended with teachers predicting what it would mean to think like a historian, a geologist, an anthropologist, and so forth. They also discussed at some length the different kinds of information one might get in an interview with a working geologist. They then considered asking those same questions to someone who taught students how to be a geologist.

The teachers were asked to do a tremendous amount of work that evening. Using the camera as a tool, they were to take pictures of "their relationship to Hawaii" from the perspective of twenty-four different knowledge systems. If their topic was fishing, then they were to explore fishing from twenty-four different perspectives such as an historian, economist, anthropologist, or lawyer, taking a picture of the dimension of fishing in which they thought someone from a particular knowledge system would be interested.

They were also asked to find and interview, face-to-face if at all possible (by telephone if it was not), an expert from any one of the disciplines. Specifically they were to explore what it meant to think in this knowledge system, taking field notes as to what kinds of data and observations were of particular interest to this expert. In addition, they were to collect a sample of some functional tool that the expert used in his or her work and, if possible, bring it to class the next day. As a parting shot, Jerry reminded participants that they would be having Editors Table: any revisions they were going to make on their Relationship to Hawaii pieces had to be completed that evening. Probably they could do these revisions, Jerry suggested, while they were getting their photographs developed at one-hour photography shops.

The next morning, on the third day, the participants came in tired but excited. They began in small groups sharing the pictures and interview data they had collected. The talk was animated and the participants engrossed. Charlene Yuen shared how she had interviewed the naturalist at the Arizona War Memorial. She had discovered a book written by another person who lived through this event. Interestingly, the book was written from the perspective of an eight-year-old child. Tears welled up in the eyes of the participants in her small group as she read the book to them. They could experience for themselves the powerful personal connections she was making. Buoyed by their interest and sensitivity, she told how the naturalist had informed her of an oral history project going on across the island in which persons who lived through the war were invited to tell their stories. She had the address and, in addition to all her other work that evening, she had driven across the island to tell her story. She was excited and shared everything she still hoped to do relative to this inquiry.

Jan Kihl had gone to the local fish market only to find that fish that had been found "full of mercury" by the local paper were still being sold over the counter. Fishermen had been told not to handle these fish for fear of ciguatera poisoning, but they were still being sold to unsuspecting customers. She drafted a petition which every class member signed after listening to her story and the sense of urgency that she conveyed.

In the afternoon participants laid out the photographs they had taken in clusters representing what they saw as particularly insightful perspectives for understanding the dimension of Hawaii their group was exploring. They did not have to use all the photographs that were taken. The only requirement was that at least six of every person's photographs were to be used. Participants were asked not to label their clusters. Instead, class members circulated around the room trying to discover the organizational framework that each group had used. Sharing conclusions was both entertaining and generative. Some of the predictions were better than the initial frameworks.

The last hour of the day was spent in a quick Editors Table and engaging in invitations. Jerry had brought twenty curricular invitations that asked participants to experience firsthand what it meant to think in a sign system or knowledge system. These invitations included engagements such as finding a piece of poetry, adding music to it, and then reflecting on how the meaning expands. Another invitation was to read a book and think about what it means; then participants were to make a symbolic representation of that meaning through music, paint, or clay. There was no particular content theme to these invitations, which in retrospect was a mistake. This would have been a more powerful demonstration had all of the invitations explored a particular topic from the perspective of various sign systems and knowledge systems.

The assignment for the evening was to develop a curricular invitation that would allow others to explore particularly important perspectives for understanding the relationship each person had to Hawaii. Invitations were to be of the type Jerry had brought in and were to be developed with directions so that class members could actually do them in class.

This phase of the course ended with a Curriculum Fair the next morning. Participants set up their invitations, and the morning was spent working through them. One invitation invited participants to listen to slack-key guitar and record the emotions it evoked in art; another invited participants to do Japanese floral arrangement by studying the plant, using its natural lines and its role in nature; still another invited participants to study the ruins of a war and reconstruct what must have happened. The Fair ended with a discussion of the invitations. In the process, a set of working criteria for planning curricular invitations in classrooms was developed.

The rest of the course was just as hectic. During the final day and a half participants worked in groups, identified a theme they wished to pursue with their class for the next year, and walked their way through a planning-to-plan document that essentially replicated the perspectives they had taken in exploring their "Relationship to Hawaii" inquiry projects. As a final culminating activity participants brought a curricular invitation to class on their new theme. In this fashion they introduced others to what it was they were thinking about doing in their classrooms. The class ended by reading aloud favorite "Relationship to Hawaii" pieces from the magazine the class had published.

The course was a tremendous experience for everyone. Student self-evaluation reports confirmed that every teacher in the group was planning to try a multiple ways-of-knowing inquiry curriculum next year with their children. Jerry was later able to check with these teachers and found that for the most part they all did try. Some had more success than others, but all were willing to try again.

By comparing these two courses, we learned the importance of embedding sign systems within inquiry. When isolated and explored on their own, the functionality of the systems is lost. Within the context of inquiry, sign systems serve an important role in expanding, more fully appreciating, and understanding a concept. In this context they aren't just frills, but tools for gaining new perspectives on our world. Although the participants in each course enjoyed their experiences, in the second course a new future for education was created and the power of a multiple ways-of-knowing inquiry curriculum versus an activity curriculum was demonstrated.

Conclusion

This chapter represents our latest thinking about curriculum as inquiry. It discusses the ways in which curricular engagements build from each other and are chained conceptually to create something new that goes beyond the effect of the individual engagements. As we wrote this chapter, there were several points that became significant to us as we thought about what it really means to view curriculum as inquiry. The first is that the core of curriculum as inquiry is personal and social knowing. This means that as teachers we must begin curriculum by listening, not by teaching.

Second, it means that others play a key role. A conducive environment for inquiry is collaborative. Our focus as teachers is not on the kinds of information we need to teach, but on offering students new perspectives on a particular theme or topic through sign systems, knowledge systems, and talk with others. Teachers find this a relief. Instead of trying to teach children everything they need to know to explore a theme, their focus is on creating an environment that offers children multiple perspectives on a topic, then giving them enough time to "wander and wonder" their way into inquiry. Teachers also need to be concerned with creating physical and social structures that encourage talk and interaction among students. This allows students to go beyond working together to thinking with each other in new ways.

A third key insight is the importance of experiencing inquiry ourselves as teachers. Once we had experienced writing in a collaborative writing group, we couldn't go back to teaching writing the old way. We've found the same to be true about inquiry. There is something magical about being caught up in your own inquiry and experiencing first-hand what it feels like to be a real learner. We can't emphasize this enough. Not only will your experience as an inquirer change your teaching, but refectively you will become part of a larger thought collective of educators who are exploring the potential of curriculum as inquiry. Margaret Brown experienced this change as a teacher and a person during a graduate course. She reflected, "This is the first time it ever occurred to me that my agenda for teaching and learning were valid. Before I always accepted everyone else's agenda—my administrator's or my professor's. Now I realize I have a right to my agenda, and I don't want to go back."

We use the theme of invitation to close this book. In the article which follows, Kathy Egawa, working with colleagues, demonstrates what it means to be a teacher-researcher using inquiry to improve teaching and learning. Chapter 5, "Maintaining a Community of Inquirers," takes our current conception of the authoring cycle and elaborates our thinking about each phase. There is always a gap between theory and practice. In some cases practice is ahead of theory; in others, theory is ahead of practice. Difference in thinking and teaching, not sameness, is your invitation to inquire and enter into conversation. We are not trying to standardize teaching and thinking, but to explore the differences and points of tension. One of the reassuring things about curriculum as collaborative inquiry is that you never have to work alone again.

The only thing that bothers us about this chapter is that it is possible for readers to walk away thinking that curriculum as inquiry is an alternative to theme cycles or units of study rather than a philosophy that permeates the entire school day. In reality, everything is inquiry—from discipline problems, to classroom organization, to reading and writing, you name it. We will explore the pervasiveness of this perspective in Chapter 5 when we attempt to answer some common concerns and questions about an inquiry curriculum and to expand our conceptions of curriculum as inquiry.

Allen- Age 9   9-22

What makes a question a good question

1. It will mak you think of other questions.
2. A good question is hard to figure out.
3. Can't just go to one place and look it up.
4. should take you far in your learning.
5. It should be something you really don't know
6. Something you really want to know.
7. It should be challenging
8. It should be something a real desire to know.
9. Something your willing to put effort into.
10. It should be something you should be able to ask others about and find a peace later.
11. Cause you to think.

Chapter Four
The Authoring Cycle as
Curricular Framework
for Inquiry

■ Kathy Egawa's educational inquiry focuses on the questions that absorb each of us as learners. She currently works with educators, parents, and a multi-age classroom of first, second, and third graders in the Seattle, Washington area. These contexts lead her to co-explore such issues as: How do microwaves make food hot and how do all those numbers work? Shouldn't we be concerned that Nicole reverses her numbers? How do I get kids to come to literature discussion groups with something significant to say? and How can educators sustain significant, theoretically-driven change in schools? This chapter chronicles part of her dissertation research with a group of colleagues in Gosport, Indiana.

When Teachers and Parents Inquire

KATHY EGAWA

with Judy Best, Debbie Edwards, Pam Hanscom, and Debbie Kavanaugh

Recently I was in the school workroom tracing children's illustrations so that I could photocopy them for a kindergarten class project. Steven was sitting in the same room as punishment for hurting another child. He soon launched into a series of questions: "Who drew that picture? Who drew that other picture? How does that machine make copies?" Without looking up, I finally remarked, "You sure have a lot of questions, don't you?" His response first made me chuckle— "That's what I think I was made for"—and then I wrote his thought down. In fact, that's exactly what I think Steven was "made for."

Although this chapter focuses on the inquiry of teachers and parents, a major function of schooling is to support *all* learners in the exploration of their own compelling questions. Steven's questions about how a copy machine works are a reminder that the potential for inquiry topics is almost limitless.

The project described here began with my commitment to work alongside several teachers who were asking questions about their teaching (Egawa, 1995). I wanted to better understand the impact of inquiry-based professional development, a purposeful, theoretically driven pursuit. The intent was to unpack the complexity and tensions involved when a group of educators inquired together rather than to simply answer or solve particular questions.

In this chapter we will define "teaching as inquiry," share several instances of how our teacher collaborative "got better at what we were doing" through inquiry, and contrast this process with alternate models of professional development.

Defining Teaching as Inquiry

Teaching as inquiry begins with the issues arising out of teachers' daily lives in classrooms and the belief that pursuing one's own concerns is essential to the work of all learners. Simply, there is no other place to begin. With that idea as a starting point, professional inquiry is defined as a personal intent "to learn deliberately" or "to do self-consciously what comes naturally" (Boomer, 1987).

Of course learning occurs all around us: skateboarders learn to "rock and roll," prospective parents learn what to expect when the baby is born, and teachers learn how to live together with students in crowded spaces. Likewise, some students learn how to "give the teacher what she wants" or how to do enough to "get by"; some teachers learn to "shut the door." There is no shortage of deliberate learning.

The distinction that pushes learning to inquiry is a melding of intentional learning and reflection on that learning in such a way that new action is a likely result. Explicit connections to one's own theory of learning are integral to the reflective process. This definition acknowledges that each of us operates from a theory of learning, implicitly or explicitly, that drives the instructional decisions we make (Watson, Burke, & Harste, 1989). Teaching as inquiry, then, is at the heart of teachers' current knowledge and beliefs as they translate their beliefs into action and then reflect on the results of that action.

As our work together began, I represented the process in Figure TA4.1, shown on the next page.

Beginning the Process of Purposeful Learning

Our involvement with inquiry began as the teachers "put me to work" in their classrooms. Because their school was in the midst of a restructuring effort and had set aside business-as-usual, each teacher was grappling with a number of immediate issues: narrative reports, multi-age groupings, and theme-based curriculum were among them. After several weeks of working together, we began to specifically discuss and write down the most pressing questions:

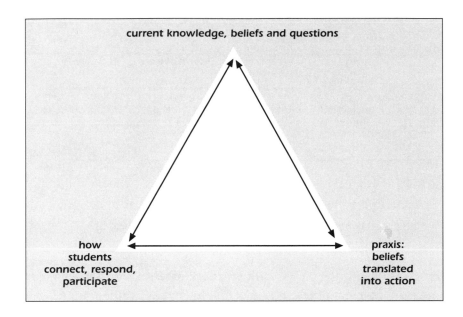

current knowledge, beliefs and questions

how
students
connect, respond,
participate

praxis:
beliefs
translated
into action

- How do I evaluate without giving a negative sense of the process? Who is evaluation really for?
- I'd feel more comfortable [with evaluating students] if I really knew what I was looking for and I could express that to parents. I just want to be credible to the parents. Or, I guess I just really want to be credible to myself. How can I do that?
- How can I teach math better—more holistically?
- How can I set up my half classroom? How can I physically set up the classroom, and how can I schedule our day so that I can implement my beliefs about learning?
- Some kids don't recognize the alphabet letters by name. I need to teach them, don't I?

Over the next sixteen months we engaged in collaborative inquiry as we explored our collective interests and questions. In our work together, we became involved in six major areas of inquiry. Figure TA4.2 lists those six areas and the specific engagements we developed through our work together. From the numerous activities, we will discuss two instances of our learning here: Working with Parents and Creating Narrative Reporting Frames.

Working with Parents

I'd feel more comfortable [with evaluating students] if I really knew what I was looking for and I could express that to parents.

1 The Teacher Study Group	2 Community Inquiry	3 Curriculum Planning	4 Classroom Organization	5 Working with Parents	6 Time for Reflexivity
▪Evaluation Parent Invitations ▪Learner profiles ▪Narrative frames ▪Strategy lessons	▪Learning wrksps ▪"Seeing what's there" group ▪Reading with young children	▪Focus Studies: math & science communication ▪Literature study ▪Mathematics	▪Day/wk schedules ▪Text sets ▪Kids' work plans ▪Class work plan ▪Classroom hlprs	▪Letters home ▪Homework ▪Goal-setting conferences ▪Parent nights	▪Journals ▪Professional Prfl ▪Conference pres ▪Journey papers

FIGURE TA4.2
Working with Parents

I just want to be credible to the parents. Or, I guess I just really want to be credible to myself. How can I do that? (Judy)

From the beginning of our work together, parent issues played a part in each of our inquiries. Whether the focus was evaluation or math curriculum or classroom organization, how to go about working with parents and respond to their concerns remained in the periphery of our conversations. Judy bravely described her struggles with several parents who were not pleased with the restructuring efforts in general and her stance as a teacher more specifically:

I think presenting myself to parents as a learner and someone who doesn't necessarily have all the answers made a few parents very uncomfortable. It soon became quite obvious that some of them didn't agree with my views on learning and because I had invited them to talk with me about it, I had to listen to them anyway. A few of the parents were concerned about the fact that their children were teaching other students. Parents had the misconception that I wasn't doing my job as a teacher. I was trying to change my role with students and encourage them to take some responsibility for their own learning. I think I was fairly successful in creating a classroom environment where that was beginning to happen. For example, when Sara read her stories to the class, she asked her classmates to comment on three things she did well and one thing she could improve. This was a strategy that I had shared with the class earlier in the year, and now Sara took it on as her own. She did not wait for me to comment on her work. Her classmates, in turn, responded to her work appropriately, and she was able to improve her story writing.

Section One
The Authoring Cycle:
Let's Talk Curriculum

Even though I had begun to create a positive learning environment for students, I wasn't able to help parents understand the value in Sara and her classmates participating in the evaluation process. To be perfectly honest, where parents were concerned, I just wasn't very articulate. The parents didn't understand my intentions, or if they understood them, they didn't see the possibility in them that I did.

Slowly, and throughout our work together, our inquiry led us to plan opportunities to include parents in our discussions, to communicate directly with them concerning curriculum, and to elicit their comments and understandings of their children as learners.

In preparation for a parent night, the group of us made a video that showed kids involved in various curricular engagements—journal writing, composing a class newspaper, literature discussion, buddy reading. We also created a handout that outlined all the places in the curriculum where kids could be found reading and writing. At the parent night we shared some of the professional texts that informed the restructured curriculum, such as *Language Stories and Literacy Lessons* (Harste, Woodward, & Burke, 1984), *Questions & Answers about Whole Language* (Cochrane, 1991), *Home: Where Reading and Writing Begin* (Hill, 1989), and *Spell by Writing* (Bean & Bouffler, 1987). We invited parents to check out these books for their own reading. We also solicited parent comments and questions. Here are several:

▪ I notice (on the video) some children just turning pages. What could a parent do to help them be more interested?
▪ How do you encourage kids to write more?
▪ If a child isn't tested, how do they learn to take tests that they will have to take in upper grades or college?
▪ Don't you feel that creative spelling is only going to confuse the kids and start some bad spelling habits?

It was helpful to directly hear the parents' comments and concerns. We too could see instances on the video where kids weren't attentive and seeing those helped us make plans to adjust several curriculum activities. Further, we learned we had to make curriculum even more explicit for parents.

We addressed this issue several months later when we planned a math parent night. Debbie Kavanaugh's inquiry focused on math, so the two of us sketched out our understanding of math theory on an overhead from which she could speak. In addition, the teachers asked several parents to bring their children to the meeting so that Debbie Edwards could actually demonstrate with them the ways math was included in composing the daily news. We chronicled all the places in the daily schedule that math was highlighted, as we had previously done for language arts and reading. Although there were only ten parents at this meeting, their comments were all positive; Debbie Edwards's work with the children had brought our opening comments to life.

Another on going contact with the parents was the weekly homework sheet and reading record. The homework sheet outlined a homework activity for Monday through Thursday nights, emphasizing activities which built from the curriculum rather than just practice sheets (i.e. Monday night: *How much did you weigh when you were born? How much would a baby weigh that would need to be placed in an incubator? Who's the largest baby that your family knows? Bring in your birth certificate if you can locate it easily*). The reading record provided a place for the family to list the book(s) they read together and to include comments about "What I noticed when we were reading together." The inclusion of this simple invitation and the parents' comments documented their increased understanding of initial reading. For example, Alan's mother commented:

> 9/92   What we do at our house is, we read a word and have him repeat it until we finish the story. We also have him try to sound out some of the easier words.
>
> 10/92   Alan tries to read but doesn't try to sound out words. I have let him read and guess what it says by looking at the pictures, then we go back and read the words. (After a note from Debbie about other strategies the mother might use in reading with Alan.)
>
> 11/92   I have noticed that Alan is watching the punctuation marks and reading accordingly! We are glad to see this and reading is more enjoyable.
>
> 1/93   Alan is getting a lot better with his reading. He inserts words when he gets stuck that make sense in the sentence. I feel he has really come along great!

These comments from Alan's mother let us know that not only was she responding to some of the comments Debbie sent home, but that she was also noting more subtle changes in his abilities to share with us. As Debbie comments:

> It's very interesting to read the comments from parents about things they notice as their child reads. Reading those comments helps me see what the parents value, and what their beliefs are about the reading process. Understanding that helps me know what kind of information to send home for parents to read. For example, I sent home a sheet about the different reading stages through which a child progresses.

Each member of the school community knows that the work between teachers, parents, and students is an ongoing process. We do feel, however, that our work together helped begin and sustain some new, substantial conversations among ourselves, as well as the larger school community.

Creating Narrative Report Frames

Months prior to the beginning of our group, the school community had decided to eliminate letter grades and replace them with narrative reports. With minimal preparation, the teachers faced blank pages and literally began to write. The first reports averaged four legal-length pages per student. The comments, organized by subjects, alternated between the reporting period curriculum activities, teacher expectations, and the student's performance. Here is an example:

Mathematics

In math class we have been working on counting, writing the numbers correctly, and the number concepts of addition and subtraction. The students do counting every day when we add a number to the days of school during the calendar activities. We are learning to count by 1s, 2s, 5s, and 10s. We even discuss the difference between even and odd numbers. Instead of doing traditional flash card and paper and pencil drill of math facts, the children are involved in exploration of math manipulatives and various hands-on games which allow them to investigate the different combinations that make up the addition and subtraction families. Leon participates fairly well when we count on the number line. If he is the leader then his participation is great. Counting by 1s and 10s seems to be easiest for him right now. Leon is making most of his numbers correctly but could use some work on neatness. He does tend to reverse the numbers 3, 4, and 5. This is common up to about eight years of age . . .

Although everyone acknowledged that they knew the children better as learners than ever before, the first narrative reports were unwieldy for both parents and teachers. The reports raised many new questions about assessment. Many parents in the community were not confident readers, and the new reporting form required a lot of reading. In addition, the information wasn't organized so that indications of the student's ability and success were clear. Despite the lengthy and informative reports, several parents continued to ask, "How is she doing?" Others expressed more confidence in letter grades. Perhaps for the first time, parents who had not previously responded to the invitation to be involved in the restructuring process came face-to-face with the evidence of substantial change. Somewhat more common, however, was a lack of response to the report cards. None of these were the expected responses after the time and energy it took to write the quarterly narratives. As teachers we knew something needed to change. We forged ahead in our inquiry, embracing what we felt was most important about documenting learning and trying to find more effective and efficient ways of implementing our beliefs about evaluation.

During the second year of the restructuring efforts, the Leadership Team responded to the teachers' wishes to schedule goal-setting conferences in the fall and spring, with the narrative reports coming out in January and June. They also followed some parents' wishes that letter grades be provided on request (an option that had always been available). The revised assessment calendar provided additional time during the fall to think more carefully about our own beliefs and expectations, as well as to consider the parents' responses. We focused our initial efforts on listing indicators for the various curricular areas of the curriculum. We worked in pairs, each teacher authoring her own curriculum expectations before combining them with others. The first draft of the mathematics section now read:

Mathematics

- is able to make connections between thinking in math and his or her own life
- can manipulate objects to represent math processes (by the teacher's direction or on his or her own)
- creates new ways to use the materials; makes connections beyond teacher directions
- begins to represent processes symbolically (with numerical equations: $8 + 6 = 14$)
- can read math symbols and understand what is written
- can perform simple number operations (addition and subtraction through 10)
- can perform more complex operations (as described)
- contributes to math focus study by: identifying math tools, explaining the use of tools, making connections with his or her own life, and using the tools and own ideas

Specific comments about each child were included below these statements. The draft shown above was used with students in the multiage first- and second-grade classrooms. The responses from parents were heartening:

Now I understand what's expected of the children!

The indicators were a great help. I've often wondered how you used each item to assess. It shows how much individual time is given! Erik doesn't have a comment so I am enclosing a couple of stories he has written at home. They are first copies but I thought you would like to see them. I would like them back. Thanks for all your hard work and time given. I'm very pleased.

I am glad to see Donny is making some progress. I'm hoping he will even do much better. We are trying to help him more at home. I do believe the way you laid out the report helped us.

In addition, one family's response to the report helped us revise the space we had provided for comments. Initially we included space for comments at the end of the report. Larry's father, however, squeezed in comments after each curriculum area. When Debbie Edwards had written that she would like to see Larry contribute more detailed news on the daily newsboard, his father responded: *I think before nobody said much about school to him therefore he didn't think school was no big deal.* When she commented that the handwriting in Larry's journal could be neater, he laughingly noted, *Larry gets in a hurry but he is getting lots better. I think he has a lot more confidence and will get better if we show we care. P.S. My handwriting is pretty sloppy too, ha ha!* Throughout the report, he responded to his son and himself as learners; he helped us better understand the larger learning context of Larry's life. We knew that Larry enjoyed writing stories about animals, but not, in addition, that *Larry loves animals, he likes to go hunting with me.*

These comments from a father brought new life and importance to the reporting frame that we had spent hours writing. We were pleased that the report almost "begged" his response and revised the format to include space for comment throughout. We were also pleased that Erik's family had sent stories he was writing at home for us to see. Conversations with parents about the students felt substantially different than they had in the past. The narrative reporting format is still being revised, as it is our goal that it be responsive to our own increased knowledge of the learning process, as well as the interests and values of parents.

Many issues and questions remained unresolved at the end of that year. First, how could we keep pushing ourselves as teachers to collect data and report learning in ways that were theoretically consistent, rather than reporting old information in a new format? This was an ongoing challenge, especially as we discussed what information was most important to gather. Second, how could the students themselves be more involved in the assessment process? We had each done an in-depth assessment of one student and included several student self-evaluations in that process. Still, the assessment process remained time-consuming and the primary responsibility of the teacher. Third, some of the parents did not understand or value the narrative reports; they voiced concern about how their kids were doing, even when the state-mandated standardized test scores showed grade level performance. Ironically, the parents of one of these students with whom we had worked closely requested grades, yet did not pick the report card up for several months. There was a general concern that a narrative reporting format would not truly replace grades until parents' fears and values were addressed and transformed. We feel hopeful that our inquiry as teachers offers this potential; nonetheless, there was criticism directed at teachers for not having all the answers, as well as for involving parents in issues that were viewed as the "teachers' responsibility." We often acknowledged that our inquiry had just begun.

What Have We Learned?

The lessons we have learned from our collaboration are as complex and extensive as the directions our inquiries took us. Here we share three lessons that we hope will be helpful for other educators involved in purposeful change:

- Meaningful change affects every area of the curriculum;
- A focus on inquiry establishes all participants as learners and helps sustain the change process;
- Collaborative inquiry is negotiated among parties with varied perspectives, talents, and agendas, yet committed to a joint project.

Meaningful Change Affects Every Area of the Curriculum

While we might agree with the many educators who urge teachers to move slowly and take small steps, our experiences differed from that advice. In fact, it was hard for the collaborators in this study to focus their energies on one or two concerns prior to talking about their beliefs. This lack of focus led them to touch briefly on spelling, devise a new format for anecdotal comments, move on to try journal writing, and then to think about what was most important to include in a narrative evaluation. From the outward appearances, the two processes (pre-inquiry, inquiry) might have looked the same—lots of change. Debbie Edwards describes it this way:

> Since I didn't take the time to really think about my beliefs and since things didn't feel very successful, I kept making changes in my room. First I would try one thing and then another. I

wouldn't give the kids enough time to see how different ways of doing things could evolve. I wasn't sure what I expected of them or myself, yet I would often get discouraged because things didn't "feel good."

Later she writes,

We ended the school year very positively (four months into the process), feeling that doors had opened and that the conversations had begun. The four of us, along with Kathy, began to talk about things that were and weren't working in our classrooms, about our learning and evaluation beliefs, about creating in-depth learning profiles of students we were concerned about, and many other issues.

The next year there was a very important difference in the Debbie who taught last year and the one who was beginning her second year in the classroom and this new program. Though I've continued to make changes throughout the year, I've come to realize that change isn't necessarily bad if you're in touch with your beliefs.

I propose the difference for Debbie, and all of us, was the focus on purposeful change and the discussion of that process with a group of other, equally invested educators. "Going slow" in this context became of secondary concern. Rather, taking an inquiry perspective and thinking through our beliefs helped us focus on the most significant issues we faced and became a lens through which we viewed our practice as a whole.

A Focus on Inquiry Establishes All Participants as Learners and Helps Sustain the Change Process

This statement rings true, especially as I consider our work with parents, teaching assistants, and colleagues whose view of traditional education had been interrupted. When considering functional spelling or Explorers Club projects (Copenhaver, 1992), for instance, there was always an intellectual difference of opinion about whether a curriculum change was necessary or worthwhile. But the conversations changed when we looked to the children and their engagement as learners over time. We learned to look at kids' work and talk about what they *could* do, leading one parent to note: "In the beginning she spelled 'have' *hv*, then *hav*, and soon she will spell it *have*." Curriculum inquiry gave us a perspective on the past, the present, and allowed us to project our continued engagement into the future.

Collaborative Inquiry Is Negotiated Among Parties with Varied Perspectives, Talents, and Agendas, Yet Committed to a Joint Project

Dewey contended that the self is in continuous formation through action of choice. He also noted that the richness and complexity of selves people create are functions of their commitments to projects they recognize as their own (Greene, 1988).

Our growing understanding of and commitment to collaborative research helped us focus on the kind of people we wanted to be together (Harste, 1994), rather than viewing our inquiry as an act of faithfulness to a set of procedures for determining "truth." By taking both a philosophical and semiotic perspective on research, no engagement in the study served a single function and no participant played a single role. Rather, learning, evaluation, and inquiry were bound together for all participants. Each of us valued the opportunity to work together. We also enjoyed thinking and writing, both together and on our own. Debbie, Judy, Pam, and Debbie have shared their new learning with their staff. They have also written conference proposals to continue including their voices in the larger professional community. We have authored articles together and separately; we also continue to regularly talk about curriculum.

Inquiry: A Significant Alternative

Teaching as inquiry is an alternative conception of what it means to engage as a professional. We believe that the questions of others are only useful in the context of learners' own efforts (Watson, Burke, & Harste, 1989). Unfortunately, most professional development programs and curriculum models are based on others' questions, not the participants'. Further, full participation in a democracy includes interrogating the values and beliefs of our collective efforts (Dewey, 1938; Freire, 1989), rather than simply putting into practice the directives of others. In other words, *why* we do what we do is as

Perspective	Teaching as Transmission	Teaching as Inquiry
On the role of schooling	...to inculcate normative values and knowledge that prepare learners for the job market	...to immerse societal members in a working democracy; to interrogate the values and beliefs that direct collective efforts
On the nature of knowledge	...fixed, objective, determinable; to be transmitted	...cultural, local and contextual; constructed by active inquirers in a community; a consequence of human activity
On the relationship between the known and an inquirer	...to stand back and observe, objectively viewing nature "as she does her thing"	...subjective; created in the transactional act of inquiry; values mediate the inquiry process
On the nature of being	...to understand one's place in the order of things; hierarchical	...all contribute to creating a more ethical world; inter subjective many connections are possible
On learning	...linear, learning as a destination focused on successful performance of pre-determined skills	...focus on accessing learners' intention, hypotheses, and broader connections made
On curriculum	...standardized, pre-determined content; cultural, disciplined knowledge to be mastered	...open-ended, fueled by phenomena that captivate learners' attention; related to the disciplined perspectives that are human creations
On research	...to better predict and control human behavior; objective, variables controlled	...collaborative, includes active and reactive participants who both raise questions and pursue temporary open-ended understandings
On implications of educational policy	...establish vehicles to transmit or interpret new expert knowledge of "what works" to practitioners	...establish structures and habits-of-mind that support continued inquiry and conversation.

FIGURE TA4.3

important as *what* we do and that conversation is one in which each of us must participate.

This perspective can be contrasted with a body of educational research focusing on teacher "change" that primarily represents research conducted to document teachers' responses to *externally mandated* change efforts (Richardson, 1990). Conceptions of learning or learners are also based on distinct beliefs—beliefs often invisible to those taking the course. Some see teachers as deficient or expert or novice; they might see students as naive, inexperienced, or gifted. Teaching as inquiry is represented and contrasted with the predominant "transmission" view of learning or teaching in the table above (Mayher, 1990, partially adapted from Berghoff [1992] & Harste

Section One
The Authoring Cycle:
Let's Talk Curriculum

[1993]). This table represents two of several theoretical or ideological positions; it is not meant to pose these positions as clear opposites.

Other educators similarly describe teaching as inquiry as "learning from teaching," or as what Rexford Brown (1991) calls a "literacy of thoughtfulness," in which all educators recognize the importance of opportunities to learn, reflect, and take risks. An inquiry process is more the cultivation of "habits of mind" than it is a strict process to be followed. It is distinguished by what learners do when they "don't know"—which determines what they ultimately will be able to know (Duckworth, 1987).

We invite you to join the conversations of other, like-minded educators who are learning the value of inquiry in their professional lives—a process that enacts the best of what we know about the learning process for both our students, their parents, *and* ourselves.

Maintaining a Community of Inquirers

"There are a lot of nice things going on, but it's not a community yet."

"What do you mean?"

"In every classroom you can infer what choices the teacher gave children. Kids haven't taken ownership of their learning."

This conversation with Karen Smith was not music to any of our ears. Along with several teachers from the Indianapolis Public Schools, Jerry had started a new school called "The Center for Inquiry." The focus of the curriculum was on multiple ways-of-knowing and inquiry. It was a K–5 public school in an inner-city neighborhood, part of the Indianapolis Select School Options Program. The setting was perfect: a blue-collar neighborhood and a fully integrated school. Parents worked hard for a living and they wanted the very best for their children. The only stipulation made by the district was that children had to take the state competency examination at the end of the year. We didn't like this, but we could live with it. Other than that, this was an opportunity to shine, to create the kind of curriculum and environment in schools that each of us had dreamed of creating. Karen's comments made it obvious that all was not well in Nirvana!

"Well, what advice do you have?"

"I'd begin by starting better literature discussions. I've found that when kids are really talking about books and sharing what is on their minds communities form naturally. Everyone's voice gets heard. Everyone's ideas get respected. Everyone comes to know for themselves the strengths of each member of the community. I think you've said something very much like this yourself, Jerry!"

Karen's comments and advice were hard medicine, but they struck the right chord. We knew something wasn't right, yet we couldn't quite put our finger on it. The year had been hectic. It was the first time many teachers had worked with multi-age classes. Although there was a school administrator for the building, the school population was kept at 100 for the first couple of years, too small to merit a principal by Indianapolis Public School standards. Instead, the school had a collaborative form of school administration in which the faculty ran the Center. Probably the teachers were right, there was too much on their plates. Probably it was time to get back to basics.

What were the basics? For us it is our belief in education as inquiry and in multiple ways-of-knowing. It is our belief that a good curriculum has to support the underlying processes in inquiry:

1. building from the known through voice and connection;
2. taking time to find questions for inquiry through observation, conversation, and selection;
3. gaining new perspectives through collaboration, investigation, and transmediation;
4. attending to difference through tension, revision, and unity;
5. sharing what was learned through transformation and presentation;
6. planning new inquiries through reflection and reflexivity; and
7. taking thoughtful new action through invitation and reposition.

We had to think about each of these processes separately but within the framework of inquiry—the big picture. We also had to think about maintaining a community of inquirers from within this theoretical frame.

This wasn't the first time that things had not worked exactly as planned. Often, as you work on a new component of the curriculum, other components—things you once had in place—suddenly aren't working like they did before. In this chapter we share common questions that teachers have had as they implement an inquiry curriculum, as well as how they use inquiry as a vehicle to further their own professional development as teachers. The questions are organized in terms of the seven underlying processes of inquiry for purposes of reminding ourselves of our beliefs and our vision of literacy. We don't wish to lose sight of the big picture. We close each section with our lingering questions and current inquiries. Although not everything is solved, educators need to learn to rebuild their ship while moving full-steam ahead on the sea of education. We wouldn't even want to dry dock our ship if we could, for it is the ongoing flow of classroom life that provides the data with which we self-correct.

Building from the Known Through Voice and Connection

Children are natural risk takers and hence learners. Parents in one moment gasp for breath as their child does something they perceive to be dangerous, and then, in the next moment, glow as they realize their child is a genius. Adults often have learned to be cautious, and with this conservatism their learning slows down. In the end we all need to take risks—to test our wings, so to speak—if we are to learn and to grow.

In a classroom for inquiry each child must see him or herself as a valuable member of the learning community. Our research suggests that a low risk environment is best. A no risk environment means that anything goes. If what we are doing is important, then there have to be consequences. A high risk environment, however, means that any error will cause stress. Under those conditions it is likely that no one will take chances.

Engagements need to be open-ended so learners can provide a variety of responses based on their own experiences. The problem with worksheets is that both the starting and ending points are fixed. An open invitation to write a Family Story, for example, is a different matter. You can write regardless of your spelling ability or the nature of your story. You can create your story through pictures and/or words. It's a low risk environment because there is neither a preconceived idea as to where one must start nor a preconceived idea as to where one must end.

Choice supports the creation of low risk environments as well as provides options for where students might begin. Choice makes it possible for students to negotiate and renegotiate a curricular invitation

"What we hear, what we say, what we read, and what we write, has everything to do with who we are, who we have shared our lives with, and the specific contexts in which we find ourselves."

Serebrin, 1994, p. 107

Chapter Five
Maintaining a
Community of Inquirers

in light of what makes personal sense to them. Cognitively, choice acts as a propeller in learning.

We often think of learning as abstract, and while this may characterize the end product, it is not the way learning begins. What we know is the base upon which we grow. Education always involves connecting the known to the unknown. As teachers we often worry when children choose familiar books to read or inquiry topics that parallel an ongoing interest. This concern is groundless. Our experience shows that familiarity pushes children beyond where they have been. They don't stay with what they already know. They pursue new perspectives and more in-depth investigation on these topics. They bring these new ideas to the class and push the class beyond what they already know.

"Up close and personal" ought to be education's new motto. No child can be allowed to slip through the cracks. Should any child appear to be at risk of failure, it is time to take a closer look. The questions we as inquirers need to ask are: How can I make Miguel the center of my curriculum today? What sign systems would have to be used? What topics would have to be discussed? On the basis of these questions we can plan new curricular invitations that both feature Miguel and invite others in the class to explore Miguel's way of knowing. No matter how frustrating we may find a child, the thing to remember is that schools are not here to silence children, but to listen to their voices.

Although there are specific curricular invitations that support children in making connections and in developing voices, much of creating a classroom where all voices can be heard is psychological and sociological. Psychologically, children have to be assured as well as shown that their voice matters. Sociologically, children need to learn to support each other and come to see classrooms as resources in their learning. From the perspective of the teacher, hearing all voices assumes that someone is listening. Because how teachers respond to children makes a difference, our mouth becomes our biggest strategy lesson. What we don't say is as important as what we do say. The one thing we know for sure is that it is a whole lot easier to intimidate a language learner than it is to support one.

Although we have learned a good deal about how to build curriculum from the known, there are lingering questions. At an intuitive level a variety of methods should serve a variety of children better than a single method. Some people interpret this to mean that while whole language will work for some children, a skills approach and a phonics approach may work with others. We disagree with this interpretation. It is why we insist that whole language be seen as a philosophy rather than just another method of teaching reading and writing. Whole language accommodates lots of methods; what it does not accommodate is violating what we know about language and learning. Some children find their way into literacy through books, others through environmental print, and still others through writing, drama, and song. Depending on how they are implemented, each of these approaches can be called whole language. Despite such flexibility and progress in our understanding of literacy, building curriculum *with* children is different than building curriculum *from* children.

Does This Curriculum Really Serve Everyone?

An inquiry curriculum is rooted in personal and social knowing. The curriculum is built from children, not prepackaged and sequenced ahead of time. The three teacher-researcher stories included here illustrate how teacher-researchers have been exploring this issue with children who, given the way schools are currently organized, are at risk of failure.

Jevon Doesn't Sit in the Back Anymore

Connie White, a kindergarten teacher in Kings County, Nova Scotia, was considered a fantastic whole language teacher. But she had

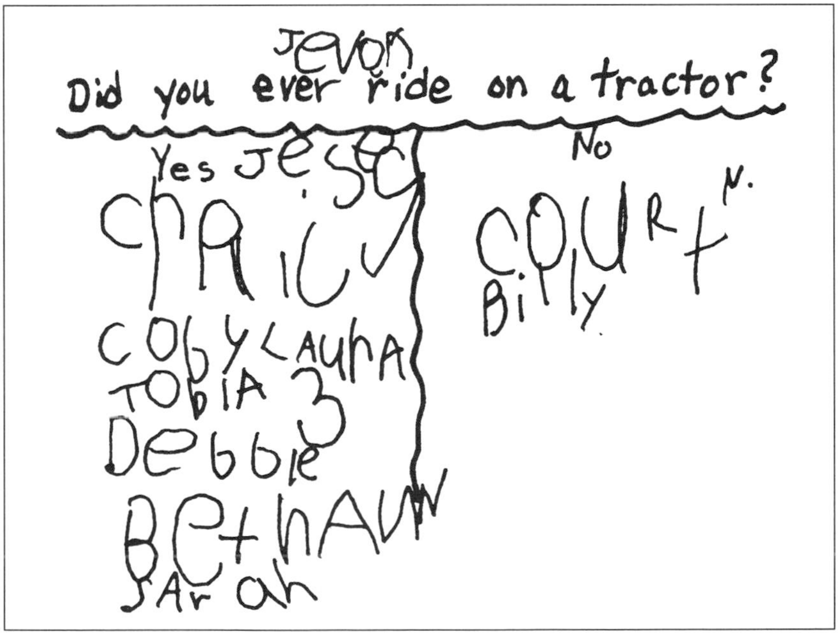

FIGURE 5.1
Survey; Jevon, Age 7
(White, 1991)

Worksheet; Jason, Age 9

Predictable Little Book ("Jason's Alphabet Book"); Jason, Age 9

reservations when Jevon, a big strapping kindergartner who lived on a neighboring farm, didn't seem to be making much progress. In her book (White, 1991), Connie tells the story of how she finally made progress by building the curriculum from Jevon. She noticed that whenever she read anything in class, Jevon was only interested in the names of the characters. At one point while reading a book to the class Jevon responded almost automatically, "Hey, that's my dad's name." Connie began to listen and learn. She took Jevon's interest in names and in farm life in general to create experiences and bring in books to get Jevon interested in reading and writing. Her book, *Jevon Doesn't Sit In The Back Anymore*, is the story of two learners inquiring together and is well worth reading.

Jason Learns to Read

Not unlike Connie White's teacher research project, Jerry received a call from a local teacher one day saying that she had a child in her third grade class who didn't know how to read. Would he help? Together with Diane Stephens he took up the challenge and built a program based on what he knew about language and learning. When they first visited the classroom, Jason was working on a worksheet. The teacher had given Jason this worksheet based on his performance on a standardized test which suggested that he could not visually discriminate the difference between letters. By asking ourselves "What's there?" we decided, despite the limited context, there were several things we knew about Jason. First, he could discriminate several letters of the alphabet, *a*, *d*, and *r*. Second, we knew he could write his name.

We made a predictable Little Book using this information and our knowledge of what makes books predictable for children to read—written language that matches the flow of oral language, pictures that support the text, repeated language patterns, information that matches what the child knows about the world. Our goal was to produce a book that we knew he could read once we had read it to him. Together we did a Shared Reading of the book, after which time Jason read the book back to us. Together we made a blank book for Jason and invited him to write his own predictable book to bring the next time we met.

We also introduced a commercially published predictable book, *I Was Walking Down the Road* (Barchas, 1975) through a Shared Reading. We talked our way through the book, the first time introducing the language patterns of the book informally as we talked about what was happening on each page and every picture. We then read the book inviting Jason, through anticipatory pauses, to chime in whenever he could. After completing this reading we talked about the book and invited Jason to take it to read to everyone and anyone he could find who would listen in his classroom and at home.

We continued with this pattern. Each session began with Jason reading the commercially published predictable book we had introduced at the last session (which was taped in order to study Jason's reading progress through miscue analysis), reading the predictable book that we had created from Jason's writing sample from the previous session, making a blank book which Jason was invited to fill building on the pattern of the Little Book we had created, and finally collecting a new writing sample evolving from a topic of Jason's choice and building on conversations that naturally came up during the session.

The second writing sample we collected was a shopping list. Jason said he added, "Race Track Car" as his last entry because often his mother would buy him a toy when she went to the grocery store; "a good deal" he said he didn't want his mother to forget about.

Shopping List; Jason, Age 9

Figure 5.2 on the next page shows the predictable Little Book we developed off of Jason's writing sample based on our notion of how to support and extend the reading process.

Diane and Jerry worked with Jason for fifteen weeks, three times a week, spending one-half hour with him at each session. At the end of this period Jason was not only reading but saw himself as a reader. The standardized test at the end of year suggested that Jason had advanced three grade levels in one year and was now reading on level.

Magic? Not really. We simply used what we knew to create the most supportive environment possible for Jason. Jerry extended the program to other children by asking preservice teachers who were early childhood majors at the university to work with a child their teacher saw at risk of failure. Over the course of the semester, the same phenomenon occurred. Every child was perceived by the end of the semester (sixteen weeks) to be reading on or about grade level—that is, like other children the teacher had in her room. While this experience was a success, what still needs to be done is to develop a partner version that capitalizes on the social nature of language and learning as children talk and collaborate together.

First Graders Pick Their Own Teacher

Vivian Vasquez and the two other first-grade teachers in her school in Toronto decided that children should have a choice in which

FIGURE 5.2
Predictable Little Book ("The
Shopping Trip"); Jason, Age 9

first-grade classroom they were assigned. Instead of allowing the principal to assign children to their rooms, they sought permission to set up their classrooms initially in terms of learning centers so that children could move freely among all three rooms. During the first week of school the teachers observed the children carefully getting to know their classmates and themselves, and asked questions such as, "When the child gets hurt, which teacher does he or she go to for comfort?" "Who works well with whom and for what purpose?" After the first month of school and on the basis of this information, first-grade children were assigned a homeroom teacher.

In many classrooms teachers have a rule that visitors participate with the children rather than permit them to be outsiders looking in. This insures that visitors understand the curriculum at a lived-though level. When Jerry visited Vivian's classroom, he was not surprised therefore to be invited immediately by the children to participate in what they were doing. At one point, not knowing that children were in the process of selecting their own teacher, he got nervous when he saw eighteen children just stroll out the door. Vivian seemed unconcerned. Jerry thought probably she hadn't seen what was going on. He interrupted and said, "Vivian, I just want you to know that eighteen children just left the room." "Oh, I know, children here are free to wander between any of the three first grade rooms they want."

At lunch, Jerry asked Vivian about her schedule and how she made scheduling decisions. "Oh," she said, "I have no schedule initially. I just set up the room and see what the children prefer to do first, second, and so on. I take notes to get some idea of how much time they need and we go from there. It appears they want books read to them right away in the morning and again around ten o'clock, so I guess that will be the start of our schedule this year."

Lingering Questions

Currently one of the programs that is being instituted across the world is Reading Recovery (Clay, 1972, 1979; DeFord, Pinnell, Lyons, & Place, 1990). Children in first grade who are viewed by teachers as at risk of failure are given intensive individual help using much of what we know about the reading process to support their growth in literacy. Reading Recovery teachers are highly trained. In the half-hour one-on-one sessions with children they reread familiar books and collect miscue-like data on the child's reading. They also write a simple sentence to focus on visual discrimination and letter-sound relationships and do a shared reading of a new predictable book. Although expensive to institute, proponents report that almost all the children return to their classroom reading on grade level after fifteen or sixteen weeks.

There are many strong aspects of this program. The teacher in-service is excellent. Teachers walk away understanding the reading process and have a theoretical frame from which they can make instructional decisions in classrooms. Further, the program is socially responsible as it fills a societal need and uses much of what we have learned about language to say that it is intolerable to let children fail.

Despite these strengths there are concerns. If we as a society could give up the idea that all children have to read by age six, there would be no need for Reading Recovery. Children selected for Reading Recovery typically have very little interest in books. Rather than come to reading on their own, the Reading Recovery instructional environment and procedures force children to attend to print whether or not they are interested (a criticism that also could be lodged about my work with Jason).

Despite this, the question becomes whether or not there aren't other ways to introduce these children to the world of literacy. One option might be multi-age whole language classrooms in which children stay for three years (Kasten, 1994, Kasten & Clark, 1993). Under these conditions—and a willingness to accept that some children might learn to read at seven and still others at eight or nine—teachers say that none of their inner-city children need Reading Recovery. They learn to read naturally.

Although other holistic educators raise additional concerns, this is the only one we will discuss here. Instead, we will use the case of Reading Recovery to raise a related concern. At present—as Reading Recovery demonstrates—there is no doubt that we know enough about the reading process to ensure that everyone learns to read. Building from what children already know, we can develop programs that get them to read and to write according to our current notions of literacy. While we have learned to accept the literacy that children bring with them to school, what is less clear is that we have learned to respect their literacy. If we did, we would not try to move the child from his or her current way-of-knowing to our way-of-knowing, but rather invite other children and ourselves to try that child's way-of-knowing on for size. In a sense we would be legitimizing lots of ways-of-knowing and using diversity to expand current conceptions of literacy. The agenda ahead of us is to explore multiple literacies which respect alternate ways-of-knowing in literacy itself as well as in other sign systems. This work is just beginning but must continue.

Taking the Time to Find Questions for Inquiry Through Observation, Conversation, and Selection

When Jerry asked a physics professor friend who was working on the development of a solar battery where he got his ideas, he replied, "Well, I just had a breakthrough this morning. I noticed that even though I was running water down the sides of the shower curtain, the bottom kept coming in towards me. I'm using that idea to solve a particular problem we're having in designing a prototype of the battery."

While it is true that Jerry still doesn't know what this has to do with a solar battery, the point is that even people involved in very abstract work think concretely using the powers of observation to solve their most theoretical work. While their work looks abstract to us, it is concrete to them, often involving very mundane metaphors and analogies. Vera John-Steiner (1981) interviewed and investigated persons who were thought to be near geniuses in their fields of study. One of the things that characterized these people was their intense powers of observation and concentration.

To be a writer is to see the world in a new way. Unless you have something new to say, no one is likely to listen. The writing process, like learning more generally, begins in observation. That's why researchers not only love to, but need to, play with their data. They know that it is through this intense observation that they are most likely to gain a new insight. Observers attend to patterns as well as surprises. It is by making sense of what others see as noise that knowledge is gained. Shirley Brice Heath (1983) says that research is a process of making the familiar strange.

As inquirers talk about the metaphors they create, language makes their ideas public and suddenly we know more. Although schools often stress written language literacy, most of what we know and learn occurs through talk. Michael Halliday (1975) predicts that as much as eighty percent of what we know is learned through talk.

David Bleich (1988) maintains that the difference between a monologue and a conversation is that in a conversation your speech lives in the speech of the person with whom you are speaking. In order to have a conversation a reciprocity is assumed. To have a successful conversation you have to listen to the other speaker and propel the conversation forward on the basis of what has been said.

Conversation is the most accessible research tool we have. It is in the give and take of conversation that we discover what we believe. Often we don't know what position we wish to take on a subject until we hear what others have to say, then suddenly we know.

Gordon Wells (1986) says what we know depends on the company we keep. Unlike early conceptions of knowledge which liken the brain to a filing cabinet, new conceptions of knowledge view it as socially constructed and ever changing. Knowledge resides between people rather than in the head of a single person.

The more we learn about cognition, the more central a role conversation seems to play in learning. By engaging in conversation

---

...The wise woman listened, and laughed. "My dear child, you have found the secret." Jenny was puzzled "How can I have found it?"

"Because, you see, the secret to wisdom is to be curious—to take the time to look closely, to use all your senses to see and touch and taste and smell and hear. To keep on wandering and wondering."

"Wandering and wondering," Jenny repeated softly.

"And if you don't find all the answers, you will surely find more to marvel at in this curving, curling world that spins around and around amid the stars."

Eve Merriam (1991)

"Meaning can come into existence only when two or more voices come into contact: when the voice of a listener responds to the voice of a speaker" (p.73).

Mikhail Bakhtin as cited in J. V. Wertsch

---

learners connect the new with what they already know. Isolated bits of information are useless to the learner. That is why you can cram for a test, get an A, and yet not remember a thing one month later. In order for knowledge to be of use it must be tied to everything else we know.

Cognitive psychologists (De Beaugrande, 1980) say we make sense of the world by breaking it up into manageable units of meaning. Some call these chunks of meaning "texts," others call them "stories." Harold Rosen (1986) sees story as the primary function of the mind and maintains that groups identify themselves through stories. Sometimes all that is needed is a one line reminder, "Remember the time Jerry hit the deer." These statements, he says, are the residual of a much longer story, the knowledge of which binds participants intellectually as well as socially.

Conversation and story play a central role in inquiry. Together they represent the primary vehicles we use to connect or integrate what we are learning to what we already know. "Storying" is the process we use to tie together, identify, and finally select a set of experiences we see as unified or meaningful. Conversation and story allow learners the opportunity to explore a theme from a variety of dimensions and, in the process, commit themselves to a position and an inquiry question which represents what they believe about the subject.

Ludwik Fleck (1979) sees knowledge as residing in thought collectives. Through conversation and story, people in particular thought collectives develop their own ways of talking as well as their own procedures for thinking through a topic. Through conversation and story learners explore various thought collectives for purposes of finding one with which they are willing to align themselves. This exploration is important as the process of selecting an inquiry question involves both the taking of a stand and the adoption of a thought collective.

In order to grow, inquirers need to position themselves intellectually in their field of work. If, instead, learners hold a variety of positions, they simply apply a different theory to each problem or question that arises. Because of their eclecticism, they have nothing to puzzle over and so experience no tension or growth in their beliefs and understandings. When inquirers take a stand intellectually in a particular set of beliefs, they notice unpredictable happenings and are forced to reconsider their beliefs in light of those happenings. To resolve these surprises, they revise their initial stance and learning results.

Inquirers rapidly learn that the key to planning an inquiry is to select a stance that allows them to tell a story they believe needs to be told and then organize everything they do to support the telling of that story. In some ways good researchers can be seen as playing a believing game (Elbow, 1981). They proceed with their research by "acting as if" certain assumptions about learning are true. Conversation is the vehicle by which they invite others collaboratively to construct this story with them. What always comes as a surprise is that the very process they set in motion more often than not forces them to reject their initial intention as well as the very question that initiated the inquiry in the first place. This is why the outcome of a productive inquiry is often a new, more powerful question.

Even if the stance a learner initially takes is wrong, it is a touchstone for growth. That's why inquirers don't have to worry about whether or not they asked the right question. History confirms the fact that most learners have asked really bad questions all along. That's why there is still so much work to do and so much more to learn. Curiosity, not correctness, propels the learning process. We need not concern ourselves if the inquiry questions that students are asking initially seem shallow to us. There is no one correct spot from which to start the journey of learning.

Having said that, let us qualify our statement. Our experience suggests that when the inquiry questions that learners ask seem shallow (My question is, "Would dogs make good pets?" [Lisa, Grade 5]), teachers have often failed to support the complexity of the topic, or students have not explored the topic from a variety of standpoints. That is why wandering and wondering are so important. Wandering and wondering allow learners time to locate a position from which they will be able to sustain prolonged inquiry. It's also why shallow questions get answered so quickly. Having made a small investment, a small return is hardly a surprise.

The demonstrations provided to learners as they have conversations and create stories with other learners are central to the learning process. Alan Koshewa (1994) conducted a study in Rise Paynter's fifth-grade classroom. He was interested in discovering how it was that children found their inquiry questions. By tape recording conversations during Explorers Club and then transcribing and analyzing these tapes, Alan found that the demonstrations provided by other learners was a key source of information. What others demonstrated they knew about electricity sparked interest, helped students see the

> "When you have a choice, it's like you never want to stop. Learning is fun when you want to do it, and you get to do it your way. When you do your own planning and you decide which days you're gonna read, this day you're gonna watch a movie, this day you're gonna do this. Well, I like doing it in any way, in any order that I can, because I do it when I need to and not when the teachers says."

Student Comment; Rachel, Age 9 (Maras & Brummett, 1995)

potential of the topic, and helped students focus their own inquiries on the topic.

Demonstrations are why it is crucial that teachers have their own inquiry projects in which they engage as the students engage in their projects. In the company of inquirers one learns not only *what* to research but *how* to research and *why*.

Although we have learned a good deal about literacy, we are just beginning to understand the process of inquiry and the classroom conditions that sustain and support inquiry. Questions of classroom organization are neither incidental nor simple. Despite progress on some fronts, as we learn more about inquiry new curricular engagements will have to be investigated and explored.

What Do I Need to Consider in Organizing My Classroom for Inquiry-Based Instruction?

Some teachers devote little thought or energy to setting up their rooms. Although it is true that children can and should be involved in creating the organization of their classroom, teachers shoulder the initial responsibility. How the classroom is organized when students enter the room makes a difference. We recommend that no teacher begin with an uninviting room. Desks in rows, a teacher's desk at the front, and no work areas says something very different from what you want to say.

In order to understand why we think the physical organization of your classroom is important, you need to understand a bit about semiotics (Eco, 1976). Semiotics is the study of how groups create meaning or make sense of their world. Semioticians are interested in how language is used in a cultural group as well as art, music, movement, gestures, and the like. There are even branches of semiotics that study architecture, asking themselves questions like why are the houses in Tucson different from the houses in Indiana, and what does that say about the lifestyles and cultures of groups that inhabit these areas.

Semiotically, you want the physical environment in your classroom to sign what it is this room is about. Since you are expecting to do different things in this classroom from what typically goes on in schools, you want children to walk in and say to themselves, "Hey, this is different." From a semiotic perspective, what you have done is set up a new expectation both for yourself and the children you teach.

Time

Over the years, teachers have told us over and over again that there just isn't enough time to do everything. They soon discover that an inquiry curriculum requires large chunks of time; it can't simply be added to what they are already doing. The net result is the realization that something has to go.

The assumption that one has to do a little bit of every subject badly every day needs serious rethinking. Researchers have found that left on their own children will eat a balanced meal (true, they eat their dessert first). Working in Rise Paynter's room, Joby Copenhaver (1992) found that children balance their inquiry diets, covering and going beyond the topics found in curriculum guides.

In setting up a conducive environment for inquiry the twin issues of time and compartmentalization need to be confronted. The issue is not how to squeeze more in an already busy schedule. In other words, we do not—and we hope readers do not—see inquiry as an additive curriculum, but rather one that replaces what currently is going on in the name of spelling, English, reading groups, creative writing, penmanship, mathematics, science, and social studies. By combining the time now consumed for these stop-and-go activities, what Graves calls the "Cha-Cha-Curriculum" (1983), large blocks of time can be retrieved.

One simple but compelling justification for why the curriculum should not be compartmentalized is that there is no evidence supporting the idea that a special part of the brain handles reading, another part handles writing, another spelling, and so on. In fact, there is extensive evidence to the contrary. We think classrooms should reflect our current knowledge base in education. To impose an organizational structure that does not reflect how the mind works seems odd.

Work time is the official way that we put uninterrupted time for reading and writing each day into the classroom. Work time is designed to send the message that we are here to learn by actively using reading, writing, and other sign systems as tools for learning. As an organizational decision, work time supports the integration of the language arts and keeps the focus of everyone's attention on learning.

"In essence, the kindergarten curriculum is everything that happens to the children from the time they step into the school building until the time they leave. The sum of all their experiences—how they're greeted, how they're instructed, how they work with each other—plays a part in forming their attitudes and motivation long after they've graduated from school" (p.92).

Lamb, B, & P. Logsdon (1991)

Rather than think about a block of time for mathematics, a block of time for science, another block of time for social studies and so on, some teachers find it helpful to have an afternoon block of time devoted to inquiry. Rise Paynter uses Explorers Clubs as her organizational device, during which individual and small groups of students pursue inquiry questions of their own choosing. Rise used to have a rotating two-week schedule. Two weeks were devoted to science, two weeks to social studies, and two weeks to the pursuit of questions of personal interest. Initially she used the units in the social studies and science textbooks to help her structure these times. Students read through a textbook unit—magnetism, for example—but then were free to pursue a topic of their own choice that related to this theme. After reassuring herself that children studied topics from a broad range of content area when left to pursue their own questions over time, she now uses free choice as her organizational device.

Schedule

It is difficult to give specific advice about daily schedules. Often specialists in art, music, and physical education come to schools at different times to work with students, a librarian schedules a library period, and without much warning whole school assemblies are called. Despite this, there are some things that help, not the least of which is beginning to think differently. While routines are important, carving a schedule in stone isn't.

In The Center for Inquiry, the first part of the day seemed hectic. Some child invariably seemed to come in upset. Lunch money needed to be collected, attendance posted, and a host of similar chores needed to get done. Carol Hall and Becky Lane, primary multi-age teachers, came up with a solution. The first hour and a half of the day is quiet time. Children come in and work on their journals. Once they are done they move to what they call DEAR Time (Drop Everything And Read). During these periods Becky and Carol finish their book work, write in their own journals, and do some reading. In addition they circulate around the room, talk privately with each child, and generally get things settled down. Around ten o'clock in the morning they have a group sharing time in which they read aloud from children's books, children share journal entries, and the class discusses the day's events. Children move from sharing time to work time, and so the day begins. While it has never occurred to us to start the day with so many quiet periods—we were always told to balance

A Sample Week in Rise Paynter's Fifth Grade

	Monday	Tuesday	Wednesday	Thursday	Friday
8:50 to 9:05	Attendance, Jobs, Lunch, Check Schedule				
9:05 to 9:45	Uninterrupted Reading, Writing, Rendering, Recording, Researching				
	▪ Extensive reading (individual books) ▪ Keep literature logs	▪ Intensive reading for dialogue (text sets, multiple copies, paired books)	▪ Book illustrating, graphic rendering, chart making, game making, sound tracking	costume designing, map making, note taking, interview transcribing, pattern seeking	▪ Individual planning ▪ Journal writing, story drafting, expert pieces
9:45 to 10:30	Collaborative Circles, Sharing, Invitations, Strategy Instruction				
	▪ Literature Circles ▪ Invitations in math, social and physical science, and humanities	▪ Writers Guild ▪ Invitations in math, social and physical science, and humanities	▪ Literature Circles ▪ Invitations in math, social & physical science, & humanities	▪ Math Engagements ▪ Research Groups	▪ Literature Response Activities (i.e. Reader's Theater, Sketch to Stretch, letters to authors...)
10:30 to 11:05	Demonstrations, Large Group Engagements				
	Inquiry Strategies	Math	Math	Language Strategies	Language Strategies
11:10 →	to 12:00 Art	to 11:35 P.E. 11:40 to 12:00 Current Events	to 12:00 Music	to 12:00 P.E.	to 11:35 Art 11:40 to 12:05 Music
12:00 to 12:20	What's on Your Mind? (large group sharing)				
12:20 to 1:00	Lunch, Recess				
1:00 →	to 1:20 Spelling Stumpers 1:20 to 1:50 Stories 1:50 to 2:00 Lockers	to 1:30 Library 1:30 to 1:50 Stories 1:50 to 2:00 Lockers	to 2:00 Math & Science Engagements	to 1:20 Math Stumpers 1:20 to 1:50 Stories 1:50 to 2:00 Lockers	to 2:00 Math & Science Sharing Research in Progress
2:00 →	to 3:00 Focused Studies: Science, Social Studies or Explorers Club 3:00 to 3:15 Reflections	to 3:00 Focused Studies: Science, Social Studies or Explorers Club 3:00 to 3:15 Reflections	to 2:30 Stories 2:30 to 2:45 Reflections 2:45 to 3:10 Recess	to 3:00 Focused Studies: Science, Social Studies or Explorers Club 3:00 to 3:15 Reflections	to 2:30 Stories 2:30 to 2:45 Reflections 2:45 to 3:10 Recess

FIGURE 5.3
Rise Paynter's Classroom
Schedule (Copenhaver, 1992)

active activities with quiet ones in planning—Becky and Carol's schedule suits their needs and those of the children they teach.

Teachers should be aware that even more radical schedules are possible, and we encourage them to experiment with various structures that fit the needs of the classroom. For example, some teachers devote one day a week for the pursuit of a single topic. As a result of a television program on ecology, children in one classroom became interested in the study of paper. Their questions—How is paper made? How do different kinds of paper react to different chemicals? How much work is it to recycle paper and what is really involved?—were used to organize learning stations through which children cycled throughout the day. The day began with each child receiving a Learning Log in which they recorded their observations and ended with a group sharing of what they had learned.

The daily schedule in most process-centered classrooms is very complex. Kittye Copeland used to schedule a farmer's market every two weeks on Friday as part of a unit on money and economy in her multi-age classroom. Some children offered to paint other students' fingernails, some sold crafts and pieces of art they developed, while still others brought in fruits and vegetables that children might eat as snacks. No specific time was scheduled during the week for students to set up a bookkeeping system, advertise, or otherwise get their stall up and running. It was just one of the options students could work on during their daily work time.

When Karen Smith was teaching sixth grade, she sat with particular literature discussion groups during work time. Because she believes it is rude to be interrupted when you are engaged in a conversation, she insisted that children develop a schedule which they posted and on which they outlined how they were going to use their time. There were no interruptions when she was involved in a literature discussion group (Harste & Jurewicz, 1991).

Debbie Manning, a second-grade teacher in Fresno, California, uses clipboards and invites students in her room to organize recurring time blocks. When Jerry recently visited her classroom, one child organized the opening group sharing time, another was in charge of putting together a two-hour radio program which her classroom broadcasts daily to people within a four-mile radius of the school, a third was planning the closing session for the day, a fourth was in charge of deciding what books were to be read by whom, and so on.

Routines are important. The keys, however, are flexibility, reviewing what needs to be done, scheduling large blocks of time and insisting students develop personal plans and take responsibility for their own learning. Semiotically, just knowing there is a block of time devoted to authoring and another to inquiry clarifies expectations. It also assures students that they will be able to collaborate and have the conversations they need to pursue projects of personal and social interest.

Space

If your room is small, you might consider removing some of the desks or cramming the desks together to create a large open work area. Many teachers arrange the desks in groups to form work tables throughout the room. If students are assigned desks for purposes of storing their materials but not as their place to sit, don't tape name tags to the desks. Use moveable name tags so that students can sit anywhere and claim that seat during a particular period by simply placing their name tag on the table or desk (Short, 1990). This resolves the problem of some other student sitting in the seat should the student be absent momentarily from the work area.

Some teachers are lucky enough not to be given desks for each child. Rise Paynter, for example, has some desks, but mostly lots of tables around which children can work. She has students buy plastic storage boxes from a local outlet store in which to keep their materials. Often students have two such boxes: One to house their general school supplies and one to house the books and materials which relate to the inquiry project on which they are currently working.

Pam Shelton, a first-grade teacher in Kings County, Nova Scotia, removed the teacher's desk from her classroom. She did not want students to use it as a place to store their work, or see it as a place where she should sit while they worked collaboratively in groups. Pam reported she was surprised with how much space became available when "the big desk" was removed. Interestingly the desk stood out in the hallway for months after she moved it out of her classroom. Obviously both the janitor and the principal needed this time to convince themselves that Pam meant business. Both were just sure she would want it back.

Functionality

Just as the secret to good teaching is to see what children are up to and then support them in doing it, the secret to classroom organizational problems lies in the same logic. We need to think functionally.

In visiting and videotaping whole language classrooms, we were struck with the simple eloquence of Carolyn Dye's first-grade classroom in Columbia, Missouri (Whole Language Umbrella Teleconference, 1993). When someone asked her how she came up with her organization and what advice she had for beginning teachers, her suggestion was that teachers begin by thinking about their room functionally in terms of what activities had to go on as well as what activities were going to go on whether they liked it or not. She said, for example, "This is a social environment. Students are going to want to talk to one another. Instead of letting this become a problem, I turned this inevitability into an integral part of my language arts program by creating a Message Board in which children are free to write notes back and forth to each other. My only rule is that no one write notes that are hurtful to another person."

Carolyn also said that she had a squirrel that lived outside her classroom window. Neither the squirrel nor the enthusiasm the children showed for watching the squirrel hours on end were a surprise to Carolyn. Instead of letting this become a problem, Carolyn created a Science Log (really just a loose leaf, three-ring binder) which she placed on the window ledge along with a set of binoculars. Children signed up to watch the squirrel and record their observations. At various times the science log was shared with the class. The questions children have about squirrels sometimes lead the class into an inquiry on other animals.

John McInerney, a first-grade teacher in Indianapolis, had a principal that liked every wall decorated. Since John hated worrying about bulletin boards, he divided several into 12" × 12" squares, assigned children their own space, and let them solve his problem for him. The children loved it. They displayed art work, created a post office and Message Center, and advertised inquiry questions in an attempt to entice others to join them on projects.

The writing-reading center evolved from our research with young children (Harste, Woodward, & Burke, 1984), which suggested that in homes where reading and writing materials were available, children engaged in many more literacy events than in homes where these things were absent or less accessible. Therefore, we developed the motto "litter the environment with print" as we attempted to apply this research finding to curricular practice. In a preschool in which Jerry was working, he recorded how certain children used the room as well as the activities in which they chose to engage. After getting this baseline data, the teachers followed our motto and pulled the reading area out of the corner and into the middle of the room. A notepad was added by the telephone in the play area, children signed in as an alternative to taking attendance, and every opportunity was taken to "litter the environment with print." The result was that children spent up to ten times more time engaged in literacy events.

The trick is to place the writing-reading center so that it is in a direct path to the door when coming into the classroom. When placed in this fashion, the center signs to visitors that something different is happening in this classroom. As children enter, opportunities for reading and writing litter their path. Recently we have been exploring with other teacher researchers what happens when this center becomes an authoring center that is filled with tools from a range of sign systems including various art materials, musical score paper, graph paper, math manipulatives, instruments, pencils, books, and so forth.

Classroom Discipline

Rise Paynter was unhappy with her sixth graders' inability to think through problems that occurred in the classroom and on the playground. Every recess someone seemed to get in a fight that ruined the atmosphere of the class and what she was trying to accomplish. In thinking through this problem she suddenly realized that the ability to think through problems was one of her major curricular objectives. Instead of viewing discipline as an "add-on" program, she began to see it as curriculum. While this wasn't the content she had initially thought of as a topic for inquiry, the context of the situation in which she found herself dictated that she rethink this decision. The curricular device she devised was called the problems journal. Whenever problems occurred in the classroom or on the playground, the students involved were invited to tell their stories in the problems journal. At the end of the day, these stories were read to the class, and students were asked to suggest solutions to the problem. Rise took notes in the journal of all the options that were suggested. Children who were experiencing the problem were asked to try any one of the solutions they thought would help. If the same problem cropped up later, a new account was written and a new set of options were generated.

Both Rise and the children were pleased with the result: Students became more thoughtful. Once problems were handled, students wanted their sheet to come out of the problems journal. They didn't want guests and parents at open house to read about what they now saw as fairly trivial matters in retrospect. The function of the problems journal was expanded when several children took this opportunity to talk about problems they were having at home and to find out how class members thought they should be handled.

One day when Jerry was visiting, he entered just as the class was in the midst of a discussion about the problems journal. The author of one of the problems was a girl who was unhappy that her mother had started work. No one was home for her after school. When it came time for suggestions, another girl in the class immediately spoke up: "Well for goodness sake, don't start doing the dishes. It will only make matters worse!"

To remain alert to the needs of students, Rise also has a suggestion box in her classroom along with a holder containing strips of paper labeled "Suggestions." When something isn't working in the class, children write a suggestion for change which is discussed at the end of the day. Rise, of course, feels free to make suggestions too. She is willing to live with the fact that some of the things she would like to see changed concern only her and not the other members of the class.

Karen Smith believes in a democratic organizational style. She handled governance by initially asking each student to write out five rules they thought should be in place in the classroom. Working in small groups and then with the group as a whole the students devised a self-government policy containing no more than ten rules. Whenever needed, she or one of the students called a town meeting in which these rules were reviewed and new strategies for handling problems were discussed.

Lingering Questions

As our understanding of inquiry grows, changes in curriculum will have to be made. One of our latest discoveries, for example, has been the important role that observation plays in learning. Not surprisingly, therefore, the thing that we are currently working on is how to more powerfully support observation in classrooms. In the past we have been guilty of assuming observation but not necessarily creating invitations and providing time for indepth observation. From what we can tell, most teachers provide precious few opportunities for children to observe their world intensely; instead, there seems to be a headlong rush to more active parts of the cycle which result in more visible products.

How to provide a classroom environment that supports observation becomes even more problematic in a multiple-ways-of-knowing curriculum. Classrooms need to be set up so that children can explore as well as experience what it means to see the world as an artist, to explore the world from the perspective of music, and so on. At present we are experimenting with Sketch Journals, studio time, and an exploration room.

Expanded versions of artists-in-residence programs and parent-community involvement programs are also needed. While experts can help us understand what it means to create meaning like an artist, one would hate to see multiple ways-of-knowing reduced to nothing more than a talent contest. The fact that success in different occupations calls on different sign systems and ways of thinking provides new ways for parents—from bricklayers to interior decorators—to work together. The true significance of sign systems lies in the fact that they represent resources available to all humans to expand our communication potential if we but know how to observe.

Gaining New Perspectives Through Collaboration, Investigation, and Transmediation

Inquirers collaborate, not just cooperate, with each other. David Heine (1987) defines the difference this way. We cooperate to get some task accomplished. You bring the coffee. I'll bring the donuts. Someone else brings the paper plates, napkins, plastic silverware, and cups. The result is that breakfast is served. Collaboration, he says, is different. In collaboration, people are changed in the process of working together. Collaborators are not the same people they were when they started the collaboration. Each has used the other as a vehicle for outgrowing their very selves.

When most people think about research they think about a systematic attempt to learn about some topic through reading books at the library. Even ignoring the fact that reading and research are equated in this formulation, the problem with this concept of research is that it does not identify the important processes involved. To say research involves reading doesn't do much. Of critical importance is what we read and the function this reading plays in our subsequent thinking. Although research may involve reading, the purpose of this reading is to find out what others know about our topic given the perspectives they have taken.

Different knowledge systems offer different perspectives on a topic. The goal of research is to gain new insights. There are lots of ways to do this in addition to reading. Researchers can interview others, observe the world closely, collect artifacts, and more.

Although not all topics are amenable to all perspectives, the more perspectives a researcher takes on a topic, the more likely the complexity of the issues surrounding the topic will be identified. For example, by taking two different theoretical perspectives in physics, light was identified as both a wave and a particle, not one or the other as originally thought. When perspectives change over time, these changes add complexity to our understandings. Although we were told that atoms were the smallest thing in the universe when we were in school, quarks now hold that honor. The issue is not truth, but realizing that what anyone knows is dependent upon the perspective that is taken. The current controversies over refugees illegally entering the United States take on new dimensions when examined from the perspectives of economics, linguistics, politics, religion, medicine, and social issues.

We will never forget an experience in an eleventh-grade class in which the students were exploring various job choices. They read about the job of their choice, interviewed people who held positions they wanted, and studied their job from a variety of perspectives—number of hours worked, salaries, level of education required and the like. One day Lisa, a special education student who was studying nursing, came up to Jerry and said, "You know, Dr. Harste, the more I learn about this job, the less I like it!" Important stuff to find out now!

Given any topic, some perspectives are more insightful than others. Although curricular invitations should be designed to help students explore major dimensions of a topic, not every learner needs to experience the same curriculum to have a good experience. As learners investigate topics from the perspective of an ecologist, a feminist, or an historian, the potential of their topic expands. Conflicting explanations force students mentally to try new ideas on for size and in conversation and collaboration critically examine which arguments can or cannot be defended logically. Ideas, not people, are put at risk.

"In reality, each reader reads only what is already within himself. The book is only a sort of optical instrument which the writer offers to the reader to enable the latter to discover in himself what he would not have found but for the aid of the book."

Holland, 1975, p. 19

Section One
The Authoring Cycle:
Let's Talk Curriculum

Invitations to present a topic through art, music, dance, and other sign systems also help students create new meanings. Transmediation is the process of moving what you know in one sign system to another sign system. Because the content plane in language is different from the content plane in art ("love" doesn't have an equivalent single expression in art), to move an idea to art means that the underlying concept needs to be reconfigured. The twin processes, reconfiguring concepts and then convincing others that your reconfiguration is a good idea, constitute fundamental processes in literacy (Siegel, 1984).

Often as learners think about their inquiry questions through other sign systems, whole new dimensions of the topic present themselves. Inviting children to represent what their topic looks like in another sign system puts them in touch with qualitative dimensions of a topic, many of which they may not have considered before.

One has to be reasonable here. Inquiry is much more than just rotating a topic through different sign systems or knowledge systems. The goal of inquiry is unpacking the complexity of the topic to find issues to pursue and trying out new perspectives on the topic to see what can be learned, not rotating topics through these systems for the sake of the activity.

What is important is that more than a single perspective be taken. Karen Smith began by asking students in her room to take at least three different knowledge system perspectives on each of their questions. She also asked students to express their meanings in three different sign systems as an attempt to support children in the use and exploration of sign systems as heuristic devices for inquiry.

Although the case can be made that our society is competitive and that schools therefore have an obligation to be competitive to prepare children for the real world, this argument does not have a lot of merit. The one thing we can be assured of is that children will experience competition. The outside world will take care of this. If schools are to contribute to a child's education then collaboration is even more important. This may be the child's first opportunity to experience what it really means to work and to learn together. We think this is an important lesson for life.

Curriculum should not so much prioritize a perspective as invite multiple perspectives. In some ways there are no guarantees. While the authoring cycle invites writers to view their writing as a reader,

"Open-mindedness is a willingness to construe knowledge and values from multiple perspectives without loss of commitment to one's own values . . . . It demands that we be conscious of how we come to our knowledge and as conscious as we can be about the values that lead us to our perspectives."

Bruner, 1990, p. 30

this may or may not happen. A teacher can create environments where students will be offered opportunities to shift perspective and plan new curricular engagements that re-invite the learner to try new ideas and engagements. Although inadequate at times, organizational decisions as well as specific strategy lessons help. Recently, we have been taking what we learned about supporting readers and writers to explore how to support students in other sign systems. While inadequate, this work is a beginning.

In Real Specific and Concrete Terms, What Can I Do to Support a Multiple Ways-of-Knowing, Inquiry Curriculum in My Classroom?

Because education as inquiry is a philosophical stance on education rather than a specific method, there are no easy answers to this question. In our pursuit of an answer to this question, we have experimented with how to create a conducive classroom environment using strategy instruction.

Creating a Conducive Classroom Environment

Organizationally our recommendation is that teachers consider having areas where tools for music, art, drama, math, and other sign systems are located. There is something semiotically very powerful about having an art easel in a sixth grade classroom!

Beth Berghoff and Sue Hamilton spent a year exploring what an inquiry-based, multiple ways-of-knowing classroom might look like (Berghoff, 1993). They found that it was extremely important to have designated areas for sign system exploration within the classroom. For the first graders in their inner-city Indianapolis classroom, just physically getting up and walking to an area helped them psychologically shift stances. They literally tried on different hats and explored different ways-of-knowing as they moved around the room. Whereas Vygotsky (1978) found that what children do psychologically (by themselves) they first learned to do socially (with others), Beth and Sue found that what children do mentally (see something through art, music, mathematics, and so on) they first learned to do physically (actually move to different areas). Beth and Sue argue for space. Children need a sense of space where they can physically go to work on a project in an ongoing fashion.

At The Center for Inquiry in Indianapolis we have a room we call The Exploration Room. In this room children are invited to explore art, music, mathematics, and other sign systems as ways-of-knowing. Occasionally the invitations in this room are organized around topics like Indiana which the school as a whole has decided to explore. Children are invited to explore Indiana by making and sharing meaning through art, music, movement, dance, and other sign systems. One advantage of a room of this sort is that it encourages the exploration of school-wide themes by all of the students in the school. A second advantage is that teachers are free to do extended kidwatching, noting which children gravitate to which invitations for what purposes.

In planning curriculum, it is important to understand that transmediation is the way of the world. Lots of whole world examples abound. Transmediation is not something added on to inquiry, but a natural part of the process itself. The only thing that makes it unique within the framework of curriculum as inquiry is that at this point teachers are helping children become consciously aware of it as a tool by which they can gain a new perspective on the topic under investigation. The issue isn't when to use each separate sign system but encouraging students to integrate and move between multiple systems.

In the classroom transmediation can take many forms, such as reading and discussing a story and then putting on a drama, drawing a picture, or identifying background music to continue to explore this story. It can also occur when students create a piece of music after viewing a piece of art. In writing, transmediation takes place when we illustrate a point we are making with a picture, chart, or sample of student's work. Making time lines, graphing data, and making analogies all constitute forms of transmediation that naturally occur during inquiry.

To support investigation, experts can be interviewed by telephone or invited to visit the classroom. Parents are a ready resource, often providing talents and information that schools have rarely tapped. Investigation means that opportunities abound in the classroom which support learners in unpacking the complexity of their topic, not necessarily finding simple answers to half-formed ideas.

Recently The Center for Inquiry at Indianapolis has been wired for interactive television. Because of the connection of the Center with the university we are hoping that children engaged in inquiry projects will be able to interview and chat with experts in various

"Perhaps, more than anything else, whole language is all about learners feeling whole and able and part of a community of learners. It is about belonging and risk taking and feeling successful as teachers and learners. It is about the power of collaboration to break down the isolation of teachers and to establish communities of belonging and learning for all students and teachers."

Routman, 1991, p. 59

<table>
<tr>
<td>1. What are appealing topics or issues? What is my personal involvement and relationship to them?</td>
<td>2. What do I most want to explore right now? A web of what I and my collaborators already know about this topic/issue.</td>
<td>3. What do I want to know about this topic? What am I wondering about? What might others want to know?</td>
</tr>
<tr>
<td>4. What knowledge systems are related to this topic? What questions, knowledge, tools or ways of researching would experts from these systems use to investigate my topic?</td>
<td>5. What can I read? Who can I talk to? What other sign systems besides language can I use to get a sense of my topic? What can I do to explore my topic?</td>
<td>6. Research Notes</td>
</tr>
</table>

FIGURE 5.4
Planning-to-Plan Journal

knowledge systems about the topics of their inquiry via this medium in the very near future.

Strategy Lessons

To support children in learning to rotate the topic of their investigation through various knowledge systems, we've developed little booklets which we called planning-to-plan (see Figure 5.4). Although our initial purpose was to support teachers in exploring the potential of future class themes, such as systems, cycles, and the like, several teachers have used an adapted version of this document with the children in their classroom. They report by the time children have worked their way through this document they have both learned a good deal and sharpened their inquiry questions.

If cameras are available, children can be invited to take pictures of their research topic from the perspective of different knowledge systems. Sharing these photographs with other class members helps stu-

Section One
The Authoring Cycle:
Let's Talk Curriculum

7. Web of focused issues and relationships related to my topic.	8. How can I share what I have learned with others?	9. What still puzzles me about my topic? What are my questions and interests?

10. What things need to be changed? What new action am I going to take?	11. If I were to study this topic again, what would I do differently?

dents clarify the potential of their topic as well as expands other students' notion of what is involved in particular inquiries. On occasion we have had groups of six children share their photographs and, using at least six photographs from each person in the group, web the kinds of connections they see between and among projects. To share their in-process learning, groups rotate from table to table, trying to reconstruct for themselves the framework of the original group.

At times, teachers may want to purposefully use transmedition to put an edge on learning. For example, to disrupt dysfunctional notions of reading Jerry and the teachers at The Center for Inquiry created a strategy lesson called Interwoven Texts. They were concerned that students saw texts as closed systems with specific meanings. They also wanted students to realize that they could move between sign systems as a resource to push their thinking. To initiate this strategy, three tradebooks that had previously been read and discussed individually in class were read aloud. To put an edge on learning and to create new tension, each book was divided into eighths and teachers interwove the reading—first one book, then another, then another, and so on—until all three books had been read. The books selected had the moon as their common theme, and included *Happy Birthday, Moon* (Asch, 1982), *The Nightgown of the Sullen Moon* (Willard, 1983), and *Grandfather Twilight* (Berger, 1984).

Rather than discuss each book separately, children were asked to think about what all three stories meant together. "What message were all three books as a whole saying about how the world works?" After reading, children first wrote down what they thought the stories meant and second expressed what they thought it meant in some other sign system—art, music, mathematics, dance, drama, movement, and so forth. Children shared their meanings by playing Save the Last Word for the Artist, an engagement which allows everyone in the group to talk about what the artist is saying before the artist gets to have the last word.

This strategy lesson is particularly valuable because inevitably different interpretations arise—some readers see the books as signifying people's unity with nature, others see the books as a scientific explanation of the harmonic relationship between the earth and the moon, still others see the books as speaking to people's need to personify innate objects, and the like. One student saw each book as telling a story of egotism, and she had a legitimate point. Different students bring different insights to the story, and these shared insights alter their first interpretations. Jerry has found that interweaving the reading of the three texts encourages students to make connections to broader themes rather than staying closely to the interpretation of any one text.

As a culminating experience, the students talked about how their understandings of these books were altered as a function of participation in the group. Since there are no right answers, children experience language as an open system of meaning, an experience which begins to help them develop a more functional notion of the reading process itself. They experience learning as a search for unity, but realize there is no one right unity that all must reach. In addition, children experience first hand the value of their voice and those of their classmates in enriching the meaning of literacy. This strategy lesson also served as a demonstration to children who later used it to create presentations for the class from their own inquiries.

Lingering Questions

One of the concerns we have in introducing a multiple-ways-of-knowing inquiry curriculum is that we do not water down the curriculum so nothing in-depth really gets understood or explored. We wonder whether expanding a writing workshop to a studio where students explore a range of sign systems will lead to students dabbling in many systems without ever exploring any system in any depth. Will students avoid the hard work of any one system by jumping from system to system?

Michael Halliday (1985) points out that in any meaningful language experience, students have the opportunity to learn language, learn through language, and learn about language. We believe the same is true for other sign systems. We have explored how to involve students in learning multiple literacies by making the tools of these systems available and encouraging them to explore. Our concern now is whether they are also using these systems to think deeply and critically about texts from different sign systems and to learn about how that system operates. In reading we want students to read widely for many purposes, but we also want them to think critically about what they read in Literature Circles and to consider how language operates through strategy lessons. How do we make these same opportunities available in other sign systems?

Another part of our concern relates to our own knowledge as educators and our inability to know everything about these different systems. Can we support students in sign systems where we have little knowledge or experience? We know that teachers who really know children's literature have quite different literature discussion groups than teachers who don't. These teachers make connections to other books, pull related materials off their shelves for students to read, and in many other ways demonstrate the power of literature which teachers not having this knowledge simply can't do. While we do not see this as an excuse not to use children's literature in the classroom in that such programs are still more powerful than basals, nonetheless, we are still concerned. Somehow we don't want a curriculum for dabblers.

The answer is, we suppose, that things will balance out. Some teachers will be quite knowledgeable in art, others in music, others in science, and so on. We know we have our work cut out for us as many teachers do not feel that "their way-of-knowing" is a legitimate focus for the curriculum. One option is to invite experts in these areas into our classrooms on a regular basis. This approach seems viable. After all, we learned a whole lot about the writing process by studying real writers as opposed to building from what it was teachers of writing thought writers should know. Without elaborating this issue further, we will close simply by saying that the curricular agenda ahead is to interact with experts in lots of fields to identify how it is they work. Using the understandings we can from these interactions, we can then adapt and create curricular engagements that enrich the quality of the literacy program being offered in schools.

Attending to Difference Through Tension, Revision, and Unity in Learning

In an effort to make sense, we chunk the world into "texts." When what we perceive makes sense in terms of what we know, understanding occurs. If what we perceive does not make sense, we try to make sense using all of the powers of logic at our disposal. Following Peirce (1931–1958) and Deely (1982), Kathy has argued that there are three forms of logic involved in inquiry and learning (Short, 1986).

Learning begins by immersing yourself into the world and observing what occurs around you. Inevitably, tensions and anomalies arise when your expectations for what should occur aren't confirmed. Something puzzles you and so you are forced to search for a different explanation or connection between the current situation and your past experiences. The creation of a new possible explanation that has never been entertained before is called abductive logic. Often abductive logic is intuitive. You can't really explain why you think a solution might work, but you intuitively think it will and so move to test it out against the world. A second form of logic involves deduction. We think about what else would have to be true if we accept the possible explanation or hypothesis. We then take what we have deduced and use inductive logic to collect data for purposes of deciding whether or not to accept the hypothesis. As a real-world activity we collect data, search for patterns, and on the basis of what we find, adjust our beliefs.

Educationally, we have always valued inductive and deductive logic. This is why most curricula teach children the scientific method. Inductive logic is stressed when children are encouraged to collect data and to make statements explaining what they found in terms of a theory of how the world works. Deductive logic is emphasized when children are given a theory and asked to think through the real world implications of that theory.

Abductive logic has been underplayed in most schools. This is unfortunate as it is only through abduction that new ideas get considered. With both deductive and inductive logic, learners use what it is they already know and make sense of it in terms of their existing theories of how the world works. Abductive logic involves the creation of new explanations and sometimes the development of a new theory. This is why Robert Carey (1982) says a good curriculum is one where abductions can occur.

Tension is what drives the abductive process. When what we project (our mental frames) does not coincide with what we perceive, tension is created, and calls for new explanations. To ignore things that surprise us, the odd tidbit, or a difference of opinion is to overlook golden opportunities for learning.

Revision forces us to think anew about what we have already learned. The implications of new ideas need to be explored both mentally and physically. New ideas not only affect how we think about this topic, but cause us, metaphorically, at least to reread past texts. Intellectually what is required is that we think through what it is we know and adjust our mental frameworks based on new insights and information.

From a cognitive perspective, thinking through the implications of what one has learned involves critical thinking. New mental connections give us new perspectives on this and other concepts we hold.

It is easy to get caught up in the specifics of a particular inquiry. It is during the process of creating a new unity that one regains a view of the big picture, instead of getting lost in the acquisition of specific pieces of information.

The inclusion of tension as a criterion for inquiry is meant to reflect a changing view of learning. Our task is not to simplify learning, but to make the normal surprising, the common complex, the everyday new and interesting. John Dewey (1938) says that the role of the teacher is to create a learning environment that has the most potential for raising anomalies for learners.

In the past, education focused on common knowledge—on what everyone should know as a result of having read a certain book, engaged in a certain science experiment, or participated in a particular course of study. The assumption, based on stimulus-response learning

> "It is possible to view life as undergoing constant revision, as individuals become aware of new possibilities. This is why groups are so important. Not just students, but all people need others when they are trying to grow."
>
> Peterson, 1992, p.96

theory, was that things should be simplified for instructional purposes so that correct responses could become automatic. Error was considered bad; an inherent problem in the learner or in the delivery system. The result of this thinking led to a proliferation of testing and labeling of children as well as the production of teacher proof instructional materials and step-by-step guidelines as to what constitutes effective teaching. Students were found to do well on test items that tested exactly what had been taught in the way it had been taught, but poorly on items that asked them to apply what they knew to new situations (Harste, 1989). A bankrupt model of learning led to a bankrupt model of teaching.

Given new insights into learning—most notably the role that tension plays—much work needs to be done in rethinking education and instruction. Although good teachers intuitively have known how to make things interesting for children by turning work into games, contests, and even competitions, with an increased understanding of the learning process new instructional principles need to be developed and explored. Instead of making what's not worthwhile teaching into an interesting activity, we need to change our teaching to focus on what is significant in children's lives.

What Are the Implications of Seeing a Theory of Difference as Both a Theory of Learning and a Theory of Education?

How we view learning makes a difference. If we see learning as occurring because of practice, then memorization and rote learning characterize instruction. Interview some of the elders in your community. Schooling for them often involved memorizing long passages of text because the mind was seen as a muscle that needed to be exercised. With a changed view of the mind came reform in education. Today we see learning as occurring functionally, with other learners providing important demonstrations from which we can learn. The result is a new attempt to make schooling real and a new emphasis on the importance of group work. This view of learning has resulted in whole language, cooperative learning, as well as holistic mathematics, hands-on science and other educational trends. Unfortunately, many of these newer trends, while moving in the right direction, still do not question the assumption that the function of education is to teach a common set of concepts to everyone.

A theory of difference challenges this view. It argues that people can have a good educational experience even though they are not learning the same thing. Not everyone has to end up knowing the same ideas. Difference is okay. This view of education is anchored in a new view of learning. In this view, learning happens at the edges. Although the implications of this view have not been fully explored, educationally this means we need to seriously rethink the role that education can and should play in a democracy. Instructionally it means using invitations to raise the intellectual ante as well as supporting students by putting an edge on their learning.

Rethinking the Role of Education in a Democracy

Despite rhetoric to the contrary, it can easily be shown that the focus of education has always been conformity and consensus. That is why we have curriculum guides, standardized tests, behavioral objectives, and national standards for the English language arts being developed. Because of this focus, education for democracy has been interpreted as meaning everyone should be the same—come out of school knowing the same things, passing the same tests, covering the same objectives, meeting the same standards.

Given that what we bring to a process strongly affects what we get out of that process, this vision of schooling is an impossibility. Students not only come into schools different, but they have different experiences in school even if they are taking the same courses. It should not surprise us that they come out different. New standards, new tests, new mandates will not change this basic fact.

In contrast to a consensus view of education, we now understand the role that difference plays in learning. It is the propeller, the result of which is tension, anomaly, and new learning. From the perspective of diversity, we wouldn't want everyone coming out of school knowing the same thing, even if this were a possibility. An even playing field would stop inquiry.

Given the multicultural nature of our society, adopting a theory of difference as our model of learning and the basis for education makes better sense than maintaining the consensus view which is now in place. All of a sudden diversity and difference are not seen as problems but as potentials for both inquiry and education.

> ". . . our theories in language education focus on individual, but our goal (if it's democracy we're after) is societal. We aim for democracy — a *societal* system dependent on equally weighted participation, on an absence of undue influence."
>
> **Edelsky, 1994, p. 255**

Using Invitations to Raise the Intellectual Ante

To support critical thinking in the classroom, some teachers plan whole class engagements and strategy lessons that invite students to explore the concepts they have acquired in new ways. In Karen

Smith's classroom, we observed a group of children having what they thought was a final discussion over *Tuck Everlasting* (Babbitt, 1975). Right before they broke up to leave, Karen passed out a published review of the book saying, "I know this review was written for teachers, but why don't you read through it and see what you think. We could meet tomorrow to discuss it."

The next day at literature group only three of the six students in the group spoke. The others said they really didn't understand the article, though as three children spoke, Karen noticed the others had comments to add, such as "Oh, so that is what that part is about." Karen was unfazed. She simply said, "Well, that was tough. Let's reread this article again tonight and come back tomorrow to talk about it again. I bet you will get a lot more out of it." Sure enough they did. The discussion was heated. Children not only talked about the book comparatively but disagreed with many of the criticisms that the reviewer was making. The videotape of this session sounded like a literature discussion group at the college level, rather than a group of fifth and sixth graders in inner-city Phoenix.

The fifth grade students in Gloria Kauffman's classroom became interested in issues of slavery as an outgrowth of their study of Christopher Columbus during the Columbus Quincentenary. They were intrigued to learn that the slave trade with Africa began because American Indians refused to become "good" slaves. They became involved in reading historical fiction, diaries, and oral accounts of slaves. One of the assumptions they made as they engaged in this research was that slavery had occurred many years ago. Gloria challenged their assumptions by choosing *Devil's Arithmetic* (Yolen, 1988) about the Holocaust as her next read-aloud book. Students began to make comparisons between 1492 and 1942 and realized that there were different kinds of enslavement and inhumanity.

When an article about slavery in the world today appeared in the local newspaper, Gloria shared it during the morning meeting. This article created surprise and anomaly and challenged students' assumptions that "things are different now." Their discussions and inquiry made a dramatic shift and students began exploring the issue of human rights; they formed inquiry groups to look at the rights of children, women, animals, and African Americans today.

Putting an Edge on Learning

When instruction becomes too routinized, learning stops. No instructional activity is immune. One of the nice things about the authoring cycle is that it is hard for it to become so routinized that learning stops, though it can happen. This is why it is important that teachers understand the function of Editors Table, the function of Authors Circle, the function of publishing, and the like. Logs and journals support children in exploring ideas, in getting in touch with what's on their mind, in taking stock of what they know, in logically thinking through problems and in making plans for the future. If they are not serving these functions—if for some reason what the children are writing appears to look more like an assignment ("We had math. We went to recess. We had fun.") than a true expression of the kind of communication you were expecting, it is time to call a halt and re-group.

Journals are a vehicle to accomplish some end and as such are re-placeable. If all of the teachers in your building have been using jour-nals and the children are tired of them, use some other device. What is important is that you have in place some curricular device or en-gagement that supports children in looking and thinking more deeply about their world. An alternative might be Sketch Journals, or a day pad that fits in your back pocket on which children record three new things that they observe about the world each day. The key is to think about the function journals serve in your program—to experi-ence writing as a heuristic device for organizing thinking—and with the children devise curricular engagements and devices which serve these ends.

Lingering Questions

As is quite evident, a theory of difference calls for a radical shift in our thinking about both curriculum and instruction. Although some theoretical work has been done (Bateson, 1979; Short, 1986; Bintz & Harste, 1994), a further explication of the theory is needed. Practi-cally educational change based on a theory of difference is just begin-ning, and often in fields far removed from elementary education.

For example, noting that medical doctors often acted routinely, ig-noring important specific information given to them by their pa-tients, the medical profession recently has been exploring what they have called "Ignorance Based Education." Rather than focus on rote memorization of symptoms and treatments, interns in this program are rewarded for identifying anomalies to what otherwise are consid-ered known treatment patterns. By attending to exceptions, doctors are encouraged to consider new conclusions and new treatments. To date this program has been successful. Doctors trained to look for points of ignorance are not only more attentive to patients but are more generative in terms of coming up with new treatments. Given the success of this program, it is not surprising to find that the program is being expanded. Currently Indiana University, for example, is exploring Ignorance Based Education as a framework for training journalists (Women Studies Seminar Series, 1993).

While programs of this sort are encouraging, we know of no similar efforts at the elementary and secondary level. Clearly the title "Ignorance Based Education" is problematic. Something more positive sounding, we believe, would help sell the idea to the public. So, while we are encouraged, the difficulties of making such a fundamental shift in our thinking on a grand scale boggles our mind.

Because of the pervasiveness of a consensus view of education, work will have to take place on many levels. Each of us must do our part. A beginning is to make every classroom a demonstration of the power of diversity in learning. Nothing demonstrates success like success. As is evident by the spread of whole language, such grass roots approaches to educational change have worked in the past.

Sharing What Was Learned Through Transformation and Presentation

One of the requirements of an inquirer is that they be able to communicate to others what it is they have discovered in such a way that it makes sense. Some of our most brilliant scholars have difficulty communicating to others. In fact there are whole tiers of professors in universities whose real claim to fame is not the discovery of new ideas, but the ability to take another person's ideas and transform them so that they make sense to other people.

The ability to take what is known and apply it to new situations is a feat of literacy which merits both respect and understanding. What is required is selection, transformation, and presentation, resulting in a multimodal text that is appropriate to the right context. We can't help but wonder if the inability of so many researchers in this country to create appropriate texts is a reflection of our lack of understanding of this underlying process in both literacy and inquiry as well as its absence in so many educational programs in the world. Rather than put in place structures that support the multiple presentations of information to a wide variety of audiences, educators have contented themselves by requiring a single artifact—typically an oral or written report—as single proof of engagement in the process of inquiry. To add insult to injury this report is often seen as the culmination of the inquiry, when clearly such thinking short-circuits what we know about the process of inquiry. Similarly, presentation is often seen as artifact rather than as process.

To make a successful presentation, the presenter must first know his or her audience. In fact the better the audience is known the more likely will be the success of the presentation. Next, the presenter has to select, given what he or she sees as the inquiry questions of the audience, ideas and information from his or her understandings that are appropriate. Even further, to be successful a range of metaphors and analogies needs to be created which support the audience in making connections between what is being presented and what is already known. While doing all this, content has to be communicated through appropriate sign systems and the whole event sequenced in a unified manner and orchestrated multimodally. Change the audience and a whole new round of transformation and inquiry necessarily takes place. How many of us have been sorely disappointed with ourselves when we misjudged our audience and they didn't understand what we had to say. The successful transformation and presentation of what it is we know is difficult but exciting literate work.

Engaging in the process of presenting is a learning event in its own right. Concepts and ideas learners understood when they first encountered them all of a sudden become unclear. Having to present what we have learned to others forces us to confront edges and more often than not supports another round of learning. Presenting increases conscious awareness of the connections that have and could be made, forcing us to push our own thinking as well as push the thinking of our thought collective. By presenting we bring our learning to a new level of knowing. What was intuitive and taken for granted has to be made public and understandable. But it is worth it. Presenting invites others to share in our celebration of learning.

> "Learning and teaching are a mutual enterprise, a search. Learning is not slabs of knowledge: It is the development of understanding. We want to demonstrate that to you and engage you in it."
>
> Smith, 1993, p. 26

How Do I Plan, Lay Out, and Share an Inquiry Curriculum When It Is Continually Evolving?

Some people interpret a child-centered curriculum as one that cannot be planned in the absence of the children themselves. Critics see this as a problem declaring that such thinking is missing the very point of what education is all about. In some important ways they are right. One definition of *curriculum* is "a course to be run." Obviously someone needs to plan "the course." Curricula are by their very nature intentful. They need to be planned so that the lived-through experience they provide matches what it is we think is valuable. Even in child-centered, inquiry-based classrooms not all experiences are equal. As educators we want certain things to happen and not others. Preplanning is important. Being unnecessarily prescriptive, however, can ruin everything. Suddenly we are on a hunting expedition, killing off predetermined objectives, rather than on a fishing expedition, exploring possibilities. How to balance these two is more than problematic though some progress has been made. To date, we have found two ideas particularly helpful. One is Dorothy Watson's "planning-to-plan" (in Watson, Burke, & Harste, 1990). The other is Carolyn Burke's work with focused studies. Teachers such as Beth Berghoff and Sue Hamilton have used her format to think about curriculum in ways that are both highly planned and yet allowed to evolve in collaboration with children.

Planning-to-Plan.   For anyone who has tried to do a unit of study in a classroom, nothing is more evident than the fact that one needs many resources related to the topic to be explored. After working with teachers on using themes as organizational devices for planning their curricula, Pat Smith (1990), a teacher educator in Australia, says her first advice is to pick topics for which there are many resources. "Think about what resources are available. If there are no resources, my recommendation is that the unit be put off until such time as resources can be gathered. And remember, children can be a tremendous source."

Building on similar experiences, Dorothy Watson has developed what she calls a "planning-to-plan" framework. In some ways planning-to-plan is nothing more than a brainstorming device. It calls for teachers to think about their class in terms of possibilities—potential themes to pursue, resources to gather, strategies which may need to be taught and so on. Figure 5.5 shows such a document. By completing the planning-to-plan document a general framework is provided within which the specifics take shape as the inquiry proceeds on a day by day basis in the classroom. By planning-to-plan teachers alert

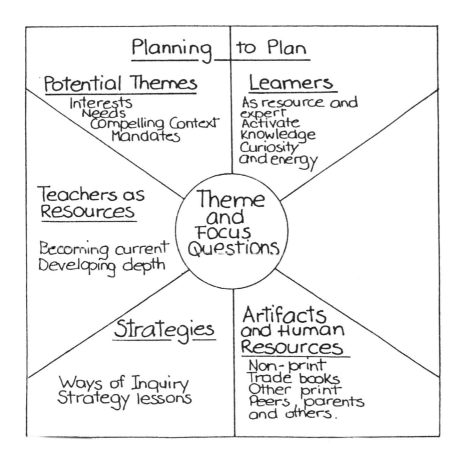

FIGURE 5.5
Planning-to-Plan (Watson,
Burke, & Harste, 1990)

themselves to possibilities so that teachable moments do not slip by unnoticed.

Using this particular document is probably not as important as realizing that all of us as teachers are responsible for careful thinking and planning of possibilities. What we have to remember is that what we create is our planning-to-plan—a set of possibilities for what might occur in the classroom. The plan itself is negotiated collaboratively with students.

Planning Focused Inquiries
Rather than focus curriculum on specific pieces of content that everyone must master, an inquiry-based curriculum supports the underlying processes of inquiry. While some experiences are ones that may be significant for all children, the importance of others depends on the specific interests and life experiences of students. The planning-to-plan format used by teachers needs to be focused as well as flexible.

Another issue is finding a format to share the curriculum teachers and students have developed with other teachers. Other teachers need, as well as want, ideas on how they might initiate a particular inquiry focus in their classrooms, but those ideas need to be shared in ways that allow others to approach the focus in a different way in their own setting. It is difficult to share the curriculum from one classroom and yet leave that curriculum open for others. Typically curriculum guides lay out objectives and activities, a product that looks closed, even though this may not have been the real intent of those who wrote those guides.

Beth Berghoff and Sue Hamilton (1993) went a long way toward solving these problems by using Carolyn Burke's planning to plan framework. This format is one teachers can use in thinking through their curriculum, yet open enough that other teachers might generate alternative engagements that make more sense to them and the children whom they teach. Beth and Sue began by thinking in terms of major curricular components: How can the focused study be initiated? What devices can be used to insure that children will be able to share as they are in the process of their inquiry? What books and text sets can be used? Given what we know about this age group and topic, what dimensions of the inquiry might children find particularly appealing? What perspectives on this topic do we think are crucial that children experience? How might children share what they have learned as a result of their personal inquiries?

Figure 5.6 shows the basic components of Carolyn's planning-to-plan curricular layout as well as gives definitions for each category.

There are several ways this planning-to-plan framework might be used. Figure 5.7 demonstrates the way in which Kathy and Gloria Kauffman used it to think about the umbrella concept of connections and the negotiation of class and personal inquiries at the beginning of the year. Figure 5.8 represents the framework as Kathy and Junardi Armstrong used it to think about a class focused study on insects. As a preplanning document, this framework helps teachers think through the important components of curriculum. The layout of the curriculum suggests alternatives, with empty slots inviting teachers doing similar focused studies to add their own possibilities and ideas and to collaboratively build the curriculum with their students. It can also be used by teachers to share their classroom inquiries with each other.

Focused Study	Can be any topic of personal and social interest. Focused studies sometimes reflect curriculum mandates, the talents and interests of a particular individual, or a compelling current event. Examples: earthquakes, systems, discovery, Indiana.
Possible Insights, Outcomes, and Questions	A listing of insights from key disciplines which this focused study affords. Can be posed as a series of focusing questions which capture key dimensions of the study from the perspectives of various knowledge systems and sign systems.
Initiating Events	Engagements which help each participant identify their relationship to the theme in terms of their own personal experience. Initiating events should support wandering and wondering as well as the development of voice and observation. Examples: field trips, writing invitations, films, etc.
Conceptually Related Texts	Materials (books, videos, posters, etc.) representing alternate perspectives which invite learners to put an edge on their learning via conversation, tension, and the making of complex connections. Examples: text sets, book and toy sets.
Devices for Organizing and Sharing	Ways to preserve relationships being explored and to share what is being learned. Should reflect research tools and methods of key knowledge systems. Examples: time lines, portfolios, sociograms, scatter plots, etc.
Invitations	Opportunities to explore key dimensions of the focused study using a variety of sign systems and texts. Should involve systematic doing.
Culminating Experiences	Engagements which help participants reflect on experiences and make plans for future engagements. Examples: learning logs, exit slips, reflection journals.

Lingering Questions

One of the requirements of an inquiry-based curriculum is that learners be permitted to pursue their own inquiry questions. Yet, this too is problematic. One of our lingering questions is the relationship of personal inquiries to class inquiries. Without adequate structures for sharing and dialogue, the concept of classroom as community could be destroyed by having each child pursue individual inquiry questions that are unrelated to a class focus. To date we have worked with teachers on both class-focused inquiry and expert-project models of curriculum. The class focus creates a shared context that pushes learners to consider new perspectives, providing many resources and opportunities for conversations. Within that class focus, students still pursue their own inquiries and questions. Students also need an opportunity to pursue their own personal questions even if they do not relate to

FIGURE 5.6
Components of Carolyn Burke's Planning-to-Plan a Focused Study

Chapter Five
Maintaining a
Community of Inquirers

Focused Study on Connections

FOCUSING QUESTION:

What does the concept of "connection" mean?

What might be possible class and personal topics of study?

INITIATING EVENTS:

Begin with engagements on relationships with each other and with families

Getting to Know You and Name Symphony

Partner Activities

Self time lines

Family time lines and Family Stories

Books on all kinds of relationships for browsing and read-aloud

Daily sharing and charting of issues about relationships

DEVICES FOR ORGANIZING AND SHARING:

Webs and charts

Diagrams and graphs

Observation logs

REFLECTIVE LEARNING EXPERIENCES AND SYSTEMATIC DOING:

Form text set groups based on student's issues related to relationships

Students discuss these issues in their groups and then present to the class

Class discussion about relationships

Create a concept map on connections using the relationship focus

Exploration Centers on a wide range of topics related to connections.

Books, activities, models, demonstrations, games, etc. on vibrations, instruments, cultural traditions, simple machines, time travel, explorers, people's connection to land, animals and thought, physical health, survival, war and peace, water cycle, food chain, plant cycle, recycling, weather, ancient civilizations, rules and democracy, and friendship

Students have one week to explore centers recording "I See" and "I Wonder" in observation journals

Sharing and charting of observations

CULMINATING EXPERIENCE:

Create a class web of possible topics/issues/themes related to connections that students might be interested in exploring this year. Negotiate the focus of the first class focused study.

FIGURE 5.7
Focused Study on Connections;
Gloria Kauffman & Kathy Short
Section One
The Authoring Cycle:
Let's Talk Curriculum

the class focus. It's not possible to plan class foci that will relate to all of the children's individual needs and interests, so some form of individual inquiry needs to be available. While we believe important differences exist between these two curricular foci, we are just now beginning to articulate what it is we are observing. Much more work and thinking need to be done before issues of this sort can be resolved. We

Focused Study on Insects

FOCUSING QUESTION:
    How does one go about field research?
    What is the cycle of life for insects?

INITIATING EVENTS:
    Read-aloud books and poetry
    Art prints of insects
    Music and sounds of insects
    Sharing past experiences with insects
    Brainstorm what we know about insects
    Observation of insects
    Exploration of books and models
    Recording and sharing observations and "wonderings"

DEVICES FOR ORGANIZING AND SHARING:
    Webs and charts
    Diagrams and graphs
    Observation logs

REFLECTIVE LEARNING EXPERIENCES AND SYSTEMATIC DOING:
    Choose and list significant questions
    Choose one question to explore in small groups by developing own experiment
    Share findings and create a chart on ways to create experiments
    Share ways children learn something at home and put on a chart
    Categorize insect questions and form six small groups
    Each group examines questions, brainstorms ways to answer those questions, lists materials
        needed, and conducts own observational research
    Invitations on insects and art
    Literature circles on Eric Carle
    Guest to demonstrate scientific drawing

CULMINATING EXPERIENCE:
    Presentations and demonstrations from small group inquiries
    Class discussion on scientific inquiry

need a deeper understanding of choice and the meaning of choice in conducive and supportive learning environments for inquiry.

FIGURE 5.8
Focused Study on Insects;
Junardi Armstrong

Planning New Inquiries Through Reflection and Reflexivity

The difference between reflection and reflexivity is that in reflection you look back, while in reflexivity you interrogate the very constructs you are using to make sense of the world. The systematic collection of artifacts during the process of inquiry supports reflection. Through examination of these artifacts learners are able to reconstruct the mental journey that they have taken. They can reflect on what they

Chapter Five
Maintaining a
Community of Inquirers

have learned (content), how they have learned (process), and why they have learned (purpose).

By reconstructing and thinking through the research process inquirers bring to conscious awareness what worked as well as what didn't work. It is this information which is crucial if thoughtful new plans of action are to be taken.

Because language is not a neutral tool but rather an artifact of our own creation, inquirers are required to step back and critically examine the constructs they have created for making sense of the world. Reflexivity as a process involves the interrogation of values. Why is it that I want to talk about the world in these new terms? Who benefits from this new construction? Whose voices will not get heard? Am I morally and ethically willing to accept these consequences?

Knowledge is never innocently "just the truth." Learners need to take responsibility for what they know as well as how this information will be used. Whether the world is a better place or a worse place is the inquirer's responsibility. Neither reflexivity nor this realization is easy, only ethical and moral, as these decisions affect what we are to become.

John Dewey (1938) said that there were two kinds of experiences—educative and miseducative. True education has a future about it; miseducation doesn't. To understand reflexivity is to understand why it is that the main goal of assessment should be helping a learner or a community of learners interrogate their values. It cannot provide truth, only a perspective on truth that supports or lends credence to certain ideas and not others. This is why the assessment procedures used in the name of Dewey's notions of education ought to help children assess their growth as inquirers and help teachers and parents assess the quality of the support they both have provided children in growing as inquirers. Assessment should also help administrators and school board members assess whether what they have been doing has supported the professional development of teachers in providing the best curriculum possible. To use such devices for purposes of labeling either teachers or students constitutes miseducation.

Too often in process-oriented classrooms children are engaged in one activity after another, with little time for reflection. To support reflection and reflexivity teachers need to schedule time for learners to think deeply about the meaning of what they have learned. Reflexivity is too important a process to rush as the products of inquiry

"If I were to travel with a ray of light, what would I see?"

"I have no special gift. I am only passionately curious."

Albert Einstein's Inquiry Question and Self-assessment of himself as a learner (Margaret Donaldson, 1992)

constitute a new stance in the world and thus a new set of interaction patterns for yourself and others. Instructionally we support these processes by including opportunities in our curriculum for children to share, reconstruct, and self-assess their learning.

There are no spectators, only participants, in educational evaluation. Teachers, administrators, school board members, parents, and other stakeholders in education need to see evaluation as an opportunity to assess as well as reassess their values and involvement. To use assessment as a device for labeling schools, teachers, or students is to misunderstand the roles that reflection and reflexivity play in everyone's learning.

How Do Holistic Educators Deal with Such Issues as Report Cards and Grading?

Although many of us have to live with both report cards and grading, these clearly are issues worth fighting over. From an inquiry perspective the only sensible evaluation is self-evaluation. Report cards and grading make it nearly impossible to have a real conversation. When one of the parties involved has the power to evaluate the performance, the other becomes intent on presenting his or her best face rather than speaking his or her mind.

The philosophy behind grading is that the act of giving students a C forces them to think about why they didn't receive a B or an A and on this basis grow. In reality grading doesn't work this way. Some students give up, others see the teacher as picking on them, and some unfortunately come to see themselves as having a C mind. Rarely does it motivate children to become better learners.

Although teachers have tried a range of strategies to deal with grades and alleviate their negative effects, these strategies are never wholly satisfactory. Grades are a violation of our beliefs about inquiry; the only effective way to deal with their effect is to eliminate them. Most teachers have put a broader system of evaluation into their classrooms so that they and their students systematically gather, record, and analyze the learning that is occurring. Through Learning Logs, self-evaluations, field notes, and checklists, teachers and students gain understandings about learning so that new curricular engagements can be planned that will push students and allow them to grow. Teachers do not take these evaluation devices and reduce them to a grade, but negotiate the grade as a separate entity with students. That's why some teachers now schedule portfolios so they do not coincide with grading periods. The message they want to send to students is that the purpose of these portfolios is reflection, not grades. While the portfolios obviously influence teachers' evaluation and reporting on students, they are not reduced to a checklist or a grade.

Many teachers are using field notes and checklists in lieu of grades and narrative reports in lieu of report cards. Each of these approaches works best when parents and students are involved in their development and use.

Field Notes and Checklists

Field notes, taking notes about the ongoing life in the classroom, is the heart of our evaluation system. We take field notes of children's talk in Literature Circles and Authors Circles, their choices and engagements during work time, their inquiry questions and "wonderings," and their research strategies. Some teachers carry clipboards for their notes, while others carry a journal. The critical issue is that the clipboard or journal is always with them so they can quickly jot down notes about events and conversations as they occur. These notes are quick jottings. Using complete sentences and thoughts is not important; capturing the essence of what is happening is.

Some teachers find it difficult to take many field notes during the day and so they reserve a time at the end of the day when they can write in a teaching journal. During the day, they jot a few notes to remind themselves of the significant events of that day. After children leave, they find a quiet corner and write a reflective account of what occurred. Other teachers schedule a time for writing in Learning Logs at the end of the day right before students leave. As students write in their logs, these teachers use the time for their own journaling.

As teachers gather field notes and artifacts from children such as written pieces, pictures, logs, webs, and charts, they need some way to analyze and make sense of children's learnings. They need to decide what they are looking for in these notes and artifacts. Checklists have become one way of delineating key processes in learning that can be used as a yardstick for indicating how well students are doing in a particular area. A checklist of reading strategies can be used to evaluate the range of strategies that particular students are currently using. They can also help teachers make decisions about curricular engagements that need to be offered to encourage students to expand those strategies.

Reading as Inquiry

- Reads for meaning
- Likes to read
- Self-selects books
- Sees him- or herself as a reader
- Makes personal connections
- Makes connections to other literature
- Appreciates different opinions and perspectives
- Expresses understanding in a variety of ways
- Actively contributes to class literature studies
- Participates in small group literature studies
- Uses a variety of strategies flexibly to overcome reading problems
- Can talk about reading and the reading process
- Selects books suited to the needs and interest of "buddy" during Buddy Reading

FIGURE 5.9
Reading as Inquiry Checklist (compliments of the teachers at The Center for Inquiry, Indianapolis)

Inquiry in Other Curricular Areas

- Uses personal experience to identify questions of interest
- Uses logic to make and seek meaningful connections
- Risks taking a stance and testing ideas
- Explores alternate perspectives on a topic through research and investigation
- Uses art, music, and movement to further sensitivity and understanding of a topic
- Attends to things that don't go as expected and uses these experiences to readjust thinking
- Can present what was learned to various audiences
- Takes time to reflect on what was learned and uses this experience to make new plans
- Takes thoughtful new actions which are reflected in attitude and behavior

FIGURE 5.10
Inquiry in Other Curricular Areas Checklist (compliments of the teachers at The Center for Inquiry, Indianapolis)

Teachers at The Center for Inquiry used the authoring cycle as a curricular frame to identify key behaviors in reading, writing, and other curricular areas. In terms of reading they set the following criteria: Makes personal connections with what is read; ties what is read to other books and experiences; uses others to gain new perspectives; and so forth. To date they have developed checklists of this sort for each major curricular area in an effort to map and report individual student progress.

The greatest value of checklists often lies in the thinking that goes into developing these lists, not in their use. In order to develop a checklist, teachers have to really think about what they value: what's of most importance to them in relation to this process or area. In fact, many teachers find that they soon abandon the checklist and begin writing narrative summaries. The checklist has served the purpose of helping them think through their criteria for analyzing artifacts and notes; now they can use these without actually filling out the checklist. Adopting someone else's checklist becomes an exercise in filling in the blanks and completely bypasses what makes these checklists a learning context for teachers.

These checklists can be collaboratively developed with students. Carolyn Burke has undergraduate students develop rubrics for assessment prior to their involvement in a curricular engagement. If, for example, they are to develop a curriculum notebook, they first discuss what they see as important components; on this basis they develop criteria for judging the final product.

One benefit of this procedure is that students can play a role in setting expectations as well as have firsthand knowledge of what is expected. On the negative side, unless students have "lived the process," the rubrics they develop can be quite shallow.

Narrative Report Cards

In her teacher article, Kathy Egawa describes how she and a study group of teachers at Gosport Elementary School worked together on the topic of evaluation. They found that what parents wanted on a report card was information on what was expected, on what went on in the classroom during the grading period involved, on how well their child did in terms of both expectation and the particular activities that had been planned, and on what it is they could do to support their child's learning.

They developed a narrative report card which was modified at The Center for Inquiry. The categories in this report are Reading as Inquiry, Writing as Inquiry, Mathematics as Inquiry, Inquiry in Other Curricular Areas, and the like. To introduce a category such as Reading as Inquiry, teachers write a paragraph about what it is that good readers do in terms of the inquiry cycle. This information is permanent and is not changed each grading period. Next teachers write a paragraph listing the specific engagements in reading from that semester. This section needs to be updated for each grading period, but it is the same for each child. Third, they write about how each child did in relationship to reading as inquiry, identifying areas of both strengths and weaknesses.

To facilitate this write up some teachers keep stenographer notebooks in which they jot observations throughout the semester, while others keep a tape recorder handy in which they make comments on specific children each day to be transcribed later. Children add their own assessment of how they are doing via a letter they write to their parents. To make this task somewhat manageable, students select different areas of the curriculum to talk about with their parents each grading period rather than talk about each and every area each time. Under each curricular area reported to parents is a blank space in which parents are invited to note any observations they made about their child relative to this curricular area. One week after the report card is sent home, parent-teacher-child conferences are held.

One of the complaints from teachers at the Center is that they needed up to fifty-four hours to complete the report cards for their class each time it was due. On the positive side they thought the report card worked extremely well. Becky Lane said one of the positive things was that it forced her to really think about curriculum in a way she had never done before. Carol Hall thought that she got to know the children in her room a whole lot better than she had ever known children in past years. Pam LaFranz said that she thought the report card made students less competitive. "They feel no pressure and don't see school in terms of doing better than someone else." Chris Collier thought that, despite the time involved, this procedure probably didn't really take all that much longer than any other report and "it was a lot more satisfying." Teachers realized that the report card was supporting home-school connections when a parent commented as she was leaving a parent-teacher-child conference, "You know, the nicest thing about this school is I don't feel like the teachers are trying to take my child away from me. In other schools I always felt like I wasn't a real part of my child's education."

Lingering Questions

Probably the most innovative approach to reflection we have seen is the procedure developed by Sunnyslope School outside of Phoenix. Teachers write reports based on kidwatching. Each narrative is written from the child's perspective about the child's appearance and actions in school, the child's interests and preferences as shown through his or her activities, the child's relationships with other children and adults, and a description of the child's learning. Negative comments about the child are never made.

Although an evaluation system of this sort is clearly the goal of the teachers at The Center for Inquiry, when they will get there is a

Dear Mama,

Mama this nine week I have improved my goal better than the last nine week. I have being writing better story and being on task and working hard. And the goal I set this week was to be on task and working hard and work on my being and ending sentence. And I think I have improved to

Love your son,

Jefferson

P.S.   My Goal this last nine week was to just about the same except my ending and being sentence. Well I got to go Lunch By

Student Self-assessment Letter to Parents as Part of Reporting System; Jefferson, Age 9 (compliments of Debbie Goodman)

matter of some debate. What we like about this system is that children are not compared against some arbitrary standard, but rather accepted as unique individuals who bring their own strengths to the world. Teachers are not there to assess so much as to learn through observation and on this basis plan supportive instruction. Inherent in the reporting system is a model of the world in which diversity, rather than consensus, is seen as a resource and strength. Conceptually, evaluation is seen as inquiry.

Another lingering question is our realization that the move to narrative report cards often does little to change our relationship with parents. Teachers are still reporting *to* parents, just in more powerful ways. We want to pursue other forms of evaluation which involve teachers, parents, and children working together in evaluating and providing the data needed to create learning environments and engagements that support children in their learning. Asking parents to write letters about their child's learning strategies and interests at the beginning of the year and exchanging Dialogue Journals where parents record their observations at home to share with the teacher open up a more equal exchange. Bringing children into this process in authentic ways through student-led conferences and self-evaluation reports with goals adds another dimension and challenge to this collaboration.

Unlike most efforts to reform evaluation, our current efforts reflect a philosophical shift which has been difficult to accomplish. We believe that evaluation is an integral part of the curricular process rather than something imposed after the fact in the name of accountability.

How such changes in thinking about evaluation can become widespread is a matter of some urgency. Currently words like portfolio assessment, performance-based assessment, outcome-based assessment, and authentic assessment pollute our landscape. For the most part these movements represent no real change in education. What is up for debate is what should be assessed. The underlying philosophy of assessment itself is never questioned. Bill Bintz and Jerry (1994) argue that these efforts still assume that we understand and can predict human development. They still ignore the use of multiple sign systems in learning, still privilege tests over kids as curricular informants, and still maintain hierarchical relationships between testers and testees. They still make student learning more vulnerable than teacher knowledge, still use performance-based tasks as criteria for and proof of learning, and still perpetuate disempowering social relationships between teachers and students. Most importantly, these efforts still conceptualize assessment as a tool for verifying existing theories of learning and confirming existing criteria for learning.

We believe a good starting point for thinking differently about the future of assessment is to interrogate our current assumptions about the nature of learning. Current assessment procedures assume that we know what inquiry questions children should be asking. They fail to allow us to identify and interrogate what lies behind children's real inquiry questions. Unfortunately, unless we can identify the intent underlying a learner's inquiry question, we have no idea how to support them instructionally. When preschoolers asked inquiry questions about Power Rangers and Ninja Turtles, their preschool teachers did not know how to support them until they realized that the intent behind their questions was an exploration of good guys versus bad guys. This realization led to a focus on folklore which gave the children the context they needed to explore good and evil.

To change assessment is to change how we think. Seeing assessment as an opportunity to inquire—to come to grips with and interrogate one's own values as a person and a community—could bring new life into assessment as well as education. We can think of few more important or more challenging goals.

Taking Thoughtful New Action Through Invitation and Reposition

Reflexivity is not just a mental exercise but a social one as well. Through this process learners decide what new stances to take as well as how it is that they are going to reposition themselves in the world.

The end result of inquiry is thoughtful new action. It is not good enough to simply know better; what is required is that we act better. It is here that inquirers invite themselves and others to take new more responsible social action. Now is the time to write a new identity by acting differently in the world. As an example, let us assume that as an inquirer you recently confronted and learned the subtle ways in which women have been discriminated against in the world. Now, then, is the time to commit yourself to acting differently in both speech and behavior. What real contributions to equity and justice are you going to make? What structures are you going to put in place to insure that the new conversations your inquiry has started are continued? What invitations are you going to offer to others that will support them in the process of coming to know for themselves what it is you have

"[Learners] may not learn what we want them to learn. They may not learn what we think we are teaching them. But they learn, if only that what we try to teach them is boring or that they are unlikely to learn what we think we are teaching. Learning is the brain continually updating its understanding of the world; we cannot stop the brain from doing this."

Smith, 1983, p.101

Chapter Five
Maintaining a
Community of Inquirers

learned? How are you, together with them, going to live the new life you want to live and be the new people you want to be?

What Are the Implications of Education as Inquiry for How We Work with Others?

Too often discussions of education begin with whatever topic is current in the media. Parents, especially, are vulnerable in that they have few other sources from which to get their information. Unfortunately, too often we inform parents of what we are doing for purposes of warding off problems rather than inviting them to become true partners in education. Education as inquiry calls for new ways of interacting with parents as well as new ways of operating as professionals.

Parent-School Partnerships

In Manitoba, Gary Kilarr and Wayne Serebrin are exploring an inquiry-based approach with parents. Based on parental concerns that phonics was not being directly taught as well as parents' genuine interest in helping their child learn to read, Wayne and Gary introduced the Burke Reading Interview (Burke, 1980). They also invited parents to collect data from their child in terms of how they view the reading process. At parent conferences they examine the data together and talk with them about how supporting the reading process is never just a matter of giving another strategy to learners, but changing their underlying beliefs about reading. Because parents were interested, Gary and Wayne introduced them to activities they might do at home to support their child's growth in reading.

A similar outreach program has been reported by Dorothy Strickland and members of her Literacy Coalition in a recent issue of *Primary Voices* devoted to the topic of meaningful change. What is significant about this effort is that not only are teachers and administrators working in a more open-ended inquiry approach, but they, in turn, are working with parents in a similar manner.

Each Wednesday afternoon the Center for Inquiry has what it calls Explorers Club. Parents with talents in a wide variety of areas—photography, drama, brick laying, karate, quilting, modern dance, jazz, nature exploration, farming—come in, organize, and lead their club. A parent of one of the children in the Center organizes the clubs that will be available during each quarter. Typically fifteen or more clubs are going at the same time, which means that the average size of the club is eight students, a number which does not intimidate most par-

"Why is it, in spite of the fact that teaching by pouring in, learning by passive absorption, are universally condemned, that they are still so entrenched in practice? That education is not an affair of 'telling' and being told, but an active and constructive process is a principle almost as generally violated in practice as conceded in theory" (p. 38).

John Dewey (1966)

Section One
The Authoring Cycle:
Let's Talk Curriculum

ents. The biggest problem so far is that parents keep volunteering to repeat their club for the next quarter, too.

Explorers clubs invite parents to participate in their child's education as well as legitimize the knowledge and various ways-of-knowing that are available in the community. Children expand their ways-of-knowing, gain a broader view of education, and come to know and respect the people in their community in new ways. Teachers learn too. Everyone, including the parents, has a new sense of values and of what really matters.

Luis Moll (1992), along with other researchers, has been involved in research on the funds of knowledge that are shared and exchanged among working-class households within social networks. These funds of knowledge represent the "essential cultural practices and bodies of knowledge that households use to survive, get ahead, or thrive" (p. 21) and are a potential social and intellectual resource for schools. Teachers have conducted visits to households to document the available funds of knowledge and then worked together to find ways to use this knowledge in the classroom. For example, one teacher developed a classroom unit on construction and building that included many library resources as well as building of models. Students' parents were invited to the classroom as experts during this study and their homework assignments encouraged them to tap the funds of knowledge in their homes and in other work sites.

Teachers as Learners

Education as inquiry is a philosophical call to see education, not as the transmission of truth but as lifelong learning. The issue, even for professionals, is not "Am I doing it right?" but "What did I learn from this attempt that I can use to improve my teaching?"

One of the most exciting movements in education has several labels—"teachers as learners," "teachers as researchers," "teachers as reflective practitioners"—depending upon with whom you are talking or what country you are in. The essence of this movement is to study one's own teaching for purposes of developing one's philosophy of teaching and then putting this philosophy into action in the classroom. Teacher-researcher study groups, sometimes under the auspices of a university (Manning & Harste, 1994), form themselves into collaboratives for purposes of sharing and reflecting on their own experience. Their goal is to develop their own personal theory of literacy instruction and, in the process, reclaim their profession. Any topic of personal interest is a starting point. Susan Settle (1994) began by keeping a reflective journal in which she noted her day-to-day concerns with implementing a process-centered reading and writing program. Jane Baskwill (1992) studied parent reaction to school decisions for purposes of better understanding the community in which she was teaching. In each case, the focus was self-help and the development of a more articulated personal theory of literacy instruction.

Teacher and principal study groups are another place where educators are able to set the agenda based on inquiry questions of personal and social significance to them (Short, Crawford, Kahn, Kaser, Klassen, & Sherman, 1992). The study group at Warren Elementary School in Tucson meets after school one afternoon a week on a biweekly basis. For these teachers, the study group supports their day-to-day living in classrooms and schools; it also provides a form of professional development that is not based on someone else's expertise and agenda. Because inquiry cannot be mandated, membership in this group is voluntary. The Warren group begins each year by brainstorming a list of issues and concerns that are critical to group members. At each meeting, the group starts by sharing concerns and successes; they then move into a discussion of their focus. They end the session by deciding what they want to discuss at their next meeting and whether or not they want to read an article or try some type of engagement or strategy in their classroom for the next meeting. For example, when teachers became interested in field notes, they all agreed to try some form of field notes in their classrooms before the next meeting. Teachers have continued taking university courses and attending conferences, but now they also have a place where they can think through these ideas with their peers as well as create their own ideas and understandings. The study group context supports them in acting to transform their teaching.

Although there have been a variety of efforts to reform undergraduate teacher education, one of the most exciting recent attempts is taking place at the University of Manitoba in Canada (Serebrin, 1994). Working with Joan Irwin, an historian and social studies professor in the School of Education, Wayne Serebrin has created a curriculum as an inquiry-based teacher preparation program for early childhood majors. Students begin with a focused inquiry into the community and end by developing playscapes for young children that invite them to explore themes of personal and social significance from a variety of perspectives. One of the unique features of the pro-

"Teaching well, like writing well, is about lingering longer to see and feel and experience things I might otherwise pass by; it's about being willing to risk failure and trusting my own voice. Like writing, teaching grows out of our passions, our sense of self, our faith in other people, our hope for the world. The way I teach has everything to do with finding a world in the backyard, feeding pigeons on the rooftop, and cherishing a fleet of orange slices on the window will. I nurture my teaching by nurturing my soul."

Calkins, 1991, p. 120

Section One
The Authoring Cycle:
Let's Talk Curriculum

gram is that preservice teachers are placed with classroom teachers. Together they become curriculum inquirers exploring topics of significance to them and the children in the room. Gone is the notion of hierarchy. In this program everyone is an inquirer. Currently the University of Manitoba is expanding this program to include all of the courses in the undergraduates' major area of study.

Lingering Questions

The question of whether an inquiry-based curriculum should be front-loaded on issues of equity and justice reflects a current debate in the field of education. Curriculum in inquiry-based classrooms is developed with the child rather than imposed on him or her. When and if children, through the course of their inquiries, raise issues of equity and justice, these naturally become the focus of curriculum, though we readily admit, not always successfully. Vivian Vasquez (1994) recently did a study of what issues her first graders raised in their journals and letters over the course of the year. Although their issues were valid (why they had to be sent to hot portable classrooms; why they had to study French when they had friends who spoke other languages they would prefer to study; why they couldn't pick their substitute teacher, and the like), all of these concerns were passed on to persons in authority but were never addressed. Adults saw their concerns as cute but not serious. So, while we have learned to accept children and their literacy, we have not learned to really respect their issues!

Because the world politically is not an even playing field—society is organized so that some issues are less likely to be addressed than others—some educators propose that issues of equity and justice need to be frontloaded onto the curriculum.

Our concern, of course, is that the direct instruction of concepts adults think important has always been the basis of curriculum and as such represents the very same thing we have been fighting against through developing the authoring cycle and inquiry-based curricula. Because issues of equity and justice are of concern to us too, this is not an easy dilemma to face. Clearly we do not want to throw away all that we have learned about the importance of building curricula from children; yet, just how one supports the exploration of such issues in an inquiry curriculum, without leaving it to unfair chance, is currently a major question for us.

Letter; Lindsey, Age 6
(Vasquez, 1994)

TRANSLATION
Dear Miss Vasquez I don't like supply (substitute) teachers because they don't let us do some of the things that you let us do and they don't let us finish our snacks and they don't let us sit on the couch and when we try and tell them we are the boss of this classroom they don't listen.

*Chapter Five
Maintaining a
Community of Inquirers*

Conclusion

"I went to a workshop the other day and learned about a new strategy to use in Literature Circles. It sort of bothers me but I can't tell why. I'm going to try it today and see. Do you want to come and watch?"

This invitation, given by Chris Collier, a teacher at The Center for Inquiry, to Karen Smith and Jerry was one they couldn't refuse.

The strategy lesson began with each child receiving a piece of paper divided into three sections with a blank space on top. Next, Chris asked each child to find a quote they liked in the chapter of the book they had read, *Charlotte's Web* (White, 1952). In the first column they wrote what they thought of the quote and drew a picture. They then passed it on to a neighbor who read the quote and what they had written; their neighbor then wrote a response which they too could illustrate if space permitted. The third turn was up to the child. Either they could write a second response or pass it on to someone else in the group for another response.

The activity proceeded smoothly. Children interacted well together. What they said was pertinent given the quote the child had chosen. Yet, all was not well. The chapter they had read was the third chapter in *Charlotte's Web* where Charlotte, one of the central characters in the whole book, is introduced. Her personality colors what happens from that point on in the book.

What the children had done, not surprisingly, was copy sentences out of the book such as, "She sucked blood out of her victims like a vampire." These were gross enough for their tastes, and you can imagine the responses that ensued. Despite the businesslike demeanor of the class, the problem was what children said had nothing to do with the chapter or their understanding of Charlotte and the role she plays in the story. The strategy lesson pulled them away from, rather than into, the book. Needless to say, once Chris saw the strategy lesson in the context of children's use of it in the classroom and in the context of a book she loved, she did not need Karen and Jerry to help her do her own critical debriefing of the strategy.

We share this story because it is easy to get in the habit of adding new activities into the curriculum with little real thought. The end result, like this experience, is often disappointing.

In lieu of this additive approach we recommend incorporating only those engagements that are theoretically consistent with the philosophy underlying your curriculum. In our case, what is central is

The authoring cycle began to drive our classrooms, our curriculum, and our own professional investigations and development. Throughout the entire year we, as teachers, were involved in our own authoring cycle. The importance of collaboration and conversation, and the powers of voice, choice, and reflection helped us examine assumptions that guide our practices as we continued to change our views of learners, learning, teaching and curriculum. Short and Burke (1991) have helped us learn that change in the classroom comes from within, not without, and that we must take responsibility for change. And, perhaps most importantly, only when learners support each other from the inside can powerful curricular changes be made. (Maras & Brummett, 1995)

FIGURE 5.11

inquiry and multiple ways-of-knowing. Because an inquiry curriculum ought to support the underlying processes of inquiry, these processes become criteria we use to judge the merits of a new engagement as well as where in the curriculum a particular engagement might best fit.

Because of the long traditions of hierarchy, competition, and individualism in schools, establishing and sustaining a new social context for learning is a difficult task. Taking an inquiry perspective is not always easy to carry out in the classroom. As teachers, we want our classrooms to operate smoothly and we often abandon experiences that are not successful. If children have difficulty writing or working in groups, we tend to say, "Well, this just isn't going to work in this class." If, instead, we operate from a theory of curriculum which says that conversation and collaboration are important, then we are willing to inquire and make hard but important changes in our own teaching practices which support our new visions for schooling, curriculum, and literacy.

Curricular Engagements

Anomalies
Graffiti Board
Webbing What's on Your Mind

Introduction

We learn from exploring "what's on our minds." As we interact with people and texts, we search for patterns that connect our current experiences to past events, texts, and feelings. It is through these connections that we are able to make sense of those experiences, to create some kind of unity that allows us to understand the relationships across our experiences. As we share what's on our minds, however, we not only search for connections but we attend to difference. It is the "yet to be understood" that fascinates us and that serves our natural desire to learn. When we are faced with an anomaly, an unexpected occurrence or surprise, our attention turns to generating hypotheses to explain that anomaly. Once we reach a working solution, our attention turns elsewhere.

This tension in learning reminds us that knowledge is always tentative. The next anomaly could cause us to make major changes in our beliefs about how the world works. Tension keeps us alert, monitoring our experiences for ambiguities, stretching ourselves and our capabilities. Only when outside forces act coercively on learners do they disregard or refuse to deal with anomalies and their own connections because the price of pursuing them is too costly.

FIGURE CE1.1
List of Anomalies for **The**
Flunking of Joshua T. Bates
(Shreve, 1984); Amy, Age 9
(Gloria Kauffman's classroom)

> Joshua J. Bates
>
> 1. Why couldn't his parents help with his reading?
> 2. Was Joshua's teacher the only one that took the time to help him? Why?
> 3. Was it his teacher that helped Joshua first or did she give him confedence in himself?
> 4. Was it fair for Mrs. Goodwin to help Joshua pass?

In schools, the focus on correct answers has led students to edit what's on their minds. They only share the responses they think the teacher wants. They are sure no teacher wants to hear or values what they are really thinking about. We need curricular engagements that encourage students to explore the connections and tensions they are thinking about so that these can be examined in conversations with other learners. These engagements legitimize the messiness that is an essential part of learning.

Materials/Procedures for Anomalies

▮ Multiple copies of a reading selection
▮ Four 3" × 5" cards or slips of paper per reader

1. Readers are asked to read the same selection or engage in the same experience. The selection or experience chosen should con-

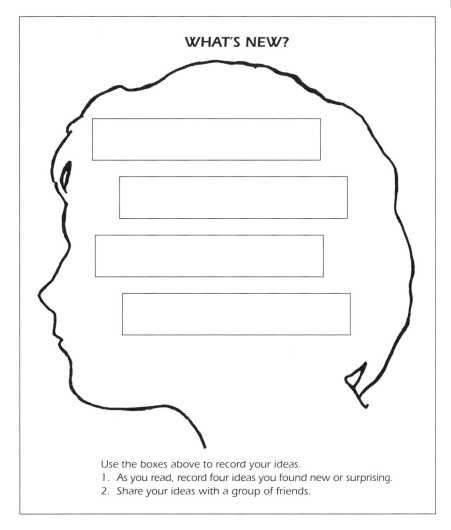

WHAT'S NEW?

Use the boxes above to record your ideas.
1. As you read, record four ideas you found new or surprising.
2. Share your ideas with a group of friends.

tain issues that are potentially controversial or new for the particular students involved.

2. Students are asked to write one quotation from the selection on
each of four 3" × 5" cards, either during or after reading. The quotations selected should be items that were new and exciting or
that caused them problems as they read. They can also be points
at which readers found themselves stopping to rethink or reread.
or
Students record the questions and issues that trouble them as they
read the selection or engage in the experience.

Anomalies
Graffiti Board
Webbing What's on
Your Mind

FIGURE CE1.3
Graffiti Board for Text Set on Other People's Beliefs About You; Chela, Tommy, Irene, Monique, Ages 10 and 11 (Gloria Kauffman's classroom)

3. As students finish writing the four cards, they rank order their four cards from most anomalous or surprising to least anomalous.

4. When students come back together in a group, each person reads his or her top anomaly to the group and shares why that item was surprising.

5. After sharing, discussion turns to why certain tensions were similar or different across the people in the group.

Materials/Procedures for Graffiti Board

▌ A large sheet of brainstorming chart paper
▌ A marker for each person

1. Students engage in some type of shared experience such as reading from a particular Text Set or shared book set, exploring a particular concept, or participating in a science observation.

2. During the shared experience, students sit in small groups at tables with a large piece of brainstorming paper in the middle of the table. At various points throughout the experience, students are invited to stop and write their observations and reflections on the paper in the form of graffiti. Each person takes his or her own corner of the paper and works alone, sketching and writing images, words, and phrases that come to mind. There is no particular order or organization to these images and words. They are simply added randomly to the graffiti board.

3. Students within each small group share their graffiti entries with each other and use these to identify issues and connections to begin a dialogue or to create a more organized web, chart, or diagram of their connections, either in the small group or as a whole class.

Materials/Procedures for Webbing What's on Your Mind

▌ A large sheet of brainstorming chart paper
▌ Markers

1. After engaging in a shared experience such as a literature discussion of a text set or initial engagements in an inquiry focus, students take the time to share their initial responses, connections, and anomalies with one another through conversation. Sometimes this sharing is supported by engagements such as Graffiti Board, Anomalies, or Sketch to Stretch. As in any brainstorming engagement, all responses are accepted.

2. When students have shared what's on their minds and want to find an in-depth focus for dialogue, they create a visual web of their connections and anomalies. One member of the group serves as the scribe and writes the focus (title of the book, the concept, or the name of the experience) in the middle of the web. The group works together to create an organized visual web of the connections and anomalies that were shared as well as any new ideas

Anomalies
Graffiti Board
Webbing What's on
Your Mind

FIGURE CE1.4
Webbing What's on Your Mind
in a Literature Log Entry;
Melissa, age 10 (Gloria
Kauffman's classroom)

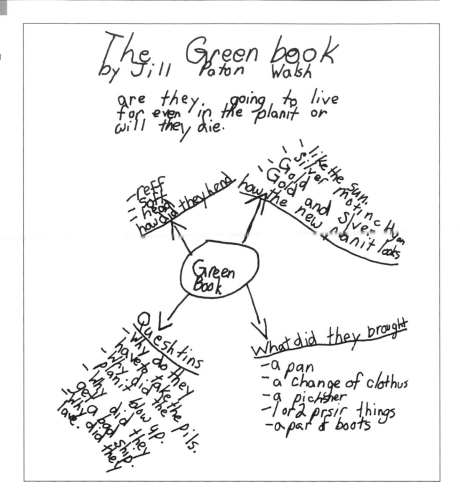

and issues that are raised through the webbing. These items are
not discussed, simply placed on the web. As ideas are suggested,
related ideas and issues are placed together on the web, although
the amount of organization into categories will vary greatly by the
group and how much they have already discussed.

3. Once the web has been created, the group examines the web
and reaches a group decision on what they want to discuss at their
next meeting. Students are then responsible for preparing for that
discussion and may spend time talking about how they will prepare.

4. As the group continues to meet, the web is always placed in the
middle of their group so that it can be referred to for other topics

Section Two
Curricular
Engagements

of discussion. New ideas and issues are added in a different color of marker as they arise. Not everything on the web is discussed in depth. The group selects from their web the issues they feel are worth examining together.

5. When the group finishes, they either add to their web in another color or create a new web showing the ways in which their thinking has changed over time. These webs can be used to share informally with the rest of the class or as the basis for deciding what ideas they want to present to others.

Establishing the Learning Context

These engagements depend on a learning environment that encourages students to take the risk of pursuing tensions and personal connections rather than looking for further support for beliefs they already hold. Depending on students' past instructional histories, they may hesitate to pursue anomalies and instead search for the "right" answer that they believe the teacher will ask them to provide. Students may need to be involved in these engagements several times to demonstrate that it really is okay to search for and think about what's really on their minds.

Variations

1. These engagements can also be used with a presentation or lecture, a piece of art, a musical composition, a dramatic presentation, or other form of communication. As students listen or observe, they write down their anomalies and connections.

2. Students can record their anomalies or connections on a worksheet highlighting that these come from what's on their minds.

3. Students can be asked to write about an experience that "caused them to think." This invitation gives writers the space to formulate as well as to generate possible alternatives for responding to a problem. When students share these pieces of writing,

Anomalies
Graffiti Board
Webbing What's on
Your Mind

others will be able to follow the mental processes of the writers to see how they resolved the tensions they felt while thinking about possible responses.

References

Harste, J.C. 1988. "What it means to be strategic: Good readers as informants." *Reading-Canada-Lecture* 6(1): 28–36.
Shreve, Susan. 1984. *The flunking of Joshua T. Bates.* New York: Knopf.

FIGURE CE1.5
Web on the meaning of confidence created when the child came across the word in a book and couldn't ask anyone what it meant; Natalia, Age 6 (Jean Schroeder's classroom)

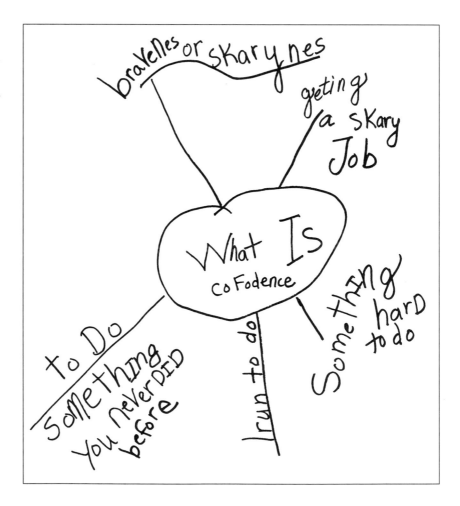

Authors Circle
Writing in the Round

Introduction

Authors Circle demonstrates to writers that their first concern is the meaning of what they want to say, not the conventions of writing. It helps them see that writing is an ongoing process that may require revision to clarify meaning. Authors Circle demonstrates the social nature of writing and helps develop a sense of audience as writers read what they have written to an audience, and the audience responds. This process gives authors the opportunity to shift from the perspective of writer to that of reader to that of critic, and thus to take a new look at their compositions.

The Authors Circle is made up of three to four authors who read aloud their writing to the group and receive responses and suggestions. Students bring their writing to an Authors Circle when they want to think about it with others. Sometimes they want to work through a particular problem; other times they bring a piece they are considering publishing and want an audience perspective. Many informal types of writing such as messages and journals never go to an Authors Circle.

Because only meaning-related questions are asked of the writer, risk taking is facilitated. Authors Circle helps writers clarify what they have written based on the audience's questions and responses.

Authors receive help on what is and is not working in their writing and what, if anything, they might consider doing next. It is important that all participants bring a piece of writing and that all leave feeling the group has been productive for them as authors. Authors should be helped to understand that the function of Authors Circle is to help them become better writers and that, as members of an Authors Circle, their role is to support the further development of themselves and each other as writers. The curricular impact of Authors Circle will be lost if it becomes another place to share rather than critique their work with others. Authors chair provides a place for those who only want to share.

Writers are encouraged to consider the reactions of others, although they are not obligated to modify what they have written. They consider privately the recommendations made and arrive at their own decisions regarding any changes in their writing. It is essential that the author retain this decision-making responsibility, thereby maintaining ownership of the piece. After leaving the Authors Circle and making decisions on revisions, authors may choose to return to another Authors Circle, take their piece to Editors Table, or put the piece back into their Authors Folder and not publish it at that time.

Materials/Procedures

■ Sign-up sheets for Authors Circle or a revision box for rough drafts ready to go to Authors Circle
■ Small round table or desks formed into a circle

Small groups of three to four writers who have a piece they want to think more about with other authors attend an Authors Circle. Several different variations of Authors Circle are presented here. All of these variations focus on supporting authors in exploring and critiquing their pieces of writing but differ according to their experience with Authors Circles and their needs as authors.

Procedure A (often used when pieces are in process)

1. Authors bring their pieces to the group, but they do not read them aloud. Instead, authors talk about what the particular piece

is, why they chose to write it, and the strategies they used as they wrote. They also indicate any particular problems that they want the group to think about with them.

2. The other participants in the group ask the author what other strategies and alternatives he or she might try with this particular piece of writing.

3. If appropriate, participants may then offer suggestions of other options the author might want to consider.

4. After everyone has had a chance to talk about their writing, the group disbands and authors continue to work on their pieces. The author later takes the piece to another Authors Circle where the piece is read aloud for response (see Procedures B, C, & D).

Procedure B (often used in beginning circles)

1. The first author reads the piece aloud to the other authors in the Authors Circle.

2. The listeners receive the piece by telling what they heard in the piece, especially focusing on what they found most effective.

3. The listeners have the opportunity to raise questions about parts that were unclear to them, areas where they felt additional information was needed, or to make any other comments about the meaning of the piece. The author can take notes to remember comments.

4. The next author reads a piece and the process continues until each author has been heard and received responses.

5. The authors leave the circle to consider the suggestions that were made and to arrive at their own decisions.

Procedure C (often used once students have experience with circles)

1. The first author tells the group what he or she likes best about the piece, identifies troublesome parts, asks for response to certain areas, and then reads the piece aloud.

Authors Circle

2. The group discusses and explores ideas on how to deal with the author's concerns. The author makes notes on the listeners' recommendations.

3. Once the group has discussed the identified areas to the author's satisfaction, they talk about parts of the piece they particularly liked and raise questions about meaning.

4. The next author continues the process in the same manner until all participants have had a chance to get a response to their writing.

5. Sometimes authors do not want to have the group immediately respond to specific parts of a piece. Instead, they want to get the group's general response. In this case, the author reads the piece to the group, who then respond with statements about what they found effective and where they have further questions or confusions. Following this discussion, the author may ask for help with specific areas if desired.

Procedure D (used when authors need help with a specific problem)

1. During writing, authors often encounter difficulty with a particular part of a draft and are unable to figure out how to deal with it, even after talking informally with other writers.

2. The author may go to an Authors Circle to help brainstorm possible ways to deal with the difficult part. The author can choose three or four particular students the author feels will be able to help think through the difficulty, ask for volunteers, or join one of the ongoing Authors Circles.

3. The author identifies the problem area and then reads the piece aloud to the group.

4. The group and the author brainstorm possible ways of handling the problem.

Establishing the Learning Context

When Authors Circles first begin, the teacher plays an essential role in setting the tone for the type of exchange that will occur. The goal is to create a supportive environment for authors. Students will initially be unsure of the types of questions to ask or how to listen to someone else's piece. Comments that are not supportive or that deal with aspects other than meaning are discouraged. Similarly, comments that deal with portions of the story that the author did not identify as problematic should play only a minor role in the discussion. The goal is to give the author ideas but to permit the author to take the lead, and to limit the majority of suggestions to what the author wishes to address.

Teachers can use the group meeting before work time begins to have the entire class respond to a student's work in order to demonstrate ways of talking and thinking about writing in Authors Circle. Scheduling an author talk time at the end of the daily work time also provides students with important demonstrations and experiences in talking about their work with others. During author talk time, students do not read pieces to each other, but meet briefly as partners, in small groups, or as a class to talk about insights or problems they encountered during their work time that day. Because author talk time occurs daily, students are encouraged to talk about their in-process work and so this sharing time can have a significant impact on re-thinking and re-visioning a piece of writing.

Like other participants at Authors Circle, teachers are free to make suggestions, but their recommendations bear no more weight than anyone else's. Students need to understand that they do not have to accept a teacher's recommendation. When teachers bring their own writing to the group, they are more likely to be seen as participants. Although teachers should not be part of every Authors Circle, the first circles should be scheduled so teachers can walk students through the process. Once students understand how to conduct Authors Circles, the teacher does not need to be present in every circle. Students may form and meet in Authors Circles by themselves, with the teacher joining the groups only occasionally or briefly.

Teachers also need to be aware of the authors' needs and experiences in developing procedures for Authors Circles that support authors in thinking about their writing with other authors. These procedures should not become so routinized that authors ask automatic questions of one another without really listening or thinking with others. Once teachers and students understand the function of Authors Circles within the authoring cycle, they can create their own variations to meet their changing needs and learning contexts.

Authors Circle

> Me and my frarand
> Kams to thes plas
> a vrey tim, i LoK at
> it tha Jis it gru
> gras and a tree
> aBehiv. A Bee stug me
> and I so 2 skorp
> ins.

Changes in the Desert

Emanuel and I went to the desert. We go there often. We just play tag and climb up trees.

The desert is all dirt with a bunch of bushes. A coyote lived in one bush. We noticed the tracks and one time we saw the coyote.

Everytime I go to the desert, it changes. I don't know why it changes.

I went to the desert after it rained. I noticed that the grass had grown.

My favorite tree had changed. Before it didn't have any branches and now it does. I'm mad because now I can't climb the tree because I get scratches. So I chopped the branches off.

Now I'm happy.

Variations

1. It may be necessary for authors, especially young children, to read their pieces through twice so that listeners get a frame for the piece and then are able to listen for meaning the second time. Young children often are better able to respond to a draft on a storyboard which has visual references they can refer to during the circle.

2. Once the Authors Circle pattern has been established, students may be encouraged to gather a few classmates informally to listen and respond to a piece. Even one or two listeners may be sufficient to meet an author's needs. In many instances, authors will select students whose opinions they value on the topic of concern to them.

3. As authors' pieces become lengthier, it may be necessary to provide copies of the drafts for each listener. This should be consid-

ered only after a tone has been set that focuses on content and not on convention.

4. *Writing in the Round:* Some teachers introduce revision by having students share their writing in small groups. Students exchange papers with one another and write one question they believe the author should consider to improve the draft. After each member of the small group has read each paper and written a question, the author gets the piece back and decides which of the questions, if any, will be considered in a second draft.

5. Students can use drama to help them think through their stories, especially if their stories involve action or dialogue. The author watches as other students either read through the story as a Readers Theatre or act out the story as a drama. Drama can be used during writing to help the author get past a difficult section, or after completing an initial draft of a story the author is considering revising.

FIGURE CE2.3
Journal Entry; Laura, Age 8
(Ruth Ann Peachy's classroom)

References

Atwell, N. 1987. *In the middle*. Portsmouth, NH: Heinemann.

Calkins, L. M. 1983. *Lessons from a child*. Portsmouth, NH: Heinemann.

——. 1991. *Living between the lines*. Portsmouth, NH: Heinemann.

——. 1994. *The art of teaching writing* new edition. Portsmouth, NH: Heinemann.

Graves, D. 1983. *Writing: Teachers and children at work*. Portsmouth, NH: Heinemann.

Murray, D. 1989. *Expecting the unexpected*. Portsmouth, NH: Heinemann.

Authors Circle

Authors Folder
Reflection Portfolio

Introduction

Writing is an ongoing process that involves constant decision making by the author on how to communicate a written message. Authors need a learning environment that provides a structure that supports them in focusing on meaning, taking risks, making choices, and keeping track of ideas and pieces of writing. Authors also need structures that allow them to reflect on their writing processes and strategies as well as reflexively to consider and critique their values and beliefs about authoring and to offer invitations for future experiences.

Authors Folders provide the organizational support that authors need for writing over time. Authors keep both current and past drafts of writing in their folders, along with lists of ideas for writing. They can thus continue to work on pieces of writing that are currently in progress and to revisit earlier drafts as they write. These folders highlight and support the role of the author as a decision maker in selecting what to write, how to write, and how long to write. Authors need varying amounts of time to develop their pieces and should not feel pressured to complete writing in one day's time. Students use their Authors Folders to select pieces of writing they want to continue working on and take through Authors Circle, Editors Table, and into informal or formal publication.

Monitoring growth as a writer is central to an author's continued development. Authors Folders and Reflection Portfolios give students a way to monitor and evaluate growth over time and to focus on process as well as mechanics. The folders provide a cumulative record of an author's pieces of writing. Authors can use the folders to take a mental trip as they remember and revisit the past, work in the present, and plan the future. These folders provide a collection from which students can select work for their Reflection Portfolios to reflexively interrogate who they are as writers. In these portfolios, they consider what they write, how they write, and why they write. Through this critical examination of who they are as writers, they are able to reposition themselves and take thoughtful new action.

Materials/Procedures for Authors Folders

▮ One or two strong manila file or pocket folders for each student
▮ Cardboard box for storing the file folders
▮ Date stamp and ink pad

1. As soon as students begin writing, they are given a folder to collect their writing over the course of the year. The writing kept in the folders consists of the stories and articles that students perceive as publishable rather than informal writing such as pen pal letters and messages. Pieces of writing in the folder are in various stages of revision; they might include jottings of ideas, pieces that are currently being written or revised, partial or completed pieces that the author has abandoned or decided not to publish, and pieces that have already been published.

2. Students date each piece of writing, staple all draft copies of a single piece together, and file the writing in the folder from oldest to newest. A list of all of the pieces is kept on one side of the folder with asterisks next to the titles of published pieces.

3. The folders are stored in a cardboard box in a set location in the classroom so that when students are going to write, they can easily get their folders. Folders are returned to the box when writing is completed for the day.

4. A brainstormed list of ideas or topics to write about is usually kept in the folder, to be changed as the author adds or uses ideas from the list. When ideas occur to students as they are involved in writing, reading, and other kinds of experiences or as they interact

Authors Folder
Reflection Portfolio

> Leah
> Who I am as a student,
> What has chaged.
> I have red a lot of books I
> use to not be a bold to read
> at all. Now I can also put my
> ideas on paper and its amazing
> how I flew, I presintate much
> much better,

with other children in the classroom, they quickly jot these ideas down on their lists for future reference.

5. Authors will often need more than one folder as their writing piles up during the year. Teachers can establish two different sets of folders for authors. The first set contains folders in which students keep work that is currently in progress as well as their lists of topics. The second set is for folders of past work that students either abandoned or completed. These folders are also a place to store notes, letters, and messages. It is important that students be able to return to past work to see how they handled problems in an earlier draft and to be able to look at their growth throughout the year. Students may also decide to reactivate an earlier piece and either continue writing a piece that had been partially completed or write a new draft of a completed piece.

6. Teachers should regularly invite students to look through their folders to reflect on the types of writing they are pursuing and their strategies as writers. Students can informally share with others in small groups or as a class. They can also write brief self-evaluations.

Materials/Procedures for Reflection Portfolios

1. Three times a year, students are encouraged reflexively to critique who they are as writers and where they want to go next.

These portfolios are usually not done at the end of a grading period so that students do not associate them with external evaluation and grades, but rather view them as a tool for their own reflection and learning.

2. To begin this process, the class brainstorms what they can gather to show who they are as writers on a large chart. This brainstorming occurs at the end of their daily uninterrupted writing time. Students are encouraged to think about the writing they do throughout the day. This brainstorming chart is hung on the wall for reference and to add additional items.

3. Students gather their writing from everywhere—Authors Folders, journals, logs, notes, letters, lists, and so forth—to create huge mounds on their desks.

4. Students browse through their mounds. Then they share their mounds and what they noticed about their writing with another person.

5. The class comes together to brainstorm their thinking on questions such as: Who are we as writers? What's important to us? What are we working on right now?

6. Students return to their mounds and select pieces of writing they feel indicate what is most important to them right now and reflect their growth, efforts, struggles, and writing process. They are *not* asked to choose favorite or best pieces of work. "Best" often signals to students that they need to use teacher criteria and "favorite" often takes them away from a focus on themselves as writers to personal issues.

Students are encouraged to be selective and to narrow down their number of choices. Journal and log entries are photocopied so they do not have to be taken out of the notebook. They also consider the items already in their portfolio. Students can decide whether the items already in their portfolios will remain. They can also decide to remove items and put them into their Authors Folder.

7. Once students have selected a limited number of writing artifacts, they share what they have chosen with a partner and talk about why they picked those pieces. If students are having difficulty, the class gathers together for a whole group sharing.

Authors Folder
Reflection Portfolio

This is the math portion of my port folio. It shows some of my work in 9 weeks time. On this paper I will talk about things that I've learned, things that I didn't learn, and things I would like to learn. Some of the things I learned were some stradigies I used during the math invitations. What I did do was to look at how much room the object took up and how much space there is. Some thing else I learned ~~from~~ ~~the~~ the math invitations. Some of the things I learned from it was how to build things and figure out the value. There are many different ways to figure out the value of the buildings. One of the way I used was to count each block as a dollar if you use hundreds tens and thousands blocks because they have little squares. There are also things I didn't learn that I would of liked to. Those things would be to learn all the different stradigies that people used because they might of been better than the ones that I used I would also like to know the process people used to get their awnsers and how did our teachers get the idea for the invitations. I still have a question that I couldn't figure out. That question is why am I learning estimation again when I was already adding subtracting multiplying and dividing at the same time. I have set some goals for myself to. Those goals were to be able to think and learn the same as a math matition and to be able to think up something and write it down without a problem.

8. Students make their final selections and write a tag for each item they select. The tag explains what the item is and why they chose it. As they write these tags, the class often gathers for informal sharing to hear what others are writing. The tags are usually written on half-sheets of paper and stapled to the writing piece.

9. Students meet with a partner to share their portfolios with each other. They share each piece and read the tag. They then talk about what they learned about themselves as writers.

10. The class meets together to talk about how students would describe themselves as writers. After a number of students have shared their descriptions, they create a brainstormed list on a chart of the kinds of goals they want to work for in their future writing.

11. Each student writes a one-page reflection which first describes how that student sees himself or herself as a writer and then establishes goals for the next period of time.

12. The one-page reflections are shared with parents and placed into the students' cumulative file to go on to other teachers. Students also sometimes choose three pieces of writing at the end of the year from the Authors Folder or portfolio to put into their cumulative folder; this is forwarded to the next year's teacher. This process gradually builds a record of the student's growth throughout elementary school for referral. The rest of the writing is sent home with the student at the end of the year.

13. The portfolio itself belongs to the student and is not shared with others outside of the class unless the student chooses to do so. The primary function of this portfolio is to support self-reflection, not for others to evaluate the student.

Establishing the Learning Context

The teacher's primary function is to work with students in creating an organizational structure that facilitates writing as an ongoing process of creating and reflecting on meaning. A location and a procedure for using the writing folders needs to be established as well as regular routines for students to reflect on writing. These folders provide a way for students to self-evaluate their writing, because they

Authors Folder
Reflection Portfolio

can look at their writing from various perspectives over time. Teachers also use the folders for evaluation and need to develop a system that allows them regularly to read through students' folders and make comments. Many teachers find it helpful to look through five or six folders at a time rather than trying to look at all the folders at one time.

Reflection Portfolios are successful only in contexts where students have had many experiences as writers and so can gather a large collection of writing from which they can select items for their portfolios. A daily emphasis on oral and written reflection is also essential in order for students to be able reflexively to critique themselves as writers and learners from the more distant stance required by the portfolio. During the portfolio experience, students need many opportunities to share with a partner and the whole class so that students are able to put their thinking into words and to consider other alternatives.

Variations

1. Large three-ring binders can be used instead of folders for students' writing from year to year. At the end of each year, the student and teacher decide which pieces will go into the binder. At the end of elementary school, the student is given the collection of writing as a graduation present.

2. Cumulative writing folders or binders can be used to demonstrate growth to curriculum coordinators and administrators and to develop handouts to orient parents to the kinds of growth they can expect in their children as a result of the process writing program. Teachers should always have these folders available for referral during parent-teacher conferences.

3. Teachers can keep a folder of their own writing to share with students. This type of file can be used to demonstrate the value of revision, to illustrate why certain attitudes are problematic to the growth of a writer, and to point out and invite students to develop their own writing styles and idiosyncrasies.

4. The portfolio process can be used to support student reflection in other areas such as thinking about who they are as readers,

artists, mathematicians, scientists, or historians. Typically only two of these areas are selected at any one time.

5. Students can put together portfolios to reflect broadly on who they are as learners. Students gather collections for these portfolios in boxes or baskets to reflect their learning both inside and outside of school. They can include a wide range of artifacts and objects rather than written materials. This type of portfolio is especially effective at the beginning of the year because it connects school and home experiences and introduces students to reflective thinking.

6. Students can use a bulletin board to create a portfolio of their development across the school year. Elena Castro takes a large bulletin board and divides it into spaces for each of her students. At the end of the first month of school, students each choose a piece of writing that they feel shows who they are as writers and put it on their space on the board. Each month they add another piece of writing to the board so that over time the board reflects a history of their development as writers. Visitors to the room often look through a particular child's drafts and get a sense of children's growth and change as writers.

References

Anthony, R. 1991. *Evaluating literacy: A perspective for change*. Portsmouth, NH: Heinemann.

Baskwill, J., & P. Whitman. 1988. *Evaluation: Whole language, whole child*. New York: Scholastic.

Bird, L., K. Goodman, & Y. Goodman. 1994. *The whole language catalog: Forms for authentic assessment*. New York: Macmillan.

Crafton, L., & C. Burke. 1994. "Inquiry-based evaluation: Teachers and students reflecting together." *Primary Voices K–6* 2(2): 2–7.

Goodman, K. 1992. *The whole language catalog: Supplement on authentic assessment*. New York: Macmillan.

Goodman, K., Y. Goodman, & W. Hood, eds. 1989. *The whole language evaluation book*. Portsmouth, NH: Heinemann.

Graves, D. 1983. *Writing: Teachers and children at work*. Portsmouth, NH: Heinemann.

Authors Folder
Reflection Portfolio

———. 1995. *A fresh look at writing*. Portsmouth, NH: Heinemann.

Graves, D., & B. Sunstein. 1992. *Portfolio portraits*. Portsmouth, NH: Heinemann.

Newkirk, T., & N. Atwell, eds. 1988. *Understanding writing: Ways of observing learning and teaching*. 2d ed. Portsmouth, NH: Heinemann.

Rhodes, L., & N. Shankin. 1993. *Windows into literacy: Assessing learners K–8*. Portsmouth, NH: Heinemann.

Short, K., & G. Kauffman. 1992. "Hearing students' voices: The role of reflection in learning." *Teachers Networking* 11(3): 1, 3–6.

Tierney, R. 1991. *Portfolio assessment in the reading-writing classroom*. Norwood, MA: Christopher-Gordon.

FIGURE CE3.3
Self-evaluation in October;
Rilea, Age 8 (Margaret
Ferguson's classroom)

I am begining to feel like 2nd grader. My favorite subject is Math, I am very good at Math. I can make alot of questions, usally I can find the answers to them. I can read very good I get alot of my ideas from books. What will the futer be like since I'me learning? Will it be bad or good? I would like to now how to be a teacher Techers seam so smart. Also I woud like toknow how to be a scien ist? Because Its fundaing experment with the mandycas.

Section Two
Curricular
Engagements

Authors Meeting Authors

Introduction

Students' recognition of themselves as authors is facilitated when they have the chance to meet professionally published authors or when they hear and read about the lives and the authoring processes of professional authors. These professional authors may be writers, poets, or illustrators. Students begin to see professional authors as real people who have to work hard at their authoring and who encounter difficulties, just as students do. Learning about and meeting authors demystifies the authoring process and opens students up to exploring different strategies in their own writing and illustrating. Students also develop a personal feeling for authors whom they have met or learned about, and so they search for that person's work at the library and begin to recognize an individual's style. As they become familiar with certain authors, they make better predictions when they read that person's work, and this, in turn, facilitates their comprehension.

Materials/Procedures

- Biographical information on authors
- Displays of the authors' books

Types of Author Studies

1. The teacher sets up regular displays in the classroom that feature a particular writer, poet, or illustrator. The display includes the

featured author's books and biographical information. If the author is an illustrator, the display can include the art media used by that illustrator so that students can try out the illustration technique.

On the first day, the author is introduced to the class by telling students briefly about the person's background and sharing personal life stories or comments the author has made about his or her work. If a video or filmstrip on the person is available, it is shown to the class (Weston Woods and Random House are the best sources).

On the following days, the teacher shares books written or illustrated by that person with the class through short book introductions, reading excerpts, or reading the entire book aloud. Students are also encouraged to choose that person's work for their own wide reading.

Once students have explored the author's work and learned more about the author as a person, they should be given an opportunity to respond in some way. This response might be at group sharing time or in Literature Circles where students talk with each other about that person's work, or the response might be whole-class, small-group, or individual projects. Students can create a drama based on a book, do various kinds of art projects, perform a Readers Theatre from one or several books, create a display based on a book, or write their own stories using characters from the books or based on the author's style. Students often write to the author asking questions that grow out of their study of the author.

2. Students should be encouraged to engage in their own research on favorite writers, poets, and illustrators. This research process involves gathering the author's books from the library and locating biographical information. Students can share what they learn in their research through displays or presentations to the class.

3. Literature Circles can be organized around a Text Set on a particular author, illustrator, or poet. The Text Set includes that person's work and biographical information. Students begin by browsing and reading in the Text Set, sharing and looking for connections and comparisons across the books. Then they examine the biographical materials before returning again to consider the books themselves. Students may also engage in further research on the author for additional information. When they finish their discussion, they present their author to other groups.

Autobiographical books for children are now available by authors such as Roald Dahl, Beverly Cleary, Laurence Yep, Betsy Byars, Jean Little, and Phyllis Naylor. A group may want to first read multiple copies in a shared book set on the biography and then read different books from a Text Set of that person's work. Another way to use these biographies is to have the teacher read aloud the autobiography while each group reads and discusses a different novel by that author.

Author Interviews

1. The class gathers and explores the author's published work and biographical information through read-aloud, browsing, wide reading, and discussions in Literature Circles.

2. Students make a list of what they already know about the author.

3. Students work in small groups to list questions about what else they want to know about this author. Before the groups are brought back together, they check their questions against the chart of known information and eliminate unneeded questions.

4. The groups then come together to compile their questions into one list. (More than one list may be needed if several interviews will be taking place.)

5. The author is invited to visit the class and is asked to share writings or drawings, samples of rough drafts, and a brief personal history. As the person shares, students should be listening carefully so they don't repeat questions that have already been addressed. If an actual visit is not possible, communication can occur through writing or through a telephone conference call.

6. After this sharing session, the students talk with the author and ask further questions. They will undoubtedly think of new questions to ask in addition to those on their lists. Students can also share any special projects they completed that were based on that person's work, or the students can share their own work.

Establishing the Learning Context

The teacher's major role is as an organizer and resource person in helping to locate resources and published writing for students who are engaging in author studies. Several good reference books that give biographical information are listed in the Appendix. Making sure that these references are readily available to students in the school and classroom library is probably the most important role of the teacher in these studies.

The teacher also needs to locate an available local author or illustrator, make arrangements for a visit, and clearly communicate what kinds of items the person should bring and what should be shared. It is important that the students have had time to explore and think about an author's work before the author visits, or the visit will not be productive. The students should have a good understanding of the author and the author's work so that their questions and comments have real depth.

Variations

1. Small groups or a single group may be assigned to compile information about a guest author and to write a biographical sketch or interview for the class newspaper. If two or more groups work independently, the two different pieces can be used as the basis for a revision session as students combine the drafts into a single piece. These written interviews can be compiled into a class guest book.

2. Students should write thank-you notes to the guest, including comments about what they learned about the author and the authoring process. The class could also work on a Group Composed Book for the person.

3. An "I Recommend" file can be created from author and illustrator studies. After a particular study, students write "I Recommend" cards for a favorite book by that author or illustrator. These are placed in a classroom library card file alphabetized by author; students can use the file to locate a book to read.

4. Writing letters to authors is a favorite follow-up activity to classroom author studies. These letters should not be written as assignments but only when children really want to communicate with a particular author. Students can also write cards to the author on holidays or on the author's birthday. Such correspondence should be sent to the publisher who is currently publishing that author's hardcover books. These publishers usually have biograph-

April 2, 1985

Dear Dr. Harste,

Thank for coming to the class room. You wright good books. I liked the book it didnt frighten me becuase I am afrad of the dark. I think there are monsters under my bed and I hare to have a light on in the house. I think there are warm dreses, mummyes, frankenstines and these litt'le deformed cild that eats raw meat.

I liked My Iky Picky Sister because my little cousin is a brat and she all was bothers my ather cousin and me. I am going to tall Bissy my cousin all about your books, by.

Your friend,
Kim

ical information sheets on authors that they will send free on request.

5. This activity should highlight authors from within the classroom, both students and the teacher, as well as outside authors. An "Author of the Week" may be designated—a particular author's work is displayed and read during the week. The author can be interviewed about the writing process and one of the author's published pieces can be used as a choice for a Literature Circle.

6. Parents should be informed about which authors or illustrators are being featured in the classroom and encouraged to look for that person's work when they take their children to the library.

Authors Meeting
Authors

Appendix A: Reference Books for Information on Writers, Poets, and Illustrators

Canadian Kit on Authors and Illustrators. Children's Books Centre, 229 College St., 5th Floor, Toronto, Ontario M5T 1R4, Canada.

Commire, A. 1971–present. *Something about the author* and *Something about the author autobiography series.* Detroit: Gale. (Excellent sets of encyclopedias on children's authors that add new volumes every year.)

Copeland, J. 1993. *Speaking of poets: Interviews with poets who write for children and young adults.* Urbana, IL: National Council of Teachers of English.

Cummins, J., ed. 1992. *Children's book illustration and design.* NY: Rizzoli.

Gallo, D., ed. 1990. *Speaking for ourselves.* Urbana, IL: National Council of Teachers of English.

———. 1993. *Speaking for ourselves, too.* Urbana, IL: National Council of Teachers of English.

Hopkins, L.B. 1987. *Pass the poetry please.* New York: Harper.

H. W. Wilson Co. 1940–78. *Junior book of authors.* (Four editions are currently available.)

Lloyd, P. 1987. *How writers write.* Portsmouth, NH: Heinemann.

Marantz, S. & K. 1992. *Artists of the page.* New York: McFarland.

McElmeel, S. 1990. *Bookpeople.* Englewood, CO: Libraries Unlimited.

———. *An author a month.* Englewood, CO: Libraries Unlimited.

Schon, I. 1994. *Contemporary Spanish-speaking writers and illustrators for children and young adults: A biographical dictionary.* Westport, CT: Greenwood.

Stott, J., & R. Jones. 1988. *Canadian books for children: A guide to authors and illustrators.* San Diego, CA: Harcourt.

Appendix B: Autobiographies of Writers, Poets, and Illustrators Written for Children

Aardema, Vera. 1992. *A bookworm who hatched.* Katonah, NY: Richard Owen.

Byars, Betsy. 1991. *The moon and I.* Englewood Cliffs, NJ: Julian Messner.

Cleary, Beverly. 1988. *A girl from Yamhill.* New York: Morrow.

Cummings, P. 1992. *Talking with artists.* New York: Bradbury.

Dahl, Roald. 1984. *Boy: Tales of childhood.* New York: Puffin.

Fox, Mem. 1992. *Dear Mem, I have read all your books even the pathetic ones. . . .* San Diego, CA: Harcourt.

Fritz, Jean. 1982. *Homesick*. New York: Dell.

———. 1992. *Surprising myself*. Katonah, NY: Richard Owen.

Gallo, D. 1993. *Presenting: Richard Peck*. New York: Dell.

Goble, Paul. 1994. *Hau kola hello friend*. Katonah, NY: Richard Owen.

Gonzalez, D. 1991. *Madeleine L'Engle: Author of A Wrinkle In Time*. New York: Dillon Press.

Hopkins, Lee. 1993. *The writing bug*. Katonah, NY: Richard Owen.

Howe, James. 1994. *Playing with words*. Katonah, NY: Richard Owen.

Hyman, Trina Schart. 1981. *Self-Portrait: Trina Schart Hyman*. New York: Addison Wesley.

Kamen, G. 1990. *Edward Lear: King of nonsense*. Ill. E. Lear & G. Kamen. New York: Atheneum.

Kerr, M. E. 1983. *Me, me, me*. New York: Harper.

Lewin, Ted. 1993. *Ted Lewin: I was a teenage professional wrestler*. New York: Orchard.

Little, Jean. 1988. *Little by Little: A writer's childhood*. New York: Viking.

Martin, Rafe. 1992. *A storyteller's story*. Katonah, NY: Richard Owen.

Meltzer, Milton. 1988. *Starting from home: A writer's beginnings*. New York: Viking.

Naylor, Phyllis R. 1987. *How I came to be a writer*. New York: Macmillan.

Paulson, Gary. 1990. *Woodsong*. New York: Bradbury.

Peck, Richard. 1991. *Anonymously yours*. Englewood Cliffs, NJ: Julian Messner.

Peet, Bill. 1989. *Bill Peet: An autobiography*. Boston: Houghton Mifflin.

Polocco, Patricia. 1994. *Firetalking*. Katonah, NY: Richard Owen.

Rosen, M., ed. 1993. *Speak! Children's book illustrators brag about their dogs*. New York: Harcourt.

Rylant, Cynthia. 1989. *But I'll be back again: An album*. New York: Orchard.

———. 1992. *Best wishes*. Katonah, NY: Richard Owen.

Turner, R. 1993. *Faith Ringgold*. Boston: Little, Brown.

Uchida, Yoshika. 1992. *The invisible thread*. Englewood Cliffs, NJ: Julian Messner.

Yolen, Jane. 1992. *A letter from Phoenix Farm*. Katonah, NY: Richard Owen.

Yep, Laurence. 1991. *The lost garden*. Englewood Cliffs, NJ: Julian Messner.

Essays by authors are published on a regular basis in *Horn Book* and *The New Advocate*. The July/August issue of *Horn Book* always contains the Newbery and Caldecott speeches and biographies. *Language Arts*, *Learning*, *Teaching*, and *Book Links* have regular feature articles on authors.

Appendix C: Audiovisual Resources on Authors

Random House
201 East 50th Street
New York, NY 10022

Weston Woods
Weston, CT 06883

Trumpet Book Club
666 Fifth Avenue
New York, NY 10103

Scholastic Book Club
P.O. Box 3720
Jefferson City, MO 65102-3720

Appendix D: Articles and Children's Books on Author Visits to Schools and Writing to Authors

Kline, S. 1993. *Mary Marony hides out*. Ill. B. Sims. New York: Putnam.

Marzollo, J. 1990. "An author's advice on author's day." *Instructor* September: 32–33.

Parker, M. 1981. "An author is coming to school: Madeleine L'Engle." *The Web* Spring: 24–26.

Phelan, C. 1981. "A visit from a poet." *Language Arts* 58(4): 448–451.

———. 1994. "Writing to authors." *Book Links* 4(2): 46–50.

Pinkwater, D. 1993. *Author's Day*. New York: Macmillan.

Bookmaking
Hardcover Books
Side Staple Covers
Little Books

Introduction

Although there are many ways to celebrate authorship, some type of publication program is clearly an important way that authors can present their authorship publicly. Publication allows authors to share and celebrate their authorship with others and gives them a real reason for moving some of their writing through the entire authoring cycle. From their many entries and drafts, authors choose documents to revise and edit for publication for a wider audience.

A published document needs a real audience that goes beyond the author and the teacher. It also needs a continuing use that keeps it alive and functional within the classroom. One type of formal publication involves making books to add to the classroom library for students to read on an ongoing basis. When a ready supply of blank books is available for student use, authorship is encouraged and involvement in the authoring cycle is seen as a functional activity. Bookmaking introduces students and teachers to an easy procedure for making durable and attractive blank books for classroom use. To emphasize that student-authored works are "real" books, this engagement focuses on making hardcover books that resemble professionally published books.

Materials/Procedures for Hardcover Books (see Figure CE5.1)

▌ Rolls of contact paper, prepasted wallpaper, or fabric
▌ Cardboard (posterboard or cereal boxes)
▌ Regular-sized white typing or copier paper
▌ Sewing machine
▌ Paper glue and scissors

1. A stack of six to ten pieces of typing or copier paper is folded in half and stitched down the center, using a sewing machine on the widest stitch possible. About 1" should be left at each end of the paper (step 1).

2. Two 6" × 9" pieces of cardboard cut from the front and back of a cereal box or from a large sheet of posterboard will form the cover.

3. A piece of contact paper or wallpaper should be cut to measure 12" × 15". Backing on the contact paper is removed; prepasted wallpaper is moistened; or fabric is glued.

4. The two cardboard pieces should be centered on the sticky side of the contact paper or wallpaper, leaving 1/8" to 1/4" between the two pieces of cardboard so the book will close (step 2). Corners are mitered by cutting off each of the four corners of the contact paper or wallpaper. All four sides of the paper are folded in over the edges of the cardboard to complete the book cover (step 3). The corners that were cut off can then be pasted over the inside corners to reinforce them.

5. The entire backs of the outside book pages are covered with paper glue.

6. The book pages are glued to the inside of the finished cardboard cover by placing the book pages so that the stitching runs between the two cardboard pieces (step 4).

FIGURE CE5.1
Hardcover Books with Center Seam

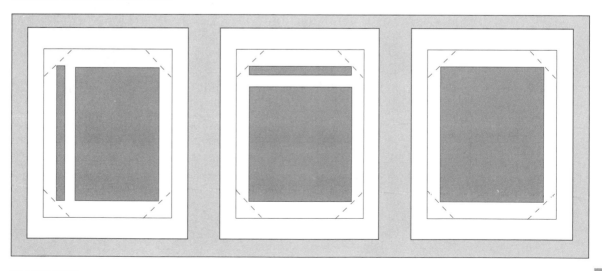

FIGURE CE5.2
Side Staple Covers

7. Students' manuscripts are typed and then cut apart and glued onto the pages of the book. Illustrations can be drawn directly into the book or drawn on pieces of paper that are then glued onto the desired page. If additional pages are needed, another sewn set of book pages is glued into the book.

8. Different-sized books can be made by keeping the following measurements in mind. The cardboard covers should each be cut 1/2" larger than the pages that have been cut and sewn. The material used to cover the cardboard should be 2" larger than the cardboard.

Materials/Procedures for Side Staple Covers

Some books, such as Group Composed Books, are too thick to be folded down the middle and sewn. The following procedure allows the pages to be stapled together so that the cover folds back easily.

1. Two covers of the same size are cut out from the cardboard. A 1/4" strip is cut off the cardboard that will serve as the book's front cover. The strip is cut from the side if the book opens on the side or from the top if the cover is to lift up (see Figure CE5.2).

2. Each piece of cardboard is covered separately with either contact paper or wallpaper. The cardboard for the front cover is placed onto the contact paper or wallpaper, leaving a small space between the strip and the rest of the cover. The contact paper or wallpaper should completely cover over the strip to connect it with the rest of the front cover.

3. The individual pages are then placed between the two covers and stapled on the strip with a heavy-duty stapler. The small space that was left between the strip and the rest of the front cover allows the front cover to bend back easily.

4. As an alternative to stapling, two holes can be punched through each cover and each page of the book. Lay a single piece of bamboo or a chop stick vertically across the holes on the front of the book. Loop a rubber band around the stick at the top hole and then string it along the back of the book. Bring it back up

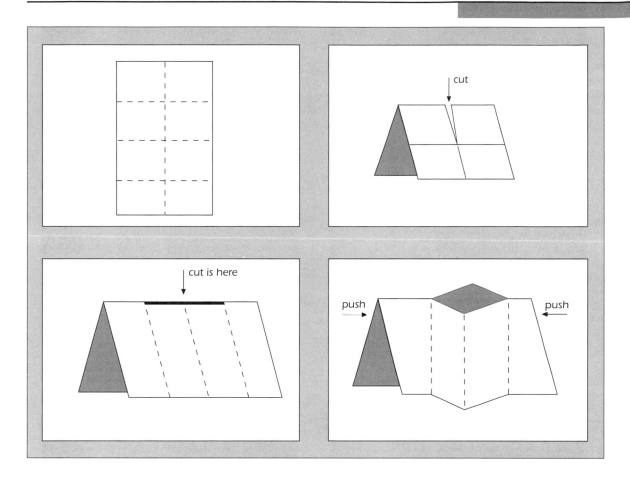

through second hole and loop it around the other end of the stick to hold the book in place.

Materials/Procedures for Little Books

▌ Sheet of typing paper 8 1/2" × 11"
▌ Pair of sissors

1. Fold typing paper in half three times as per Figure CE5.3.

2. Unfold paper and then holding it vertically (the 11" side should be up and down) let it fold in half. Make a cut down the center fold line until you come to the first cross fold. When unfolded this time, the paper will end up having a slit in the center.

FIGURE CE5.3
Directions for Making a Stapleless One-Page Book out of a Single Sheet of Typing Paper (compliments of Jan Nakamora)

Bookmaking

3. Unfold the paper and refold it horizontally. Push both ends towards the center to make a tent. The center will first form a star and then collapse into a 4-page little book.

Establishing the Learning Context

Many teachers have a Parents Night when parents are invited to make blank books for the classroom. Other teachers send home the materials for parents to make blank books. Stacks of finished covers and sewn pages are then put into the writing-reading center. When students have a typed manuscript, they glue the book pages into the cover; they then cut out and glue their manuscript into the book. Students will need demonstrations on how to make decisions about cutting apart a story and deciding what goes on each page.

Once students have finished making the book, teachers need to provide a time for sharing and celebrating that book with others at authors chair. Student-authored books should be treated as real literature by providing time for these works to be read aloud and by placing student books into the class library to be read by other students. Authors often want to take the books home first to share with family members, but these books should then be placed in the classroom library for class members to read. The books are returned to the authors to take home at the end of the year.

Variations

1. There are many other creative ways in which books can be designed including accordion-fold books, circle books, triangle books, scrolls, flap and fold-out books, and pop-up books. The design of the book is an essential aspect of the bookmaking process and needs to be considered in relation to the book's meaning. A list of reference books for alternative designs is included.

2. If the school system has a Young Authors Conference, students can look through all the books they have written to choose one to take to the conference. The chosen book can be taken as originally published, or the author may decide to rework the text, illustrations, or book design and publish a revised version for the conference.

3. Students can be invited to make two copies of several of their books during the year. One copy is theirs to keep, and the other copy is added to the permanent collection of the classroom or school library.

4. This same Bookmaking process can be used to make various kinds of Group Composed Books including birthday books, messages to a favorite author, thank-yous to a special guest, group composed stories, a collection of reports or short stories on the same theme, and stories based on a certain structural pattern from a predictable book.

5. Other types of publications include classroom newspapers or magazines, game boards, bulletin board displays, posters, and so on. See Classroom Newspapers and Magazines for further information.

References

The basic hardback version of bookmaking we report here was adapted from procedures first introduced to us by Vera Milz. We were first introduced to Little Books in Hawaii, thanks to Jan Nakamura. The bamboo/chop stick alternative to binding class composed books was first shared with us by Jocelyn Mokulehua.

Johnson, P. 1990. *A book of one's own*. Portsmouth, NH: Heinemann.
————. 1993. *Literacy through the book arts*. Portsmouth, NH: Heinemann.
Milz, V. 1980. "The comprehension-centered classroom: Setting it up and making it work." In D. Strickler & B. Farr, eds. *Handbook, Reading comprehension videotape series*. Portsmouth, NH: Heinemann.

Appendix A: Children's Literature on Bookmaking and Creating Stories

Aliki. 1986. *How a book is made*. New York: Crowell.
Brookfield, K. 1993. *Book*. New York: Knopf.
Chapman, G., & P. Robson. 1991. *Making books: A step-by-step guide to your own publishing*. Brookfield, CT: Millbrook.
Cobb, V. 1989. *Writing it down*. Ill. M. Hafner. New York: Lippincott.

Bookmaking

Conford, E. 1989. *Jenny Archer, author.* Ill. D. Palmisciano. Boston: Little, Brown.

Delton, J. 1982. *The goose who wrote a book.* Ill. C. Cleary. Minneapolis, MN: Carolrhoda.

Duke, K. 1992. *Aunt Isabel tells a good one.* New York: Dutton.

Edwards, M. 1990. *Dora's book.* Minneapolis, MN: Carolrhoda.

Guthrie, D., N. Bentley, & K. Arnsteen. 1994. *The young author's do-it-yourself book: How to write, illustrate and produce your own book.* Ill. K. Arnsteen. Brookfield, CT: Millbrook.

Irvine, J. 1987. *How to make pop-ups.* Ill. B. Reid. Toronto, Canada: Kids Can Press.

Kehoe, M. 1993. *A book takes root: The making of a picturebook.* Minneapolis, MN: Carolrhoda.

Leigh, N. 1993. *Learning to swim in Swaziland: A child's eye-view of a Southern African country.* New York: Scholastic.

Little, J., & M. De Vries. 1991. *Once upon a golden apple.* Ill. P. Gilman. New York: Viking.

Martin, R. 1981. *The making of a picture book.* Ill. J. Siow. Milwaukee, WI: Gareth Stevens.

Mitgutsch, A. 1986. *From picture to picture book.* Minneapolis, MN: Carolrhoda.

Nixon, J. 1988. *If you were a writer.* Ill. B. Degen. New York: Four Winds.

Stowell, C. 1994. *Step-by-step: Making books.* Ill. J. Robins. New York: Kingfisher.

Suhr, M. 1994. *Making books.* New York: Thompson Learning.

Surat, M. 1983. *Angel child, dragon child.* Ill. V. Mai. New York: Scholastic.

Williams, V. 1986. *Cherries and cherry pits.* New York: Greenwillow.

Classroom Newspapers and Magazines

Introduction

A publication program encourages authorship and makes involvement in the authoring cycle a functional activity. The essential criteria for publication is that the published document have a real audience and a continuing use that keeps it alive and purposeful in the classroom or for a wider audience. Two types of published documents that students have usually seen adults read outside of school are newspapers and magazines. Publishing a classroom newspaper or magazine to be read by class members, other students in the school, and family members provides students with many more outlets for their writing that are less involved than publishing a book. In addition, publishing a newspaper or magazine can involve students in many different roles, including reporters, editors, cartoonists, artists, typists, and layout designers.

Materials/Procedures

- Various kinds of articles and artwork
- Scissors and tape
- Typewriter or computer

1. The first decision that must be made is the type of newspaper or magazine to publish and whether the publication will be

school-wide or classroom-based. Once that decision has been made, students need time to examine similar publications to make lists of the kinds of articles and features that are typically found in the publication. From this list, they make decisions about what they will include in their publication. Here are some options for types of publications to consider:

a. Students can create a newspaper containing a range of articles and topics such as found in local newspapers. Students first examine local papers and brainstorm a list of possible topics and types of articles they want to have in their newspaper. These could include news reports, messages, announcements, cartoons, puzzles, want ads, movie and book reviews, letters to the editors, and so on.

b. Themes related to classroom study can be used in constructing a newspaper or magazine. For example, a newspaper can publish various reports on a class field trip and on class projects and studies relating to that trip. If the class is involved in a specific unit of study, articles and stories related to that unit can be used to produce a theme newspaper or magazine.

c. If class members have been involved in a special writing experience, such as Getting to Know You or Family Stories, these can be collected and published in a newspaper or magazine.

d. The newspaper can be used to report school occurrences to parents. Reports on school activities, messages to parents, future plans, and information such as school menus can be included.

e. A literary magazine can be published with a collection of student writing drawn from Authors Folders or published books.

f. Many areas now have a local magazine that has feature articles on people, places, and events of interest to people living in that area and visitors. For example, Tucson has a magazine with articles on local businesses and restaurants, human interest stories and interviews, articles on events and places, and lists of events, restaurants, stories and local attractions. Students can examine this magazine and create their own version for their local community and school.

2. Once the type of newspaper or magazine has been decided, calls for writing to be submitted to the publication are made. A box in a specific location is designated for students' submissions. A sign-up sheet or chart can be created for students to show the articles or other work they intend to submit.

3. Positions that need to be filled are also announced. Sign-up sheets for editors, assistant editors, cartoonists, reporters, and typists can be posted on the Message Board, or students can fill out applications for particular positions. These jobs should rotate among students for each issue of the paper.

4. The class should decide on a name for the publication and create a masthead.

5. Once the copy for the paper has been collected, either from already existing writing or from writing done especially for the publication, outside editors edit the pieces. The articles are then given to the managing editor (usually a teacher or parent) for typing.

6. The layout designers cut and arrange the typed copy and artwork onto master sheets.

7. The newspaper or magazine is then copied and assembled by students for distribution to the class, family members, or other students in the school.

8. The publication should include an invitation for readers to respond with letters to the editors, suggesting improvements for the next issue and responding to the content of the current issue. These letters to the editors open the way for changes and improvements in subsequent issues and help students to be more aware of their audience. A box or Message Board should be designated for these letters. Subsequent issues should publish both the letters and the editors' responses.

9. The next issue of the newspaper or magazine should be announced so that students can begin to identify and write pieces for it.

Establishing the Learning Context

Many different examples of newspapers and magazines are gathered for students to examine in order to make decisions about the type of publication and features they want. Teachers will need to work with students in establishing an ongoing structure for determining how students will volunteer for particular roles and in making sure that writing is being submitted. Although teachers may feel that it is easier to carry out the publication themselves, it is important that students, as much as possible, carry out the responsibilities and assigned roles. Problems and mistakes in the first publication are learning situations that students can deal with in subsequent issues.

The elaborateness and frequency of a classroom newspaper or magazine will vary greatly from classroom to classroom. Some classrooms publish a weekly or biweekly news sheet that is brief and quickly put together, while others publish more elaborate newspapers and magazines several times a year. Teachers need to look at their publishing program as a whole and the needs of students to determine what kind of publishing program will best fit the students in a particular classroom. Some classrooms with extensive book publishing programs only publish several newspapers a year. Others put their focus on newspaper or magazine publishing and publish fewer books.

The same type of newspaper does not need to be published throughout the year. The class may do a newsletter one time, a topic-centered newspaper another time, and a standard magazine format another time. However, staying with the same type of newspaper or magazine over several issues allows students to use what they have learned from one issue to the next. Teachers should participate along with students in submitting work to be published.

Variations

1. Some teachers have each student produce an individual magazine as a semester-long or year-long project. Each magazine contains samples of the various types of writing that the student has taken through the authoring cycle. Students make enough copies of their magazine so that everyone in the class gets a copy of everyone else's magazine.

2. Individual students or small groups of students may decide to publish a newspaper or magazine focused on their particular interests. For example, a small group of fourth-grade boys decided to publish a newspaper of jokes once a month because of their interest in collecting jokes and riddles. They handled the entire

The Class News

Wedneday June 7 — days of school 171

Editors: Egawa, Nesvig, Tensen

Family Literature Night
Friday June 9 6-9pm
Barbeque 5-6pm

Everyone's getting ready! Hope you and your family can come! Our weather surveyors report a decent forecast for Friday afternoon so we're on for the barbeque. Please send $1.00 as soon as possible for each family member who will be eating. That will cover plates, hotdogs, chips, beans, pop, coffee. Do I have any good sports who would make potatoe or macaroni salad? Let me know. See you at 5! or 6! or when you get here! "

Acsident
by Reid

A twp car Acsident bloced both lanes Nerows brige This Morning. It was an ingeree accsident.

The Talent Show
by Ryan

Try-outs: June 7. 14 acts Show: June 21 morning Kind of acts: piano, lipsync, singing, karate, more. My sister is going to be in it.

___ of us are coming for hotdogs!
___ of us are coming for the literature sharing at ___ pm
More? Write on back ☺!   Family name _____

Classroom Newspapers
& Magazines

process of writing and publishing on their own and then distributed copies to class members.

3. Newspapers can be made more participatory by leaving blank spaces where readers can write or draw their own responses to articles or drawings in the newspaper. For example, if the newspaper includes a picture, a blank space can be provided below it for readers to draw their own picture.

4. Newspapers created by preschool children can include both the child's original writing for child audiences and, below that, a conventional version for adult audiences.

5. Newsletters can be created on a weekly or daily basis. Kathy Short and her first grade students ended the afternoon by reflecting on that day's experiences. Students then dictated a paragraph on what had been most significant to them about that day. These were written on a sheet divided into five sections and copied for parents at the end of the week. The back side of the newsletter contained a letter from the teacher and a feature on the Child of the Week. Kathy Egawa uses an overhead to write down the thoughts of her first graders at the end of the day. A child adds a drawing to the bottom of the overhead. The overhead is photocopied and sent home on a daily basis. Sometimes blank boxes are included for parents to write back. In both rooms, children wrote their own text later in the year instead of using dictation.

6. Students can create a video "newspaper" by taping news reports in which they read news articles that they wrote themselves about local or national news. These news reports are then made available for viewing in other classes at school.

7. Teachers may want to create a special bulletin board or sharing time for students to bring in articles of interest from the local newspaper for sharing and critiquing. Teachers may also want to have a newspaper delivered to the school for students to read. Many newspapers are willing to provide free newspapers to classrooms for students' use. Students may want to rewrite newspaper items they bring in and publish their own news magazine for other students to read and critique.

8. Parents and other people in the school or community can be invited to submit articles, ads, and other items to the newspaper.

9. The teacher should check other newspapers and magazines that publish students' work. Some school districts publish a newspaper or magazine at the district level. Sometimes local newspapers include some writing by children in a weekly section or in a special section during "Newspaper in Education Week" (usually held nationwide the first week in March). *Stone Soup*, a national periodical for children, consists of artwork and stories by children. (Send pieces to Stone Soup, Children's Art Foundation, 915 Cedar Street, Santa Cruz, CA 95060.) *Skipping Stones* is an international, multicultural magazine that publishes children's work. (Send pieces to Skipping Stones, PO Box 3939, Eugene, OR 97403-0939).

10. See Bookmaking for further discussion of other ways to publish.

References

Several computer software programs are available to help in preparing Classroom Newspapers:

Children's Writing & Publishing Center. 1994. The Learning Company, Fremont, CA.
Newsroom. 1984. Springboard Software, Minneapolis, MN.

References on children's magazines:

Brawner, L. 1994. "Magazines for children." *Book Links* July: 50–55.
Richardson, S. 1991. *Magazines for children: A guide for parents, teachers, and librarians.* 2nd ed. Chicago, IL: American Library Association.
Stoll, D., ed. 1994. *Magazines for kids and teens.* 2nd ed. Newark, DE: International Reading Association.

Appendix A: Children's Literature on Newspapers and Magazines

Gibbons, G. 1987. *Deadline! From news to newspaper.* New York: Crowell.
Granfield, L. 1993. *Extra! extra! The who, what, where, when and why of newspapers.* Ill. B. Slavin. New York: Orchard.

Cloning an Author
Generating Written Discourse
Storyboards
Picture Setting
Schema Stories

Introduction

Successful reading and writing involve the creation of a text world in which meaning is organized and unified. Although language users must take ownership of this process, they may need support in considering a range of organizations and story structures as they read and write.

Successful comprehension involves synthesizing what is read into a set of key ideas. Readers must be actively involved in this process, by bringing meaning to, as well as constructing meaning from, the text. Good readers understand that key ideas are a function of the text, the context, and their own purposes for reading. Readers create their own unified meaning rather than trying to replicate the author's unified meaning. Participants "clone" the activities of *an* author; they construct their own meaning, not reconstruct the author's meaning.

Writing is a decision-making process guided by the author's attempt to create an overall framework for meaning. The writer then uses this structure to add more specific pieces of information and to generate the text itself. Generating Written Discourse and Storyboards support writers in focusing on the more global aspects of constructing texts, which creates structures more flexible than those generated by more traditional methods, such as using an outline. Generating Written Discourse especially supports writers of expository or persuasive texts where there is no story plot for them to follow, as in narrative texts. The need to move parts of the text around and to try various organizations therefore becomes especially important for these authors. Authors of picture books also need a more flexible organization such as a Storyboard that allows them to think about and plan the relationships between print and pictures and across pages. The writing process involves being able to shift ideas around within an evolving text, juxtaposing parts to strengthen the organization of the whole.

Both as readers and writers, students need to develop a sense of the conventions our society has developed for how particular kinds of texts or genres are structured. Picture Setting and Schema Stories help students become more aware of story elements and structures that they can use to create meaning as they read and write. These structures are not meant to restrict, but to support meaning. Authors often choose to adapt and change these structures to create new meaning potentials. Picture Setting also helps students identify topics for writing that grow out of their personal experiences.

Materials/Procedures for Cloning an Author

▮ Multiple copies of a selection to read
▮ Stack of eight 3″ × 5″ cards or slips of paper for each student

1. Students are given a stack of eight cards and a copy of the article to be read. When used as an ongoing activity, different color cards should be used for each selection read or the ends of each set of cards marked with a different color marker (see Variations).

2. Students are asked to identify what *they* see as the eight key concepts in the selection and to put each concept on a separate

Cloning an Author
Generating Written
Discourse
Storyboards
Picture Setting
Schema Stories

FIGURE CE7.1
Two Sets of Cloning an Author
Cards for **Little Humpback
Whale** (McGovern, 1979); Billy
(Set A) and Sam (Set B), Age 9
(compliments of Mary Lynn
Woods' classroom)

A humpback whale is the biggest jumping whale.

The big whales are gulp a million krill in one mouth full.

A humpedback is 17 meters or 55 feet.

The big whales are gulp a million krill in one mouth full.

When a father of a baby whale sends out a sound that can be heard a hundred miles in the ocean.

The smallest whale is 10 fill long and that a Pigmy Sperm whale.

every six months a humpback whale moves to a diffrent home

A bull is a male whale.
A cow is a female whale.
A calf is a young whale.

A baby whale has two enemies which are a shark and a killer whale.

Humpback whales eat little fish, shrimp called krill.

A   B

card. Students may complete these cards as they are reading or immediately after they finish reading the selection. Students need not write in complete sentences, but rather write just enough to remind them of the concept.

3. Once students have completed their cards, they select what they see as the five key concepts and discard the remaining cards. (While this may initially seem cruel, we have found that throwing cards away encourages decision making and active reading.)

4. Having reduced their stack of cards to five, students identify the idea they see as most central to the selection they have read. They place this card in the center of their desk or tabletop. If stu-

Section Two
Curricular
Engagements

dents cannot find such a card, they are invited to cross out one of their entries and write a card that they believe fills this function.

5. Once this center card has been selected, students place the remaining cards around it, reflecting how they see the concepts tied to the central concept and to each other.

6. Working in pairs, students take turns explaining to their partners their reasons for selecting the center card and for the placement of the other cards.

7. As a group, students discuss what commonalities as well as differences existed across readers and why such variation is an expected event in reading.

Materials/Procedures for Generating Written Discourse

■ Large pile of small file cards or pieces of paper
■ Large, clear surface on which to lay out the cards

1. After students have explored and researched topics they want to write about using an informational or persuasive text, they take several small cards and write one idea per card. These ideas represent what they feel they have to say that's important or new. These ideas do not have to be in complete sentences. The cards serve as placeholders for meanings students want to remember during their writing, and so they must make decisions about what to write to jog their memory.

2. Once they have their ideas on different cards or slips of paper, they share these with a partner to see if they need to make any changes in the ideas.

3. Each student takes his or her cards and tries out different arrangements that reflect how each of these ideas relate to one another. Idea cards are added or deleted, including a center card that reflects the idea the student sees as most central to what they want to write about the topic. Cards are also added that are summaries for a cluster of ideas or examples of ideas or points the writer wants to make by showing, not telling.

cooking

my Mother taught me to bake	When I started to bake I starty in My Easy Make oven	I like to make sand wiches for guest.	I like to bake cakes	Ponuts	I like to cook chicken even when you have to wash it of.
Every time I bake I My Molter has to help me	when you bake in my oven kit its small cakes	The kind of cakes I like are streusel cakes	When I make sand wiches I like to have enough everything on it.	It's funny when you wash chicken the feel slime	when I make donuts I bake It in a ponut Make They taste like they came from the bakn

Monica

When I first learned to bake it was bacon my mother taught me to bake. But still when I bake my my mother help me. I got me Basy Bake oven for Christmas & the cakes or so small you can eat it in a second. The reason why I like to make sandwiches is because my mother goes to the store and buys everything. Of course when I cooked it I cooked bacon too but I forgot how to turn it over. and I cooked hot dogs all buy my self. left in the after-

one day I think cooking is going to be my hobey my mother didn't let me cook but she did let me wash the chicken. my mother says the cakes she makes or so simple that I could make it buy my self but she never let's me. I he got the donut maker from some one after she makes them she puts cinnamon on them! In fact the last time I cooked all by my self was scrambled eggs It was sunday

FIGURE CE7.2
Cards and Articles Produced
Using Generating Written
Discourse Strategy (Kucer,
1983)

Section Two
Curricular
Engagements

430

4. Once students are satisfied with their arrangements, they meet in pairs and take turns explaining their placement of the cards.

5. Students then use their cards to support the writing of their text.

Materials/Procedures for Storyboards

▌ Large sheet of paper

▌ Small squares of paper and tape or large Post-it notes

the

Bear

by Abraham

one day a Bear Was in a Forst.

and a rver Bear Came And They Startd to fit.

FIGURE CE7.3
First Two Pages of a
Storyboard; Abraham, Age 10
(Gloria Kauffman's classroom)

1. Storyboards are used by authors who are creating picture books and so need to be able to work with a rough draft which includes both print and pictures. Storyboards allow students to see where pages are in relation to each other and the broader whole of the book.

2. The squares of paper are taped onto the large sheet of paper to create the number of pages that will be in the book. Most picture books have a standard thirty-two page format so sixteen squares are often used in four rows of four. Young children have difficulty following the rows and may work better on a long strip of paper.

3. The author begins sketching and writing the story on the squares to determine the flow of the book. The focus is on creating a map of the story; the exact wording of the story and elaborate sketches are not the focus. Stick figures and short sentences are used to capture quickly how the story will unfold.

4. Some authors find it best to work on the beginning of the story and then move to the end of the story before going back to the middle to figure out what needs to happen in order to get to the desired ending.

Cloning an Author
Generating Written
Discourse
Storyboards
Picture Setting
Schema Stories

5. Throughout this process, squares can be moved around or discarded as needed. Young children using a long strip can cut their strip apart and add additional squares as needed.

6. Once the basic structure of the story has been planned, the author considers which meanings can be best conveyed through art and which through language. The words should not just describe the pictures, but convey meanings which are not in the pictures. By the same token, the pictures can show colors, actions, and so on that do not need to be included in the written text. The author makes revisions based on these considerations.

7. The storyboard is shared just like any other rough draft with other authors at an Authors Circle and then revised and used to put together a published picture book.

Materials/Procedures for Picture Setting

▍ Wide selection of pictures without people or animals for settings
▍ Construction paper, both 8–1/2″ × 11″ and 3″ × 3″
▍ Stapler or tape, scissors, paper, pencils, crayons

1. Students are asked to go home and look through magazines to identify a picture of a setting that reminds them of an important moment or event in their lives. They should focus on events they see as significant and disregard whether they believe others would see it as significant. If students forget to bring a picture, they can look through and select a picture from a pile the teacher has provided. This picture becomes the setting for their story.

2. The teacher calls a group of six to eight students together for Picture Setting. Other students are engaged in reading or in working on other pieces of writing. The Picture Settings are trimmed and stapled on pieces of 8–1/2″ × 11″ construction paper.

3. Using small (3″ × 3″) pieces of construction paper, students at Picture Setting are asked to draw and color the characters (people and animals) involved in the story they want to write. Thinking about the color of the clothes that various persons were wearing is an important part of the experience that often helps put writers in touch with their feelings and emotions.

The neighborhood

The Graveyard 1

One day in a nice neighbor hood there was a big house and only a woman and boy lived there. The womans name was Mary and the boys name was Bryan, his father had died when he was 7 months old and he lives with his mother, Mary Bryan liked to ride bicycles a lot But one day he was thinking how his father looked when he was alive. Then after a while he got off his bed and

asked his mother, "Whats my father's name? Then his mother said John That afternoon Bryan went on his bicycle to the graveyard and looked for the name John Mcfee. After two hours he found his father's grave and then he heard a voice say you are not suppose to be here; It was a gentle voice after Bryan heard that voice he ran as fast as he can till he got back home; Then his mother asked 2

have you been Bryan? Then Bryan said playing with the other boys; we were racing With the bicycles and that took a long time. Then him mother said how come your wheels are muddy. Then his mother said again The truth, The truth Bryan and then Bryan Said to the 3

Graveyard. Then his mother said to the what to the Graveyard again. Then his mother said do you want to hear a tape of your fathers voice Then Bryan said, " Yeeees", And when he heard the voice it was the same and he told his mothe and the went to that grave-yard Every Day. 4

4. Students cut out their characters so they can physically move the characters around as they orally share with the group what they are thinking about writing.

5. After everyone has had an opportunity to share what they are thinking about writing, uninterrupted time for writing is scheduled.

6. After an extended period of writing, or after some students have finished writing, everyone can be asked to share what they have written up to that point and how they plan to finish their pieces.

7. Once students finish their drafts, they can decide whether to put them back into their Authors Folder, share them at authors chair, or continue working on the draft for publication.

Materials/Procedures for Schema Stories

▮ Text that is cut into parts (narrative text works best)
▮ Original copy of the text

1. Select a text that is narrative in form and has an easily identifiable beginning, plot development, and ending. The key text segments are identified and the text is cut apart just before or after the segment. Cutting between the segments facilitates students' predictions about what must follow or precede the segment. Each segment should be long enough (at least a complete paragraph) to give readers something substantial to read. Depending on the text complexity and readers' abilities, three to ten sections can be created. Glue the segments onto cards so they are more easily manipulated.

2. Each student in a small group takes one segment of text and reads it silently, thinking about what might have happened before or after that segment.

3. Assembling the text begins by asking who thinks he or she has the beginning of the text. That student should read the segment aloud. The other students decide if they agree that this is the first segment and try to find the next segment. The group continues with each reader reading a segment aloud when he or she thinks it comes next in the text, with the others listening and agreeing or disagreeing with the reader. Disagreements are negotiated by having students refer to the events in the segments and to what

makes sense given their understandings of the story structure and content. Variations in the order of the text are accepted as long as they create a story that has unity and makes sense.

4. Once the students have assembled the text to their satisfaction, the entire text is read aloud as a unit, with each person reading his or her segment aloud to the group.

5. The original copy of the text can be distributed to the students so they can see how their story compares to the original text, not to see if they are "correct" but simply to compare the two versions if they are different.

6. The students reflect on this experience and what they learned about the structure of the particular text type or genre involved.

7. While this engagement should be introduced with texts that have easily identifiable structures such as folklore and fables, other kinds of texts can then be used such as cartoons, poetry, recipes, songs, other narrative stories, wordless books, and informational texts.

Establishing the Learning Context

Teachers should participate in these different engagements to provide a demonstration to students that proficient readers and writers engage in the same kind of thinking and that there is no one interpretation of a book or organization for a piece of writing. The class may need to come together at particular points throughout these engagements to share what they are thinking and doing. A whole-class discussion following the engagements can help students reflect on these engagements as possible strategies they can use on their own.

Variations for Cloning an Author

1. Student pairs may exchange stacks of cards and lay out what they believe to be the other's organization. The original author of the card stack listens to what the new student did with the cards and then shares his or her original organization scheme. Rather than insist that theirs is the "correct" organization, authors should be encouraged to explore the organizational possibilities demonstrated by their partner's decisions.

2. Different colored cards can be used by students for each related reading experience (white for Reading Experience 1, green for Reading Experience 2, and so on). Different sets of cards can be made for each chapter in a longer book or for different reading selections. Once each student has several sets of cards, these cards can be combined into one set. For example, if two selections have been read, students can be asked to take their five white cards from Reading Experience 1 and their five green cards from Reading Experience 2, shuffle them, and select a new set (approximately seven cards) from which to create a map covering both selections read. Students share these new maps with their fellow students and discuss differences and similarities. Using colored cards allows students to go back to their original sets.

3. Participants can engage in Cloning an Author after reading a variety of related selections in a unit of study. After all selections have been read, all cards are shuffled and participants select the five to seven key concepts they see as central in this unit of study. Results can either be shared orally or written in an uninterrupted writing session.

4. Students should be encouraged to use this engagement as a way of summarizing materials they have read. College students have found it to be an excellent device to prepare for class discussions and essay examinations.

5. With kindergarten and elementary school children, students can be encouraged to write down or draw pictures of what they want to remember as they read the story. Once they have done this they can put their cards in the order they wish and use them during author talk time or in their Literature Circles. In primary classrooms, children's story retellings are not only much longer, but qualitatively improved using this engagement.

Variations for Generating Written Discourse

1. There are several variations that authors can use if they are having difficulty considering alternate ways of structuring meaning. Instead of immediately starting to write, authors may want to shuffle the ideas together. The following day, the author takes out the ideas and tries out several different organizations. The author

could also give the shuffled cards to another student and ask that person to put them into an organization that makes sense. The student then explains the order to the author and gives reasons for that ordering. The author puts the cards into the original order and explains that to the student.

2. Generating Written Discourse can be used to generate multiple-authored writing. Two or three authors work together in writing ideas on cards and then organizing them. The students could then each write their own sections or could work together as a group in writing each part.

3. Authors who have written a draft and are dissatisfied with how the ideas are coming together can cut their piece into "idea units" and use Generating Written Discourse to create a new structure for that piece.

Variations for Picture Setting

1. Students can be asked to find pictures of people or objects that remind them of particular experiences. Participants would then draw the setting before writing their selection.

2. Rather than identifying settings that remind them of a personal experience, participants can be asked to find settings that they think would make a good backdrop for a fictional story.

3. Students can use dioramas or small puppet stages, either student-made or commercially made, to create background settings in which to place their characters and stories.

4. A group of students can create a large mural background with moveable characters (characters are cut out and taped onto straws or sticks) to use in creating a group Picture Setting story.

5. Students can be given pieces of construction paper and asked to symbolically represent major characters and objects from stories they have read. By placing these objects on an overhead projector, they can be invited to retell a story they have either written or read. In her dissertation, Pat Enciso (1990) also asked students to make a symbol which represented themselves as a reader and to position themselves in relation to the story being told.

Cloning an Author
Generating Written
Discourse
Storyboards
Picture Setting
Schema Stories

Variations for Schema Stories

1. Each student can be given a complete set of the segments of the text. Students can work individually or in pairs to put the text in the order that they feel makes sense and then compare their version of the story with others in the group.

2. If cuts are made at points of transition in the story, texts can be reconstructed in a variety of ways. Students can see how many different ways they can construct a story and still have it make sense.

3. One or two blank slots can be provided with the text segments, either to replace particular sections of the story or to add an additional segment to the story. As students construct the story, they make a decision about where to put the blank slots and what should go in them.

4. Students can use Schema Stories as a revision strategy for their own writing when experiencing difficulty with the organization of a piece of writing. The author makes a photocopy of the draft and cuts it into sections, giving the sections to someone else to put together. The author then compares this organization with the one they originally developed for the piece and decides whether or not to make changes.

References

Cloning an Author was initially developed by Jerome Harste. Generating Written Discourse is an adaptation of an engagement initially developed by Stephen Kucer and Myriam Revel-Wood. Schema Stories was originally developed by Dorothy Watson. Picture Settings was originally developed by Stephen Kucer and Carolyn Burke.

Enciso, P. 1990. "The nature of engagement in reading: Profiles of three fifth-graders' engagement strategies and stances." Ph.D. diss., The Ohio State University.

Kucer, S. 1983. "Using text comprehension as a metaphor for understanding text production: Building bridges between reading and writing." Ph.D. diss., Indiana University, Bloomington.

McGovern, A. 1979. *Little humpback whale*. New York: Scholastic.

Shulevitz, U. 1985. *Writing with pictures*. New York: Watson-Guptill.

Editors Table

Introduction

Because the function of written language is to communicate a message, writers need first to focus on getting their meaning down. When an author decides to take a manuscript to formal publication, however, it is edited for convention to show the author's regard for readers. Conventions are needed to construct meaning by outside readers, not authors who already know what their pieces say. Editors Table allows writers to attend to meaning rather than to be overly concerned with conventions early in the writing process. It also helps them develop a personal strategy for self-editing and editing of other's texts.

The editing process consists of both semantic editing and editing for convention. Semantic editing by outside readers focuses on the identification of unclear or confusing portions of the text. It extends the focus on meaning by encouraging authors to take another perspective on their writing. Editing for convention occurs after semantic editing to highlight the notion that control of conventions is not a prerequisite to production of meaningful messages. Instead, it is a final concern for manuscripts that the author chooses to make public. After editing, the text goes to the typist who serves as a final check on conventions.

The editing process provides a demonstration of an effective strategy used by published authors for dealing with aspects of convention. Serving as editors of one another's texts helps students develop an appreciation of audience and the communicative commitment they make to their readers.

Materials/Procedures

- Table
- Box for writers' rough drafts
- Blackboard or chart paper on which to write editing rules
- Visors, armbands, or buttons to identify editors
- Variety of regular and colored pencils or highlighter pens
- Scrap paper
- Dictionary, spelling dictionary, thesaurus, English stylebook, and other useful reference books
- Typewriter or computer
- Folders or boxes for texts in process of being edited or typed
- Tape, scissors, paper glue, and blank paper for pasting up galleys
- Examples of publications similar to those being published

1. Before the editorial board is set up, it is important to establish a need for publication in the authoring cycle. Writers must have drafts that they have shared in Authors Circles. Authors will choose only some of their pieces to go to formal publication. Pieces which are being informally published are not usually submitted to Editors Table.

2. Establish an editors box in the classroom where students can place pieces that they want to have published that have gone through an Authors Circle.

3. Volunteers can be asked to serve as editors for the first publication. It is helpful to include children of different ages and ability levels on the editorial board. This process will be repeated for subsequent publications so that others have an opportunity to serve as editors. Decisions regarding length of board membership should be based on frequency and type of publication.

4. An editorial board meeting should be called. Badges, visors, or armbands can be distributed to identify students during their terms as editors.

5. The editorial board should examine and discuss published documents similar to the ones that the class will publish (trade books, newspapers, etc.) and discuss what an editor does. The board compiles a list that reflects the dual responsibilities of editors: editing for meaning and editing for convention. Text ownership should be discussed by taking a rough draft from the editors box, then talking about, "Whose paper is this?" The idea that it is the author's text and that no one except the author has the right to change the meaning or structure of the text should be clearly established.

6. The teacher may wish to prepare a student text in advance for use on the overhead projector to assist students in generating and applying editorial rules. It may be helpful if each editor has a copy of that student text. The editors should establish enough rules and symbols to enable them to begin the editing process. It is quite likely that other rules will evolve as the need arises. The list should be considered as a set of working guidelines that are subject to change. One of the participants acts as scribe, recording the suggestions (preferably on a chalkboard to emphasize the tentative nature of the decisions). Markings should be easily identifiable, yet small, so the author's manuscript is marked as little as possible.

7. These rules should be posted in the editors corner and added to and changed when suggestions are made by the editorial board.

8. Editing may not be necessary for all pieces in a publication or for all types of informal publications. The teacher and/or editors may decide to exclude some pieces from the editing process and print them as submitted (e.g., letters to the editor, artwork, personal ads, and other pieces whose original form is an integral part of the message).

9. Once the editorial board has decided on the rules and symbols, they should begin the editing process with a rough draft.

   a. Semantic editing: The editors' primary focus is identifying and marking with the agreed-on symbols any portions of a text that require additional information to be understood, that seem

Editors Table

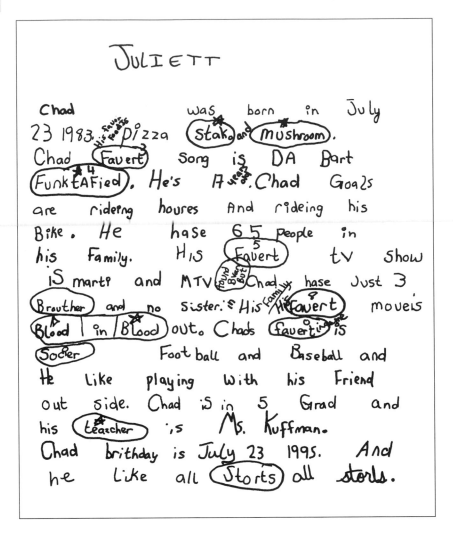

confused, or that need clarification. The teacher should stress the cardinal rule: No one has the right to alter the structure or meaning of a text except the author.

b. Semantic meeting: If questions regarding meaning arise, the editor must confer with the author. The editor should locate the author and ask questions based on the semantic editing. The author decides whether to make any changes and, if so, makes them during the conference.

c. Editing for conventions: Once all questions regarding meaning have been resolved with the author, the editor rereads the rough draft to edit for conventions such as spelling, punctuation, and capitalization. These changes are marked right in the text. Highlighter pens can be used to mark words that the editor feels are functionally spelled, and the conventional spelling of the word can be written above any misspelled word. If unsure of the conventional spelling, the editor might write out alternative spellings on a piece of paper, look up the word in the dictionary, or consult with other editors, including the teacher. If the editor is still unsure of the spelling, the word can be left highlighted for the managing editor or final typist (usually the teacher or a parent volunteer) to resolve.

d. Typing of manuscript: The rough draft is given to the typist, who may make final changes in spelling, punctuation, or capitalization if nonconventional forms would embarrass either the teacher, the child, or the school.

10. At the end of the first editing session, it is important for editors to regroup and discuss problems and issues that have arisen. This is a good opportunity to revise and add to editorial rules and policies.

Establishing the Learning Context

Editors Table is the one part of the authoring cycle that teachers often drop, feeling that students cannot handle editing or that there is not enough time for Editors Table. Editors Table should always be part of the cycle, even for young children, because of its role in allowing students to explore conventions. The role of conventions is more obvious in another person's writing than in your own, which is why many authors have difficulty proofreading their own work. Through Editors Table, students are able to learn about the role of conventions and to develop understandings they can take back to their own work. While less proficient writers will identify fewer editing changes, they often learn the most from this process.

If the editing process is initially too overwhelming for students, teachers may want to limit the amount of editing that each editor is expected to do. For example, editors may look only for misspelled words or punctuation instead of editing for all conventions. Young children may only be asked to circle words they think might be misspelled. Students may want to begin by editing in pairs, rather than working alone.

Variations

1. When a second editorial board is established, procedures 1–5 may be repeated during the initial meeting. Because a set of editorial rules already exists, step 6 will involve the sharing of current working rules for the editing process, rather than the generation of a new list. Former editors may be enlisted to explain existing policies. The tentativeness of these guidelines should be emphasized so that editors will feel comfortable in suggesting changes and refining policies.

2. Editing texts for publication is only one responsibility of editors. They may also be involved in making decisions about layout, organization of a collection of pieces, assembly and distribution of the publication, and types of future publications. As editors take responsibility for the entire publication process, it may be necessary to create specialized editorial positions to deal with these aspects of publication.

3. Editors may find readers' comments useful in shaping their next publication. Reexamining an assortment of published materials may provide editors with ideas for responding to a wide range of reader requests. For instance, newspaper editors may receive requests for new types of articles, or for the addition of illustrations and artwork to make the document more interesting and appealing to readers. If publishing books, editors may receive suggestions concerning such features as a dedication or a table of contents. As the editors make decisions about their responses to such suggestions, they may wish to make applications available for new staff positions designed to respond to these reader-identified problem areas (cartoonists, artists, etc.).

4. As the authoring cycle continues to operate over time and with various kinds of publications, the role taken by editors will change. The Editors Table, as initially implemented, serves as a demonstration of editing to students. As they become familiar with the editing process, students gradually begin to self-edit and to edit informally with other authors.

5. The role of the editor in publishing books is discussed in *How a Picture Book Is Made* (Kellogg & Blantz, 1976), a filmstrip from Weston Woods, and *How a Book Is Made* (Aliki, 1986). Additional references are found in Bookmaking.

References

Editors Table was initially developed by Carolyn Burke and then further developed by Jean Anne Clyde, Deborah Rowe, and Kathy Short. Additional references include:

Calkins, L. 1994. *The art of teaching writing* new edition. Portsmouth, NH: Heinemann.

Graves, D. 1983. *Writing: Teachers and children at work*. Portsmouth, NH: Heinemann.

Family Stories
Remember When Stories
Historical Family Stories
Scary Stories

Introduction

Learning is always a process of connecting our current experiences to our past stories. The more we know and explore our past stories, the more potential exists for making richer and more complex ties with our current experiences—which, in turn, enhances learning. One important source of past stories are stories that families tell over and over again about events that happened to family members. These stories are an insightful source of how families and cultures interpret their experiences and what they value. Both oral and written traditions of storytelling are valued in this engagement.

Gathering Family Stories engages students in a process of research as they learn techniques of interviewing, notetaking, oral storytelling, and writing a story from the data they collect. These stories are a good introduction to research because students care about the subject and already have a great deal of knowledge about it. They use the research process and primary sources for information, instead of copying reports from encyclopedias.

> I Fel owt of the truk
> I Was olea 2 yir's old and
> my Dad was olea 19 yir's old.
> I was wiring a dipr and a srt
> and me and my Dad was
> kuming bak frum kolneline and.
> we wr haf wa home and
> I opind the dor and fel out,
> of the truk and I wit kboum
> on the rod. My dipr got tor up
> topecis The End.

Materials/Procedures

▌ Paper for notetaking and writing stories

Procedure A: Remember When Stories

1. The teacher should talk with students about the important stories that everyone carries around inside of them. Some of these stories are family stories or "remember when" stories that family members tell over and over again about things that happened a long time ago to them or to other people in their family. The children are going to become researchers and collect these family stories over the next several weeks.

Family Stories
Remember When Stories
Historical Family Stories
Scary Stories

2. Students are asked to interview family members about these stories and to take notes on the stories so they can share them with the class. The focus is on gathering the oral literature of that family.

3. During the next several weeks, each day students orally share any family stories they have collected. As students tell stories, they are asked to reflect on connections across their stories as well as on ways they can improve the telling of their stories.

4. While the major focus is on oral storytelling, as a variation students can list the family stories they have collected and place this list into their Authors Folder as ideas for written drafts. These drafts can be published in individual books, class books, or a class newspaper. In one classroom, students each published individual collections and then chose their favorite story to put in a class newspaper that was sent home.

5. Children's books where family members tell stories to each other can be shared (see Appendix A).

6. Students discuss the various strategies they used for notetaking, interviewing, and creating oral stories and how they can use these strategies in other situations when they need to do research.

Procedure B: Family Stories

1. *The Relatives Came* by Cynthia Rylant (1985) is read aloud to the class and students respond with their own connections and responses. The teacher then initiates a discussion of stories about particular family experiences that reflect that family's culture—its way of living and thinking in the world.

2. Students are invited to write stories about what it is like to grow up in their family and what experiences define who they are as a family. In order to write these stories, students spend time observing their family life and writing notes as well as thinking about past experiences that might reflect and capture what life in their family is like.

3. To support students in thinking about these stories, other children's literature is read aloud and is available for browsing and Literature Circles (see Appendix B).

My Family Tradition

Before I was born my family started Christmas traditions that continue each year. Early on Christmas morning we get up and open our presents from Santa Claus and then at about 1p.m. we go over to my Grandparents' house. My Grandmother always makes a standing rib roast and my Dad always carves it into pieces. Each dinner starts with a prayer that everyone says a part of. After the prayer has gone around the table we eat dinner. After dinner we get to open presents from our family. It is fun! My uncle Mike has always played Santa Claus. He passes out the presents one at a time by name. Before a present is opened you put the bow on your head and then you rip it open. Everyone claps at what you got, and someone always takes pictures. After we are all done opening presents, the cousins put on a circus show with bike tricks and skits. This part of the day is only two years old and was my sister Amanda's idea! When everyone is worn out, we have raspberry ribbon pie, which my grandmother only makes at Christmas. After we are done with our pie, we hug everyone and say thank you one more time before we go home tired and happy!

Family Story; Stephanie, Age 9 (Gloria Kauffman's classroom)

When my Grandpa was little, he and his brothers would make mud pies and throw them at each other. They would get in trouble and had to get sprayed by the hose. Then they would go right back and do it again. Their faces were muddy and they would get in trouble even more.

When they came in their Mom looked at them and screamed bloody murder. Her face would get red as a flower and they knew that she was mad. They would run out the door and she would chase them with her broom.

They would hide from her in the bushes and she found them. The others would run in the house and she would chase them and they would shut the bedroom door. One of the kids would stand in front of the door and hold it so she could not get in.

Finally she put the broom down and went half way in the kitchen and ran and the door fell. The kids were underneath the door and she was jumping up and down on the door. The other kids were laughing at their mom, and then she got off.

Then they went and had some hot chocolate and she was not mad at all.

Historical Family Story; Kelly, Age 9 (Gloria Kauffman's classroom)

Procedure C: Historical Family Stories

1. Students read an historical family story such as *Sarah, Plain and Tall* (MacLachlan, 1985) or *Aurora Means Dawn* (Sanders, 1989); see Appendix C. The book can be read aloud to them or multiple copies can be purchased so they can read the book in pairs using Say Something.

2. After sharing initial responses and connections, students can be invited to interview family members to find the seeds for their own

Family Stories
Remember When Stories
Historical Family Stories
Scary Stories

historical family stories. The afterwords in both books describe how the author took a family memory and expanded it to create a story about what might have happened. Sometimes the author stays fairly close to the original story and sometimes the author creates a new story that is only peripherally related to the original family story. Other times, only a small fragment of the story remains and so the author must take that small piece and create a story around it.

Procedure D: Scary Stories

▌ 4 sheets of construction paper for each student (red, black, white, and purple)

1. Another type of story which is told over and over again are scary stories. These stories often involve vivid images and strong feelings and so are especially powerful when told through art.

2. Using the book *Picture This* (Bang, 1991), introduce students to a few basic principles about the use of shape, color, space, and line to communicate strong emotions.

3. Encourage students to share stories about times in their lives when they have been afraid. Children's literature about fears may also be shared (see Appendix D).

4. Give each student the four sheets of construction paper and ask them to create a scary picture using all four colors. They are not given glue.

For the first experience, you may want to use the strategy Bang suggests and have students choose to make a scary picture of either a shark or a bird so they have a common point of comparison for discussing visual composition and revision.

5. Give students a relatively short period of time (ten to twenty minutes) and then ask them to carefully carry their pictures to the center of an open area in the room.

6. Place the pictures in the center of the area and gather in a circle around them. First ask students to identify pictures they find visually scary. Talk about each picture and what makes it visually frightening.

7. Ask students to identify pictures they think could be more frightening. Talk as a group about what could be done to increase their scariness. Since the parts are not glued down, pieces can be moved to try out ideas that are suggested.

8. Students take their pictures and return to their desks to revise them so they more powerfully tell their scary stories.

9. The pictures are again returned to the center of the room for another discussion of the ways in which authors used visual elements such as color, shape, space, and line to communicate scariness and stories.

10. Following this discussion, students take their pictures and return to their desks for one last revision and then glue their pictures. These pictures are displayed against a black background in the classroom.

11. As a followup, students may want to write their stories.

Family Stories
Remember When Stories
Historical Family Stories
Scary Stories

Establishing the Learning Context

Teachers need to engage in the same process of researching their own Family Stories to show students that these stories are important to all of us and to demonstrate the research process. Once students get to the point of telling or writing their stories, it is helpful if the teacher chooses one of his or her own stories and goes through the process of using notes to create an oral or written story.

Students will need class time for oral sharing of these stories. This is a crucial part of the process as children gain experience in how to tell these stories. Also, as they hear others' stories, they are reminded of additional stories in their own families and are motivated to do more interviewing. During this sharing, the class can explore similarities and differences that run across their stories. Guests who have family stories to tell can be invited to the classroom so that students can hear oral literature. Collecting the oral traditions of families has become quite popular; teachers should be able to locate people in the community who have made family stories their focus. Senior citizens are often a rich source of these stories.

Students also will need many pieces of literature available to them that can be shared through read aloud, wide reading, and Literature Circles. Students can be involved in studying and reading the work of authors, such as Pat Hutchins, who write books based on things that happened to their families (see appendices).

Variations

1. Students can research and write community stories or tales of long ago from elderly people in the community.

2. Students can explore folktales, looking at both oral storytelling and what happens to these stories when they are written down.

3. Students can become involved in researching other ways in which cultures and communities tell their stories including art, music, and dance.

4. Students may want to research literacy and language use in their community. Denny Taylor (1990) suggests engaging in Literacy Digs on a particular person or place. To do this dig, every piece of literacy is gathered, cataloged, and then analyzed to de-

termine the types and uses of reading and writing in that place or that person's life. For example, students may want to do a literacy dig on their bedrooms or their desks at school. They might choose a person such as a grandparent, documenting and collecting all the ways that person uses literacy. Students could also interview family and community members about literacy issues such as how they feel about being bilingual and for what purpose and under what conditions they use various languages. Or they might make observations and write up their findings about how various groups of people in the community use reading and writing.

5. Students can become involved in many other projects using original research. For example, students may research why a local creek has a particular name or write to grandparents to find out how they celebrated certain holidays. They can survey the community to identify possible places of historical significance and use this information to prepare a history book on the sites in their community. They might also do ethnographic research about the funds of knowledge in their own households which their families use to survive and function (Moll, 1992). They might interview family and community members about what it means to be literate in the community in which they live and how various groups use reading and writing.

6. Alternative ways to present research to others, including art, drama, and oral traditions, can be explored instead of always relying on a written report. In addition, when the class becomes involved in writing expository reports, the teacher should introduce various kinds of nonfiction so that they are aware of some of the options that are available for this type of writing.

References

This strategy was developed by Jerome Harste, Kathy Short, and Gloria Kauffman. Scary Stories was developed by Molly Bang and is described in her book *Picture This* (1991).

Bang, M. 1991. *Picture this: Perception and composition*. Boston: Little, Brown.
Moll, L. 1992. "Bilingual classroom studies and community analyses: Some recent trends." *Educational Researcher* 21(2): 21–24.

Family Stories
Remember When Stories
Historical Family Stories
Scary Stories

Taylor, D. 1990. "Teaching without testing: Assessing the complexity of children's literacy learning." *English Education* 22(1): 4–74.

Wigginton, E. 1986. *Sometimes a shining moment: The Foxfire experience.* New York: Doubleday.

Appendix A: "Remember When" Stories

Ackerman, K. 1990. *Just like Max.* Ill. G. Schmidt. New York: Knopf.

Bornstein, R. 1990. *A beautiful seashell.* New York: Harper & Row.

Dionetti, M. 1991. *Coal mine peaches.* Ill. A. Riggio. New York: Orchard.

Friedman, I. 1984. *How my parents learned to eat.* Ill. A. Say. Boston: Houghton Mifflin.

Greenfield, E. 1980. *Grandma's joy.* Ill. C. Byard. New York: Philomel.

Havill, J. 1992. *Treasure nap.* Ill. E. Savadier. Boston: Houghton Mifflin.

Hest, A. 1990. *The ring and the window seat.* Ill. D. Haeffele. New York: Scholastic.

Howard, E. 1991. *Aunt Flossie's hats (and crab cakes later).* Ill. J. Ransome. New York: Clarion.

Howard, K. 1994. *In wintertime.* New York: Lothrop.

Johnson, A. 1989. *Tell me a story, Mama.* Ill. D. Soman. New York: Orchard.

Lyon, G. E. 1990. *Basket.* Ill. M. Szilagyi. New York: Orchard.

MacLachlan, P. 1982. *Mama one, Mama two.* Ill. R. Bornstein. New York: HarperCollins.

McDonald, M. 1991. *The potato man.* Ill. T. Lewin. New York: Orchard.

McLerran, A. 1991. *Roxaboxen.* Ill. B. Cooney. New York: Lothrop.

Milstein, L. 1994. *Miami-Nanny stories.* Ill. O. Han. New York: Tambourine.

Moss, M. 1994. *In America.* New York: Dutton.

Nobisso, J. 1990. *Grandma's scrapbook.* Ill. M. Hyde. San Marcos, CA: Green Tiger Press.

Oberman, S. 1994. *The always prayer shawl.* Ill. T. Lewin. Honesdale, PA: Boyds Mill.

Polacco, P. 1988. *The keeping quilt.* New York: Simon & Schuster.

Pomerantz, C. 1989. *The chalk doll.* Ill. F. Lessac. New York: HarperCollins.

Porte, B. 1993. *When Grandma almost fell off the mountain and other stories.* Ill. M. Chambliss. New York: Orchard.

Ringgold, F. 1991. *Tar beach.* New York: Crown.

Rogers, P. 1987. *From me to you.* Ill. J. Johnson. New York: Orchard.

Rylant, C. 1987. *Birthday presents*. Ill. S. Stevenson. New York: Orchard.

Scott, A. 1990. *Grandmother's chair*. Ill. M. Aubrey. New York: Clarion.

Turner, A. 1990. *Through moon and stars and night skies*. Ill. J. Hale. New York: HarperCollins.

Waddell, M. 1989. *Once there were giants*. Ill. P Dale. New York: Delacorte.

———. 1990. *Grandma's Bill*. Ill. J. Johnson. New York: Orchard.

Appendix B: Family Stories

Breckler, R. 1992. *Hoang breaks the lucky teapot*. Ill. A. Frankel. Boston: Houghton Mifflin.

Caines, J. 1982. *Just us women*. Ill. P. Cummings. New York: Harper & Row.

Carson, J. 1990. *Pulling my leg*. Ill. J. Downing. New York: Orchard.

Crews, D. 1991. *Bigmama's*. New York: Greenwillow.

Fiday, B. & D. 1990. *Time to go*. Ill. T. Allen. New York: Gulliver.

Flournoy, V. 1985. *The patchwork quilt*. Ill. J. Pinkney. New York: Dial.

Garza, C. L. 1990. *Family pictures: Cuadros de familia*. San Francisco: Children's Book Press.

Hill, E. 1967. *Evan's corner*. Ill. S. Speidel. New York: Viking.

Hutchins, P. 1971. *Titch*. New York: Macmillan.

Isadora, R. 1991. *At the crossroads*. New York: Greenwillow.

Johnson, A. 1992. *The leaving morning*. Ill. D. Soman. New York: Orchard.

Mennen, I. 1994. *One round moon and a star for me*. Ill. N. Daly. New York: Orchard.

Otey, M. 1990. *Daddy has a pair of striped shorts*. New York: Farrar, Straus and Giroux.

Rylant, C. 1985. *The relatives came*. Ill. S. Gammell. New York: Bradbury.

Say, A. 1989. *The lost lake*. Boston: Houghton Mifflin.

Sonneborn, R. 1970. *Friday night is Papa night*. Ill. E. McCully. New York: Puffin.

Soto, G. 1993. *Too many tamales*. Ill. E. Martinez. New York: Putnam.

Waddell, M. 1994. *The big big sea*. Ill. J. Eachus. Cambridge, MA: Candlewick.

Williams, D. 1990. *Walking to the creek*. Ill. T. Allen. New York: Knopf.

Appendix C: Historical Family Stories

Cech, J. 1991. *My grandmother's journey*. Ill. S. McGinley-Nally New York: Bradbury Press.

Coats, L. 1991. *The almond orchard*. New York: Macmillan.

Cooney, B. 1982. *Miss Rumphius*. New York: Viking.

Grifalconi, A. 1986. *The village of round and square houses*. Boston: Little, Brown.

Harvey, B. 1986. *My prairie year: Based on the diary of Elenore Plaisted*. Ill. D. Ray. New York: Holiday.

Houston, G. 1992. *My great-aunt Arizona*. Ill. S. C. Lamb. New York: HarperCollins.

Johnston, T. 1988. *Yonder*. Ill. L. Bloom. New York: Dial.

Levinson, R. 1985. *Watch the stars come out*. Ill. D. Goode. New York: Dutton.

MacLachlan, P. 1985. *Sarah, plain and tall*. New York: HarperCollins.

———. 1991. *Three names*. Ill. A. Pertzoff. New York: HarperCollins.

Mitchell, M. 1993. *Uncle Jed's barbershop*. Ill. J. Ransome. New York: Simon & Schuster.

Polacco, P. 1988. *The keeping quilt*. New York: Simon & Schuster.

Sanders, S. 1989. *Aurora means dawn*. Ill. J. Kastner. New York: Bradbury.

Shevrin, A. 1991. *Around the table: Family stories of Sholom Aleichem*. Ill. T. Gowing. New York: Scribner's.

Taylor, M. 1987. *The gold Cadillac*. Ill. M. Hays. New York: Dial.

Williams, D. 1993. *Grandma Essie's covered wagon*. Ill. W. Sadowski. New York: Knopf.

Yep, L. 1991. *The starfisher*. New York: Morrow.

Appendix D: Text Set on Fear

Adoff, A. 1977. *Tornado!* Ill. R. Himler. New York: Delacorte.

Booth, B. 1991. *Mandy*. Ill. J. Lamarche. New York: Lothrop.

Carle, E. 1977. *The grouchy ladybug*. New York: Crowell.

Crowe, R. 1976. *Clyde monster*. Ill. K. Chorao. New York: Dutton.

———. 1980. *Tyler toad and the thunder*. Ill. K. Chorao. New York: Dutton.

Emberley, E. 1992. *Go away, big green monster!* Boston: Little, Brown.

Freschet, B. 1973. *Bear mouse*. Ill. D. Carrick. New York: Scholastic.

Gackenback, D. 1977. *Harry and the terrible whatzit*. New York: Scholastic.

Goss, J., & J. Harste. 1981. *It didn't frighten me*. Ill. S. Romney. New York: Scholastic.

Hoban, R. 1960. *Bedtime for Francis*. Ill. G. Williams. New York: Harper.

Hoellwarth, C. 1990. *The underbed*. Ill. S. Gerig. Intercourse, PA: Good Books.

Lee, J. 1987. *Ba-nam*. New York: Holt.

Martin, B., Jr., & J. Archambault. 1985. *The ghost-eye tree*. Ill. T. Rand. New York: Holt.

Mayer, M. 1968. *There's a nightmare in my closet*. New York: Dial.

Morris, W. 1990. *What if the shark wears tennis shoes*. Ill. B. Lewin. New York: Atheneum.

Mossmann, B. 1991. *The night lion*. Ill. W. Farber. Boston: Houghton Mifflin.

Polacco, P. 1990. *Thunder cake*. New York: Philomel.

Stolz, M. 1988. *Storm in the night*. Ill. P. Cummings. New York: Harper & Row.

Van Allsburg, C. 1981. *Jumanji*. Boston: Houghton Mifflin.

Viorst, J. 1973. *My mama says there aren't any zombies, ghosts, vampires, creatures, demons, monsters, fiends, goblins, or things*. Ill. K. Chorao. New York: Atheneum.

Waber, B. 1972. *Ira sleeps over*. New York: Houghton Mifflin.

Family Stories
Remember When Stories
Historical Family Stories
Scary Stories

Getting to Know You
Life Story Time Lines

Introduction

To become an effective language user, all learners need many opportunities to use language with other people for real purposes. Getting to Know You facilitates social interaction as each person learns something about another individual. Because the activity is informal, the language user's attention is focused on meaning. The reading and writing that occur are motivated by the need to record and convey meaning to others. In addition, this engagement focuses on the interrelationship of reading, writing, listening, and speaking.

Getting to Know You allows reluctant writers to see written language as a useful vehicle for helping them remember information. Because no one else reads their interview notes, the language users are encouraged to risk using functional spellings. This engagement allows language users to discover the convenience of written language literacy as a vehicle in exploring their world. It also effectively introduces students to the authoring cycle by quickly moving their writing from a rough draft to a publication in the classroom.

Life Story Time Lines can also be used as an introductory strategy to writing. Working with a partner students take turns reflecting back on their day, sharing what happened as well as relating any stories that their reflections trigger. In looking back over their time lines

Meet Camille

A girl named Camille that likes trampolines, quiche and Sister-Sister was my partner. Successfully born at Saint Joe, she has gone to pre-school and she now made it to 4th grade.

On South Calle Angosta, she lives in a house. Brown hair, brown eyes, born 1985, she spends her time swimming.

She is nine years old, lives in Tucson with 5 people in her family.

By Michael

students begin to identify stories, essays, or other pieces that they might elaborate in writing. This engagement supports students in identifying personal topics for writing.

Materials/Procedures for Getting to Know You

▌ Paper and pencils

1. Students are told that they will be interviewing each other to produce a class newspaper or magazine that will introduce them to parents, visitors, or pen pals as well as to each other. There must be some real purpose for producing the newspaper.

Meet Zachary

Ashley: What kind of work do you do?
Zach: Feed fish

Ashley: What food do you eat?
Zach: Banana bread.

Ashley: Do you have a hobby?
Zach: Yes I do. Fighting.

Ashley: Who are the members of your family?
Zach: Two grandmas

Ashley: What is your favorite color?
Zach: Blue

Ashley: Tell us about your pets.
Zach: The girl bird layed eggs.

By Ashley

Getting to Know You
Life Story Time Lines

Meet Mario

Mario likes school. He has two brothers and two sisters. He is loving and kind. He plays with his three dogs. His name is Mario. His favorite color is green. He used to make books. He takes a bath. He is playful. He is bashful. He is not married. He would like to be married. He is six years old and in the first grade. May 28th is Mario's birthday.

By Melinda

2. Interviews from previous years or from magazines and newspapers are read and discussed.

3. The class brainstorms questions to ask during the interviews.

4. Once students have some ideas of questions to ask, they pair up and conduct their interviews. They are encouraged to take notes during their interviews so they will be able to remember the information. They each make the decision, however, about how much and what to write down. The notes taken during interviewing can consist of drawings as well as words or phrases.

5. Students use their notes to write or dictate an article about the person they interviewed.

6. Once the students produce rough drafts, they take them to Authors Circle to get suggestions for revision. It is better if the person who is the subject of the interview is not part of the Authors Circle, because this tends to take ownership of the text away from the writer.

7. Following the Authors Circle, the interview is revised and sent to the Editors Table and then put into a publication that is shared with others.

Materials/Procedures for Life Story Time Lines

▌ Paper and pencils
▌ Overhead transparency and overhead transparency marking pens

1. Work on the overhead, walking students through the events in your day and making notes on the overhead to recall what happened. The time and the event are listed on these notes.

6:00   Awoke
        Make coffee, read the paper
        Need a half hour to wake up
        Hate intrusions

7:00   Took shower, got ready for the day
        Needed to take car into the body shop to get fixed
        Children's driving record
        On first name basis with Bob, the manager of the body
        shop

7:35   Arrived at the office
        Hate E-Mail (Consider it an abuse)
        Hate Voice Mail (Consider it an abuse)
        Hate Faxes (Consider it an abuse)

2. Once you have completed your time line, go back through it identifing events or ideas that you might develop into some type of writing, such as a narrative, essay, informational piece, and so on.

In this instance circle the entries on the body shop and E-Mail, Voice Mail, and Faxes saying: "I might write about how I got to be on a first name basis with Bob, the body shop manager. I could easily make this into a humorous piece."

"I could also write an essay on all of the ways that our privacy is being invaded by our need to communicate instantaneously. I could, in other words, tell the other side of the story to what many see as modern day conveniences—the fax, voice mail, electronic mail, etc."

3. Invite students to work in pairs and take turns walking each other through their day, creating their own time lines and relaying any stories that are triggered by their reflection. In order to get a whole day, students usually do the previous day. If this is difficult, teachers may want to give students a log for keeping track of a day and then use this to construct a time line. It often helps to keep track of several days, one of which is on a weekend.

4. Ask pairs to go back through their time lines and identify stories or essays that they could develop into some type of piece of writing.

As an introduction to inquiry, children were asked on the first day of school to make a paper-plate self-portrait and then, using 3 ×5 cards, find out as much as they could about each other. What they learned was stapled to a ribbon and suspended from the plate (compliments of Carol Hall)

461

5. Have student pairs introduce each other to the class sharing one thing that they found out about their partner that they believe would be of interest to the class.

6. As a culminating experience ask students to select one of the stories or essays that they could write and take it to rough draft form. Have students put their time lines in their Authors Folders for reference should they have difficulty finding topics to write about in the future.

Establishing the Learning Context

Establishing a real reason for conducting these interviews is essential to this engagement. The teacher should participate in these interviews along with the students and write an interview for publication. After the interviews are published, the class discusses the experience together and talks about the authoring cycle and its various components.

Variations of Getting to Know You

1. Instead of writing up the interviews, students can use their notes to introduce their partner orally to the rest of the group or to create some kind of collage or visual display introducing the person.

2. Extensions of this engagement include interviews with community members on some local civic issue; interviews with authors, athletes, police officers, doctors, or others about their occupations; surveys of class members on specific topics; and collections of family stories.

3. "Shoebox" biographies can be used to introduce class members to each other. The teacher introduces the engagement by bringing in five to ten personal items in a shoebox. These items are used to share a personal experience or interest. The students are then asked to interview each other and to use that interview to assemble items that reflect that person's interests into a shoebox biography. Once the shoeboxes are assembled, the students use them to

introduce the people they interviewed. Instead of shoeboxes, students could use a large bag or knapsack to make a "me bag."

4. Students can create Reflection Portfolios on who they are as learners. They take a box or bag and gather items from both home and school that reflect who they are as learners. These collections then go through the portfolio process (see Reflection Portfolios) and students write a description of themselves as learners which they share with others.

5. Students can put together Personal Text Sets containing books that reflect their personalities, interests and experiences. One way in which we have used these Text Sets is to have students place their sets out on display, but withhold their names from the display. The rest of the class walks around, examines each set, and records who they think a particular set represents. It's best to introduce this engagement and then give students some time to gradually put together their Text Set lists as they encounter books. They can then pull together their sets to share with others.

Variations of Life Story Time Lines

1. Life Story Time Lines can be used to capture what students see as important moments in their lives—times when they learned the most, or people who have influenced them. Time lines of this sort can support students in finding topics for writing.

2. Once introduced to these time lines, students can use them to keep a Reflective Journal by simply thinking back over the day to recall each event and note key ideas or thoughts they had along the way. To begin their Reflective Journal students are invited to select several of these thoughts and elaborate their thinking in terms of what it meant to them as well as how this idea affects their beliefs and behavior.

Reference

Getting to Know You was originally developed by Carolyn Burke and Mary Lynn Woods. Life Story Time Lines was adapted from Donald Graves.

Sunday
September 11

2:00 A.M. = Woke up/had friend Natalie over

8:30 A.M. = Watched t.v.

9:00 A.M.- Played Sega Gerasis

9:30 A.M.= Ate Breakfast

10:00 A.M.= Got dressed/Got ready for the day

11:00 A.M.= Left for Washington, In.

12:30 P.M.=Arrived at Park in Washington In.

1:00 P.M.= Ate Lunch

1:30 P.M. = Played at Park

4:30 Went to Grandma's, then Home

6:30 P.M.= Got Home

7:00 P.M= Ate Supper

7:30 P.M.= Dropped Natalie at Home

FIGURE CE10.4
Life Story Time Line including time line of day, selection of topic, expansion of topic through webbing, and first draft of narrative; Shannon, Age 11 (compliments of Carol Hardin)

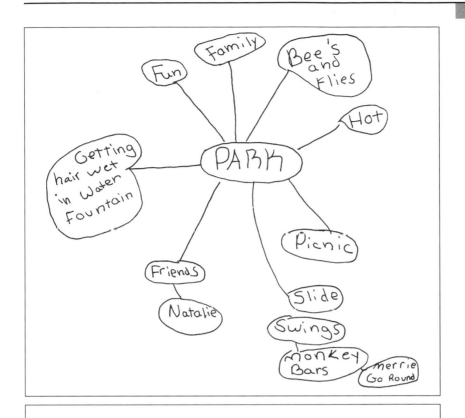

My friend Natalie came over Saturday. She spent the night. The following morning she went with us to Washington Indiana. It was a family picnic at a big park down in Washington. We played with my cousins and family. We played games lik football and frisbee, and things like that. It was getting really hot, so we dunked our heads in the water fountain wich cooled us down. We were going to get in the paddle boats, but they were closed.

Learning Logs
Literature Logs
Inquiry Logs
Class Observation Logs
Math Logs
Exit Cards
Personal Journals
Sketch Journals
Writer's Notebooks

Introduction

Successful learners have learned that the very process of writing and sketching produces growth and new understandings. Putting thoughts, feelings, images, and ideas into words and sketches is not simply a representation of what one knows, but an extension of that knowing. Learners discover new ideas as well as reflect on and re-vision what they already know. Writing and art are tools for think-

I was going home with my water bottle
I saw a teraele hole. I put water
in it but noting came out. I look
in side and a big big teraele.
The big ternsela biger dan the
in our class room.

I'm hungey

ing and reflecting through which learners construct meaning and grow.

Writing plays many different functions in our lives; students should experience those different functions in the writing they do in the classroom. Personal Journals can fulfill both an informal personal function and a recording function for the writer. In a journal, a writer makes a personal record of thoughts, feelings, happenings, plans, and problems. The content of a journal is thus open to each writer to decide. The journal can take on a personal diary function, or can become a Writer's Notebook. The notebook is used to observe the world through collecting "bits of life." These entries can serve as a natural place for writers to find topics they want to develop into drafts. A Sketch Journal plays a similar function to the notebook but emphasizes collecting bits and pieces of life through using art as a way to observe and reflect on thoughts, feelings, images, and experiences.

Learners also need time to reflect on their learning experiences in school and the processes they have used in that learning. When learners reflect, they come to value the strategies they are developing by engaging in authoring through reading, writing, and art and through observing the demonstrations of other learners around them. Learning Logs provide learners with the opportunity to reflect on both the process and content of their authoring and their various inquiry studies. Learning Logs thus give teachers, parents, and students another source of information and evaluation on what students are learning. Students often fail to recognize the small steps they are making in learning. Learning Logs provide students with an opportunity

Learning Logs
Personal Journals
Sketch Journals
Writer's Notebooks

to reflect on the day's activities and to ask themselves, "What have I learned today?" These logs can take a variety of forms.

All of these logs and journals provide writers and sketchers with an informal and safe situation in which they can focus on their own thoughts, images, and feelings and on meaning and fluency, rather than on assigned topics or on conventions. They are informal and personal, and so learners concentrate on thinking and reflecting, not correct spelling or grammar. In contrast to various kinds of Dialogue Journals, these logs and journals are not primarily a place to explore the communicative function of authoring, but authoring as a tool for thinking.

Materials/Procedures for Learning Logs

❚ Pencils or pens
❚ Spiral notebooks or paper stapled into covers
❚ Date stamp

1. At the end of a particular engagement, a morning, or an entire day, students take out their Learning Logs, stamp or write the date, and make an entry. It may sometimes be helpful to have a brief discussion of the day's events before students write to encourage them to select from the entire day rather than the most recent event.

2. Students are asked to write about something new they learned that day at school. They can respond either to what they learned—content—or how they went about learning it—process. If students have difficulty focusing on something new that was learned, the entries can be introduced as writing a reaction or response to the day or to a particular activity. Students should also be encouraged to make connections in their entries between the new learning and what they already know.

Questions that can be used to help students think about their entries are: What did I understand about the work I did in class today? What didn't I understand? At what point did I get confused or did I begin to understand? What do I know now that I didn't know when I got to school today? What can I do better today than I could yesterday? What do I have questions about or wonder about?

3. After students have written for about ten minutes, they can be invited to share their entries with each other. This sharing is especially important when Learning Logs are first introduced. Later on, the sharing may occur only occasionally.

4. Students can have one Learning Log where they reflect broadly across the day or a specific form of the log can be developed. Some of these types of logs are:

a. **Literature Logs**: Logs in which students write about their responses to a particular piece of literature—literature they read independently, the class read-aloud book, or literature for Literature Circles. Students should be encouraged to write their reactions, connections, and questions rather than a summary of the story. Their entries can be webs, sketches, charts, favorite quotes, and diagrams as well as written reflections. These logs can also take the form of Post-it notes, bookmarks, or Little Books that are placed in the book to record the student's thoughts while reading.

b. **Inquiry Logs**: Logs used by students to record their explorations, experiments, interviews, and so on during a particular inquiry focus as students explore a topic and then research a particular question or issue within that topic. In these logs, students record notes on what they are learning, "wonderings" and questions, their process of research, and possible sources to pursue. The log can include their reflections about their initial understandings and interests in a topic and their reflections after completing the inquiry as well as in-process research notes and reflections.

c. **Class Observation Logs**: A class log can be kept next to classroom animals or a particular classroom experiment such as growing plants. Anyone can make an entry in this class log. Another type of class log is a Class History Log (see Visitors Corner).

d. **Math Logs:** Math logs can be used for students to work through their thinking about particular mathematical concepts or problems. After participating in mathematical experiences, they first write about the meaning and practical implications of

Math Journal: Survey of the Pets People Own; Tyrone, Age 7 (Tim O'Keefe's classroom)

Learning Logs
Personal Journals
Sketch Journals
Writer's Notebooks

> All pigs on deck
>
> I think that The Indians should have been left alone. I think that the only reason for trying to sail to the indies is for gold. I don't know why gold is so valuble. I think someone said that gold could make you rich. and they belived that person.
>
> I think Clumbus was trying to make cakes and everything for the Indians is to see if they would trade it for gold. I think that Clumbus was selfish because all he wanted was the Indicn's gold. I think that the Indians are lucky because they had peace with each other

the solution they developed and then reflect on their strategies and understandings.

e. **Exit Cards**: At the end of the day or a particular class period, students fill out exit cards (half sheets of paper or file cards) on which they write one thing they learned and one question they have. These cards are their "exit slips" that are handed to the teacher before leaving class.

5. At the end of each grading period or at the end of the year, students can be asked to look back through their Learning Log entries and to write a self-evaluative entry about their learning during that time period.

Materials/Procedures for Personal Journals

- Pens, pencils, or other writing materials
- Spiral-bound notebooks or paper stapled into construction paper or wallpaper covers
- Date stamp

1. Introduce the journal to the class by bringing in actual diaries or books that contain diaries, such as *Dear Mr. Henshaw* (Cleary, 1983) or *A Gathering of Days* (Blos, 1979). These books can be read to students or used as a set in Literature Circles. Another source is historical documents, such as the journals of historical figures like Benjamin Franklin or Anne Frank. The private function of journals is often an unfamiliar one in the lives of students and their families, so initially they may not know what to write in their journals. Teachers should talk about the function that journals will play in the classroom and describe some of the things students might write in their journals.

2. Each day at a designated time students get their journals, write or stamp the date at the top of the page, and write their entry. Entries can include drawings or sketches as well as writing. It is important to find a time of day that works for a particular group of students. Many teachers have students begin their day by writing in their journals, because it provides a quiet reflective transition from home to school.

3. Journals are returned to the box or space where they are stored. In some classrooms, students are invited to share from their journals during a class meeting. This sharing is especially important when first beginning journals because many students are uncertain about what to write. These journals are private, and so students are never required to share that journal with others unless they choose to do so.

4. If teachers occasionally read through the journals, some system needs to be worked out for entries that the student does not want

Learning Logs
Personal Journals
Sketch Journals
Writer's Notebooks

anyone to read. Such pages can be marked VP (very private), folded over, or stapled shut. Some teachers do not read the journals at all but simply do a quick check or page count to see that the student is writing entries.

Materials/Procedures for Sketch Journals

▪ Colored pencils, charcoal pencil, watercolors, crayons, and other art materials
▪ Some type of sketch book or bound blank book
▪ Date stamp

1. Because the function of the Sketch Journal is to support learners in observing their world more closely, the Sketch Journal should be introduced by inviting students to sketch one new thing they have observed in the world each day. Introduce the Sketch Journal by sharing your journal or ask an artist to share the journal they use for rough sketches with the class. Also share quotes from illustrators and artists about their use of sketch journals to observe and reflect on the world around them. *Talking with Artists* (Cummings, 1992) is a good source as well as children's books such as *A Crack in the Wall* (Haggerty, 1993) where characters use sketching as part of their life (see Appendix B).

2. Students need to find just the right kind of notebook or sketch pad and collect art materials that they can easily carry with them.

3. Each day students spend time looking through and sketching in their journals. A regular time for sketching in the journals, such as right after lunch or at the end of the day, should be scheduled, but students also carry the journals throughout the day and at home. Procedures need to be established so that students always have the journals at school.

4. When students first begin sketching in their journals, invitations and demonstrations should constantly be available on the types of sketches they can make. Many of their sketches will be observations and reflections on the events occurring around them and their feelings and emotions as well as past images and memories. Another important use of the sketch journal is as a place to explore techniques and rough draft sketches for an illustrated book. It may be necessary to offer specific strategy lessons on how

to draw a figure or use of perspective to support students. Many will be unsure and uncomfortable with sketching at first. Books such as *Drawing on the Right Side of the Brain* (Edwards, 1989) and *Watercolor for the Artistically Undiscovered* (Hurd & Cassidy, 1992) are helpful in finding invitations for the classroom.

5. Establish an art studio center which contains many different kinds of art materials, papers, and techniques for students to explore, as well as art prints and picture books. The center can also include rotating invitations to try a particular technique such as scratchboard or sprinkling salt on watercolor or to explore a particular element of art such as color, line, or perspective.

6. Illustrator or artist studies can support students as they try to understand art as a way of making sense of the world and their lives. Students particularly connect with studies of their favorite illustrators. They can discuss Text Sets of these illustrators in Literature Circles and try out that illustrator's technique in their Sketch Journal or the art studio. Copying a favorite picture by a particular illustrator is often a strategy that students use to explore how an illustrator has constructed that picture.

7. While the major focus of this journal is on sketching as a tool for thinking and reflecting, students often also add written comments along the side of their sketches for particular thoughts or quotes that they cannot put into their sketch.

Sketch Journal, Portrait of a Fellow Student; Lynice, Age 8 (Gloria Kauffman's classroom)

8. Students will need regular times to share and reflect on the journals with a partner or small group, keeping in mind that they always have the choice of keeping particular entries private.

9. The Sketch Journal can be used as a place for students to find a topic or idea they want to pursue in a piece of writing and/or art. They look for themes, connections, interests, or images that they want to use to create a draft and possibly publish in a more formal way for an audience.

Materials/Procedures for Writer's Notebooks

- Pens, pencils, or other writing materials
- Some type of notebook or blank bound book
- Date stamp

Learning Logs
Personal Journals
Sketch Journals
Writer's Notebooks

1. Introduce Writer's Notebook by sharing your notebook or Jean Little's book, *Hey World, Here I Am!* (1986). Also share quotes from various authors and illustrators about how they collect ideas and quotes in journals, diaries, bureau drawers, and files. These bits and pieces of life are the "seed bed" from which they look for topics and ideas for their major pieces of writing. Most of their time is spent observing life, collecting ideas, and writing short entries, not writing drafts for publication. *Shoptalk* (Murray, 1990) and *How Writers Write* (Lloyd, 1987) are good sources of these quotes (see Authors Meeting Authors for a list of other sources).

2. Students each need to find just the right kind of notebook—a looseleaf notebook, composition book, bound blank book, or spiral notebook.

3. Each day students spend time reading through their notebooks and writing entries. The notebooks are highlighted during uninterrupted writing, but students also carry them throughout the day and at home. Procedures need to be established so that students always have the notebooks at school for work time.

4. When students first begin writing in their notebooks, invitations and demonstrations should constantly be available on the types of entries they can make. These entries can be observations of something or someone, memories, favorite quotes, clippings, lists, ramblings, experiences from their lives, an unforgettable scene, responses to literature, research notes, family stories, and so on. The notebooks are a place for students to observe and make sense of their world.

5. Having regular times to share and reflect on the notebooks is very important. Time should be scheduled for students to meet with a partner or small group and share their entries with each other, keeping in mind that they always have the choice of keeping particular entries private.

6. Sharing quotes and strategies from professional authors of children's books will support students as they search for the kind of entries they want to make. Students should also become engaged in their own author studies where they explore particular writers, poets, and illustrators and what these authors have said about their work.

7. About once a month, students are encouraged to read and reflect on their entries in order to find a topic or idea they want to pursue in a piece of writing. They look for themes, connections, interests, or images that they might want to use for a topic. They are not looking for a particular entry to revise, but use the entries as a place to discover a topic or idea for a draft. These drafts are usually not written in the notebook but are kept in the student's Authors Folder.

Establishing the Learning Context

All of these journals and logs require a classroom environment where students feel safe. They will be unwilling to explore their personal observations and reflections on their life and learning and to take risks in writing and sketching what's really on their minds if they do not trust the teacher and other students. Establishing a strong sense of community is essential. It is also essential that students have the right to keep any entries private and that teachers never correct the entries for grammar or spelling. In general, teachers should not write in these logs and journals, unless that response is invited by the student and, even then, the response should be written on a separate piece of paper or Post-it note.

Many students initially will have difficulty observing and reflecting on their learning and life experiences because they have not been asked to reflect in this way before. They've lived the experience, not thought about it. Establishing an environment where students are constantly asked to reflect orally on their engagements in brief whole class discussions supports students in seeing reflection as a natural part of living and learning. It also gives them experiences and demonstrations on reflection. Taking five minutes at various points throughout the day to ask students to talk quickly about what they are doing and thinking will be of tremendous benefit. Having brief sharing times when students can choose to share their logs, notebooks, and journals is also critical in providing demonstrations of other ways they can reflect.

Both teachers and students need to recognize that it may take a period of time for students to develop their own purposes for these logs and journals and be able to use them to observe carefully and reflect on their lives and learning. Journals will play differing roles in the lives of students. Some students will write or sketch long, involved

Learning Logs
Personal Journals
Sketch Journals
Writer's Notebooks

entries, while others will have brief entries or say they have nothing to write or sketch. Sometimes a student will have brief entries for several weeks (or months) and then will suddenly create long entries. Teachers need to have patience and support students having difficulty with journals, as well as to allow for individual variation in the role that journals and logs play for students.

While it may be tempting to assign students topics for journal or log entries because of the difficulties students experience in getting started, assignments defeat the very function of these logs and journals. Students need many demonstrations, but they need to find their own purposes. Through sharing, author and illustrator studies, and specific invitations, teachers can provide support for students without assigning topics.

Teachers should keep the same kind of log, notebook, or journal as students to provide demonstrations that adults use these same personal functions for writing and sketching in their lives. Keeping a journal also gives teachers greater insights into the process of thinking and observing that is being asked of students. Adults often assume that particular engagements are easy for children until they try them for themselves.

One of the major issues is the overuse of different kinds of logs, notebooks, and journals in the same classroom. While several kinds may be used at the same time in the classroom, teachers need to consider carefully students' needs and the curriculum to make choices of which kinds to introduce into the classroom at any one point in time. These may change over the course of the year. Also one notebook can be used for a variety of functions and entries or students may have different notebooks for different kinds of logs and journals. No matter what types are used, students need a sufficient amount of time on a regular basis in the schedule for writing and sketching. Students need to be able to predict when journals will occur so they can be thinking about what they want to write or sketch.

References

Cummings, P. 1992. *Talking with artists*. New York: Bradbury.

Edwards, B. 1989. *Drawing on the right side of the brain*. New York: Putnam.

Ernst, K. 1994. *Picturing learning: Artists and writers in the classroom*. Portsmouth, NH: Heinemann.

Fulwiler, T. 1987. *The journal book*. Portsmouth, NH: Heinemann.

Hurd, T., & J. Cassidy. 1992. *Watercolor for the artistically undiscovered*. Palo Alto, CA: Klutz Press.

Little, J. 1986. *Hey world, here I am!* Toronto, Canada: Kids Can Press.

Lloyd, P. 1987. *How writers write*. Portsmouth, NH: Heinemann.

Kiefer, B. 1994. *The potential of picturebooks: From visual literacy to aesthetic understanding*. Englewood Cliffs, NJ: Merrill.

Murray, D. 1990. *Shoptalk*. Portsmouth, NH: Heinemann.

Appendix A: Children's Books That Contain Diaries

Baylor, B. 1986. *I'm in charge of celebrations*. Ill. P. Parnall. New York: Scribners.

Blos, J. 1979. *A gathering of days: A New England girl's journal, 1830–32*. New York: Aladdin.

Cleary, B. 1983. *Dear Mr. Henshaw*. New York: Morrow.

Cooney, B. 1994. *Only Opal: The diary of a young girl*. New York: Philomel.

Filipovic, Z. 1994. *Zlata's diary: A child's life in Sarajevo*. New York: Viking.

Fitzhugh, L. 1964. *Harriet the spy*. New York: Dell.

Frank, A. 1967. *Anne Frank: The diary of a young girl*. New York: Doubleday.

Gottlieb, D. 1991. *My stories by Hildy Calpurnia Rose*. New York: Knopf.

Greenfield, E. 1974. *Sister*. Ill. M. Barnett. New York: Harper & Row.

Harvey, B. 1986. *My prairie year: Based on the diary of Elenore Plaisted*. Ill. D. Ray. New York: Holiday.

Klein, R. 1983. *Penny Pollard's diary*. Ill. A. James. Melbourne, Australia: Oxford University Press.

Knight, A. S. 1993. *The way west: Journal of a pioneer woman*. Ill. M. McCurdy. New York: Simon & Schuster.

Lester, J. 1968. *To be a slave*. Ill. T. Feelings. New York: Dial.

Little, J. 1986. *Hey world, here I am!* Ill. S. Truesdell. New York: HarperCollins.

Lowry, L. 1979. *Anastasia Krupnik*. Boston: Houghton Mifflin.

Roop, P. & C., eds. 1993. *Off the map: The journals of Lewis and Clark*. Ill. T. Tanner. New York: Walker.

Stevens, C. 1993. *A book of your own: Keeping a diary or journal*. New York: Clarion.

Thaxter, C. 1992. *Celia's island journal*. Ill. L. Krupinski. Boston: Little, Brown.

Learning Logs
Personal Journals
Sketch Journals
Writer's Notebooks

Williams, V. 1993. *Scooter*. New York: Greenwillow.

Wilson, B. 1990. *Jenny*. Ill. D. Johnson. New York: Macmillan.

Appendix B: Children's Books Where Children Use Sketching

Bulla, C. 1987. *The chalk box kid*. Ill. T. Allen. New York: Random House.

Byars, B. 1978. *The cartoonist*. Ill. R. Cuffari. New York: Puffin Books.

Carle, E. 1992. *Draw me a star*. New York: Philomel.

Cazet, D. 1987. *Frosted glass*. New York: Bradbury.

Christiana, D. 1990. *Drawer in a drawer*. Canada: HarperCollins.

Collins, D. 1992. *I am an artist*. Ill. R. Brickman. Brookfield, CT: Millbrook.

Drescher, H. 1982. *Simon's book*. New York: Lothrop.

Fleischman, P. 1988. *Rondo in C*. Ill. J. Wentworth. New York: Harper & Row.

Garaway, M. 1989. *Ashkii and his Grandfather*. Ill. H. Warren. Tucson, AZ: Treasure Chest Publications.

Greenfield, E. 1981. *Daydreamers*. Ill. T. Feelings. New York: Dial.

Haggerty, M. 1993. *A crack in the wall*. Ill. R. de Anda. New York: Lee & Low.

Hoban, R. 1989. *Monsters*. Ill. Q. Blake. New York: Scholastic.

Lionni, L. 1991. *Matthew's dream*. New York: Knopf.

Markun, P. *The little painter of Sabana Grande*. Ill. R. Casilla. New York: Bradbury.

Moss, M. 1990. *Regina's big mistake*. Boston: Houghton Mifflin.

Paulsen, G. 1988. *The island*. New York: Orchard.

————. 1991. *The monument*. New York: Delacorte.

Stanley, D. 1994. *The gentleman and the kitchen maid*. Ill. D. Nolan. New York: Dial.

Testa, F. 1983. *If you look around you*. New York: Dial.

Toll, N. 1993. *Behind the secret window: A memoir of a hidden childhood during World War Two*. New York: Dial.

Williams, H. 1991. *Stories in art*. Brookfield, CT: Millbrook.

Williams, V. 1986. *Cherries and cherry pits*. New York: Greenwillow.

See also: Anomalies, Webbing What's on Your Mind, Graffiti Board, Authors Meeting Authors, Family Stories, Sketch to Stretch, Dialogue Journals

Literature Circles

Introduction

Readers need time to read both extensively for enjoyment and information and intensively to think deeply about life. Extensive reading engagements such as read-aloud and uninterrupted reading allow readers to read widely and gain reading proficiency. These engagements need to be balanced with intensive experiences such as Literature Circles that support readers in thinking critically about books. When readers talk about books with others, they can savor a book so that it becomes a significant part of their life experiences. Through conversation and dialogue, readers have the opportunity to explore their own half-formed ideas, to expand their understandings through hearing others' interpretations, and to become critical and inquiring thinkers. Readers need to understand that a variety of interpretations exist for any piece of literature and that they can collaboratively explore their interpretations with one another to reach new understandings. Literature Circles help readers become literate.

Literature Circles support reading as a transaction, a process in which readers actively construct meaning from a text by bringing meaning to as well as taking meaning from a text (Rosenblatt, 1978). The reader brings his or her understandings and experiences to a book and engages in a "lived-through" experience with that book that results in the reader constructing an interpretation of that book. This interpretation is a new text that the reader can continue to explore and change over time through interactions with other readers.

There is no one meaning to be determined, but many meanings to be explored and critiqued within a community of readers. Readers do not come to a Literature Circle to answer the teacher's questions, give a summary of the book, or fill in a worksheet. Readers do not engage with books to determine literary elements or extract a piece of information, but rather, first and foremost, to learn about and experience life.

Readers bring their "rough draft" understandings about the book to a discussion and think collaboratively with other readers to create new and more complex understandings. In Literature Circles, readers are not simply working together cooperatively. They are not assigned particular roles and tasks. Everyone must be involved equally in listening and thinking with each other so that everyone is pushed to outgrow their current selves. The dialogue in these circles leads to new perspectives on literature, life, and literacy.

Materials/Procedures

▌ Shared book sets (multiple copies of a piece of literature), Text Sets (sets of different books that are conceptually related to each other), or Paired Books (two books on the same topic but with some kind of opposition to each other)

▌ Literature logs and chart paper for Webbing What's on Your Mind

1. Based on classroom themes and inquiries, shared book sets, Text Sets, or Paired Books are put together by teachers and students. These sets are related to each other and to the topics and themes being explored in the classroom at that time.

   a. Use quality literature that will support an intensive consideration. High interest series books for middle grade readers and the highly predictable books that young children read usually do not have issues that children can discuss in depth with each other. These books are to be read for enjoyment and fluency, not discussion.

   b. Use a range of literature including picture books, novels, short stories, poetry, informational books, and books authored by children from the classroom.

   c. Literature can be shared through films and video.

2. The sets are introduced to the class through short book talks. Students then have time to browse through the books for a day or two. For young children, the teacher may read each choice aloud to the class.

3. Students decide which Literature Circle they want to join. This choice can be indicated by signing up "first come/first served" on a chart or by having students mark their first and second choices on a ballot that they give to the teacher, who then forms the groups. These groups should have four to six members.

4. There are different variations of how students go about reading the literature depending on their reading proficiencies and the length and difficulty of the book.

a. In most cases, students read the literature before beginning their Literature Circles. Students reading longer chapter books meet to determine how many pages they need to read a day in order to finish the book in one week. Anyone who does not get the reading done during school completes it as homework. Children may also want to meet each day in mini-circles for ten to fifteen minutes where they share with each other about what they read the previous day and set their goals for how far they will read that day.

b. Sometimes, students meet in their Literature Circles as they read the book. This usually occurs when the book is especially long and difficult, students are reading in their second or third language and need to process the book with each other as they read, or students need support in maintaining their interest and enthusiasm in a book. When they finish the book, they meet for several more days to discuss it as a whole.

c. Students cannot always independently read the books they choose to discuss in circles. Usually students having difficulty will partner read with someone from the group. Sometimes teachers have put the book on tape for a reader.

d. Young children (K–1) are usually unable to read the books independently for their circles. Their literature circles focus on quality picture books which need to be read aloud to them by a teacher, buddy reader, or family member. Young children also often need to hear the story several times before they are able

Literature Circles

to discuss it in a Literature Circle. Some teachers read the books aloud to the entire class, put the books out for independent browsing and at the listening center, and then again read the book to the group right before the discussion. Sometimes the books are sent home in a special packet for several days with a request for a family member to read the book aloud the next several evenings. The child is also asked to draw or write a response on a piece of paper and put a Post-it note on their favorite page before bringing it back to the group.

e. As students read, they are encouraged to write or sketch their connections, questions, and responses so they will be ready to share with their group members. These responses can be in a Literature Log, Sketch Journal, or on Post-it notes placed in the book. Sometimes students use a particular engagement such as Sketch to Stretch and Save the Last Word for Me as they read.

f. Students who finish reading ahead of the rest of the group are encouraged to read from a set of books related to their Literature Circle books. These can be books by the same author or on the same theme.

5. Literature Circles usually last anywhere from two days to two weeks, depending on the length of the book and the depth of the discussion about the book. Sometimes only half the class is involved in Literature Circles at any one time, and the others are doing extensive reading, Shared Reading, writing, and so on.

6. The Literature Circle discussions are open-ended and provide time for readers to share their initial responses with each other and then explore several issues in more depth. Literature Circles often follow this general pattern:

a. Students begin by asking each other, "What did you think about as you read this story?" They share their initial responses by talking about their favorite parts, discussing sections they found confusing, retelling parts they enjoyed, talking about the illustrations, making connections to their lives and to other books, telling stories of their own experiences, and engaging in social chatter. Their talk resembles a conversation that "mucks about" and wanders around to many different topics without focusing on any one topic for any length of time. Students do not necessarily listen well to each other because everyone wants to share what's on their minds about this book.

Students can also share their entries from the literature logs or the pages they marked with a Post-it note reminder. If they used a particular engagement such as Sketch to Stretch, Cloning an Author, or Save the Last Word for Me as they read, they begin their circle by sharing their sketches or quotes. Another initial sharing engagement is Graffiti Board.

This initial sharing can last anywhere from fifteen minutes to several days. Sometimes groups have a lot to say; other times they sit and stare at each other. The sharing provides a chance for the students to put forth a wide range of ideas and connections from which they can choose issues for further discussion.

b. Based on their initial sharing, students move into a focused dialogue on one or more issues related to their interpretations of the literature. Sometimes this transition occurs naturally when an issue is raised that catches everyone's attention. Many times, however, groups reach a point where they either consider themselves finished or begin repeating the same comments over and over again.

c. Students take a large chart paper and place it in the middle of their group to create a web of all the issues and connections that came up as they shared. They are asked, "What could you talk about with this book? What ideas, connections, and questions do you have related to this book?" Teachers usually serve as scribes for this brainstorming with young children and at the beginning of the year with older students. As members of the group, teachers can add their ideas to the webs also.

d. The group reads through their brainstormed web of "what's on their minds" and negotiate to choose an issue or question from the web to begin their discussion the next day. Once they have decided what they will discuss, they also talk about how they will prepare for that discussion— rereading certain sections of the book, writing in their literature logs, thinking about the issue, engaging in further research, or trying a particular way of responding such as Sketch to Stretch, Save the Last Word for Me, or Anomalies.

Literature Circles

e. Each day the group begins by talking about the issue agreed upon on the previous day and then refers back to the web if they run out of ideas to discuss. They add other issues and questions as they arise. The web is a list of possibilities and the group does not need to discuss everything on the web or limit themselves to only those topics. The web is used only if the group needs this support for moving to a focus for in-depth dialogue.

f. If the teacher is a member of the group, then he or she should participate as a reader, not a question-asker. Instead of asking questions to keep the group talking, teachers need to share their interpretations and comments as part of the group process. When teachers do ask questions, they should be questions about issues the teacher truly does not understand or wants to know what others think or questions to encourage students to explain their thinking (e.g. when a student says "The book was stupid," asking the student to talk about what made it seem stupid to them). Teachers prepare for these groups in the same way as students, by reading and writing about what's on their minds in their literature logs.

7. Particularly at the beginning of the year, the class should meet together for a class meeting after the Literature Circles for that day are finished. At this meeting, they first share *what* they talked about that day. They then talk about *how* the groups went that day and discuss ways to solve any problems that groups are experiencing.

8. As students finish their discussions in Literature Circles, they find a way to present to the class. They may choose to share informally during a class sharing time by simply standing up as a group and telling the class about their book and what they discussed and perhaps sharing their web. They can also choose to put together a formal presentation by using the following process:

a. Students are asked to make a web or list to answer the question, "What do you want others to understand about your book and discussion? What is most important to you about this Literature Circle?" This discussion supports students in thinking about what they want to communicate through their presentation and prevents problems with "cute" projects that have little to do with the book.

b. The group then brainstorms a list of the different ways they might present their Literature Circle to others. Students are pushed to create a list with many different ideas, not just one or two. They are also encouraged to share their ideas through another sign system such as drama, art, mathematics, and music. Supplies for the various kinds of presentations should be located in a center for easy access by students. A brainstormed list of possible ways to present a book should also be in the center.

Presentations might involve creating murals, dioramas, roller TV shows, paintings, papier-mâché, collage, sculpture, mobiles, and posters; performing dramatized versions or puppet shows; writing or performing a new ending, a different story with the same theme or characters, or telling the story from a different character's point of view; writing journals or letters from the point of view of characters in the book; creating a newspaper based on the time period and events in the book; developing a Readers Theatre; creating a game for others to play (board games or TV game shows); setting up displays or learning centers; and making a comparison chart.

c. The group then compares their list of presentation ideas with the list of what they want to communicate and decide on their presentation. They reach a decision on a presentation and work to put it together.

d. As soon as a group is ready, they present to the class. The class receives the presentation by talking about what was effective and asking the students questions about the book and/or their discussion.

9. Groups will finish at different times with their discussions and presentations. As each group finishes their presentation, they return to reading books of their choice and other kinds of reading and writing experiences. Literature Circles demand hard thinking and so students often need time off to read broadly from high interest books before another set of circles start. This time between groups can be a week or two of extensive reading engagements for

Literature Circles

older readers. For younger students, teachers often offer many Shared Reading and small group guided reading engagements to focus on fluency and reading strategies with highly predictable books for a week or two.

Establishing the Learning Context

For Literature Circles to be successful, there needs to be a classroom environment already established that supports risk taking and varied constructions of meaning from reading. If students feel that they must reproduce what the teacher thinks is *the* meaning of a piece of literature, the Literature Circles will not be productive. Students who have a long literacy history of basal reading groups may initially treat Literature Circles as basal reader discussions and focus on the text to come up with the "right" interpretation. They are used to sitting back and answering the teacher's questions and may not know how to talk and work collaboratively with other students. The teacher will need to provide other kinds of curricular engagements to establish a learning environment that supports Literature Circles and should not be discouraged if students say little when they first become involved in these discussions.

Some curricular engagements that will help establish a supportive learning atmosphere include Sketch to Stretch, Say Something, Save the Last Word for Me, Written Conversation, Literature Logs, Readers Theatre, Uninterrupted Reading and Writing, and so on. It is essential that students have time daily to read widely from many different kinds of reading materials. They also need to be authors who have published their own writing and participated in Authors Circles. The discussions in Authors Circles have a major impact on Literature Circles. The teacher should be reading aloud to the class and using the whole-class discussions after reading aloud to demonstrate the types of questions and topics that the students can focus on in Literature Circles. In addition, students should be involved in responding over time in a variety of ways to literature including art, music, drama, and writing.

Literature Circles should be connected to other parts of the curriculum. Students have many more connections to bring to their discussions if the groups are related to each other and to the broader class curriculum. Even high quality literature can have difficulty standing on its own. If students are focusing on a study of families or different cultures, then literature can be chosen that deals with family situations or the clash of cultures. If students are reading a particular genre, such as folktales, they should be invited to try writing their own folktales; or if students are going to be writing some type of nonfiction report, Literature Circles can focus on nonfiction.

The depth of discussion in Literature Circles depends on the rich history of stories to which the pieces of literature being discussed are connected. There are various ways that this rich history can be built: Use of familiar stories that students have heard over and over, multiple readings of the same story in the classroom, relating the book to other books read previously in the classroom through topic, genre, theme, or author, or relating the literature to themes or topics being discussed in the classroom. If students are unfamiliar with and dislike books, it may be necessary to begin with many extensive reading engagements before moving to circles.

During the initial circles, the teacher should demonstrate the types of comments, questions and discussion behaviors that are appropriate to establish a supportive context for sharing and constructing interpretations of literature. Varied interpretations are accepted as long as the reader can support them. Readers are asked to support and explain what they say, rather than simply making statements about their reading experience with a particular book ("I like it"). The teacher also encourages readers to explore each others' interpretations and collaboratively to build new understandings of the literature during the Literature Circle. Literature Circles are a time of exploration with one another, not a time to present a formal or final interpretation of a particular piece of literature. Readers need to listen to each other (that includes the teacher) and to build off each others' comments. Both the students and the teacher should reply to one another rather than assess; this helps avoid cutting off discussion.

Literature Circles can be organized in a variety of ways so that teachers and students share in the control of these groups. Although the groups will probably begin with the teacher taking an active role, the teacher needs to allow students to take over and direct the discussion. Because of the teacher's greater experience and knowledge, the teacher's presence in Literature Circles influences the dynamics of the group. Teachers can change their role from leader to member by waiting for student responses rather than dominating the discussion

Literature Circles

and by occasionally offering their own opinions about what is being discussed rather than asking questions. Teachers can offer differing amounts of support and share control with students by trying different variations of the circles in which they are sometimes present and at other times circulate from group to group, or not join the group at all.

The teacher needs to obtain multiple copies of books, especially if the books are chapter books. Picture books can be easily shared among the group members, but students need their own copies of the longer books. Check libraries, other teachers, Chapter I and resource teacher collections, and closets. Use the bonus points from paperback book clubs, ask the school to substitute literature for textbook or workbook money, and check with the parent-teacher organization for money. Short stories and poems can be photocopied. Remember that picture books are not just for young children but can be used productively with older readers.

Variations

The following variations particularly support children who are having difficulty knowing how to talk and think together in Literature Circles:

1. Ask students to choose a picture book for the teacher to read to the class from a stack of books which were previously read aloud. During the second reading, an easel is placed next to the authors chair. During the read-aloud, the teacher stops periodically to ask students, "What's on your mind?" Student comments are quickly jotted down on the chart. At the end of the read-aloud, students choose several of the comments to discuss in depth.

2. Encourage students to talk and work together as partners in as many different ways as possible. Say Something and Written Conversation are especially effective partner strategies that encourage children to talk and listen to each other. Teachers can also read aloud a book and then ask students to work as partners and respond to the book using engagements such as Sketch to Stretch and Save the Last Word for Me. The class can then come together for a whole group discussion of the book.

3. Teachers can introduce students to different ways of responding through read-alouds and Literature Logs. During the first chapter

book read-aloud, teachers ask students to respond to the book several times a week in their Literature Logs. Each time, a different way of responding is introduced such as webs, charts, sketches, questions, quotes, and connections through different engagements such as Sketch to Stretch and Save the Last Word. Students share their log entries with each other so they can see how others used that way of responding. When students begin Literature Circles, they can use their logs to remind them of their different options for response.

4. Classes may want occasionally to use a whole class set where everyone in the classroom reads and discusses the same book. A whole class set can be used at the beginning of the year or as a shared experience to introduce a long-term inquiry focus in the classroom. Whole class sets should be used only occasionally because they eliminate choice and whole group discussions allow only a few children to talk. If used, teachers should move back and forth between whole group and small group discussions of the book.

5. When teachers have read aloud a chapter book to which the class has responded in positive ways, that experience can be extended into reflective literature circles (Kahn, 1994). After finishing the read-aloud, the class spends several days creating a brainstormed list of all of the issues and connections they see in this book. They then put together this list and group related issues and connections and sign up for a Literature Circle to discuss one of the groups of issues. After discussing the issues for several days, they share their discussions with the rest of the class.

6. Text Sets often work well as a first experience with older students who are not willing to talk in the groups. Because each person is the only one who has read a particular book in the set, each needs to retell that book to the group. Paired Books work well with both younger and older students in supporting initial discussions because the children can focus on comparisons across the two books.

7. Students can also engage in Literature Circle experiences that use other sign systems to explore interpretation such as reflective drama. After reading a book or poem several times, students can use the following types of engagements as part of a reflective drama:

a. Work as partners with one person playing the role of the reporter and the other a character from the book who is being interviewed by the reporter.

b. The reporter arranges the character into a still life or frozen pose that summarizes what the reporter learned about the character. The reporters then walk around the room, commenting on the various frozen poses and what they are thinking and doing. They may even create dialogue for what they might be saying. The frozen characters are not allowed to speak. The class then meets together and the children who were frozen talk about what they were thinking.

c. The children form groups of four and create a still life scene with characters from the book. They create a scene in which there is some kind of opposition in what characters are saying or doing. Half of the class walks around and discusses the other still life scenes and then returns to take their poses while the others walk around.

d. The class meets together in a meeting led by the teacher as a character related to the book. The meeting is to discuss some kind of problem posed by the book and to extend the book beyond the storyline.

References

The engagement of Literature Circles was developed by Kathy Short and Gloria Kauffman based on Karen Smith's work with literature studies.

Other references include:

Barnes, D. 1975. *From communication to curriculum*. New York: Penguin.

Cullinan, B. 1993. *Children's voices: Talk in the classroom*. Newark, DE: International Reading Association.

Edmiston, B., P. Enciso, & M. King. 1987. "Empowering readers and writers through drama: Narrative theater." *Language Arts* 64(2): 219–228.

Holland, K., R. Hungerford, & S. Ernst, eds. 1993. *Journeying: Children responding to literature*. Portsmouth, NH: Heinemann.

Kahn, L. 1994. "Mathematics as life: Children's responses to literature." Ed.S. Thesis, University of Arizona.

O'Neill, C., & A. Lambert. 1982. *Drama structures*. Portsmouth, NH: Heinemann.

Peterson, R., & M. Eeds. 1991. *Grand conversations*. New York: Scholastic.

Pierce, K., & C. Gilles, eds. 1993. *Cycles of meaning*. Portsmouth, NH: Heinemann.

Rosenblatt, L. 1978. *The reader, the text, and the poem: The transactional theory of the literary work*. Carbondale, IL: Southern Illinois University Press.

Short, K., & K. Pierce, eds. 1991. *Talking about books*. Portsmouth, NH: Heinemann.

Sloan, G. 1993. *The child as critic*. 3rd ed. New York: Teachers College Press.

Vandergrift, K. 1980. *Child and story*. New York: Neal-Schuman.

Appendix A: Literature for Shared Book Sets (multiple copy sets)

Picture Books

Ackerman, K. 1988. *Song and dance man*. Ill. S. Gammell. New York: Scholastic.

Aliki. 1979. *Mummies are made in Egypt*. New York: Harper.

Baker, J. 1987. *Where the forest meets the sea*. New York: Scholastic.

Bang, M. 1985. *The paper crane*. New York: Mulberry.

Begay, S. 1992. *Ma'ii and Cousin Horned Toad*. New York: Scholastic.

Birdseye, T. 1988. *Airmail to the moon*. Ill. S. Gammell. New York: Holiday.

Bunting, E. 1988. *How many days to America?* Ill. B. Peck. New York: Trumpet Club.

———. 1989. *The Wednesday surprise*. Ill. D. Carrick. New York: Trumpet Club.

Burningham, J. 1987. *John Patrick Norman McHennessy—the boy who was always late*. New York: Trumpet Club.

Cherry, L. 1990. *The great Kapok tree*. New York: Trumpet Club.

Clifton, L. 1983. *Everett Anderson's goodbye*. Ill. A. Grifalconi. New York: Trumpet Club.

Cohen, B. 1983. *Molly's Pilgrim*. Ill. M. Deraney. New York: Bantam.

Cole, J. 1986. *The magic schoolbus at the waterworks*. Ill. B. Degan. New York: Scholastic.

Cooney, B. 1982. *Miss Rumphius*. New York: Trumpet Club.

de Paola, T. 1975. *Strega Nona*. New York: Scholastic.

Literature Circles

————. 1981. *Now one foot, now the other*. New York: Trumpet Club.

————. 1989. *The art lesson*. New York: Trumpet Club.

Dorros, A. 1991. *Abuela*. Ill. E. Kleven. New York: Trumpet Club.

Fox, M. 1984. *Wilfrid Gordon McDonald Partridge*. Ill. J. Vivas. New York: Trumpet Club.

————. 1988. *Koala Lou*. Ill. P. Lofts. New York: Trumpet Club.

Friedman, I. 1984. *How my parents learned to eat*. Ill. A. Say. Boston: Houghton Mifflin.

Fritz, J. 1969. *George Washington's breakfast*. Ill. P. Galdone. New York: Trumpet Club.

Goble, P. 1978. *The girl who loved wild horses*. New York: Aladdin.

Hayes, J. 1987. *La Llorona: The weeping woman*. Ill. V. Hill. El Paso, TX: Cinco Punto Press.

Hazen, B. 1979. *Tight times*. Ill. T. Hyman. New York: Puffin.

Heide, F., & J. Gilliland. 1990. *The day of Ahmed's secret*. Ill. T. Lewin. New York: Scholastic.

Hodges, M. 1984. *Saint George and the dragon*. Ill. T. Hyman. Boston: Little, Brown.

Hoffman, M. 1991. *Amazing Grace*. Ill. C. Binch. New York: Scholastic.

Huck, C. 1989. *Princess Furball*. Ill. A. Lobel. New York: Scholastic.

Hutchins, P. 1968. *Rosie's walk*. New York: Aladdin.

Isadora, R. 1979. *Ben's trumpet*. New York: Scholastic.

————. 1991. *At the crossroads*. New York: Scholastic.

Levine, E. 1989. *I hate English*. Ill. S. Bjorkman. New York: Scholastic.

Lionni, L. 1959. *Little blue and little yellow*. New York: Scholastic.

————. 1967. *Frederick*. New York: Trumpet Club.

Lobel, A. 1970. *Frog and toad are friends*. New York: Harper & Row.

————. 1980. *Fables*. New York: Scholastic.

Lowell, S. 1992. *The three little javelinas*. Ill. J. Harris. New York: Scholastic.

Louie, A. 1982. *Yeh-Shen: A Cinderella story from China*. Ill. E. Young. New York: Philomel.

Macaulay, D. 1973. *Cathedral: The story of its construction*. Boston: Houghton Mifflin.

Martin, B., Jr., & J. Archambault. 1985. *The ghost-eye tree*. Ill. T. Rand. New York: Scholastic.

McKissak, P. 1988. *Mirandy and Brother Wind*. Ill. J. Pinkney. New York: Knopf.

Morris, A. 1989. *Hats hats hats*. Ill. K. Heyman. New York: Scholastic.

Polacco, P. 1992. *Mrs. Katz and Tush*. New York: Scholastic.

Ringgold, F. 1991. *Tar beach*. New York: Scholastic.

Rylant, C. 1985. *The relatives came*. Ill. S. Gammell. New York: Scholastic.

Schwartz, D. 1985. *How much is a million?* Ill. S. Kellogg. New York: Scholastic.

Scieszka, J. 1989. *The true story of the three little pigs*. Ill. L. Smith. New York: Scholastic.

———. 1991. *The frog prince continued*. Ill. S. Johnson. New York: Trumpet Club.

Sendak, M. 1963. *Where the wild things are*. New York: Harper.

Sheldon, D. 1990. *The whale's song*. Ill. G. Blythe. New York: Scholastic.

Spier, P. 1977. *Noah's ark*. New York: Trumpet Club.

———. 1982. *Rain*. New York: Trumpet Club.

Steig, W. 1969. *Sylvester and the magic pebble*. New York: Trumpet Club.

Steptoe, J. 1969. *Stevie*. New York: HarperTrophy.

———. 1972. *The story of jumping mouse*. New York: Mulberry.

———. 1987. *Mufaro's beautiful daughters*. New York: Scholastic.

Stolz, M. 1988. *Storm in the night*. Ill. P. Cummings. New York: Harper.

Surat, M. 1983. *Angel child, dragon child*. Ill. V. Mai. New York: Scholastic.

Tsuchiya, Y. 1951. *Faithful elephants*. Ill. T. Lewin. New York: Trumpet Club.

Turner, A. 1987. *Nettie's trip South*. Ill. R. Himler. New York: Scholastic.

Van Allsburg, C. 1981. *Jumanji*. New York: Scholastic.

Viorst, J. 1992. *Alexander and the terrible, horrible, no good, very bad day*. Ill. R. Cruz. New York: Scholastic.

Williams, K. 1990. *Galimoto*. Ill. C. Stock. New York: Trumpet Club.

Williams, V. 1982. *A chair for my mother*. New York: Mulberry.

Winter, T. 1988. *Follow the drinking gourd*. New York: Trumpet Club.

Yashima, T. 1965. *Crow boy*. New York: Scholastic.

Yolen, J. 1981. *Sleeping ugly*. Ill. J. Stanley. New York: Scholastic.

———. 1987. *Owl Moon*. Ill. J. Schoenherr. New York: Scholastic.

Young, E. 1989. *Lon Po Po*. New York: Scholastic.

———. 1992. *Seven blind mice*. New York: Scholastic.

Chapter Books

Avi. 1991. *Nothing but the truth*. New York: Avon.

Babbitt, N. 1975. *Tuck everlasting*. New York: Trumpet Club.

Bauer, M. 1986. *On my honor*. New York: Yearling.

Bishop, C. 1980. *Twenty and ten*. New York: Puffin.

Buck, P. 1947. *The big wave*. New York: Harper.

Buss, F. 1991. *Journey of the sparrows*. New York: Dell.

Byars, B. 1977. *The pinballs*. New York: Scholastic.

Cleary, B. 1983. *Dear Mr. Henshaw*. New York: Yearling.

———. 1988. *A girl from Yamhill*. New York: Dell.

Coerr, E. 1977. *Sadako and the thousand paper cranes*. New York: Yearling.

Collier, J., & C. Collier. 1974. *My brother Sam is dead*. New York: Scholastic.

Dahl, R. 1984. *Boy: Tales of childhood*. New York: Puffin.

de Angeli, M. 1949. *The door in the wall*. New York: Scholastic.

Estes, E. 1971. *The hundred dresses*. New York: Harcourt.

Fleischman, S. 1986. *The whipping boy*. New York: Greenwillow.

Fox, P. 1973. *The slave dancer*. New York: Dell.

———. 1984. *One-eyed cat*. New York: Yearling.

———. 1991. *Monkey island*. New York: Dell.

Freedman, R. 1987. *Lincoln: A photobiography*. New York: Scholastic.

Fritz, J. 1977. *Can't you make them behave, King George?* Ill. T. de Paola. New York: Scholastic.

George, J. 1972. *Julie of the wolves*. New York: Harper.

Hobbs, W. 1989. *Bearstone*. New York: Avon.

King-Smith, D. 1980. *Pigs might fly*. New York: Scholastic.

Konigsburg, E. 1987. *From the mixed-up files of Mrs. Basil E. Frankweiler*. New York: Dell.

L'Engle, M. 1962. *A wrinkle in time*. New York: Dell.

Le Guin, U. 1968. *A wizard of Earthsea*. New York: Bantam.

———. 1988. *Catwings*. Ill. S. Schindler. New York: Scholastic.

Lester, J. 1968. *To be a slave*. New York: Scholastic.

Lewis, C. S. 1950. *The lion, the witch and the wardrobe*. New York: Scholastic.

Little, J. 1972. *From Anna*. New York: Trumpet Club.

———. 1989. *Little by Little: A writer's education*. New York: Puffin.

Lord, B. 1984. *In the year of the boar and Jackie Robinson*. New York: Harper.

Lowry, L. 1989. *Number the stars*. New York: Yearling.

MacLachlan, P. 1985. *Sarah, plain and tall*. New York: Harper.

———. 1991. *Journey*. New York: Dell.

Majorian, M. 1981. *Good night, Mr. Tom*. New York: Harper.

Mathis, S. 1975. *The hundred penny box*. Ill. L. & D. Dillon. New York: Scholastic.

McKinley, R. 1978. *Beauty*. New York: Pocket Books.

————. 1982. *The blue sword*. New York: Ace Books.

Miles, B. 1980. *Maudie and me and the dirty book*. New York: Bullseye.

Naidoo, B. 1986. *Journey to Jo'burg*. New York: Harper.

Naylor, P. 1991. *Shiloh*. New York: Yearling.

O'Brien, R. 1971. *Mrs. Frisby and the rats of NIMH*. New York: Aladdin.

O'Dell, S. 1960. *Island of the blue dolphins*. New York: Dell.

————. 1970. *Sing down the moon*. Boston: Laurel Leaf.

Nhuong, H. 1982. *The land I lost*. New York: Harper & Row.

Paterson, K. 1977. *Bridge to Terabithia*. New York: Trumpet Club.

————. 1978. *The great Gilly Hopkins*. New York: Trumpet Club.

————. 1988. *Park's quest*. New York: Puffin Books.

————. 1991. *Lyddie*. New York: Trumpet Club.

Paulsen, G. 1987. *Hatchet*. New York: Trumpet Club.

————. 1989. *The winter room*. New York: Dell.

————. 1991. *The monument*. New York: Dell.

Pearson, K. 1987. *A handful of time*. New York: Puffin.

Peet, B. 1989. *Bill Peet: An autobiography*. Boston: Houghton Mifflin.

Pitts, P. 1988. *Racing the sun*. New York: Avon.

Roberts, W. 1977. *Don't hurt Laurie*. New York: Aladdin.

Rylant, C. 1964. *But I'll be back again*. New York: Orchard.

————. 1992. *Missing May*. New York: Yearling.

Sachs, M. 1971. *The bear's house*. New York: Avon.

Shreve, S. 1984. *The flunking of Joshua T. Bates*. New York: Scholastic.

Smith, D. B. 1973. *A taste of blackberries*. New York: Harper.

Soto, G. 1990. *Baseball in April and other stories*. San Diego, CA: Harcourt.

Speare, E. 1958. *The witch of Blackbird pond*. New York: Dell.

————. 1983. *The sign of the beaver*. New York: Dell.

Spinelli, J. 1990. *Maniac Magee*. New York: Scholastic.

Tate, E. 1987. *The secret of Gumbo Grove*. New York: Bantam.

Taylor, M. 1981. *Let the circle be unbroken*. New York: Bantam.

————. 1984a. *Roll of thunder hear my cry*. New York: Bantam.

————. 1984b. *Song of the trees*. New York: Bantam.

————. 1987. *The friendship and the gold Cadillac*. New York: Bantam.

————. 1990. *Mississippi bridge*. New York: Bantam.

Taylor, T. 1969. *The cay*. New York: Avon.

Uchida, Y. 1981. *A jar of dreams*. New York: Aladdin.

Voigt, C. 1982. *Dicey's song*. New York: Fawcett.

————. 1983. *A solitary blue*. New York: Scholastic.

Walsh, T. 1982. *The green book*. Sunburst.

Literature Circles

Watisky, M. 1980. *A boat to nowhere*. New York: Signet.

White, E. B. 1952. *Charlotte's web*. Ill. G. Williams. New York: Harper.

Yep, L. 1977. *Child of the owl*. New York: Harper.

———. 1991. *The star fisher*. New York: Puffin.

Yolen, J. 1977. *The hundreth dove and other tales*. Ill. D. Palladini. New York: Schocken Books.

———. 1988. *The devil's arithmetic*. New York: Trumpet Club.

Poetry

Fleischman, P. 1988. *Joyful noises*. Ill. E. Beddows. New York: Trumpet Club.

Giovanni, N. 1985. *Spin a soft black song*. Ill. G. Martins. Sunburst Books.

Greenfield, E. 1978. *Honey, I love*. Il. D. & L. Dillon. New York: Harper & Row.

———. 1988. *Nathaniel talking*. Ill. J. Gilchrist. New York: Black Butterfly Children's Books.

Griego, M., B. Bucks, S. Gilbert, & L. Kimball. 1981. *Tortillas para mama*. Ill. B. Cooney. New York: Holt.

Little, J. 1986. *Hey world, here I am!* Ill. S. Truesdell. New York: Harper & Row.

Merriam, E. 1962. *Jamboree: Rhymes for all times*. Ill. W. Gaffney-Kessell. New York: Yearling.

Sneve, V. 1989. *Dancing teepees*. Ill. S. Gammell. New York: Holiday.

Soto, G. 1992. *Neighborhood odes*. Ill. D. Diaz. New York: Scholastic.

See Text Sets (pages 549–567) for examples of different types of sets of literature:

1. Variations of the same folktale
2. Versions of the same folktale
3. Books by one author or illustrator
4. Books on a certain theme or topic
5. Books in the same genre or text type
6. The same text with different illustrators
7. Books with similar literary elements
8. Books with the same characters
9. Books focused around a particular aspect of culture
10. Books focused around artistic elements

See Paired Books for examples of paired book sets.

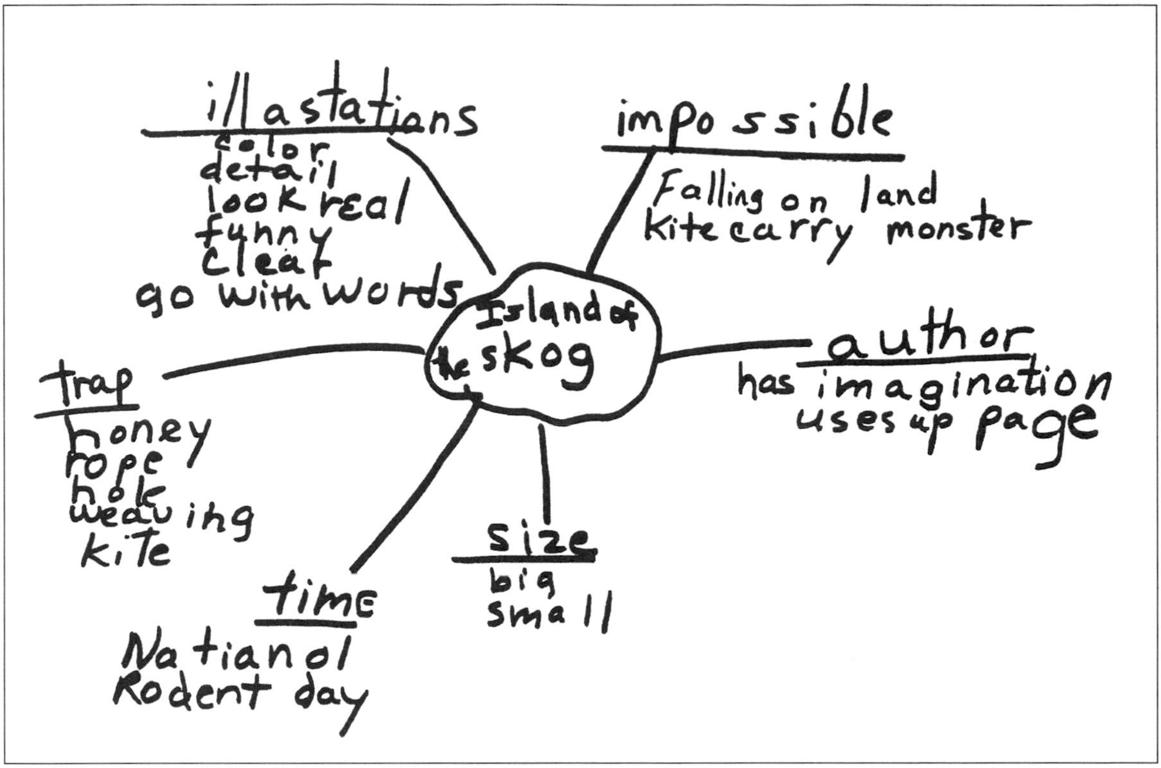
illastations
color
detail
look real
funny
clear
go with words
impossible
Falling on land
Kite carry monster
Island of the skog
author
has imagination
uses up page
trap
honey
rope
hok
weaving
kite
size
big
small
time
Natianol
Rodent day

FIGURE CE12.1
Webbing What's on Your Mind; Third grade Literature Circle (Gloria Kauffman's classroom)

For further information on curricular engagements that support talk and response to literature see: Anomalies, Webbing What's on Your Mind, Graffiti Board, Authors Meeting Authors, Cloning an Author, Learning Logs, Save the Last Word for Me, Say Something, Sketch to Stretch, Written Conversation.

Readers Theatre
Choral Reading
What Music Adds
Acting It Out

Introduction

Readers Theatre focuses on bringing stories and characters alive through oral interpretation. Unlike plays, there is little or no costuming or movement, no stage sets, and no memorized lines. The focus in Readers Theatre is instead on meaning or interpretation. Literature becomes a living experience for both the readers and the audience through the use of facial expressions, voice, and a few gestures. As groups try several different readings of the same story, these readings highlight multiple interpretations of texts. Choral Reading highlights the rhythm and flow of language through the oral interpretation of poetry.

What Music Adds and Acting It Out are additional invitations which focus on extending the meaning of stories through the use of other sign systems. In What Music Adds readers are asked to select a favorite poem and then add music to enrich and extend the meaning. Learners can physically feel the meaning of the piece expand as music is added. In Acting It Out readers are asked to enact a story and through movement step into the story and relive the tale as a lived-through experience.

Each of these engagements focus the reader's attention on meaning. When used in combination with each other, different engagements highlight different dimensions of meaning. Participants come to see text as a meaning potential and the key to reading as interpretation. Students walk away knowing strategies they can use to get a new perspective on a piece that they are reading, as well as having experienced, firsthand, reading as an open process of meaning making.

Materials/Procedures for Readers Theatre

▮ Multiple copies of literature or scripts
▮ A few simple props, such as chairs or stools and hats

1. The literature chosen for Readers Theatre should have a great deal of dialogue, interesting characters, rich and rhythmic language, and a story line with suspense or conflict and an element of humor or surprise. Folktales and short stories are good sources.

2. The literature can be adapted to make a Readers Theatre script. The adaptations can include omitting extraneous parts, shortening long speeches or descriptive sections, and using a narrator to make connections between scenes. Most adaptations can be done with only minimal rewriting. Many times the original story can be used by just crossing off phrases such as "he said."

3. Copies of the literature should be available for each reading part. Each reader should use a highlighter on his or her copy to indicate the parts to be read. Usually there are one or two narrators and then the character speaking parts.

4. Readers may occasionally use a tape of background music during Readers Theatre. The group would need to decide what kind of music best fits their script.

5. Readers decide whether to stand or sit and how they will position themselves in relation to one another.

6. Readers Theatres can be presented formally or informally. Informal presentations are quickly planned and presented to the

Readers Theatre
Choral Reading
What Music Adds
Acting It Out

class or a small group. Often several groups present the same script, critique the presentations, and then make changes to improve the oral interpretation. In formal presentations, the group usually gives a practice session with a small group so they can revise their performance. During a performance, readers sit or stand facing the audience and read their parts from the scripts, using their vocal expressions to bring life to the story. Sometimes readers turn their backs to the audience when they are not reading.

7. After students participate in a Readers Theatre, a class discussion can be held about the success of the program. Readers can describe how they made decisions, the audience can respond to what was and was not effective, and a revised performance may then be held.

8. As a follow-up experience, students may become involved in writing their own scripts for Readers Theatre.

9. A Readers Theatre file can be compiled to list the selection, characters, and story line for future reference. Actual scripts can also be stored for others to use. Readers Theatres can be one of the choices during an uninterrupted reading time.

Materials/Procedures for Choral Reading

▌ Multiple copies of poetry or nursery rhymes

1. Each student should have a copy of a poem or rhyme.

2. To introduce students to different kinds of choral arrangements, take a familiar rhyme such as "Hickory Dickory Dock" and, working as a class and in small groups, try out as many different arrangements as possible. The following can be varied:

a. The arrangement of the poem in terms of who speaks: unison (everyone reading at the same time); refrains (whole group reads together on refrains, other parts are read individually, line-a-child or line-a-group); antiphonal (two groups who go back and forth); cumulative (more and more voices are added on each line or stanza); rounds (two to three groups with each group starting one line behind the others). Arrangements can be solo, partner, small group, or whole group.

b. The voice quality can be changed in terms of the loudness or softness of the voice; the smoothness (reading in a flowing voice) versus staccato, the speed of the voice; where pauses are placed; which words are emphasized; different tones and pitches of voice in dialogues.

c. Chants or body movements can be added in the background while another group reads the poem or rhyme chorally.

3. Each day the teacher or a student brings in a poem. The class works in small groups and each one creates and performs an arrangement for the class.

4. The class discusses the readings and which were most effective.

Materials/Procedures for What Music Adds

- A variety of musical instruments
- A Text Set of poetry

1. Students are asked to work with a partner in reading poetry to find a poem they particularly like. Once they have selected a poem, they develop an effective Choral Reading of the poem.

2. Students experiment with the musical instruments to find musical sounds that they can add to the Choral Reading to enhance the sounds and meanings of various lines of the poem.

3. Students share their final production with classmates by first chorally reading the poem without music and then with music added.

4. The class discusses how the meaning of the poem changed as a function of the music that was added.

Materials/Procedures for Acting It Out

- A selection of wordless picture books (Appendix B)
- Box of costumes and props with a list of cast members for each book. For example, The box for **The Bear and The Fly** (Winter, 1976) could include a flyswatter, dresses, and shirts.

Readers Theatre
Choral Reading
What Music Adds
Acting It Out

1. Students select the wordless book they wish to act out.

2. They look through the book to see how many characters are needed and then invite friends to cast the play.

3. Together the group reads through the book, creating their own story based on the pictures. Usually students first look through the entire book, looking at the pictures together and commenting on what is happening. They go through the book several more times, creating their own story about the illustrations.

4. Students then use the props to act out their story.

5. The play can stay at an informal level or be performed for class members.

Establishing the Learning Context

The teacher may wish to introduce these engagements through storytelling. The story *Something from Nothing* (Gilman, 1992) is an easy way to begin as the changes in this story can be written on tagboard and in this way the structure of the story easily maintained. From these kinds of engagments, students walk away understanding their role as authors in the reading process and are willing to risk sharing their interpretation of a story. All responses should be accepted and authors invited to share what it was they were trying to do regardless of the effectiveness of their oral interpretation. A spirit of inquiry rather than correctness should be maintained.

To further enhance the use of art, music, and drama as forms of meaning making, the teacher might consider setting up art, music, and drama areas in the classrooms. As children read and write they should be invited to explore these areas as aids to story revision and interpretation.

References

What Music Adds was originally developed by Esther Gray.

Gilman, P. 1992. *Something from nothing*. Ontario, Canada: North Winds.

The following are good resources on Readers Theatre:

Coger, L. I., & M. R. White. 1973. *Readers theatre handbook: A dramatic approach to literature*. Rev. ed. Glenview, IL: Scott, Foresman.
Readers Theatre Script Service. P.O. Box 178333, San Diego, CA 92117.

Sloyer, S. 1982. *Readers theatre: Story dramatization in the classroom*. Urbana, IL: National Council of Teachers of English.

Appendix A: Poetry for Choral Reading

Adoff, A. 1979. *Eats*. Ill. S. Russo. New York: Lothrop, Lee & Sons.

Booth, D., ed. 1990. *Voices on the wind: Poems for all seasons*. Ill. M. Lemieux. New York: Morrow.

Brenner, B., ed. 1994. *The Earth is painted green: A garden of poems about our planet*. New York: Scholastic.

Bryan, A. 1992. *Sing to the sun*. New York: HarperCollins.

Ciardi, J. 1962. *You read to me, I'll read to you*. Ill. E. Gorey. New York: Harper & Row.

de Regniers, B., E. Moore, M. White, & J. Carr, eds. 1988. *Sing a song of popcorn*. New York: Scholastic.

Dunning, S., E. Lueders, & H. Smith, eds. 1966. *Reflections on a gift of watermelon pickle . . . : And other modern verse*. New York: Scholastic.

Fleischman, P. 1985. *I am Phoenix: Poems for two voices*. Ill. K. Nutt. New York: HarperTrophy.

———. 1988. *Joyful noise: Poems for two voices*. Ill. E. Beddows. New York: Harper & Row.

Giovanni, N. 1971. *Spin a soft black song*. Ill. G. Martins. New York: Hill & Wang.

Greenfield, E. 1972. *Honey, I love*. Ill. D. & L. Dillon. New York: Crowell.

———. 1988. *Nathaniel talking*. Ill. J. Gilchrist. New York: Black Butterfly Children's Books.

Hoberman, M. 1981. *Yellow butter, purple jelly, red jam, black bread*. New York: Viking.

Hopkins, L. B., ed. 1988. *Side by side: Poems to read together*. Ill. H. Knight. New York: Simon & Schuster.

Kennedy, X. J., ed. 1992. *Talking like the rain: A first book of poems*. Boston: Little, Brown.

Kuskin, K. 1980. *Dogs & dragons, trees & dreams*. New York: Harper & Row.

Larrick, N., ed. 1968. *Piping down the valleys wild*. Ill. E. Raskin. New York: Dell.

———. 1991. *To the moon and back*. Ill. C. O'Neill. New York: Delacorte.

Lee, D. 1963. *Alligator pie*. Ill. F. Newfeld. Toronto, Canada: Macmillan of Canada.

Merriam, E. 1962. *Jamboree: Poems for all times*. Ill. W. Gaffney-Kessell. New York: Dell.

Readers Theatre
Choral Reading
What Music Adds
Acting It Out

————. 1964. *A sky full of poems.* Ill. W. Gaffney-Kessell. New York: Dell.

Nye, N., ed. 1992. *This same sky.* New York: Four Winds.

Pomerantz, C. 1982. *If I had a paka: Poems in eleven languages.* New York: Greenwillow.

Prelutsky, J. 1984. *The new kid on the block.* Ill. J. Stevenson. New York: Greenwillow.

————. 1990. *Something big has been here.* Ill. J. Stevenson. New York: Greenwillow.

————. 1991. *For laughing out loud: Poems to tickle your funnybone.* Ill. M. Priceman. New York: Knopf.

————, ed. 1983. *The Random House book of poetry for children.* Ill. A. Lobel. New York: Random House.

Rosen, M. 1983. *Quick, let's get out of here.* Ill. Q. Blake. New York: Puffin.

Schwartz, A., ed. 1992. *And the green grass grew all around.* Ill. S. Truesdell. New York: HarperCollins.

Westcott, N., ed. 1994. *Never take a pig to lunch: And other poems about the fun of eating.* New York: Orchard.

Worth, V. 1972. *Small poems.* New York: Farrar, Straus & Giroux.

Appendix B: Wordless Books for Acting It Out

Alexander, M. 1970. *Bobo's dream.* New York: Dial.

Mayer, M. 1974. *Frog goes to dinner.* New York: Dial.

Prater, J. 1985. *The gift.* New York: Penguin.

Spier, P. 1982. *Peter Spier's rain.* New York: Doubleday.

————. 1986. *Dreams.* New York: The Trumpet Club.

Tafuri, N. 1987. *Do not disturb.* New York: Greenwillow.

Turkle, B. 1976. *Deep in the forest.* New York: Dutton.

Appendix C: Other Wordless Books

Anno, M. 1977. *Anno's journey.* New York: Philomel.

Bang, M. 1980. *The grey lady and the strawberry snatcher.* New York: Four Winds.

Briggs, R. 1978. *The snowman.* New York: Random.

Brouillard, A. 1992. *Three cats.* Charlottesville, VA: Thomasson-Grant.

Carle, E. 1987. *Do you want to be my friend.* New York: Crowell.

Day, A. 1985. *Good dog, Carl.* New York: Green Tiger Press.

de Paola, T. 1978. *Pancakes for breakfast.* New York: Harcourt.

———. 1981. *The hunter and the animals*. New York: Holiday.

Dupasquier, P. 1987. *Our house on the hill*. New York: Puffin.

Goodall, J. 1990. *The story of the seashore*. New York: Macmillan.

Hoban, T. 1988. *Look! look! look!* New York: Greenwillow.

Hutchins, P. 1971. *Changes, changes*. New York: Macmillan.

Martin, R. 1989. *Will's mammoth*. Ill. S. Gammell. New York: Putnam.

Mayer, M. 1971. *A boy, a dog, a frog and a friend*. New York: Dial.

———. 1973. *Frog on his own*. New York: Dial.

Ormerod, J. 1981. *Sunshine*. New York: Lothrop.

Sara. 1990. *Across town*. New York: Orchard.

Spier, P. 1977. *Noah's ark*. The Trumpet Club.

Tafuri, N. 1988. *Junglewalk*. New York: Greenwillow.

Vagin, V. & F. Asch. 1989. *Here comes the cat!* New York: Scholastic.

Ward, L. 1973. *The silver pony*. Boston: Houghton Mifflin.

Wiesner, D. 1988. *Free fall*. New York: Lothrop.

———. 1991. *Tuesday*. New York: Houghton Mifflin.

Winter, P. 1976. *The bear & the fly*. New York: Scholastic.

Young, E. 1983. *Up a tree*. New York: HarperCollins.

———. 1984. *The other bone*. New York: HarperCollins.

Save the Last Word for Me
Save the Last Word for the Artist

Introduction

Reading is an active process in which the reader constructs meaning from a text. Because readers bring differing experiences and knowledge to a reading experience, each reader will construct a different interpretation of a text. Readers need to be encouraged to take an active stance in their reading, asking questions and looking for points of agreement or disagreement with the author as they read. This active stance in reading is facilitated when readers interact with other readers and discuss their differing questions and interpretations of a book.

Less proficient readers often believe that proficient readers understand everything they read and that there is one "right" interpretation of every text. Save the Last Word for Me demonstrates to them that all readers work at constructing their own interpretations of what they read through relating their life experiences to the text as well as through discussing the text with other readers. When students are encouraged to share their interpretations through art, they must transmediate their understandings into a new sign system and so they come to deeper and more complex understandings of the text.

FIGURE CE14.1
Save the Last Word for Me Card
for **Bridge to Terabithia**
(Paterson, 1977); Angie, Age
12 (Sue Robinson's classroom)

Side 1

pg. 27

"He hadn't even won his heat. There was no cheering at either end of the field. The rest of the boys seemed as stunned as he."

Side 2

Jesse

Jesse was scared cause he was beaten in a race by a girl. He was not afraid of the girl. It was the boys he was afraid of. Of what they were going to say.

Materials/Procedures for Save the Last Word for Me

- Multiple copies of a text
- 3" × 5" cards or slips of scrap paper

1. Each student individually reads the text.

2. As the students read, they write on the first side of the cards or slips of paper any segments of the text words, phrases, or sentences that particularly catch their attention. These segments or quotes can be items that they find interesting and want to discuss later or

Save the Last Word for Me, Save the Last Word for the Artist

FIGURE CE14.2

Save the Last Word for Me Card
for **What's Whole in Whole
Language** (Goodman, 1986);
Adult (Carolyn Burke's Summer
Workshop)

Side 1

"From the earliest preschool learning and throughout life, it is important for people to have the opportunities to present what they know, to share it through language, and in the course of this presentation, to complete the learning." p. 16

Side 2

All our ideas and thoughts are the result of talking with others and they have no "body" till that discussion takes place beyond the internal dialogue of other voices + your own. In sharing, we gain our voice and our sense of knowing.

that they particularly agree or disagree with. Students should also record the page number of that segment.

3. On the other side of the cards or slips of paper, the students write out what they want to say about each quote they have selected. This can include questions and points of agreement or disagreement they have with the text segment.

4. Once students have completed the reading and writing of the cards, they gather in small groups or in a single group to share their cards.

5. Before the group discussion, students go through their cards and put them in order from most important to least important in terms of their desire to discuss them. During sharing, if someone else uses the same top quote, the person who has not yet shared will choose his or her next quote.

6. Each student reads the quote on a card to the group. The other members of the group have a chance to react to what was read. The student who read the quote then has the last word about why that segment of text was chosen and bases the remarks both on what he or she wrote on the back of the card and on the preceding discussion.

Materials/Procedures for Save the Last Word for the Artist

▮ A short story
▮ An "odds and ends" box of art materials (pipe cleaners, toilet paper rolls, clay, string, rubber bands, paper plates, balloons, ribbon), and other art supplies (construction paper, glue, scissors, and so on).

1. The teacher either reads aloud the short story to the class or multiple copies of the story are distributed so that each student can read the story on their own.

2. In groups of five or six, students discuss what they think the story means.

3. Each group is asked to use the art materials to collaboratively create a sketch that symbolizes what their group thinks the story means.

Instead of the box of materials, students can be given a large sheet of paper and markers and asked to create a Sketch to Stretch of the meaning of the story.

4. Each group displays their art piece for the class, but does not talk about it. The group remains silent while members of the other groups say what it is they think the group was trying to say in their art piece.

5. After everyone has said what they think the piece of art represents, the creators of the piece get to talk about what they saw each symbol as representing and the overall meaning of their piece.

6. The engagement proceeds with each group presenting their piece of art, everyone else predicting what was meant, and the artists, themselves, getting the last word.

7. Once all groups have shared, the teacher may wish to have students take five minutes to reflect on the experience in terms of what they learned about the reading process and the role of the reader in that process.

8. Students may also individually create their own pieces of art and then share these in small groups.

Establishing the Learning Context

The teacher will want to introduce this engagement using texts that are provocative and have the potential for strong response from students. Save the Last Word for Me works best with texts that are particularly powerful in their use of language. Save the Last Word for the Artist works well with texts that are ambiguous and tend to leave readers confused so they feel a need to think and talk about the text with other readers.

The teacher should participate in making and sharing cards or art pieces along with the students. Initially, the teacher may need to play a major role in demonstrating what can be written on the cards and how to go about discussing the cards or art pieces in the groups.

Variations

1. Students work in groups of three to six. Each student silently reads the text material and then chooses one quotation from the text. The students exchange their quotations with each other, and each person responds to the quotation he or she now has. The student who chose the original quotation is not given the last word but does get to see how someone else responds to the quotation he or she chose.

2. Instead of having an oral discussion, students can pass their cards around with a sheet of paper in a variation of Writing in the Round (see Say Something). Each person chooses one card to pass around the small group. Students read the card and write their comments about the quotation on the piece of paper. The next person responds both to the card and to the comments.

3. In collage reading, students highlight powerful words, phrases, and sentences in a book or poem as they read. When the class gathers together, an invitation is given for the group to create their own interpretation of the book or poem by reading quotes out loud. One person begins and then others join in reading their highlighted words, phrases, and sentences so that they play off of what the previous person read. Certain quotes may be read repeatedly to create a refrain.

4. In text rendering, students highlight quotes that they consider significant or powerful as they read. These quotes are then read aloud during a whole class meeting. The person who reads the quote also makes a comment about their interpretation of the quote and then another person reads a quote. Text rendering works well with informational and professional reading.

5. As a further variation of Save the Last Word for the Artist, different groups of students can be assigned different sign systems. For example, one group can be asked to symbolically represent their meaning through art, another through music, a third through pantomine, a fourth through drama, a fifth through mathematics, and so on. As a culminating experience students can explore how the system in which they worked contributed to as well as highlighted various dimensions of the story's meaning.

References

Save the Last Word for Me was originally developed by Carolyn Burke. Save the Last Word for the Artist is an extension of Sketch to Stretch and owes its origins to Carolyn Burke, Jerome Harste, Marjorie Siegel, and Karen Feathers.

Goodman, K. 1986. *What's whole in whole language?* New York: Scholastic.
Paterson, K. 1977. *Bridge to Terabithia.* New York: Dell.

Save the Last Word for Me, Save the Last Word for the Artist

Say Something

Introduction

Language did not develop because of the presence of one person but because two people wished to communicate. Language and language learning are inherently social events. Say Something highlights the social nature of language and demonstrates that understanding develops and evolves from our interactions with others. Participants are able to see that partnership enhances meaning, and that as constraints normally operating in reading are altered, so are involvement and the kind of thinking that becomes possible.

Say Something is designed to help readers develop a more functional view of reading. Participants learn to respond in terms of what the passage meant to them and how it does or does not relate to their own experiences, rather than in terms of what they think the teacher wants. This engagement is particularly supportive for students who are having difficulty knowing what to talk about in a Literature Circle.

Say Something also supports readers who view the reading process as an inactive process where they either race or plow slowly through the reading and then decide what the text meant. These readers view comprehension as an act that is completed once the text is finished. As readers engage in Say Something, they are involved in the same active process of chunking a text, asking questions, finding connections, and making predictions that characterize the processes of proficient readers. Readers thus become aware of alternative reading strategies they can use as they read independently without the support of another reader.

Materials/Procedures

▌ Multiple copies of a reading selection

1. Students are asked to choose a partner, and each pair is given a single copy of a reading selection.

2. Before reading, each pair of participants is asked to decide whether they will read the selection aloud or silently. If reading orally, the two share one text and take turns reading aloud the sections of text.

3. Students are informed that as they read the selection, they will discuss what they have read with their partner. After they read the first several paragraphs, they are to stop to "say something" to each other about what they have read. After each exchange of this sort, the partnership reads the next several paragraphs and again each "says something" to the other before going on to the next paragraph, and so on through the text. Students can comment on what was just read, make predictions about what will happen next, share connections and experiences related to the selection, or ask a question about something that is confusing them.

Establishing the Learning Context

Teachers demonstrate that successful language users engage in Say Something by choosing a partner and participating in this activity with students. Throughout the group discussion, the teacher works at establishing a context in which students feel that their interpretations are accepted and that there is no one "right" answer. Any interpretation is accepted as long as the student can support it. "Why" should be a frequent response.

After the first several times that Say Something is used with a group, the teacher should engage the students in a group discussion aimed at helping them become aware of how they can use this strategy in their own reading. The students can discuss what reading strategies were used to make sense of this reading, and how and under what conditions students might find Say Something a helpful strategy

Say Something

for them to use as readers in the future. They can also talk about how successful readers use procedures similar to Say Something when encountering difficulty in reading texts and that if they experience difficulty reading any of the materials for the class, Say Something is an alternative reading strategy they can use to solve their problem.

Variations

1. A group Say Something can be used with a small group of students. Each student has a copy of the text. They look through the entire text as a group and decide where they will stop reading to "say something" to one another. These stopping points are marked with a pencil. Each person then begins reading silently. When a reader comes to a stopping point, the reader stops and waits until the others in the group are also ready. Group members then each say something about the section they just read before going on to read the next section silently.

2. Say Something can be used with a read-aloud book. The teacher reads aloud, stopping at particular points. Students are encouraged to "say something" and after several comments, the teacher begins reading again. Instead of responding as a whole group, the students can instead turn and say something to a partner every time the teacher stops reading aloud. This variation works well with young children and to introduce the engagement to the class.

3. Written Conversations can be substituted for oral conversations during Say Something. Writing, however, is more constrained. We have found that it is not wise to introduce this alternative until after students feel free to respond to text at a more personal "what it meant to me" level.

4. Instead of making a group web, each pair of students can write a brief summary/response after reading and discussing the selection. These summaries can then be shared with other pairs who have read the same selection and written their own summaries. Students could also do sketches that are then shared with other pairs.

5. A variation of Say Something used to give responses to writing is Writing in the Round. Writers attach a blank sheet of paper to a

draft, asking for responses to their writing. The draft is circulated to three or four different readers. Each reader reads the draft and previous readers' comments and then makes suggestions for revisions of meaning. This same activity can be used to get responses to artwork projects and oral reports.

6. A similar procedure, Reading in the Round, involves a student writing a response to a reading selection. This response is circulated among other students who write their own comments about the reading selection and about the reactions already written on the sheet by other readers. Instead of beginning with a response, the sheet could have on it several key statements selected from the reading material. As the sheet is passed around, readers respond to one another and to the key statements.

7. Students should be encouraged to use Say Something whenever they say they are having difficulty understanding what they are reading. This procedure should be continued until students naturally engage in this strategy on their own. Say Something can be used with informational books as well as fiction. If students are reading science or social studies textbooks, it helps them process the different sections instead of being overwhelmed by the number of concepts covered in most textbook chapters. Students also often choose to use Say Something when beginning a chapter book for a Literature Circle. Reading the first chapter or two with Say Something gets them into the book and they then finish the reading on their own.

References

Say Something was developed by Jerome Harste, Carolyn Burke, and Dorothy Watson. Writing in the Round was developed by Jeff Ducer and Paul Crowley.

Shared Reading
Shared Reading of Predictable Books
Partner Reading
Popcorn Reading
Group Composed Books
Twice Told Tales

Introduction

Reading is a social activity that involves the construction of meaning. Readers are supported in the reading process when they can share in the reading of meaningful, predictable texts with other readers. This strategy is based on the belief that we learn to read by reading and that reading can be learned in much the same way as speech is learned. Reading and rereading familiar and predictable stories with others provide successful and enjoyable reading experiences. As students reread stories over and over, they are able to attend to different demonstrations in the stories each time, and they develop a feeling of competence in themselves as readers because they are able to read the stories all the way through fluently. Because the language and structure of these stories become familiar to them, they are able to draw from these stories in understanding new stories that they read and in their writing of stories.

Shared Reading is a useful strategy for all readers, but it is particularly useful for less fluent readers. Less proficient readers need to read in an atmosphere that supports their initial reading experiences and encourages them to take risks and to make predictions based on meaning and structure as they read, rather than focusing their attention on isolated aspects of the reading process. The different variations of Shared Reading are characterized by multiple rereadings in which readers support each other through reading orally together, often sharing the reading of highly predictable books, poems, songs, and rhymes.

Writers are also supported in the writing process when they share in writing texts with other writers. Through a shared writing process, writers are able to offer demonstrations to each other about strategies they use while composing. Less proficient writers are supported by the group process, use of predictable language, and story patterns. They also feel less overwhelmed by the amount of writing they need to contribute to the book.

Twice Told Tales asks readers to take what they have read and recast it in terms of the structure of a more familiar and predictable story they know. This engagement supports readers in making connections between texts they have read as well as in rereading texts in terms of the past texts they have encountered.

Materials/Procedures for Shared Reading

▌ Predictable books, both regular size and big books

Procedure A: Shared Reading of Predictable Books

1. The teacher introduces the story by reading the title and having the students predict what the story might be about based on the title and the cover illustration.

2. The teacher then reads the story to the students. Students must be able to see the print as the teacher reads the story. This can be accomplished through having a "big book" with enlarged print so that an entire group can see the print, or through each student having a copy of the story to follow along as the teacher reads. If

Shared Reading
Group Composed
Books
Twice Told Tales

the teacher is reading from a big book, the teacher should point to the words while reading.

3. Students should be encouraged to begin to join in on repeating phrases or sentences as soon as they recognize the predictable parts of the story. With some stories, the teacher may want to pause to let the pupils predict what comes next or to take time to examine how the text and illustrations support each other.

4. After the first reading, students can share their feelings about the story, confirm their predictions, and elaborate on certain parts of the story that they especially liked.

5. If possible, a second reading should immediately follow the discussion. If not, this story should be the first one read during the next Shared Reading period. In the second reading, the students should be encouraged to take more responsibility for reading the repetitive parts or the words that are highly predictable from the meaning and structure of the story.

6. If the students remain interested in the story, it can be read a third time, with the students taking on still more of the reading in chorus. The number of times a story is reread depends on the response of the group—on whether they are enjoying the story and asking for it during Shared Reading, and on how well they are able to join in reading.

7. The story should then be placed in the library corner for students to read independently or with another child, and in the listening corner for those who still need support in reading the story. The students should be given many opportunities to reread the story so that they are able to read it fluently.

8. Each Shared Reading should involve the children's selection of old favorites that they again want to read together as a group and the introduction of new stories, songs, and poems that are predictable.

9. Once a story has been read and enjoyed a number of times, teachers and students may want to look at it together to talk about different aspects of words, letter-sound relationships, sentence and story structures, or reading strategies.

10. Predictable books usually provide story structures that easily lead to a variety of additional activities. These activities should

focus attention on the meaning of the story. Some stories may be dramatized as the students read the parts of the characters. Some follow a pattern that can be used to write a new story. Some stories can be cut apart into several meaningful chunks and then students can put the story back together in sequence (see Schema Stories). Other stories can be responded to and interpreted through art or music.

11. This same engagement can be used with small groups of students and is usually called guided reading in this context.

Procedure B: Partner Reading

1. During uninterrupted reading, students are allowed to choose whether they will read alone or with one or two other children.

2. The sharing of the reading can take different forms: One person can read to the other person, each can read every other page, one person can read the first half of the book and the other can finish the book, each can read a book to the other person, the two can read in unison, the book can be read chorally with each taking different parts, and other variations.

3. Partner reading can occur between students of different grade levels as well as at the same grade level. Students can share books they have read or authored with each other.

When older students read with younger students, they can enter into discussions about reading strategies and how to support beginning readers. If older students read with the same younger partner over a period of time, the students can be invited to use their knowledge about their partner to write a book for him or her.

Procedure C: Popcorn Reading

1. Each reader should have a copy of the text to be read.

2. One person starts reading aloud, then stops reading at any point.

3. As soon as one reader stops, another person quickly jumps in and takes over. Whoever jumps in first continues reading as long as desired, then suddenly stops, and another reader quickly pops in. Whoever jumps in first gets to continue reading. No one is

forced to read, and there is no order determining how the readers take over. If one person is dominating or reads too far, he or she may be asked to let others have a turn.

4. If there is only one copy of the text, the reader simply passes the text on to another person at whatever point he or she chooses to stop reading.

Materials/Procedures for Group Composed Books

▌ *Paper and writing supplies*

1. The content of a Group Composed Book should grow out of class studies or engagements that are part of classroom life. The books may be initiated by the teacher or a student.

a. Students can use the language pattern or plot structure of a favorite predictable book or a favorite author's book to create their own text. For example, they may use the pattern from *The Very Hungry Caterpillar* (Carle, 1969) to write "The Very Hungry Tadpole" that changes from tadpole to frog through eating each day or "The Very Healthy Person" who changes from unhealthy to healthy person through exercises each day.

b. Students can create an information book in which each page contains information about a topic the class has been studying ("What We Know About ———").

c. Students can put together birthday books or thank-you books that contain letters and messages for a child having a birthday or for a guest speaker.

d. The class can create collections that include favorite nursery rhymes, songs, jump rope rhymes, environmental print, commercials, and so on.

2. Either the teacher or a student issues an invitation for class members to join a group to write a book together on a particular topic.

3. The students who join the group discuss their ideas for what they want to write. Time is spent raising and exploring ideas and thinking about how to express those ideas.

First-Grade Group Book based on *Rosie's Walk* (Hutchins, 1968), First Three Pages (Gloria Kauffman's classroom)

Section Two

Curricular

Engagements

4. The students in the group each write a page for the group book, and these are then gathered together to make the book. The process of writing can occur in two ways:

a. After a group discussion about the topic of the book, each student individually writes and illustrates a page. These are then compiled and stapled into the book.

b. After the group discusses what they might write about, one person—either the teacher or a student—acts as a scribe to write down the story on the chalkboard as the group develops it together. Individual students may still compose a certain page, but they do so knowing what the other pages say and with the support of the rest of the group. After the story is finished, each student is responsible for copying one page of the book from the chalkboard.

5. See Bookmaking for suggestions on binding these large books together.

6. The finished book is read to the class with each student reading his or her contribution to the book which is then placed into the classroom library.

Materials/Procedures for Twice Told Tales

▮ A selection of familiar predictable books with strong repetitive patterns
▮ A new piece of literature

1. Read the new piece of literature aloud to the group or provide copies so they can read it by themselves. Have a literature discussion about their initial responses and connections to the book.

2. Invite interested students to retell the new story using the structure of a familiar predictable book. Students first must make the decision of which predictable book pattern they want to use and then work together to write a new version using that pattern.
   For example, if Cinderella is the new story and *Brown Bear, Brown Bear* is the familiar predictable book that students select, then participants might begin with "Cinderella, Cinderella, Who do you see? I see three ugly sisters looking at me," and continue building and retelling the story from this point.

Shared Reading
Group Composed
Books
Twice Told Tales

Fortunately, James had too marvelous parents.

Unfortunately his parents were gobbled up by a loose rhinoserous.

3. The group shares their retelling with the class and they discuss the changes in the story's meaning.

Establishing the Learning Context

Many different kinds of predictable books are needed for these engagements. Books are predictable for a particular group of students because they build on familiar reader experiences and because of the text organization. The text organization is predictable because of the language, story line, and structure rather than because of controlled vocabulary or phonetic regularity. Features such as rhyme, rhythm, familiar sequences, repetitive patterns or refrains, familiar concepts or story lines, and a good match between the text and illustrations can help make a text predictable. Although repetitive patterns characterize predictable books for younger children, books for older children are predictable when they are about familiar topics or issues from a student's daily life, or from a series or genre in which the student has done a lot of reading. Any book that a student has read or listened to several times becomes a predictable book for that student.

Teachers should provide opportunities for students to read texts in unison or to do choral reading. Reading and rereading chorally or in unison provide support for readers who are at different levels of proficiency in reading. During unison reading, some children will be reading the print, while others cannot read the print but can join in on the repeating parts, and still others sit and listen. No one is embarrassed or made to feel inadequate, but everyone simply joins in as able.

In writing a Group Composed Book, a great deal of coordination and cooperation must occur among writers. The teacher needs to attend to the group dynamics and help students develop decision-making strategies as they struggle to reach consensus as a group, especially when the group works together to compose the book. In general, avoid taking a vote and having the majority rule and instead work to have the group reach a consensus that takes into consideration the differing perspectives of group members. Majority rule often leads to disgruntled children and simplistic solutions to problems, while consensus involves dialogue negotiation.

As the group works to write a Group Composed Book, students should be encouraged to observe and discuss one another's composing strategies or to notice certain aspects of the written message. The group composing process can provide important demonstrations to writers. Be careful, however, of overdoing the talk about composing and thereby losing the focus on the story being developed.

Variations

1. A traveling story can be created. One person begins to write a story and then passes the paper on to the next person, who adds to the story and then passes it on to another writer. This continues until the last person receives the story and writes an ending.

2. Teachers can take pictures of classroom events, either daily activities or special events. These pictures are then placed in Photo Group Composed Books and individual students either write or dictate a description or story about what they were doing in each picture.

3. A group can be invited to write multiple story line books following the pattern of various "Choose Your Own Adventure" books.

References

Twice Told Tales was developed by Karen Feathers. The person most closely associated with big books and Shared Reading is Don Holdaway. Others have also written about predictable books and shared reading and have provided bibliographies of predictable books:

Shared Reading
Group Composed Books
Twice Told Tales

Atwell, M. 1985. "Predictable books for adolescent readers." *Journal of Reading* 29(1):18–22.

Dahl, R. 1961. *James and the giant peach*. New York: Knopf.

Hart-Hewins, L., & J. Wells. 1990. *Real books for reading: Learning to read with children's literature*. Portsmouth, NH: Heinemann.

Heald-Taylor, G. 1987a. "How to use predictable books for K–2 language arts instruction." *The Reading Teacher* 40(7):656–661.

———. 1987b. "Predictable literature selections and activities for language arts instruction." *The Reading Teacher* 41(1):6–12.

Holdaway, D. 1979. *The foundations of literacy*. Portsmouth, NH: Heinemann.

———. 1982. "The big book trend—A discussion with Don Holdaway." *Language Arts* (8):815–821.

Rhodes, L. 1981. "I can read! Predictable books as resources for reading and writing instruction." *The Reading Teacher* 34(5):511–518.

Slaughter, J. 1993. *Beyond storybooks: Young children and the shared book experience*. Newark, DE: International Reading Association.

Appendix A: A Beginning List of Predictable Books

Aardema, V. 1975. *Why mosquitoes buzz in people's ears*. Ill. L. & D. Dillon. New York: Dial.

———. 1981. *Bringing the rain to Kapiti Plain*. Ill. B. Vidal. New York: Dial.

Allen, P. 1982. *Who sank the boat?* New York: Dell.

Aylesworth, J. 1992. *Old black fly*. Ill. S. Gammel. New York: Holt.

Baer, G. 1989. *Thump, thump, rat-a-tat-tat*. Ill. L. Ehlert. New York: HarperCollins.

Barchas, S. 1975. *I was walking down the road*. Ill. J. Kent. New York: Scholastic.

Barrett, J. 1970. *Animals should definitely not wear clothing*. New York: Atheneum.

Becker, J. 1973. *Seven little rabbits*. Ill. B. Cooney. New York: Scholastic.

Brown, M. W. 1947. *Goodnight moon*. Ill. C. Hurd. New York: Harper & Row.

———. 1949. *The important book*. Ill. L. Weisgard. New York: HarperCollins.

Brown, R. 1981. *A dark dark tale*. New York: Dutton.

Browne, A. 1989. *Things I like*. New York: Knopf.

Burningham, J. 1970. *Mr. Gumpy's outing*. New York: Holt.

Campbell, R. 1982. *Dear zoo*. New York: Viking.

Cameron, A. 1993. *The cat sat on the mat*. Ill. C. Jones. Boston: Houghton Mifflin.

Carle, E. 1969. *The very hungry caterpillar*. New York: Philomel.

———. 1984. *The very busy spider*. New York: Philomel.

Charlip, R. 1964. *Fortunately*. New York: Four Winds.

Cole, K. 1981. *Golly Gump swallowed a fly*. Ill. B. Weissman. New York: Parents Magazine.

Cuyler, M. 1991. *That's Good! That's Bad!* Ill. D. Catrow. New York: Holt.

de Regniers, B. 1964. *May I bring a friend?* New York: Aladdin.

Fox, M. 1986. *Hattie and the fox*. Ill. P. Mullins. New York: Bradbury.

———. 1988. *Koala Lou*. Ill. P. Lofts. New York: Gulliver.

Galdone, P. 1972. *The three bears*. New York: Clarion.

———. 1973a. *The little red hen*. New York: Clarion.

———. 1973b. *The three billy goats gruff*. New York: Clarion.

Ginsburg, M. 1972. *The chick and the duckling*. Ill. J. & A. Aruego. New York: Macmillan.

Goss, J., & J. Harste. [1981]1985. *It didn't frighten me!* Worthington, OH: Willowisp.

Grossman, B. 1988. *Donna O'Neeshuck was chased by some cows*. Ill. S. Truesdall. New York: Harper.

Guarino, D. 1989. *Is your mama a llama?* Ill. S. Kellogg. New York: Scholastic.

Helen, N. 1988. *The bus stop*. New York: Orchard.

Hutchins, P. 1968. *Rosie's walk*. New York: Macmillan.

———. 1971. *Titch*. New York: Greenwillow.

———. 1976. *Don't forget the bacon*. New York: Greenwillow.

———. 1986. *The doorbell rang*. New York: Greenwillow.

Joosse, B. 1991. *Mama, do you love me?* Ill. B. Lavallee. New York: Chronicle.

Kalan, R. 1981. *Jump, frog, jump*. Ill. B. Barton. New York: Greenwillow.

Kaler, R. 1993. *Blueberry Bear*. Bloomington, IN: Inquiring Voice Press.

Kovalski, M. 1987. *The wheels on the bus*. Toronto, Canada: Kids Can Press.

Kraus, R. 1945. *The carrot seed*. Ill. C. Johnson. New York: Harper & Row.

———. 1970. *Whose mouse are you?* Ill. J. Aruego. New York: Macmillan.

Lindbergh, R. 1987. *The midnight farm*. Ill. S. Jeffers. New York: Dial.

Lobel, A. 1984. *The rose in my garden*. Ill. A. Lobel. New York: Scholastic.

Martin, B., Jr. 1967. *Brown bear, brown bear, what do you see?* Ill. E. Carle. New York: Holt.

Shared Reading
Group Composed
Books
Twice Told Tales

————. 1991. *Polar bear, polar bear, what do you hear?* Ill. E. Carle. New York: Holt.

Mayer, M. 1973. *What do you do with a kangaroo?* New York: Scholastic.

Numeroff, L. 1985. *If you give a mouse a cookie.* Ill. F. Bond. New York: HarperCollins.

————. 1991. *If you gave a moose a muffin.* Ill. F. Bond. New York: Harper-Collins.

Oppenheim, J. 1986. *You can't catch me.* Ill. A. Shachat. Boston: Houghton Mifflin.

Peek, M. 1941. *Mary wore her red dress and Henry wore his green sneakers.* New York: Clarion.

Preston, E. 1978. *Where did my mother go?* Ill. C. Conover. New York: Scholastic.

Robart, R. 1986. *The cake that Mack ate.* Ill. M. Kovalski. Toronto, Canada: Kids Can Press.

Rosen, M. 1989. *We're going on a bear hunt.* Ill. H. Oxenbury. New York: Macmillan.

————. 1990. *Little Rabbit Foo Foo.* Ill. A. Robins. New York: Simon & Schuster.

Saunders, D. & J. 1990. *Dibble and Dabble.* New York: Bradbury.

Shaw, N. 1991. *Sheep in a shop.* Ill. M. Apple. Boston: Houghton Mifflin.

Slobodkina, E. 1940. *Caps for sale.* New York: Scholastic.

Stevens, J. 1985. *The house that Jack built.* New York: Holiday.

Stow, J. 1992. *The house that Jack built.* New York: Dial.

Tolstoy, A. 1968. *The great big enormous turnip.* Ill. H. Oxenbury. London: Piccolo Picture Books.

Van Laan, N. 1990a. *A mouse in my house.* Ill. M. Priceman. New York: Knopf.

————. 1990b. *Possum come a-knockin'.* Ill. G. Booth. New York: Knopf.

————. 1992. *This is the hat.* Ill. H. Meade. Boston: Little, Brown.

Ward, C. 1988. *Cookie's week.* Ill. T. de Paola. New York: Scholastic.

Weissman, A. 1987. *The castle of Churumbel: El castillo de Churumbel.* Ill. S. Bailyn. Tucson, AZ: Hispanic Books Distributors, Inc.

Westcott, N. 1980. *I know an old lady who swallowed a fly.* Boston: Little, Brown.

————. 1987. *Peanut butter and jelly: A play rhyme.* Boston: Little, Brown.

————. 1988. *The lady with the alligator purse.* Boston: Little, Brown.

————. 1989. *Skip to my Lou.* Boston: Little, Brown.

————. 1990. *There's a hole in the bucket.* New York: HarperCollins.

Williams, L. 1986. *The little old lady who was not afraid of anything*. Ill. M. Lloyd. New York: HarperCollins.

Wood, A. 1984. *The napping house*. Ill. D. Wood. New York: Harcourt.

Appendix B: Predictable Sets of Books

Bill Martin Instant Readers and *Sounds of Language* Reading Series. New York: Holt, Rinehart, & Winston.

Reading Systems and *Reading Unlimited*. Glenview, IL: Scott, Foresman.

Ready to Read Books. Katonah, NY: Richard Owen.

Rigby Readers. Mount Prospect, IL: Jostens Learning Systems.

Wright Group Story Box. San Diego, CA: Wright Group.

Pinata. Miami, FL: DDL Books.

Appendix C: Books about Environmental Print

Collins, P. 1984. *Don't tease the guppies*. Ill. M. Hafner. New York: Putnam.

Goor, R. & N. 1983. *Signs*. New York: Crowell.

Hoban, T. 1983. *I read signs*. New York: Greenwillow.

———. 1984. *I walk and read*. New York: Greenwillow.

Hutchins, P. 1980. *The tale of Thomas Mead*. New York: Greenwillow.

Sketch to Stretch
Sketch Me a Story
Interwoven Texts
Song Maps

Introduction

These engagements help language users realize that we can create meaning in many sign systems. By taking what we know in one sign system and recasting it in terms of another system—language, art, movement, mathematics, music, and so forth—new signs and new forms of expression are created, and new knowledge generated. This process of recasting is called "transmediation," and is a fundamental process of what it means to be literate.

These engagements encourage students to go beyond a literal understanding of what they have experienced. By becoming involved in this strategy, students who are reluctant to take risks or who have dysfunctional notions of language see that not everyone has the same response to a selection. Although much of the meaning is shared, variations in interpretation add new meanings and new insights.

Often, as students sketch, they generate new insights of their own. They are faced with a problem because the meanings they had constructed for the selection through language cannot be transferred into a sketch. As they deal with this problem, they usually come to under-

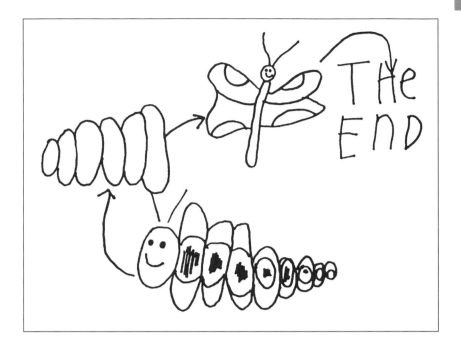

stand the selection at a different level than when they first read the book. Sometimes students discuss and explore aspects of meaning they may have captured in art that they were not aware of having understood verbally or musically.

Materials/Procedures for Sketch to Stretch

▮ Multiple copies of a reading selection
▮ Pencil, paper, and crayons or colored markers

1. Students work in small groups of four or five. They first read the selection, individually or as a group.

2. After reading the selection, students think about what they read and draw a sketch of "what this story means to you." Encourage students not to draw an illustration of the story, but to think about the meaning of the story and see if they can find a way to visually sketch that meaning. It also helps to ask students to draw their own connections to this story.

Teachers can help students understand these directions by sharing several examples of Sketch to Stretch with them before they are asked to create their own. Either examples from previous students or the ones included in this engagement can be used.

Sketch to Stretch
Interwoven Texts
Song Maps

FIGURE CE17.2
A Sketch for **Ira Sleeps Over**
(Waber, 1972); Matt, Age 10
(Siegel, 1984)

A Sketch for **Nana Upstairs,
Nana Downstairs** (de Paola,
1973); Lisa, Age 10 (Siegel,
1984)

3. Students should be told there are many ways of representing the meaning of an experience and they are free to experiment with their interpretation. Students should not be rushed but given ample time to read and draw.

4. When the sketches are complete, each person in the group shows his or her sketch to the others in that group. The group participants study the sketch and say what they think the artist is attempting to say.

5. Once everyone has been given the opportunity to hypothesize an interpretation, the artist, of course, gets the last word.

6. Sharing continues in this fashion until all group members have shared their sketches. Each group can then identify one sketch in the group to be shared with the entire class. This sketch is put on an acetate sheet for the overhead projector.

Materials/Procedures for Interwoven Texts

▮ A Text Set of three books related by theme (see Appendix A)
▮ A box of art materials—pipe cleaners, clay, string, ribbons, ballons, paper plates, and the like—and art supplies—construction paper, glue, scissors, and so forth

1. As a class, read and discuss each of the three books separately over several days.

2. The teacher divides each book into eight sections.

3. Before reading, the class is invited to listen for the meanings that cut across all three books. Encourage them to attend to the messages of each book and to the tone and feel of the books individually and together.

4. To read, invite three people to read the books in an interwoven fashion. Person 1 reads the first portion of his or her book, Person 2 reads the first portion of his or her book, Person 3 reads the first portion of his or her book, Person 1 then reads the second portion of his or her book, Person 2 reads the second portion of his or her book, and so on until all books are complete.

5. After reading, students are asked to individually jot down what they see as the messages or meanings cutting across all three books.

6. Working in small groups of five or six, students share their interpretations of the stories. They then decide as a group on one interpretation that they think is interesting and decide how they might symbolically represent that meaning in an artistic form.

7. Each group shares their art pieces with the rest of the class by using the strategy Save the Last Word for the Artist.

Materials/Procedures for Song Maps

- Several pieces of classical music like Beethoven's Fifth, and a Bach Concerto.
- Blank sheets of paper and crayons
- Overhead transparencies and markers

1. Play a piece of music inviting participants to listen for recurring patterns in the music.

2. Share a song map for the piece of music that was created by previous students or use the song map included in this engagement. A song map is an artistic and mathematical representation using line and pattern to show the deep structure or musical meaning of a song.

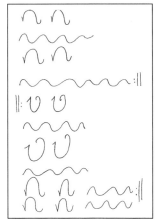

Songmap to **Gavotte** by
J. S. Bach

Sketch to Stretch
Interwoven Texts
Song Maps

FIGURE CE17.3
Sketch to Stretch; Picture
created while listening to
Mozart's **Seranade #10 in B
flat;** Laura, Masters Student
(compliments of Virginia
Woodward)

A clear, dark stary night!

3. Invite students to follow along on the song map as they relisten to the musical selection. Talk together about the difference between capturing the surface structure of the musical notes and the deep structure of "musical waves" in the song.

4. Play and replay another musical selection asking participants to create song maps for that selection. They can work alone or in small groups.

5. Ask students to share their song maps of the deep structure for that musical piece by sketching their maps on overheads for sharing and discussion.

Establishing the Learning Context

Teachers may need to help students focus on interpretation rather than on their artistic talents. Teachers should do their own Sketch to Stretch and share it with the group of students they are working with at an appropriate time. Students often initially have difficulty understanding the directions to "draw what the story means to you," and will draw their favorite scene. Don't give up on the engagement. The

Stars sparkleing in the sky at night.
By Monica

FIGURE CE17.4
Sketch to Stretch: Picture created while listening to Mozart's **Seranade #10 in B flat**; Monica, Age 9 (compliments of Virginia Woodward)

students will need several opportunities to try this engagement before they begin to play with the meanings they are creating through sketching and to get beyond their initial limited interpretations of what a sketch should be.

After using the engagement several times, the students should discuss: 1. why various readers have different interpretations; 2. why there is no correct reading or sketch but rather that what each reader focused on depended on the reader's interest and background; and 3. how and under what conditions Sketch to Stretch might be a particularly useful strategy for readers to use with time line

Sketch to Stretch
Interwoven Texts
Song Maps

selections or stories, floor plans in mysteries, complex descriptions of cell reproduction, etc.

Variations

1. Sketches can be compiled and published in a class book (see Bookmaking). In addition, a Message Board could be developed for students to share sketches they make from self-selected books they are reading. These sketches can serve as advertisements for particular books.

2. Students can read different selections that are related in some way (see Text Sets) and make sketches. As they discuss their sketches, they can make hypotheses about how their different selections are related.

3. Once students have written a first draft or have experienced a writer's block, they can be asked to shift to another sign system. Students can be asked how else they might represent their meaning. Their choice of pantomime, drama, math, music, art, or other system should be honored. Students return to writing once they have expressed their meaning in an alternate system. Often they will find that they have gained new insights into the topic at hand.

4. This procedure for Sketch to Stretch highlights written language. Art is secondary and seen as supportive of written language growth. However, this relationship can be reversed by having students move from math to writing or art to reading and then back to art or math. To this end, students should be helped to see that shifts in sign systems help learners gain new perspectives and insights. Such shifting is one of several strategies that they and other successful language learners might employ in a variety of learning situations.

5. Students can create story maps. A story map pictures the events that took place within the story in one large mural.

6. Students can sketch what they think the author looks like after reading a number of books by a particular author, and then compare their sketches.

7. *Sketch Me a Story*—Students can be given sheets of paper and asked to sketch scenes they "see" as the teacher reads aloud a book. On a second reading they can be asked to post their scenes in sequential order. After discussion, students can be invited to fill in missing scenes on a third reading. Pictures can be assembled in the form of a class composed book and can be used by even young children to recreate the story from memory. This variation provides access to the reading process for very young readers. It also provides a functional context for the reading and rereading of a complex story.

References

Interwoven Texts and Sketch Me a Story were developed by Mary Lynn Woods and Carol Hall. Sketch to Stretch was originally developed by Jerome Harste, Carolyn Burke, Marjorie Siegel, and Karen Feathers. It was the focus of a research study by Marjorie Siegel (1984).

Carle, E. 1969. *The very hungry caterpillar.* New York: Philomel.
de Paola, T. 1973. *Nana upstairs and nana downstairs.* New York: Putnam's.
Siegel, M. G. 1984. "Reading as signification." Unpublished doctoral dissertation. Bloomington, IN: Indiana University.
Waber, B. 1972. *Ira sleeps over.* Boston: Houghton Mifflin.

See Sketch Journals for a bibliography of children's books where children use sketches.

Upitis, R. 1990. *This too is music.* Portsmouth, NH: Heinemann.
———. 1992. *Can I play you my song?* Portsmouth, NH: Heinemann.

Appendix A: Text Sets for Interwoven Text Strategy

Asch, F. 1982. *Happy birthday, moon.* New York: Simon & Schuster.
Berger, B. 1984. *Grandfather Twilight.* New York: Philomel.
Willard, N. 1983. *The nightgown of the sullen moon.* Ill. D. McPhail. New York: Harcourt.

Sketch to Stretch
Interwoven Texts
Song Maps

Bunting, E. 1989. *The Wednesday surprise*. Ill. D. Carrick. New York: Clarion.

Isadora, R. 1979. *Ben's trumpet*. New York: Greenwillow.

Rylant, C. 1988. *All I see*. Ill. P. Catalanotto. New York: Orchard.

Fox, M. 1988. *Koala Lou*. Ill. P. Lofts. San Diego: Harcourt.

Joose, B. 1991. *Mama, do you love me*. Ill. B. Lavallee. New York: Chronicle Books.

Munsch, R. 1986. *Love you forever*. Ill. S. McGraw. Ontario, Canada: Firefly.

Hall, D. 1979. *Ox-cart man*. Ill. B. Cooney. New York: Viking.

Rylant, C. 1993. *The relatives came*. Ill. S. Gammell. New York: Aladdin.

Sanders, R. 1989. *Aurora means dawn*. Ill. J. Kastner. New York: Bradbury.

Hoffman, M. 1991. *Amazing Grace*. Ill. C. Binch. New York: Dial.

Isadora, R. 1979. *Ben's trumpet*. New York: Scholastic.

Schick, E. 1992. *I have another language: The language is dance*. New York: Macmillan.

Reference for piece of music in the songmap—*Gavotte*, J.S. Bach, Ouverturen/Suites BWV 1068–1069. English Baroque Soloists, John Eliot Gardiner. Germany: Erato-Disques s.a. 1985

Text Sets
Paired Books
Book and Toy Sets

Introduction

Learning is a process of searching for patterns that connect. We learn something new when we can make a connection to something we already know. When there are few or no connections, learning is difficult and easily forgotten. We do not, however, want to stay too close to what we already know. We need to stay in sight of what we know, but consider new perspectives and connections that build deeper and more complex understandings. While this process of making connections is a natural way of learning for young children, schools are organized around isolated subjects, books, and information. Nothing is connected and so students no longer search for the connections that would facilitate learning. Text Sets and Paired Books highlight the making of connections and considering new perspectives. Through these engagements, students develop both an expectation for connection and strategies for making the search for connections more productive and wide ranging.

When readers read two or more texts that are related in some way, they are encouraged to share and extend their understandings of each text differently than if only one text had been read and discussed.

Readers are able to understand what they read only because of the intertextual connections they make between the current book and their past experiences, which include previous books they have read or written. As readers make connections between texts, they begin to see the reading event as an experience in itself. A reader can read one text to prepare for reading and better understanding a second text. The focus is not on what readers have to do to get ready to read, but on what happens when readers read one text to facilitate their understanding of other, related texts.

In addition, reading related texts encourages discussion among a group of students in Literature Circles. Because they have read different texts, they have a real reason for sharing their books with one another. It is one of the few times when they have a real reason for retelling a book. The contributions of all students are needed and valued. Differences in reading proficiencies and the types of materials each person has read are not a problem, but rather are an asset. Text Sets also present students with a much wider range of perspectives and so are particularly appropriate when beginning an inquiry focus or engaging in research. Book and Toy Sets extend the types of materials in these sets and allow children to intertextualize books and toys in their play.

Materials/Procedures for Text Sets

▮ Five to fifteen texts that are conceptually related in some way, such as similar themes, text types, topics, and so on (see Appendices)

1. A large theme set of books are collected from various libraries and placed in the classroom for student browsing over several days or weeks. This theme set consists of many different books and other reading materials related to a class topic or focus that is just beginning. As students browse, read, and share from this broad theme set, ideas are discussed for smaller and more focused Text Sets. Sometimes teachers create these Text Sets by watching to see which books most appeal to students and taking field notes on the connections and issues that students make during sharing time after browsing and read-aloud. Other times, students form these sets by brainstorming possible categories for grouping books.

2. Initial text sets should be kept small (five to six books) with close relationships across the books to facilitate connections for students in their discussion. The sets gradually grow in size and complexity as students develop strategies for making connections.

3. The Text Sets are carefully constructed to reflect a variety of perspectives. The following criteria are considered:

a. Degree of familiarity: Some of the books in the set should meet students' expectations for the topic of the text set and connect closely to their current background experiences. There should be one or two books that will contradict their assumptions and possibly raise anomalies for them.

b. Range of genres and reading materials: The texts in the set should cut across poetry, fiction, and information books. They should also include maps, newspapers, song books, articles, recipe books, and pamphlets as appropriate to the set. This range allows students to see that they can read about a topic across a wide range of reading materials. Each kind of material and genre offers different potentials for understandings about the focus of the set.

c. Nonprint Texts: Add an art print, a tape of music, or a video of a dance or drama as appropriate to the focus of the set. Crossing sign systems allows students to take a different perspective on the topic because different meanings can be created from each system.

d. Knowledge Systems: Consider whether the texts cut across different knowledge systems such as history, ecology, psychology, economics, etc., since each knowledge system represents an alternative way of viewing the world.

e. Cultural Perspectives and Language: The set should reflect a range of cultural perspectives, including books that reflect a range of ethnic and international perspectives. Look for books written by insiders—not just a book about another country, but a book written by someone from that country. Remember that culture refers broadly to specific ways of living and thinking in the world; it includes such aspects as gender, socioeconomic status, community, and religion as well as ethnicity and race. If

Text Sets
Paired Books
Book and Toy Sets

possible, bilingual books or a book written in another language should be part of the set.

If the sets are used in a bilingual classroom, each set should be bilingual with books in both primary languages so that students are not placed into separate groups by language.

f. Difficulty of Text: The books should reflect a range of difficulty for readers of different proficiencies. Some books in the set may be used for browsing or reference while others are for students to read in entirety.

4. Once the Text Sets have been put together, they are introduced to students who browse through the sets and then sign up for the set they want to discuss.

5. The groups begin by browsing through the books in their set and then each person chooses one or two books from the set that they want to read. The sets are usually stored in a basket or box so the group can easily take their set to the table or area where they are working.

6. The group meets to share their books with each other through brief retellings so that others can get a sense of what the book was about, particularly in relation to the topic of their set. Sometimes the group members spontaneously begin making comparisons across the books and other times the group stays with retellings.

7. The group makes a decision about how to proceed with reading and discussing their Text Set based on the amount of time and purpose for the group and the students' interests in the books. Some groups continue reading and sharing the books over the next several days or week until they have read all or most of the books in their set. Other groups stop their reading at this point and begin discussing the connections across their books.

8. Once students have finished sharing, they move to comparisons across their books. The group discusses the similarities and differences across the texts. They can discuss similarities and differences in content as well as in how the texts were written. If they are reading informational books, they focus on what kinds of in-

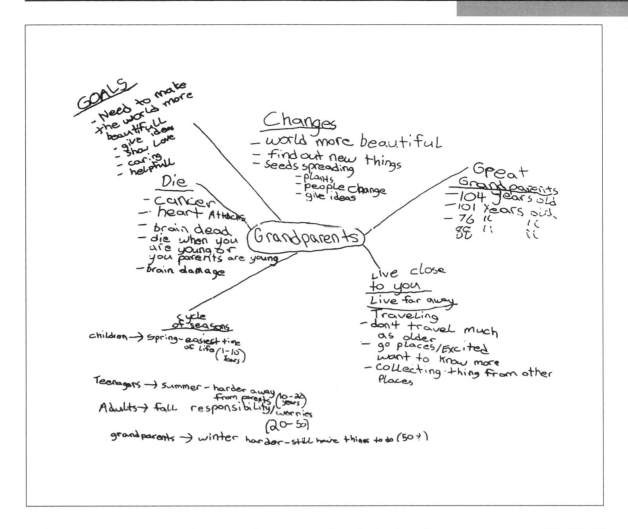

The web contains the following handwritten content:

GOALS
- Need to make the world more beautifull
- give Love
- show Love
- caring
- helpfull

Changes
- world more beautiful
- find out new things
- seeds spreading
  - plants
  - people change
  - give ideas

Great Grandparents
- 104 years old
- 101 years old
- 76 "
- 38 "

Die
- cancer
- heart Attacks
- brain dead
- die when you are young or you parents are young
- brain damage

Grandparents

Live close to you
Live far away
Traveling
- don't travel much as older
- go places/Excited want to know more
- collecting things from other places

cycle of seasons
children → spring - easiest time of life (1-10 years)
Teenagers → summer - harder away from parents (10-20 years)
Adults → fall responsibility/worries (20-50)
grandparents → winter harder - still have things to do (50 +)

formation were presented in more than one book and whether the books presented contradictory information.

9. Students brainstorm as many different connections across their books as possible. Because of their focus on connections, they naturally bring in many life experiences as well as connections to the books themselves. Often students create a web to organize the connections they are considering across these books and their lives.

10. The groups move to consider more intensely several of these connections or comparisons in more depth. They may do this by

FIGURE CE18.1
Web of Connections and Discussion Topics for Grandparents Text Set; Third graders (Gloria Kauffman's classroom)

Text Sets
Paired Books
Book and Toy Sets

choosing an area from their web of possible connections for discussion. At the end of each day's discussion, students choose what they want to discuss from their web for the following day and students are responsible for preparing for that discussion by revisiting their Text Set.

11. Some groups create a comparison chart of the comparisons that they want to look at closely. They choose four or five books from their set to list on the left-hand side of the chart and four or five categories to list across the top of the chart. They choose the categories based on the comparisons they think are most important to examine within their books. It is important not to use a comparison chart too early in the Text Set discussion. Students need to have already discussed the range of possible connections in order to determine the categories for their chart. Charts can become "fill-in-the-blank" exercises when teachers determine the categories early in the process.
   The charts will be more attractive if students use both words and pictures to record how each text fits in a particular category. Working together on the chart is facilitated if each student is given a small square of paper to draw or write on, and then the student glues that square onto the large chart.

12. At any point during the initial or in-depth discussions of the Text Set, students may add other books to the set, either books with which they are familiar or books they locate through library research.

13. At the end of their Literature Circle, the Text Set group brainstorms what they want others to understand about their set and discussion and puts together a presentation to give to the class such as writing a drama, Readers Theatre, or story related to the theme of their Text Set, creating a game or display, or making a mural or diorama. The students may also choose to share informally by describing their set and sharing their web or chart.
   See Literature Circles for a discussion of how to support student talk in these groups and for more information on how to organize the groups and support presentations.

TAXI a book of city words	the Year at Maple Hill Farm	
city	farm	setting illustrations story discribe illustrations noise
taxi	animals	
words	month	
people	seasons	
bridge	people	
loud + nosy	quiet + soft	

FIGURE CE18.2
Comparison Chart of Paired Book Set; Daniel and Justin, Age 9 (compliments of Carol Burke)

Materials/Procedures for Paired Books

▌ Two books that are conceptually related to each other, but set up some kind of opposition to each other

1. The basic procedures for Paired Books are the same as Text Sets. Paired Books are created out of a broader theme set and often reflect comparisons and oppositions that students notice as they browse through the books or that students discuss as they engage in experiences related to the class focus. Any of the criteria

Text Sets
Paired Books
Book and Toy Sets

discussed for Text Sets can be used to form Paired Books. Students sign up for the Paired Books they want to discuss.

2. The two books in the set can be read by everyone in the group and then compared using the same procedures discussed under Text Sets. The discussion is much more focused because the students only have two books to compare. Many teachers have used Paired Books as a way to introduce Text Sets to students. They also use Paired Books to highlight a particular comparison that the class has decided to examine in more depth.

3. Another strategy for reading and comparing the books is to form groups of four students for each pair of books. Two students in the group take one of the books to read and discuss and the other two students take the other book. Each pair of student partners read the book and discuss it together. After several days, the two pairs of students come together, and each pair describes their book. The group then searches for similarities and differences across their books.

4. Just as with Text Sets, students may want to use webs and comparison charts to examine their comparisons in more depth. After completing their discussions, they share their comparisons through informal sharing or a presentation.

Materials/Procedures for Book and Toy Sets

❚ Books and toys that are conceptually related to each other

1. Teachers of young children observe the themes and topics that are important in the lives of those children and that they consistently pursue in various experiences and areas around the classroom.

2. Based on children's use of different toys and books around the room, these books and toys are reorganized so that they are placed together in the same area. For example, books about machines are placed on the shelf next to the dump trucks, pickups, and bulldozers while books about zoo animals are placed next to the zoo animal collection. Students are encouraged to incorporate the books into their play and to incorporate the toys into their browsing of the books or when adults are reading aloud the books to them. The sets may be stored in boxes.

Establishing the Learning Context

When teachers ask a group to read several books in a Text Set before meeting and discussing these books, the groups develop different strategies for how they conduct these discussions. Some groups read only those two or three books and spend their time drawing comparisons between them. Some groups decide to take one book that everyone reads, or a certain subset of books in the set each day to focus on in the discussion. Some groups continue reading as they discuss so that students have read most or all of the books by the end of their discussion. Some groups generate a web or list of possible comparisons or questions, and then use this list to guide their discussion. Others find one theme and pursue that across all of the books. Some groups actually physically sort books into different stacks. All groups have to find some way to focus their discussion of the set. We have found it helpful during the first Text Set discussions to brainstorm possible ways of handling these discussions with students, but then each group develops its own discussion strategy. The group meetings allow students to share the different ways they are reading and sharing their books and their strategies for making comparisons across their books. These reflections support students in using the Text Sets without dictating a particular procedure that everyone must use.

Variations

1. Young children have difficulty dealing with Text Sets because they are unable to read most of the books independently. Kindergarten and first grade teachers have tried a number of variations:

   a. One book from the Text Set or Paired Books is read aloud to the class each day. Students can then discuss the book as a whole group, or they can break into small groups for a short discussion and then come back together as a class to share their comparisons. A chart, web, or list is created on a large sheet of chart paper and the different connections and comparisons from these discussions are recorded.

   b. Students begin in shared book sets groups where each group has only one book to read or have read to them and discuss. For example, each group may have a book by Pat Hutchins or a

Text Sets
Paired Books
Book and Toy Sets

particular version of "Little Red Riding Hood." After each group has had time to discuss their book in depth, the groups are reformed so that each new group has one child from each of the previous groups. These new groups are now Text Set groups because each child has read a different Pat Hutchins book or "Little Red Riding Hood" version.

2. Students can be invited to write their own text that would fit in the same Text Set or to develop a drama that uses the characteristics of the Text Set. If the Text Set involved analyzing illustrations, students could try some of the illustrating techniques in their own work. When these are shared in Authors Circle, other students comment on whether the student has used the major characteristics of the Text Set.

3. A Caldecott or Newbery Award Text Set can be created. Students first read through a set of books that won one of these awards in previous years. They use these books to generate criteria for winning the award. The students are then given the books that received the award or an honorable mention for the current year. They are told that these books were nominated for the award and are asked to look through them and decide which book should win the award, and why it should win. Once they have made and defended their choice, they are told which book received the medal. If the book they chose did not win, the students discuss why they think the award was given to another book and decide whether they agree with the committee.

4. Text Sets of three or four books can be put in book bags for students to check out to take home as homework to be read with and to family members.

5. Paired Books and Text Sets are excellent to use in Literature Circles to facilitate discussion, especially among students who are reluctant to talk (see Literature Circle).

6. The Text Set engagement has been used by teachers who are required to use the basal reader or content area textbook in some way. One possibility is to place a basal story or textbook chapter as one choice within the Text Set. Another is to take a group of stories or chapters and treat them as a Text Set. Each student reads one story or chapter, and then the group comes together to share

and make connections across those stories or chapters, thus covering a great deal of the basal or textbook in a short period of time. A third possibility is to read the textbook or basal unit quickly as an overview on a particular theme or topic and then use that reading to brainstorm topics for Text Sets in order to pursue that theme or topic in greater depth.

7. Read-a-Book-a-Day is a variation that involves tearing apart a paperback copy of a chapter book by chapters. The teacher reads the first chapter to a small group and then gives each person in the group a chapter to read independently. After the students have read their chapters, they come back together as a group to share their individual chapters and discuss how they are related and fit together. This variation can be used with informational books that have chapters or with fiction books that are episodic stories. Episodic stories have chapters that can be understood fairly well without the other chapters having been read. Instead of each chapter being highly connected to the next, each chapter relates another adventure of the characters. Examples of episodic books are *Homer Price* (McCloskey, 1943), *Wind in the Willows* (Grahame, 1940), *Frog and Toad Together* (Lobel, 1972), and the Ramona stories by Beverly Cleary.

8. Paired Books can also be used as a discussion strategy along with Text Sets. After students have spent time reading and discussing their Text Set, they can be invited to look back through their set and see if they can put together any Paired Books that establish some kind of opposition to each other.

9. Text Sets can be a browsing engagement used at the beginning of a new class focus to encourage students to consider a broader range of possibilities in relation to that focus and to find questions they want to pursue through inquiry. Students may have sharing discussions about these books, but the sets are not used for in-depth Literature Circles. Text Sets can also be put together to support students' research once they have chosen a particular question to pursue. The set provides them with a range of materials and perspectives as they research their question. This set may be used as a reference set or discussed in depth through a Literature Circle.

Text Sets
Paired Books
Book and Toy Sets

10. In order to familiarize students with a set of books that she collected on a particular theme, Pat Heine created a strategy she calls "Pass." Students are initially each given a book and allowed thirty seconds to look at it after which time they "pass" it on to their neighbor. Every thirty seconds "pass" is called; after as many turns as there are students the strategy is terminated. At this point students may go back to a book they found interesting and begin reading either alone or with others (if it was selected by more than one person). In addition to providing time for students to find their own inquiry question, one of the advantages of this strategy is that students begin to get familiar with the materials that are available in the room.

References

Dorothy Watson initially developed the notion of conceptually related texts. As presented here, Text Sets were developed by Kathy G. Short based on other variations by Carolyn Burke, Linda Crafton, and Lynn Rhodes. To the best of our knowledge the Pass Strategy was initially developed by Patricia Heine.

Grahame, K. 1940. *The wind in the willows*. New York: Scribner's.

Lobel, A. 1971. *Frog and Toad together*. New York: Harper.

McCloskey, R. 1943. *Homer Price*. New York: Viking.

Appendix A: Subject Bibliographies of Children's Literature

Barstow, B., & J. Riggle. 1989. *Beyond picture books: A guide to first readers*. New York: R. R. Bowker.

Jensen, J. M., & N. L. Roser, eds. 1993. *Adventuring with books: A booklist for pre-K–grade 6*. 10th ed. Urbana, IL: National Council of Teachers of English.

Lima, C. W., & J. A. Lima. 1993. *A to Zoo: Subject access to children's picture books*. 4th ed. New Providence, NJ: R. R. Bowker.

Miller-Lachmann, L. 1992. *Our family, our friends, our world: An annotated guide to signficant multicultural books for children and teenagers*. New Providence, NJ: R. R. Bowker.

The Web, published by The Ohio State University, and *Book Link*, by the American Library Association, both include extensive book lists by subjects and themes.

Appendix B: Types of Text Sets

Story Variants (different cultural variants of the same story) and Story Versions (same story in different retellings)

1. Cinderella Variants

Climo, S. 1989. *The Egyptian Cinderella*. Ill. R. Heller. New York: Harper.

————. 1993. *The Korean Cinderella*. Ill. R. Heller. New York: HarperCollins.

Cole, B. 1987. *Prince Cinders*. New York: Putnam's.

Compton, J. 1994. *Ashpet*. Ill. K. Compton. New York: Holiday.

Delamare, D. 1994. *Cinderella*. New York: Green Tiger.

Greeves, M. 1990. *Tattercoats*. Ill. M. Chamberlain. New York: Potter.

Hooks, W. 1987. *Moss gown*. Ill. D. Carrick. New York: Clarion.

Huck, C. 1989. *Princess Furball*. Ill. A Lobel. New York: Greenwillow.

Louie. A. 1982. *Yeh-Shen: A Cinderella story from China*. Ill. E. Young. New York: Philomel.

Martin, R. 1992. *The Rough-Face girl*. Ill. D. Shannon. New York: Putnam.

Perrault, C. 1985. *Cinderella*. Ill. S. Jeffers. New York: Dial Books.

San Souci, R. 1989. *The talking eggs*. Ill. J. Pinkney. New York: Dial.

————. 1994. *Sootface: An Ojibwa Cinderella story*. Ill. D. San Souci. New York: Doubleday.

Steptoe, J. 1987. *Mufaro's beautiful daughters*. New York: Lothrop.

Winthrop, E. 1991. *Vasilissa the beautiful*. Ill. A. Koshkin. New York: HarperCollins.

2. Little Red Riding Hood Versions and Variants

Coady, C. 1991. *Red Riding Hood*. New York: Dutton.

de Regniers, B. 1972. *Red Riding Hood*. New York: Aladdin.

Delaney, A. 1988. *The gunnywolf*. New York: Harper.

Emberley, M. 1990. *Ruby*. Boston: Little, Brown.

Goodall, J. 1988. *Little Red Riding Hood*. New York: McElderry.

Grimm, J. & W. 1983. *Little Red Cap*. Ill. L. Zwerger. Natick, MA: Picture Book Studio.

————. 1993. *Little Red Cap*. Ill. M. Laimgruber. New York: North-South Books.

Hyman, T. S. 1983. *Little Red Riding Hood*. New York: Holiday.

Laird, D. 1985. *'Ula Li'i and the magic shark*. Ill. C. Jossem. Honolulu, HI: Barnaby Books.

Text Sets
Paired Books
Book and Toy Sets

Marshall, J. 1987. *Red Riding Hood*. New York: Dial.

Montressor, B. 1991. *Little Red Riding Hood*. New York: Doubleday.

Perrault, C. 1983. *Little Red Riding Hood*. Ill. S. Moon. Mankato, MN: Creative Education.

Richardson, L. 1985. *Little Red Riding Hood*. Ill. S. Holt. Carmel, CA: ShirLee.

3. Snow White Versions and Variants

French, F. 1986. *Snow White in New York*. Oxford: Oxford University Press.

Heins, P. 1974. *Snow White*. Ill. T. Hyman. Boston: Little, Brown.

Jarrell, R. 1972. *Snow White and the seven dwarfs*. Ill. N. Burkert. Toronto: Colins.

Littledale, F. 1980. *Snow White and the seven dwarfs*. Ill. S. Jeffers. New York: Scholastic.

O'Brien, K., & A. Dempster. 1948. *Snow White and the seven dwarfs*. Ill. Walt Disney Studio. New York: Golden.

4. Modern Variants of The Frog Prince

Berenzy, A. 1989. *A frog prince*. New York: Holt.

Bos, B. 1990. *Prince Valentino*. Ill. H. de Beer. New York: North-South.

Gwynne, F. 1990. *Pondlarker*. New York: Simon & Schuster.

Priceman, M. 1989. *Friend of frog*. Boston: Houghton Mifflin.

Scieszka, J. 1991. *The frog prince continued*. Ill. S. Johnson. New York: Trumpet Club.

Tarcov, E. 1974. *The frog prince*. Ill. J. Marshall. New York: Scholastic.

Vesey, A. 1985. *The princess and the frog*. New York: Puffin.

Zemach, H. & K. 1975. *The princess and froggie*. Ill. M. Zemach. New York: Sunburst.

5. Jack in the Beanstalk Versions and Variants

Briggs, R. 1970. *Jim and the beanstalk*. New York: Puffin.

Cauley, L. 1983. *Jack and the beanstalk*. New York: Putnam.

Cole, B. 1986. *The giant's toe*. New York: Dell.

Compton, K. & J. 1993. *Jack and the giant chaser: An Appalachian tale*. New York: Holiday.

Galdone, P. 1974. *Jack and the beanstalk*. New York: Clarion.

Haley, G. 1986. *Jack and the bean tree*. New York: Crown.

Kellogg, S. 1991. *Jack and the beanstalk*. New York: Trumpet.

Laird, D. 1982. *Keaka and the liliko'i vine*. Ill. C. Jossem. Honolulu, HI: Barnaby.

Paulson, T. 1990. *The beanstalk incident*. Ill. M. Corcoran. New York: Birch Lane.

Pearson, S. 1989. *Jack and the beanstalk*. Ill. J. Warhola. New York: Simon & Schuster.

6. Variants of The Three Little Pigs

Campbell, J. 1993. *Three little pigs*. Ill. G. DiCiccio. New York: Disney.

Celsi, T. 1990. *The fourth little pig*. Ill. D. Cushman. Austin, TX: Raintree Steck-Vaughn.

Galdone, P. 1970. *The three little pigs*. New York: Scholastic.

Hooks, W. 1989. *The three little pigs and the fox*. Ill. S.D. Schindler. New York: Macmillan.

Laird, D. 1981. *The three little Hawaiian pigs and the magic shark*. Ill. C. Jossem. Honolulu, HI: Barnaby Books.

Lowell, S. 1992. *The three little javelinas*. Ill. J. Harris. New York: Scholastic.

Marshall, J. 1989. *The three little pigs*. New York: Scholastic.

Ross, T. 1983. *The three little pigs*. New York: Pantheon.

Rounds, G. 1992. *The three little pigs and the big bad wolf*. New York: Trumpet Club.

Scieszka, J. 1989. *The true story of the 3 little pigs*. Ill. L. Smith. New York: Viking.

Trivizas, E. 1993. *The three little wolves and the big bad pig*. Ill. H. Oxenbury. New York: McElderry.

7. Rumpelstiltskin Variants

Galdone, P. 1985. *Rumpelstiltskin*. Boston: Houghton Mifflin.

Hastings, S. 1985. *Sir Gawain and the loathly lady*. Ill. J. Wijngaard. New York: Mulberry.

Moser, B. 1994. *Tucker Pfeffercorn*. Boston: Little, Brown.

Ness, E. 1978. *The Devil's bridge*. New York: Scribner.

Ness, E. 1965. *Tom Tit Tot*. New York: Dutton.

Zelinsky, P. 1986. *Rumpelstiltskin*. New York: Dutton.

Zemach, H. & M. 1973. *Duffy and the devil*. New York: Sunburst.

Literary Elements: Plot Structure, Point of View, Flashback, Symbolism, Setting, etc.

1. Point of View (these books tell a story from multiple points of view or offer an alternative perspective on a well known story)

Aardema, V. 1975. *Why mosquitoes buzz in people's ears*. Ill. L. & D. Dillon. New York: Scholastic.

Text Sets
Paired Books
Book and Toy Sets

Ahlberg, J. & A. 1986. *The jolly postman*. Boston: Little, Brown.

Anno, M. 1993. *Anno's twice told tales*. New York: Philomel.

Blume, J. 1974. *The pain and the great one*. Ill. I. Trivas. New York: Bradbury.

Lionni, L. 1970. *Fish is fish*. New York: Knopf.

MacLachlan, P. 1991. *Journey*. New York: Dell.

Schwartz, A. 1982. *Bea and Mr. Jones*. New York: Puffin.

Scieszka, J. 1989. *The true story of the 3 little pigs*. Ill. L. Smith. New York: Scholastic.

Shorto, R. 1990. *Cinderella*. Ill. T. Lewis. New York: Citadel.

Stolz, M. 1960. *A dog on Barkham street*. New York: Harper.

———. 1963. *The bully of Barkham street*. Ill. L. Shortall. New York: Harper.

Turkle, B. 1976. *Deep in the forest*. New York: Trumpet Club.

Viorst, J. 1974. *Rosie and Michael*. Ill. L. Tomei. New York: Atheneum.

Williams, B. 1974. *Albert's toothache*. Ill. K. Chorao. New York: Trumpet Club.

Yolen, J. 1992. *Encounter*. Ill. D. Shannon. San Diego, CA: Harcourt.

2. Cumulative Story Structure   (In these texts, there is a cumulative pattern where one thing causes another thing to happen)

Aardema, V. 1975. *Why mosquitoes buzz in people's ears*. Ill. L. & D. Dillon. New York: Scholastic.

———. 1981. *Bringing the rain to Kapiti Plain*. Ill. B. Vidal. New York: Dial.

Allison, D. 1992. *This is the key to the kingdom*. Boston: Little, Brown.

Caldecott, R. 1989. *The house that Jack built*. Poole, Sorset U.K.: New Orchard.

Carle, E. 1977. *The grouchy ladybug*. New York: Scholastic.

Hogrogian, N. 1971. *One fine day*. New York: Trumpet Club.

Hutchins, P. 1968. *Rosie's walk*. New York: Scholastic.

Kalan, R. 1981. *Jump, frog, jump*. Ill. B. Barton. New York: Scholastic.

Lobel, A. 1984. *The rose in my garden*. Ill. A. Lobel. New York: Scholastic.

Neitzel, S. 1989. *The jacket I wear in the snow*. Ill. N. Parker. New York: Mulberry.

Noble, T. 1980. *The day Jimmy's boa ate the wash*. Ill. S. Kellogg. New York: Scholastic.

Robart, R. 1986. *The cake that Mack ate*. Ill. M. Kovalski. Toronto: Kids Can Press.

Stern, R. 1991. *The house that Bob built*. New York: Rizzoli.

Stevens, J. 1985. *The house that Jack built*. Ill. J. Stevens. New York: Holiday.

Stow, J. 1992. *The house that Jack built*. New York: Puffin.

Weissman, A. 1987. *The castle of Churumbel*. Ill. S. Bailyn. Tucson, AZ: Hispanic Books Distributors.

Wood, A. 1984. *The napping house*. Ill. D. Wood. San Diego, CA: Harcourt.

Zolotow, C. 1963. *The quarreling book*. Ill. A. Lobel. New York: Harper.

Characters

1. Same Character   (Any set of books that contains stories about the same set of characters)

Frog and Toad series by Arnold Lobel

Amelia Bedelia series by Peggy Parish

Nate the Great series by Marjorie Sharmat

Peter and his friends series by Ezra Jack Keats

Rosa and her family series by Vera Williams

Jim and his friends series by Miriam Cohen and Lilian Hoban

Grandpa series by James Stevenson

Anastasia series by Lois Lowry

Tillerman series by Cynthia Voigt

Rinko and her family series by Yoshiko Uchida

Ramona, Henry Huggins, and *Ralph* series by Beverly Cleary

2. Same Type of Character   (A set of books involving the same kind of character such as a princess, wolf, pig, musician, etc.)

Pig Text Set

Axelrod, A. 1994. *Pigs will be pigs*. Ill. S. McGinley-Nally. New York: Four Winds.

Browne, A. 1986. *Piggybook*. New York: Knopf.

Dunn, J. 1987. *The little pig*. Ill. P. Dunn. New York: Random House.

Geisert, A. 1986. *Pigs from a to z*. Boston: Houghton Mifflin.

Hawkins, C. & J. 1985. *This little pig*. London: Macmillan.

Johnson, A. 1993. *Julius*. Ill. D. Pilkey. New York: Orchard.

King-Smith, D. 1993. *All pigs are beautiful*. Ill. A. Jeram. Cambridge, MA: Candlewick.

Krause, U. 1989. *Pig surprise*. New York: Puffin.

Lobel, A. 1979. *A treeful of pigs*. Ill. A. Lobel. New York: Scholastic.

Text Sets
Paired Books
Book and Toy Sets

———. 1983. *The book of pigericks*. New York: Harper & Row.

Munsch, R. 1989. *Pigs*. Ill. M. Martchenko. Toronto, Canada: Annick.

Rayner, M. 1976. *Mr and Mrs Pig's evening out*. London: Macmillan.

Retan, W. 1993. *Piggies piggies piggies*. Ill. S.D. Schindler and others. New York: Simon & Schuster.

Yolen, J. 1987. *Piggins*. Ill. J. Dyer. San Diego, CA: Harcourt.

Text Types (books which are the same genre or type of text such as fables, tall tales, experiment books, mysteries, imaginary kingdoms, etc.)

1. Time Travel (chapter books in which the character travels into the past or future)

Conrad, P. 1990. *Stonewords: A ghost story*. New York: Harper.

Greer, G., & B. Ruddick. 1988. *Max and me and the wild West*. New York: Harper.

L'Engle, M. 1962. *A wrinkle in time*. New York: Dell.

Lunn, J. 1981. *The root cellar*. New York: Puffin.

Park, R. 1980. *Playing Beatie Bow*. New York: Puffin.

Pearce, P. 1959. *Tom's midnight garden*. New York: Lippincott.

Pearson, K. 1987. *A handful of time*. New York: Puffin.

Sauer, J. 1943. *Fog magic*. New York: The Trumpet Club.

Slepian, J. 1993. *Back to before*. New York: Scholastic.

Vick, H. 1993. *Walker of time*. Tucson, AZ: Harbinger.

Walsh, J. 1978. *A chance child*. Sunburst.

Yolen, J. 1988. *The devil's arithmetic*. New York: Puffin.

2. Fables (brief, didactic tales in which animals speak as human beings)

Anderson. H. 1965. *The nightingale*. Ill. N. Burkert. New York: Harper & Row.

Anno, M. 1987. *Anno's Aesop*. New York: Orchard.

Bader, B. 1991. *Aesop & company: With scenes from his legendary life*. Ill. A. Geisert. Boston: Houghton Mifflin.

Brown, M. 1961. *Once a mouse*. New York: Aladdin.

———. 1977. *The blue jackal*. New York: Scribner.

Cooney, B. 1958. *Chanticleer and the fox*. Ill. B. Cooney. New York: Crowell.

Kraus, R. 1994. *Fables Aesop never wrote*. New York: Viking.

Lionni, L. 1967. *Frederick*. New York: Knopf.

———. 1968. *The biggest house in the world*. New York: Knopf.

Lobel, A. 1980. *Fables*. New York: Scholastic.

Lowell, S. 1994. *The tortoise and the jackrabbit*. Ill. J. Harris. Flagstaff, AZ: Northland.

MacDonald, S. 1990. *Once upon another: The tortoise and the hare; the lion and the mouse*. New York: Dial.

Paxton, T. 1990. *Belling the cat and other Aesop's fables*. Ill. R. Rayevsky. New York: Morrow.

Plante, P., & D. Bergman. 1981. *The turtle and the two ducks*. Ill. A. Rockwell. New York: Crowell.

Steig, W. 1971. *Amos & Boris*. New York: Puffin.

Young, E. 1992. *Seven blind mice*. New York: Philomel.

Topics (Any set of books focused around a specific topic growing out of class and individual inquiries)

1. Weaving

Beskow, E. 1972. *Pelle's new suit*. New York: Scholastic.

Blood, C., & M. Link. 1976. *The goat in the rug*. Ill. N. Parker. New York: Four Winds.

Castaneda, O. 1993. *Abuela's weave*. Ill. E. Sanchez. New York: Lee and Low.

de Paola, T. 1973. *Charlie needs a cloak*. New York: Scholastic.

Dorros, A. 1991. *Tonight is carnival*. Ill. Club de Madres Virgen del Carmen. New York: Dutton.

Hest, A. 1986. *The purple coat*. Ill. A. Schwartz. New York: Four Winds.

Lattimore, D. 1990. *The dragon's robe*. New York: Harper.

Lecher, D. 1992. *Angelita's magic yarn*. New York: Farrar, Straus & Giroux.

Macaulay, D. 1983. *Mill*. Boston: Houghton Mifflin.

Miles, M. 1971. *Annie and the old one*. Ill. P. Parnall. Boston: Little, Brown.

O'Reilly, S. 1993. *Arts & crafts: Weaving*. New York: Thompson Learning.

Ziefert, H. 1986. *A new coat for Anna*. Il. A. Lobel. New York: Scholastic.

2. Rain and Storms

Aardema, V. 1981. *Bringing the rain to Kapiti Plain*. Ill. B. Vidal. New York: Scholastic.

Adoff, A. 1976. *Tornado!* Ill. R. Himler. New York: Delacorte.

Text Sets
Paired Books
Book and Toy Sets

Bauer, C. 1986. *Rainy day: Stories and poems*. Ill. M. Chessare. New York: Lippincott.

Branley, F. 1988. *Tornado alert*. New York: Harper & Row.

Cole, J. 1986. *The magic schoolbus at the waterworks*. Ill. B. Degan. New York: Scholastic.

Kalan, R. 1978. *Rain*. Ill. D. Crews. New York: Mulberry.

Lee, J. 1985. *Toad is the uncle of heaven*. New York: Holt.

Martin, B., & B. Archambault. 1988. *Listen to the rain*. Ill. J. Endicott. New York: Holt.

Peters, L. 1991. *Water's way*. Ill. T. Rand. New York: Arcade.

Polacco, P. 1990. *Thunder cake*. New York: Scholastic.

Robbins, K. 1994. *Water: The elements*. New York: Holt.

Shulevitz, U. 1969. *Rain rain rain*. New York: Sunburst.

Simon, S. 1989. *Storms*. New York: Morrow.

Spier, P. 1982. *Rain*. Garden City, NY: Doubleday.

———. 1989. *Noah's ark*. New York: Trumpet Club.

Stolz, M. 1988. *Storm in the night*. Ill. P. Cummings. New York: Harper & Row.

Zolotow, C. 1952. *The storm book*. Ill. M. Graham. New York: Harper & Row.

3. Alaska and the Arctic

Andrews, J. 1985. *Very last first time*. Ill. I. Wallace. New York: Atheneum.

Carlstrom, N. 1992. *Northern lullaby*. Ill. L. & D. Dillon. New York: Philomel.

Cartwright, S. 1990. *Alaska's three bears*. Ill. S. Gill. Homer, AK: Paws IV.

De Armond, D. 1985. *Berry Woman's children*. New York: Greenwillow.

Dunphy, M. 1993. *Here is the Arctic winter*. Ill. A. Robinson. New York: Hyperion.

Ekoomiak, N. 1988. *Arctic memories*. New York: Holt.

Hoyt-Goldsmith, D. 1992. *Arctic hunter*. New York: Holiday.

Jenness, A., & A. Rivers. 1989. *In two worlds: A Yup'ik Eskimo family*. Boston: Houghton Mifflin.

Kalman, B., & W. Belsey. 1988. *An Arctic community*. New York: Crabtree.

Kendall, R. 1992. *Eskimo boy: Life in an Eskimo village*. New York: Scholastic.

Luenn, N. 1994. *Nessa's story*. Ill. N. Waldman. New York: Atheneum.

Schenherr, J. 1991. *Bear*. New York: Philomel.

Scott, A. 1972. *On mother's lap*. Ill. G. Coalson. New York: Clarion.

Service, R. 1986. *The cremation of Sam McGee*. Ill. T. Harrison. New York: Greenwillow.

Themes   (books which have similar underlying broad themes)

1. Living at Peace with Others

Aaseng, N. 1963. *The peace seekers: The Nobel Peace Prize*. Minneapolis: Lerner.

Abells, C. 1983. *The children we remember*. New York: Greenwillow.

Aliki. 1963. *The story of Johnny Appleseed*. New York: Prentice Hall.

Bunting, E. 1990. *The wall*. Ill. R. Himler. New York: Clarion.

Coerr, E. 1993. *Sadako*. Ill. E. Young. New York: Putnam.

de Paola, T. 1980. *The knight and the dragon*. New York: Putnam.

Dolphin, L. 1993. *Oasis of peace*. New York: Scholastic.

Durell, A., & M. Sachs, eds. 1990. *The big book for peace*. New York: Dutton.

Eco, U., & E. Carmi. 1989. *The three astronauts*. San Diego, CA: Harcourt.

Fitzhugh, L. 1969. *Bang bang you're dead*. Ill. S. Scoppettone. New York: Harper.

Gallaz, C., & R. Innocenti. 1985. *Rose Blanche*. Mankato, MN: Creative Education.

Heide, F., & J. Gilliland. 1992. *Sami and the time of the troubles*. Ill. T. Lewin. New York: Clarion.

Kellogg, S. 1973. *The island of the skog*. New York: Dial.

Lattimore, D. 1987. *The flame of peace*. New York: Harper.

Leaf, M. 1936. *The story of Ferdinand*. Ill. R. Lawson. New York: Scholastic.

MacDonald, M. 1992. *Peace tales*. Hamden, CT: Linnet Books.

Maruki, T. 1980. *Hiroshima no pika*. New York: Lothrop.

Mochizuki, K. 1993. *Baseball saved us*. Ill. D. Lee. New York: Lee & Low.

Pomerantz, C. 1974. *The princess and the admiral*. Ill. T. Chen. New York: The Feminist Press.

Raschka, C. 1993. *Yo! Yes?* New York: Scholastic.

Reesink, M. 1967. *The two windmills*. Ill. G. Apol. New York: Harcourt.

Scholes, K. 1989. *Peace begins with you*. Ill. R. Ingpen. Boston: Little, Brown.

Seuss, Dr. 1984. *The butter battle book*. New York: Random.

Text Sets
Paired Books
Book and Toy Sets

Tsuchiya, Y. 1988. *Faithful elephants*. Ill. T. Lewin. Boston: Houghton Mifflin.

Vagin, V. 1989. *Here comes the cat!* Ill. F. Asch. New York: Scholastic.

2. Breaking Stereotypes

Adoff, A. 1982. *All the colors of the race*. Ill. J. Steptoe. New York: Lothrop.

Browne, A. 1986. *Piggy book*. Great Britain: Little Mammoth.

Bunting, E. 1992. *Summer wheels*. Ill. T. Allen. San Diego, CA: Harcourt.

Cole, B. 1986. *Princess Smartypants*. New York: Putnam.

de Paola, T. 1979. *Oliver Button is a sissy*. San Diego, CA: Harcourt.

Escudie, R. 1988. *Paul and Sebastian*. Ill. U. Wensell. Brooklyn, NY: Kane/Miller.

Golenbock, P. 1990. *Teammates*. Ill. P. Bacon. San Diego, CA: Harcourt.

Lee, J. 1987. *Ba-nam*. New York: Holt.

McKee, D. 1979. *Tusk tusk*. Brooklyn, NY: Kane/Miller.

Morris, A. 1990. *Loving*. New York: Lothrop.

Osofsky, A. 1992. *My buddy*. Ill. T. Rand. New York: Holt.

Otey, M. 1990. *Daddy has a pair of striped shorts*. New York: Farrar, Straus & Giroux.

Quinlan, P. 1987. *My dad takes care of me*. Ill. V. Van Kampen. Toronto: Annick Press.

Scieszka, J. 1989. *The true story of the 3 little pigs*. Ill. L. Smith. New York: Scholastic.

Spier, P. 1980. *People*. New York: Trumpet Club.

Stamm, C. 1991. *Three strong women: A tall tale from Japan*. Ill. J. & M. Tseng. New York: Viking.

Surat, M. 1983. *Angel child, dragon child*. Ill. V. Mai. New York: Scholastic.

Vagin, V. 1989. *Here comes the cat!* Ill. F. Asch. New York: Scholastic.

Williams, B. 1975. *Kevin's grandma*. Ill. K. Chorao. New York: Dutton.

Yashima, T. 1955. *Crow boy*. New York: Viking.

Zolotow, C. 1972. *William's doll*. Ill. W. Du Bois. New York: Harper & Row.

Different Illustrators of the Same Text (the same text is illustrated by different illustrators)

Adams, P. 1973. *There was an old lady who swallowed a fly*. Wilts, England: Child's Play.

Bantock, N. 1990. *There was an old lady*. New York: Viking.

Bonne, R. 1961. *I know an old lady.* Ill. A. Graboff. New York: Scholastic.

Hawkins, C. & J. 1987. *I know an old lady who swallowed a fly.* New York: Putnam.

Karas, G. 1994. *I know an old lady.* New York: Scholastic.

Pienkowski, J. 1989. *Oh my a fly!* Ill. M. Stajewski & D. Meyer. Los Angeles, CA: Price Stern Sloan.

Rounds, G. 1990. *I know an old lady who swallowed a fly.* New York: Holiday.

Westcott, N. 1980. *I know an old lady who swallowed a fly.* Boston: Little, Brown.

Other examples include *The Wind in the Willows* and *The Night Before Christmas*.

Authors, Illustrators, and Poets (Any set of books written by the same author or poet or illustrated by the same illustrator)

A set of picture books by Tomie de Paola, Pat Hutchins, Eric Carle, Chris Van Allsburg, William Steig, Lois Ehlert, Ed Young, Anno Mitsumasa, Peter Catalanotto, Tana Hoban, David Macaulay, George Ella Lyons, Gail Gibbons, Vera Williams, Brian Pinkney, Ronald Himler, Aliki, John Burningham, Mem Fox, Allen Say, Molly Bang, Faith Ringgold, Shonto Begay, Pat Mora, Lulu Delacre, Alma Flor Ada, Paul Goble, Michael Lacapa.

A set of chapter books by Betsy Byars, Roald Dahl, Gary Paulson, Katherine Paterson, Cynthia Voigt, Jean Fritz, Robin McKinley, Virginia Hamilton, Walter Dean Myers, Russell Freedman, Michael Dorris, Gary Soto, Laurence Yep, Yoshiko Uchida, Mildred Taylor, Jean Little, Patricia MacLachlan, Paula Fox.

Other authors such as Cynthia Rylant, Jane Yolen, Paul Fleischman, Eve Bunting, and Pam Conrad write both picture books and chapter books.

A set of poetry books by Karla Kuskin, Arnold Adoff, Eve Merriam, David McCord, Valerie Worth, Michael Rosen, Dennis Lee, Jack Prelutsky, Myra Cohn Livingston, Eloise Greenfield, Ashley Bryan, Diane Siebert.

Text Sets
Paired Books
Book and Toy Sets

Culture   (books which highlight a particular aspect of culture such as race, ethnicity, region or country, gender, community, family structure, socio-economic status, religion, etc.)

1. Living in the Inner City

Brisson, P. 1994. *Wanda's roses*. Ill. M. Cocca-Leffler. Honesdale, PA: Boyds Mill Press.

Clifton, L. 1973. *The boy who didn't believe in Spring*. Ill. B. Turkle. New York: Dutton.

DiSalvo-Ryan, D. 1991. *Uncle Willie and the soup kitchen*. New York: Morrow.

Greenfield, E. 1988. *Nathaniel talking*. Ill. J. Gilchrist. New York: Black Butterfly.

Haggerty, M. 1993. *A crack in the wall*. Ill. R. De Anda. New York: Lee & Low.

Isadora, R. 1983. *City seen from a to z*. New York: Trumpet Club.

Johnson, A. 1992. *The leaving morning*. Ill. D. Soman. New York: Orchard.

Jones, R. 1991. *Matthew and Tilly*. Ill. B. Peck. New York: Dutton.

Keats, E. 1971. *Apt. 3*. New York: Aladdin.

Ringgold, F. 1991. *Tar beach*. New York: Crown.

Rush, K. 1994. *Friday's journey*. New York: Orchard.

Soentpiet, C. 1994. *Around town*. New York: Lothrop.

Taylor, C. 1992. *The house that crack built*. Ill. J. Thompson. San Francisco: Chronicle.

Thomas, A. 1991. *Life in the ghetto*. Kansas City, MO: Landmark.

Torres, L. 1993. *Subway sparrow*. New York: Farrar, Straus & Giroux.

Weisman, J. 1993. *The storyteller*. Ill. D. Bradley. New York: Rizzoli.

Wild, M. 1992. *Space travelers*. Ill. G. Rogers. New York: Scholastic.

2. Growing up Navajo

Begay, S. 1995. *Navajo visions and voices across the mesa*. New York: Scholastic.

Crowder, J. 1986. *Tonibah and the rainbow*. Bernalillo, NM: Upper Strata.

Doherty, C. & K. 1991. *The Apaches and Navajos*. New York: Franklin Watts.

Franklin, K. 1994. *The shepherd boy*. Ill. J. Kastner. New York: Atheneum.

Garaway, M. 1989. *Ashkii and his grandfather*. Ill. H. Warren. Tucson, AZ: Treasure Chest.

Green, T. 1991. *Mystery of Navajo moon*. Flagstaff, AZ: Northland.

Hoffman, V. 1974. *Lucy learns to weave: Gathering plants*. Ill. H. Denetsosie. Chinle, AZ: Rough Rock Press.

Morgan, W. 1988. *Navajo coyote tales*. Ill. J. Lind. Santa Fe, NM: Ancient City Press.

Osinski, A. 1987. *A new true book: The Navajo*. Chicago: Childrens Press.

Roessel, M. 1993. *Kinaalda: A Navajo girl grows up*. Minneapolis, MN: Lerner.

Rucki, A. 1992. *Turkey's gift to the people*. Flagstaff, AZ: Northland.

Illustration

1. Element of Art: Light and Dark   (These sets highlight elements of art such as line, color, light and dark, shape, space)

Ackerman, K. 1988. *Song and dance man*. Ill. S. Gammell. New York: Knopf.

Brown, R. 1981. *A dark tale*. New York: Dial Books.

Lyon, G. 1992. *Who came down that road?* Ill. P. Catalanotto. New York: Orchard.

Martin, B., Jr., & J. Archambault. 1985. *The ghost-eye tree*. Ill. T. Lewin. New York: Holt.

McCully, E. 1992. *Mirette on the high wire*. New York: Putnam.

Sheldon, D. 1990. *A whale's song*. Ill. G. Blythe. New York: Scholastic.

Shulevitz, U. 1974. *Dawn*. New York: Farrar, Straus & Giroux.

Wood, A. 1985. *King Bidgood's in the bathtub*. Ill. D. Wood. San Diego, CA: Harcourt.

———. 1987. *Heckedy peg*. Ill. D. Wood. San Diego, CA: Harcourt.

Yolen, J. 1987. *Owl moon*. Ill. J. Schoenherr. New York: Philomel.

Young, E. 1989. *Lon Po Po*. New York: Scholastic.

2. Illustration Technique: Pastels   (These sets highlight particular techniques used for illustration such as scratchboard, colored pencils, pen and ink, pastels, crayon, watercolor, opaque paint, charcoal, photography, clay, collage, paper and fabric, and printmaking)

Booth, B. 1991. *Mandy*. Ill. J. Lamarche. New York: Lothrop.

Breckler, R. 1992. *Hoang breaks the lucky teapot*. Ill. A. Frankel. Boston: Houghton Mifflin.

Text Sets
Paired Books
Book and Toy Sets

Brouillard, A. 1990. *Three cats*. Charlottesville, VA: Thomasson-Grant.

Bunting, E. 1988. *How many days to America?* Ill. B. Peck. New York: Trumpet Club.

Greenfield, E. 1988. *Nathaniel talking*. Ill. J. Gilchrist. New York: Black Butterfly Children's Books.

Higginson, W. 1991. *Wind in the long grass*. Ill.S. Speidel. New York: Simon & Schuster.

Lewis, R. 1988. *In the night, still dark*. Ill. E. Young. New York: Atheneum.

Louie, A. 1982. *Yeh-Shen: A Cinderella story from China*. Ill. E. Young. New York: Philomel.

Scott, A. 1972. *On mother's lap*. Ill. G. Coalson. New York: Clarion.

Van Allsburg, C. 1983. *The wreck of the Zephyr*. New York: Puffin.

Wild, M. 1992. *Space travellers*. Ill. G. Rogers. New York: Scholastic.

3. Bookmaking and Design Elements: Borders   (These sets highlight different aspects of the design of the book such as unusual formats, formal and informal text placement, kinds of paper and print, borders, book jackets, covers, front matter, endpaper, and pop-ups)

Brett, J. 1989. *The mitten*. New York: Scholastic.

Cherry, L. 1992. *A river ran wild*. San Diego, CA: Harcourt.

Dragonwagon, C. 1990. *Home place*. Ill. J. Pinkney. New York: Macmillan.

Kamal, A. 1989. *The bird who was an elephant*. Ill. F. Lessac. New York: Lippincott.

Lawrence, J. 1968. *Harriet and the promised land*. New York: Simon & Schuster.

Lindbergh, R. 1990. *Johnny Appleseed*. Ill. K. Jakobsen. Boston: Little, Brown.

Ringgold, F. 1991. *Tar beach*. New York: Crown.

Williams, V. 1982. *A chair for my mother*. New York: Greenwillow.

Yorinks, A. 1986. *Hey, Al*. Ill. R. Egielski. New York: Farrar, Straus & Giroux.

Young, E. 1983. *Up a tree*. New York: Harper & Row.

4. Illustration Style: Surrealism   (These sets highlight particular styles such as graphic design, cartoons, surrealism, folk art, realistic, impressionism, and expressionism)

Browne, A. 1990. *Changes*. London: Julia MacRae.

Desimini, L. 1993. *Moon soup*. New York: Hyperion.

Drescher, H. 1983. *Simon's book*. New York: Scholastic.

Scieszka, J. 1989. *The true story of the 3 litle pigs*. Ill. L. Smith. New York: Viking.

Sendak, M. 1981. *Outside over there*. New York: Harper.

Smith, L. 1991. *The big pets*. New York: Viking.

Van Allsburg, C. 1981. *Jumanji*. Boston: Houghton Mifflin.

Wiesner, D. 1991. *Tuesday*. New York: Clarion Books.

Broad Concept: Sense of Place   (The following text sets are all related to the broad umbrella concept of sense of place)

1. Scary Places/Comforting Places

Andrews, J. 1985. *Very last first time*. Ill. I. Wallace. New York: Atheneum.

Baylor, B. 1974. *Everybody needs a rock*. Ill. P. Parnall. New York: Aladdin.

Crews, D. 1991. *Bigmama's*. New York: Greenwillow.

Heide, F., & J. Gilliland. 1992. *Sami and the time of the troubles*. Ill. T. Lewin. New York: Clarion.

Hill, E. 1991. *Evan's corner*. Ill. S. Speidel. New York: Viking.

Hoellwarth, C. 1990. *The underbed*. Ill. S. Gerig. Intercourse, PA: Good Books.

Isadora, R. 1991. *At the crossroads*. New York: Scholastic.

Martin, B., Jr., & J. Archambault. 1985. *The ghost-eye tree*. Ill. T. Rand. New York: Scholastic.

Oppenheim, S. 1992. *The lily cupboard*. Ill. R. Himler. New York: Charlotte Zolotow.

2. Dream Places

Baylor, B. 1974. *Everybody needs a rock*. Ill. P. Parnall. New York: Aladdin.

Dragonwagon, C. 1990. *Home place*. Ill. J. Pinkney. New York: Scholastic.

Feelings, T. 1981. *Daydreamers*. Ill. E. Greenfield. New York: Dial.

Fiday, B. & D. 1990. *Time to go*. Ill. T. Allen. San Diego, CA: Gulliver Books.

Keats, E. 1974. *Dreams*. New York: Collier.

Lyon, G. E. 1993. *Dreamplace*. Ill. P. Catalanotto. New York: Orchard.

Mazer, A. 1991. *The salamander room*. Ill. S. Johnson. New York: Trumpet Club.

Parnall, P. 1993. *Spaces*. Brookfield, CT: Milbrook.

Pryor, B. 1992. *Lottie's dream*. Ill. M. Graham. New York: Simon & Schuster.

Text Sets
Paired Books
Book and Toy Sets

Ringgold, F. 1991. *Tar Beach*. New York: Scholastic.

Say, A. 1989. *The lost lake*. Boston: Houghton Mifflin.

Shefelman, J. 1992. *A peddler's dream*. Ill. T. Shefelman. Boston: Houghton Mifflin.

3. Sense of Place Within Family

Bruchac, J. 1993. *Fox song*. Ill. P. Morin. Toronto: Oxford University.

Havill, J. 1992. *Treasure nap*. Ill. E. Savadier. Boston: Houghton Mifflin.

Johnson, A. 1990. *When I am old with you*. Ill. D. Soman. New York: Orchard.

MacLachlan, P. 1982. *Mama one, mama two*. Ill. R. Bornstein. New York: Harper & Row.

Martel, C. 1976. *Yagua days*. Ill. J. Pinkney. New York: Dial.

Nobisso, J. 1990. *Grandma's scrapbook*. Ill. M. Hyde. San Marcos, CA: Green Tiger.

Rylant, C. 1987. *Birthday presents*. Ill. S. Stevenson. New York: Orchard.

Scott, A. 1990. *Grandmother's chair*. Ill. M. Aubrey. New York: Clarion.

Spohn, K. 1994. *Broken umbrellas*. New York: Viking.

Waddell, M. 1989. *Once there were giants*. Ill. P. Dale. New York: Delacorte.

4. Sense of Place When Cultures Meet

Bode, J. 1989. *New kids in town: Oral histories of immigrant teens*. New York: Scholastic.

Friedman, I. 1984. *How my parents learned to eat*. Ill. A. Say. Boston: Houghton Mifflin.

Hewett, J. 1990. *Hector lives in the United States now*. New York: Lippincott.

Jenness, A., & A. Rivers. 1989. *In two worlds: A Yup'ik Eskimo family*. Boston: Houghton Mifflin.

Keegan, M. 1991. *Pueblo boy: Growing up in two worlds*. New York: Dutton.

Kuklin, S. 1992. *How my family lives in America*. New York: Bradbury.

Levine, E. 1989. *I hate English*. Ill. S. Bjorkman. New York: Scholastic.

Polacco, P. 1992. *Mrs. Katz and Tush*. New York: Bantam.

Say, A. 1990. *El Chino*. Boston: Houghton Mifflin.

Surat, M. 1983. *Angel child, dragon child*. Ill. V. Mai. New York: Scholastic.

Williams, K. 1991. *When Africa was home*. Ill. F. Cooper. New York: Orchard.

Yolen, J. 1992. *Encounter*. Ill. D. Shannon. San Diego, CA: Harcourt.

5. People and Animals Sharing Spaces

Brett, J. 1985. *Annie and the wild animals*. Boston: Houghton Mifflin.

Cooper, H. 1993. *The house cat*. New York: Scholastic.

Cowcher, H. 1990. *Antarctica*. New York: Farrar, Straus & Giroux.

Locker, T. 1991. *The land of gray wolf*. New York: Dial.

MacGill-Callahan, S. 1991. *And still the turtle watched*. Ill. B. Moser. New York: Dial.

Martin, R. 1993. *The boy who lived with the seals*. Ill. D. Shannon. New York: Putnam.

McCloskey, R. 1969. *Make way for ducklings*. New York: Viking.

Murphy, J. 1993. *Backyard bear*. Ill. J. Greene. New York: Scholastic.

Paraskevas, B. 1993. *The strawberry dog*. Ill. M. Paraskevas. New York: Dial.

Rand, G. 1992. *Prince William*. Ill. T. Rand. New York: Holt.

Yolen, J. 1987. *Owl moon*. Ill. J. Schoenherr. New York: Scholastic.

Yorinks, A. 1987. *Company's coming*. Ill. D. Small. New York: Scholastic.

6. Places to Live: Houses and Homes

Blos, J. 1987. *Old Henry*. Ill. S. Gammell. New York: Mulberry.

Bour, D. 1985. *The house from morning to night*. Brooklyn, NY: Kane/Miller.

Buchanan, K. 1991. *This house is made of mud*. Ill. L. Tracy. Flagstaff, AZ: Northland Publishing.

Burton, V. 1942. *The little house*. Boston: Houghton Mifflin.

Carle, E. 1987. *A house for hermit crab*. Saxonville, MA: Picture Book Studio.

Dewey, J. 1991. *Animal architecture*. New York: Orchard.

Emberley, R. 1990. *My house: A book in two languages*. Boston: Little, Brown.

Gibbons, G. 1990. *How a house is built*. New York: Scholastic.

Hoberman, M. 1978. *A house is a house for me*. Ill. B. Fraser. New York: Scholastic.

Isaacson, P. 1988. *Round buildings, square buildings and buildings that wiggle like a fish*. New York: Knopf.

Katz, A. 1979. *Tortoise solves a problem*. New York: HarperCollins.

Thompson, C. 1992. *Pictures of home*. New York: Green Tiger.

7. Searching for a Place: Homelessness

Berck, J. 1992. *No place to be: Voices of homeless children*. Boston: Houghton Mifflin.

Bunting, E. 1988. *How many days to America?* Ill. B. Peck. New York: Clarion.

———. 1991. *Fly away home*. Ill. R. Himler. New York: Clarion.

Chalofsky, M., G. Finland, & J. Wallace. 1992. *Changing places: A kid's view of shelter living*. Ill. I. Klass. Mt. Rainier, MD: Gryphon House.

Text Sets
Paired Books
Book and Toy Sets

DiSalvo-Ryan, D. 1991. *Uncle Willie and the soup kitchen*. New York: Morrow.

Garland, S. 1993. *The lotus seed*. Ill. T. Kiuchi. San Diego, CA: Harcourt.

Hammond, A. 1993. *This home we have made: Esta casa que hemos hecho*. New York: Crown.

Hathorn, L. 1994. *Way home*. Ill. G. Rogers. New York: Crown.

Joosse, B. 1992. *Nobody's cat*. Ill. M. Sewall. New York: HarperCollins.

Paraskevas, B. 1993. *Strawberry Dog*. Ill. M. Paraskevas. New York: Dial.

Seymour, T. 1993. *Pole dog*. Ill. D. Soman. New York: Orchard.

8. Changing Places

Baker, J. 1987. *Where the forest meets the sea*. Sydney: Julia McRae.

———. 1991. *Window*. New York: Puffin.

Dugan, B. 1993. *Leaving home with a pickle jar*. Ill. K. Baker. New York: Greenwillow.

Hopkinson, D. 1993. *Sweet Clara and the freedom quilt*. Ill. J. Ransome. New York: Knopf.

Levinson, R. 1993. *Soon, Amanda*. Ill. J. Downing. New York: Orchard.

Rosen, M. 1993. *Moving*. Ill. S. Williams. New York: Viking.

Ryder, J. 1993. *The goodbye walk*. Ill. D. Haeffele. New York: Lodestar.

Von Tscharner, R., R. Fleming, & Townscape Institute. 1987. *New Providence*. Ill. D. Orloff. San Diego, CA: Harcourt.

Wheatley, N. 1987. *My place*. Ill. D. Rawlins. Melbourne, Australia: Collins Dove.

Whelan, G. 1992. *Bringing the farmhouse home*. Ill. J. Rowland. New York: Simon & Schuster.

Winter, J. 1992. *Klara's new world*. New York: Knopf.

9. A Place in History: Japan and World War II

Coerr, E. 1993. *Sadako*. Ill. E. Young. New York: Putnam.

Hamanaka, S. 1990. *The journey*. New York: Orchard.

Maruki, T. 1980. *Hiroshima no pika*. New York: Lothrop.

Mochizuki, K. 1993. *Baseball saved us*. Ill. D. Lee. New York: Lee & Low.

Morimoto, J. 1987. *My Hiroshima*. New York: Viking.

Newton, D. 1992. *Cities at war: Tokyo*. New York: New Discovery.

Say, A. 1982. *The bicycle man*. Boston: Houghton Mifflin.

Stein, R. 1992. *The USS Arizona*. Chicago: Childrens Press.

Takashima, S. 1971. *A child in prison camp*. Plattsburgh, NY: Tundra Books.

Tsuchiya, Y. 1951. *Faithful elephants*. Ill. T. Lewin. New York: Trumpet Club.

Uchida, Y. 1991. *The invisible thread*. Englewood Cliffs, NJ: Julian Messner.
———. 1993. *The bracelet*. Ill. J. Yardley. New York: Philomel.

Appendix C: Paired Books

1. Books by the Same Author

Clifton, L. 1978. *Everett Anderson's nine month long*. Ill. A. Grifalconi. New York: Holt.
———. 1983. *Everett Anderson's goodbye*. Ill. A. Grifalconi. New York: Holt.

Macaulay, D. 1987. *Why the chicken crossed the road*. Boston: Houghton Mifflin.
———. 1990. *Black and white*. Boston: Houghton Mifflin.

Rylant, C. 1984. *Waiting to waltz*. Ill. S. Gammell. New York: Bradbury.
———. 1991. *Appalachia: The voices of sleeping birds*. Ill. B. Moser. San Diego, CA: Harcourt.

2. Traditional and Modern Variants

Cole, B. 1987. *Prince Cinder*. New York: Putnam.
Perrault, C. 1985. *Cinderella*. Ill. S. Jeffers. New York: Dial.

Emberley, M. 1990. *Ruby*. Boston: Little, Brown.
Hyman, T. 1983. *Little Red Riding Hood*. New York: Holiday.

Lattimore, D. 1989. *Why there is no arguing in Heaven: A Mayan myth*. New York: Harper & Row.
Rohmer, H., & M. Anchonodo. 1988. *How we came to the fifth world*. San Francisco: Children's Book Press.

Martin, R. 1985. *Foolish rabbit's big mistake*. Ill. E. Young. New York: Scholastic.
Kellogg, S. 1985. *Chicken Little*. New York: Mulberry.

Yagawa, S. 1979. *The crane wife*. Ill. S. Akaba. New York: Mulberry.
Bang, M. 1983. *Dawn*. New York: Morrow.

Text Sets
Paired Books
Book and Toy Sets

Cooney, B. 1981. *Tortillas para Mama*. New York: Holt.

Wyndham, R. 1968. *Chinese mother goose rhymes*. Ill. E. Young. New York: Philomel.

3. Books with Similar Story Structures/Text Types

Garza, C. L. 1990. *Family pictures*. San Francisco: Children's Book Press.

Ekoomiak, N. 1988. *Arctic memories*. New York: Holt.

Stevens, J. 1985. *The house that Jack built*. New York: Holiday.

Wood, A. 1984. *The napping house*. Ill. D. Wood. San Diego, CA: Harcourt.

Polacco, P. 1988. *The keeping quilt*. New York: Simon & Schuster.

Rogers, P. 1987. *From me to you*. Ill. J. Johnson. New York: Orchard.

4. Books with Similar Topics or Themes

Crowe, R. 1976. *Clyde monster*. Ill. K. Chorao. New York: Dutton.

Morris, W. 1990. *What if the shark wears tennis shoes?* Ill. B. Lewin. New York: Atheneum.

Flack, M. 1933. *The story about Ping*. Ill. K. Wiese. New York: Scholastic.

Van Allsburg, C. 1988. *Two bad ants*. Boston: Houghton Mifflin.

Bash, B. 1989. *The desert giant*. Boston: Little, Brown.

Takeshita, F. 1989. *The park bench*. Ill. M. Suzuki. New York: Kane/Miller.

Hutchins, P. 1972. *Good-night owl*. New York: Puffin.

Tafuri, N. 1987. *Do not disturb*. New York: Greenwillow.

Ramonova, N. 1983. *Once there was a tree*. Ill. G. Spirin. New York: Dial.

Silverstein, S. 1964. *The giving tree*. New York: Harper & Row.

Baker, J. 1991. *Window*. New York: Greenwillow.

Burton, V. 1942. *The little house*. Boston: Houghton Mifflin.

Steptoe, J. 1969. *Stevie*. New York: Scholastic.

Turkle, B. 1969. *Thy friend, Obadiah*. New York: Puffin.

McKenzee 4/19

Today we read versoin five of _The Three Billy Goats Gruff._ It was realy deffrent because one of the billy goats said please mag I cross your brige. Also instead of them wanting to cross the brige for grass they wanted to cross the brige to eat comquats. I thout that was funny.

Sharmat, M. 1980. _Gila monsters meet you at the airport._ Ill. B. Barton. New York: Puffin.

Vagin, V., & F. Asch. 1989. _Here comes the cat!_ New York: Scholastic.

Blood, C., & M. Link. 1976. _The goat in the rug._ Ill. N. Parker. New York: Four Winds.

Ziefert, H. 1986. _A new coat for Anna._ Ill. A. Lobel. New York: Knopf.

Carle, E. 1969. _The very hungry caterpillar._ New York: Scholastic.

Gibbons, G. 1989. _Monarch butterfly._ New York: Holiday.

Aardema, V. 1981. _Bringing the rain to Kapiti Plain._ Ill. B. Vidal. New York: Scholastic.

Lee, J. 1985. _Toad is the uncle of heaven._ New York: Holt.

Baker, J. 1987. _Where the forest meets the sea._ London: Julia MacRae.

Cowcher, H. 1990. _Antarctica._ New York: Farrar, Straus & Giroux.

Sharmat, M. 1980. _Gila monsters meet you at the airport._ Ill. B. Barton. New York: Puffin.

Gray, N. 1988. _A country far away._ Ill. P. Dupasquier. New York: Orchard.

Text Sets
Paired Books
Book and Toy Sets

Written Conversation
Message Board
Pen Pals
Dialogue Journals
Walking Journals
Problems Journal

Introduction

Classroom writing experiences need to reflect the many types and functions of writing which are part of everyday life. While Personal Journals, Writer's Notebooks, and Learning Logs often take on personal, private, and reflective uses of writing as a tool for thinking, another function of writing is a tool for communication with others. Sometimes writing is used to communicate in formal ways through business letters, persuasive essays, and published fiction and nonfiction. Other times writing is a form of informal communication between acquaintances and friends who send each other notes, messages, and letters.

These engagements provide an informal writing environment in which students and teachers are encouraged to explore meaning with each other. Because the focus is on informal communication with another person, the engagements are supportive in helping language users overcome their insecurities about putting their ideas down on paper and in drawing their attention to consideration of audience. In this case, the audience is someone with whom they have some kind of personal relationship and from whom they can receive an immediate response, not a distant outside audience.

Through the process of sending and receiving written messages, readers and writers, particularly young or inexperienced ones, come to understand that literacy is a multimodal communicative process. These engagements help learners understand that written language as well as oral language involves social interaction. Although written language differs from oral language, what children know about oral language can be used to support their move into writing. These engagements build on this support by making minimal distinctions between oral language and written language. In these engagements, writing takes on the form of an informal conversation with another person and that conversation—not grammar or spelling or correct story structures—receives attention. Not only does oral language support written language, but also reading and writing support each other. What one language participant writes is read by a second participant and can be used to support what that participant writes, and vice versa.

Materials/Procedures for Written Conversation

■ Paper (any scrap will do) and a pencil

1. Written Conversation is introduced as just like an oral conversation, except that instead of talking orally with a neighbor or friend, students will do their talking on paper. The following options can be used as a first experience:

a. Some teachers have announced a "Written Conversation Day" during which students can do as much talking as they wish, but on paper rather than orally.

b. Other teachers begin by having a public Written Conversation with one student using the overhead projector. Students

Written Conversation
Message Board
Pen Pals
Dialogue Journals

FIGURE CE19.1
**Written Conversation Between
Two Special Education
Students; Billy and Bobbie,
Age 11 (compliments of Pat
Tefft Cousin)**

TRANSLATION
Glen, do you have a girl
friend?
No.
Why not?
I don't like girls!
Why not?
Because they got me in
trouble!
How do they do that?
They write letters to you
and they talk to you
when you are not supposed to!

are then asked to pair up and have similar conversations with each other.

c. Another strategy is simply for the teacher to begin informally sitting next to various children and having a Written Conversation, and then encouraging them to try this engagement with others.

3. The first participant writes a question on a sheet of paper and hands the paper and the pencil to the second participant.

4. The second participant reads the question, writes a response to it, and returns the paper to the first participant. The participants proceed in this fashion, changing roles in asking questions and making responses, until the conversation is terminated by one of the participants.

When using Written Conversation for young children whose writing is unconventional and difficult for others to read, each

Melinda and Tommy,
did you like Amelia's
Road? a little bite I
Like When Amelia's fond
the Road. I didnt like it.
Wath parkt did you
like? when she left. how
come you liked When
she left. I did
not like When she
left. Maybe I dont like what
you like do you like the
Gake K-Pot tree? its
a pretty cool book. Amelia's
Road chnts to me
Because I foned
a Place were I
Like to go to
after school. Do
you? No. Do you
Wish that you
did? not Relly Woth
did you like in
the Great Kupok tree?
when the snake Talked to
him. So did I
but my bust Part
was When all
the amelas tode
hem not to wipe
down the Great
Kapok Tree.

participant, whether adult or child, writes a message and then reads whatever was written to the other participant.

5. Once students have had experience using Written Conversation to have a conversation with a friend, the engagement can be used in various ways throughout the curriculum:

Written Conversation
Message Board
Pen Pals
Dialogue Journals

a. After reading a selection, students can be asked to discuss, via Written Conversation, their understanding of that selection with another student. Although these conversations could be collected by the teacher, they are best used and introduced to students as simply a device they can use to organize their thinking before engaging in a group discussion.

b. Students can read different variations of the same story such as Cinderella variants and then engage in Written Conversations with one another to compare the similarities and differences in their versions.

c. Students can be invited to have a Written Conversation with another student on a topic they want to write about as a strategy for helping them think about their topic before beginning the draft.

d. Written Conversation can be used to discuss disputes and disruptive behavior in the class or on the playground. Having the students who were involved write about what happened often calms tempers and gives students time to organize and support their view of the experience.

Materials/Procedures for Message Board

- Bulletin board in a central location
- Ample supply of various sizes of paper and envelopes
- Writing instruments
- Thumbtacks

1. To initiate the Message Board, the teacher may write a message to the entire class or to a particular student and place it on the board.

2. When the students discover the message, they are invited to write messages to one another and/or to the teacher. The only restriction is that messages must be signed. Each message may be hung publicly, folded over with the recipient's name on the outside, or sealed in an envelope. Both art and writing can be used to send messages to others.

3. A trip to the grocery store or other local businesses may provide useful examples of ways adults use bulletin boards to advertise goods and services for sale and to post lost-and-found notices.

FIGURE CE19.3
Student Messages Sent to
Their Teacher via the Message
Board; Ben, Anne, and Saul,
Age 10 (Myriam Revel-Wood's
classroom)

Mrs. Wood,

Stephanie wrote a cuss word on my writing book she will probably erase it but I think you should talk to her.

Sincerely,
Ben

Mrs. Wood,   4/10/25

Something is wrong with the pencil sharpener. I found that out at, 2:43 during Archeology.

Anne

Mrs. Wood do you want a small frog about this big?

Saul

4. A variety of types of messages can be posted on the Message Board by teachers, students, and parents, including personal messages, announcements, records of class assignments, invitations, jokes or riddles for class members to respond to, items to sell, current events, sign-up sheets for classroom activities such as songs, drama, or sharing stories—anything that needs to be communicated with others. Messages can also be exchanged between

Written Conversation
Message Board
Pen Pals
Dialogue Journals

classrooms. As the Message Board gets crowded, students may wish to divide the board into categories based on the general types of messages being posted.

5. The function of Message Board changes according to classroom needs and students' interests. The following are some variations:

a. In one classroom of young children, the teacher used Message Board in conjunction with sharing time. Children who had something they wanted to share with the rest of the class during the class sharing time wrote their message on a piece of paper and posted it on the Message Board. At the end of the day, everyone came together for sharing time, and the children who had earlier put messages on the board read them to the class. Only children with written messages were allowed to share. Because each child read his or her own message, it did not matter if the message was written conventionally.

b. Several teachers have used a special Message Board to manage their classroom newspaper or magazine. Sign-up sheets for different positions on the newspaper, notices and requests for certain kinds of articles, and articles for the newspaper were all posted on the Message Board.

c. One classroom decided to use their Message Board during the second half of the year to send messages to the "Students of the Week." Each week, several students' names were drawn from a hat, and each person in the class wrote messages to the selected students and posted them on the board. At the end of the week, the messages were taken down and given to the Students of the Week.

d. Message Board provides a functional way to handle some of the mundane business of school. Other tasks, such as handling lunch money and taking attendance, can also become functional language activities that involve the students. In one preschool, the children learn to write their names through signing in each morning as a way to take attendance. The board can also be used by students to post messages to the teacher instead of interrupting the teacher during class time.

e. As an extension of Message Board and Pen Pals (see next page) a school-wide postal system can be established. Each day, several children serve as school postal workers to gather and deliver mail to each classroom and the office. Once the mail is delivered to a classroom, several children in that room are responsible for putting the mail into individual mailboxes. Each classroom needs to have a box or bag where mail is placed to be delivered and individual mailboxes for all class members.

Materials/Procedures for Pen Pals

▌ Various kinds of stationery and envelopes

1. Establish various kinds of pen pal exchanges:

   a. Long-distance pen pals allow students to communicate with someone from a different community and culture, but usually the exchanges occur infrequently.

   b. Arrange a pen pal exchange with another class from a nearby school so that letters can be exchanged frequently on a regular basis. Choose a teacher who lives on or near the route between home and school each day so that the letters can be easily exchanged.

   c. If there is a nearby college, an exchange can be set up with undergraduate students in a language arts methods class.

   d. Contact a nearby senior citizen facility or nursing home to establish an exchange.

   e. Exchange letters with children from another classroom in the same school but who are several grades apart.

2. Establish procedures for how often the exchanges will occur and how they will occur. These procedures make the difference in whether or not the exchange will be successful. If students do not receive and return letters on a regular basis, they lose interest.

3. When first choosing pen pals, one group often sends a "Getting to Know You" newspaper to the other group so that they can read through each person's interview and choose the person whom they want as a pen pal.

4. When students receive a letter, they are given a certain period of time for writing a letter and putting it in the mailbag. Teachers

Written Conversation
Message Board
Pen Pals
Dialogue Journals

Dear Kimberly,
I'me ok. I tdd you but anywa,
I am right handed. I want to play piano
wheen I grew up and now! I have 1 sister.
She is 1 year old her name is Samantha
I liked Amber On The Mountan because
Amber taught herself to write and
Surprised Anna. The Three Billy Goats
Gruff is aboat goats who save themselves.
I wont to be a fire fighter when I grow up
Do you have a job? If so what? If not,
What do you want to do? Are you marred?
Childlren perhaps? Grand father Journey
is about a family who Like othercou ty's be
sides thier home.
P.S.
I liked Love,
Grandfather Journey Rilea - Jane

announce when the mail pouch will be leaving the room and students are responsible for getting their letters into the bag. Various
kinds of stationery and envelopes should be available.

5. Whenever possible, arrange for pen pals to meet each other
sometime during the exchange. Instead of waiting until the end of
the year, meeting part way through the year can rekindle enthusiasm for writing to the pen pal. If it is not possible to meet, a video
of the two groups of pen pals can be exchanged between the groups.

6. Students can keep their pen pal's letters in a pocket folder and
then use them to examine language use, content, form, conven-

tions, etc. This is especially effective if children are exchanging with adults or a group of older students are corresponding with young children.

7. Usually the content of the pen pal letters is determined by the children. Sometimes, however, the exchange has a particular focus. Children have exchanged letters about books that are being read in both classrooms or students may be writing to ask questions of senior citizens about "long ago" in their community.

Materials/Procedures for Dialogue Journals

■ Some type of journal, often a spiral notebook

1. Dialogue Journals are a form of written dialogue between two people, usually either the teacher or classmates. Usually students write daily in their journals about their experiences at home or at school and then exchange the journal for response. Some type of system is needed for the exchange. Teachers often color code the journals so that they can take one color each day for response. By the end of the week, they have responded to everyone's journal. Sometimes students place their journals on a table and anyone who chooses can take the journal to write a response. Other times, students hand their journal to another person for response.

2. Dialogue Journals can be used as way to converse about books students are reading independently. Their entries take the form of a letter to the teacher or another student in which they discuss what they think and feel about what they read, what they like and don't like, and what the book means to them. In addition, they ask questions, request help, or respond to previous comments. The responder writes letters back commenting on both the student's letter and the book itself.

3. A variation of dialogue journals is to have students write their journal entries as homework each evening. Students write about their own topics, or the class agrees on a particular topic. Each morning the students place their journals on a table. During the day, each student (and the teacher) responds to two other journals.

4. *Walking Journals* are a more public variation of Dialogue Journals. Students organize themselves into groups of three or four and

Written Conversation
Message Board
Pen Pals
Dialogue Journals

> Are you finished with your fairy tale? I really like the way you are having the Knight defeat the dragon. How is Aaron's story coming?
>
> 3-1 We did it get to it yesterday. Erin asxy de tiy steped on his crun box. and then I had to git.
>
> Sounds like you had a lot of trouble yesterday. Some days are like that. I hope today goes better for you.
>
> 3-8 Michael sede to me that you don't like us.
>
> Michael is having some problems and he's feeling bad right now. It has nothing to do with you. I like the whole class, including you and Michael.

share one journal. A schedule is established so that the journal rotates from person to person with the teacher being an additional member of each group and receiving the journal on a particular day. Each person has one or two days to read the previous set of entries from the different group members, write a response, and pass the journal on to the next person. The journal thus becomes a conversation among a small group rather than only two people.

> *My stuff is being stolen. I can't get my stuff back. We think we know who stole it but we arn't posative. What can we do?*
>
> 1. Tell the person you think stole your stuff that you would like your stuff back. Be sure to keep this private and not mean.
>
> 2. One thing you should do is not tell the person you think is stealing and be really sure that your things were not misplaced.
>
> 3. Maybe we need to store extra supplies in a cabinet in the room.
>
> 4. If you did take something you could put it in someone's locker or mailbox when no one's in the room.
>
> 5. Maybe someone has gone to the wrong locker by accident.

FIGURE CE19.6
Problems Journal Entry;
Kim, Age 10 (Rise Paynter's
classroom)

5. Another form of Walking Journal is a class journal on a particular issue or events. At various times students are invited to share their thinking about class projects, events, or problems. The Walking Journal can be different journals, each one on a particular issue, that are passed around from person to person; each person has the opportunity to write in the journal, sharing thoughts on the topic being discussed as well as responding to previous entries. The teacher takes a turn just like everyone else.

6. *Problems Journal* is a Dialogue Journal which Rise Paynter developed to help students think through problems and become critical thinkers. As problems occurred on the playground or in class, students were invited to write their complaint in this journal. At the end of each day, the whole class listened to the complaint and then generated alternative solutions to the problem. Rise played the role of scribe. Students were invited to select any one of the solutions offered. If the problem reoccurred, it was again reported in the Problems Journal and again discussed.

> When I was helping michael Michael was thow bloks, at me.

Problems Journal Entry;
Kate, Age 8 (Mary Pietsch's
classroom)

Written Conversation
Message Board
Pen Pals
Dialogue Journals

Rise also used this journal to talk about things she felt were not working in the classroom. Because of its effectiveness, students brought in problems from home and elsewhere for discussion. No attempt was made to force solutions on participants, but rather the Problems Journal was seen as time for discussion, collaboration, and inquiry.

Establishing the Learning Context

Written Conversation can be introduced as a natural way for class members (including the teacher) to exchange comments and yet not disturb others who are working. Teachers can engage in Written Conversations with students as frequently as possible, often electing a Written Conversation over an oral conversation if such a choice can be made. Teachers should also encourage students to engage in Written Conversations with one another whenever appropriate.

Message Boards often seem to go through cycles of use by the students. When teachers see that students' use of the board is dying down, they can encourage new types of uses. Teachers can continuously demonstrate and encourage use of the board by the messages they send on it. One particularly effective use of the board by teachers is to send notes complimenting children on their use of new reading or writing strategies.

Because young children's knowledge of conventional representations is sometimes limited, functional spelling may dominate, and some children may have difficulty reading messages from their classmates. The teacher can encourage the reader to predict "indecipherable" portions of the message from the portions that have been read. If the functional spelling is particularly difficult to understand, the reader may be encouraged to see the author of the message for clarification. Here, common sense rules—what would you do if you wanted to read the message and couldn't quite make it out?

References

Written Conversation and Message Board were initially developed by Carolyn Burke. Walking Journals were first developed by David Heine. The Problems Journal is the creation of Rise Paynter.

Atwell, N. 1984. "Writing and reading literature from the inside out." *Language Arts* 61(3):240–252.

———. 1987. *In the middle: Writing, reading, and learning with adolescents.* Portsmouth, NH: Boynton/Cook.

Staton, J., R. Shuy, J. Kreeft, & L. Reed. 1986. *Interactive writing in dialogue journals.* Norwood, NJ: Ablex.

Appendix A: Children's Literature Involving Letters

Ada, A.F. 1994. *Dear Peter Rabbit*. Ill. L. Tryon. New York: Atheneum.

Ahlberg, J. & A. 1986. *The jolly postman*. Boston: Little, Brown.

Asch, F., & V. Vagin. 1992. *Dear Brothers*. New York: Scholastic.

Berger, M. & G. 1994. *Where does the mail go? A book about the postal system*. Ill. G. Brittingham. Nashville, TN: Ideals.

Brisson, P. 1989. *Your best friend, Kate*. Ill. R. Brown. New York: Macmillan.

———. 1990. *Kate heads West*. Ill. R. Brown. New York: Bradbury.

———. 1992. *Kate on the coast*. Ill. R. Brown. New York: Bradbury.

Campbell, R. 1982. *Dear zoo*. New York: Four Winds.

Caseley, J. 1991. *Dear Annie*. New York: Mulberry.

Harrison, M. 1991. *Lizzie's list*. Ill. B. Matthews. Cambridge, MA: Candlewick.

Hesse, K. 1992. *Letters from Rifka*. New York: Holt.

Hoban, L. 1976. *Arthur's pen pal*. New York: Harper & Row.

James, S. 1991. *Dear Mr. Blueberry*. New York: Macmillan.

Kidd, D. 1989. *Onion tears*. Ill. L. Montgomery. New York: Orchard.

Marshak, S. 1990. *Hail to mail*. Ill. V. Radunsky. New York: Holt.

Selway, M. 1992. *Don't forget to write*. Nashville, TN: Ideals.

———. 1994. *I hate Roland Roberts*. Nashville, TN: Ideals.

Silverberg, R. 1990. *Letters from Atlantis*. Ill. R. Gould. New York: Atheneum.

Toll, N. 1993. *Behind the secret window: A memoir of a hidden childhood during World War Two*. New York: Dial.

Turner, A. 1987. *Nettie's trip South*. Ill. R. Himler. New York: Macmillan.

Va, L. 1987. *A letter to the King*. New York: HarperCollins.

Wild, M. 1991. *Thank you, Santa*. Ill. K. Argent. New York: Scholastic.

Williams, V. 1988. *Stringbean's trip to the shining sea*. Ill. J. & V. Williams. New York: Greenwillow.

Woodruff, E. 1994. *Dear Levi*. Ill. B. Peck. New York: Knopf.

Written Conversation
Message Board
Pen Pals
Dialogue Journals

Visitors Corner
Class History Log
Curriculum Notebook
Visitors Folder
Picture Reflections

Introduction

Students and teachers in each classroom need to establish their own sense of identity and history together. They need a way to preserve and share this history with each other and with others who visit their classroom. Visitors Corner contains a variety of logs, notebooks, and artifacts that serve a range of purposes in a classroom. For the students in that classroom, putting together the items for the Visitors Corner helps them create and preserve a history of their time together in that classroom and to gain a sense of connectedness and rootedness as a community. Through these ties to history and classroom community, they gain a sense of who they are and of stability in a changing world. They can add to and revisit this history throughout the year.

When visitors such as parents, administrators, or visiting teachers come to the classroom, the Visitors Corner is the first place they go.

> We did choice time this morning because we didn't have it yesterday, and it woud be to cazy this afternoon. Today was the TRAK MEET and we went out to see all the things that were going on.
>
> Steph S.
> 3-19

The items in that corner give them a sense of what this classroom is all about and let them know that they are expected to be active members of the classroom, even though they are only visiting for a short period of time.

Materials/Procedures

- A small corner in the classroom with a table, bulletin board, and small shelving unit
- Various kinds of notebooks, scrapbooks, and logs
- Camera

Any or all of the following items can be found in a Visitors Corner:

1. *Class History Log:* This daily log is used by students to keep track of the significant events occurring in the classroom. The entries can be generated as a group at the end of the day and then written into the log by the teacher or a student. Another option is to have a student be responsible each day to add an entry to the log and then share it with the class. This log can include photographs of special events.

Visitors Corner

FIGURE CE20.2
Guest Book (Gloria Kauffman's classroom)

The Class History Log can be used to create a class time line of the most significant events occurring in the classroom. At particular intervals of time, such as once a month, the Class History Log is reread and students make a decision of which events were so significant that they need to be recorded on the class time line.

2. *Curriculum Notebook*: A Curriculum Notebook contains pictures and descriptions of each of the major curricular components in that classroom. At the beginning of the year, teachers take pictures of the different engagements occurring in the classroom. These pictures are then organized according to the major curricular components that are part of the classroom and the types of engagements that occur across the day. The notebook might be organized according to certain time blocks such as journals, wide reading, group meeting, work time, author talk time, lunch, etc., or according to the curricular framework of the authoring cycle. Next to each picture, quotes from students are placed that explain what is occurring during that time of the day and what kinds of learning and thinking that engagement is supporting.

How We Do the Inquiry Process and Journals

We think about our favorite ideas or our interests and we list them. We can keep adding new ideas to our list.

We pick the one we want to pick for this time.

We write what we already know.

We tell our questions and we ask other people their questions.

And then what we find out from friends and big buddies and other kids in the room and books and TV, we write in our inquiry journal. We put some of our ideas on the computer. We paint and do art.

We share our inquiry journals. We show the pictures we painted, a book from our topic, and some new things we learned that we put in our inquiry journal.

We think of new ideas.

Putting this notebook together helps students sort out and understand the underlying structures and routines of the classroom. Once it is put together, it becomes an important document for visitors in introducing them to the classroom.

3. *Visitors Folder*: This folder contains a letter welcoming visitors to the classroom, telling them briefly how the classroom operates, and letting them know the expectations for their participation in the classroom. If the school has a handbook or statement of philosophy, this can also be added to the folder.

The folder should also contain a form on which each visitor is invited to write their response to the classroom at the end of their visit. These responses are then put into a Visitors Response Book which is kept in the corner.

4. *Picture Reflections*: Picture Reflections are children's reflections about photographs of themselves in various engagements around the classroom. Underneath each picture, several children write their reflections on "What were we doing?" and "Why were we doing this?"

5. Other items that might be found in the Visitors Corner include:

a. Guest book: a log in which visitors sign in and out.

b. Visitors' Reading: a set of professional articles and short books that parents or other interested visitors to the classroom can check out to read.

Visitors Corner

Name Zachary Date 6-8

Picture Reflection

What is the picture of?

me michael, Jason and Adam made a volcano out of a blue shet and rolers and tape

What does it show about you as a learner?

What we know about volcanos. That we can make a volcano.

Why is this important?

Its an easyer way to show what you maen something You dent have to tall by a pice of paper.

c. Student of the Week Display

d. Student files: cumulative files where students place pictures, writing, etc., that they want to keep but are not currently working on.

e. Class directory: a picture directory of each person in the room along with their "Getting to Know You" interview.

f. Other items such as past copies of classroom newspapers and magazines, student portfolios, letters or notes from past visitors, displays related to pen pals, classroom mailboxes, class books, scrapbooks on special events such as a field trip, experience charts, awards given to any class member, student collections, class surveys, and postcards.

g. Any of these same items but from previous years.

Establishing the Learning Context

It is important that students begin the year with a sense that this classroom has a history. By placing murals, books, pictures, and stories from students who were in the classroom previously all around the room, students entering the room already have a sense of the kind of place this classroom will be and of a history to which they will connect. Throughout the year, students should have continuous access to previous books and projects. Literature is not read aloud or used for a particular inquiry and then disappears from the room. It simply moves to another part of the room where students can continue to revisit those books throughout the year.

When visitors enter the room, several students should have the responsibility for giving those visitors a tour of the room in which they explain the different parts of the room and how the classroom operates. The tour should end at the Visitors Corner with a request for the visitor to sign in and spend some time browsing the materials in that corner.

Picture Reflection; Kelly, Age 5 (compliments of Heidi Mills)

References

The Curriculum Notebook and Picture Reflections were developed by Carolyn Burke.

Visitors Corner

References

Anderson, R. C., & P. D. Pearson. 1984. *A schema-theoretic view of basic processes in reading comprehension.* Technical Report No. 306. Champaign, IL: University of Illinois, Center for the Study of Reading.

Anderson, R., P. Wilson, & L. Fielding. 1988. "Growth in reading and how children spend their time outside of school." *Reading Research Quarterly* 23(3):285–303.

Asch, F. 1982. *Happy birthday, moon.* New York: Simon & Schuster.

Atwell, N. 1984. "Writing and reading literature from the inside out." *Language Arts* 61(3):240–52.

———. 1987. *In the middle: Writing, reading, and learning with adolescents.* Portsmouth, NH: Boynton/Cook.

———. 1991. *Side by side: Essays on teaching to learn.* Portsmouth, NH: Heinemann.

Babbitt, N. 1975. *Tuck everlasting.* New York: Farrar, Straus & Giroux.

Bang, M. 1991. *Picture this: Perception and composition.* Boston: Little Brown.

Barchas, S. E. 1975. *I was walking down the road.* Ill. J. Kent. New York: Scholastic.

Barnes, D. 1975. *From communication to curriculum.* New York: Penguin.

Baskwill, J. 1992. "Finding common ground: Building a dialogic community." Honors Degree diss., Mount Saint Vincent University, Halifax.

Bateson, G. 1979. *Mind and nature: A necessary unity.* New York: Bantam.

Baylor, B. 1963. *Amigo.* New York: Macmillan.

Bean, W., & C. Bouffler. 1987. *Spell by writing.* Rozelle, NSW, Australia: Primary English Teachers Association.

Benedict, S., & L. Carlisle, eds. 1992. *Beyond words: Picture books for older readers and writers.* Portsmouth, NH: Heinemann.

Berger, B. 1984. *Grandfather Twilight.* New York: Philomel.

Berghoff, B. 1993. "Moving toward aesthetic literacy in the first grade." In *Examining central issues in literacy research, theory, and practice,*

Forty-second Yearbook of The National Reading Conference, edited by D. Leu & C. Kinzer. Chicago, IL: NRC.

Berghoff, B., & S. Hamilton. 1993. "Curriculum as inquiry." Presentation given at the Indiana Summer Reading Conference, Bloomington.

Berghoff, B., & J. C. Harste. 1992. "Teacher as researcher. Classrooms that support teacher and student inquiry." Speech presented at Annual Meeting of Whole Language Umbrella. NY: Niagara Falls.

Bintz, W., & J. C. Harste. 1994. "Revisioning evaluation and assessment." In *Assessment and evaluation in whole language programs* 2d ed., edited by B. Harp. Norwood, MA: Christopher Gordon.

Birdseye, T. 1988. *Airmail to the moon.* Ill. S. Gammell. New York: Holiday.

Bleich, D. 1988. *The double perspective: Language, literacy, and social relations.* New York: Oxford University Press.

Boomer, G. 1987. "Addressing the problem of elsewhereness: A case for action research in schools." In *Reclaiming the Classroom,* edited by D. Goswami & P. Stillman. Portsmouth, NH: Heinemann.

Brown, M. W. 1947. *Goodnight moon.* Ill. C. Hurd. New York: Harper & Row.

Brown, R. 1991. "The politics of literacy." Presentation given at the Annual Meeting of the National Reading Conference, Austin.

Bruner, J. 1990. *Acts of meaning.* Cambridge, MA: Harvard University Press.

Bunting, E. 1989. *The Wednesday surprise.* Ill. D. Carrick. New York: Clarion.

Burke, C. 1980a. "The Burke Reading Interview." In *The reading comprehension resource guide,* edited by D. J. Strickler. Bloomington, IN: Language Education.

———. 1980b. The Burke Writing Interview. In "The evolution of text: The interrelationship of reading and writing in the composing process" by M. Atwell. Ph.D. diss., Indiana University, Bloomington.

———. 1989. "The inquiry cycle." Unpublished manuscript, Indiana University, Bloomington.

———. 1991a. "Great concepts in language: Curriculum and cognition." Bloomington, IN: Doctoral seminar, Indiana University.

———. 1991b. "The inquiry cycle." Speech presented at the Eisenhower Grant Institute, Columbia, SC.

Buss, F. L. 1991. *The journey of the sparrows.* New York: Lodestar.

Byars, B. 1977. *The pinballs.* New York: Harper.

Calkins, L. 1991. *Living between the lines.* Portsmouth, NH: Heinemann.

———. 1994. *The art of teaching writing* new edition. Portsmouth, NH: Heinemann.

Carey, R. F. 1982. "Toward holistic theory." Paper presented at the Annual Meeting of the International Reading Association, Chicago, IL.

Carle, E. 1969. *The very hungry caterpillar*. Cleveland, OH: Collins World.

Church, S. M. 1994. "Is whole language really warm and fuzzy?" *The Reading Teacher* 47(5):168–76.

Clay, M. 1972. *Reading: The patterning of complex behaviour* 1st ed. Auckland, NZ: Heinemann.

———. 1979. *Reading: The patterning of complex behaviour* 2d ed. Auckland, NZ: Heinemann.

———. 1985. *The early detection of reading difficulties* 3d ed. Portsmouth, NH: Heinemann.

Cleary, B. 1983. *Dear Mr. Henshaw*. New York: Morrow.

Clyde, J. A. 1986. "A collaborative venture: Exploring the socio-psycho-linguistic nature of literacy." Ph.D. diss., Indiana University, Bloomington, IN.

Cochrane, O. 1991. *Questions & answers about whole language*. Winnipeg, Manitoba: Blue Frog Press/WLU.

Cole, B. 1987. *The goats*. New York: HarperCollins.

Commire, A. 1971–present. Something about the Author series. Detroit, MI: Gale.

Copenhaver, J. 1992. "Instances of inquiry." *Primary Voices*, K–6 Premiere Issue: 6–12.

Crafton, L., & C. Burke. 1994. "Inquiry-based evaluation: Teachers and students reflecting together." *Primary Voices K–6* 2(2):2–7.

Crawford, K., M. Ferguson, G. Kauffman, J. Laird, J. Schroder, & K. Short. 1994. "Exploring historical and multicultural perspectives through inquiry." In *If this is social studies, why isn't it boring?* edited by S. Steffey & W. Hood. York, ME: Stenhouse.

Cummings, P., ed. 1992. *Talking with artists*. New York: Bradbury.

De Beaugrande, R. 1980. *Text, discourse, and process*. Norwood, NJ: Ablex.

Deely, J. 1982. *Introducing semiotic: Its history and doctrine*. Bloomington, IN: Indiana University Press.

DeFord, D. E., G. S. Pinnell, C. A. Lyons, & A. W. Place. 1990. *Report of the follow-up student* Vol. II. Columbus, OH: Ohio Reading Recovery Project.

Dewey, J. 1938. *Experience and education*. New York: Collier.

———. 1966. *Democracy and education: An introduction to the philosophy of education*. New York: Collier-Macmillan.

Doake, D. 1986. *Whole language principles and practices in reading development with special emphasis on reading recovery.* Videotape. Ontario, Canada: Scholastic TAB.

Donaldson, M. 1978. *Children's minds.* New York: Norton.

Duckworth, E. 1986. "Teaching as research." *Harvard Educational Review* 56(4):481–95.

———. 1987. *"The having of wonderful ideas" and other essays on teaching and learning.* New York: Teachers College Press.

Dufrensne, J. 1991. "The Freezer Jesus." *The way that water enters stone.* New York: Norton.

Eco, U. 1976. *A theory of semiotics.* Bloomington, IN: Indiana University Press.

Edelsky, C. 1992. "Let's talk: About whole language." In *The whole language catalog: Supplement on authentic assessment,* edited by K. S. Goodman, L. B. Bird, & Y. M. Goodman. Santa Rosa, CA: American School Publishers.

———. 1994. "Education for democracy." *Language Arts* 71(1):252–57.

Edelsky, C., & K. Smith. 1984. "Is that writing—or are those marks just a figment of your curriculum?" *Language Arts* 67(1):192–205.

Egawa, K. 1995. "When teachers inquire." Unpublished doctoral dissertation, Indiana University.

Einstein, A. 1942. *The evolution of physics.* New York: Simon & Schuster.

Eisner, E. W. 1982. *Cognition and curriculum.* New York: Longman.

Elbow, P. 1981. *Contraries and inquiry.* New York: Oxford University Press.

Ericksen, F. 1985. "Qualitative research on teaching." In *Handbook on research in teaching* 3d ed., edited by M. C. Wittrock. New York: Macmillan.

Everett, G. 1993. *John Brown.* Ill. J. Lawrence. New York: Rizzoli.

Fischetto, L. 1991. *All pigs on deck.* New York: Delacorte.

Fleck, L. [1935]1979. *Genesis and development of a scientific fact.* Chicago: University of Chicago Press.

Forbes, E. 1946. *Johnny Tremain.* Boston: Houghton Mifflin.

Fox, P. 1984. *One eyed cat.* New York: Dell.

Franklin, K. 1992. *The old, old man and the very little boy.* Ill. T. Shaffer. New York: Atheneum.

Freeman, J. 1992. *Books kids will sit still for: The complete read-aloud guide* 2nd ed. New York: R. R. Bowker.

Freire, P. 1985. *The politics of education.* South Hadley, MA: Bergin & Garvey.

———. 1989. *Pedagogy of the oppressed.* New York: Continuum.

Fulghum, R. 1988. "A bag of possibilities and other matters of the mind." *Newsweek* 887:88–92.

Galdone, P. 1985. *The three bears*. New York: Clarion.

Gardner, H. 1993. *Multiple intelligences: The theory into practice*. New York: Basic Books.

Gentry, J. R. 1987. *Spel . . . is a four-letter word*. Portsmouth, NH: Heinemann.

Gilman, P. 1993. *Something from nothing*. New York: Scholastic.

Goodman, K. S. 1967. "Reading: A psycholinguistic guessing game." *Journal of the Reading Specialist* 4(1):126–35.

———. 1984. "Unity in reading." In *Becoming readers in a complex society*, edited by A. C. Purves & O. Niles. (Part I: 83rd Yearbook of the National Society for the Study of Education.) Chicago, IL: University of Chicago Press.

Goodman, K. S., E. B. Smith, R. Meredith, & Y. M. Goodman. 1987. *Language and thinking in school*. Katonah, NY: Richard C. Owen.

Goodman, Y. M. 1978. "Kidwatching: An alternative to testing." *Journal of National Elementary School Principals* 57(4):22–27.

———. 1992. "Retrospective miscue analysis." Speech presented at the National Council of Teachers of English, Indianapolis, IN.

Goodman, Y. M., & C. L. Burke. 1972. *Reading miscue inventory*. New York: Macmillan.

Goodman, Y. M., B. Altwerger, & A. Marek. 1989. *Print awareness in preschool children: The development of literacy in preschool children, research, and review*. Tucson, AZ: Program in Language and Literacy, University of Arizona.

Goodman, Y. M., C. L. Burke, with B. Sherman. 1980. *Strategies in reading: Focus on comprehension*. New York: Holt, Rinehart & Winston.

Goodman, Y. M., D. Watson, & C. L. Burke. 1987. *Reading miscue inventory: Alternate procedures*. Katonah, NY: Richard C. Owen.

Goor, R. & N. 1983. *Signs*. New York: Crowell.

Goss, J. L., & J. C. Harste. [1981] 1985. *It didn't frighten me!* Worthington, OH: Willowisp.

Graves, D. 1983. *Writing: Teachers and children at work*. Portsmouth, NH: Heinemann.

———. 1989. *Investigate nonfiction*. Portsmouth, NH: Heinemann.

———. 1992. *Explore poetry*. Portsmouth, NH: Heinemann.

———. 1994. "Inviting diversity through writing." Keynote address given at the 4th Annual Meeting of the Whole Language Umbrella, San Diego, CA.

Graves, D., & J. Hansen. 1983. "The author's chair." *Language Arts* 60(2):176–83.

Greene, M. 1988. *The dialectic of freedom*. New York: Teachers College Press.

———. 1993. "Professional ethics and morality." Speech given at the Annual Meeting of the National Reading Conference, Charleston.

Haggerty, M. 1993. *A crack in the wall*. Ill. R. De Anda. New York: Lee & Low.

Hakes, D. T. 1980. *The development of metalinguistic abilities in children*. New York: Springer-Verlag.

Halliday, M. A. K. 1975. *Learning to mean—Explorations in the development of language*. London: Edward Arnold.

———. 1985. "Three aspects of children's language development: Learn language, learn about language, learn through language." Unpublished manuscript, Department of Linguistics, University of Sydney.

Hanssen, E. 1990. "Planning for literature circles: Variations in focus and structure." In *Talking about books: Creating literate communities*, edited by K. Short & K. Pierce. Portsmouth, NH: Heinemann.

Harste, J. C. 1986. "What it means to be strategic: Good readers as informants." Paper presented at the National Reading Conference, Austin, TX.

———. 1989a. "Foreword." In *Critical thinking* by A. Neilsen. Monographs on Teaching Critical Thinking No. 2. Bloomington, IN: ERIC/NCTE.

———. 1989b. *New policy guidelines for reading: Connecting research and practice*. Urbana, IL: ERIC/NCTE.

———. 1993a. "Literacy as curricular conversations about knowledge, inquiry, and morality." In *Theoretical models and processes of reading* 4th ed., edited by M. Ruddell & R. Ruddell. Newark, DE: IRA.

———. 1993b. "Response to Ridgeway, Dunston, & Qian: Standards for instructional research." *Reading Research Quarterly* 28(4):356–58.

———. 1994. "Whole language: Celebrating our success." *Whole Language Umbrella Newsletter* 5(2):1–10.

Harste, J. C., & C. L. Burke. 1977. "A new hypothesis for reading teacher education research: Both the teaching and learning of reading are theoretically based." In *Reading: Research, theory, and practice*. Twenty-sixth Yearbook of the National Reading Conference. Minneapolis, MN: Mason.

Harste, J. C., & R. F. Carey. 1979. "Comprehension as setting." In *New perspectives on comprehension*, edited by J. C. Harste & R. F. Carey. Indiana University Monographs in Language and Reading Studies. Bloomington, IN: Indiana University, School of Education Publications.

Harste, J. C., host and developer & E. Jurewicz, producer and director. 1985. *The Authoring Cycle: Read Better, Write Better, Reason Better*. Videotape series. Portsmouth, NH: Heinemann.

————. 1991–94. *Visions of literacy*. Videotape series. Portsmouth, NH: Heinemann.

————. 1992. *Literature guilds*. Videotape. Portsmouth, NH: Heinemann.

Harste, J. C., C. L. Burke, & V. A. Woodward. 1981. *Children, their language and world: Initial encounters with print*. Final Report NIE–G–79–0132. Bloomington, IN: Indiana University, Language Education Department.

————. 1983a. *Children, their language and world: The pragmatics of written language use and learning*. Final Report NIE–G–80–0121. Bloomington, IN: Indiana University, Language Education Department.

————. 1983b. *The young child as writer-reader and informant*. Final Report NIE–G–80–0121. Bloomington, IN: Indiana University, Language Education Department.

Harste, J. C., K. G. Short, with C. L. Burke. 1988. *Creating classrooms for authors: The reading-writing connection*. Portsmouth, NH: Heinemann.

Harste, J. C., V. A. Woodward, & C. L. Burke. 1984. *Language stories & literacy lessons*. Portsmouth, NH: Heinemann.

Heath, S. B. 1983. *Ways with words: Language, life and work in communities and classrooms*. Cambridge, MA: Cambridge University Press.

Heine, D. 1987. "A collaborative study of school change." Ph.D. diss., Indiana University, Bloomington.

Hepler, S. I. 1982. "Patterns of response to literature: A one-year study of a fifth- and sixth-grade classroom." Ph.D. diss., Ohio State University, Columbus.

Hickman, J. 1978. *Zoar Blue*. New York: Macmillan.

————. 1981. "A new perspective on response to literature: Research in an elementary school setting." *Research in the Teaching of English* 13(4):343–54.

Hill, M. W. 1989. *Home: Where reading and writing begin*. Portsmouth, NH: Heinemann.

Hoban, T. 1983. *I read signs*. New York: Greenwillow.

————. 1984. *I walk and read*. New York: Greenwillow.

Holdaway, D. 1979. *The foundations of literacy*. Portsmouth, NH: Heinemann.

Holland, N. 1975. *Five readers reading*. New Haven, CT: Yale University Press.

Home Box Office. 1993. *Shadowland* [call number 90968]. Distributed by Blockbusters, Dallas, TX.

Hotze, S. 1991. *A circle unbroken*. New York: Clarion.

Howard, E. 1991. *Aunt Flossie's Hats*. New York: Clarion.

Hutchins, P. 1968. *Rosie's walk*. New York: Macmillan.

Innocenti, R. 1985. *Rose Blanche*. Mankato, MN: Creative Education.

Jennings, P. 1992. *Grandad's gifts*. Ill. P. Gouldtorpe. Ringwood, Victoria: Penguin Books Australia.

John-Steiner, V. 1981. *Notebooks of the mind*. Albuquerque, NM: University of New Mexico Press.

Johnson, P. 1992. *A book of one's own: Developing literacy through making books*. Portsmouth, NH: Heinemann.

———. 1993. *Literacy through the book arts*. Portsmouth, NH: Heinemann.

Johnson, T., & D. R. Louis. 1987. *Literacy through literature*. Portsmouth, NH: Heinemann.

Kahn, L. 1994. "Mathematics as life: Children's responses to literature." Ed.S. Thesis, University of Arizona.

Kaser, S. 1994. "Exploring cultural identity: Creating a learning environment that invites cultural connections through family studies, inquiry and children's literature." Ed.S. Thesis, University of Arizona.

Kasten, W. C. 1994. "Compelling reasons for multi-age classrooms." *Talking Points* 5(1):2–5.

Kasten, W. C., & B. K. Clarke. 1993. *The multi-age classroom: A family of learners*. Katonah, NY: Richard C. Owen.

Kauffman, G., & K. G. Short. 1990. "Teachers and students as decision makers: Creating a classroom for authors." In *Portraits of whole language classrooms: Learning for all ages*, edited by H. Mills & J. A. Clyde. Portsmouth, NH: Heinemann.

———. 1993. "Self-evaluation portfolios: A device to empower learners." In *Windows into literacy: Assessing learners K–8*, edited by L. Rhodes & N. Shanklin. Portsmouth, NH: Heinemann.

Kauffman, G., & K. Yoder. 1990. "Celebrating authorship: A process of collaborating and creating meaning." In *Talking about books: Creating literate communities*, edited by K. Short & K. Pierce. Portsmouth, NH: Heinemann.

Kintsch, W. 1977. "On comprehending stories." In *Cognitive processes in comprehension*, edited by M. A. Just & P. A. Carpenter. Hillsdale, NJ: Erlbaum.

Kirby, D., & C. Kuykendall. 1991. *Mind matters: Teaching for thinking*. Portsmouth, NH: Heinemann.

Koshewa, A. 1994. *Curriculum as inquiry: What's central?* Independent Study Final Report, Indiana University, Bloomington.

Kunhardt, D. 1940. *Pat the bunny*. New York: Golden Press.

Lamb, B., & P. Logsdon. 1991. *Positively kindergarten*. Rosemont, NJ: Modern Learning Press.

Langer, S. 1980. *Philosophy in a new key: A study in the symbolism of reason, rite and art* 3rd ed. Cambridge, MA: Harvard University Press.

Liestman, V. 1991. *Columbus Day*. Minneapolis, MN: Carolrhoda.

Leland, C., & J. C. Harste. 1994. "Multiple ways of knowing: Curriculum in a new key." *Language Arts* 71(5):337–45.

Levi, R. 1991a. "Art and music as composing processes." Ph.D. diss., Wayne State University.

———. 1991b. "Emerging stories and developing motives: An interdisciplinary approach to the composing process." Speech given at the Annual Meeting of the National Council of Teachers of English, Seattle, WA.

Lipson, E. 1991. *The New York Times parents' guide to the best books for children* Revised and updated. New York: Times Books.

Lloyd, P. 1987. *How writers write*. Portsmouth, NH: Heinemann.

Lopez, B. 1992. *The rediscovery of America*. New York: Random House.

Lyon, G. E. 1990. *Basket*. Ill. M. Szilagyi. New York: Orchard.

———. 1992. *Who came down that road?* Ill. P. Catalanotto. New York: Orchard.

MacLachlan, P. 1985. *Sarah, plain and tall*. New York: Harper & Row.

Manning, A., & J. C. Harste. 1994. Teacher research: Demonstrations of possibilities. *Reading* 28(1):2–5.

Manning, A., & A. Neilsen. 1991. "Teacher as informant: Examining dilemmas in teaching." Internal Grant Proposal, Mount Saint Vincent University, Halifax.

Maras, L., & B. Brummett. 1995. "Time for a change: Presidential Elections in a Grade 3–4 Multi-age Classroom." In *Endless Possibilities: Generating Curriculum in Social Studies and Literacy*, edited by P. Cordeiro. Portsmouth, NH: Heinemann.

Martin, B., Jr. [1970] 1983. *Brown bear, brown bear, what do you see?* New York: Holt, Rinehart & Winston.

———. 1982. *Whistle, children, whistle*. New York: Holt.

Maruki, T. 1980. *Hiroshima no pika*. New York: Lothrop, Lee, & Shepard.

Mayher, J. 1990. *Uncommon Sense*. Portsmouth, NH: Heinemann.

McCracken, M. J., & R. A. McCracken. 1979. *Reading, writing, and language: A practical guide for primary teachers*. Winnipeg, Canada: Peguis Publishers Limited.

Merriam, E. 1991. *The wise woman and her secret*. New York: Simon & Schuster.

Mills, H., & J. A. Clyde, eds. 1990. *Portraits of whole language classrooms*. Portsmouth, NH: Heinemann.

Mills, H., T. O'Keefe, & D. Stephens. 1992. *Looking closely: Exploring the role of phonics in one whole language classroom*. Urbana, IL: NCTE.

Milz, V. 1980. *Comprehension-centered classroom: Making it work*. Videotape. Portsmouth, NH: Heinemann.

Mochizuki, K. 1993. *Baseball saved us*. New York: Lee & Low.

Moll, L. 1992. "Bilingual classroom studies and community analysis: Some recent trends." *Educational Researcher* 21(2):21–24.

Morrow, L. M. 1991. "Promoting voluntary reading." In *Handbook of research on teaching the English language arts*, edited by J. Flood, J. Jensen, D. Lapp, & J. Squire. New York: Macmillan.

Murray, D. 1984. *Write to learn*. New York: Holt, Rinehart & Winston.

———. 1989. *Expecting the unexpected: Teaching myself—and others—to read and write*. Portsmouth, NH: Heinemann.

Naidoo, B. 1986. *Journey to Jo'burg*. New York: Lippincott.

Naylor, P. 1991. *Shiloh*. New York: Dell.

Numeroff, L. J. 1985. *If you give a mouse a cookie*. Ill. F. Bond. New York. Harper & Row.

O'Dell, S. 1980. *Sarah Bishop*. Boston, MA: Houghton Mifflin.

O'Neill, C., & Lambert, A. 1982. *Drama structures*. Portsmouth, NH: Heinemann.

Pappas, C. C., & E. Brown. 1988. "The development of children's sense of the written story language register: An analysis of the texture of 'pretend reading.'" *Linguistics and Education* 52(1):45–79.

Paterson, K. 1988. *Gates to excellence*. Toronto, Ontario: Fitzhenery & Whiteside.

Patterson, F. 1987. *Koko's story*. New York: Scholastic.

Peirce, C. S. 1931–58. *Collected papers*. Cambridge, MA: Harvard University Press.

Peterson, R. 1992. *Life in a crowded place*. Portsmouth, NH: Heinemann.

Peterson, R., & M. Eeds. 1990. *Grand conversations*. New York: Scholastic.

Piaget, J. 1976. *The grasp of consciousness: Action and concept in the young child*. Cambridge, MA: Harvard University Press.

Pierce, K. M. 1986. "Curriculum as collaboration: Toward practical theory." Ph.D. diss., Indiana University, Bloomington.

Pierce, K. M., & C. Gilles, eds. 1994. *Cycles of meaning: Exploring the potential of talk in learning communities*. Portsmouth, NH: Heinemann.

Rhodes, L. 1981. "I can read! Predictable books as resources for reading and writing instruction." *Reading Teacher* 34(5):511–18.

———. 1983. *Extended literature activities*. Denver, CO: University of Colorado.

Richardson, V. 1990. "Significant and worthwhile change in teaching practice." *Educational Researcher* 19(7):10–18.

Rosen, H. 1986. *Stories and meanings*. London: National Association for the Teaching of English.

Rosenblatt, L. 1978. *The reader, the text, and the poem: The transactional theory of the literary work*. Carbondale, IL: Southern Illinois University Press.

Routman, R. 1988. *Transitions*. Portsmouth, NH: Heinemann.

———. 1991. *Invitations: Changing as teachers and learners K–12*. Portsmouth, NH: Heinemann.

Rowe, D. W. 1986. "Literacy in the child's world: Preschoolers' explorations of alternate sign systems." Ph.D. diss., Indiana University, Bloomington.

———. 1993. "Learning about literacy and the world: Two-year-olds' and teachers' enactments of a thematic inquiry curriculum." Paper presented at the National Reading Conference, Charleston, SC.

Ruwe, M. 1971. *Ten little bears*. Ill. D. Csanady. Glenview, IL: Scott, Foresman.

Rylant, C. 1986. *The relatives came*. Ill. S. Gammell. New York: Bradbury.

Schwartz, A. 1984. *In a dark, dark room and other scary stories*. New York: Scholastic.

Serebrin, W. 1994. "Empowering ourselves to inquire: Preservice teacher education as a collaborative enterprise." Ph.D. dissertation, Indiana University, Bloomington.

Settle, S. 1994. "Becoming real: A teacher researcher's journey." *Reading* 28(1):5–9.

Shannon, P. 1993. "Developing democratic voices." *The Reading Teacher* 47(2):86–94.

Sheppard, L. 1990. "Our class knows Frog and Toad: An early childhood literature-based classroom." In *Talking about books: Creating literate communities*, edited by K. G. Short & K. M. Pierce. Portsmouth, NH: Heinemann.

Sherman, B. 1979. "Reading for meaning: Don't let word study blind your students." *Learning* 60(1):41–44.

Short, K. G. 1986. "Literacy as a collaborative experience." Ph.D. diss., Indiana University, Bloomington.

———. 1990. "Creating a community of learners." In *Talking about books: Creating literate communities*, edited by K. G. Short & K. M. Pierce. Portsmouth, NH: Heinemann.

———. 1992. "Making connections across literature and life." In *Journeying: Children responding to literature*, edited by K. Holland, R. Hungerford, & S. Ernst. Portsmouth, NH: Heinemann.

———. 1993. "Curriculum for the 21st Century: A redefinition." Speech given at the Annual Meeting of the National Council of Teachers of English, Pittsburgh, PA.

Short, K. G., & J. Armstrong. 1993. "Moving toward inquiry: Integrating literature into the science curriculum." *The New Advocate* 6(3):183–99.

Short, K. G., & C. L. Burke. 1991. *Creating curriculum: Teachers and students as a community of learners*. Portsmouth, NH: Heinemann.

Short, K. G., & G. Kauffman. 1992. "Hearing students' voices: The role of reflection in learning." *Teachers Networking* 11(3):1, 3–6.

———. 1995. "So what do I do? The role of the teacher in literature circles." In *Book talk and beyond: Children and teachers respond to literature*, edited by N. Roser & M. Martinez. Newark, DE: IRA.

Short, K. G., & C. Klassen. 1993. "Literature circles: Hearing children's voices." In *Children's voices: Talk in the classroom*, edited by B. Cullinan. Newark, DE: IRA.

Short, K. G., & K. M. Pierce, eds. 1990. *Talking about books: Creating literate communities*. Portsmouth, NH: Heinemann.

Short, K. G., K. Crawford, L. Kahn, S. Kaser, C. Klassen, & P. Sherman. 1992. "Teacher study groups: Exploring issues through collaborative dialogue." In *Literacy research, theory, and practice: Views from many perspectives*, edited by C. Kinzer & D. Leu. Forty-first Yearbook of the National Reading Conference. Chicago, IL: National Reading Conference.

Shulevitz, U. 1985. *Writing with pictures*. New York: Watson-Guptill.

Siegel, M. G. 1984. "Reading as signification." Ph.D. diss., Indiana University, Bloomington.

Smith, F. 1981. "Demonstrations, engagement, and sensitivity: A revised approach to the language arts." *Language Arts* 52(1):103–112.

———. 1983. *Essays into literacy*. Portsmouth, NH: Heinemann.

———. 1993. *Whose language? What power? A universal conflict in a South African setting*. New York: Teachers College Press.

Smith, K. 1990. "Entertaining a text: A reciprocal process." In *Talking about books: Creating literate communities*, edited by K. G. Short & K. M. Pierce. Portsmouth, NH: Heinemann.

———. 1993. "A descriptive analysis of the responses of six students and their teacher in literature study sessions." Ph.D. dissertation, Arizona State University, Phoenix, AZ.

Smith, P. 1990. *Expert interview*. Field footage videotapes. Bloomington, IN: Language Education and Radio & Television.

Spiro, R. J., B. C. Bruce, & W. F. Brewer, eds. 1980. *Theoretical issues in reading comprehension*. Hillsdale, NJ: Erlbaum.

Steig, W. 1969. *Sylvester and the magic pebble*. New York: Windmill.

Stein, N. L, & C. G. Glenn. 1978. "An analysis of story comprehension in elementary school children." In *Advances in discourse processing* vol. 2, New Directions, edited by R. O. Freedle. Norwood, NJ: Ablex.

Taylor, D. 1983. *Family literacy*. Portsmouth, NH: Heinemann.

Taylor, D., & C. Dorsey-Gaines. 1988. *Growing up literate: Learning from inner-city families*. Portsmouth, NH: Heinemann.

Taylor, M. 1976. *Roll of thunder, hear my cry*. New York: Dial.

Taylor, T. 1969. *The cay*. New York: Doubleday.

Tierney, R. J., J. LaZansky, & D. Schallert. 1981. "Secondary social studies and biology students' use of textbooks." Unpublished manuscript, University of Illinois at Urbana-Champaign.

Trelease, J. 1989. *The new read-aloud handbook*. New York: Penguin.

Turkle, B. 1969. *Thy friend, Obadiah*. New York: Viking.

Vargus, N. R. 1982. "Letter writing over time: Socio-cognitive constraints in transition." Ph.D. diss., Indiana University, Bloomington.

Vasquez, V. 1994. "A step in the dance of critical literacy." *Reading* 28(1):39–42.

Voigt, C. 1984. *Building blocks*. New York: Fawcett.

Vygotsky, L. S. [1934] 1962. *Thought and language*. Cambridge, MA: MIT Press.

———. 1978. *Mind in society: The development of higher psychological processes*, edited by M. Cole, V. John-Steiner, S. Scribner, & E. Souberman. Cambridge, MA: Harvard University Press.

Watson, D. J. 1982. "What is a whole-language reading program?" *The Missouri Reader* 7(1):8–10.

Watson, D. J., C. L. Burke, & J. C. Harste. 1989. *Whole language: Inquiring voices*. Toronto, Canada: Scholastic TAB.

Weaver, C. 1990. *Understanding whole language: From principles to practice*. Portsmouth, NH: Heinemann.

Wells, G. 1986. *The meaning makers: Children learning language and using language to learn*. Portsmouth, NH: Heinemann.

Wertsch, J. V. 1991. *Voices of the mind: A sociocultural approach to mediated action*. Cambridge, MA: Harvard University Press.

White, C. 1990. *Jevon doesn't sit at the back anymore*. Toronto, Canada: Scholastic TAB.

White, E. B. 1952. *Charlotte's Web*. New York: Harper & Row.

Whitin, D., & S. Wilde. 1993. *Read any good math lately?* Portsmouth, NH: Heinemann.

Whitin, D. J., H. Mills, & T. O'Keefe. 1990. *Living and learning mathematics: Stories and strategies for supporting mathematical literacy*. Portsmouth, NH: Heinemann.

Whole Language Umbrella Teleconference. 1993. *Moving in and through whole language* videotape. Stillwater, OK: Oklahoma State University.

Wilde, S. 1991. *You kan red this! Spelling and punctuation for whole language classrooms, K–6*. Portsmouth, NH: Heinemann.

Willard, N. 1983. *The nightgown of the sullen moon*. Ill. D. McPhail. New York: Harcourt Brace Jovanovich.

Winter, P. 1976. *The bear & the fly*. New York: Crown.

Women Studies Seminar Series. 1993. "Ignorance-based education: Implications for the future." Women Studies Program, Indiana University, Bloomington.

Wray, D., & J. Medwell. 1991. *Literacy and language in the primary years*. New York: Routledge.

The Writing Center. 1994. Fremont, CA: The Learning Company.

Yolen, J. 1988. *Devil's arithmetic*. New York: Viking.

———. 1992. *Encounter*. Ill. D. Shannon. San Diego, CA: Harcourt.

Zutell, J. 1978. "Some psycholinguistic perspectives on children's spelling." *Language Arts* 55:(8)44–50.

Index

Index

Index

Index